PRENTICE HALL

SCIENCE EXPLORER

Earth Science

Prentice
Hall

Needham, Massachusetts
Upper Saddle River, New Jersey
Glenview, Illinois

PRENTICE HALL

SCIENCE EXPLORER

Earth Science

Program Resources

Student Edition
Annotated Teacher's Edition
Unit Resource Books, including:
- Chapter Project Support
- Lesson Plans
- Section Summaries
- Review and Reinforce Worksheets
- Enrich Worksheets
- Laboratory Worksheets

Laboratory Manual, Student Edition
Laboratory Manual, Teacher's Edition
Chapter and Unit Tests
Performance Assessment
Standardized Test Preparation Book
Inquiry Skills Activity Book
Student-Centered Science Activity Books
Guided Reading and Study Workbook
Reading in the Content Area with Literature Connections
Science Explorer Interdisciplinary Explorations
Prentice Hall Interdisciplinary Explorations series
Product Testing Activities by Consumer Reports™
How to Manage Instruction in the Block
How to Assess Student Work

Media/Technology

Interactive Student Tutorial CD-ROM
Computer Test Bank Book with CD-ROM
Resource Pro® (Teaching Resources on CD-ROM)
Internet Site at www.phschool.com (includes www.PlanetDiary.com)
Color Transparencies
Section Summaries on Audio CD
Spanish Section Summaries on Audio CD and Book
Lab Activity Video Library
Science Explorer Videotape Library
Science Explorer Spanish Videotape Library
Science Explorer Videodisc Library (English/Spanish)
Interactive Physics Software

Materials Kits

Consumable Materials Kit
Nonconsumable Materials Kit
Materials List CD-ROM

Acknowledgments

Activities on pages 198–199 and 657 are from *Exploring Planets in the Classroom*, copyright © Hawaii Space Grant Consortium. Used with permission.

ISBN 0-13-050622-2
4 5 6 7 8 9 10   03 02 01

Prentice
Hall

Cover: The Colorado River formed the spectacular rock formations of the Grand Canyon in Arizona.

Program Authors

Michael J. Padilla, Ph.D.
Professor
Department of Science Education
University of Georgia
Athens, Georgia

Michael Padilla is a leader in middle school science education. He has served as an editor and elected officer for the National Science Teachers Association. He has been principal investigator of several National Science Foundation and Eisenhower grants and served as a writer of the National Science Education Standards.

As lead author of *Science Explorer,* Mike has inspired the team in developing a program that meets the needs of middle grades students, promotes science inquiry, and is aligned with the National Science Education Standards.

Ioannis Miaoulis, Ph.D.
Dean of Engineering
College of Engineering
Tufts University
Medford, Massachusetts

Martha Cyr, Ph.D.
Director, Engineering
   Educational Outreach
College of Engineering
Tufts University
Medford, Massachusetts

Science Explorer was created in collaboration with the College of Engineering at Tufts University. Tufts has an extensive engineering outreach program that uses engineering design and construction to excite and motivate students and teachers in science and technology education.

Faculty from Tufts University participated in the development of *Science Explorer* chapter projects, reviewed the student books for content accuracy, and helped coordinate field testing.

Book Authors

Joseph D. Exline, Ed.D.
Former Director of Science
Virginia Department of Education

Jay M. Pasachoff, Ph.D.
Professor of Astronomy
Williams College
Williamstown, Massachusetts

Barbara Brooks Simons
Science Writer
Boston, Massachusetts

Carole Garbuny Vogel
Science Writer
Lexington, Massachusetts

Thomas R. Wellnitz
Science Teacher
The Paideia School
Atlanta, Georgia

Contributing Writers

W. Russell Blake, Ph.D.
Planetarium Director
Plymouth Community
    Intermediate School
Plymouth, Massachusetts

Alfred B. Bortz, Ph.D.
School of Education
Duquesne University
Pittsburgh, Pennsylvania

Rose-Marie Botting
Science Teacher
Broward County School District
Fort Lauderdale, Florida

Jeffrey C. Callister
Science Teacher
Newburgh Free Academy
Newburgh, New York

Colleen Campos
Science Teacher
Laredo Middle School
Aurora, Colorado

Holly Estes
Science Teacher
Hale Middle School
Stow, Massachusetts

Edward Evans
Former Science Teacher
Hilton Central School
Hilton, New York

Greg Hutton
Science and Health Curriculum
    Coordinator
School Board of Sarasota County
Sarasota, Florida

Jan Jenner, Ph.D.
Science Writer
Talladega, Alabama

Lauren Magruder
Science Teacher
St. Michael's Country Day School
Newport, Rhode Island

Steve Miller
Science Writer
State College, Pennsylvania

Emery Pineo
Science Instructor
Barrington Middle School
Barrington, Rhode Island

Karen Riley Sievers
Science Teacher
Callanan Middle School
Des Moines, Iowa

Sharon M. Stroud
Science Teacher
Widefield High School
Colorado Springs, Colorado

Reading Consultant

Bonnie B. Armbruster, Ph.D.
Department of Curriculum
    and Instruction
University of Illinois
Champaign, Illinois

Interdisciplinary Consultant

Heidi Hayes Jacobs, Ed.D.
Teachers College
Columbia University
New York, New York

Safety Consultants

W. H. Breazeale, Ph.D.
Department of Chemistry
College of Charleston
Charleston, South Carolina

Ruth Hathaway, Ph.D.
Hathaway Consulting
Cape Girardeau, Missouri

Content Reviewers

Tufts University Program Reviewers

Behrouz Abedian, Ph.D.
Department of Mechanical
  Engineering

Wayne Chudyk, Ph.D.
Department of Civil and
  Environmental Engineering

Eliana De Bernardez-Clark, Ph.D.
Department of Chemical
  Engineering

Anne Marie Desmarais, Ph.D.
Department of Civil and
  Environmental Engineering

David L. Kaplan, Ph.D.
Department of Chemical
  Engineering

Paul Kelley, Ph.D.
Department of Electro-Optics

George S. Mumford, Ph.D.
Professor of Astronomy, Emeritus

Jan A. Pechenik, Ph.D.
Department of Biology

Livia Racz, Ph.D.
Department of Mechanical
  Engineering

Robert Rifkin, M.D.
School of Medicine

Jack Ridge, Ph.D.
Department of Geology

Chris Swan, Ph.D.
Department of Civil and
  Environmental Engineering

Peter Y. Wong, Ph.D.
Department of Mechanical
  Engineering

Teacher Reviewers

Stephanie Anderson
Sierra Vista Junior
  High School
Canyon Country,
  California

John W. Anson
Mesa Intermediate School
Palmdale, California

Pamela Arline
Lake Taylor Middle School
Norfolk, Virginia

Lynn Beason
College Station Jr. High
  School
College Station, Texas

Richard Bothmer
Hollis School District
Hollis, New Hampshire

Jeffrey C. Callister
Newburgh Free Academy
Newburgh, New York

Judy D'Albert
Harvard Day School
Corona Del Mar,
  California

Betty Scott Dean
Guilford County Schools
McLeansville,
  North Carolina

Sarah C. Duff
Baltimore City Public
  Schools
Baltimore, Maryland

Melody Law Ewey
Holmes Junior High
  School
Davis, California

Sherry L. Fisher
Lake Zurich Middle
  School North
Lake Zurich, Illinois

Melissa Gibbons
Fort Worth ISD
Fort Worth, Texas

Debra J. Goodding
Kraemer Middle School
Placentia, California

Jack Grande
Weber Middle School
Port Washington,
  New York

Steve Hills
Riverside Middle School
Grand Rapids, Michigan

Sandra M. Justin
Swift Junior High School
Oakville, Connecticut

Carol Ann Lionello
Kraemer Middle School
Placentia, California

Jaime A. Morales
Henry T. Gage Middle
  School
Huntington Park,
  California

Patsy Partin
Cameron Middle School
Nashville, Tennessee

Deedra H. Robinson
Newport News Public
  Schools
Newport News, Virginia

Bonnie Scott
Clack Middle School
Abilene, Texas

Charles M. Sears
Belzer Middle School
Indianapolis, Indiana

Barbara M. Strange
Ferndale Middle School
High Point,
  North Carolina

Jackie Louise Ulfig
Ford Middle School
Allen, Texas

Kathy Usina
Belzer Middle School
Indianapolis, Indiana

Heidi M. von Oetinger
L'Anse Creuse Public
  School
Harrison Township,
  Michigan

Pam Watson
Hill Country Middle
  School
Austin, Texas

Activity Field Testers

Nicki Bibbo
Russell Street School
Littleton, Massachusetts

Connie Boone
Fletcher Middle School
Jacksonville Beach, Florida

Rose-Marie Botting
Broward County
    School District
Fort Lauderdale, Florida

Colleen Campos
Laredo Middle School
Aurora, Colorado

Elizabeth Chait
W. L. Chenery Middle
    School
Belmont, Massachusetts

Holly Estes
Hale Middle School
Stow, Massachusetts

Laura Hapgood
Plymouth Community
    Intermediate School
Plymouth, Massachusetts

Sandra M. Harris
Winman Junior High
    School
Warwick, Rhode Island

Jason Ho
Walter Reed Middle School
Los Angeles, California

Joanne Jackson
Winman Junior High
    School
Warwick, Rhode Island

Mary F. Lavin
Plymouth Community
    Intermediate School
Plymouth, Massachusetts

James MacNeil, Ph.D.
Concord Public Schools
Concord, Massachusetts

Lauren Magruder
St. Michael's Country
    Day School
Newport, Rhode Island

Jeanne Maurand
Glen Urquhart School
Beverly Farms, Massachusetts

Warren Phillips
Plymouth Community
    Intermediate School
Plymouth, Massachusetts

Carol Pirtle
Hale Middle School
Stow, Massachusetts

Kathleen M. Poe
Kirby-Smith Middle
    School
Jacksonville, Florida

Cynthia B. Pope
Ruffner Middle School
Norfolk, Virginia

Anne Scammell
Geneva Middle School
Geneva, New York

Karen Riley Sievers
Callanan Middle School
Des Moines, Iowa

David M. Smith
Howard A. Eyer Middle
    School
Macungie, Pennsylvania

Derek Strohschneider
Plymouth Community
    Intermediate School
Plymouth, Massachusetts

Sallie Teames
Rosemont Middle School
Fort Worth, Texas

Gene Vitale
Parkland Middle School
McHenry, Illinois

Zenovia Young
Meyer Levin Junior
    High School (IS 285)
Brooklyn, New York

Contents

Earth Science

Unit 2 Inside Earth

PRENTICE HALL
SCIENCE EXPLORER
EARTH SCIENCE

Unit 3   Earth's Changing Surface

Unit 4　Earth's Waters

PRENTICE HALL
SCIENCE
EXPLORER
EARTH SCIENCE

Unit 5   Weather and Climate

Unit 6　Astronomy

PRENTICE HALL
SCIENCE EXPLORER
EARTH SCIENCE

Reference Section

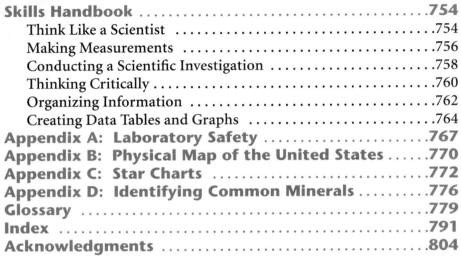

Activities

DISCOVER
Exploration and inquiry before reading

Sharpen your *Skills*

Practice of specific science inquiry skills

TRY THIS
Reinforcement of key concepts

Skills Lab
In-depth practice of inquiry skills

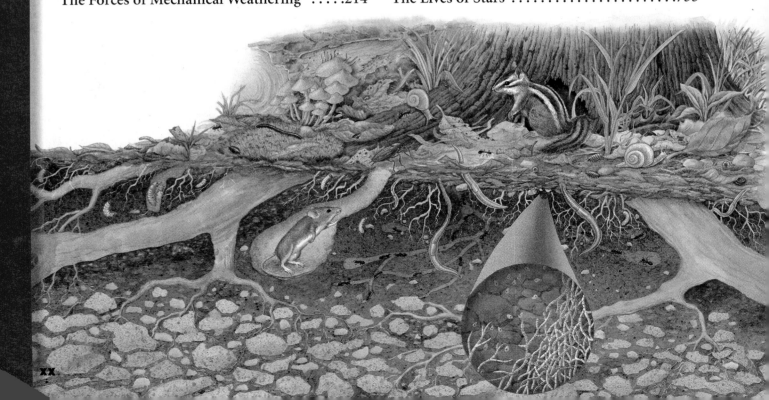

Interdisciplinary Activities

Connection

Searching for the home of
COMETS

It's a long way from astronomer Jane Luu's office in the Netherlands to the mountaintop in Hawaii where she searches the night sky. But astronomers need dark skies, far from city lights. They also need clean, clear air to see deep into the solar system. That's why Jane Luu travels all the way to the high mountain observatory in Hawaii. Jane Luu has traveled long distances before. Born in Vietnam, she came to the United States at the age of 12.

"As a kid in Vietnam," she says, "I didn't have a single class in science. But after studying physics in college, I got a job at the Jet Propulsion Laboratory, the place where they track all the unmanned space missions. It was a summer job, pretty unimportant stuff. But when I saw the pictures taken by *Voyager I* and *Voyager II* in the mid-1980s, I thought they were spectacular. Those pictures of the planets were what made me go to graduate school in planetary astronomy."

Object in the
Kuiper Belt

Dr. Jane Luu
arrived in the United States from Vietnam as a young girl. Dr. Luu studied physics at Stanford University in California and astronomy at the Massachusetts Institute of Technology. She now works at Leiden University in the Netherlands.

TALKING WITH DR. JANE LUU

What Jane Luu looks at now lies just beyond the farthest planets in our solar system. It's a ring made of millions of pieces of ice-rock that circle the sun. Luu and her co-worker David Jewitt first discovered these objects in 1992. The rocky planet Pluto is the biggest object in this ring, which is called the Kuiper (KY pur) Belt. Pluto travels through space along with thousands of other objects that Luu and Jewitt have named "Plutinos" (little Plutos). Objects in the Kuiper Belt sometimes escape from the belt and approach the sun. The sun's heat then makes them light up and they become comets.

Q *Why did you start searching for the Kuiper Belt?*

A There were two reasons. We wanted to know if there was anything beyond Neptune besides Pluto. Why should that space be empty when there were so many planets and smaller objects nearer the sun? Scientists had predicted there would be a group of comets not too far beyond Neptune, but no one had seen these objects. There were other people trying to find the same thing, so it was a bit of a race. We're glad we won it.

Q *Where did you start looking?*

A Most things in the solar system are in a plane, a basically flat disk where the planets and the sun are. So you start looking there. Then, you want to look opposite the sun. Also, you look at a time of the year when the Milky Way, our home galaxy, isn't in the part of the sky you're

These color-enhanced images of Jupiter (above), Saturn (right), and Neptune (below) were taken from a *Voyager* spacecraft.

searching. That's so the light of all those stars doesn't make it hard to see.

Q *Once you knew where to look, what did you do?*

A We took pictures. We started in 1987 and saw the first object in 1992, five years later. In the beginning we didn't have a computer at the telescope that was fast enough to analyze the pictures. So we'd make three pictures and then take them home to analyze. We'd take images, say a half-hour apart, of the same piece of sky. Then we'd look to see if any point of light had moved

1

These observatories are located on top of Mauna Kea, an inactive volcano in Hawaii.

The Kuiper Belt lies beyond the part of the solar system where the planets revolve around the sun. Objects in the Kuiper Belt revolve far from Earth and the sun. Pluto's orbit is on a different plane from the other planets.

between the three pictures. If it moves, we know it's near us in the solar system, and not a distant star. Since our first discovery in 1992, scientists have found many more objects in the Kuiper Belt. David and I have found about two thirds of those.

Q *Do you stay up all night?*

A Yes, we have to. Telescope time is valuable so you don't want to waste a single minute. We observe for a week or so, staying up for 5 or 6 nights in a row. It's hard work, switching from a daytime to a nighttime schedule. In Hawaii, we observe on top of Mauna Kea volcano at 14,000 feet. So we have to add an extra night at the beginning to get used to the altitude and thin air.

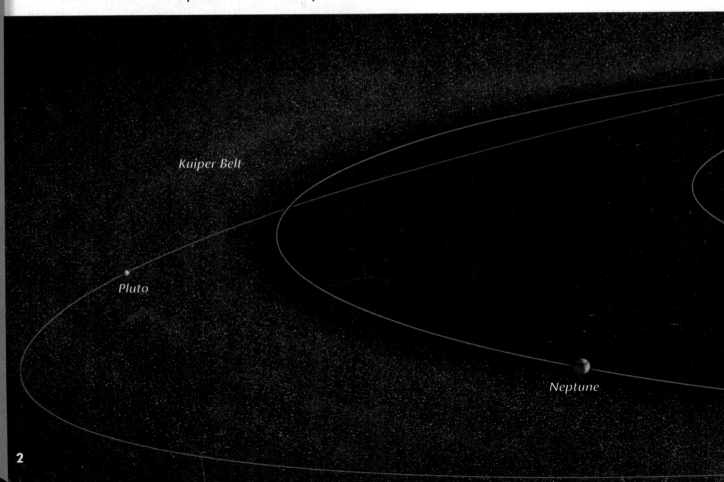

Kuiper Belt

Pluto

Neptune

Q *Five years is a long time to wait for a discovery. Didn't you get discouraged?*

A We told ourselves that after we'd covered a certain part of the sky without finding anything, we would stop. We were pretty near that limit. But the newer cameras could take bigger pictures of the sky. They helped us do in a month what at first had taken two years. We could see something and know right away where to look the next night.

Because I've been lucky, I've participated in discoveries. There's such a satisfaction you get when you solve a puzzle, when you find out something that nobody has known before. And it's really fun after a lot of hard work, when you've finally found what you wanted to find.

In Your Journal

Jane Luu describes working night after night for five years, observing and recording data for one part of the night sky. "It was so time-consuming, and we didn't know if anything was going to come from it." Fortunately, in the end, she was rewarded. How did Jane Luu's persistence, as well as her skill, energy, and step-by-step reasoning, lead to her success?

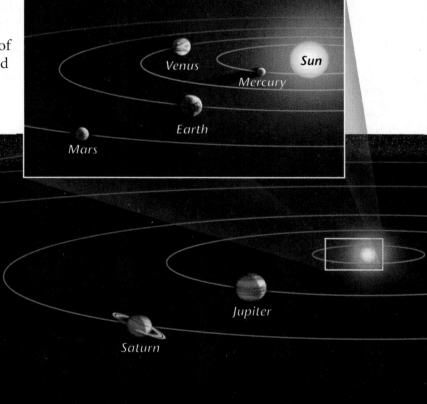

What is SCIENCE?

GUIDE FOR READING

◆ What is science?

◆ What methods do scientists use?

◆ What are the branches of Earth science?

Reading Tip Before you begin reading, make a list of boldfaced terms. As you read, write the definition for each term.

Astronomer Jane Luu's search for the home of comets began with curiosity. Her curiosity led her to ask many questions: Where do comets come from? What is at the outer edge of the solar system? In asking these questions, Dr. Luu was acting like a scientist, a person who studies the natural world.

Science is a way of learning about the natural world and the knowledge gained through that process. The word science comes from a Latin word that means "knowing." The natural world includes not just Earth, but everything in the universe.

As they study the natural world, scientists use scientific inquiry. **Scientific inquiry** is the diverse ways in which scientists explore problems and seek to answer questions about the natural world. Scientific inquiry involves how scientists think as well as the techniques they use.

About 500 years ago, the astronomer Copernicus developed this model of the solar system. *Comparing and Contrasting How does this model compare with the modern one on pages 2–3?* ▶

4

Using a telescope designed for the purpose, this student can safely observe a solar eclipse.

Thinking Like a Scientist

As you study science, you will need to think like a scientist. In fact, you probably have used some kinds of scientific thinking already. For example, as you get ready for school in the morning, you may observe that the sky is cloudy. Then you infer, or make an inference, that rain is likely. Observation and inference are just two of the skills that scientists use.

Observation involves using sight, hearing, smell, and sometimes taste to gather information. An **inference** is an interpretation based on your observation and prior knowledge. See the Skills Handbook on pages 754–766 to learn more about observing, inferring, and other skills that will help you think like a scientist.

To find answers to her questions Jane Luu used observation and inference. She also used other kinds of scientific thinking, including predicting and making models.

Years before Jane Luu made her discovery, a scientist named Gerard Kuiper predicted that there might be comets at the outer edge of the solar system. Kuiper based his prediction on the idea that some material may have been left over after the solar system formed. Kuiper thought that this leftover material would be found in the form of icy comets beyond the orbit of Neptune. Jane Luu wanted to find out if Kuiper's prediction was correct.

Before Dr. Luu's discovery of the Kuiper belt, scientists' model of the solar system showed empty space between Neptune and Pluto. After Dr. Luu's discovery, scientists changed their model of the solar system to include the Kuiper belt. Scientists named the Kuiper belt in honor of Gerard Kuiper, who had predicted its existence.

✓ *Checkpoint* *What is the difference between an observation and an inference?*

Scientific Methods

Scientists use many methods as they search for answers to questions about the natural world. **Scientific methods generally include posing questions, developing and testing hypotheses, and drawing conclusions. Scientists often test hypotheses by conducting controlled experiments.**

In the 1800s, scientists applied scientific methods to the study of glaciers. Glaciers are usually found on and around high mountains, such as the Alps in Switzerland. Two hundred years ago, scientists knew very little about glaciers. Some scientists thought that glaciers could move. But others claimed that it was impossible for such huge masses of ice to move. To settle this dispute, some scientists in Switzerland decided to investigate.

Posing Questions
Scientists begin with a question about something that is unexplained. The Swiss scientists studying glaciers asked, "Do glaciers move?"

Developing Hypotheses
After posing a question, scientists often gather information or make observations. They then use this information to form a hypothesis. A **hypothesis** is a possible explanation for observations that relate to a scientific question. A hypothesis can be tested by observation or experiment. Scientists do not accept a hypothesis after just one test. Repeated tests must provide evidence that supports the hypothesis.

People in the Alps had long observed boulders in the valleys below glaciers. Did that mean that moving ice had carried the boulders? Such observations led scientists to the hypothesis that glaciers move slowly over the land.

☑ *Checkpoint* *What is a hypothesis?*

Designing a Controlled Experiment
The controlled experiment is an important method that scientists use to test hypotheses. A **controlled experiment** is a test of a hypothesis under conditions established by the scientist. In a controlled

The Gorner glacier winds down from high peaks in the Swiss Alps. The dark bands in the glacier are pieces of rock broken off and picked up by the moving ice.

experiment, a scientist determines how one particular variable affects the outcome of the experiment. A **variable** is one of the factors that can change in an experiment.

The variable that a scientist changes is called the **manipulated variable.** The manipulated variable is also called the independent variable. The variable that changes because of the manipulated variable is the **responding variable,** or dependent variable.

In a controlled experiment, scientists control, or keep constant, all other variables. Controlling variables enables the scientist to eliminate the effects of the other variables as factors in the results of the experiment. You will design and conduct controlled experiments at many points in this textbook. You can learn more about controlled experiments in the Skills Handbook on pages 758–759.

Testing Hypotheses
In the real world, conducting a controlled experiment in Earth science is often difficult or impossible. The objects studied by Earth scientists can be very large. And Earth scientists often study processes that take millions of years! Earth scientists usually test hypotheses through observation and measurement, as did the Swiss scientists who studied glaciers. The figure above shows how these scientists measured the movement of a glacier.

Collecting and Interpreting Data
The facts, figures, and other evidence gained through observation are called **data.** Observation often involves measurements to obtain data that can be expressed as numbers. Scientists then interpret the data to determine whether or not the data support their hypothesis.

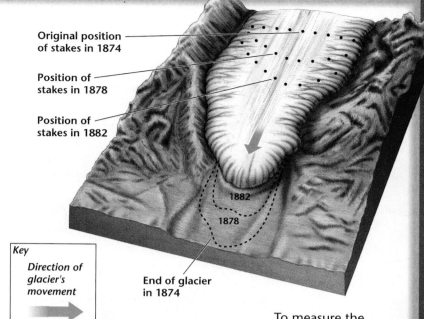

Original position of stakes in 1874

Position of stakes in 1878

Position of stakes in 1882

Key
Direction of glacier's movement

1882
1878

End of glacier in 1874

To measure the movement of a glacier, scientists drove a row of stakes into the glacier. They then measured how much the stakes moved in relation to the rocky sides of the valley. *Interpreting Diagrams Which part of the glacier appears to be moving the fastest? How can you tell?*

Measuring Measurement enables scientists to record what they observe in a way that others can understand easily. That's because units of measurement used by scientists are the same worldwide. This system of measurement is the International System of Units, also called SI units. For more about measurement and SI units, see pages 756–757 of the Skills Handbook.

Drawing Conclusions Once scientists have reviewed their data, they are ready to draw a conclusion. The data may support the hypothesis or show that the hypothesis was incorrect. Sometimes, no conclusion can be reached, and more data are needed.

The Swiss scientists studying glaciers concluded that their data supported their hypothesis. Glaciers do indeed move slowly. But the scientists' data also revealed a surprise. As the glacier was moving downhill, it was also melting back at its lower end. A surprising finding like this one can lead scientists to form new hypotheses.

You can practice developing hypotheses in the Skills Lab on page 9. Review Appendix A before you begin.

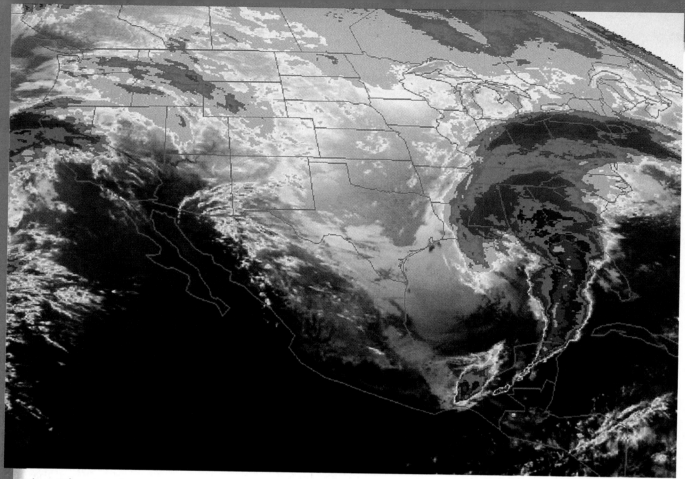

A weather map is a model of changing conditions in Earth's atmosphere. This map, based on satellite data, shows a storm over the eastern United States. *Interpreting Maps Which color on the map do you think represents areas of heavy rain? Explain your answer.*

Models and Simulations To test a hypothesis, Earth scientists may also create models or simulations. A simulation is a model that imitates something in the real world. Scientists compare the results obtained from a simulation with known facts. This helps them decide whether this evidence supports the hypothesis.

Today, scientists know much more than they did during the 1800s about how glaciers move. For example, scientists working in laboratories have used simulations to model how glaciers move. The scientists studied samples of hot metal to see how the metal changed shape when under great pressure. The metal served as a model of the slowly flowing ice in a glacier. Studying such models helps scientists develop new hypotheses and ways of testing them. Above, you can see another type of model: a weather map.

Scientific Theories

Since the 1800s, scientists studying glaciers have made repeated observations of glacial movement. These observations confirmed the Swiss scientists' work. For a hypothesis to be widely accepted, other scientists must be able to repeat an experiment and obtain the same results.

As scientists study the natural world, they do more than just collect facts. Their goal is to develop concepts that explain their observations. These concepts are called scientific theories. A **scientific theory** is a well-tested scientific concept that explains a wide range of observations. An accepted theory has withstood repeated tests. But if tests fail to support a theory, scientists change the theory or abandon it.

✓ Checkpoint What is a scientific theory?

Speeding Up Evaporation

Evaporation is the process by which water vapor enters Earth's atmosphere from the ocean and other surface waters. Rates of evaporation determine the amount of moisture in the atmosphere. Atmospheric moisture in turn affects the formation of clouds and helps to determine whether it will rain.

Problem

What factors increase the rate at which water evaporates?

Materials (per student)

water	plastic dropper
2 plastic petri dishes	1 petri dish cover
3 index cards	paper towels
stopwatch	lamp

Procedure

Part 1 Effect of Heat

1. How do you think heating a water sample will affect how fast it evaporates? Record your hypothesis.
2. Place each petri dish on an index card.
3. Add a single drop of water to each of the petri dishes. Try to make the two drops the same size.
4. Position the lamp over one of the dishes as a heat source. Turn on the light. Make sure the light does not shine on the other dish. **CAUTION:** The light bulb will become very hot. Avoid touching the bulb or getting water on it.
5. Observe the dishes every 3 minutes to see which sample evaporates faster. Record your result.

Part 2 Effect of Wind

6. How do you think fanning the water will affect how fast it evaporates? Record your hypothesis.
7. Dry both petri dishes and place them over the index cards. Add a drop of water to each dish as you did in Step 3.
8. Use an index card to fan one of the dishes for 5 minutes. Be careful not to fan the other dish.
9. Observe the dishes to see which sample evaporates faster. Record your result.

Analyze and Conclude

1. Did the evidence support both hypotheses? If not, which hypothesis was not supported?
2. Make a general statement about factors that increase the rate at which water evaporates.
3. **Think About It** What everyday experiences helped you make your hypotheses at the beginning of the experiment? Explain how hypotheses differ from guesses.

Design an Experiment

How do you think increasing the surface area of a water sample will affect how fast it evaporates? Write your hypothesis and then design an experiment to test it. Check your plan with your teacher before you begin.

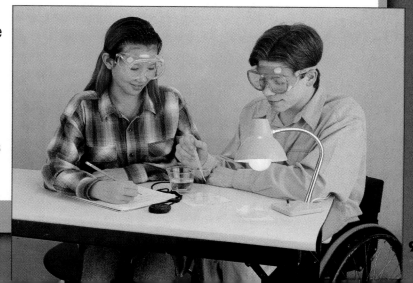

Laboratory Safety

As you use this textbook, you will conduct many Earth science experiments and other activities. In experiments and activities, it is very important to think about safety. Always follow your teacher's instructions on safety in the laboratory. Before conducting any experiments, review with your teacher the Science Safety Rules in Appendix A on pages 767–769. Also watch for the safety symbols that appear at the beginning of a lab or activity. The symbols alert you to needed precautions, such as wearing goggles to protect your eyes. Learn to recognize the safety symbols and know what precautions they require you to take. The safety symbols are listed in Appendix A on page 767.

Technology and the Internet in Earth Science

Today, many Earth scientists use the latest technology to explore Earth's surface and outer space. Computers, robots, satellites, and space probes are just some of the tools used by Earth scientists. For example, many different satellites constantly scan Earth's surface, collecting data for Earth scientists.

Technology helps scientists collect data. But technology also helps scientists communicate their discoveries to other scientists and to the public. You can find large amounts of information about current research and discoveries in Earth science on the Internet. Web sites maintained by several United States government agencies such as NASA, the U.S. Geological Survey (USGS), and the National Oceanic and Atmospheric Administration (NOAA) are often excellent sources of information. The Web sites of private research institutes and scientific associations also can be very helpful. These Web sites provide data about everything from earthquakes and volcanoes to hurricanes.

Branches of Earth Science

Throughout history, people have observed the Earth around them and the skies above them. Over thousands of years, scientists have built a body of knowledge based on these observations. **Earth science** is the term for this knowledge about Earth and its place in the universe.

Earth science has several different branches. **In this book, you will learn about geology, oceanography, meteorology, and astronomy.**

Geology The first three units of this book deal mainly with geology. Geology is the study of the solid Earth. **Geologists** study the forces that have shaped Earth throughout its long history. Geologists study the chemical and physical characteristics of rock,

These Earth science students are using the Internet to find information on oceanography.

the material that forms Earth's hard surface. Geologists describe land-forms, the features sculptured in rock and soil by water, wind, and waves.

Oceanography In Unit 4, you will learn about the water that covers about 75 percent of Earth's surface. Oceanography is the study of Earth's oceans. **Oceanographers** study every-thing from the chemistry of ocean water to the shape of the ocean floor to living things in the ocean's depths. Scientists in related fields study Earth's fresh water in lakes, rivers, and glaciers and beneath the surface.

Meteorology Unit 5 presents meteorology. Meteorology is the study of Earth's atmosphere. Meteorologists do much more than just forecast tomorrow's weather. **Meteorologists** are scientists who gather information about conditions in the atmosphere from around the world. Scientists in related fields study the forces that slowly change Earth's climate.

Astronomy Astronomy, the study of the universe beyond Earth, is the subject of Unit 6. Some **astronomers,** like Jane Luu, focus on the solar system. Other astronomers observe stars and galaxies in an effort to under-stand the universe and its history.

Environmental Science Some Earth scientists, called **environmental scientists,** study Earth's environment and resources. Environmental scientists work together to determine the effects of human activities on Earth's land, air, water, and living things. They try to solve problems, such as pollution, that result from the use of resources. Throughout the first five units of this textbook, you will find examples of how environ-mental science relates to the other Earth sciences.

As you can see in *Exploring Careers in Earth Science,* Earth scien-tists do many different things.

☑ *Checkpoint* What is Earth science?

Chandra X-ray Observatory is a satellite placed in orbit in 1999 to detect X-rays given off by distant stars and galaxies.
Posing Questions
What do you think are some questions that astronomers would like to answer with data from Chandra's *observations?*

EXPLORING Careers in Earth Science

If you worked as an Earth scientist, you might release a weather balloon into the atmosphere. Or you might pilot a submersible deep beneath the ocean or chip samples of rock from a mountain top.

Geologists

The work of geologists often takes them outdoors—from caves beneath the surface (above) to mountainsides (below).

Oceanographers

These oceanographers have donned scuba gear to observe the interactions of living things with the environment on a measured square of ocean floor.

Astronomers

Astronomers use radio telescopes like this one in New Mexico to detect radio waves from distant stars and galaxies.

Meteorologists

Meteorologists use data from weather satellites to monitor storms such as hurricanes. Computers are important in processing and displaying weather data.

Environmental Scientists

These environmental scientists are gathering data by testing water samples to find evidence of environmental change or pollution.

Study Guide

Key Ideas

◆ Science is a way of learning about the natural world and the knowledge gained from that process.

◆ Scientific methods generally include posing questions, developing and testing hypotheses, and drawing conclusions. Scientists often test hypotheses by conducting controlled experiments.

◆ A scientific theory is a well-tested scientific concept that explains a wide range of observations.

◆ The System of International Units (SI) is the standard system of measurement in science.

◆ In experiments and activities, it is very important to think about safety. Always follow your teacher's instructions on safety in the laboratory.

◆ Earth science has several branches, including geology, the study of the solid Earth, and oceanography, the study of the oceans. Meteorology is the science concerned with Earth's atmosphere and the processes that cause the weather. Astronomy is the exploration of the origin and structure of planets, moons, stars, and galaxies.

Key Terms

science	responding variable
scientific inquiry	data
observation	scientific theory
inference	Earth science
hypothesis	geologists
controlled	oceanographers
experiment	meteorologists
variable	astronomers
manipulated variable	environmental scientists

Reviewing Content

 For more review of key concepts, see the Interactive Student Tutorial *CD-ROM.*

True or False

If the statement is true, write true. If it is false, change the underlined word or words to make the statement true.

1. A <u>variable</u> is an interpretation of an observation.
2. The information that a scientist obtains through observation is called <u>data</u>.
3. If an experiment fails to support a <u>scientific theory</u>, scientists will change the theory or abandon it.
4. <u>Meteorologists</u> are scientists who study stars, planets, and other bodies in space.
5. <u>Environmental scientists</u> study the effects of human activities on Earth's land, air, water, and living things.

Multiple Choice

Choose the answer that best completes the sentence.

6. Scientists seek to answer questions about the natural world in a process of
   a. modeling.   **b.** scientific inquiry.
   c. predicting.   **d.** developing hypotheses.
7. An explanation that can be tested by observation or experiment is called a(n)
   a. experiment.   **b.** scientific theory.
   c. scientific fact.   **d.** hypothesis.
8. One of the factors that can change in an experiment is called a(n)
   a. variable.   **b.** theory.
   c. hypothesis.   **d.** observation.
9. One way in which scientists test a hypothesis is by
   a. asking questions.
   b. drawing conclusions.
   c. interpreting data.
   d. conducting a controlled experiment.
10. An Earth scientist who studies the chemical and physical characteristics of rock is a(n)
    a. oceanographer.
    b. geologist.
    c. meteorologist.
    d. environmental scientist.

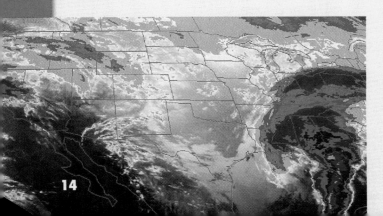

Checking Concepts

11. In your own words, explain briefly what science is.
12. Give an example of an observation of the natural world that you have made. Then give an example of an inference that you made based on that observation. Explain.
13. Why is it often difficult to use controlled experiments to test hypotheses in Earth science? Explain.
14. What is the difference between a hypothesis and a scientific theory?
15. Explain how a scientist would use the data gathered through a controlled experiment.
16. Explain the importance of following safety rules in laboratory experiments.
17. Which kind of Earth scientist would you consult to find out what a certain rock is made of and how it formed?

Thinking Critically

18. **Problem Solving** You may have heard the saying, "Red sky at night/Sailor's delight." This expression is a hypothesis: A colorful red sunset means there will be fair weather the next day. Describe a scientific method of testing this hypothesis.
19. **Relating Cause and Effect** In a controlled experiment, why do scientists try to control all of the variables except one?
20. **Making Judgments** As a result of just one experiment, a scientist finds evidence that supports a hypothesis. Should other scientists around the world accept this hypothesis? Explain your answer.
21. **Classifying** Which Earth science would investigate the surface temperature of a star? Water temperature at the bottom of the sea? Air temperature at the top of a mountain?

Test Preparation

Use these questions to prepare for standardized tests.

Read the passage. Then answer Questions 22–25.

It may surprise you to learn that the climate in a large city can be different from the climate just outside the city. Climate is the average, year-to-year, weather conditions in a region. Meteorologists have collected data on these climate differences. The data show that the climate in a city is often warmer and wetter than the climate in the nearby countryside. Cities are also less sunny and windy than the country around them.

Why are cities warmer? One reason is that buildings and paved surfaces absorb and store more of the sun's energy than do grass, crops, and trees. Another reason is that cars, factories, heating, and air conditioning in cities all give off heat.

Scientists think several factors cause increased rainfall in cities. One hypothesis is that the built-up areas of a city form an obstacle to passing storms. As a result, the storms take longer to move over the city, allowing more rain to fall.

22. The best title for this reading selection is
    a. Sunny Weather Ahead
    b. Meteorologists at Work
    c. The Climates of Cities
    d. What Causes Storms?
23. Meteorologists found that the climate in a city differs from the climate in the country by
    a. asking city residents.
    b. collecting data.
    c. observing clouds.
    d. performing controlled experiments.
24. How would you predict a city could lower its outdoor temperature in the summer?
    a. by building more factories
    b. by having more parks with grass and trees
    c. by putting more cars on the road
    d. by adding more air conditioners
25. The idea that a city's buildings can increase rainfall by slowing down a passing storm is an example of a(n)
    a. variable.   b. scientific theory.
    c. determining factor. d. hypothesis.

CHAPTER
1 Mapping Earth's Surface

WEB ACTIVITY www.phschool.com

SECTION 1 Exploring Earth's Surface

Discover **What Is the Land Like Around Your School?**

SECTION 2 Models of Earth

Discover **How Can You Flatten the Curved Earth?**
Try This **Where in the World?**
Real-World Lab **A Borderline Case**

Integrating Technology

SECTION 3 Maps in the Computer Age

Discover **Can You Make a Pixel Picture?**
Science at Home **Maps in the News**

Getting on the Map

A shining river winds across a green plain. A plain is one of Earth's landforms. In this chapter, you will learn about plains and other landforms such as mountains and plateaus. You will also learn how to read and use maps that show the shape, height, and slope of Earth's surface. For this chapter project, you will select a small piece of land and draw a map of its physical features.

Your Goal To create a scale map of a small area of your neighborhood.

To complete this project you must
◆ work with your teacher or an adult family member
◆ choose and measure a small square or rectangular piece of land
◆ use a compass to locate north and draw a map to scale
◆ use symbols and a legend to represent natural and human-made features of the land

Get Started Start looking for a suitable site. Your site should be about 300 to 1,000 square meters in area. It could be part of a park, playground, or backyard. Look for an area that includes interesting natural features such as trees, a stream, and changes in elevation or slope. There may be some human-made structures on your site, such as a park bench or sidewalk.

Check Your Progress You'll be working on this project as you study this chapter. To keep your project on track, look for Check Your Progress boxes at the following points.
Section 1 Review, page 24: Choose a site, measure the boundaries, and sketch all the physical features.
Section 2 Review, page 30: Brainstorm ideas for symbols to include on your map.
Section 4 Review, page 39: Complete the final draft of your map, including a key and map scale.

Present Your Project At the end of this chapter (page 43), you will present your map to the class.

The Cheyenne River flows through Buffalo Gap National Grassland near Red Shirt, South Dakota.

SECTION 4 Topographic Maps

Discover Can a Map Show Relief?
Sharpen Your Skills Interpreting Data
Skills Lab A Map in a Pan

SECTION
1 Exploring Earth's Surface

DISCOVER · ACTIVITY · · ·

What Is the Land Like Around Your School?

1. On a piece of paper, draw a small square to represent your school.

2. Choose a word that describes the type of land near your school, such as flat, hilly, or rolling. Write the word next to the square.

3. Use a magnetic compass to determine the general direction of north. Assume that north is at the top of your piece of paper.

4. If you travel due north 1 kilometer from your school, what type of land do you find? Choose a word to describe the land in this area. Write that word to the north of the square.

5. Repeat Step 4 for areas located 1 kilometer east, south, and west of your school.

Think It Over
Forming Operational Definitions What phrase could you use to describe the land in your area?

GUIDE FOR READING

◆ What determines the topography of Earth's surface?

◆ What are the main types of landforms?

◆ What are the four "spheres" that make up Earth's surface?

Reading Tip Before you read, preview *Exploring Landforms* on page 21. Make a list of questions you have about landforms.

I n 1804, an expedition set out from St. Louis to explore the land between the Mississippi River and the Pacific Ocean. The United States had just purchased a part of this vast territory, called Louisiana, from France. Before the Louisiana Purchase, the United States stretched from the Atlantic coast westward to the Mississippi River. Few United States citizens had traveled west of the Mississippi. None had ever traveled over land all the way to the Pacific.

Led by Meriwether Lewis and William Clark, the expedition traveled up the Missouri River, crossed the Rocky Mountains, followed the Columbia River to the Pacific Ocean—and then returned. The purpose of the expedition was to map America's interior and discover resources.

Topography

On the journey to the Pacific, the Lewis and Clark expedition traveled more than 5,000 kilometers across the continent of North America. As they traveled, Lewis and Clark observed many changes in topography. **Topography** is the shape of the land. An area's topography may be flat, sloping, hilly, or mountainous.

Figure 1 While traveling down the Columbia River, the Lewis and Clark expedition met the Chinook people.

The topography of an area is determined by the area's elevation, relief, and landforms. The desktop where you do homework probably has piles of books, papers, and other objects of different sizes and shapes. Your desktop has both elevation and relief!

Elevation The height above sea level of a point on Earth's surface is its **elevation.** When Lewis and Clark started in St. Louis, they were about 140 meters above sea level. By the time they reached Lemhi Pass in the Rocky Mountains, they were more than 2,200 meters above sea level.

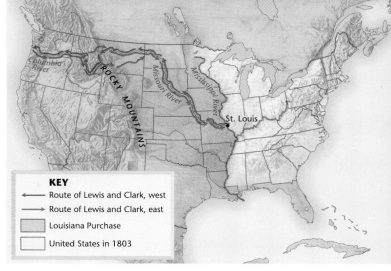

Figure 2 The Lewis and Clark expedition followed major rivers, except when crossing the Rocky Mountains.

Relief The difference in elevation between the highest and lowest parts of an area is its **relief.** As the Lewis and Clark expedition entered the Rocky Mountains, the relief of the land changed from flat or rolling land with low relief to huge mountains with high relief.

Landforms If you followed the route of the Lewis and Clark expedition, you would see many different landforms. A **landform** is a feature of topography formed by the processes that shape Earth's surface. All landforms have elevation and relief. A large area of land where the topography is similar is called a **landform region.** Figure 3 shows the landform regions of the United States, not including Alaska and Hawaii.

☑ *Checkpoint* *What is the difference between elevation and relief?*

Figure 3 The United States has many different landform regions. *Interpreting Maps In what regions are Charleston, Topeka, Santa Fe, and Walla Walla located?*

Landform Regions of the United States

KEY
- Coastal plains
- Interior plains or lowlands
- Mountains
- Plateaus or highlands
- Plains and mountains

Figure 4 The Great Plains of western North America include a vast area of flat or rolling land. The Great Plains are interior plains. *Predicting What do you think would be some differences between interior plains and coastal plains?*

Types of Landforms

Landforms can vary greatly in size and shape—from level plains extending as far as the eye can see, to low, rounded hills that you could climb on foot, to jagged mountains that would take you days to walk around. **There are three main types of landforms: plains, mountains, and plateaus.**

Plains A **plain** is a landform made up of flat or gently rolling land with low relief. A plain that lies along a seacoast is called a coastal plain. In North America, a coastal plain wraps like an apron around the continent's eastern and southeastern shores. Coastal plains have both low elevation and low relief.

A plain that lies away from the coast is called an interior plain. Although interior plains have low relief, their elevation can vary. The broad interior plain of North America is called the Great Plains.

The Great Plains extend from Texas north into Canada. From their eastern border in the states of North and South Dakota, Nebraska, Kansas, Oklahoma, and Texas, the Great Plains stretch west to the Rocky Mountains. At the time of the Lewis and Clark expedition, the Great Plains were a vast grassland.

Figure 5 The Bitterroot Mountains in Idaho are part of the Rocky Mountains system.

Mountains A **mountain** is a landform with high elevation and high relief. Mountains usually occur as part of a mountain range. A **mountain range** is a group of mountains that are closely related in shape, structure, and age. After crossing the Great Plains, the Lewis and Clark expedition crossed a rugged mountain range in Idaho now called the Bitterroot Mountains.

The different mountain ranges in a region make up a mountain system. The Bitterroot Mountains are one mountain range in the mountain system known as the Rocky Mountains.

Mountain ranges and mountain systems in a long, connected chain form a larger unit called a mountain belt. The Rocky Mountains are part of a great mountain belt that stretches down the western sides of North America and South America.

Plateaus A landform that has high elevation and a more or less level surface is called a **plateau.** A plateau is rarely perfectly smooth on top. Streams and rivers may cut into the plateau's surface. The Columbia Plateau in Washington State is an example. The Columbia River, which the Lewis and Clark expedition followed, slices through this plateau. The many layers of rock that make up the Columbia Plateau are about 1,500 meters thick.

☑ *Checkpoint* *What types of landforms have low relief?*

EXPLORING *Landforms*

Mountains, plains, and plateaus are just a few of the many landforms that make up the topography of Earth's surface.

Mountains
A mountain's base usually covers an area of at least several square kilometers, but its peak may rise to a point. Mountains often have steeply sloping sides.

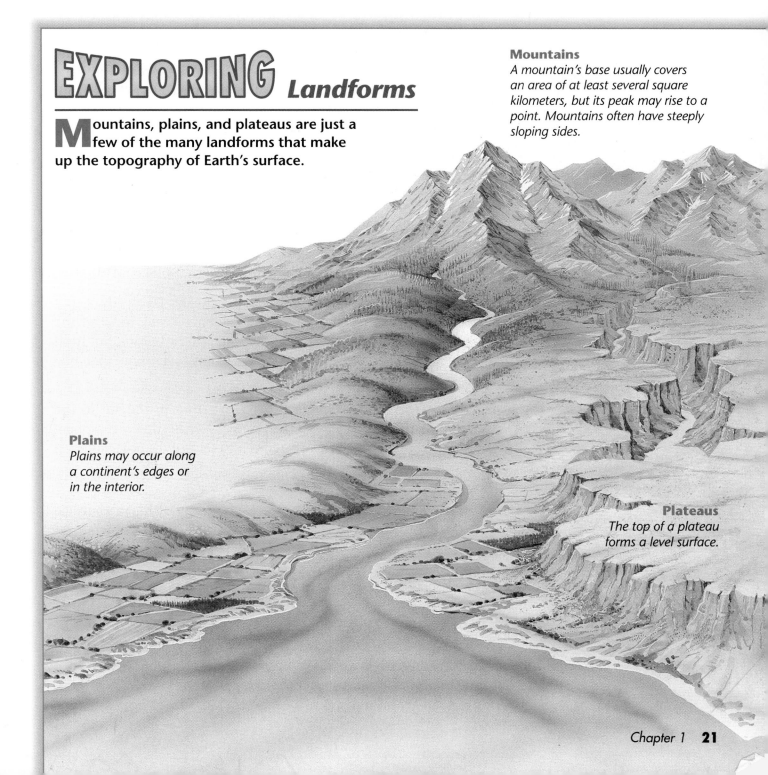

Plains
Plains may occur along a continent's edges or in the interior.

Plateaus
The top of a plateau forms a level surface.

Earth's Four Spheres

Lewis and Clark's two-year journey took them across western North America. Along the way, they observed the land, water, air, and living things. Together, these four things make up everything that is on and around planet Earth. **Scientists divide Earth into four spheres: the lithosphere, atmosphere, hydrosphere, and biosphere.** In this book, you will learn mainly about the lithosphere and how it is affected by each of the other spheres.

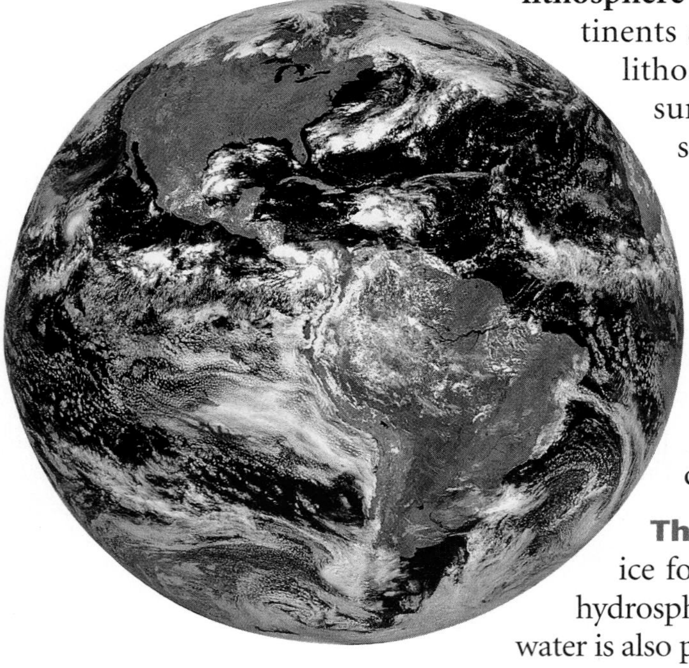

The Lithosphere Earth's solid, rocky outer layer is called the **lithosphere** (LITH uh sfeer). The lithosphere is made up of continents as well as smaller landmasses called islands. The lithosphere extends under the entire ocean floor. Its surface varies from place to place. It ranges from smooth plains to wrinkled hills and valleys to jagged mountain peaks.

The Atmosphere The outermost sphere is the atmosphere (AT muh sfeer), the mixture of gases that surrounds the planet. By far the most abundant gases are nitrogen and oxygen, but the atmosphere also contains water vapor, carbon dioxide, and other gases. When water vapor condenses, it forms the droplets that make up clouds.

The Hydrosphere Earth's oceans, lakes, rivers, and ice form the hydrosphere (HY druh sfeer). Most of the hydrosphere consists of the salt water in the oceans, but fresh water is also part of the hydrosphere. Oceans cover more than two thirds of Earth.

The Biosphere All living things—whether in the air, in the oceans, or on and beneath the land surface—make up the biosphere (BY uh sfeer). The biosphere extends into each of the other spheres.

Earth's Structure

You probably know very well the topography of Earth's surface around your home and school. But what do you know about what's inside Earth? Throughout much of human history, Earth's interior was the subject of myths and unsupported theories. In the 1800s, for example, some people actually thought that Earth was hollow! Then, during the 1900s, scientists determined Earth's overall structure.

As you can see in Figure 7, the dense **core** forms the center of Earth. The core is divided into two layers: the solid inner core and the hot, liquid outer core. Surrounding the core is a thick layer called the **mantle**. The mantle is made of hot but solid

Figure 6 A view from space shows all four of Earth's spheres—the atmosphere, hydrosphere, biosphere, and lithosphere. *Observing What evidence of each of the spheres can you see in the photograph?*

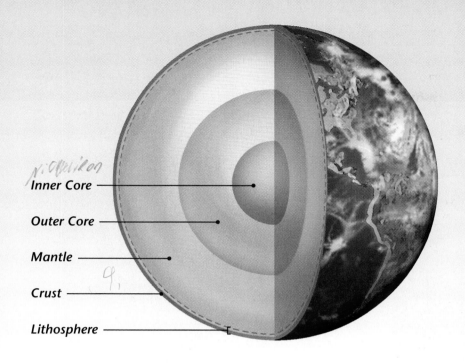

Inner Core

Outer Core

Mantle

Crust

Lithosphere

Figure 7 Earth has a layered structure. In this cutaway view, the mantle and core are shown to scale. But the thickness of the crust has been greatly exaggerated.

material that is less dense than the material that makes up the core. Like a giant golf ball, Earth has a rigid outer covering—the lithosphere. The **crust** is the thin, outer layer of the lithosphere that forms Earth's surface. The crust is made up of hard material called **rock.** The lithosphere also includes part of the upper mantle. You will learn more about the structure of Earth's interior in Chapter 4.

The Development of Geology

The modern science of **geology** began in the late 1700s. Geologists of that time studied the rocks on the surface. These geologists concluded that Earth's past, present, and future are the work of natural forces that slowly build up and wear down the land.

Although these early geologists did not have modern equipment to study Earth, their conclusions were correct. Throughout our planet's long history, its surface has been lifted up, pushed down, bent, and broken by forces beneath the surface. Although the resulting movements of the surface are usually too small and too slow to be directly observed, they are constantly changing Earth's appearance. Thus Earth looks different today from the way it did millions of years ago.

Today, geologists divide the forces that change the surface into two groups: constructive forces and destructive forces. Constructive forces shape the surface by building up mountains and land areas. Destructive forces are those that slowly wear away mountains and, eventually, every other feature on the surface.

Figure 8 The formation of the island of Surtsey is an example of Earth's constructive forces at work. In 1963, a volcanic eruption began in the ocean near Iceland. Within several years, the volcano added 2.5 square kilometers of new land to Earth's surface—the new island of Surtsey.

Two hundred years ago, the science of geology was young. Then, geologists knew only a few facts about Earth's surface. They knew that Earth is a sphere with a radius at the equator of more than 6,000 kilometers. They knew that there are seven continents surrounded by oceans. They knew that the continents were made up of layers of rock that they could sometimes see on the walls of cliffs and the sides of valleys. They began to explore high mountain ranges. However, many riddles remained: How old is Earth? How has Earth's surface changed over time? Why are there oceans, and how did they form? For the past 200 years, geologists have tried to answer these and other questions about the planet.

Section 1 Review

1. What three factors determine the topography of a region?
2. What are the most common types of landforms?
3. Which is larger, a mountain belt or a mountain system?
4. What are the main layers that form Earth's structure?
5. **Thinking Critically Comparing and Contrasting** How are mountains and plateaus similar? How are they different?

Check Your Progress
CHAPTER PROJECT

Choose a site that is as square or rectangular as possible. **CAUTION:** *Make sure to obtain permission from the property owner before you begin.* To start mapping your site, mark the four corners with stakes, stones, or other markers. Measure the boundaries and record the distances on a rough sketch. Your sketch should show your site's topography, plus natural and human-made features. Include a north arrow on your sketch. How can you determine which direction is north?

SECTION
2 Models of Earth

DISCOVER ···ACTIVITY···

How Can You Flatten the Curved Earth?

1. Using a felt-tip pen, make a rough sketch of the outlines of the continents on the surface of an orange or grapefruit.

2. ✂ Using a plastic knife, carefully peel the orange. If possible, keep the peel in one large piece so that the continents remain intact.

3. Try to lay the pieces of orange peel flat on a table.

Think It Over

Observing What happens to the continents when you try to flatten the pieces? What adjustments would you need to make to the shapes of the continents to get them to match their shape and position on a sphere?

You want to invite relatives from out of town to a sports event at your school. You could use words to explain how to find the school: Take the third exit off the highway, turn left at the first traffic light, and so on. But verbal directions can be hard to follow. Instead, you might sketch a map of the best route to your school. Maps use a picture instead of words to tell where things are.

Maps and Globes

Maps and globes show the shape, size, and position of Earth's surface features. A **map** is a model on a flat surface of all or part of Earth's surface as seen from above. A **globe** is a sphere that represents Earth's entire surface. A globe correctly shows the relative size and shape of landmasses and bodies of water, much as if you were viewing Earth from space.

Maps and globes are drawn to scale and use symbols to represent topography and other features on Earth's surface. A map's **scale** relates distance on a map to a distance on Earth's surface. Scale is often given as a ratio. For example, one unit on the map equals 25,000 units on the ground. So one centimeter on the map represents 0.25 kilometers. This scale, "one to twenty-five thousand," would be written "1 : 25,000." Figure 9 shows three ways of giving a map's scale.

GUIDE FOR READING

◆ How do maps and globes represent Earth's surface?

◆ How are latitude and longitude used to locate points on Earth's surface?

Reading Tip Before you read, rewrite the headings in the section as *how, why,* or *what* questions. As you read, look for answers to these questions.

Figure 9 Here are three ways to show scale on a map.

Ratio scale 1:100,000
Bar scale
0 1 2 3 4 5 km
0 1 2 3 mi
Equivalent units scale
1 cm = 1 km   1 inch = 1.58 miles

Mapmakers use pictures called **symbols** to stand for features on Earth's surface. A symbol can represent a physical feature, such as a river, lake, mountain, or plain. A symbol also can stand for a human-made feature, such as a highway, a city, or an airport. A map's **key,** or legend, is a list of all the symbols used on the map with an explanation of their meaning.

Maps also include a compass rose or north arrow. The compass rose helps the map user to relate directions on the map to directions on Earth's surface. North usually is located at the top of the map.

☑ *Checkpoint* *Where can you find the meaning of the symbols on a map?*

Maps and Technology

Centuries ago, people invented instruments for determining compass direction, latitude, and longitude. Mapmakers developed techniques to show Earth's surface accurately.

1154 Sicily

The Arab mapmaker Al-Idrisi made several world maps for King Roger of Sicily. Idrisi's maps marked a great advance over other maps of that time. They showed the Arabs' grasp of scientific mapmaking and geography. But unlike modern maps, these maps placed south at the top!

1100	1200	1300	1400

AROUND 1100 China

Because the needle of a magnetic compass points north, ships at sea could tell direction even when the sun and stars were not visible. Arabs and Europeans adopted this Chinese invention by the 1200s.

AROUND 1300 Spain

Lines representing wind directions criss-crossed a type of map called a portolan chart. These charts also showed coastlines and harbors. A sea captain would use a portolan chart and a compass when sailing from one harbor to another in the Mediterranean Sea.

An Earth Reference System

When you play chess or checkers, the grid of squares helps you to keep track of where each piece should be. To find a point on Earth's surface, you need a reference system like the grid of squares on a checkerboard. Of course, Earth itself does not have grid lines, but most maps and globes show a grid. The grid is based on two imaginary lines: the equator and the prime meridian.

The Equator Halfway between the North and South poles, the **equator** forms an imaginary line that circles Earth. The equator divides Earth into the Northern and Southern hemispheres. A **hemisphere** (HEH mih sfeer) is one half of the sphere that makes up Earth's surface.

In Your Journal

Choose one period on the time line to learn more about. Use the library to find information about maps in that time. Who used maps? Why were they important? Share what you learn in the form of a letter written by a traveler or explorer who is using a map of that period.

1595 England

To find latitude, sailors used a variety of instruments, including the backstaff. The navigator sighted along the backstaff's straight edge to measure the angle of the sun or North star above the horizon. Later improvements led to modern instruments for navigation.

1684 France

On land, mapmakers developed new ways of measuring land areas accurately. Philippe de La Hire's map of France proved that the country was actually smaller than people had thought. The king of France said that he lost more land because of this map than he would have lost through losing a war.

| 1500 | 1600 | 1700 | 1800 |

1569 Belgium

Flemish mapmaker Gerardus Mercator invented the first modern map projection, which bears his name. Mercator and his son, Rumold, also made an atlas and maps of the world such as the one shown below.

1763 England

John Harrison, a carpenter and mechanic, won a prize from the British navy for building a highly accurate clock called a chronometer. Harrison's invention made finding longitudes quicker and easier. With exact longitudes, mapmakers could greatly improve the accuracy of their maps.

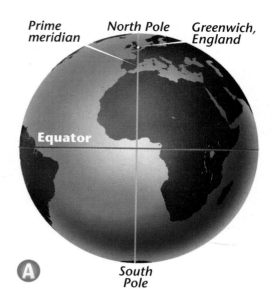

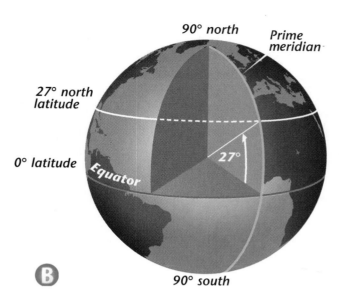

A South Pole

B 90° south

Figure 10 A. The equator and the prime meridian divide Earth's surface into hemispheres. B. Latitude measures distances north or south of the equator. C. Longitude measures distances east or west of the prime meridian. D. Cairo, Egypt, is located where the latitude line 30° N crosses the longitude line 31° E.

The Prime Meridian Another imaginary line, called the **prime meridian,** makes a half circle from the North Pole to the South Pole. The prime meridian passes through Greenwich, England. Places east of the prime meridian are in the Eastern Hemisphere. Places west of the prime meridian are in the Western Hemisphere.

Measurements on a Sphere To measure distances around a circle, scientists use units called degrees. A **degree** (°) is $\frac{1}{360}$ of the way around a full circle. As you can see in Figure 8, each degree is a measure of the angle formed by lines drawn from the center of Earth to points on the surface. If you started at the prime meridian and traveled west along the equator, you would travel through 360 degrees before returning to your starting point. If you started at the equator and traveled to one of the poles, you would travel 90 degrees—one quarter of the distance in a full circle.

☑ *Checkpoint* *In what two hemispheres is the United States located?*

Locating Points on Earth's Surface

Using the equator and prime meridian, mapmakers have constructed a grid made up of lines of latitude and longitude. **You can use lines of latitude and longitude to find locations anywhere on Earth.**

Latitude The equator is the starting line for measuring **latitude,** or distance in degrees north or south of the equator. Between the equator and both poles are evenly spaced lines called lines of latitude. All lines of latitude are parallel to the equator. Latitude is measured from the equator, which is at 0°. The latitude of each pole is 90° north or 90° south.

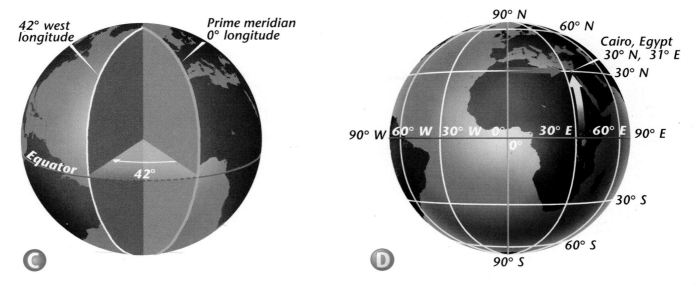

42° west longitude

Prime meridian 0° longitude

Equator

42°

C

90° N
60° N
Cairo, Egypt
30° N, 31° E
30° N
90° W 60° W 30° W 0° 30° E 60° E 90° E
0°
30° S
60° S
90° S

D

Longitude The distance in degrees east or west of the prime meridian is called **longitude.** There are 360 lines of longitude that run from north to south, meeting at the poles. Each line represents one degree of longitude. The prime meridian, which is the starting line for measuring longitude, is at 0°. Each longitude line crosses the latitude lines, including the equator, at a right angle.

As Figure 11 shows, the longitude lines in each hemisphere are numbered up to 180 degrees. This is one half the total number of degrees in a circle. At 180 degrees east or 180 degrees west lies a single longitude line directly opposite the prime meridian.

Figure 11 Every point on Earth's surface has a particular latitude and longitude.
Interpreting Maps What are the latitude and longitude of New Orleans? Of Sydney?

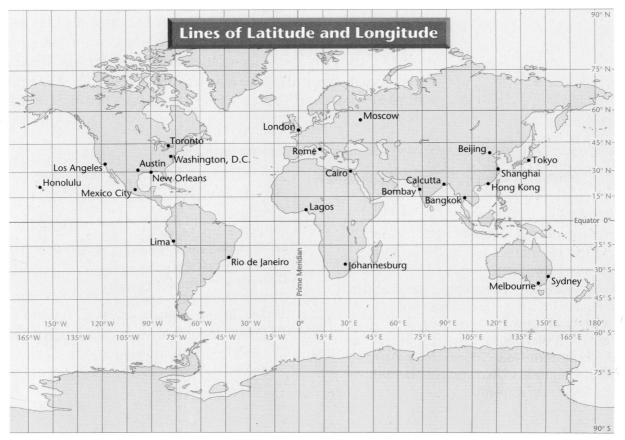

Lines of Latitude and Longitude

Moscow
London
Toronto
Rome
Beijing
Washington, D.C.
Tokyo
Austin
Shanghai
Los Angeles
Cairo
Honolulu
New Orleans
Calcutta
Hong Kong
Mexico City
Bombay
Bangkok
Lagos
Lima
Rio de Janeiro
Johannesburg
Melbourne Sydney

Prime Meridian

90° N
75° N
60° N
45° N
30° N
15° N
Equator 0°
15° S
30° S
45° S
60° S
75° S
90° S

150°W 120°W 90°W 60°W 30°W 0° 30°E 60°E 90°E 120°E 150°E 180°
165°W 135°W 105°W 75°W 45°W 15°W 15°E 45°E 75°E 105°E 135°E 165°E

29

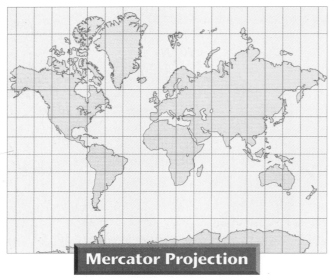

Mercator Projection

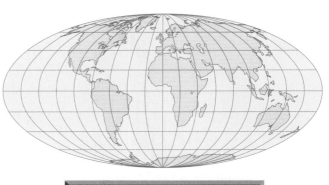

Equal-Area Projection

Figure 12 On a Mercator projection (left), lines of longitude are parallel, so shapes near the poles are distorted. An equal-area projection (right) shows areas correctly, but distorts some shapes around its edges. *Comparing and Contrasting Why does Greenland appear larger on the Mercator projection than on the equal-area projection?*

Map Projections

To show Earth's curved surface on a flat map, mapmakers use map projections. A **map projection** is a framework of lines that helps to show landmasses on a flat surface.

On a Mercator projection, the lines of latitude and longitude all appear as straight, parallel lines that form a rectangle. On a Mercator projection, the size and shape of landmasses near the equator are distorted only a little. But as you go toward the poles, size and shape become more and more distorted. The reason for this distortion is that the lines of longitude do not come together at the poles as they do on a globe. As you can see in Figure 12, this projection also changes the relative sizes of landmasses.

To solve the problem of distortion on Mercator projections, mapmakers developed equal-area projections. An equal-area projection correctly shows the relative sizes of Earth's landmasses. But an equal-area projection also has distortion. The shapes of landmasses near the edges of the map appear stretched and curved.

Section 2 Review

1. What information does a map's scale provide?
2. What do latitude and longitude each measure?
3. What are the advantages and disadvantages of an equal-area projection?
4. **Thinking Critically** **Measuring** Look at the map in Figure 11. If you fly due east from New Orleans, through how many degrees of longitude must you travel to reach Shanghai? If you flew west from New Orleans, how many degrees of longitude would you pass before reaching Shanghai? Explain.

Check Your Progress

CHAPTER PROJECT

Choose an appropriate scale for your map. Make a list of the types of natural and human-made features for which you will need symbols. Examine the samples of maps in the chapter and those provided by your teacher. Brainstorm ideas for symbols to include. If possible, return to your site and add more detail to your map.

You may have wondered how people first decided where to locate the borders between states.

Problem

Which was more important in locating state borders: lines of latitude and longitude or physical features?

Skills Focus

drawing conclusions, observing, inferring

Materials

United States map with latitude, longitude, and state borders

tracing paper   paper clips   colored pencils

Procedure

1. Lay the tracing paper on top of a map of the United States and secure it with paper clips.
2. Trace over the Pacific and Atlantic coasts of the United States with a blue pencil.
3. Using the blue pencil, trace all Great Lakes shorelines that reach nearby states.
4. Trace all state borders that go exactly north-south with a red pencil. (*Hint:* Some straight-line borders that appear to run north-south, such as the western border of Maine, do not follow lines of longitude.)
5. Use a green pencil to trace all state borders or sections of state borders that go exactly east-west. (*Hint:* Straight-line borders that are slanted, such as the southern border of Nevada, do not follow lines of latitude.)
6. Now use a blue pencil to trace the borders that follow rivers.
7. Use a brown pencil to trace any borders that are not straight lines or rivers.

Analyze and Conclude

1. How many state boundaries are completely defined by longitude and latitude? How many are partially defined by longitude and latitude?
2. What feature is used to define a state border when longitude and latitude are not used? Give examples of specific states.
3. Study the physical map of the United States in Appendix B. What other physical features are used to define borders? Which state borders are defined by these features?
4. Which was used more often in locating state borders: longitude or latitude?
5. How many states do not use longitude and latitude for the location of their borders?
6. **Apply** In which region of the country were lines of latitude and longitude most important in determining state borders? What do you think is the reason for this?

More to Explore

Research the history of your state to find out when and how its borders were established. Are your state's borders based on longitude and latitude, landforms and topography, or both?

Review a map of your county or state. Are any features, other than the state's border, related to longitude and latitude? Which features seem to follow landforms and topography?

SECTION 3 Maps in the Computer Age

DISCOVER ··· ACTIVITY

Can You Make a Pixel Picture?

1. With a pencil, draw a square grid of lines spaced 1 centimeter apart. The grid should have 6 squares on each side.

2. On the grid, draw the outline of a simple object, such as an apple.

3. Using a different color pencil, fill in all squares that are completely inside the apple. If a square is mostly inside the apple, fill it in completely. If it is mostly outside, leave it blank.

4. Each square on your grid represents one pixel, or bit of information, about your picture. Looking at your pixel picture, can you recognize the shape you started with?

Think It Over

Predicting How would the pixel picture change if you drew the object smaller? How would the pixel picture look if you used graph paper with squares that are smaller than your grid?

GUIDE FOR READING

◆ How are satellites and computers used in mapmaking?

Reading Tip Before you read, preview Figures 14 and 15. Predict how computers have affected mapmaking.

Figure 13 A satellite image is made up of many pixels. This enlargement of a satellite image shows Tampa Bay and St. Petersburg, Florida.

For centuries, mapmakers slowly gathered data and then drew maps by hand. Explorers made maps by sketching coastlines as seen from their ships. Mapmakers sometimes drew the land based on reports from people who had traveled there. More accurate maps were made by locating points on the surface in a process called surveying.

During the twentieth century, people learned to make highly accurate maps using photographs taken from airplanes. These photographs are called aerial photographs. Aerial photographs are still important in many types of mapmaking.

Since the 1970s, information gathered by satellites has revolutionized mapmaking. Powerful computers use the satellite data to make maps quickly and accurately.

Satellite Mapping

Beginning in 1972, the United States launched a series of Landsat satellites designed to observe Earth's surface. Landsat uses electronic devices to collect information about the land surface in the form of computer data. **Satellite images** are pictures of the surface based on these data. As Landsat orbits Earth, it collects and stores information about a strip of the surface that is

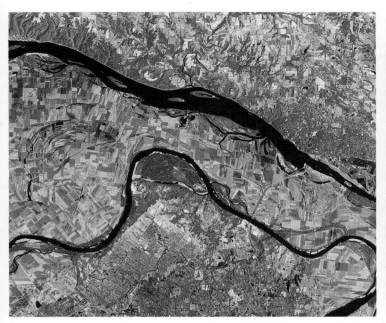

185 kilometers wide. The satellite relays the data back to a station on Earth, where computers create images of the surface.

Pictures made by Landsat show what covers the land surface—plants, soil, sand, rock, water, or snow and ice. Large human-made features, such as cities, are also visible.

Printing Satellite Images Unlike a photograph, a satellite image is made up of thousands of tiny dots called **pixels.** A painting made of pixels would have many separate dots of color. Each pixel in a satellite image contains information on the color and brightness of a small part of Earth's surface. This information is stored on a computer as a series of 0's and 1's. When the satellite image is printed, the computer translates these numbers into colors.

Interpreting Satellite Images Scientists learn to identify **INTEGRATING ENVIRONMENTAL SCIENCE** specific features by the "signature," or combination of colors and shapes, that the feature makes on a satellite image. In a satellite image, areas covered by grass, trees, or crops are often shown as red, water as black or blue, and cities as bluish gray. Landsat images may show features such as grasslands, forests, and agricultural crops, as well as desert areas, mountains, or cities. By comparing one image with another made at an earlier time, scientists can see changes due to drought, forest fires, or floods. Figure 14 shows satellite images taken before and during a flood in the Mississippi River valley.

✓ *Checkpoint* *What information does a pixel in a satellite image contain?*

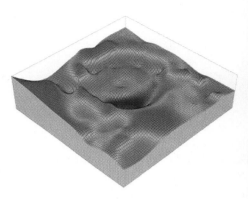

Figure 15 Today computers are an essential tool in making accurate maps. A computer produced the digital model shown above.

Computer Mapping

With computers, mapmakers have new ways of storing and displaying map data. Computer mapmakers use up-to-the-minute data to produce maps quickly and easily.

All of the data used in computer mapping must be in numbers, just like the pixels in a satellite image. The process by which mapmakers convert the location of map points to numbers is called **digitizing.** Once the map data have been digitized, they can be displayed on a computer screen, modified, and printed out in map form.

Computers can automatically create three-dimensional views that might take a person hundreds of hours to draw by hand. The computer image in Figure 15, for example, was made to help geologists search for oil.

Section 3 Review

1. Describe how Landsat collects data about Earth's surface.
2. What are the two ways in which computers are useful in making maps?
3. How are the data for a map put in a form that a computer can use?
4. **Thinking Critically Making Generalizations** In your own words, describe how computers and satellites have improved the accuracy of maps.

Science at Home

Maps in the News Most of the maps that you see today in newspapers and magazines are made using computers. With family members look through newspapers and news magazines. How many different types of maps can you find? Explain to your family the map's scale, symbols, and key. After you have studied the map, try to state the main point of the information shown on the map.

SECTION 4 Topographic Maps

DISCOVER ·· ACTIVITY

Can a Map Show Relief?

1. ✂ Carefully cut the corners off 8 pieces of cardboard so that they look rounded. Each piece should be at least 1 centimeter smaller than the one before.

2. Trim the long sides of the two largest pieces so that the long sides appear wavy. Don't cut any more than one-half centimeter into the cardboard.

3. Trace the largest cardboard piece on a sheet of paper.

4. Trace the next largest piece inside the tracing of the first. Don't let any lines cross.

5. Trace the other cardboard pieces, from largest to smallest, one inside the other, on the same paper.

6. Stack the cardboard pieces in the same order they were traced beside the paper. Compare the stack of cardboard pieces with your drawing. How are they alike? How are they different?

Think It Over

Making Models If the cardboard pieces are a model of a landform, what do the lines on the paper represent?

You are an engineer planning a route for a highway over a mountain pass. You need to consider many different factors. To design a safe highway, you need a route that avoids the steepest slopes. To protect the area's water supply, the highway must stay a certain distance from rivers and lakes. You also want to find a route that avoids houses and other buildings. How would you find the best route? You could start by studying a topographic map.

Mapping Earth's Topography

A **topographic map** is a map showing the surface features of an area. Topographic maps use symbols to portray the land as if you were looking down on it from above. **Topographic maps provide highly accurate information on the elevation, relief, and slope of the ground surface.**

GUIDE FOR READING

◆ What is a topographic map?
◆ How do mapmakers represent elevation, relief, and slope?
◆ What is the Global Positioning System?

Reading Tip As you read, make a list of main ideas and supporting details about topographic maps.

Figure 16 Topographic maps provide the data necessary for the planning of highways, bridges, and other large construction projects.

Math TOOLBOX

Scale and Ratios

A ratio compares two numbers by division. For example, the scale of a map given as a ratio is 1 : 250,000. At this scale, the distance between two points on the map measures 23.5 cm. How would you find the actual distance? Begin by writing the scale as a fraction.

$$\frac{1}{250,000}$$

Next, write a proportion. Let d represent the actual distance between the two points.

$$\frac{1}{250,000} = \frac{23.5 \text{ cm}}{d}$$

Then write the cross products.

$$1 \times d = 250,000 \times 23.5 \text{ cm}$$
$$d = 5,875,000 \text{ cm}$$

(*Hint:* To convert cm to km, divide d by 100,000.)

Uses of Topographic Maps People find many uses for topographic maps. Businesses use them to help decide where to build new stores, housing, or factories. Cities and towns use them to decide where to build new schools. Topographic maps have recreational uses, too. If you were planning a bicycle trip, you could use a topographic map to see whether your trip would be flat or hilly.

Scale Topographic maps usually are large-scale maps. A large-scale map is one that shows a close-up view of part of Earth's surface. In the United States, most topographic maps are at a scale of 1 : 24,000, or 1 centimeter equals 0.24 kilometers. At this scale, a map can show the details of elevation and features such as rivers and coastlines. Large buildings, airports, and major highways appear as outlines at the correct scale. Symbols are used to show houses and other small features.

Coverage Most nations have a government agency that is responsible for making topographic maps. In the United States, that agency is the U. S. Geological Survey, or USGS. The USGS has produced about 57,000 topographic maps at scales of either 1 : 24,000 or 1 : 25,000. The maps cover all of the United States, except for parts of Alaska. Each map covers an area of roughly 145 square kilometers.

Symbols Mapmakers use a great variety of symbols on topographic maps. If you were drawing a map, what symbols would you use to represent woods, a campground, an orchard, a swamp, or a school? Look at Figure 17 to see the symbols that the USGS uses for these and other features.

☑ *Checkpoint* *In the United States, what agency is responsible for producing topographic maps?*

Figure 17 Maps made by the U.S. Geological Survey use more than 150 symbols.

Commonly Used Map Symbols

Contour line: elevation		Primary highway		River	
Contour line: depression		Secondary highway		Stream	
Building		Divided highway		Waterfall or rapids	
School; church		Railroad tracks		Marsh or swamp	
Built-up area		Airport		Rock or coral reef	
Campground; picnic area		Woods		Breakwater; wharf	
Cemetery		Orchard		Exposed wreck	

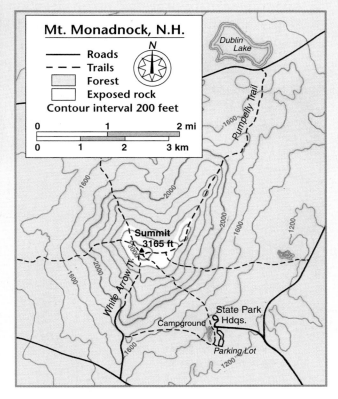

Figure 18 The contour lines on a topographic map represent elevation and relief. *Comparing and Contrasting What information does the topographic map provide that the photograph does not?*

Showing Relief on Topographic Maps

To represent elevation, relief, and slope on topographic maps, mapmakers use contour lines. On a topographic map, a **contour line** connects points of equal elevation.

The change in elevation from contour line to contour line is called the **contour interval.** The contour interval for a given map is always the same. For example, the map in Figure 18 has a contour interval of 200 feet. If you start at one contour line and count up 10 contour lines, you have reached an elevation 2,000 feet above where you started. Usually, every fifth contour line is darker and heavier than the others. These lines are labeled with the elevation in round units, such as 1,600 or 2,000 feet above sea level. Most USGS maps give contour intervals in feet rather than meters.

Looking at a topographic map with many squiggly contour lines, you may feel as if you are gazing into a bowl of spaghetti. But if you follow the rules listed in *Exploring Topographic Maps* on the following page, you can learn to read contour lines. Reading contour lines is the first step toward "seeing" an area's topography by looking at a topographic map.

Interpreting Data

ACTIVITY

You are planning to hike up Mt. Monadnock. Use the topographic map in Figure 18 to determine which route is steeper: the White Arrow Trail or the Pumpelly Trail. What is the difference in elevation between the park headquarters and the summit?

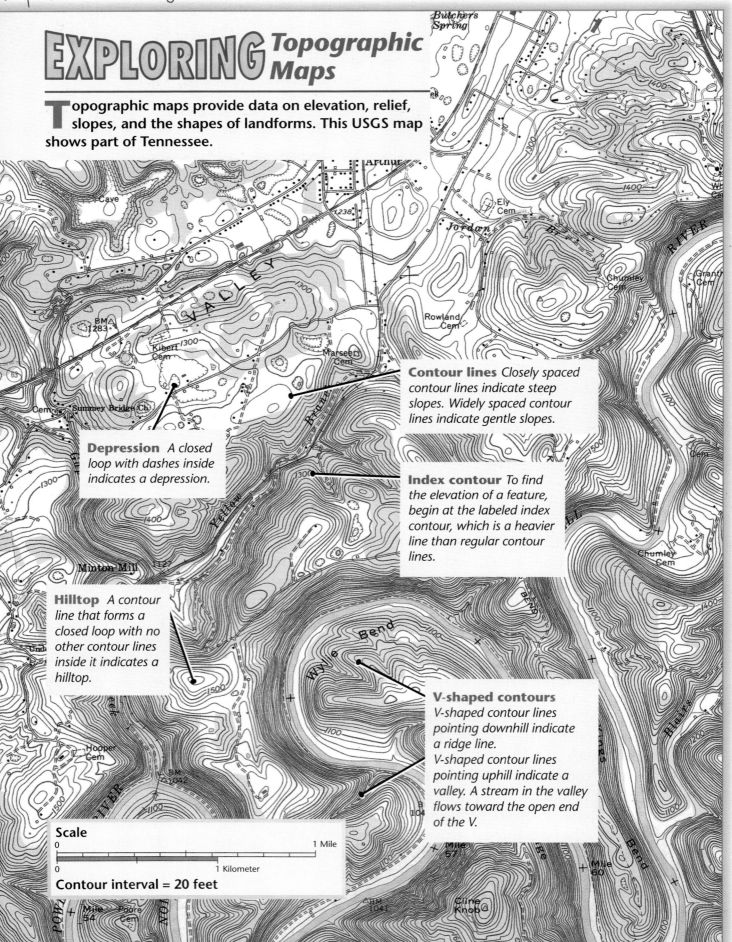

Stephen Jaremczuk

EXPLORING Topographic Maps

Topographic maps provide data on elevation, relief, slopes, and the shapes of landforms. This USGS map shows part of Tennessee.

Contour lines *Closely spaced contour lines indicate steep slopes. Widely spaced contour lines indicate gentle slopes.*

Depression *A closed loop with dashes inside indicates a depression.*

Index contour *To find the elevation of a feature, begin at the labeled index contour, which is a heavier line than regular contour lines.*

Hilltop *A contour line that forms a closed loop with no other contour lines inside it indicates a hilltop.*

V-shaped contours *V-shaped contour lines pointing downhill indicate a ridge line. V-shaped contour lines pointing uphill indicate a valley. A stream in the valley flows toward the open end of the V.*

Scale

0   1 Mile

0   1 Kilometer

Contour interval = 20 feet

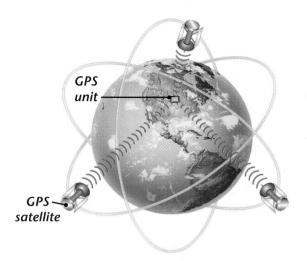

GPS
unit

GPS
satellite

Figure 19 The GPS network includes 24 satellites. Three satellites (left) must be above the horizon to pinpoint the location of the user (right). The user's latitude and longitude appear on the screen of a portable GPS unit like the one in the photograph.

Global Positioning System

INTEGRATING TECHNOLOGY Today, surveyors, pilots, and mapmakers around the world rely on the **Global Positioning System,** or GPS, to determine locations precisely. **The Global Positioning System is a method of finding latitude, longitude, and elevation of points on Earth's surface using a network of satellites.** At any given moment, there are between five and eight GPS satellites above the horizon in a given area. A hand-held unit the size of a cellular phone picks up signals broadcast by these satellites. A computer inside the GPS unit then calculates the user's location and elevation.

Engineers can use GPS to locate points on the ground for a construction project. Airplanes, ships, and hikers can use GPS to navigate. Some cars now contain both a GPS unit and a digital road map stored in a computer. Using GPS, the computer determines the car's location and suggests a route to your destination.

Section 4 Review

1. What kind of information does a topographic map provide about landforms?
2. How do topographic maps represent elevation and relief?
3. What would the highest and lowest points in an area look like on a topographic map?
4. What is the role of satellites in the Global Positioning System?
5. **Thinking Critically** **Interpreting Maps** Look at the map on page 38. Where is the highest elevation? Where do you find the steepest slopes? The gentlest slopes?

Check Your Progress CHAPTER PROJECT

On a large piece of paper, draw your map to scale. Locate all natural and human-made features on the map using the measurements you recorded on your rough sketch and the symbols you brainstormed earlier. Include a north arrow, a legend, and scale on your map. Show the topography of the land by using contour lines or other symbols that show how the land slopes.

A Map in a Pan

A topographic map is a two-dimensional model of three-dimensional landforms.

Problem

How can you make a topographic map?

Materials

deep-sided pan
marking pencil
clear, hard sheet of plastic
sheet of unlined white paper
1 L water
rigid cardboard
modeling clay
metric ruler

Procedure

1. Cut a piece of cardboard to fit the bottom of a deep-sided pan.
2. On the cardboard, shape some clay into a model of a hill.
3. Place the model in the pan. Pour colored water into the pan to a depth of 1 centimeter to represent sea level.
4. Place a sheet of hard, clear plastic over the container.
5. Trace the outline of the pan on the plastic sheet with a marking pencil. Then, looking straight down into the pan, trace the outline the water makes around the edges of the clay model. Remove the plastic sheet from the pan.

6. Add another centimeter of water to the pan, bringing the depth of the water to 2 centimeters. Replace the plastic sheet exactly as before, then trace the water level again.
7. Repeat Step 6 several times. Stop when the next addition of water would completely cover your model.
8. Remove the plastic sheet. Trace the outlines that you drew on the plastic sheet onto a sheet of paper.

Analyze and Conclude

1. Looking at your topographic map, how can you tell which parts of your model hill have a steep slope? A gentle slope?
2. How can you tell from the map which point on the hill is the highest?
3. Where on your map would you be likely to find a stream? Explain.
4. Is there any depression on your map where water would collect after it rained? What symbol should you use to identify this depression?
5. **Think About It** Compare your map with the clay landform. How are they alike? How are they different? How could you improve your map as a model of the landform?

More to Explore

Obtain a topographic map that includes an interesting landform such as a mountain, canyon, river valley, or coastline. After studying the contour lines on the map, make a sketch of what you think the landform looks like. Then build a scale model of the landform using clay or layers of cardboard or foamboard. How does your model landform compare with your sketch?

SECTION 1

Exploring Earth's Surface

Key Ideas

◆ Earth's topography is made up of landforms that have elevation and relief, such as plains, mountains, and plateaus.

◆ The atmosphere, hydrosphere, and biosphere surround Earth's rocky outer layer, the lithosphere.

Key Terms

topography	plain	core
elevation	mountain	mantle
relief	mountain range	crust
landform	plateau	rock
landform region	lithosphere	geology

 SECTION 2

Mapping Earth's Surface

Key Ideas

◆ Maps and globes are drawn to scale to show features on Earth's surface as seen from above.

◆ The grid of latitude and longitude lines can be used to locate points on Earth's surface.

Key Terms

map	key	degree
globe	equator	latitude
scale	hemisphere	longitude
symbols	prime meridian	map projection

 SECTION 3

Maps in the Computer Age

INTEGRATING TECHNOLOGY

Key Ideas

◆ Instruments carried aboard satellites in orbit around Earth make pictures of the surface called satellite images.

◆ Computers are used to store and display the information used in making maps.

Key Terms

satellite image   digitizing
pixel

 SECTION 4

Topographic Maps

Key Ideas

◆ Topographic maps portray the elevation, relief, and slope of the landforms in an area.

◆ Contour lines are used on a topographic map to show elevation and relief.

◆ The contour interval of a topographic map is the amount that elevation increases or decreases between contour lines.

◆ In addition to showing elevation and relief, topographic maps include a variety of other natural and human-made features.

Key Terms

topographic map	contour interval
contour line	Global Positioning System

Organizing Information

Concept Map Copy the concept map about landforms onto a separate piece of paper. Then complete it and add a title. (For more on concept maps, see the Skills Handbook.)

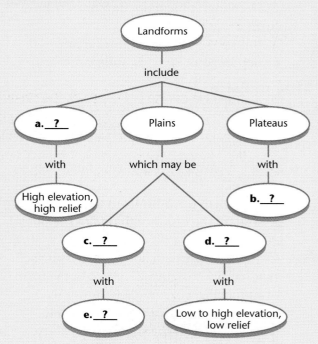

Reviewing Content

 For more review of key concepts, see the Interactive Student Tutorial CD-ROM.

Multiple Choice
Choose the letter of the best answer.

1. A landform that has high elevation but a mostly flat surface is a
   a. coastal plain.   b. mountain.
   c. mountain belt.   d. plateau.
2. The thin, outer layer of the lithosphere that forms Earth's surface is the
   a. outer core.   b. inner core.
   c. crust.   d. mantle.
3. Latitude is a measurement of distance north or south of the
   a. hemispheres.   b. equator.
   c. axis.   d. prime meridian.
4. To show the continents without distorting their relative sizes and shapes, a mapmaker would choose a
   a. Mercator projection.
   b. globe.
   c. equal-area projection.
   d. topographic map.
5. On a topographic map, the contour lines form a V at a
   a. hilltop.   b. level area.
   c. depression.   d. valley.

True or False
If the statement is true, write true. If it is false, change the underlined word or words to make the statement true.

6. <u>Relief</u> measures a landform's height above sea level.
7. Going north or south from the <u>prime meridian</u>, the distance to one of the poles is 90 degrees.
8. Computers use data about Earth's surface that has been <u>digitized</u>, or put in the form of numbers.
9. If contour lines on a slope are spaced <u>wide apart</u>, then the slope is very steep.
10. Contour lines that form a closed loop marked with dashes indicate a <u>depression</u>.

Checking Concepts

11. What do geologists call an area where there is mostly one kind of topography?
12. What is a mountain range?
13. Compare the elevation of a coastal plain to that of an interior plain.
14. The South Island of New Zealand lies at about 170° E. What hemisphere is it in?
15. Could contour lines on a map ever cross? Explain.
16. Which would be more likely to show a shallow, 1.5-meter-deep depression in the ground: a 1-meter contour interval or a 5-meter contour interval? Explain.
17. **Writing to Learn** With your family, you make a car trip across the United States along the latitude line 35° N. Write a series of postcards to friends describing the landforms that you see on your trip. Use Appendix B to determine what the land is like along your route.

Thinking Critically

18. **Applying Concepts** Earth's diameter is about 13,000 kilometers. If a globe has a diameter of 0.5 meter, write the globe's scale as a ratio. What distance on Earth would 1 centimeter on the globe represent?
19. **Inferring** An airplane flies directly west at 1,000 kilometers per hour. Without changing direction, the plane returns to its starting point in just one hour. What can you infer about the plane's route with regard to lines of latitude and longitude? Explain.
20. **Observing** Using an atlas, find the latitude and longitude of San Francisco, California; Wichita, Kansas; and Richmond, Virginia. What do these three cities have in common?
21. **Comparing and Contrasting** How is mapmaking with computers different from earlier mapmaking techniques?
22. **Problem Solving** Your community has decided to build a zoo for animals from many regions of Earth. How could you use topographic maps of your area to help decide on the best location for the zoo?

Applying Skills

This map shows part of Acadia National Park in Maine. The contour interval is 20 feet. Use the map to answer Questions 23–25.

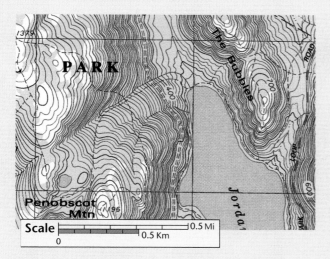

23. Interpreting Maps

A. What is the elevation of the large lake?

B. Which of the two Bubbles is higher?

24. Calculating Use the map scale to calculate the distance from the top of Penobscot Mountain to the large lake.

25. Inferring How can you tell whether the streams flow into or out of the large lake?

Performance CHAPTER PROJECT **Assessment**

Present Your Project Present your map to the class. Discuss the natural and physical features found on your site. What symbols did you use to represent these features? How did you measure and locate them on your map? How accurate is your map? Ask your classmates how you could improve your map.

Reflect and Record Write an evaluation of your map. What would you change about it? What would you keep the same? Does your map give others a clear idea of what the land looks like?

Test Preparation

Use these questions to prepare for standardized tests.

The map shows part of Earth's surface with a grid of latitude and longitude lines. Study the map. Then answer Questions 26–30.

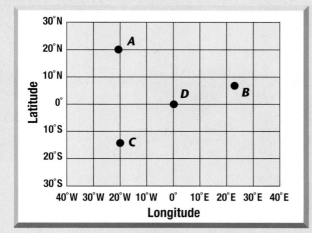

26. The horizontal line labeled 0° is called the
a. horizon line.　　b. equator.
c. prime meridian.　d. contour line.

27. The latitude and longitude of point B is best given by
a. 25°S 7°W.　　b. 7°N 25°W.
c. 7°E 25°N.　　d. 7°N 25°E.

28. In which two hemispheres is point C located?
a. western and southern hemispheres
b. northern and eastern hemispheres
c. eastern and western hemispheres
d. western and northern hemispheres

29. The north-south distance in degrees from point A to Point C is about
a. 15°.　　b. 35°.
c. 25°.　　d. 0°.

30. Suppose you start at point D and travel southwest to point C. Through how many degrees of longitude have you traveled?
a. 20°　　b. 15°
c. 60°　　d. 30°

CHAPTER 2 Minerals

WEB ACTIVITY www.phschool.com

Growing a Crystal Garden

Everyone has wondered at the beauty of minerals. Minerals occur in an amazing variety of colors and crystal shapes—from clear, tiny cubes of halite (table salt) to precious rubies and sapphires. Some crystals look like dandelion puffs. In this project, you will grow crystals to see how different types of chemicals form different crystal shapes.

Your Goal To design and grow a crystal garden.
To complete this project successfully, you must
◆ create a three-dimensional garden scene as a base on which to grow crystals
◆ prepare at least two different crystal-growth solutions
◆ observe and record the shapes and growth rates of your crystals
◆ follow the safety guidelines in Appendix A.

Get Started Begin by deciding what materials you will use to create your garden scene. Your teacher will suggest a variety of materials and also describe the types of crystal-growth solutions that you can use.

Check Your Progress You'll be working on this project as you study this chapter. To keep your project on track, look for Check Your Progress boxes at the following points.
Section 1 Review, page 54: Design and build a setting for your crystal garden and add the solutions.
Section 2 Review, page 60: Observe and record the growth of the crystals.

Present Your Project At the end of the chapter (page 71), display your finished crystal garden to your class. Be prepared to describe your procedure, observations, and conclusions.

These aurichalcite (oh rih KAL syt) crystals were found in a copper mine in Mexico. This mineral is formed from the metals zinc, copper, and other elements.

1 Properties of Minerals

What Is the True Color of a Mineral?

1. Examine samples of magnetite and black hematite. Both minerals contain iron. Describe the color and appearance of the two minerals. Are they similar or different?

2. Rub the black hematite across the back of a porcelain or ceramic tile. Observe the color of the streak on the tile.

3. Wipe the tile clean before you test the next sample.

4. Rub the magnetite across the back of the tile. Observe the color of the streak on the tile.

Think It Over

Observing Does the color of each mineral's streak match its color? How could this streak test be helpful in identifying them as two different minerals?

GUIDE FOR READING

◆ What are the characteristics of a mineral?

◆ How are minerals identified?

Reading Tip As you read, use the headings to make an outline showing what minerals are and how they can be identified.

If you visit a science museum, you might wander into a room named the "hall of minerals." There you would see substances you have never heard of. For example, you might see deep-red crystals labeled "sphalerite" (SFAL uh ryt). You might be surprised to learn that sphalerite is a source of zinc and gallium. These metals are used in products from "tin" cans to computer chips! Although you may never have seen sphalerite, you are probably familiar with other common minerals. For example, you have probably seen turquoise, a blue-green mineral used in jewelry.

Figure 1 The Hall of Minerals at the American Museum of Natural History in New York City contains one of the world's largest collections of minerals.

Figure 2 **A.** Red crystals of the mineral sphalerite are called ruby zinc. **B.** Borax is a mineral that forms in dry lake beds. **C.** Coal is not a mineral because it is made of the remains of ancient plants. *Comparing and Contrasting How are sphalerite and borax similar? How are they different?*

What Is a Mineral?

Sphalerite and turquoise are just two of more than 3,000 minerals that geologists have identified. Of all these minerals, only about 100 are common. Most of the others are harder to find than gold. About 20 minerals make up most of the rocks of Earth's crust. These minerals are known as rock-forming minerals. Appendix B at the back of this book lists some of the most common rock-forming minerals.

A mineral is a naturally occurring, inorganic solid that has a crystal structure and a definite chemical composition. For a substance to be a mineral, it must have all five of these characteristics. In Figure 2, you can compare sphalerite with another mineral, borax, and with coal, which is not a mineral.

Naturally Occurring To be classified as a mineral, a substance must occur naturally. Cement, brick, steel, and glass all come from substances found in Earth's crust. However, these building materials are manufactured by people. Because they are not naturally occurring, such materials are not considered to be minerals.

Inorganic A mineral must also be **inorganic.** This means that the mineral cannot arise from materials that were once part of a living thing. For example, coal forms naturally in the crust. But geologists do not classify coal as a mineral because it comes from the remains of plants and animals that lived millions of years ago.

Solid A mineral is always a solid, with a definite volume and shape. The particles that make up a solid are packed together very tightly, so they cannot move like the particles that make up a liquid. A solid keeps its shape because its particles can't flow freely.

Crystal Structure The particles of a mineral line up in a pattern that repeats over and over again. The repeating pattern of a mineral's particles forms a solid called a **crystal.** A crystal has flat sides, called faces, that meet at sharp edges and corners.

Sometimes, the crystal structure is obvious from the mineral's appearance. In other minerals, however, the crystal structure is visible only under a microscope. A few minerals, such as opal, are considered minerals even though their particles are not arranged in a crystal structure.

Definite Chemical Composition A mineral has a definite chemical composition. This means that a mineral always contains certain elements in definite proportions. An **element** is a substance composed of a single kind of atom. All the atoms of the same element have the same chemical and physical properties.

Almost all minerals are compounds. In a **compound,** two or more elements are combined so that the elements no longer have distinct properties. The elements that make up a compound are said to be chemically joined. For example, a crystal of the mineral quartz has one atom of silicon for every two atoms of oxygen. Each compound has its own properties, which usually differ greatly from the properties of the elements that form it. Figure 3 compares the mineral cinnabar to the elements that make it up.

INTEGRATING CHEMISTRY

Figure 3 Minerals are usually a compound of two or more elements. **A.** Mercury is a metal that is a silvery liquid at room temperature. **B.** The element sulfur is bright yellow. **C.** The mineral cinnabar is a compound of the elements mercury and sulfur. Cinnabar has red crystals.

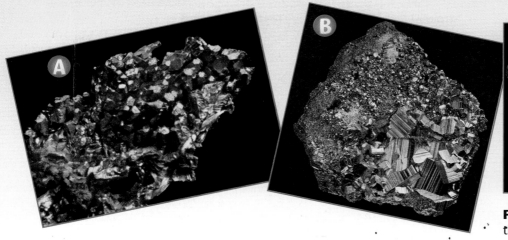

Figure 4 An old saying warns "All that glitters is not gold." **A.** Real gold can occur as a pure metal. **B.** Pyrite, or fool's gold, contains iron and sulfur. **C.** Chalcopyrite is a compound of copper, iron, and sulfur. *Observing These minerals are similar in color. But do you notice any differences in their appearance?*

Some elements occur in nature in a pure form, not as part of a compound with other elements. These elements, such as copper, silver, and gold, are considered to be minerals. Almost all pure elements are metals.

☑ *Checkpoint* **What does it mean to say that a mineral has a definite chemical composition?**

Identifying Minerals

During the California Gold Rush of 1849, thousands of people headed west to find gold in the California hills. Some found gold, but most found disappointment. Perhaps the most disappointed of all were the ones who found pyrite, or "fool's gold." All three minerals in Figure 4 look like gold, yet only one is the real thing.

Because there are so many different kinds of minerals, telling them apart can be a challenge. The color of a mineral alone often provides too little information to make an identification. **Each mineral has its own specific properties that can be used to identify it.** When you have learned to recognize the properties of minerals, you will be able to identify many common minerals around you.

You can see some of the properties of a mineral just by looking at a sample. To observe other properties, however, you need to conduct tests on that sample. As you read about the properties of minerals, think about how you could use them to identify a mineral.

Hardness When you identify a mineral, one of the best clues you can use is the mineral's hardness. In 1812, Friedrich Mohs, an Austrian mineral expert, invented a test to describe and compare the hardness of minerals. Called the **Mohs hardness scale,** this scale ranks ten minerals from softest to hardest. Look at the

Sharpen your Skills

Classifying

ACTIVITY

1. Use your fingernail to try to scratch talc, calcite, and quartz. Record which minerals you were able to scratch.

2. Now try to scratch the minerals with a penny. Were your results different? Explain.

3. Were there any minerals you were unable to scratch with either your fingernail or the penny?

4. How would you classify the three minerals in order of increasing hardness?

Figure 5 Mohs hardness scale rates the hardness of minerals on a scale of 1 to 10. *Drawing Conclusions* *You find a mineral that can be scratched by a steel knife, but not by a copper penny. What is this mineral's hardness on the Mohs scale?*

Mohs Hardness Scale		
Mineral	**Rating**	**Testing Method**
Talc	1	Softest known mineral. It flakes easily when scratched by a fingernail.
Gypsum	2	A fingernail can easily scratch it.
Calcite	3	A fingernail cannot scratch it, but a copper penny can.
Fluorite	4	A steel knife can easily scratch it.
Apatite	5	A steel knife can scratch it.
Feldspar	6	Cannot be scratched by a steel knife, but it can scratch window glass.
Quartz	7	Can scratch steel and hard glass easily.
Topaz	8	Can scratch quartz.
Corundum	9	Can scratch topaz.
Diamond	10	Hardest known mineral. Diamond can scratch all other substances.

table in Figure 5 to see which mineral is the softest and which is the hardest. A mineral can scratch any mineral softer than itself, but will be scratched by any mineral that is harder. How would you determine the hardness of a mineral not listed on the Mohs scale, such as sphalerite? If you try to scratch sphalerite with talc, gypsum, and calcite, you would find that none of them scratch sphalerite. But apatite, the mineral rated 5 on the scale, does scratch sphalerite. Therefore, you would conclude that sphalerite's hardness is about 4 on Mohs hardness scale.

Figure 6 Quartz comes in many colors.

Color The color of a mineral is an easily observed physical property. But color can be used to identify only those few minerals that always have their own characteristic color. The mineral malachite is always green. The mineral azurite is always blue. No other minerals look quite the same as these. Many minerals, however, like the quartz in Figure 6, can occur in a variety of colors.

Streak A streak test can provide a clue to a mineral's identity. The **streak** of a mineral is the color of its powder. You can observe a streak by rubbing a mineral against a piece of unglazed tile called a streak plate. Even though the color of the mineral may vary, its streak does not. Surprisingly, the streak color

Figure 7 **A.** Galena, which contains lead, has a metallic luster. **B.** Malachite, which contains copper, has a silky luster.

and the mineral color are often different. For example, although pyrite has a gold color, it always produces a greenish black streak. Real gold, on the other hand, produces a golden yellow streak.

Luster Another simple test to identify a mineral is to check its luster. **Luster** is the term used to describe how a mineral reflects light from its surface. Minerals containing metals are often shiny. For example, galena is an ore of lead that has a bright, metallic luster. You can compare the luster of galena with the luster of malachite in Figure 7. Other minerals, such as quartz, have a glassy luster. Some of the other terms used to describe luster include earthy, waxy, and pearly.

Density Each mineral has a characteristic density. Recall from Chapter 1 that density is the mass in a given space, or mass per unit volume. No matter what the size of a mineral sample, the density of that mineral always remains the same.

You can compare the density of two mineral samples of about the same size. Just pick them up and heft them, or feel their weight, in your hands. You may be able to feel the difference between low-density quartz and high-density galena. If the two samples are the same size, the galena is almost three times as heavy as the quartz.

But heft provides only a rough measure of density. When geologists measure density, they use a balance to determine precisely the mass of a mineral sample. The mineral is also placed in water to determine how much water it displaces. The volume of the displaced water equals the volume of the sample. Dividing the sample's mass by its volume gives the density of the mineral.

☑ *Checkpoint* How can you determine a mineral's density?

Crystal Systems The crystals of each mineral grow atom by atom to form that mineral's particular crystal structure. Geologists classify these structures into six groups based on the number and angle of the crystal faces. These groups are called crystal systems. For example, all halite crystals are cubic. Halite crystals have six sides that meet at right angles, forming a perfect cube. Sometimes you can see that a crystal has the particular crystal structure of its mineral. Crystals that grow in an open space can be almost perfectly formed. But crystals that grow in a tight space are often incompletely formed. Figure 8 shows minerals that belong to each of the six crystal systems.

Figure 8 This chart lists some common minerals and their properties. *Interpreting Data Which mineral is lowest in density and hardness? Which mineral could you identify by using a compass?*

Properties and Uses of Minerals

Name	 Magnetite	 Quartz	 Rutile	 Sulfur	 Azurite	 Microcline Feldspar
Hardness	6	7	$6 - 6\frac{1}{2}$	2	$3\frac{1}{2} - 4$	6
Color	Black	Transparent or in a range of colors	Black or reddish brown	Lemon yellow to yellowish brown	Blue	Green, red-brown, pink, or white
Streak	Black	Colorless	Light brown	White	Pale blue	Colorless
Crystal System	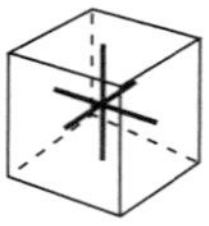 Cubic	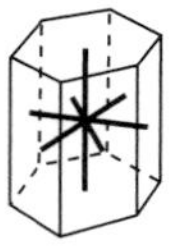 Hexagonal	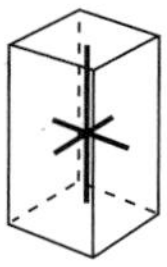 Tetragonal	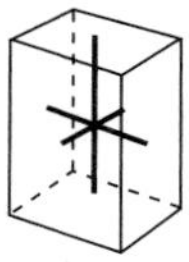 Orthorhombic	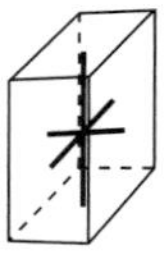 Monoclinic	 Triclinic
Luster	Metallic	Glassy	Metallic or gemlike	Greasy	Glassy to dull or earthy	Glassy
Special Properties	Magnetic	Fractures like broken glass	Not easily melted	Melts easily	Reacts to acid	Cleaves well in two directions
Density (g/cm³)	5.2	2.6	4.2–4.3	2.0–2.1	3.8	2.6
Uses	A source of iron used to make steel	Used in making glass and electronic equipment, or as a gem	Contains titanium, a hard, light-weight metal used in aircraft and cars	Used in fungicides, industrial chemicals, and rubber	A source of copper metal; also used as a gem	Used in pottery glaze, scouring powder, or as a gem

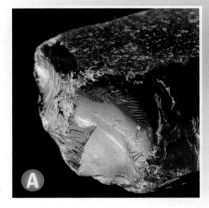

Figure 9 A. When quartz fractures, the break looks like the inside of a seashell. B. A piece of feldspar cleaves at right angles. C. Mica cleaves into thin, flat sheets that are almost transparent. *Applying Concepts* How would you test a mineral to determine its cleavage and fracture?

Cleavage and Fracture The way a mineral breaks apart can help to identify it. A mineral that splits easily along flat surfaces has the property called **cleavage.** Whether a mineral has cleavage depends on how the atoms in its crystals are arranged. Depending on the arrangement of atoms in the mineral, it will break apart more easily in one direction than another. Look at the minerals in Figure 9. Mica separates easily in only one direction, forming flat sheets. Feldspar splits at right angles, producing square corners. These minerals have cleavage.

Most minerals do not split apart evenly. Instead, they have a characteristic type of fracture. **Fracture** describes how a mineral looks when it breaks apart in an irregular way. Geologists use a variety of terms to describe fracture. For example, quartz has a shell-shaped fracture. When quartz breaks, it produces curved, shell-like surfaces that look like chipped glass. Pure metals, like copper and iron, have a hackly fracture—they form jagged points. Some soft minerals that crumble easily like clay have an earthy fracture. Minerals that form rough, irregular surfaces when broken have an uneven fracture.

✓ *Checkpoint* How are cleavage and fracture similar? How are they different?

Crystal Hands

You can grow two different kinds of salt crystals.

1. Put on your goggles.

2. ☠ Pour a solution of halite (table salt) into one shallow pan and a solution of Epsom salts into another shallow pan.

3. Put a large piece of black construction paper on a flat surface.

4. Dip one hand in the halite solution. Shake off the excess liquid and make a palm print on the paper. Repeat with your other hand and the Epsom salt solution, placing your new print next to the first one. **CAUTION:** *Do not do this activity if you have a cut on your hand.* Wash your hands after making your hand prints.

5. Let the prints dry overnight.

Observing Use a hand lens to compare the shape of the crystals. Which hand prints have more crystals?

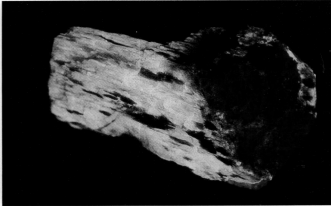

Figure 10 Scheelite looks quite ordinary in daylight, but glows with brilliant color under ultraviolet light.

Special Properties Some minerals can be identified by special physical properties. For example, minerals that glow under ultraviolet light have a property known as **fluorescence** (floo RES uns). The mineral scheelite is fluorescent. Magnetism occurs naturally in a few minerals. Lodestone, which is a form of magnetite, acts as a natural magnet. Early magnets—such as compass needles—were made by striking a piece of iron with lodestone. Uraninite and a few other minerals are radioactive. They set off a Geiger counter. Some minerals react chemically to acid. Calcite, a compound of calcium, carbon, and oxygen, fizzes and gives off carbon dioxide when a drop of vinegar is placed on it.

A few minerals, such as quartz, have electrical properties. Pressure applied to these crystals produces a small electric current. In addition, these crystals vibrate if they come in contact with an electric current. Because of these properties, quartz crystals are used in microphones, radio transmitters, and watches.

Section 1 Review

1. What characteristics must a substance have to be considered a mineral?
2. Describe how you can test a mineral to determine its hardness, density, and streak.
3. What is the major difference between an element and a compound?
4. **Thinking Critically Classifying** According to the definition of a mineral, can water be classified as a mineral? Explain your answer.
5. **Thinking Critically Making Generalizations** Explain why you can't rely on any single test or property when you are trying to identify a mineral.

Check Your Progress

CHAPTER PROJECT

Select a container for your crystal garden such as a plastic shoe box or a large-mouth jar. Make a sketch showing the shapes and locations of the "plants" you plan to grow. When you have designed your garden, decide what materials to put in the box for the crystals to grow on. Decide what crystal-growth solutions you will use. Halite, Epsom salts, and alum are possibilities. Check with your teacher to make sure the chemicals you plan to use are safe.

The Density of Minerals

In this lab, you will use water to help you measure the density of minerals.

Problem

How can you compare the density of different minerals?

Materials (per student)

graduated cylinder, 100 mL
3 mineral samples: pyrite, quartz, and galena
water
balance

Procedure

1. Check to make sure the mineral samples are small enough to fit in the graduated cylinder.
2. Copy the data table into your notebook. Place the pyrite on the balance and record its mass in the data table.
3. Fill the cylinder with water to the 50-mL mark.
4. Carefully place the pyrite into the cylinder of water. Try not to spill any of the water.
5. Read the level of the water on the scale of the graduated cylinder. Record the level of the water with the pyrite in it.
6. Calculate the volume of water displaced by the pyrite. To do this, subtract the volume of water without the pyrite from the volume of water with the pyrite. Record your answer.
7. Calculate the density of the pyrite by using this formula.

$$\text{Density} = \frac{\text{Mass of mineral}}{\text{Volume of water displaced by the mineral}}$$

(Note: Density is expressed as g/cm^3. One mL of water has a volume of 1 cm^3.)

8. Remove the water and mineral from the cylinder.
9. Repeat steps 2–8 for quartz and galena.

Analyze and Conclude

1. Which mineral had the highest density? The lowest density?
2. How does finding the volume of the water that was displaced help you find the volume of the mineral itself?
3. Why won't the procedure you used in this lab work for a substance that floats or one that dissolves in water?
4. **Apply** Pyrite is sometimes called "fool's gold" because its color and appearance are similar to real gold. How could a scientist determine if a sample was real gold?
5. **Think About It** Does the shape or size of a mineral sample affect its density? Explain.

More to Explore

Repeat the activity by finding the density of other minerals or materials. Then compare the densities of these materials with pyrite, quartz, and galena.

DATA TABLE	Pyrite	Quartz	Galena
Mass of Mineral (g)			
Volume of Water without Mineral (mL)	50 mL	50 mL	50 mL
Volume of Water with Mineral (mL)			
Volume of Water Displaced (mL)			
Density (g/cm^3)			

DISCOVER · ACTIVITY · · ·

How Does the Rate of Cooling Affect Crystals?

1. Put on your goggles. Use a plastic spoon to place a small amount of salol near one end of each of two microscope slides. You need just enough to form a spot 0.5 to 1.0 cm in diameter.

2. Carefully hold one slide with tongs. Warm it gently over a lit candle until the salol is almost completely melted. **CAUTION:** *Move the slide in and out of the flame to avoid cracking the glass.*

3. Set the slide aside to cool slowly.

4. While the first slide is cooling, hold the second slide with tongs and heat it as in Step 2. Cool the slide quickly by placing it on an ice cube. Carefully blow out the candle.

5. Observe the slides under a hand lens. Compare the appearance of the crystals that form on the two slides.

6. Wash your hands when you are finished.

Think It Over
Relating Cause and Effect
Which sample had larger crystals? If a mineral forms by rapid cooling, would you expect the crystals to be large or small?

GUIDE FOR READING

◆ What are the processes by which minerals form?

Reading Tip Before you read, rewrite the headings of the section as how, why, or what questions. As you read, look for answers to these questions.

Imagine digging for diamonds. At Crater of Diamonds State Park in Arkansas, that's exactly what people do. The park is one of the very few places in the United States where diamonds can be found. Visitors are permitted to prospect, or search, for diamonds. Since the area became a park in 1972, visitors have found more than 20,000 diamonds!

How did the diamonds get there? Millions of years ago, a volcano began to form in the mantle at a depth of 120 kilometers or more. At that depth, great

Diamonds ▶

pressure and heat changed carbon atoms into the hardest known substance—diamond. Then the volcano erupted, carrying diamonds and other materials toward the surface. Today, geologists recognize the remains of this type of volcano as an area of unusual bluish-colored rock made up of a variety of minerals, including diamond. Such rock containing diamonds is found in only a few places on Earth. Most occurs in South Africa and Australia, where many of the world's diamonds are mined today.

Processes That Form Minerals

You probably have handled products made from minerals. But you may not have thought about how the minerals formed. The minerals that people use today have been forming deep in Earth's crust or on the surface for several billion years. **In general, minerals can form in two ways: through crystallization of melted materials, and through crystallization of materials dissolved in water.** Crystallization is the process by which atoms are arranged to form a material with a crystal structure.

Minerals From Magma

Minerals form as hot magma cools inside the crust, or as lava hardens on the surface. **Magma** is molten material from the mantle that hardens to form rock. **Lava** is magma that reaches the surface. Lava also forms rock when it cools and hardens. When these liquids cool to the solid state, they form crystals. The size of the crystals depends on several factors. The rate at which the magma cools, the amount of gas the magma contains, and the chemical composition of the magma all affect crystal size.

When magma remains deep below the surface, it cools slowly over many thousands of years. Slow cooling leads to the formation of large crystals. If the crystals remain undisturbed while cooling, they grow by adding atoms according to a regular pattern.

Magma closer to the surface cools much faster than magma that hardens deep below ground. With more rapid cooling, there is no time for magma to form large crystals. Instead, small crystals form. If magma erupts to the surface and becomes lava, the lava will also cool quickly and form minerals with small crystals.

Figure 11 The gray crystal of the mineral spodumene is 24 cm long. But it's not the largest crystal. Spodumene crystals the size of telephone poles have been found in South Dakota. *Inferring Under what conditions did such large crystals probably form?*

Figure 12 **A.** Silver sometimes occurs as a pure metal, forming delicate, treelike crystals. **B.** Solutions containing dissolved metals form veins like the ones in this silver mine in Idaho.

Minerals From Hot Water Solutions

Sometimes, the elements that form a mineral dissolve in hot water. Magma has heated the water to a high temperature beneath Earth's surface. These dissolved minerals form solutions. A **solution** is a mixture in which one substance dissolves in another. When a hot water solution begins to cool, the elements and compounds leave the solution and crystallize as minerals. The silver shown in Figure 12A formed by this process.

Pure metals that crystallize underground from hot water solutions often form veins. A **vein** is a narrow channel or slab of a mineral that is much different from the surrounding rock. Deep underground, solutions of hot water and metals often follow cracks within the rock. Then the metals crystallize into veins that resemble the streaks of fudge in vanilla fudge ice cream. Figure 12B shows a vein of silver in a mine.

Many minerals form from solutions at places where there are cracks in the crust forming the ocean floor. First, ocean water

Figure 13 Many minerals form at chimneys in the ocean floor. *Interpreting Diagrams What is the energy source for this process?*

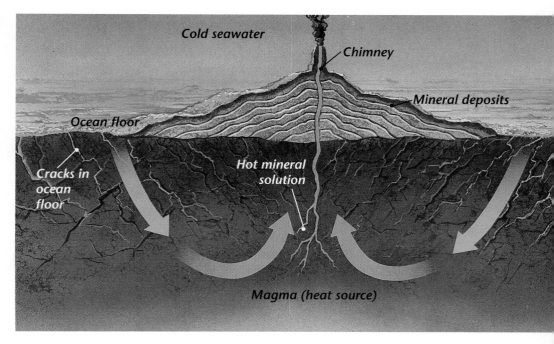

Cold seawater

Chimney

Mineral deposits

Ocean floor

Cracks in ocean floor

Hot mineral solution

Magma (heat source)

Figure 14 In Death Valley, California, water carries dissolved minerals from the surrounding mountains into the valley. When the water evaporates under the blazing desert sun, the minerals form a crust on the valley floor.

seeps down through cracks in the crust. There, the water comes in contact with magma that heats it to a very high temperature. The heated water dissolves minerals from the crust and rushes upward. This hot solution then billows out of vents, called "chimneys." When the hot solution hits the cold sea, minerals crystallize and settle to the ocean floor.

Minerals Formed by Evaporation

Minerals can also form when solutions evaporate. You know that if you stir salt crystals into a beaker of water, the salt dissolves, forming a solution. But if you allow the water in the solution to evaporate, it will leave salt crystals on the bottom of the beaker. In a similar way, thick deposits of the mineral halite formed over millions of years when ancient seas slowly evaporated. In the United States, such halite deposits occur in the Midwest, the Southwest, and along the Gulf Coast.

Several other useful minerals also form by the evaporation of seawater. These include gypsum, used in making building materials; calcite crystals, used in microscopes; and minerals containing potassium, used in making fertilizer.

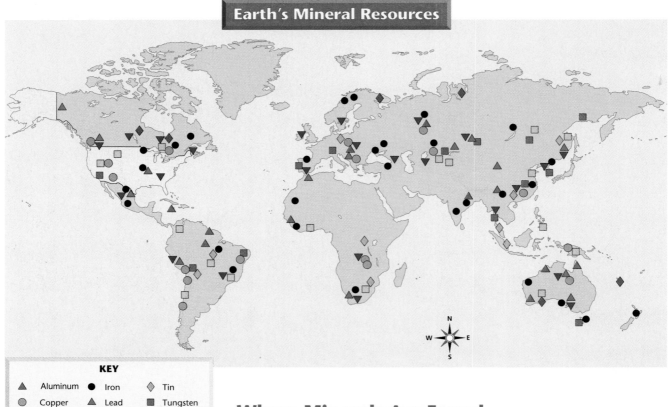

KEY

▲ Aluminum	● Iron	◆ Tin	
● Copper	▲ Lead	■ Tungsten	
▢ Gold	◆ Nickel	▼ Zinc	

Figure 15 The map shows where important mineral resources are found throughout the world. *Interpreting Maps Which metals are found in the United States? Which ones must be imported from other countries?*

Where Minerals Are Found

Earth's crust is made up mostly of the common rock-forming minerals combined in various types of rock. Less common and rare minerals, however, are not distributed evenly throughout the crust. Instead, there are several processes that concentrate minerals, or bring them together, in deposits. Look at the map of the world's mineral resources in Figure 15. Do you see any patterns in the distribution of minerals such as gold and copper? Many valuable minerals are found in or near areas of volcanic activity and mountain building. For example, rich copper deposits are found along the Andes mountains in Chile.

Section 2 Review

1. What are the two main ways in which minerals form?
2. Describe how the cooling rate of magma affects the size of the mineral crystals formed.
3. What are the steps by which mineral deposits form around chimneys on the ocean floor?
4. **Thinking Critically Relating Cause and Effect** A miner finds a vein of silver. Describe a process that could have formed the vein.

Check Your Progress

CHAPTER PROJECT

Remember to record your daily observations of how your crystal garden grows. Sketch the shapes of the crystals and describe how the crystals grow. Compare the shapes and growth rates of the crystals grown from the various solutions. (*Hint:* If crystals do not begin growing, add more of the correct solution.)

Who Owns the Ocean's Minerals?

Rich mineral deposits lie on and just beneath the ocean floor. Many nations would like to mine these deposits. Coastal nations already have the right to mine deposits near their shores. Today, they are mining materials such as tin, titanium, diamonds, and sulfur from the continental shelf— the wide area of shallow water just off the shores of continents.

But the ocean floor beyond the continental shelves is open for all nations to explore. Mineral deposits in volcanic areas of the ocean floor include manganese, iron, cobalt, copper, nickel and platinum. Who owns these valuable underwater minerals?

▲ This sample from the floor of the Pacific Ocean near New Guinea may contain copper and gold.

The Issues

Who Can Afford to Mine? Although the ocean floor is open to all for exploration, mining the ocean floor will cost a huge amount of money. New technologies must be developed to obtain mineral deposits from the ocean floor.

Only wealthy industrial nations such as France, Germany, Japan, and the United States will be able to afford these costs. Industrial nations that have spent money and effort on mining think that they should be allowed to keep all the profits. However, developing nations that lack money and technology disagree. Landlocked nations that have no coastlines also object.

What Rights Do Other Nations Have? As of 1996, 87 nations had signed the Law of the Sea treaty. Among other things, this treaty stated that ocean mineral deposits are the common property of all people. It also stated that mining profits must be shared among all nations.

Some people think that, because of the treaty, wealthy nations should share their technology and any profits they get from mining the ocean floor.

How Can the Wealth Be Shared? What can nations do to prevent conflict over mining the ocean floor? They might arrange a compromise. Perhaps wealthy nations should contribute part of their profits to help developing or landlocked nations. Developing nations could pool their money for ocean-floor mining. Whatever nations decide, some regulations for ocean-floor mining are necessary. In the future, these resources will be important to everyone.

You Decide

1. **Identify the Problem**
   In your own words, state the controversy about ocean mineral rights.

2. **Analyze the Options**
   Compare the concerns of wealthy nations with those of developing nations. How could you reassure developing nations that they will not be left out?

3. **Find a Solution**
   Look at a map of the world. Who should share the mineral profits from the Pacific Ocean? From the Atlantic Ocean? Write one or two paragraphs stating your opinion. Support your ideas with facts.

SECTION 3 Mineral Resources

GUIDE FOR READING

◆ How are minerals used?
◆ What are the three types of mines?
◆ How are ores processed to obtain metals?

Reading Tip As you read, draw a concept map that explains how metal ores are located, mined, and smelted.

More than a thousand years ago, the Hopewell people lived in the Mississippi River valley. These ancient Native Americans are famous for the mysterious earthen mounds they built near the river. There these people left beautiful objects made from minerals: tools chipped from flint (a variety of quartz), the shape of a human hand cut out of a piece of translucent mica, or a flying bird made from a thin sheet of copper.

To obtain these minerals, the Hopewell people traded with peoples across North America. The copper, for example, came from near Lake Superior. There, copper could be found as a pure metal. Because copper is a soft metal, this copper was easy to shape into ornaments or weapons.

The Uses of Minerals

Figure 16 The copper to make this Hopewell ornament may have come from an area in Michigan that is still a source of copper ore.

Like the Hopewell people, people today use minerals. You are surrounded by materials that come from minerals—for example, the metal body and window glass of a car. **Minerals are the source of metals, gemstones, and other materials used to make many products.** Are you familiar with any products that are made from minerals? You might be surprised at how important minerals are in everyday life.

Gemstones Beautiful gemstones such as rubies and sapphires have captured the imagination of people throughout the ages. Usually, a **gemstone** is a hard, colorful mineral that has a brilliant or glassy luster. People value gemstones for their color, luster, and durability—and for the fact that they are rare. Once a gemstone is cut and polished, it is called a gem. Gems are used mainly for jewelry and decoration. They are also used for mechanical parts and for grinding and polishing.

Metals Some minerals are the sources of metals such as aluminum, iron, copper, or silver. Metals are useful because they can be stretched into wire, flattened into sheets, and hammered or molded without breaking. Metal tools and machinery, the metal filament in a light bulb, even the steel girders used to frame office buildings—all began as minerals inside Earth's crust.

Figure 17 Gems like these red rubies and blue and yellow sapphires are among the most valuable minerals. These precious gems are varieties of the mineral corundum.

Other Useful Minerals There are many other useful minerals besides metals and gems. People use materials from these minerals in foods, medicines, fertilizers, and building materials. The very soft mineral talc is ground up to make talcum powder. Fluorite is important in making aluminum and steel. Clear crystals of the mineral calcite are used in optical instruments such as microscopes. Quartz, a mineral found in sand, is used in making glass as well as in electronic equipment and watches. Kaolin occurs as white clay, which is used for making high-quality china and pottery. Gypsum, a soft, white mineral, is used to make wallboard, cement, and stucco. Corundum, the second hardest mineral after diamond, is often used in polishing and cleaning products.

✓ *Checkpoint* *What is a gemstone? Why are gemstones valuable?*

Ores

A rock that contains a metal or economically useful mineral is called an **ore**. Unlike the copper used by the Hopewell people, most metals do not occur in a pure form. A metal usually occurs as a mineral that is a combination of that metal and other elements. Much of the world's copper, for example, comes from ores containing the mineral chalcopyrite (kal kuh PY ryt). Before metals, gemstones, and other useful minerals can be separated from their ores, however, geologists must find them.

Prospecting

A prospector is anyone who searches, or prospects, for an ore deposit. Geologists prospect for ores by looking for certain features on Earth's surface. These geologists observe what kind of rocks are on the land surface. They examine plants growing in an area and test stream water for the presence of certain chemicals.

Geologists also employ some of the tools used to study Earth's interior. In one technique, they set off explosions below ground to create shock waves. The echoes of these shock waves are used to map the location, size, and shape of an ore deposit.

Mining

The geologist's map of an ore deposit helps miners decide how to mine the ore from the ground. **There are three types of mines: strip mines, open pit mines, and shaft mines.** In strip mining,

SCIENCE & History

Advances in Metal Technology

For thousands of years, people have been inventing and improving methods for smelting metals and making alloys.

4000 B.C. Cyprus

The island of Cyprus was one of the first places where copper was mined and smelted. In fact, the name of the island provided the name of the metal. In Latin, *aes cyprium* meant "metal of Cyprus." It was later shortened to *cuprum*, meaning "copper." The sculptured figure is carrying a large piece of smelted copper.

| 4000 B.C. | 2500 B.C. | 1000 B.C. |

3500 B.C.
Mesopotamia

Metalworkers in Sumer, a city between the Tigris and Euphrates rivers, made an alloy of tin and copper to produce a harder metal—bronze. Bronze was poured into molds to form statues, weapons, or vessels for food and drink.

1500 B.C.
Turkey

The Hittites learned to mine and smelt iron ore. Because iron is stronger than copper or bronze, its use spread rapidly. Tools and weapons could be made of iron. This iron dagger was made in Austria several hundred years after the Hittites' discovery.

earthmoving equipment scrapes away soil to expose ore. In open pit mining, miners use giant earthmoving equipment to dig a tremendous pit. Miners dig an open pit mine to remove ore deposits that may start near the surface, but extend down for hundreds of meters. Some open pit mines are more than a kilometer wide and nearly as deep. For ore deposits that occur in veins, miners dig shaft mines. Shaft mines often have a network of tunnels that extend deep into the ground, following the veins of ore.

INTEGRATING ENVIRONMENTAL SCIENCE Mining for metals and other minerals can harm the environment. Strip mining and pit mining leave scars on the land. Waste materials from mining can pollute rivers and lakes. In the United States, laws now require that mine operators do as little damage to the environment as possible. To restore land damaged by strip mining, mine operators grade the surface and replace the soil.

In Your Journal

When people discover how to use metals in a new way, the discovery often produces big changes in the way those people live. Choose a development in the history of metals to research. Write a diary entry telling how the discovery happened and how it changed people's lives.

A.D. 1860s
England

Steel-making techniques invented by Henry Bessemer and William Siemens made it possible to produce steel cheaply on a large scale. Siemens' invention, the open-hearth furnace, is still widely used, although more modern methods account for most steel production today.

A.D. 500   **A.D. 2000**

A.D. 600s
Sri Lanka

Sri Lankans made steel in outdoor furnaces. Steady winds blowing over the top of the furnace's front wall created the high temperatures needed to make steel. Because their steel was so much harder than iron, the Sri Lankans were able to trade it throughout the Indian Ocean region.

A.D. 1960s TO THE PRESENT
United States

Scientists working on the space program have developed light and strong alloys for use in products ranging from bicycles to soda cans. For example, a new alloy of nickel and titanium can "remember" its shape. It is used for eyeglasses that return to their original shape after being bent.

Smelting

Ores must be processed before the metals they contain can be used. **After miners remove ore from a mine, smelting is necessary to remove the metal from the ore.** In the process of **smelting,** an ore is melted to separate the useful metal from other elements the ore contains. People around the world have used smelting to obtain metals from ores. Look at the time line in *Science and History* to see how this technology has developed from ancient times to the present.

How does smelting separate iron metal from hematite, a common form of iron ore? In general, smelting involves mixing an ore with other substances and then heating the mixture to a very high temperature. The heat melts the metal in the ore. The heat also causes the metal to separate from the oxygen with which it is combined. Metalworkers can then pour off the molten metal. Follow the steps in *Exploring Smelting Iron Ore.*

Figure 18 Plain steel rusts easily. But stainless steel—an alloy of iron, chromium, and nickel—doesn't rust. The chromium and nickel slow down the process by which the oxygen in the air combines with iron in the steel to form iron oxide, or rust.

After smelting, additional processing is needed to remove impurities from the iron. The result is steel, which is harder and stronger than iron. Steel is an **alloy,** a solid mixture of two or more metals. Steelmakers mix iron with other elements to create alloys with special properties. For stronger steel, the metal manganese and a small amount of carbon are added. For rust-resistant steel, the metals chromium and nickel are added. You can compare plain steel with rust-resistant stainless steel in Figure 18.

Section 3 Review

1. What are some of the ways that people use gems and metals?
2. Describe three different kinds of mines.
3. What process is used to separate useful metals from ores?
4. What are alloys, and why are they useful?
5. **Thinking Critically** In smelting, what causes a metal to separate from its ore?

Science at Home

Rust Protection You can demonstrate to your family how rust damages objects that contain iron. Obtain three iron nails. Coat one of the nails with petroleum jelly and coat the second nail with clear nail polish. Do not put anything on the third nail. Place all the nails in a glass of water with a little vinegar. (The vinegar speeds up the rusting process.) Allow the nails to stand in the glass overnight. Which nails show signs of rusting? Explain these results to your family.

EXPLORING Smelting Iron Ore

Iron usually occurs as the ores hematite or magnetite. Iron ores must be smelted to separate the iron from the oxygen and other substances in the ores. Then the iron is refined and processed into steel.

1. Iron ore is crushed and then mixed with crushed limestone and coke (baked coal), which is rich in carbon.

2. The coke and iron ore mixture is placed in a blast furnace, where extremely hot air is blown through, making the coke burn easily.

3. As the coke burns, chemical changes in the mixture produce carbon dioxide gas and molten iron.

4. The iron sinks to the bottom of the furnace. Impurities left in the ore combine with the limestone to create slag.

5. The slag and molten iron are poured off through taps in the blast furnace.

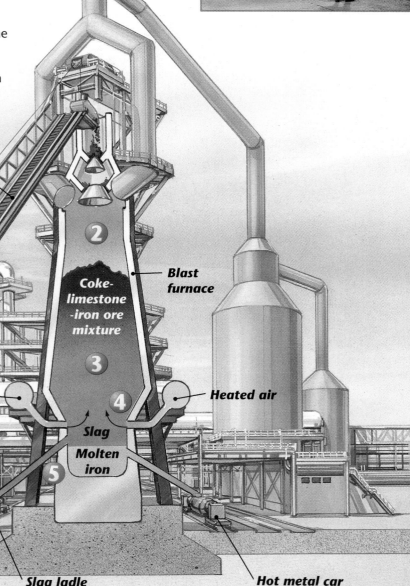

Skip hoist

Coke-limestone-iron ore mixture

Blast furnace

Heated air

Heated air

Coke

Slag

Molten iron

Iron ore and limestone

Slag ladle

Hot metal car

COPPER RECOVERY

I f you were a mining engineer, one of your tasks would be to make mining and processing ores more efficient. When copper ore is processed at copper mines, waste water containing copper sulfate is produced. Mining engineers have invented a way to recover copper metal from the waste water. They make the waste water flow over scrap iron.

Problem

How is copper recovered from a solution?

Skills Focus

observing, inferring, developing hypotheses

Materials

copper sulfate, 3 g	beaker, 400 mL
triple-beam balance	5 iron nails
graduated cylinder, 200 mL	

Procedure

1. Place 3 g of copper sulfate in a beaker. **CAUTION:** *Copper sulfate is poisonous. Handle it with care.*
2. Add 50 mL of water to the beaker to dissolve the copper sulfate. Observe the color of the solution.
3. Add the iron nails to the beaker. The nails act as scrap iron. Describe the color of the solution after the nails have been added to the solution.
4. Follow your teacher's instructions for proper disposal. Wash your hands when you are finished.

Analyze and Conclude

1. What happened to the nails after you placed them in the solution? What is the material on the nails? Explain your answer.
2. How does the material on the nails compare with the copper sulfate?
3. Form a hypothesis that describes how a mine might recover copper from mine water using the method that you have just tried.
4. What additional step would you have to perform to obtain copper useful for making copper wire or pennies?
5. **Apply** Why do you think the operator of a copper mine would want to collect copper from the waste water?

More to Explore

Repeat the experiment. This time test the solution with litmus paper both before and after you add the nails. Litmus paper indicates if a solution is acidic, basic, or neutral. Record your results. Why do you think a mining engineer would test the water from this process before releasing it into the environment?

SECTION 1 Properties of Minerals

Key Ideas

◆ A mineral is a naturally occurring inorganic solid that has a distinct chemical composition and crystal shape.
◆ Each mineral can be identified by its own physical and chemical properties.
◆ Some of the properties of minerals include hardness, color, streak, luster, density, cleavage and fracture, and crystal structure. Hardness is measured by the Mohs hardness scale.
◆ Minerals usually consist of two or more elements joined together in a compound.

Key Terms

mineral	Mohs hardness scale
inorganic	streak
crystal	luster
element	cleavage
compound	fracture
	fluorescence

SECTION 2 How Minerals Form

Key Ideas

◆ Minerals form inside Earth through crystallization as magma or lava cools.
◆ Minerals form on Earth's surface when materials dissolved in water crystallize through evaporation.
◆ Mineral deposits form on the ocean floor from solutions heated by magma. The hot-water solutions containing minerals erupt through chimneys on the ocean floor, then crystallize when they come in contact with cold sea water.

Key Terms

magma
lava
solution
vein

SECTION 3 Mineral Resources

INTEGRATING TECHNOLOGY

Key Ideas

◆ Minerals are useful as the source of all metals, gemstones, and of many other materials.
◆ Geologists locate ore deposits by prospecting—looking for certain features on and beneath Earth's surface.
◆ Ores can be removed from the ground through open pit mines, strip mines, or shaft mines.
◆ Smelting is the process of heating an ore to extract a metal.

Key Terms

gemstone
ore
smelting
alloy

Organizing Information

Venn Diagram Copy the Venn diagram comparing the mineral hematite and the human-made material brick onto a separate piece of paper. Then complete it and add a title. (For more on Venn diagrams, see the Skills Handbook.)

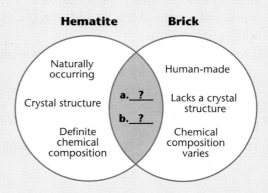

Hematite — Brick

Naturally occurring
Crystal structure
Definite chemical composition

a. _?_
b. _?_

Human-made
Lacks a crystal structure
Chemical composition varies

Reviewing Content

 For more review of key concepts, see the Interactive Student Tutorial CD-ROM.

Multiple Choice

Choose the letter of the answer that best completes each statement.

1. In a mineral, the particles line up in a repeating pattern to form
   a. an element.   **b.** a crystal.
   c. a mixture.   **d.** a compound.

2. The softest mineral in the Mohs hardness scale is
   a. quartz.   **b.** talc.
   c. apatite.   **d.** gypsum.

3. Halite is a mineral formed by
   a. chimneys on the ocean floor.
   b. cooling of magma.
   c. evaporation.
   d. cooling of lava.

4. Metals are useful for tools because they
   a. are compounds.
   b. have a metallic luster.
   c. are hard yet can be easily shaped.
   d. are elements.

5. Minerals from which metals can be removed in usable amounts are called
   a. gemstones.
   b. crystals.
   c. alloys.
   d. ores.

True or False

If the statement is true, write true. If it is false, change the underlined word or words to make the statement true.

6. <u>Luster</u> is the term that describes how a mineral reflects light from its surface.

7. A piece of unglazed tile is used to test a mineral's <u>hardness</u>.

8. If magma cools very slowly, minerals with <u>small</u> crystals will form.

9. Minerals form from <u>hot-water solutions</u> at chimneys on the ocean floor.

10. The process of removing an ore deposit from the ground is known as <u>prospecting</u>.

Checking Concepts

11. What is the difference in composition between most minerals and a pure element?

12. How can the streak test be helpful in identifying minerals?

13. Compare cleavage and fracture.

14. Describe two different ways that minerals can form.

15. Describe the process used to extract metal from hematite ore. What metal would be obtained?

16. **Writing to Learn** You are a prospector searching for gold. In a letter home, describe where you plan to look, how you will know if you have found gold, and how you will feel about your discovery.

Thinking Critically

17. **Comparing and Contrasting** Color and luster are both properties of minerals. How are these properties similar? How are they different? How can each be used to help identify a mineral?

18. **Classifying** Obsidian forms when magma cools very quickly, creating a type of glass. In glass, the particles are not arranged in an orderly pattern as in a crystal. Obsidian is a solid, inorganic substance that occurs naturally in volcanic areas. Should it be classified as a mineral? Explain why or why not.

19. **Relating Cause and Effect** Describe how a vein of ore forms underground. What is the energy source for this process?

20. **Applying Concepts** Explain the roles of elements, solutions, and compounds in the process that forms minerals around chimneys on the ocean floor.

21. **Predicting** What would happen if steelmakers forgot to add enough chromium and nickel to a batch of stainless steel?

Applying Skills

Working as a geologist, you have found a sample of the mineral wulfenite. Testing the wulfenite reveals that it has a hardness of about 3 on the Mohs hardness scale and a density of 6.8 grams per cubic centimeter. You also determine that the mineral contains oxygen as well as the metals lead and molybdenum.

Wulfenite

22. **Observing** Describe wulfenite's color, luster, and crystal structure.

23. **Inferring** Did the wulfenite form slowly or quickly? Explain your answer.

24. **Drawing Conclusions** Is wulfenite hard enough for use as a gem? What would you use these crystals for? Explain.

Performance ▼ CHAPTER PROJECT Assessment

Present Your Project Before you present your crystal garden to the class, share it with a classmate. Can your classmate identify which solution created which crystals? Do your data show differences in crystal growth rates? What conclusions can you draw from your data? Now you are ready to present your project to your class.

Reflect and Record In your journal, identify any changes that would improve your crystal garden. Which materials worked best for crystals to grow on? Which ones did not work well?

Test Preparation
Use these questions to prepare for standardized tests.

Study the table. Then answer Questions 25–29.

Properties of Six Minerals				
Mineral	Hardness	Density (g/cm³)	Luster	Streak
Corundum	9.0	4.0	glassy	white
Quartz	7.0	2.6	glassy	white
Magnetite	6.0	5.2	metallic	black
Copper	2.8	8.9	metallic	red
Galena	2.5	7.5	metallic	lead gray
Talc	1.0	2.8	pearly	white

25. Which mineral in the table could be scratched by all the others?
 a. quartz
 b. galena
 c. copper
 d. talc

26. The mineral in the table with the greatest density is
 a. copper.
 b. galena.
 c. magnetite.
 d. talc.

27. To be suitable as a gemstone, a mineral usually must be very hard and have a glassy luster. Which mineral on the list would probably make the best gemstone?
 a. copper
 b. corundum
 c. magnetite
 d. galena

28. Quartz and talc both produce a white streak and have similar density. What property or properties could you easily test to tell them apart?
 a. hardness and luster
 b. streak only
 c. density only
 d. none of the above

29. Suppose that you have found a dense, dark-colored mineral with a metallic luster. What property would you test quickly and easily to determine if the mineral were copper rather than galena?
 a. hardness
 b. luster
 c. streak
 d. density

WEB ACTIVITY
www.phschool.com

CHAPTER 3 PROJECT

Collecting Rocks

Each rock, whether a small pebble or a giant boulder, tells a story. By observing a rock's characteristics, geologists learn about the forces that shaped the portion of Earth's crust where the rock formed. The rocks in your own community tell the story of Earth's crust in your area.

In this chapter, you will learn how three different types of rocks form. You can apply what you learn about rocks to create your own rock collection and explore the properties of these rocks.

Your Goal To make a collection of the rocks in your area.

To complete this project, you must
- ◆ collect samples of rocks, keeping a record of where you found each sample
- ◆ describe the characteristics of your rocks, including their color, texture, and density
- ◆ classify each rock as igneous, sedimentary, or metamorphic
- ◆ create a display for your rock collection
- ◆ follow the safety guidelines in Appendix A

Get Started With your classmates and teacher, brainstorm locations in your community where rocks are likely to be found. Are there road cuts, outcroppings of bedrock, riverbanks, or beaches where you could safely and legally collect your rocks?

Check Your Progress You will be working on this project as you study the chapter. To keep your project on track, look for Check Your Progress boxes at the following points.

Section 1 Review, page 77: Plan your rock-hunting expeditions.
Section 3 Review, page 86: Collect your rocks.
Section 4 Review, page 89: Begin to describe, test, and catalog your rock collection.
Section 6 Review, page 95: Classify your rocks and plan your presentation.

Present Your Project At the end of the chapter (page 99), prepare a display of your rock collection. Be prepared to discuss the properties of the rocks you collected, how the rocks formed, and how people can use them.

Hikers cross a landscape of rock in the Cascade Range, a mountain range in Washington state.

Integrating Life Science

SECTION 4 Rocks From Reefs
Discover What Can You Conclude From the Way a Rock Reacts to Acid?

SECTION 5 Metamorphic Rocks

Discover How Do the Grain Patterns of Gneiss and Granite Compare?
Try This A Sequined Rock
Skills Lab Mystery Rocks

SECTION 6 The Rock Cycle

Discover Which Rock Came First?
Real-World Lab Testing Rock Flooring

SECTION
1 Classifying Rocks

DISCOVER

How Are Rocks Alike and Different?

1. Look at samples of marble and conglomerate with a hand lens.

2. Describe the two rocks. What is the color and texture of each?

3. Try scratching the surface of each rock with the edge of a penny. Which rock seems harder?

ACTIVITY

4. Hold each rock in your hand. Allowing for the fact that the samples aren't exactly the same size, which rock seems denser?

Think It Over

Observing Based on your observations, how would you compare the physical properties of marble and conglomerate?

GUIDE FOR READING

◆ What characteristics are used to identify rocks?

◆ What are the three major groups of rocks?

Reading Tip Before you read, use the headings to make an outline about rocks. Then fill in details as you read.

Between 1969 and 1972, the Apollo missions to the moon returned to Earth with pieces of the moon's surface. Space scientists eagerly tested these samples. They wanted to learn what the moon is made of. They found that the moon's surface is made of material very similar to the material that makes up Earth's surface—rock. Some moon samples are dark rock called basalt. Other samples are light-colored rock made mostly of the mineral feldspar.

Figure 1 Geology students collect and study samples of rocks.

How Geologists Classify Rocks

For both Earth and its moon, rocks are important building blocks. On Earth, rock forms mountains, hills, valleys, beaches, even the ocean floor. Earth's crust is made of rock. Rocks are made of mixtures of minerals and other materials, although some rocks may contain only a single mineral. Granite, shown in Figure 2, is made up of the minerals quartz, feldspar, mica, and hornblende, and sometimes other minerals. Feldspar is not a single mineral, but a group of similar minerals. The term mica also refers to a group of minerals that are related in composition and crystal structure.

Geologists collect and study samples of rock in order to classify them. Imagine that you are a geologist exploring a

Figure 2 Granite is made up of quartz, mica, feldspar, and hornblende. It may also contain other minerals.
Observing Which mineral seems most abundant in the sample of granite shown?

mountain range for the first time. How would you study a particular type of rock found in these mountains? You might use a camera or notebook to record information about the setting where the rock was found. Then, you would use a chisel or the sharp end of a rock hammer to remove samples of the rock. Finally, you would break open the samples with a hammer to examine their inside surfaces. You must look at the inside of a rock because the effects of water and weather can change the outer surface of a rock.

When studying a rock sample, geologists observe the rock's color and texture and determine its mineral composition. Using these characteristics, geologists can classify a rock according to its origin, or where and how it formed.

Texture

As with minerals, color alone does not provide enough information to identify a rock. A rock's texture, however, is very useful in identifying the rock. To a geologist, a rock's **texture** is the size, shape, and pattern of the rock's grains. Some rocks are smooth and glassy. Others are rough or chalky. Most rocks are made up of particles of minerals or other rocks, which geologists call **grains.** A rock's grains give the rock its texture.

Fine-grained
Slate

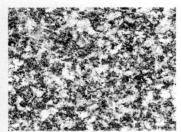

Coarse-grained
Diorite

No visible grain
Flint

Grain Size Often, the grains in a rock are large and easy to see. Such rocks are said to be coarse-grained. In other rocks, the grains are so small that they can only be seen with a microscope. These rocks are said to be fine-grained. Notice the difference in texture between the fine-grained slate and the coarse-grained diorite at left.

Grain Shape The grains in a rock vary widely in shape. Some grains look like tiny particles of fine sand. Others look like small seeds or exploding stars. In some rocks, such as granite, the grain results from the shapes of the crystals that form the rock. In other rocks, the grain shape results from fragments of other rock. These fragments can be smooth and rounded, like the fragments in conglomerate, or they can be jagged, like the fragments in breccia. You can compare conglomerate and breccia below.

Grain Pattern The grains in a rock often form patterns. Some grains lie in flat layers that look like a stack of pancakes. Other grains form wavy, swirling patterns. Some rocks have grains that look like rows of multicolored beads, as in the sample of gneiss shown below. Other rocks, in contrast, have grains that occur randomly throughout the rock.

No Visible Grain Some rocks have no grain, even when they are examined under a microscope. Some of these rocks have no crystal grains because when they form, they cool very quickly. This quick cooling gives these rocks the smooth, shiny texture of a thick piece of glass. Other rocks with no visible grain are made up of extremely small particles of silica that settle out of water. One familiar rock that forms in this manner is flint.

☑ *Checkpoint* *What terms describe a rock's texture?*

Jagged grain
Breccia

Rounded grain
Conglomerate

Nonbanded
Quartzite

Banded
Gneiss

Mineral Composition

Often, geologists must look more closely at a rock to determine its mineral composition. By looking at a small sliver of a rock under a microscope, a geologist can observe the shape and size of crystals in the rock and identify the minerals it contains. To prepare a rock for viewing under the microscope, geologists cut the rock very thin, so that light can shine through its crystals.

In identifying rocks, geologists also use some of the tests that are used to identify minerals. For example, testing the rock's surface with acid determines whether the rock includes minerals made of compounds called carbonates. Testing with a magnet detects the elements iron or nickel.

Origin

There are three major groups of rocks: igneous rock, sedimentary rock, and metamorphic rock. These terms refer to how the rocks in each group formed.

Rock belonging to each of these groups forms in a different way. **Igneous rock** forms from the cooling of molten rock—either magma below the surface or lava at the surface. Most **sedimentary rock** forms when particles of other rocks or the remains of plants and animals are pressed and cemented together. Sedimentary rock forms in layers below the surface. **Metamorphic rock** is formed when an existing rock is changed by heat, pressure, or chemical reactions. Most metamorphic rock forms deep underground.

Figure 4 A scientist is preparing to cut a thin slice from a piece of moon rock. He will then examine it under a microscope to determine its composition.

Section 1 Review

1. What three characteristics do geologists use to identify a rock sample?
2. What are the three groups into which geologists classify rocks?
3. What is a rock's texture?
4. What methods do geologists use to determine the mineral composition of a rock?
5. **Thinking Critically Comparing and Contrasting** What do the three major groups of rocks have in common? How are they different?

Check Your Progress

CHAPTER PROJECT

Your neighborhood might be a good place to begin your rock collection. Look for gravel and crushed rock in flower beds, driveways or parking lots, and beneath downspouts. **CAUTION:** *If the area you choose is not a public place, make sure that you have permission to be there.* Begin to collect samples of rocks with different colors and textures. Plan with your teacher or an adult family member to visit other parts of your community where you could collect rocks.

SECTION 2 Igneous Rocks

DISCOVER — ACTIVITY

How Do Igneous Rocks Form?

1. Use a hand lens to examine samples of granite and obsidian.
2. Describe the texture of both rocks using the terms coarse, fine, or glassy.
3. Which rock has coarse-grained crystals? Which rock has no crystals or grains?

Think It Over

Inferring Granite and obsidian are igneous rocks. Given the physical properties of these rocks, what can you infer about how each type of rock formed?

GUIDE FOR READING

◆ What characteristics are used to classify igneous rocks?

Reading Tip As you read, make a list of the characteristics of igneous rocks. Write one sentence describing each characteristic.

You are in a spacecraft orbiting Earth 4.6 billion years ago. Do you see the blue and green globe of Earth that astronauts today see from space? No—instead, Earth looks like a glowing piece of charcoal from a barbecue, or a charred and bubbling marshmallow heated over the coals.

Soon after Earth formed, the planet became so hot that its surface was a glowing mass of molten material. Hundreds of millions of years passed before Earth cooled enough for a crust to solidify. Then lava probably flowed from Earth's interior, spread over the surface, and hardened. The movement of magma and lava has continued ever since.

Figure 5 A lava flow soon cools and hardens to form igneous rock.

Characteristics of Igneous Rock

The first rocks to form on Earth probably looked much like the igneous rocks that harden from lava today. Igneous rock (IG nee us) is any rock that forms from magma or lava. The name "igneous" comes from the Latin word *ignis*, meaning "fire."

Most igneous rocks are made of mineral crystals. The only exceptions to this rule are the different types of volcanic glass—igneous rock that lacks minerals with a crystal structure. **Igneous rocks are classified according to their origin, texture, and mineral composition.**

Origin Geologists classify igneous rocks according to where they formed. **Extrusive rock** is igneous rock formed from lava that erupted onto Earth's surface. **Basalt** is the most common extrusive rock. Basalt forms much of the crust, including the crust beneath the ocean floor.

Intrusive rock is igneous rock that formed when magma hardened beneath Earth's surface. **Granite** is the most abundant intrusive rock in the part of the crust that makes up the continents. Granite forms the core of many mountain ranges.

Texture The texture of an igneous rock depends on the size and shape of its mineral crystals. Igneous rocks may be similar in mineral composition and yet have very different textures. The texture of an igneous rock may be fine-grained, coarse-grained, glassy, or porphyritic. Rapid cooling lava forms fine-grained igneous rocks with small crystals. Slow cooling magma forms coarse-grained rock with large crystals.

Intrusive and extrusive rocks usually have different textures. Intrusive rocks have larger crystals than extrusive rocks. If you examine a coarse-grained rock such as granite, you can easily see that the crystals vary in size and color.

Some intrusive rocks have a texture like a gelatin dessert with chopped-up fruit mixed in. A rock with large crystals scattered on a background of much smaller crystals has a **porphyritic texture** (pawr fuh RIT ik). How can a rock have two textures?

Figure 6 Igneous rocks can vary greatly in texture.
A. Rhyolite is a fine-grained igneous rock with a mineral composition similar to granite.
B. Pegmatite is a very coarse-grained variety of granite.
C. Porphyry has large crystals surrounded by fine-grained crystals.
Relating Cause and Effect What conditions caused rhyolite to have a fine-grained texture?

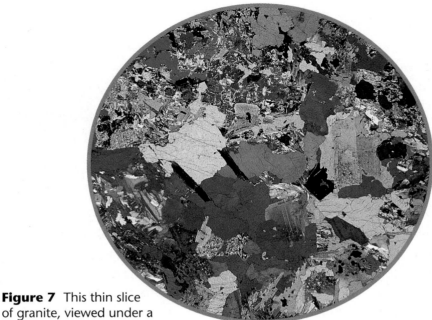

Figure 7 This thin slice of granite, viewed under a microscope, contains quartz, feldspar, mica, and other minerals.

Porphyritic rocks form when intrusive rocks cool in two stages. As the magma begins to cool, large crystals form slowly. The remaining magma, however, cools more quickly, forming small crystals. The change in the rate of cooling may occur as magma moves nearer to the surface.

Extrusive rocks have a fine-grained or glassy texture. Basalt is an extrusive rock. It consists of crystals too small to be seen without a microscope.

Mineral Composition Most of Earth's minerals contain **silica,** a material formed from oxygen and silicon. The silica content of magma and lava affects the types of rock they form. Lava that is low in silica usually forms dark-colored rocks such as basalt. Basalt contains feldspar as well as certain dark-colored minerals, but does not contain quartz.

INTEGRATING CHEMISTRY Magma that is high in silica usually forms light-colored rocks, such as granite. However, granite comes in many shades and colors. Granite can be dark to light gray, red, and pink. Granite's color changes along with its mineral composition. Granite that is rich in reddish feldspar is a speckled pink. But granite rich in hornblende and dark mica is light gray with dark specks. Quartz crystals in granite add light gray or smoky specks. Geologists can make thin slices of granite and study each type of crystal in the rock to determine its mineral composition more exactly.

✓ *Checkpoint* *Describe three ways in which igneous rocks differ.*

Uses of Igneous Rocks

Many igneous rocks are hard, dense, and durable. For this reason, people throughout history have used igneous rock for tools and building materials. For example, ancient Native Americans used obsidian for making very sharp tools for cutting and scraping.

Granite, one of the most abundant igneous rocks, has a long history as a building material. More than 3,500 years ago, the ancient Egyptians used granite for statues like the one shown in Figure 8. About 600 years ago, the Incas of Peru carefully fitted together great blocks of granite and other igneous rocks to build a fortress near Cuzco, their capital city. In the United States during the 1800s and early 1900s, granite was widely used to build bridges and public buildings and for paving streets with cobblestones. Thin, polished sheets of granite are still used in decorative stonework, curb-stones, and floors.

Igneous rocks such as basalt, pumice, and obsidian also have important uses. Basalt is crushed to make gravel that is used in construction. The rough surface of pumice makes it a good abrasive for cleaning and polishing. Perlite, formed from the heating of obsidian, is often mixed with soil for starting vegetable seeds.

Figure 8 The ancient Egyptians valued granite for its durability. This royal couple at a temple in Luxor, Egypt, was carved in granite.

Section 2 Review

1. What are the three major characteristics that geologists use to identify igneous rocks?
2. What is the difference between extrusive and intrusive rocks? Give an example of each.
3. Explain what causes an igneous rock to have a fine-grained or coarse-grained texture.
4. Why are some igneous rocks dark and others light?
5. **Thinking Critically Comparing and Contrasting** How are basalt and granite different in their origin, texture, and mineral composition? How are they similar?

Science at Home

Products from Rocks When you and a family member visit a pharmacy or large food store, observe the various foot-care products. What kinds of foot products are available that are made from pumice? How do people use these products? Check other skin and body care products to see if they contain pumice or other igneous rocks. Explain to your family how pumice is formed.

DISCOVER · ACTIVITY · · ·

How Does Pressure Affect Particles of Rock?

1. Place a sheet of paper over a slice of soft bread.

2. Put a stack of several heavy books on the top of the paper. After 10 minutes, remove the books. Observe what happened to the bread.

3. Slice the bread so you can observe its cross section.

4. Carefully slice a piece of fresh bread and compare its cross section to that of the pressed bread.

Think It Over

Observing How did the bread change after you removed the books? Describe the texture of the bread. How does the bread feel? What can you predict about how pressure affects the particles that make up sedimentary rocks?

GUIDE FOR READING

◆ How do sedimentary rocks form?

◆ What are the three major types of sedimentary rocks?

Reading Tip Before you read, preview the headings in the section and predict how you think sedimentary rocks form.

Visitors to Arches National Park in Utah see some of the strangest scenery on Earth. The park contains dozens of natural arches sculpted in colorful rock that is layered like a birthday cake. The layers of this cake are red, orange, pink, or tan. One arch, named Landscape Arch, is nearly 90 meters across and about 30 meters high. Delicate Arch looks like the legs of a striding giant. The forces that wear away rock on Earth's surface have been carving these arches out of solid rock for 100 million years. The arches are made of sandstone, one of the most common sedimentary rocks.

From Sediment to Rock

Sedimentary rocks form from particles deposited by water and wind. If you have ever walked along a stream or beach you may have noticed tiny sand grains, mud, and pebbles. These are some of the sediments that form sedimentary rock. **Sediment** is small, solid pieces of material that come from rocks or living things. Water, wind, and ice can carry sediment and deposit it in layers. But what turns these sediments into solid rock?

◀ Delicate Arch, Arches National Park, Utah

82

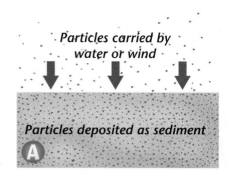

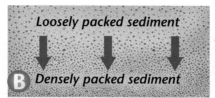

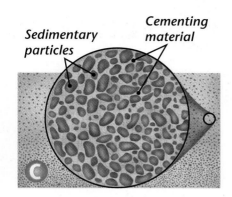

Figure 9 Sedimentary rocks form through the deposition, compaction, and cementation of sediments. **A.** Water or wind deposits sediment. **B.** The heavy sediments press down on the layers beneath. **C.** Dissolved minerals flow between the particles and cement them together.
Relating Cause and Effect What conditions are necessary for sedimentary rock to form?

Erosion Destructive forces are constantly breaking up and wearing away all the rocks on Earth's surface. These forces include heat and cold, rain, waves, and grinding ice. **Erosion** occurs when running water or wind loosen and carry away the fragments of rock.

Deposition Eventually, the moving water or wind slows and deposits the sediment. If water is carrying the sediment, rock fragments and other materials sink to the bottom of a lake or ocean. **Deposition** is the process by which sediment settles out of the water or wind carrying it. **After sediment has been deposited, the processes of compaction and cementation change the sediment into sedimentary rock.**

In addition to particles of rock, sediment may include shells, bones, leaves, stems, and other remains of living things. Over time, any remains of living things in the sediment may slowly harden and change into fossils trapped in the rock.

Compaction At first the sediments fit together loosely. But gradually, over millions of years, thick layers of sediment build up. These layers are heavy and press down on the layers beneath them. Then compaction occurs. **Compaction** is the process that presses sediments together. Year after year more sediment falls on top, creating new layers. The weight of the layers further compacts the sediments, squeezing them tightly together. The layers often remain visible in the sedimentary rock.

Cementation While compaction is taking place, the minerals in the rock slowly dissolve in the water. The dissolved minerals seep into the spaces between particles of sediment. **Cementation** is the process in which dissolved minerals crystallize and glue particles of sediment together. It often takes millions of years for compaction and cementation to transform loose sediments into solid sedimentary rock.

☑ *Checkpoint* *What are the processes that change sediment to sedimentary rock?*

Rock Absorber

Find out if water can soak into rock.

1. Using a hand lens, observe samples of sandstone and shale. How are they alike? How are they different?

2. Use a balance to measure the mass of each rock.

3. Place the rocks in a pan of water. Observe the samples. Which sample has bubbles escaping? Predict which sample will gain mass.

4. Leave the rocks submerged in the pan overnight.

5. The next day, remove the rocks from the pan and find the mass of each rock.

Drawing Conclusions How did the masses of the two rocks change after soaking? What can you conclude about each rock based on your observations?

Types of Sedimentary Rock

Geologists classify sedimentary rocks according to the type of sediments that make up the rock. **There are three major groups of sedimentary rocks: clastic rocks, organic rocks, and chemical rocks.** Different processes form each of these types of sedimentary rocks.

Clastic Rocks

Most sedimentary rocks are made up of the broken pieces of other rocks. A **clastic rock** is a sedimentary rock that forms when rock fragments are squeezed together. These fragments can range in size from clay particles too small to be seen without a microscope to large boulders too heavy for you to lift. Clastic rocks are grouped by the size of the rock fragments, or particles, of which they are made.

Shale One common clastic rock is shale. Shale forms from tiny particles of clay. For shale to form, water must deposit clay particles in very thin, flat layers, one on top of another. No cementation is needed to hold clay particles together. Even so, the spaces between the particles in the resulting shale are so small that water cannot pass through them. Shale feels smooth, and splits easily into flat pieces.

Sandstone Sandstone forms from the sand on beaches, on the ocean floor, in riverbeds, and in sand dunes. Sandstone is a clastic rock formed from the compaction and cementation of small particles of sand. Most sand particles consist of quartz. Because the cementation process does not fill all the spaces between sand grains, sandstone contains many small holes. Sandstone can easily absorb water through these holes.

Conglomerate and Breccia Some sedimentary rocks contain a mixture of rock fragments of different sizes. The fragments can range in size from sand and pebbles to boulders. If the fragments have rounded edges, they form a clastic rock called conglomerate. A rock made up of large fragments with sharp edges is called breccia (BRECH ee uh).

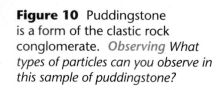

Figure 10 Puddingstone is a form of the clastic rock conglomerate. *Observing What types of particles can you observe in this sample of puddingstone?*

Organic Rocks

INTEGRATING LIFE SCIENCE Not all sedimentary rocks are made from particles of other rocks. **Organic rock** forms where the remains of plants and animals are deposited in thick layers. The term "organic" refers to substances that once were part of living things or were made by living things. Two important organic sedimentary rocks are coal and limestone.

Coal Coal forms from the remains of swamp plants buried in water. As layer upon layer of plant remains build up, the weight of the layers squeezes the decaying plants. Over millions of years, they slowly change into coal.

Limestone The hard shells of living things produce some kinds of limestone. How does limestone form? In the ocean, many living things, including coral, clams, oysters, and snails, have shells or skeletons made of calcite. When these animals die, their shells pile up as sediment on the ocean floor. Over millions of years, these layers of sediment can grow to a depth of hundreds of meters. Slowly, the pressure of overlying layers compacts the sediment. Some of the shells dissolve, forming a solution of calcite that seeps into the spaces between the shell fragments. Later, the dissolved material comes out of solution, forming calcite. The calcite cements the shell particles together, forming limestone.

Everyone knows one type of limestone: chalk. Chalk forms from sediments made of the skeletons of microscopic living things found in the oceans.

☑ *Checkpoint* *What are two important organic sedimentary rocks?*

Figure 11 When broken apart, a piece of shale from a coal mine may reveal the impression of an ancient plant. Geologists estimate that it takes about 20 meters of decayed plants to form a layer of coal about one meter thick.

Figure 12 These limestone cliffs are along the Eleven Point River in Missouri.

Chemical Rocks

Chemical rock forms when minerals that are dissolved in a solution crystallize. For example, limestone can form when calcite that is dissolved in lakes, seas, or underground water comes out of solution and forms crystals. This kind of limestone is considered a chemical rock.

Chemical rocks can also form from mineral deposits left when seas or lakes evaporate. Rock salt is a chemical rock made of the mineral halite, which forms by evaporation. Gypsum is another chemical rock formed by evaporation. Large deposits of rocks formed by evaporation form only in dry climates.

Figure 13 These rock "towers" in Mono Lake, California, are made of tufa, a type of limestone. Tufa forms from solutions containing dissolved minerals. *Classifying What type of sedimentary rock is tufa?*

Uses of Sedimentary Rocks

For thousands of years, people have used sandstone and limestone as building materials. Both types of stone are soft enough to be easily cut into blocks or slabs. You may be surprised to learn that the White House in Washington, D.C., is built of sandstone. Builders today use sandstone and limestone for decorating or for covering the outside walls of buildings.

Limestone also has many industrial uses. Recall from Chapter 4 that limestone is important in smelting iron ore. Limestone is also used in making cement.

Section 3 Review

1. Once sediment has been deposited, what processes change it into sedimentary rock?
2. What are the three major kinds of sedimentary rocks?
3. Describe two ways in which limestone can form.
4. **Thinking Critically Comparing and Contrasting** Compare and contrast shale and sandstone. Include what they are made of and how they form.

Check Your Progress

CHAPTER PROJECT

With an adult, visit an area where you can collect samples of rocks. As you collect your samples, observe whether the rock is loose on the ground, broken off a ledge, or in a stream. Begin to classify your rocks into groups. Do any of your rocks consist of a single mineral? Do you recognize any of the minerals in these rocks? Notice the texture of each rock. Did you find any rocks made of pieces of other rocks?

4 Rocks From Reefs

DISCOVER ···ACTIVITY····

What Can You Conclude From the Way a Rock Reacts to Acid?

1. Using a hand lens, observe the color and texture of samples of limestone and coquina.

2. Put on your goggles and apron.

3. Obtain a small amount of dilute hydrochloric acid from your teacher. Hydrochloric acid is used to test rocks for the presence of the mineral calcite.

4. Using a plastic dropper, place a few drops of dilute hydrochloric acid on the limestone. **CAUTION**: *Hydrochloric acid can cause burns.*

5. Record your observations.

6. Repeat Steps 2 through 4 with the sample of coquina and observe the results.

7. Rinse the samples of limestone and coquina with lots of water before returning them to your teacher. Wash your hands.

Think It Over
Drawing Conclusions
How did the color and texture of the two rocks compare? How did they react to the test? A piece of coral reacts to hydrochloric acid the same way as limestone and coquina. What could you conclude about the mineral composition of coral?

O ff the coast of Florida lies a "city" in the sea. It is a coral reef providing both food and shelter for many sea animals. The reef shimmers with life—clams, sponges, sea urchins, starfish, marine worms and, of course, fish. Schools of brilliantly colored fish dart in and out of forests of equally colorful corals. Octopuses lurk in underwater caves, scooping up crabs that pass too close. A reef forms a sturdy wall that protects the shoreline from battering waves. This city was built by billions of tiny, soft-bodied animals that have outer skeletons made of calcite.

GUIDE FOR READING

◆ How do coral reefs form?

◆ How do coral reefs become organic limestone deposits on land?

Reading Tip As you read, make a list of main ideas and supporting details about coral.

Figure 14 A coral reef in the Florida Keys provides food and shelter for many different kinds of living things.

Living Coral

Coral animals are tiny relatives of jellyfish that live together in vast numbers. Most coral animals are the size of your fingernail, or even smaller. Each one looks like a small sack with a mouth surrounded by tentacles. These animals use their tentacles to capture and eat microscopic creatures that float by. They produce skeletons that grow together to form a structure called a **coral reef.**

Coral reefs form only in the warm, shallow water of tropical oceans. Coral animals cannot grow in cold water or water low in salt. Reefs are most abundant around islands and along the eastern coasts of continents. In the United States, only the coasts of southern Florida and Hawaii have coral reefs.

Tiny algae grow within the body of each coral animal. The algae provide substances that the coral animals need to live. In turn, the coral animals provide a framework for the algae to grow on. Like plants, algae need sunlight. Below 40 meters, not enough light penetrates the water for the algae to grow. For this reason, almost all growth in a coral reef occurs within 40 meters of the water's surface.

How a Coral Reef Forms

Coral animals absorb the element calcium from the ocean water. The calcium is then changed into calcite and forms their skeletons. **When coral animals die, their skeletons remain, and more corals build on top of them.** Over thousands of years, reefs may grow to be hundreds of kilometers long and hundreds of meters thick. Reefs usually grow outward toward the open ocean. If the sea level rises or if the sea floor sinks, the reef will grow upward, too.

Figure 15 Coral animals feed on even smaller living things carried their way by the movement of ocean water. (This view has been magnified to show detail.)

Figure 16 The island of Bora Bora in the South Pacific Ocean is ringed by a fringing reef. Someday, erosion will wear away the island, leaving an atoll. *Inferring As the sea floor beneath an atoll sinks, what happens to the living part of the coral reef?*

There are three types of coral reefs: fringing reefs, barrier reefs and atolls. Fringing reefs lie close to shore, separated from land by shallow water. Barrier reefs lie farther out, at least 10 kilometers from the land. The Great Barrier Reef that stretches 2,000 kilometers along the coast of Australia is a barrier reef. An **atoll** is a ring-shaped coral island found far from land. An atoll develops when coral grows on top of a volcanic island that has sunk beneath the ocean's surface.

 Checkpoint **What are the three types of coral reefs?**

Limestone Deposits From Coral Reefs

A coral reef is really organic limestone. Over time, coral may be buried by sediments. Like modern-day coral animals, ancient coral animals thrived in warm, tropical oceans. Their limestone fossils are among the most common fossils on Earth. **Limestone that began as coral can be found on continents in places where uplift has raised ancient sea floors above sea level.**

In parts of the United States, reefs that formed under water millions of years ago now make up part of the land. Forces inside Earth slowly uplifted the ocean floor where these reefs grew until the ocean floor became dry land. There are exposed reefs in Wisconsin, Illinois, and Indiana, as well as in Texas, New Mexico, and many other places.

Figure 17 A striking band of white rock tops El Capitan Peak in the Guadalupe Mountains of Texas. This massive layer of limestone formed from coral reefs that grew in a warm, shallow sea more than 250 million years ago.

Section 4 Review

1. Explain how coral reefs form.
2. How can coral become limestone on land?
3. Why are living coral animals only found in water that is less than 40 meters deep?
4. **Thinking Critically** **Predicting** The Amazon is a great river that flows through the tropical forests of Brazil. The river dumps huge amounts of fresh water, made cloudy by particles of sediment, into the South Atlantic Ocean. Would you expect to find coral reefs growing in the ocean near the mouth of the Amazon? Explain your answer.

Check Your Progress
CHAPTER PROJECT
Begin to make an information card for each of your rocks, and decide how to store the rocks. Each rock's card should include the following information: where and when the rock was found; the type of geologic feature where you found the rock; a description of the rock's texture; a description of the minerals that make up the rock; and the results of any tests you performed on the rock. Are any of your rocks organic rocks? How could you tell?

SECTION 5 Metamorphic Rocks

DISCOVER •• ACTIVITY

How Do the Grain Patterns of Gneiss and Granite Compare?

1. Using a hand lens, observe samples of gneiss and granite. Look carefully at the grains or crystals in both rocks.

2. Observe how the grains or crystals are arranged in both rocks. Draw a sketch of both rocks and describe their textures.

Think It Over

Inferring Within the crust, some granite becomes gneiss. What do you think must happen to cause this change?

GUIDE FOR READING

◆ Under what conditions do metamorphic rocks form?

◆ How do geologists classify metamorphic rocks?

Reading Tip Before you read, rewrite the headings in the section as questions. As you read, look for answers to those questions.

Every metamorphic rock is a rock that has changed its form. In fact, the word *metamorphic* comes from the Greek words *meta*, meaning "change," and *morphosis*, meaning "form." But what causes a rock to change into metamorphic rock? The answer lies inside Earth.

How Metamorphic Rocks Form

Heat and pressure deep beneath Earth's surface can change any rock into metamorphic rock. When rock changes into metamorphic rock, its appearance, texture, crystal structure, and mineral content change. Metamorphic rock can form out of igneous, sedimentary, or other metamorphic rock.

Sometimes, forces inside Earth can push the rock down toward the heat of the mantle. Pockets of magma rising through the crust also provide heat that can produce metamorphic rocks.

The deeper rock is buried in the crust, the greater the pressure on that rock. Under pressure hundreds or thousands of times greater than at Earth's surface, the minerals in a rock can change into other minerals. The rock has become a metamorphic rock.

Figure 18 Great heat and pressure can change one type of rock into another. Granite becomes gneiss, shale becomes slate, and sandstone changes to quartzite. *Observing How does quartzite differ from sandstone?*

Granite   *Gneiss*

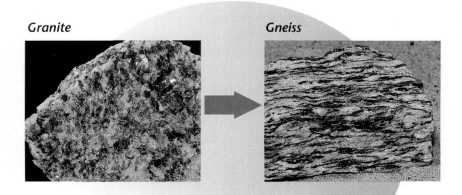

Classifying Metamorphic Rocks

While metamorphic rocks are forming, high temperatures change the size and shape of the grains, or mineral crystals, in the rock. In addition, tremendous pressure squeezes rock so tightly that the mineral grains may line up in flat, parallel layers. **Geologists classify metamorphic rocks by the arrangement of the grains that make up the rocks.**

Metamorphic rocks that have their grains arranged in parallel layers or bands are said to be **foliated.** The term *foliated* comes from the Latin word for "leaf." It describes the thin, flat layering found in most metamorphic rocks. Foliated rocks—including slate, schist, and gneiss—may split apart along these bands. In Figure 18, notice how the crystals in granite have been flattened to create the foliated texture of gneiss.

One common foliated rock is slate. Heat and pressure change the sedimentary rock shale into slate. Slate is basically a denser, more compact version of shale. During the change, new minerals such as mica and hornblende form in the slate.

Sometimes metamorphic rocks are nonfoliated. The mineral grains in these rocks are arranged randomly. Metamorphic rocks that are nonfoliated do not split into layers. Marble and quartzite both have a nonfoliated texture. Quartzite forms out of sandstone. The weakly cemented quartz particles in the sandstone recrystallize to form quartzite, which is extremely hard. Notice in Figure 18 how much smoother quartzite looks than sandstone.

☑ *Checkpoint* *What is a foliated rock?*

A Sequined Rock

1. Make three balls of clay about 3 cm in diameter. Gently mix about 25 sequins into one ball.
2. Use a 30-cm piece of string to cut the ball in half. How are the sequins arranged?
3. Roll the clay with the sequins back into a ball. Stack the three balls with the sequin ball in the middle. Set these on a block of wood. With another block of wood, press slowly down until the stack is about 3 cm high.
4. Use the string to cut the stack in half. Observe the arrangement of the sequins.

Making a Model What do the sequins in your model rock represent? Is this rock foliated or nonfoliated?

Shale

Slate

Sandstone

Quartzite

Figure 19 The pure white marble for the Taj Mahal came from a quarry 300 kilometers away. It took 20,000 workers more than 20 years to build the Taj Mahal.

Visual Arts
CONNECTION

The architect of the Taj Mahal used symmetry and repetition to design a beautiful building. Notice how the left side mirrors the right side, creating balance. Also notice how different parts of the building, such as domes, arches, and minarets (towers), are repeated. Repetition of these shapes creates rhythms as you look at the building.

In Your Journal

Write a letter to a friend describing what you feel walking toward the Taj Mahal. Explain how the building's symmetry and other features help to create this effect.

Uses of Metamorphic Rock

Marble and slate are two of the most useful metamorphic rocks. Marble usually forms when limestone is subjected to heat and pressure deep beneath the surface. Because marble has a fine, even grain, it is relatively easy to cut into thin slabs. And marble can be easily polished. These qualities have led architects and sculptors to use marble for many buildings and statues. For example, one of the most beautiful buildings in the world is the Taj Mahal in Agra, India. An emperor of India had the Taj Mahal built during the 1600s as a memorial to his wife, who had died in childbirth. The Taj Mahal, shown in Figure 19, is made of gleaming white marble.

Slate, because it is foliated, splits easily into flat pieces that can be used for flooring, roofing, outdoor walkways, or chalkboards. Like marble, slate comes in a variety of colors, including gray, black, red, and purple, so it has been used as trim for stone buildings.

Section 5 Review

1. Describe the process by which metamorphic rocks form.
2. What characteristics are used to classify metamorphic rocks?
3. Which properties of a rock may change as the rock becomes metamorphic?
4. How does pressure change rock?
5. **Thinking Critically** Relating Cause and Effect Why are you less likely to find fossils in metamorphic rocks than in sedimentary rocks?

Science at Home

Made of Rock How are rocks used in your neighborhood? Take a walk with your family to see how many uses you can observe. Identify statues, walls, and buildings made from rocks. Can you identify which type of rock is used? Look for limestone, sandstone, granite, and marble. Share a list of the rocks you found with your class. For each rock, include a description of its color and texture, where you observed the rock, and how it was used.

MYSTERY ROCKS

Problem

What properties can be used to classify rocks?

Materials

1 "mystery rock"   hand lens
2 unknown igneous rocks
2 unknown sedimentary rocks
2 unknown metamorphic rocks

Procedure

1. For this activity, you will be given six rocks and one sample that is not a rock. They are labeled A through G.
2. Copy the data table into your notebook.
3. Using the hand lens, examine each rock for clues that show the rock formed from molten material. Record the rock's color and texture. Observe if there are any crystals or grains in the rock.
4. Use the hand lens to look for clues that show the rock formed from particles of other rocks. Observe the texture of the rock to see if it has any tiny, well-rounded grains.
5. Use the hand lens to look for clues that show the rock formed under heat and pressure. Observe if the rock has a flat layer of crystals or shows colored bands.
6. Record your observations in the data table.

Analyze and Conclude

1. Infer from your observations which group each rock belongs in.
2. Decide which sample is not a rock. How did you determine that the sample you chose is not a rock? What do you think the "mystery rock" is? Explain.
3. Which of the samples could be classified as igneous rocks? What physical properties do these rock share with the other samples? How are they different?
4. Which of the samples could be classified as sedimentary rocks? How do you think these rocks formed? What are the physical properties of these rocks?
5. Which of the samples could be classified as metamorphic rocks? What are their physical properties?
6. **Think About It** What physical property was most useful in classifying rocks? Why?

More to Explore

Can you name each rock? Use a field guide to rocks and minerals to find the specific name of each rock sample.

Sample	Color (dark, medium, light, or mixed colors)	Texture (fine, medium, or coarse-grained)	Foliated or Banded	Rock Group (igneous, metamorphic, sedimentary)
A				
B				

The Rock Cycle

Which Rock Came First?

1. Make sketches of the quartzite, granite, and sandstone below on three index cards.

2. In your sketches, try to portray the color and texture of each rock. Look for similarities and differences.

3. To which major group does each rock belong?

Think It Over

Developing Hypotheses How are these three rocks related? Arrange your cards in the order in which you think the rocks formed. Over time, what might happen to the third rock in your series?

Quartzite

Granite

Sandstone

GUIDE FOR READING

◆ What is the rock cycle?

Reading Tip **Before you read, preview Figure 20 on page 95. Write a list of questions you have about the rock cycle. Then look for answers to the questions as you read.**

Earth's rocks are not as unchanging as they seem. **Forces inside Earth and at the surface produce a rock cycle that builds, destroys, and changes the rocks in the crust.** The **rock cycle** is a series of processes on and beneath Earth's surface that slowly change rocks from one kind to another.

A Cycle of Many Pathways

Figure 20 shows that the rock cycle can follow many different pathways. Here is one possible pathway: the igneous rock granite formed beneath the surface millions of years ago. Then, the forces of mountain building slowly pushed the granite upward, forming a mountain. Slowly, water and weather wore away the granite through the process of erosion. These granite particles became sand, carried by streams to the ocean.

Over millions of years, layers of sandy sediment piled up on the ocean floor. Slowly, the sediments were pressed together and cemented to form sandstone, a sedimentary rock.

Over time, more and more sediment piled up on the sandstone. As the sandstone became deeply buried, pressure on the rock increased. The rock became hot. Heat and pressure changed the rock's texture from gritty to smooth. After millions of years, the sandstone changed into the metamorphic rock quartzite.

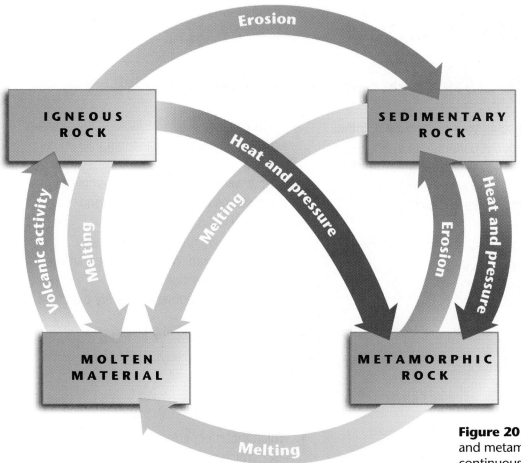

Figure 20 Igneous, sedimentary, and metamorphic rocks change continuously through the rock cycle. *Interpreting Diagrams* What steps in the rock cycle could change a sedimentary rock into an igneous rock?

Metamorphic rock does not end the rock cycle. Sometimes, forces inside Earth push all three types of rock many kilometers beneath the surface. There the heat of Earth's interior melts the rock. This molten material can form new igneous rock.

☑ *Checkpoint* How can a rock change from one form to another?

 Section 6 Review

1. What process gradually changes rocks from one form to another?
2. What rock comes before quartzite in the rock cycle? What rock or rocks could come just after quartzite in the rock cycle? Explain your answer.
3. **Thinking Critically Applying Concepts** Describe what happens as you follow a grain of sand through the rock cycle until it returns to a beach as a grain of sand again.

Check Your Progress CHAPTER PROJECT

Now that you have collected, described, tested, and recorded your rocks, classify them as igneous, sedimentary, or metamorphic. Are any of your rocks foliated? Try to identify specific types of rock. Compare your rock samples with pictures of rocks in a field guide or other library reference sources.

TESTING ROCK FLOORING

You are building your own house. For the kitchen floor, you want to use some building stones such as granite, marble, or limestone. You need to know which material is easiest to maintain and keep clean.

Problem

What kind of building stone makes the best flooring?

Skills Focus

designing experiments, forming operational definitions drawing conclusions

Suggested Materials

steel nail   wire brush   water
plastic dropper   hand lens
samples of igneous, sedimentary, and metamorphic rocks with flat surfaces
materials that form stains, such as ink and paints
greasy materials such as butter and crayons

Procedure

1. Brainstorm with your partner the qualities of good flooring. For example, good flooring should resist stains, scratches, and grease marks, and be safe to walk on when wet.
2. Predict what you think is the best building stone for a kitchen floor. Why?
3. Write the steps you plan to follow to answer the problem question. As you design your plan, consider the following factors:
   ◆ What igneous, sedimentary, and metamorphic rocks will you test? (Pick at least one rock from each group.)
   ◆ What materials or equipment will you need to acquire, and in what amounts?

◆ What tests will you perform on the samples?
◆ How will you control the variables in each test?
◆ How will you measure each sample's resistance to staining, grease, and scratches?
◆ How will you measure slipperiness?
4. Review your plan. Will it lead to an answer to the problem question?
5. Check your procedure and safety plan with your teacher.
6. Create a data table that includes a column in which you predict how each material will perform in each test.

Analyze and Conclude

1. Which material performed the best on each test? Which performed the worst on each test?
2. Which material is best for the kitchen flooring? Which material would you least want to use?
3. Do your answers support your initial prediction? Why or why not?
4. The person installing the floor might want stone that is easy to cut to the correct size or shape. What other qualities would matter to the flooring installer?
5. **Apply** Based on your results for flooring, what materials would you use for kitchen counters? How might the qualities needed for countertops differ from those for flooring?

More to Explore

Find out the cost per square meter of some materials used to build kitchen floors in your community. How does cost influence your decision on which material to use? What other factors can influence the choice of materials?

SECTION 1 **Classifying Rocks**

Key Ideas

◆ A rock is a hard piece of Earth's crust.
◆ Geologists classify rocks according to their color, texture, mineral composition, and origin.
◆ The three kinds of rocks are igneous, sedimentary, and metamorphic.

Key Terms

texture   igneous rock   metamorphic rock
grain   sedimentary rock

 SECTION 2 **Igneous Rocks**

Key Ideas

◆ Igneous rocks form from magma or lava.
◆ Igneous rocks are classified according to their origin, texture, and composition.

Key Terms

extrusive rock   intrusive rock   porphyritic texture
basalt   granite   silica

 SECTION 3 **Sedimentary Rocks**

Key Ideas

◆ Most sedimentary rocks form from sediments that are compacted and cemented together.
◆ The three types of sedimentary rocks are clastic rocks, organic rocks, and chemical rocks.

Key Terms

sediment   compaction   organic rock
erosion   cementation   chemical rock
deposition   clastic rock

 SECTION 4 **Rocks From Reefs**

INTEGRATING LIFE SCIENCE

Key Ideas

◆ When corals die, their skeletons remain. More corals grow on top of them, slowly forming a reef.

Key Terms

coral reef   atoll

 SECTION 5 **Metamorphic Rocks**

Key Ideas

◆ In a process that takes place deep beneath the surface, heat and pressure can change any type of rock into metamorphic rock.
◆ Geologists classify metamorphic rock according to whether the rock is foliated or nonfoliated.

Key Term

foliated

 SECTION 6 **The Rock Cycle**

Key Ideas

◆ The series of processes on and beneath Earth's surface that change rocks from one type of rock to another is called the rock cycle.

Key Term

rock cycle

Organizing Information

Cycle Diagram Construct a cycle diagram that shows one pathway through the rock cycle. Include the following steps in your diagram in the correct order: sediments build up; igneous rock wears away; sedimentary rock forms; igneous rock forms from magma and lava; lava erupts. (For tips on making cycle diagrams, see the Skills Handbook.)

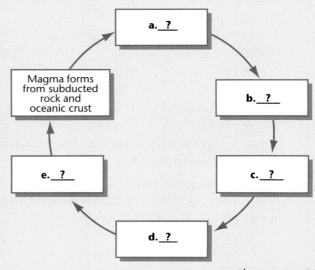

Reviewing Content

 For more review of key concepts, see the Interactive Student Tutorial CD-ROM.

Multiple Choice
Choose the letter of the best answer.

1. Which of the following sedimentary rocks is a chemical rock?
   a. shale
   b. sandstone
   c. rock salt
   d. breccia
2. Metamorphic rocks can be formed from
   a. igneous rocks.
   b. sedimentary rocks.
   c. metamorphic rocks.
   d. all rock groups.
3. The rock formed when granite changes to a metamorphic rock is
   a. marble.   b. basalt.
   c. gneiss.   d. pumice.
4. Which of the following helps create both metamorphic and sedimentary rocks?
   a. cementation   b. pressure
   c. evaporation   d. heat
5. Millions of years ago, a deposit of organic limestone was probably
   a. a swampy forest.   b. a lava flow.
   c. a coral reef.   d. an intrusive rock.

True or False
If the statement is true, write true. If it is false, change the underlined word or words to make the statement true.

6. Igneous rocks are classified by how they formed and by their color, texture, and shape.
7. Granite is a fine-grained igneous rock.
8. Sedimentary rocks that form when minerals come out of solution are classified as porphyritic.
9. A barrier reef is a ring-shaped coral island found in the open ocean.
10. The series of processes that slowly change rocks from one kind to another is called the rock cycle.

Checking Concepts

11. What is the relationship between an igneous rock's texture and where it was formed?
12. Why can water pass easily through sandstone but not through shale?
13. Describe how a rock can form by evaporation. What type of rock is it?
14. How do the properties of a rock change when the rock changes to metamorphic?
15. What are the sources of the heat that helps metamorphic rocks to form?
16. **Writing to Learn** You are a camp counselor taking your campers on a mountain hike. One of your campers cracks open a rock and finds a fossil fish inside. The camper wants to know how a fish fossil from the sea floor ended up on the side of a mountain. What explanation would you give the camper?

Thinking Critically

17. **Applying Concepts** The sedimentary rocks limestone and sandstone are used as building materials. However, they wear away more rapidly than marble and quartzite, the metamorphic rocks that are formed from them. Why do you think this is so?
18. **Inferring** As a geologist exploring for rock and mineral deposits, you come across an area where the rocks are layers of coal and shale. What kind of environment probably existed in this area millions of years ago when these rocks formed?
19. **Comparing and Contrasting** How are clastic rocks and organic rocks similar? How are they different?
20. **Relating Cause and Effect** In the rock cycle, igneous, metamorphic, and sedimentary rocks can all become magma again. What step in the rock cycle causes this to happen? Explain your answer.

Applying Skills

Answer Questions 21–23 using the photos of three rocks.

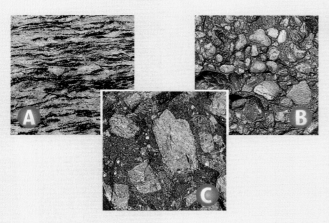

21. Observing How would you describe the texture of each rock?

22. Classifying Which of the three rocks would you classify as a metamorphic rock? Explain your answer.

23. Inferring A rock's texture gives clues about how the rock formed. What can you infer about the process by which rock B formed?

Performance ▼ CHAPTER PROJECT **Assessment**

Present Your Project Construct a simple display for your rocks. Your display should clearly give your classification for each of your rock samples. In your presentation, describe where you went hunting for rocks and what kinds of rocks you found. Describe which of your discoveries surprised you the most.

Reflect and Record In your journal, write about how you developed your rock collection. Were there any rocks that were hard to classify? Did you find rocks from each of the three major groups? Can you think of any reason why certain types of rocks would not be found in your area?

Test Preparation

Use these questions to prepare for standardized tests.

Use the diagram to answer Questions 24–28.

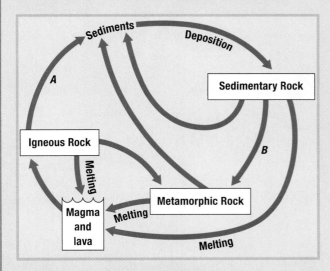

24. A good title for this diagram is
 a. Different Kinds of Rock
 b. Deposition of Sediment
 c. How Metamorphic Rock Forms
 d. Pathways of the Rock Cycle

25. The process shown by letter A is called
 a. extrusion. **b.** crystallization.
 c. erosion. **d.** intrusion.

26. The process shown by letter B involves
 a. cementation only.
 b. heat and pressure.
 c. erosion and deposition.
 d. compaction only.

27. According to the diagram, metamorphic rock forms from
 a. igneous rock and sedimentary rock.
 b. sedimentary rock only.
 c. magma and lava.
 d. melting rock.

28. According to the diagram, magma and lava may form through the melting of
 a. any type of rock.
 b. metamorphic rock only.
 c. sediments.
 d. igneous rock only.

The Noble Metal

You can find it . . .

- on people's wrists and on their ears
- in your computer ◆ around the edge of some dinner plates ◆ in outer space—on satellites and in spacesuits ◆

What is this mysterious substance? It's the rare, beautiful—and very useful— metal called *Gold*

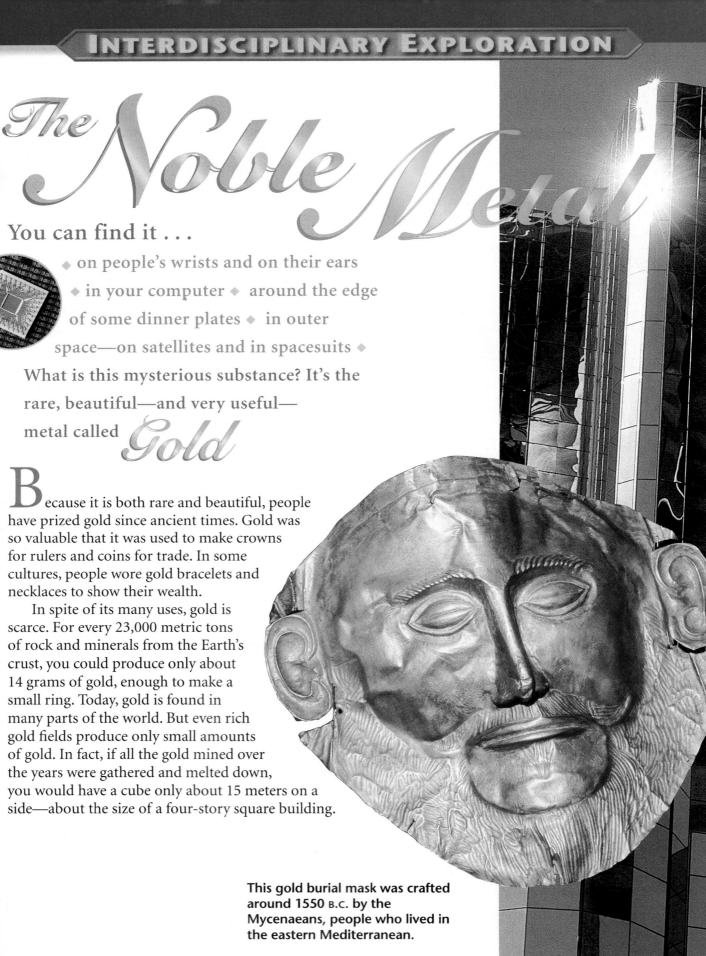

Because it is both rare and beautiful, people have prized gold since ancient times. Gold was so valuable that it was used to make crowns for rulers and coins for trade. In some cultures, people wore gold bracelets and necklaces to show their wealth.

In spite of its many uses, gold is scarce. For every 23,000 metric tons of rock and minerals from the Earth's crust, you could produce only about 14 grams of gold, enough to make a small ring. Today, gold is found in many parts of the world. But even rich gold fields produce only small amounts of gold. In fact, if all the gold mined over the years were gathered and melted down, you would have a cube only about 15 meters on a side—about the size of a four-story square building.

This gold burial mask was crafted around 1550 B.C. by the Mycenaeans, people who lived in the eastern Mediterranean.

Properties of Gold

Why is gold used for everything from bracelets to space helmets to medicine? You'll find the answers in this precious metal's unusual chemical and physical properties. Gold is deep yellow in color and so shiny, or lustrous, that its Latin name, *aurum*, means "glowing dawn." Gold's chemical symbol—*Au*—comes from that Latin word.

Gold is very stable. Unlike iron, gold doesn't rust. It also doesn't tarnish in air as silver does, so its luster can last forever. Ancient chemists thought that gold was superior to other metals. They classified it as one of the "noble" metals.

Gold is very soft and malleable. That is, it's easy to bend or hammer into shapes without breaking. It can be pounded into very thin sheets called gold leaf. In fact, you can pound 30 grams of gold into a sheet that's large enough to cover the floor of a small room. Gold is also the most ductile metal. You can draw out 30 grams of gold into a fine thread as long as 8 kilometers without breaking it.

Ancient people of Egypt, Greece, and China found ways to dig gold from mines. But most of the gold that people have used in the last 6,000 years has come from Earth's surface, often from streams and riverbanks. Gold is very heavy—one of the densest metals. Over centuries, mountain streams have washed away dirt and pebbles from veins of gold-bearing rocks and minerals and left the heavy gold in the streambeds.

Gold reflects heat and, when combined with other materials, filters sunlight. For this reason, gold is used in spacesuits and face visors. This astronaut wears a face visor coated with gold. The window glass in some skyscrapers is tinted with gold to keep out heat and protect people's eyes.

Science Activity

Many of the gold hunters who flocked to California during the Gold Rush of 1849 were searching for gold in streams and rivers. Although they had very simple equipment, their technique worked because gold is so dense. Using pans, miners washed gold-bearing gravel in running water. Try your own gold panning.

Procedure:
Set up your own model of gold panning, using a large pan, a gravel mixture, and a very dense material as a substitute for gold. Use a sink trap. Under running water, shake and swirl the pan until the lighter materials wash away. What's left is your "gold."

◆ Why is "gold" left in the pan while other materials are washed away?

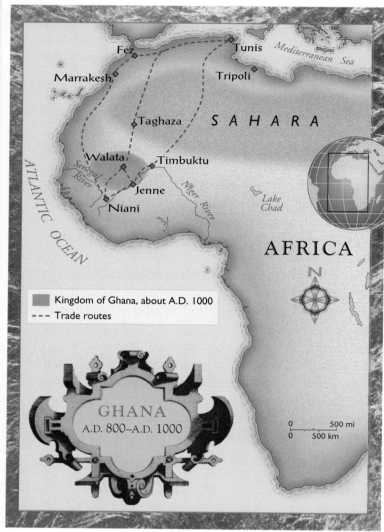

Kingdom of Ghana, about A.D. 1000
--- Trade routes

GHANA
A.D. 800–A.D. 1000

Golden Trade Routes

In West Africa nearly 1,000 years ago, salt was said to be worth its weight in gold. If you get your salt from the supermarket shelf, it may be hard to imagine how valuable this mineral was to people. But if you lived in a very hot, dry climate, you would need salt. It would be as valuable to you as gold. In West Africa, salt and gold were the most important goods traded in a busy north-south trade.

Camel caravans crossed the desert going south, carrying slabs of salt from mines in the desert. Trade centers, such as Jenne and Timbuktu, flourished. In the area around Taghaza, people built houses with walls of salt slabs. But several hundred kilometers south in the Kingdom of Ghana, salt was scarce and gold was plentiful. Salt traders from the north traveled deep into the forests of Ghana to trade salt for gold.

African gold became the basis for several rich cultures and trading empires that grew up in West Africa between 800 and 1400. At that time, most of the gold that Europeans used for crowns, coins, and jewelry was carried north from Africa.

Around 1100, Arab travelers in Africa wrote about the fabulous wealth of the Kingdom of Ghana. The most popular tale was that the salt traders and gold miners never met, as a way of keeping secret the location of gold mines. Traders from the north left slabs of salt in an agreed-upon trading place, pounded their drums to indicate a trade, and then withdrew. Miners from the south arrived, left an amount of gold that seemed fair, and withdrew. The salt traders returned. If they thought the trade was fair, they took the gold and left. If they were not satisfied, the silent trade continued.

Social Studies Activity

How would you succeed as a gold or salt trader? Find out by carrying out your own silent trade. Work in teams of Salt Traders and Gold Miners. Before trading, each team should decide how much a bag of gold or a block of salt is worth. Then, for each silent trade, make up a situation that would change the value of gold or salt, such as, "Demand for gold in Europe increases."

◆ Suppose you are selling a product today. How would the supply of the product affect the value or sale price of the product?

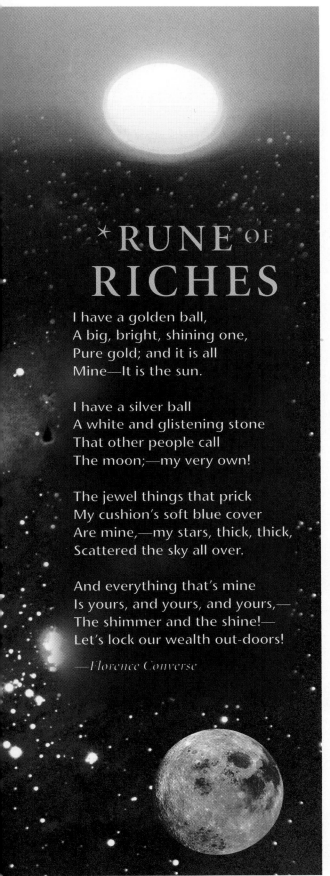

* RUNE OF RICHES

I have a golden ball,
A big, bright, shining one,
Pure gold; and it is all
Mine—It is the sun.

I have a silver ball
A white and glistening stone
That other people call
The moon;—my very own!

The jewel things that prick
My cushion's soft blue cover
Are mine,—my stars, thick, thick,
Scattered the sky all over.

And everything that's mine
Is yours, and yours, and yours,—
The shimmer and the shine!—
Let's lock our wealth out-doors!

—Florence Converse

Go for the gold

What do these sayings have in common?

◆ It's worth its weight in gold.

◆ Speech is silver, silence is golden.

◆ All that glitters is not gold.

◆ Go for the gold!

All of these sayings use gold as a symbol of perfection and value. Because gold has always been beautiful and scarce, it has for centuries been a symbol of excellence and richness—things that people want and search for. When writers use *gold* or *golden,* they are referring to something desirable, of value or worth. These words may also represent the beauty of gold.

In literature, writers and poets often use *gold* to make a comparison in a simile or metaphor. Similes and metaphors are figures of speech.

◆ A simile makes a comparison between two things, using *like* or *as* in the comparison. Here's an example: "An honest person's promise is as good as gold."

◆ A metaphor is a comparison without the use of like or as, such as, "When you're in trouble, true friends are golden."

Look for similes and metaphors in the poem by Florence Converse.

◆ What similes or metaphors has Converse made?

◆ What would this poem be like without the comparisons?

*A rune is a song or poem.

Language Arts Activity

What does gold symbolize for you? Think of some comparisons of your own in which you use gold in a simile or metaphor. After jotting down all of your ideas, choose one (or more) and decide what comparison you will make. Write a short saying, a proverb, or a short poem that includes your own simile or metaphor.
◆ How does your comparison make your saying or poem more interesting?

Measuring Gold

People often say that something is "worth its weight in gold." But how do you measure the weight of gold? Most gold that's mined today is used to make jewelry. But modern-day jewelry is seldom made of pure gold. Because gold is so soft, it is usually mixed with another metal to form an alloy—a mixture of two or more metals.

Most commonly the other metal in a gold alloy is copper, although alloys of gold can also contain silver, zinc, or other metals. A gold alloy keeps most of the properties of gold but is harder and resists denting and scratching. The other metals affect the color. More copper produces "red gold," while "white gold" may contain gold and copper along with nickel, palladium, or silver.

Suppose you are shopping for a gold ring. You see two rings that look the same and are exactly the same size. How do you decide which one to buy? If you look carefully at the gold jewelry, you'll probably see small letters that read "18 K," "20 K," "14 K," or "12 K." The "K" here stands for karat. That's the measure of how pure an alloy of gold is. Pure gold—used very rarely—is 24 karat. Gold that is 50 percent pure is $\frac{12}{24}$ gold, or 12 karat. The greater the amount of gold in a piece of jewelry, the higher the value.

Look at the display of rings above. The 18-karat ring has copper in it. What percent of the 18 K gold ring is gold? What percent is copper?

Analyze. You know that pure gold is $\frac{24}{24}$ gold. In order to find out what percent of an 18 K ring is gold, you need to write a proportion.

Write the proportion.

$$\frac{\text{number of gold parts} \rightarrow}{\text{number of parts in the whole} \rightarrow} \frac{18}{24}$$

Simplify and solve.

$$\frac{18}{24} = \frac{3}{4} = 75\%$$

Think about it. If 75% of the ring is gold, then 25% of the ring must be copper.

Math Activity

Look at the other gold rings to determine what percent of each is gold.

◆ What percent of the 14 K gold ring is gold? What percent is another metal? Round decimals to the nearest hundredth.

◆ What percent of the 12 K ring is gold? What percent of the 20 K ring is gold?

◆ Which ring would you like to own— the 12 K or the 20 K? Why?

◆ Which ring in the display would probably be the most expensive?

Tie It Together

Gold Producers

1. South Africa
2. United States
3. Australia
4. Canada
5. Russia
6. China

A Treasure Hunt

Work in small groups to make a World Treasure Map of one of the countries where gold is mined today. Use the information above to get you started. Then use the library to learn about these gold-producing countries.

On a large map of the world, use push pins to mark the location of the gold sites. In the United States and Canada, mark the states and provinces that are the largest producers. Make up fact sheets with information that will answer questions such as the following:

◆ Where are gold sites located in each country?

◆ When was gold first discovered there?

◆ Did a gold rush influence the history of that area?

If possible, collect photographs to illustrate gold products in each country. Post your pictures and fact sheets at the side of the World Treasure Map.

CHAPTER
4 Plate Tectonics

This is a satellite image of the San Francisco Bay area. The row of lakes below marks the line of the San Andreas fault, a crack in Earth's crust.

www.phschool.com

Cut-Away Earth

Along the San Andreas fault in California, two vast pieces of Earth's crust slowly slide past each other. In this chapter, you will learn how movements deep within Earth cause movements on the surface. These movements help to create mountains and other surface features. You will build a model that shows Earth's interior and how the interior affects the planet's surface.

Your Goal To build a three-dimensional model that shows Earth's surface features as well as a cutaway view of Earth's interior.

To complete this project, you must

◆ build a scale model of the layers of Earth's interior
◆ include at least three of the plates that form Earth's surface, as well as two landmasses or continents
◆ show how the plates push together, pull apart, or slide past each other and indicate their direction of movement
◆ label all physical features clearly
◆ follow the safety guidelines in Appendix A

Get Started Begin now by previewing the chapter to learn about Earth's interior. Brainstorm a list of the kinds of materials that could be used to make a three-dimensional model. Start a project folder in which you will keep your sketches, ideas, and any information needed to design and build your model.

Check Your Progress You will be designing and building your model as you study this chapter. To keep your project on track, look for Check Your Progress boxes at the following points.

Section 1 Review, page 114: Begin sketching and designing your model.

Section 4 Review, page 129: Revise your design and start building the base of your model.

Section 5 Review, page 137: Complete the final construction of your model.

Present Your Project At the end of the chapter (page 141), you will present your completed model to the class and discuss the features you included.

SECTION 4 Sea-Floor Spreading

Discover What Is the Effect of a Change in Density?
Try This Reversing Poles
Skills Lab Making Models: Modeling Sea-Floor Spreading

SECTION 5 The Theory of Plate Tectonics

Discover How Well Do the Continents Fit Together?
Sharpen Your Skills Predicting
Skills Lab Observing: Hot Plates

SECTION
① Earth's Interior

DISCOVER

How Do Scientists Determine What's Inside Earth?

1. Your teacher will provide you with three closed film canisters. Each canister contains a different material. Your goal is to determine what is inside each canister—even though you can't directly observe what it contains.

2. Stick a label made from a piece of tape on each canister.

3. To gather evidence about the contents of the canisters, you may tap, roll, shake, or weigh them. Record your observations.

4. What differences do you notice between the canisters? Apart from their appearance on the outside, are the canisters similar in any way? How did you obtain this evidence?

Think It Over

Inferring Based on your observations, what can you infer about the contents of the canisters? How do you think scientists gather evidence about Earth's interior?

GUIDE FOR READING

◆ What are the characteristics of Earth's crust, mantle, and core?

Reading Tip Before you read, rewrite the headings in the section as what, how, or why questions. As you read, look for answers to these questions.

One of the most difficult questions that geologists have tried to answer is, What's inside Earth? Much as geologists might like to, they cannot dig a hole to the center of Earth. The extreme conditions in Earth's interior prevent exploration far below the surface. The deepest mine in the world, a gold mine in South Africa, reaches a depth of 3.8 kilometers. But it only scratches the surface.

Finding Indirect Evidence

Geologists cannot observe Earth's interior directly. They must rely on indirect methods of observation. Have you ever hung a heavy picture on a wall? If you have, you know that you can knock on the wall to locate the wooden beam underneath the plaster that will support the picture. When you knock on the wall, you listen carefully for a change in the sound.

When geologists want to study Earth's interior, they also use an indirect method. But instead of knocking on walls, they use seismic waves. When earthquakes occur, they produce **seismic waves** (SYZ mik). Geologists record the seismic waves and study how they travel through Earth. The speed of these seismic waves and the paths they take reveal how the planet is put together. Using data from seismic waves, geologists have learned that Earth's interior is made up of several layers. Each layer surrounds the layers beneath it, much like the layers of an onion.

☑ *Checkpoint* What kind of indirect evidence do geologists use to study the structure of Earth?

A Journey to the Center of the Earth

Imagine taking a trip to the center of Earth. That's what happens in a novel written by French author Jules Verne in 1864. At that time, scientists knew almost nothing about Earth's interior. Was it solid or hollow? Hot or cold? People speculated wildly. Verne's novel, called *Journey to the Center of the Earth,* describes the adventures of a scientific expedition to explore a hollow Earth. Today, of course, scientists know that Earth's interior is not hollow!

But if you really could travel through Earth's layers all the way to the center, what would your trip be like? To begin, you would need a vehicle that could travel through solid rock. The vehicle would carry scientific instruments to record changes in temperature and pressure as you descend toward the center of Earth.

Temperature As you start to tunnel beneath the surface, you might expect the rock around you to be cool. At first, the surrounding rock is cool. Then at about 20 meters down your instruments report that the surrounding rock is getting warmer. For every 40 meters that you descend from that point, the temperature rises 1 Celsius degree. This rapid rise in temperature continues for several kilometers. After that, the temperature increases more slowly, but steadily.

Pressure During your journey to the center of Earth, your instruments also record an increase in pressure in the surrounding rock. The deeper you go, the greater the pressure. **Pressure** is the force pushing on a surface or area. Because of the weight of the rock above, pressure inside Earth increases as you go deeper.

As you go toward the center of Earth, you travel through several different layers. **Three main layers make up Earth's interior: the crust, the mantle, and the core. Each layer has its own conditions and materials.** You can see these layers in *Exploring Earth's Interior* on pages 112–113.

Figure 1 This cave in Georgia may seem deep. But even a deep cave is only a small nick in Earth's surface.

The Crust

Your journey to the center of Earth begins in the crust. The **crust** is a layer of rock that forms Earth's outer skin. On the crust you find rocks and mountains. But the crust also includes the soil and water that cover large parts of Earth's surface.

This outer rind of rock is much thinner than what lies beneath it. In fact, you can think of Earth's crust as being similar to the paper-thin skin of an onion. The crust includes both the dry land and the ocean floor. It is thinnest beneath the ocean and thickest under high mountains. The crust ranges from 5 to 40 kilometers thick.

The crust beneath the ocean is called oceanic crust. Oceanic crust consists mostly of dense rocks such as basalt. As you can see in Figure 2, basalt is dark, dense rock with a fine texture. Continental crust, the crust that forms the continents, consists mainly of less dense rocks such as granite. Granite is a rock that has larger crystals than basalt and is not as dense. It usually is a light color and has a coarse texture.

Figure 2 Two of the most common rocks in the crust are basalt and granite. **A.** The dark rock is basalt, which makes up much of the oceanic crust. **B.** The light rock is granite, which makes up much of the continental crust.

The Mantle

Your journey downward continues. At a depth of between 5 and 40 kilometers beneath the surface, you cross a boundary. Above this boundary are the basalt and granite rocks of the crust. Below the boundary is the solid material of the **mantle,** a layer of hot rock.

The crust and the uppermost part of the mantle are very similar. The uppermost part of the mantle and the crust together form a rigid layer called the **lithosphere.** In Greek, *litho* means "stone." The lithosphere averages about 100 kilometers thick.

Figure 3 At the surface, Earth's crust forms peaks like these in the Rocky Mountains of Colorado. Soil and plants cover much of the crust.

Next you travel farther into the mantle below the lithosphere. There your vehicle encounters material that is hotter and under increasing pressure. In general, temperature and pressure in the mantle increase with depth. The heat and pressure make the part of the mantle just beneath the lithosphere less rigid than the rock above. Like road tar softened by the heat of the sun, the material that forms this part of the mantle is somewhat soft—it can bend like plastic.

This soft layer is called the **asthenosphere** (as THEHN uh sfeer). In Greek, *asthenes* means "weak." Just because *asthenes* means weak, you can't assume this layer is actually weak. But the asthenosphere is soft. The material in this layer can flow slowly.

The lithosphere floats on top of the asthenosphere. Beneath the asthenosphere, solid mantle material extends all the way to Earth's core. The mantle is nearly 3,000 kilometers thick.

☑ *Checkpoint* *How does the material of the asthenosphere differ from the material of the lithosphere?*

The Core

After traveling through the mantle, you reach the core. Earth's core consists of two parts—a liquid outer core and a solid inner core. The metals iron and nickel make up both parts of the core. The **outer core** is a layer of molten metal that surrounds the inner core. In spite of enormous pressure, the outer core behaves like a thick liquid. The **inner core** is a dense ball of solid metal. In the inner core, extreme pressure squeezes the atoms of iron and nickel so much that they cannot spread out and become liquid.

The outer and inner cores make up about one third of Earth's mass, but only 15 percent of its volume. The inner and outer cores together are just slightly smaller than the moon.

Sharpen your Skills

Creating Data Tables

ACTIVITY

Imagine that you have invented a super-strong vehicle that can resist extremely high pressure as it bores a tunnel deep into Earth's interior. You stop several times on your trip to collect data using devices located on your vehicle's outer hull. To see what conditions you would find at various depths on your journey, refer to *Exploring Earth's Interior* on pages 112–113. Copy the table and complete it.

Depth	Name of Layer	What Layer Is Made Of
20 km		
150 km		
2,000 km		
4,000 km		
6,000 km		

EXPLORING Earth's Interior

Earth's interior is divided into layers: the crust, mantle, outer core, and inner core. Although Earth's crust seems stable, the extreme heat of Earth's interior causes changes that slowly reshape the surface.

CRUST

The crust is Earth's solid and rocky outer layer, including both the land surface and the ocean floor. The crust averages 32 km thick. At the scale of this drawing, the crust is too thin to show up as more than a thin line.

Composition of crust:
oxygen, silicon, aluminum, calcium, iron, sodium, potassium, magnesium

Inner core

Outer core Mantle Crust
1,200 km 2,250 km 2,900 km 5–40 km

MANTLE

A trip through Earth's mantle goes almost halfway to the center of Earth. The chemical composition of the mantle does not change much from one part of the mantle to another. However, physical conditions in the mantle change because pressure and temperature increase with depth.

Composition of mantle:
silicon, oxygen, iron, magnesium

CORE

Scientists estimate that temperatures within Earth's outer core and inner core, both made of iron and nickel, range from about 2,000°C to 5,000°C. If these estimates are correct, then Earth's center may be as hot as the sun's surface.

Composition of core:
iron, nickel

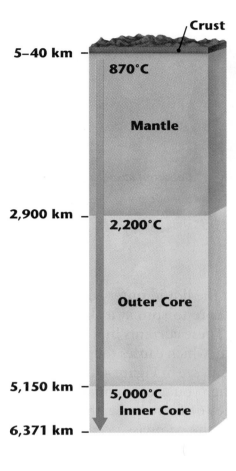

5–40 km —

Crust

870°C

Mantle

2,900 km —

2,200°C

Outer Core

5,150 km —

5,000°C
Inner Core

6,371 km —

◀ CROSS-SECTION FROM SURFACE TO CENTER

From Earth's surface to its center, the layers of Earth's interior differ in their composition, temperature, and pressure. Notice how temperature increases toward the inner core.

CRUST-TO-MANTLE

The rigid crust and lithosphere float on the hot, plastic material of the asthenosphere. Notice that continental crust, made mostly of granite, is several times thicker than oceanic crust, made mostly of basalt. ▼

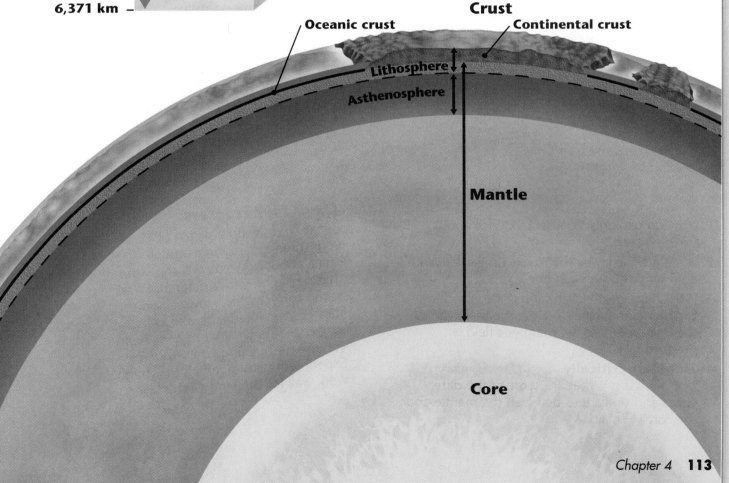

Oceanic crust

Crust

Continental crust

Lithosphere

Asthenosphere

Mantle

Core

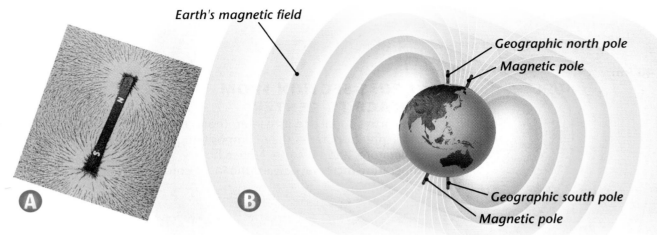
Earth's magnetic field

Geographic north pole
Magnetic pole

Geographic south pole
Magnetic pole

Figure 4 A. The pattern of iron filings was made by sprinkling them on paper placed over a bar magnet. B. Like a magnet, Earth's magnetic field has north and south poles. *Relating Cause and Effect If you shifted the magnet beneath the paper, what would happen to the iron filings?*

Earth's Magnetic Field

INTEGRATING PHYSICS Currents in the liquid outer core force the solid inner core to spin at a slightly faster rate than the rest of the planet. These currents in the outer core also create Earth's magnetic field, which causes the planet to act like a giant bar magnet. As you can see in Figure 4, the magnetic field affects the whole Earth. When you use a compass, the compass needle aligns with the lines of force in Earth's magnetic field. The north-seeking end of the compass needle points to Earth's magnetic north pole.

Consider an ordinary bar magnet. If you place it beneath a piece of paper and sprinkle iron filings on the paper, the iron filings line up with the bar's magnetic field. If you could cover the entire planet with iron filings, they would form a similar pattern.

Section 1 Review

1. How do geologists gather evidence about Earth's interior?
2. What are the layers that make up Earth? Write a sentence about each one.
3. What happens in Earth's interior to produce Earth's magnetic field? Describe the layers of the interior where the magnetic field is produced.
4. **Thinking Critically Comparing and Contrasting** What are some of the differences and similarities between the mantle and the core? Explain.

Check Your Progress

CHAPTER PROJECT

Begin by drawing a sketch of your three-dimensional model. Think about how you will show the thicknesses of Earth's different layers at the correct scale. How can you show Earth's interior as well as its surface features? What materials can you use for building your model? Experiment with materials that might work well for showing Earth's layers.

INTEGRATING **PHYSICS**

SECTION
2 Convection Currents and the Mantle

DISCOVER ·······························ACTIVITY····

How Can Heat Cause Motion in a Liquid?

1. ⚠ Carefully pour some hot water into a small, shallow pan. Fill a clear, plastic cup about half full with cold water. Place the cup in the pan.

2. Allow the water to stand for two minutes until all motion stops.

3. Fill a plastic dropper with some food coloring. Then, holding the dropper under the water surface and slightly away from the edge of the cup, gently squeeze a small droplet of the food coloring into the water.

4. Observe the water for one minute.

5. Add another droplet at the water surface in the middle of the cup and observe again.

Think It Over

Inferring How do you explain what happened to the droplets of food coloring? Why do you think the second droplet moved in a way that was different from the way the first droplet moved?

E arth's molten outer core is nearly as hot as the surface of the sun. To explain how heat from the core affects the mantle, you need to know how heat is transferred in solids and liquids. If you have ever touched a hot pot accidentally, you have discovered for yourself (in a painful way) that heat moves. In this case, it moved from the hot pot to your hand. The movement of energy from a warmer object to a cooler object is called **heat transfer**.

Heat is always transferred from a warmer substance to a cooler substance. For example, holding an ice cube will make your hand begin to feel cold in a few seconds. But is the coldness in the ice cube moving to your hand? Since cold is the absence of heat, it's the heat in your hand that moves to the ice cube! **There are three types of heat transfer: radiation, conduction, and convection.**

Radiation

The transfer of energy through empty space is called **radiation.** Sunlight is radiation that warms Earth's surface. Heat transfer by radiation takes place with no direct contact between a heat source and an object. Radiation enables sunlight to warm Earth's surface. Other familiar forms of radiation include the heat you feel around a flame or open fire.

GUIDE FOR READING

◆ How is heat transferred?

◆ What causes convection currents?

Reading Tip As you read, draw a concept map of the three types of heat transfer. Include supporting ideas about convection.

Figure 5 In conduction, the heated particles of a substance transfer heat to other particles through direct contact. That's how the spoon and the pot itself heat up.

Conduction

Heat transfer by direct contact of particles of matter is called **conduction.** What happens as a spoon heats up in a pot of soup? Heat is transferred from the hot soup and the pot to the particles that make up the spoon. The particles near the bottom of the spoon vibrate faster as they are heated, so they bump into other particles and heat them, too. Gradually the entire spoon heats up. When your hand touches the spoon, conduction transfers heat from the spoon directly to your skin. Then you feel the heat. Look at Figure 5 to see how conduction takes place.

Convection

Conduction heats the spoon, but how does the soup inside the pot heat up? Heat transfer involving the movement of fluids—liquids and gases—is called convection. **Convection** is heat transfer by the movement of a heated fluid. During convection, heated particles of fluid begin to flow, transferring heat energy from one part of the fluid to another.

Heat transfer by convection is caused by differences of temperature and density within a fluid. **Density** is a measure of how much mass there is in a volume of a substance. For example, rock is more dense than water because a given volume of rock has more mass than the same volume of water.

When a liquid or gas is heated, the particles move faster. As the particles move faster, they spread apart. Because the particles of the heated fluid are farther apart, they occupy more space. The density decreases. But when a fluid cools, its particles move more slowly and settle together more closely. As the fluid becomes cooler, its density increases.

If you look at Figure 6, you can see how convection occurs when you heat soup on a stove. As the soup at the bottom of the pot gets hot, it expands and therefore becomes less dense. The warm, less dense soup moves upward and floats over the cooler, more dense soup. At the surface, the warm soup spreads out and cools, becoming denser. Gravity then pulls this cooler, denser soup back down to the bottom of the pot, where it is heated again.

Figure 6 In this pot, the soup close to the heat source is hotter and less dense than the soup near the surface. These differences in temperature and density cause convection currents.

A constant flow begins as the cooler soup continually sinks to the bottom of the pot and the warmer soup rises. A **convection current** is the flow that transfers heat within a fluid.

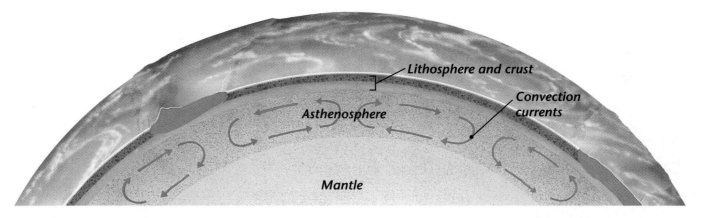

Lithosphere and crust

Asthenosphere

Convection currents

Mantle

The heating and cooling of the fluid, changes in the fluid's density, and the force of gravity combine to set convection currents in motion. Convection currents continue as long as heat is added. What happens after the heat source is removed? Without heat, the convection currents will eventually stop when all of the material has reached the same temperature.

☑ *Checkpoint* *What is convection?*

Convection in Earth's Mantle

Like soup simmering in a pot, Earth's mantle responds to heat. Notice in Figure 7 how convection currents flow in the asthenosphere. The heat source for these currents is heat from Earth's core and from the mantle itself. Hot columns of mantle material rise slowly through the asthenosphere. At the top of the asthenosphere, the hot material spreads out and pushes the cooler material out of the way. This cooler material sinks back into the asthenosphere. Over and over, the cycle of rising and sinking takes place. Convection currents like these have been moving inside Earth for more than four billion years!

Figure 7 Heat from Earth's mantle and core causes convection currents to form in the asthenosphere. Some geologists think convection currents extend throughout the mantle. *Applying Concepts What part of Earth's interior is like the soup in the pot? What part is like the burner on the stove?*

Section 2 Review

1. What are the three types of heat transfer?
2. Describe how convection currents form.
3. In general, what happens to the density of a fluid when it becomes hotter?
4. What happens to convection currents when a fluid reaches a constant temperature?
5. **Thinking Critically** **Predicting** What will happen to the flow of hot rock in Earth's mantle if the planet's core eventually cools down? Explain your answer.

Science at Home

Convection and Home Heating
Convection currents may keep the air inside your home at a comfortable temperature. Air is made up of gases, so it is a fluid. Regardless of the type of home heating system, heated air circulates through a room by convection. You may have tried to adjust the flow of air in a stuffy room by opening a window. When you did so, you were making use of convection currents. With an adult family member, study how your home is heated. Look for evidence of convection currents.

How Are Earth's Continents Linked Together?

1. Find the oceans and the seven continents on a globe showing Earth's physical features.

2. How much of the globe is occupied by the Pacific Ocean? Does most of Earth's "dry" land lie in the Northern or Southern hemisphere?

3. Find the points or areas where most of the continents are connected. Find the points at which several of the continents almost touch, but are not connected.

4. Examine the globe more closely. Find the great belt of mountains running from north to south along the western side of North and South America. Can you find another great belt of mountains on the globe?

Think It Over

Posing Questions What questions can you pose about how oceans, continents, and mountains are distributed on Earth's surface?

GUIDE FOR READING

◆ What is continental drift?

◆ Why was Alfred Wegener's theory rejected by most scientists of his day?

Reading Tip As you read, look for evidence that supports the theory of continental drift.

Five hundred years ago, the sea voyages of Columbus and other explorers changed the map of the world. The continents of Europe, Asia, and Africa were already known to mapmakers. Soon mapmakers were also showing the outlines of the continents of North and South America. Looking at these world maps, many people wondered why the coasts of several continents matched so neatly.

Look at the modern world map in Figure 8. Notice how the coasts of Africa and South America look as if they could fit together like jigsaw-puzzle pieces. Could the continents have once been a single landmass? In the 1700s, the first geologists thought that the continents had remained fixed in their positions throughout Earth's history. Early in the 1900s, however, one scientist began to think in a new way about this riddle of the continents. His theory changed the way people look at the map of the world.

World map drawn by Juan Vespucci in 1526. ▶

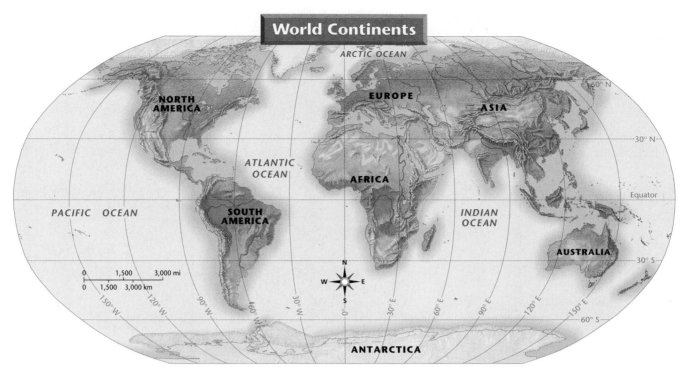

World Continents

Figure 8 Today's continents provide clues about Earth's history. *Observing* Which coastlines of continents seem to match up like jigsaw-puzzle pieces?

The Theory of Continental Drift

In 1910, a young German scientist named Alfred Wegener (VAY guh nur) became curious about the relationship of the continents. He formed a hypothesis that Earth's continents had moved! **Wegener's hypothesis was that all the continents had once been joined together in a single landmass and have since drifted apart.**

Wegener named this supercontinent **Pangaea** (pan JEE uh), meaning "all lands." According to Wegener, Pangaea existed a few hundred million years ago. This was the time when reptiles and winged insects first appeared. Great tropical forests, which later formed coal deposits, covered large parts of Earth's surface.

Over tens of millions of years, Pangaea began to break apart. The pieces of Pangaea slowly moved toward their present-day locations, becoming the continents as they are today. Wegener's idea that the continents slowly moved over Earth's surface became known as **continental drift.**

Have you ever tried to persuade a friend to accept a new idea? Your friend's opinion probably won't change unless you provide some convincing evidence. Wegener gathered evidence from different scientific fields to support his ideas about continental drift. In particular, he studied landforms, fossils, and evidence that showed how Earth's climate had changed over many millions of years. Wegener published all his evidence for continental drift in a book called *The Origin of Continents and Oceans*, first published in 1915.

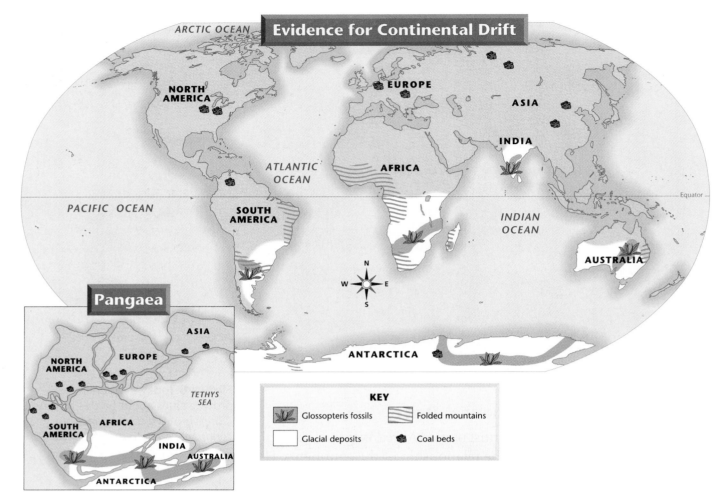

Evidence for Continental Drift

ARCTIC OCEAN

NORTH AMERICA

EUROPE

ASIA

INDIA

ATLANTIC OCEAN

AFRICA

Equator

PACIFIC OCEAN

SOUTH AMERICA

INDIAN OCEAN

AUSTRALIA

N
W   E
S

ANTARCTICA

KEY

Glossopteris fossils   Folded mountains

Glacial deposits   Coal beds

Pangaea

ASIA

NORTH AMERICA

EUROPE

TETHYS SEA

SOUTH AMERICA

AFRICA

INDIA

AUSTRALIA

ANTARCTICA

Figure 9 Wegener used several types of evidence to support his idea that the continents were once joined in a single landmass called Pangaea. *Inferring According to Wegener's theory, what does the presence of similar mountain ranges in Africa and South America indicate?*

Figure 10 Fossils of *Glossopteris* are found on continents in the Southern Hemisphere and in India.

Evidence from Landforms Mountain ranges and other features on the continents provided evidence for continental drift. For example, when Wegener pieced together maps of Africa and South America, he noticed some remarkable things. A mountain range running from east to west in South Africa lines up with a mountain range in Argentina. European coal fields match up with similar coal fields in North America. Wegener compared matching these features to reassembling a torn-up newspaper. If the pieces could be put back together, the "words" would match.

Evidence From Fossils Wegener also used fossils to support his argument for continental drift. A **fossil** is any trace of an ancient organism that has been preserved in rock. *Glossopteris* (glaw SAHP tuh ris) was a fernlike plant that flourished 250 million years ago. As shown in Figure 10, *Glossopteris* fossils have been found in rocks in Africa, South America, Australia, India, and Antarctica. The occurrence of *Glossopteris* on these widely separated landmasses convinced Wegener that the continents had once been united.

INTEGRATING LIFE SCIENCE The seedlike structures of *Glossopteris* could not have traveled the great distances that separate the continents today. The "seeds" were too large to have been carried by the wind and too fragile to have survived a trip by ocean waves. How did *Glossopteris* develop on such widely separated continents? Wegener inferred that the continents at that time were joined as the supercontinent Pangaea.

Evidence From Climate Wegener used evidence of climate change to support his theory—for example, from the island of Spitsbergen. Spitsbergen lies in the Arctic Ocean north of Norway. This island is ice-covered and has a harsh polar climate. But fossils of tropical plants are found on Spitsbergen. When these plants lived about 300 million years ago, the island must have had a warm and mild climate. According to Wegener, Spitsbergen must have been located closer to the equator.

Thousands of kilometers to the south, geologists found evidence that at the same time it was warm in Spitsbergen, the climate was much colder in South Africa. Deep scratches in rocks showed that continental glaciers once covered South Africa. Continental glaciers are thick layers of ice that cover hundreds of thousands of square kilometers. But the climate of South Africa is too mild today for continental glaciers to form. Wegener concluded that, when Pangaea existed, South Africa was much closer to the South Pole.

According to Wegener's theory, Earth's climate has not changed. Instead, the positions of the continents have changed. As a continent moves toward the equator, its climate becomes warmer. As a continent moves toward the poles, its climate becomes colder. But the continent carries with it the fossils and rocks that formed at its previous location. These clues provide evidence that continental drift really happened.

☑ *Checkpoint* *What were the three types of evidence Wegener used to support his theory of continental drift?*

Reassembling the Pieces

ACTIVITY

Assembling a puzzle can reveal a hidden meaning.

1. Working with a partner, obtain one sheet of newspaper per person.
2. Tear your sheet of newspaper into six to eight large pieces. Trade your pieces with your partner.
3. Try to fit the pieces of newspaper together.

Making Models What evidence did you use to put the pieces together? How do your pieces of newspaper serve as a model of the theory of continental drift?

Figure 11 As evidence of continental drift, Wegener pointed to scratches on rocks made by glaciers. These scratches showed that places with mild climates today once had climates cold enough for glaciers to form.

Scientists Reject Wegener's Theory

Wegener did more than provide a theory to answer the riddle of continental drift. He attempted to explain how drift took place. He even offered a new explanation for how mountains form. Wegener thought that when drifting continents collide, their edges crumple and fold. The folding continents slowly push up huge chunks of rock to form great mountains.

Unfortunately, Wegener could not provide a satisfactory explanation for the force that pushes or pulls the continents. Because Wegener could not identify the cause of continental drift, most geologists rejected his idea. In addition, for geologists to accept Wegener's idea, they would need new explanations of what caused continents and mountains to form.

Many geologists in the early 1900s thought that Earth was slowly cooling and shrinking. According to this theory, mountains formed when the crust wrinkled like the skin of a dried-up apple. Wegener said that if the apple theory were correct, then mountains should be found all over Earth's surface. But mountains usually occur in narrow bands along the edges of continents. Wegener thought that his own theory better explained where mountains occur and how they form.

For nearly half a century, from the 1920s to the 1960s, most scientists paid little attention to the idea of continental drift. Then new evidence about Earth's structure led scientists to reconsider Wegener's bold theory.

Figure 12 Although scientists rejected his theory, Wegener continued to collect evidence on continental drift and to update his book. He died in 1930 on an expedition to explore Greenland's continental glacier.

Section 3 Review

1. What was Wegener's theory of continental drift?
2. How did Wegener use evidence based on fossils to support his theory that the continents had moved?
3. What was the main reason scientists rejected Wegener's theory of continental drift?
4. **Thinking Critically Inferring** Coal deposits have also been found beneath the ice of Antarctica. But coal only forms in warm swamps. Use Wegener's theory to explain how coal could be found so near the poles.

Science at Home

Moving the Continents You can demonstrate Wegener's idea of continental drift. Use the map of the world in Figure 8. On a sheet of tracing paper, trace the outlines of the continents bordering the Atlantic Ocean. Label the continents. Then use scissors to carefully cut the map along the eastern edge of South America, North America, and Greenland. Next, cut along the western edge of Africa and Europe (including the British Isles). Throw away the Atlantic Ocean. Place the two cut-out pieces on a dark surface and ask family members to try to fit the two halves together. Explain to them about the supercontinent Pangaea and its history.

4 Sea-Floor Spreading

DISCOVER   ACTIVITY

What Is the Effect of a Change in Density?

1. Partially fill a sink or dishpan with water.

2. Open up a dry washcloth in your hand. Does the washcloth feel light or heavy?

3. Moisten one edge of the washcloth in the water. Then gently place the washcloth so that it floats on the water's surface. Observe the washcloth carefully (especially at its edges) as it starts to sink.

4. Remove the washcloth from the water and open it up in your hand. Is the mass of the washcloth the same as, less than, or greater than when it was dry?

Think It Over

Observing How did the washcloth's density change? What effect did this change in density have on the washcloth?

Deep in the ocean, the temperature is near freezing. There is no light, and living things are generally scarce. Yet some areas of the deep-ocean floor are teeming with life. One of these areas is the East Pacific Rise, a region of the Pacific Ocean floor off the coasts of Mexico and South America. Here, ocean water sinks through cracks, or vents, in the crust. The water is heated by contact with hot material from the mantle and then spurts back into the ocean.

Around these hot-water vents live some of the most bizarre creatures ever discovered. Giant, red-tipped tube worms sway in the water. Nearby sit giant clams nearly a meter across. Strange spiderlike crabs scuttle by. Surprisingly, the geological features of this strange environment provided scientists with some of the best evidence for Wegener's theory of continental drift.

GUIDE FOR READING

◆ What is the process of sea-floor spreading?

◆ What happens to the ocean floor at deep ocean trenches?

Reading Tip Before you read, preview the art and captions looking for new terms. As you read, find the meanings of these terms.

Figure 13 Tube worms cluster near hot water vents in the ocean floor.

Figure 14 Scientists use sonar to map the ocean floor.

Mapping the Mid-Ocean Ridge

The East Pacific Rise is just one part of the **mid-ocean ridge,** the longest chain of mountains in the world. In the mid-1900s, scientists mapped the mid-ocean ridge using sonar. **Sonar** is a device that bounces sound waves off underwater objects and then records the echoes of these sound waves. The time it takes for the echo to arrive indicates the distance to the object.

The mid-ocean ridge curves like the seam of a baseball along the sea floor, extending into all of Earth's oceans. Most of the mountains in the mid-ocean ridge lie hidden under hundreds of meters of water. However, there are places where the ridge pokes above the surface. For example, the island of Iceland is a part of the mid-ocean ridge that rises above the surface in the North Atlantic Ocean. A steep-sided valley splits the top of the mid-ocean ridge for most of its length. The valley is almost twice as deep as the Grand Canyon. The mapping of the mid-ocean ridge made scientists curious to know what the ridge was and how it formed.

☑ *Checkpoint* *What device is used to map the ocean floor?*

Figure 15 The mid-ocean ridge is more than 50,000 kilometers long.

Earth's Ocean Floor

ASIA

NORTH AMERICA

EUROPE

ASIA

ATLANTIC OCEAN

AFRICA

PACIFIC OCEAN

INDIAN OCEAN

SOUTH AMERICA

AUSTRALIA

KEY
— Mid-ocean ridge
— Deep-ocean trench

ANTARCTICA

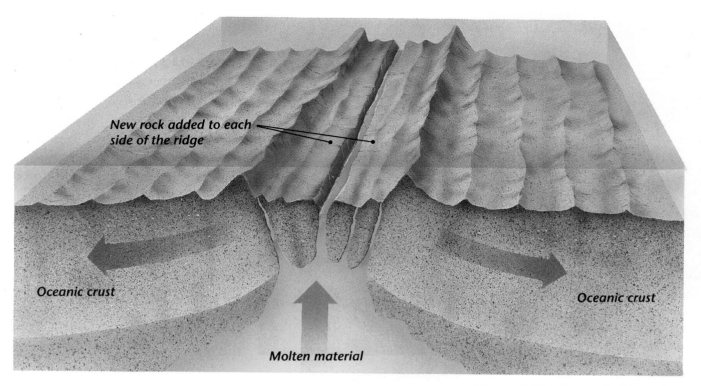

New rock added to each side of the ridge

Oceanic crust

Oceanic crust

Molten material

Figure 16 Molten material erupts though the valley that runs along the center of the mid-ocean ridge. This material hardens to form the rock of the ocean floor. *Applying Concepts What happens to the rock along the ridge when new molten material erupts?*

Evidence for Sea-Floor Spreading

Harry Hess, an American geologist, was one of the scientists who studied the mid-ocean ridge. Hess carefully examined maps of the mid-ocean ridge. Then he began to think about the ocean floor in relation to the problem of continental drift. Finally, he reconsidered an idea that he previously had thought impossible: Maybe Wegener was right! Perhaps the continents do move.

In 1960, Hess proposed a radical idea. He suggested that the ocean floors move like conveyor belts, carrying the continents along with them. This movement begins at the mid-ocean ridge. The mid-ocean ridge forms along a crack in the oceanic crust. **At the mid-ocean ridge, molten material rises from the mantle and erupts. The molten material then spreads out, pushing older rock to both sides of the ridge.** As the molten material cools, it forms a strip of solid rock in the center of the ridge. Then more molten material flows into the crack. This material splits apart the strip of solid rock that formed before, pushing it aside.

Hess called the process that continually adds new material to the ocean floor **sea-floor spreading.** He realized that the sea floor spreads apart along both sides of the mid-ocean ridge as new crust is added. Look at Figure 16 to see the process of sea-floor spreading.

Several types of evidence from the oceans supported Hess's theory of sea-floor spreading—evidence from molten material, magnetic stripes, and drilling samples. This evidence also led scientists to look again at Wegener's theory of continental drift.

Figure 17 The submersible *Alvin* photographed pillow lava along the mid-ocean ridge. These "pillows" form under water when cold ocean water causes a crust to form on erupting molten material. Each pillow expands until it bursts, allowing molten material to flow out and form the next pillow.

Evidence From Molten Material In the 1960s, scientists found evidence that new material is indeed erupting along the mid-ocean ridge. The scientists dived to the ocean floor in *Alvin,* a small submersible built to withstand the crushing pressures four kilometers down in the ocean. In the central valley of the mid-ocean ridge, *Alvin*'s crew found strange rocks shaped like pillows or like toothpaste squeezed from a tube. Such rocks can form only when molten material hardens quickly after erupting under water. The presence of these rocks showed that molten material has erupted again and again from cracks along the central valley of the mid-ocean ridge.

Evidence From Magnetic Stripes When scientists studied

INTEGRATING PHYSICS patterns in the rocks of the ocean floor, they found more support for sea-floor spreading. In Section 1 you read that Earth behaves like a giant magnet, with a north pole and a south pole. Evidence shows that Earth's magnetic poles have reversed themselves. This last happened 780,000 years ago. If the magnetic poles suddenly reversed themselves today, you would find that your compass needle pointed south. Scientists discovered that the rock that makes up the ocean floor lies in a pattern of magnetized "stripes." These stripes hold a record of reversals in Earth's magnetic field.

Figure 18 Magnetic stripes in the rock of the ocean floor show the direction of Earth's magnetic field at the time the rock hardened.
Interpreting Diagrams How are these matching stripes evidence of sea-floor spreading?

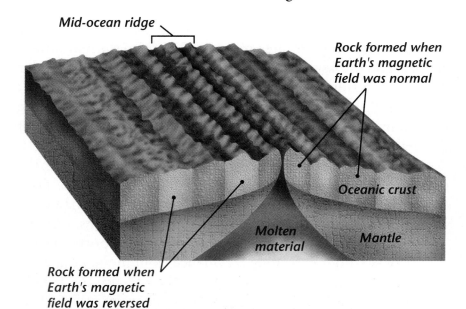

Mid-ocean ridge

Rock formed when Earth's magnetic field was normal

Oceanic crust

Molten material

Mantle

Rock formed when Earth's magnetic field was reversed

The rock of the ocean floor, which contains iron, began as molten material. As the molten material cooled, the iron bits inside lined up in the direction of Earth's magnetic poles. When the rock hardened completely, it locked the iron bits in place, giving the rocks a permanent "magnetic memory." You can think of it as setting thousands of tiny compass needles in cement.

Using sensitive instruments, scientists recorded the magnetic memory of rocks on both sides of the mid-ocean ridge. They found that a stripe of rock that shows when Earth's magnetic field pointed north is followed by a parallel stripe of rock that shows when the magnetic field pointed south. As you can see in Figure 19, the pattern is the same on both sides of the ridge. Rock that hardens at the same time has the same magnetic memory.

Evidence From Drilling Samples The final proof of sea-floor spreading came from rock samples obtained by drilling into the ocean floor. The *Glomar Challenger*, a drilling ship built in 1968, gathered the samples. The *Glomar Challenger* sent drilling pipes through water six kilometers deep to drill holes in the ocean floor. This feat has been compared to using a sharp-ended wire to dig a hole into a sidewalk from the top of the Empire State Building.

Samples from the sea floor were brought up through the drilling pipes. Then the scientists determined the age of the rocks in the samples. They found that the farther away from the ridge the samples were taken, the older the rocks were. The youngest rocks were always in the center of the ridges. This showed that sea-floor spreading really has taken place.

☑ *Checkpoint* **What evidence did scientists find for sea-floor spreading?**

Reversing Poles

1. Cut six short pieces, each **ACTIVITY** about 2.5 cm long, from a length of audiotape.

2. Tape one end of each piece of audiotape to a flat surface. The pieces should be spaced 1 cm apart and line up lengthwise in a single line.

3. Touch a bar magnet's north pole to the first piece of audiotape. Then reverse the magnet and touch its south pole to the next piece.

4. Repeat Step 3 until you have applied the magnet to each piece of audiotape.

5. Sweep one end of the magnet about 1 cm above the line of audiotape pieces. Observe what happens.

Making Models What characteristic of the ocean floor did you observe as you swept the magnet along the line of audiotape pieces?

Figure 19 The *Glomar Challenger* was the first research ship designed to drill samples of rock from the deep-ocean floor.

Subduction at Deep-Ocean Trenches

How can the ocean floor keep getting wider and wider? The answer is that the ocean floor generally does not just keep spreading. Instead, the ocean floor plunges into deep underwater canyons called **deep-ocean trenches.** A deep-ocean trench forms where the oceanic crust bends downward.

Where there are deep-ocean trenches, subduction takes place. **Subduction** (sub DUK shun) is the process by which the ocean floor sinks beneath a deep-ocean trench and back into the mantle. Convection currents under the lithosphere push new crust that forms at the mid-ocean ridge away from the ridge and toward a deep-ocean trench.

New oceanic crust is hot. But as it moves away from the mid-ocean ridge, it cools and becomes more dense. Eventually, as shown in Figure 20, gravity pulls this older, denser oceanic crust down beneath the trench. The sinking crust is like the washcloth in the Discover activity at the beginning of this section. As the dry washcloth floating on the water gets wet, its density increases and it begins to sink.

At deep-ocean trenches, subduction allows part of the ocean floor to sink back into the mantle, over tens of millions of years. You can think of sea-floor spreading and subduction together as if the ocean floor were moving out from the mid-ocean ridge on a giant conveyor belt.

Figure 20 Oceanic crust created along the mid-ocean ridge is destroyed at a deep-ocean trench. In the process of subduction, oceanic crust sinks down beneath the trench into the mantle.
Drawing Conclusions Where would denser oceanic crust be found?

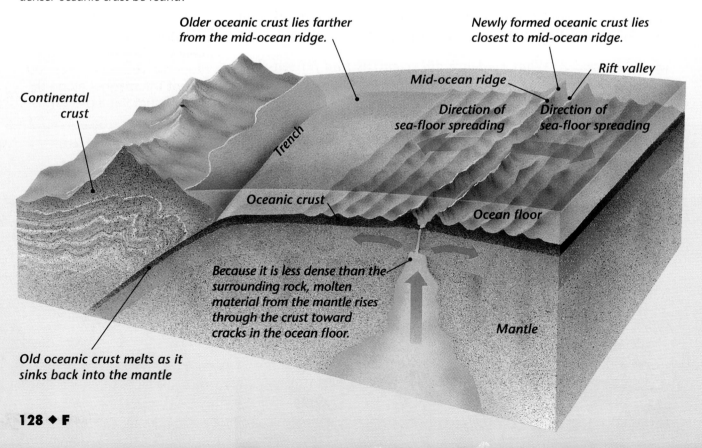

Older oceanic crust lies farther from the mid-ocean ridge.

Newly formed oceanic crust lies closest to mid-ocean ridge.

Rift valley

Continental crust

Mid-ocean ridge

Direction of sea-floor spreading

Direction of sea-floor spreading

Trench

Oceanic crust

Ocean floor

Because it is less dense than the surrounding rock, molten material from the mantle rises through the crust toward cracks in the ocean floor.

Mantle

Old oceanic crust melts as it sinks back into the mantle

Subduction and Earth's Oceans

The processes of subduction and sea-floor spreading can change the size and shape of the oceans. Because of these processes, Earth's ocean floor is renewed about every 200 million years. That is the time it takes for new rock to form at the mid-ocean ridge, move across the ocean, and sink into a trench.

Subduction in the Pacific Ocean The vast Pacific Ocean covers almost one third of the planet. And yet it is shrinking. How could that be? Sometimes a deep ocean trench swallows more oceanic crust than the mid-ocean ridge can produce. Then, if the ridge does not add new crust fast enough, the width of the ocean will shrink. This is happening to the Pacific Ocean, which is ringed by many trenches.

Subduction in the Atlantic Ocean The Atlantic Ocean, on the other hand, is expanding. Unlike the Pacific Ocean, the Atlantic Ocean has only a few short trenches. As a result, the spreading ocean floor has virtually nowhere to go. In most places, the oceanic crust of the Atlantic Ocean floor is attached to the continental crust of the continents around the ocean. So as the Atlantic's ocean floor spreads, the continents along its edges also move. Over time, the whole ocean gets wider. The spreading floor of the North Atlantic Ocean and the continent of North America move together like two giant barges pushed by the same tugboat.

Figure 21 It is cold and dark in the deep ocean trenches where subduction occurs. But even here, scientists have found living things, such as this angler fish.

Section 4 Review

1. What is the role of the mid-ocean ridge in sea-floor spreading?
2. What is the evidence for sea-floor spreading?
3. Describe the process of subduction at a deep-ocean trench.
4. **Thinking Critically** **Relating Cause and Effect** Where would you expect to find the oldest rock on the ocean floor? Explain your answer.
5. **Thinking Critically** **Predicting** As you can see in Figure 15, the mid-ocean ridge extends into the Red Sea between Africa and Asia. What do you think will happen to the Red Sea in the future? Explain your answer.

> **CHAPTER PROJECT**
>
> **Check Your Progress**
> Now that you have learned about sea-floor spreading, draw a revised sketch of your model. Include examples of sea-floor spreading and subduction on your sketch. Show the features that form as a result of these processes. How will you show what happens beneath the crust? Improve your original ideas and add new ideas. Revise your list of materials if necessary. Begin building your model.

MODELING SEA-FLOOR SPREADING

A long the entire length of Earth's mid-ocean ridge, the sea floor is spreading. Although this process takes place constantly, it is difficult to observe directly. You can build a model to help understand this process.

Problem

How does sea-floor spreading add material to the ocean floor?

Materials

scissors
metric ruler
2 sheets of unlined paper
colored marker

Procedure

1. Draw stripes across one sheet of paper, parallel to the short sides of the paper. The stripes should vary in spacing and thickness.
2. Fold the paper in half lengthwise and write the word "Start" at the top of both halves of the paper. Using the scissors, carefully cut the paper in half along the fold line to form two strips.
3. Lightly fold the second sheet of paper into eighths. Then unfold it, leaving creases in the paper. Fold this sheet in half lengthwise.

4. Starting at the fold, draw lines 5.5 cm long on the middle crease and the two creases closest to the ends of the paper.

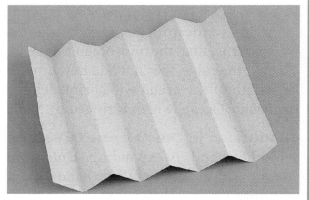

5. Now carefully cut along the lines you drew. Unfold the paper. There should be three slits in the center of the paper.

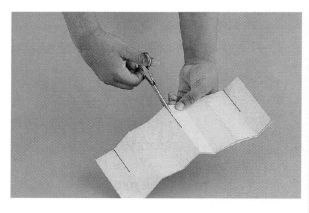

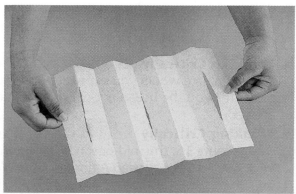

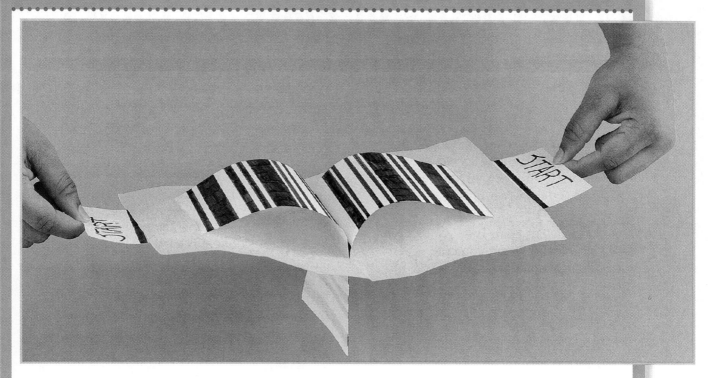

6. Put the two striped strips of paper together so their Start labels touch one another. Insert the Start ends of the strips up through the center slit and then pull them toward the side slits.

7. Insert the ends of the strips into the side slits. Pull the ends of the strips and watch what happens at the center slit.

8. Practice pulling the strips through the slits until you can make the two strips come up and go down at the same time.

Analyze and Conclude

1. What feature of the ocean floor does the center slit stand for? What prominent feature of the ocean floor is missing from the model at this point?

2. What do the side slits stand for? What does the space under the paper stand for?

3. How does the ocean floor as shown by the part of a strip close to the center slit differ from the ocean floor as shown by the part near a side slit? How does this difference affect the depth of the ocean?

4. What do the stripes on the strips stand for? Why is it important that your model have an identical pattern of stripes on both sides of the center slit?

5. Explain how differences in density and temperature provide some of the force needed to cause sea-floor spreading and subduction.

6. **Think About It** Use your own words to describe the process of ocean-floor spreading. What parts of the process were not shown by your model?

More to Explore

Imagine that so much molten rock erupted from the mid-ocean ridge that an island formed there. How could you modify your model to show this island? How could you show what would happen to it over a long period of time?

The Theory of Plate Tectonics

How Well Do the Continents Fit Together?

1. Using a world map in an atlas, trace the shapes of the continents North America, South America, Africa, and Europe, including Great Britain and Ireland.

2. ✂ Carefully cut apart the landmasses. When you cut out Europe, leave Britain and Ireland attached to Europe.

3. Piece together these landmasses as they may have looked before Pangaea split apart, creating the Atlantic Ocean.

4. Attach your partial reconstruction of Pangaea to a piece of paper.

NORTH AMERICA

Continental shelf

ATLANTIC OCEAN

5. Obtain a map that shows the continental shelf. The continental shelf is the apron of continental crust that extends underwater around the edges of the continents. Trace around the continental shelves of the same continents used in Step 1.

6. Repeat Steps 2 through 4.

Think It Over
Drawing Conclusions Do your observations support the idea that the continents were once joined together? When did they fit together better: when you cut them out along their coastlines or along their continental shelves? Explain.

GUIDE FOR READING

◆ What is the theory of plate tectonics?

◆ What are the three types of plate boundaries?

Reading Tip Before you read, preview *Exploring Plate Tectonics* on pages 134–135. Write a list of any questions you have about plate tectonics. Look for answers as you read.

Have you ever dropped a hard-boiled egg? If so, you may have noticed that the eggshell cracked in an irregular pattern of broken pieces. Earth's lithosphere, its solid outer shell, is not one unbroken layer. It is more like that cracked eggshell. It's broken into pieces separated by jagged cracks.

A Canadian scientist, J. Tuzo Wilson, observed that there are cracks in the continents similar to those on the ocean floor. In 1965, Wilson proposed a new way of looking at these cracks. According to Wilson, the lithosphere is broken into separate sections called **plates.** The plates fit closely together along cracks in the lithosphere. As shown in Figure 23, the plates carry the continents or parts of the ocean floor, or both.

Figure 22 The Great Rift Valley in east Africa is a crack in Earth's crust where two pieces of crust are pulling apart. The photograph shows one side of the Rift Valley.

A Theory of Plate Motion

Wilson combined what geologists knew about sea-floor spreading, Earth's plates, and continental drift into a single theory—the theory of plate tectonics (tek TAHN iks). A **scientific theory** is a well-tested concept that explains a wide range of observations. **Plate tectonics** is the geological theory that states that pieces of Earth's lithosphere are in constant, slow motion, driven by convection currents in the mantle. **The theory of plate tectonics explains the formation, movement, and subduction of Earth's plates.**

How can Earth's plates move? The plates of the lithosphere float on top of the asthenosphere. Convection currents rise in the asthenosphere and spread out beneath the lithosphere. Most geologists think that the flow of these currents causes the movement of Earth's plates.

No plate can budge without affecting the other plates surrounding it. As the plates move, they collide, pull apart, or grind past each other, producing spectacular changes in Earth's surface. These changes include volcanoes, mountain ranges, and deep-sea trenches.

Sharpen your Skills

Predicting

Study the map of Earth's plates in Figure 23. Notice the arrows that show the direction of plate movement. Now find the Nazca plate on the map. Which direction is it moving? Find the South American plate and describe its movement. What do you think will happen as these plates continue to move?

ACTIVITY

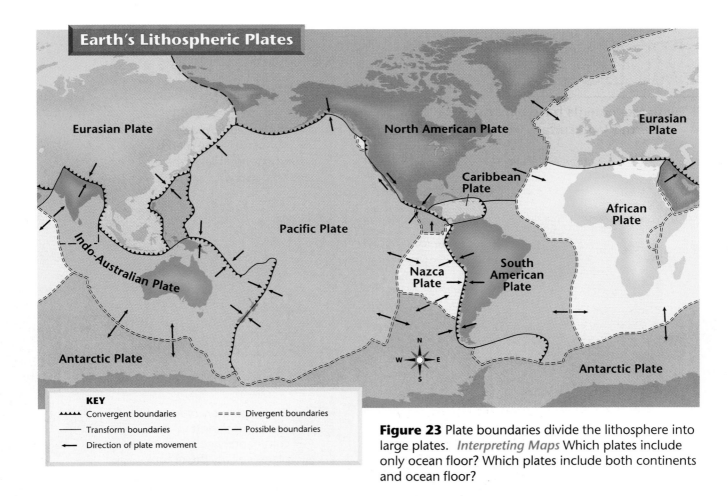

Earth's Lithospheric Plates

Eurasian Plate

North American Plate

Eurasian Plate

Caribbean Plate

African Plate

Pacific Plate

Indo-Australian Plate

Nazca Plate

South American Plate

Antarctic Plate

Antarctic Plate

KEY
- ⌃⌃⌃⌃ Convergent boundaries
- ==== Divergent boundaries
- —— Transform boundaries
- – – Possible boundaries
- ← Direction of plate movement

Figure 23 Plate boundaries divide the lithosphere into large plates. *Interpreting Maps* Which plates include only ocean floor? Which plates include both continents and ocean floor?

Plate Boundaries

The edges of different pieces of the lithosphere—Earth's rigid shell—meet at lines called plate boundaries. Plate boundaries extend deep into the lithosphere. **Faults**—breaks in Earth's crust where rocks have slipped past each other—form along these boundaries. There are three kinds of plate boundaries: transform boundaries, divergent boundaries, and convergent boundaries. For each type of boundary, there is a different type of plate movement.

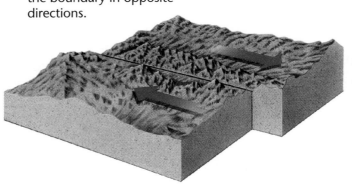

Figure 24 At a transform boundary, two plates move along the boundary in opposite directions.

Transform Boundaries Along transform boundaries, crust is neither created nor destroyed. A **transform boundary** is a place where two plates slip past each other, moving in opposite directions. Earthquakes occur frequently along these boundaries. Look at Figure 24 to see the type of plate movement that occurs along a transform boundary.

EXPLORING *Plate Tectonics*

Plate movements have built many of the features of Earth's land surfaces and ocean floors.

Diverging oceanic plates
The mid-ocean ridge marks a divergent boundary where plates move apart.

Mid-ocean ridge

Trench

Trench

Subduction zone

Oceanic crust

Oceanic crust

Converging oceanic plates When two oceanic plates collide, one plate is subducted through a trench.

Converging oceanic and continental plates When continental and oceanic plates collide, the oceanic plate is subducted.

Lithosphere

Magma

Divergent Boundaries The place where two plates move apart, or diverge, is called a **divergent boundary** (dy VUR junt). Most divergent boundaries occur at the mid-ocean ridge. In Section 4, you learned how oceanic crust forms along the mid-ocean ridge as sea-floor spreading occurs.

Divergent boundaries also occur on land. When a divergent boundary develops on land, two of Earth's plates pull apart. A deep valley called a **rift valley** forms along the divergent boundary. For example, the Great Rift Valley in east Africa marks a deep crack in the African continent that runs for about 3,000 kilometers. Along this crack, a divergent plate boundary is slowly spreading apart. The rift may someday split the eastern part of Africa away from the rest of the continent. As a rift valley widens, its floor drops. Eventually, the floor may drop enough for the sea to fill the widening gap.

✓ *Checkpoint* *What is a rift valley? How are rift valleys formed?*

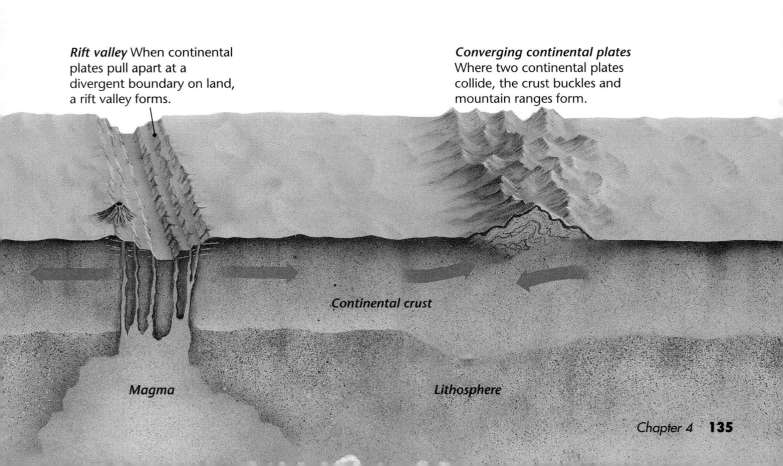

Rift valley When continental plates pull apart at a divergent boundary on land, a rift valley forms.

Converging continental plates Where two continental plates collide, the crust buckles and mountain ranges form.

Continental crust

Magma

Lithosphere

225 million years ago
All Earth's major landmasses were joined in the super-continent Pangaea before plate movements began to split it apart.

180–200 million years ago
Pangaea continued to split apart, opening narrow seas that later became oceans.

Convergent Boundaries The place where two plates come together, or converge, is called a **convergent boundary** (kun VUR junt). When two plates converge, the result is called a collision. Collisions may bring together oceanic crust and oceanic crust, oceanic crust and continental crust, or continental crust and continental crust.

When two plates collide, the density of the plates determines which one comes out on top. Oceanic crust, which is made mostly of basalt, is more dense than continental crust, which is made mostly of granite. And oceanic crust becomes cooler and denser as it spreads away from the mid-ocean ridge.

Where two plates carrying oceanic crust meet at a trench, the plate that is more dense dives under the other plate and returns to the mantle. This is the process of subduction that you learned about in Section 4.

Sometimes a plate carrying oceanic crust collides with a plate carrying continental crust. The less dense continental crust can't sink under the more dense oceanic crust. Instead, the oceanic plate begins to sink and plunges beneath the continental plate.

When two plates carrying continental crust collide, subduction does not take place. Both continental plates are mostly low-density granite rock. Therefore, neither plate is dense enough to sink into the mantle. Instead, the plates crash head-on. The collision squeezes the crust into mighty mountain ranges.

Checkpoint *What types of plate movement occur at plate boundaries?*

Figure 25 A collision between two continental plates produced the majestic Himalayas. The collision began 50 million years ago, when the plate that carries India slammed into Asia.

135 million years ago Gradually, the landmasses that became today's continents began to drift apart.

Earth today
Note how far to the north India has drifted—farther than any other major landmass.

65 million years ago
India was still a separate continent, charging toward Asia, while Australia remained attached to Antarctica.

The Continents' Slow Dance

The plates move at amazingly slow rates: from about one to ten centimeters per year. The North American and Eurasian plates are floating apart at a rate of 2.5 centimeters per year—that's about as fast as your fingernails grow. This may not seem like much, but these plates have been moving for tens of millions of years.

About 260 million years ago, the continents were joined together in the supercontinent that Wegener called Pangaea. Then, about 225 million years ago, Pangaea began to break apart. Figure 26 shows how Earth's continents and other landmasses have moved since the breakup of Pangaea.

Figure 26 It has taken about 225 million years for the continents to move to their present locations. *Posing Questions What questions would you need to answer in order to predict where the continents will be in 50 million years?*

Section 5 Review

1. What is the theory of plate tectonics?
2. What are the different types of boundaries found along the edges of Earth's plates?
3. What major event in Earth's history began about 225 million years ago? Explain.
4. **Thinking Critically Predicting** Look at Figure 23 on page 133 and find the divergent boundary that runs through the African plate. Predict what could eventually happen along this boundary.

Check Your Progress

CHAPTER PROJECT

Now that you have learned about plate tectonics, add examples of plate boundaries to your model. If possible, include a transform boundary, a convergent boundary, and a divergent boundary. Complete the construction of your model by adding all the required surface features. Be sure to label the features on your model. Include arrows that indicate the direction of plate movement.

HOT PLATES

I n this lab, you will observe a model of convection currents in Earth's mantle.

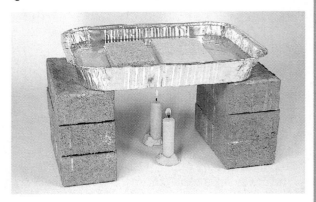

Problem

How do convection currents affect Earth's plates?

Materials

1 aluminum roasting pan
2 candles, about 10 cm long
clay to hold the candles up
6 bricks
2 medium-sized kitchen sponges
10 map pins
2 L water

Procedure

1. Stick ten pins about halfway into a long side of one of the sponges.
2. Place an aluminum pan on top of two stacks of bricks. **CAUTION:** *Position the bricks so that they fully support both ends of the pan.*
3. Fill the pan with water to a depth of 4 cm.
4. Moisten both sponges with water and float them in the pan.
5. Slowy nudge the two sponges together with the row of map pins between them. (The pins will keep the sponges from sticking together.)
6. Carefully let go of the sponges. If they drift apart, gently move them back together again.
7. Once the sponges stay close together, place the candles under opposite ends of the pan. Use clay to hold up the candles.
8. Draw a diagram of the pan, showing the starting position of the sponges.
9. Carefully light the candles. Observe the two sponges as the water heats up.
10. Draw diagrams showing the position of the sponges 1 minute and 2 minutes after placing the candles under the pan.

Analyze and Conclude

1. What happens to the sponges as the water heats up?
2. What can you infer is causing the changes you observed?
3. What material represents the mantle in this activity? What represents Earth's plates?
4. What would be the effect of adding several more candles under the pan?
5. **Think About It** How well did this activity model the movement of Earth's plates? What type of plate movement did you observe in the pan? How could you modify the activity to model plate movement more closely?

More to Explore

You can observe directly the movement of the water in the pan. To do this, squeeze a single drop of food coloring into the pan. After the drop of coloring has sunk to the bottom, place a lit candle under the pan near the colored water. How does the food coloring move in the water? How does this movement compare with convection currents in the mantle?

SECTION

1 Earth's Interior

Key Ideas

◆ Earth's interior is divided into the crust, the mantle, the outer core, and the inner core.

◆ The lithosphere includes the crust and the rigid upper layer of the mantle; beneath the lithosphere lies the soft layer of the mantle called the asthenosphere.

Key Terms

seismic wave   lithosphere
pressure   asthenosphere
crust   outer core
mantle   inner core

 SECTION

2 Convection Currents and the Mantle

INTEGRATING PHYSICS

Key Ideas

◆ Heat can be transferred in three ways: radiation, conduction, and convection.

◆ Differences of temperature and density within a fluid cause convection currents.

Key Terms

heat transfer   convection
radiation   density
conduction   convection current

 SECTION

3 Drifting Continents

Key Ideas

◆ Alfred Wegener developed the idea that the continents were once joined and have since drifted apart.

◆ Most scientists rejected Wegener's theory because he could not identify a force that could move the continents.

Key Terms

Pangaea
continental drift
fossil

 SECTION

4 Sea-Floor Spreading

Key Ideas

◆ In sea-floor spreading, molten material forms new rock along the mid-ocean ridge.

◆ In subduction, the ocean floor sinks back to the mantle beneath deep ocean trenches.

Key Terms

mid-ocean ridge   deep-ocean trench
sonar   subduction
sea-floor spreading

SECTION

5 The Theory of Plate Tectonics

Key Ideas

◆ The theory of plate tectonics explains plate movements and how they cause continental drift.

◆ Plates slip past each other at transform boundaries, move apart at divergent boundaries, and come together at convergent boundaries.

Key Terms

plate   transform boundary
scientific theory   divergent boundary
plate tectonics   rift valley
fault   convergent boundary

Organizing Information

Cycle Diagram To show the processes that link a trench and the mid-ocean ridge, copy the cycle diagram into your notebook and fill in the blanks.

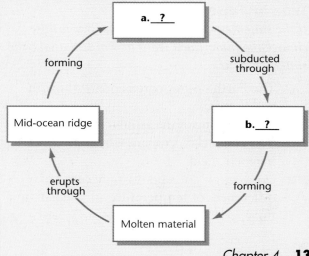

Reviewing Content

 For more review of key concepts, see the Interactive Student Tutorial CD-ROM.

Multiple Choice
Choose the letter of the answer that best completes each statement.

1. The layer of the upper mantle that can flow is the
   a. asthenosphere.
   b. lithosphere.
   c. inner core.
   d. continental crust.

2. Most scientists rejected Wegener's theory of continental drift because the theory failed to explain
   a. coal deposits in Antarctica.
   b. formation of mountains.
   c. climate changes.
   d. how the continents move.

3. Subduction of the ocean floor takes place at
   a. the lower mantle.
   b. mid-ocean ridges.
   c. rift valleys.
   d. trenches.

4. The process that powers plate tectonics is
   a. radiation.   b. convection.
   c. conduction.   d. subduction

5. Two plates collide with each other at
   a. a divergent boundary
   b. a convergent boundary
   c. the boundary between the mantle and the crust.
   d. a transform boundary.

True or False
If the statement is true, write true. If it is false, change the underlined word or words to make the statement true.

6. The Earth's <u>outer core</u> is made of basalt and granite.

7. The spinning of the <u>asthenosphere</u>, made of iron and nickel, explains why Earth has a magnetic field.

8. <u>Convection currents</u> form because of differences of temperature and density in a fluid.

9. <u>Magnetic stripes</u> on the ocean floor are places where oceanic crust sinks back to the mantle.

10. When two continental plates <u>converge</u>, a rift valley forms.

Checking Concepts

11. How is the inner core different from the outer core?

12. Why are there convection currents in the mantle? Explain.

13. What evidence of Earth's climate in the past supports the theory of continental drift?

14. What was the importance of the discovery that molten rock was coming out of cracks along the mid-ocean ridge?

15. How do magnetic stripes form on the ocean floor? Why are these stripes significant?

16. What happens when a plate of oceanic crust collides with a plate of continental crust? Why?

17. **Writing to Learn** Imagine that Alfred Wegener is alive today to defend his theory of continental drift. Write a short interview that Wegener might have on a daytime talk show. You may use humor.

Thinking Critically

18. **Classifying** Classify these layers of Earth as liquid, solid, or solid but able to flow slowly: crust, lithosphere, asthenosphere, outer core, inner core.

19. **Comparing and Contrasting** How are oceanic and continental crust alike? How do they differ?

20. **Relating Cause and Effect** What do many geologists think is the driving force of plate tectonics? Explain.

21. **Making Generalizations** State in one sentence the most significant discovery that geologists established through their study of plate tectonics.

Applying Skills

Geologists think that a new plate boundary is forming in the Indian Ocean. The part of the plate carrying Australia is twisting away from the part of the plate carrying India.

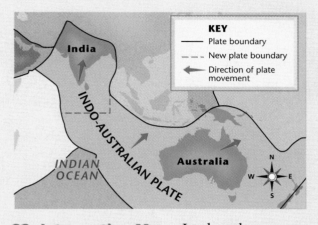

KEY
— Plate boundary
- - - New plate boundary
← Direction of plate movement

22. Interpreting Maps Look at the arrows showing the direction of plate motion. In what direction is the part of the plate carrying Australia moving? In what direction is the part carrying India moving?

23. Predicting As India and Australia move in different directions, what type of plate boundary will form between them?

24. Inferring On the map you can see that the northern part of the Indo-Australian plate is moving north and colliding with the Eurasian plate. What features would occur where these plates meet? Explain.

Performance CHAPTER PROJECT Assessment

Presenting Your Project Present your model to the class. Point out the types of plate boundaries on the model. Discuss the plate motions and landforms that result in these areas. What similarities and differences exist between your model and those of your classmates?

Reflect and Record In your journal, write an evaluation of your project. What materials would you change? How could you improve your model?

Test Preparation
Use these questions to prepare for standardized tests.

Use the diagram to answer Questions 25–28.

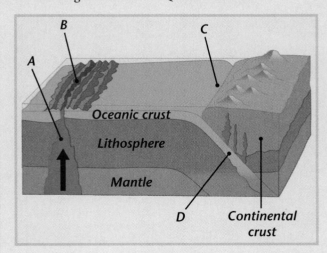

Oceanic crust
Lithosphere
Mantle
Continental crust

25. The arrow at A represents
  a. a transform boundary.
  b. continental crust.
  c. a subduction zone.
  d. molten magma rising from the mantle.

26. What is occurring at the feature labeled B?
  a. New rock is being added to the oceanic plate.
  b. The ocean floor is sinking.
  c. Subduction is occurring.
  d. Two plates are colliding.

27. As sea-floor spreading occurs, the oceanic plate
  a. does not move.
  b. moves from C toward B.
  c. moves from B toward C.
  d. floats higher on the mantle.

28. What is occurring at D?
  a. New material is rising from the mantle.
  b. The oceanic plate is melting as it sinks into the mantle.
  c. Sedimentary rock is being added to the plate.
  d. The oceanic plate is pushing the continental plate into the mantle.

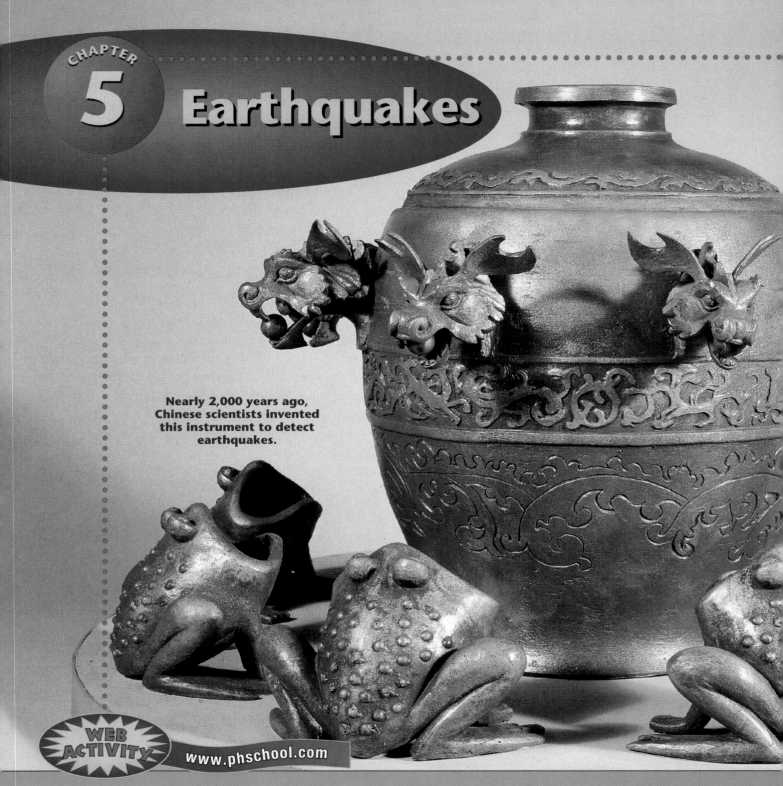

Nearly 2,000 years ago, Chinese scientists invented this instrument to detect earthquakes.

WEB ACTIVITY www.phschool.com

Shake, Rattle, and Roll

The ground shakes ever so slightly. A bronze dragon drops a ball into the mouth of the frog below. Nearly 2,000 years ago in China, that's how an instrument like this one would have detected a distant earthquake. Earthquakes are proof that our planet is subject to great forces from within. Earthquakes remind us that we live on the moving pieces of Earth's crust. In this chapter, you will design a structure that will withstand earthquakes.

Your Goal To design, build, and test a model structure that is earthquake resistant.

Your model should
- be made of materials that are approved by your teacher
- be built to specifications agreed on by your class
- be able to withstand several simulated earthquakes of increasing intensity
- be built following the safety guidelines in Appendix A

Get Started Before you design your model, find out how earthquakes cause damage to structures such as homes, office buildings, and highway overpasses. Preview the chapter to find out how engineers design structures to withstand earthquakes.

Check Your Progress You will be working on this project as you study this chapter. To keep your project on track, look for Check Your Progress boxes at the following points.
Section 1 Review, page 151: Design your model.
Section 2 Review, page 159: Construct, improve, and test your model.
Section 4 Review, page 171: Test your model again, and then repair and improve it.

Present Your Project At the end of the chapter (page 175), you will demonstrate how well your model can withstand the effects of a simulated earthquake and predict whether a building that followed your design could withstand a real earthquake.

SECTION 4

Integrating Technology

Monitoring Faults

Discover Can Stress Be Measured?

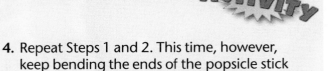

How Does Stress Affect Earth's Crust?

1. Put on your goggles.

2. Holding a popsicle stick at both ends, slowly bend it into an arch.

3. Release the pressure on the popsicle stick and observe what happens.

4. Repeat Steps 1 and 2. This time, however, keep bending the ends of the popsicle stick toward each other. What happens to the wood?

Think It Over
Predicting Think of the popsicle stick as a model for part of Earth's crust. What do you think might eventually happen as the forces of plate movement bend the crust?

GUIDE FOR READING

◆ How do stress forces affect rock?

◆ Why do faults form and where do they occur?

◆ How does movement along faults change Earth's surface?

Reading Tip Before you read, use the headings to make an outline about stress in the crust, faults, and mountain building.

You are sitting at the kitchen table eating breakfast. Suddenly you notice a slight vibration, as if a heavy truck were rumbling by. At the same time, your glass of orange juice jiggles. Dishes rattle in the cupboards. After a few seconds, the rattling stops. Later, when you listen to the news on the radio, you learn that your region experienced a small earthquake. Earthquakes are a reminder that Earth's crust can move.

Stress in the Crust

An **earthquake** is the shaking and trembling that results from the movement of rock beneath Earth's surface. The movement of Earth's plates creates powerful forces that squeeze or pull the rock in the crust. These forces are examples of **stress,** a force that acts on rock to change its shape or volume. (Volume is the amount of space an object takes up.) Because stress is a force, it adds energy to the rock. The energy is stored in the rock until the rock either breaks or changes shape.

Figure 1 Stress in the crust folded this rock like a sheet of ribbon candy.

Types of Stress

Three different kinds of stress occur in the crust—shearing, tension, and compression. **Shearing, tension, and compression work over millions of years to change the shape and volume of rock.** These forces cause some rocks to become brittle and snap. Other rocks tend to bend slowly like road tar softened by the heat of the sun.

Stress that pushes a mass of rock in two opposite directions is called **shearing.** Shearing can cause rock to break and slip apart or to change its shape.

The stress force called **tension** pulls on the crust, stretching rock so that it becomes thinner in the middle. The effect of tension on rock is somewhat like pulling apart a piece of warm bubble gum. Tension occurs where two plates are moving apart.

The stress force called **compression** squeezes rock until it folds or breaks. One plate pushing against another can compress rock like a giant trash compactor.

Any change in the volume or shape of Earth's crust is called **deformation.** Most changes in the crust occur so slowly that they cannot be observed directly. But if you could speed up time so a billion years passed by in minutes, you could see the deformation of the crust. The crust would bend, stretch, break, tilt, fold, and slide. The slow shift of Earth's plates causes this deformation.

☑ *Checkpoint* *How does deformation change Earth's surface?*

Figure 2 Deformation pushes, pulls, or twists the rocks in Earth's crust. *Relating Cause and Effect* *Which type of deformation tends to shorten part of the crust?*

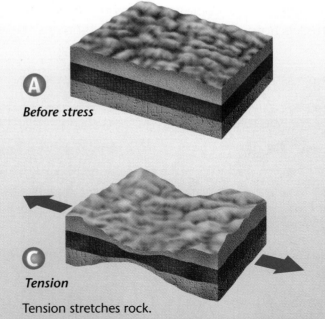

Ⓐ **Before stress**

Ⓒ **Tension**
Tension stretches rock.

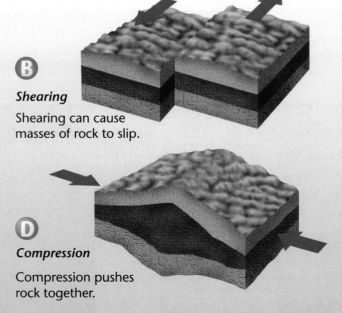

Ⓑ **Shearing**
Shearing can cause masses of rock to slip.

Ⓓ **Compression**
Compression pushes rock together.

Strike-slip fault

Figure 3 A strike-slip fault that is clearly visible at the surface is the San Andreas Fault in California.

Kinds of Faults

If you try to break a caramel candy bar in two, it may only bend and stretch at first. Like a candy bar, many types of rock can bend or fold. But beyond a certain limit, even these rocks will break. And it takes less stress to snap a brittle rock than it does to snap one that can bend.

When enough stress builds up in rock, the rock breaks, creating a fault. A **fault** is a break in the crust where slabs of crust slip past each other. The rocks on both sides of a fault can move up or down or sideways. **Faults usually occur along plate boundaries, where the forces of plate motion compress, pull, or shear the crust so much that the crust breaks.** There are three main types of faults: strike-slip faults, normal faults, and reverse faults.

Strike-Slip Faults Shearing creates strike-slip faults. In a **strike-slip fault,** the rocks on either side of the fault slip past each other sideways with little up-or-down motion. Figure 3 shows the type of movement that occurs along a strike-slip fault. A strike-slip fault that forms the boundary between two plates is called a transform boundary. The San Andreas fault in California is an example of a strike-slip fault that is a transform boundary.

Normal Faults Tension forces in Earth's crust cause normal faults. In a **normal fault,** the fault is at an angle, so one block of rock lies above the fault while the other block lies below the fault. The half of the fault that lies above is called the **hanging wall.** The half of the fault that lies below is called the **footwall.** Look at Figure 4 to see how the hanging wall lies above the

Figure 4 A normal fault created the Sandia Mountains in New Mexico.

Footwall

Hanging Wall

Normal fault

Key
Force deforming the crust ➡
Movement along the fault ➤

footwall. When movement occurs along a normal fault, the hanging wall slips downward. Tension forces create normal faults where plates diverge, or pull apart. For example, normal faults occur along the Rio Grande rift valley in New Mexico, where two pieces of Earth's crust are diverging.

Reverse Faults Compression forces produce reverse faults. A **reverse fault** has the same structure as a normal fault, but the blocks move in the opposite direction. Look at Figure 5 to see how the rocks along a reverse fault move. As in a normal fault, one side of a reverse fault lies at an angle above the other side. The rock forming the hanging wall of a reverse fault slides up and over the footwall. Reverse faults produced part of the Appalachian Mountains in the eastern United States.

A type of reverse fault formed the majestic peaks in Glacier National Park in Montana shown in Figure 5. Over millions of years, a huge block of rock slid along the fault, moving up and over the surface rock. Parts of the overlying block then wore away, leaving the mountain peaks.

✓ *Checkpoint* *What are the three types of fault? What force of deformation produces each?*

Key
→ Force deforming the crust
➤ Movement along the fault

Reverse fault

Figure 5 A reverse fault formed Mt. Gould in Glacier National Park, beginning 60 million years ago.
Inferring Which half of the reverse fault slid up and across to form this mountain, the hanging wall or the footwall? Explain.

Figure 6 The San Andreas fault extends from the Salton Sea in southern California to the point in northern California where the plate boundary continues into the Pacific Ocean.

Friction Along Faults

INTEGRATING PHYSICS How rocks move along a fault depends on how much friction there is between the opposite sides of the fault. Friction is the force that opposes the motion of one surface as it moves across another surface. Friction exists because surfaces are not perfectly smooth.

Where friction along a fault is low, the rocks on both sides of the fault slide by each other without much sticking. Where friction is moderate, the sides of the fault jam together. Then from time to time they jerk free, producing small earthquakes. Where friction is high, the rocks lock together and do not move. In this case, stress increases until it is strong enough to overcome the friction force. A powerful quake results.

The San Andreas fault forms a transform boundary between the Pacific plate and the North American plate. In many places along the San Andreas fault, friction is high and the plates lock. Stress builds up until an earthquake releases the stress and the plates slide past each other.

Mountain Building

The forces of plate movement can build up Earth's surface. **Over millions of years, fault movement can change a flat plain into a towering mountain range.**

Mountains Formed by Faulting When normal faults uplift a block of rock, a **fault-block mountain** forms. You can see a diagram of this process in Figure 7. How does this process begin?

Figure 7 Two normal faults can form fault-block mountains, such as the Teton Range near the border of Wyoming and Idaho.

Where two plates move away from each other, tension forces create many normal faults. When two of these normal faults form parallel to each other, a block of rock is left lying between them. As the hanging wall of each normal fault slips downward, the block in between moves upward. When a block of rock lying between two normal faults slides downward, a valley forms.

If you traveled by car from Salt Lake City to Los Angeles you would cross the Great Basin, a region with many ranges of fault-block mountains separated by broad valleys, or basins. This "basin and range" region covers much of Nevada and western Utah.

Mountains Formed by Folding   Under certain conditions, plate movement causes the crust to fold. Have you ever skidded on a rug that wrinkled up as your feet pushed it across the floor? Much as the rug wrinkles, rock stressed by compression may bend slowly without breaking. **Folds** are bends in rock that form when compression shortens and thickens part of Earth's crust.

The collisions of two plates can cause compression and folding of the crust. Some of the world's largest mountain ranges, including the Himalayas in Asia and the Alps in Europe, formed when pieces of the crust folded during the collision of two plates. Such plate collisions also lead to earthquakes, because folding rock can fracture and produce faults.

Individual folds can be only a few centimeters across or hundreds of kilometers wide. You can often see small folds in the rock exposed where a highway has been cut through a hillside.

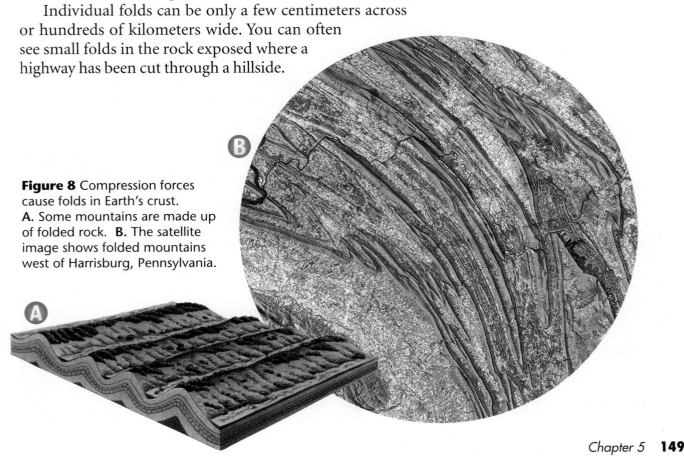

Figure 8 Compression forces cause folds in Earth's crust.
A. Some mountains are made up of folded rock. **B.** The satellite image shows folded mountains west of Harrisburg, Pennsylvania.

Anticlines and Synclines Geologists use the terms anticline and syncline to describe upward and downward folds in rock. You can compare anticlines and synclines in the diagram in Figure 9. A fold in rock that bends upward into an arch is an **anticline.** A fold in rock that bends downward in the middle to form a bowl is a **syncline.** Anticlines and synclines are found on many parts of Earth's surface where compression forces have folded the crust.

One example of an anticline is the Black Hills of South Dakota. The Black Hills began to form about 65 million years ago. At that time, forces in Earth's crust produced a large dome-shaped anticline. Over millions of years, a variety of processes wore down and shaped the rock of this anticline into the Black Hills.

You may see a syncline where a valley dips between two parallel ranges of hills. But a syncline may also be a very large feature, as large as the state of Illinois. The Illinois Basin is a syncline that stretches from the western side of Indiana about 250 kilometers across the state of Illinois. The basin is filled with soil and rock that have accumulated over millions of years.

Figure 9 **A.** Over millions of years, compression and folding of the crust produce anticlines, which arch upward, and synclines, which dip downward. **B.** The folded rock layers of an anticline can be seen on this cliff on the coast of England.

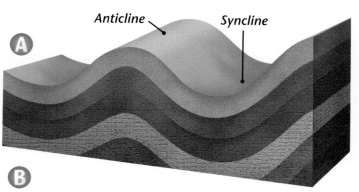

Anticline

Syncline

A

B

Figure 10 The flat land on the horizon is the Kaibab Plateau, which forms the North Rim of the Grand Canyon in Arizona. The Kaibab Plateau is part of the Colorado Plateau.

Plateaus The forces that raise mountains can also raise plateaus. A **plateau** is a large area of flat land elevated high above sea level. Some plateaus form when vertical faults push up a large, flat block of rock. Like a fancy sandwich, a plateau consists of many different flat layers, and is wider than it is tall.

Forces deforming the crust uplifted the Colorado Plateau in the "Four Corners" region of Arizona, Utah, Colorado, and New Mexico. The Colorado Plateau is a roughly circular area of uplifted rock more than 500 kilometers across. This vast slab of rock once formed part of a sea floor. Today, much of the plateau lies more than 1,500 meters above sea level.

Section 1 Review

1. What are the three main types of stress in rock?
2. Describe the movements that occur along each of the three types of faults.
3. How does Earth's surface change as a result of movement along faults?
4. **Thinking Critically** **Predicting** If plate motion compresses part of the crust, what landforms will form there in millions of years? Explain.

Check Your Progress CHAPTER PROJECT
Discuss with your classmates the model you plan to build. What materials could you choose for your earthquake-resistant structure? Sketch your design. Does your design meet the guidelines provided by your teacher? How will you use your materials to build your model? (*Hint*: Draw the sketch of your model to scale).

MODELING MOVEMENT ALONG FAULTS

Faults are cracks in Earth's crust where masses of rock move over, under, or past each other. In this lab, you will make a model of the movements along faults.

Problem

How does the movement of rock along the sides of a fault compare for different types of faults?

Materials

Modeling compound in two or more colors
Marking pen
Plastic butter knife

Procedure

1. Roll some modeling compound into a sheet about 0.5 centimeter thick and about 6 centimeters square. Then make another sheet of the same size and thickness, using a different color.

2. Cut each square in half and stack the sheets on top of each other, alternating colors.
   CAUTION: *To avoid breaking the plastic knife, do not press too hard as you cut.* The sheets of modeling compound stand for different layers of rock. The different colors will help you see where similar layers of rock end up after movement occurs along the model fault.

3. Press the layers of modeling compound together to form a rectangular block that fits in the palm of your hand.

4. Use the butter knife to slice carefully through the block at an angle, as shown in the photograph.

5. Place the two blocks formed by the slice together, but don't let them stick together.

6. Review the descriptions and diagrams of faults in Section 1. Decide which piece of your block is the hanging wall and which is the footwall. Using the marking pen, label the side of each block. What part of your model stands for the fault itself?

7. What part of the model stands for the land surface? Along the top surface of the two blocks, draw a river flowing across the fault. Also draw an arrow on each block to show the direction of the river's flow. The arrow should point from the footwall toward the hanging wall.

8. Make a table that includes the headings Type of Fault, How the Sides of the Fault Move, and Changes in the Land Surface.

Type of Fault	How the Sides of the Fault Move	Changes in the Land Surface

9. Using your blocks, model the movement along a strike-slip fault. Record your motion and the results on the data table.
10. Repeat Step 9 for a normal fault.
11. Repeat Step 9 for a reverse fault.

Analyze and Conclude

Refer to your data table to draw a chart that will help you answer questions 1 through 4.

1. On your chart, show the direction in which the sides of the fault move for each type of fault.
2. On your chart, show how movement along a strike-slip fault is different from movement along the other two types of fault.
3. Add to your chart a column that shows how the river on the surface might change for each type of fault.
4. Assuming that the river is flowing from the footwall toward the hanging wall, which type of fault could produce small waterfalls in the surface river? (*Hint:* Recall how you tell which block is the hanging wall and which block is the footwall.)
5. If you could observe only the land surface around a fault, how could you tell if the fault is a strike-slip fault? A normal fault?
6. If you slide the hanging wall of your fault model upward in relation to the footwall, what type of fault forms? If this movement continues, where will the slab of rock with the hanging wall end up?

7. From an airplane, you see a chain of several long, narrow lakes along a fault. What type of fault would cause these lakes to form?
8. **Think About It** In what ways does the model help you picture what is happening along a fault? In what ways does the model not accurately reflect what happens along a fault? How is the model still useful in spite of its inaccuracies?

More to Explore

On Earth's surface, individual faults do not exist all by themselves. With one or more of your classmates, combine your models to show how a fault-block mountain range or a rift valley could form. (*Hint:* Both involve normal faults.) How could you combine your models to show how reverse faults produce a mountain range?

SECTION
2 Measuring Earthquakes

DISCOVER •••ACTIVITY••••

How Do Seismic Waves Travel Through Earth?

1. Stretch a spring toy across the floor while a classmate holds the other end. Do not overstretch the toy.

2. Gather together about 4 coils of the spring toy and release them. In what direction do the coils move?

3. Once the spring toy has stopped moving, jerk one end of the toy from side to side once. In what direction do the coils move? Be certain your classmate has a secure grip on the other end.

Think It Over

Observing Describe the two types of wave motion that you observed in the spring toy.

GUIDE FOR READING

◆ How does the energy of an earthquake travel through Earth?

◆ What are the different kinds of seismic waves?

◆ What are the scales used to measure the strength of an earthquake?

Reading Tip Before you read, rewrite the headings in the section as what, how, or why questions. As you read, look for answers to these questions.

Earth is never still. Every day, worldwide, there are about 8,000 earthquakes. Most of them are too small to notice. But when an earthquake is strong enough to rattle dishes in kitchen cabinets, people sit up and take notice. "How big was the quake?" and "Where was it centered?" are two questions just about everyone asks after an earthquake.

To know where an earthquake was centered, you need to know where it began. Earthquakes always begin in rock below the surface. Most earthquakes begin in the lithosphere within 100 kilometers of Earth's surface. An earthquake starts at one particular point. The **focus** (FOH kus) is the point beneath Earth's surface where rock that is under stress breaks, triggering an earthquake. The point on the surface directly above the focus is called the **epicenter** (EHP uh sen tur).

Seismic Waves

If you have ever played a drum, you know that the sound it makes depends on how hard you strike it. Like a drumbeat, an earthquake produces vibrations called waves. These waves carry energy as they travel outward through solid material. During an earthquake, seismic waves race out from the focus in all directions. **Seismic waves** are vibrations that travel through Earth carrying the energy released during an earthquake. The seismic waves move like ripples in a pond. Look at Figure 11 to see how seismic waves travel outward in all directions from the focus.

154

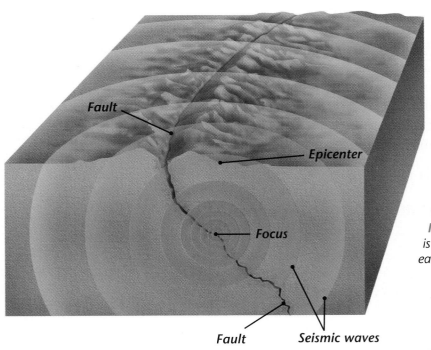

Figure 11 An earthquake occurs when rocks fracture at the focus, deep in Earth's crust. *Interpreting Diagrams* What point is directly above the focus of the earthquake?

Seismic waves carry the energy of an earthquake away from the focus, through Earth's interior, and across the surface. The energy of the seismic waves that reach the surface is greatest at the epicenter. The most violent shaking during an earthquake, however, may occur kilometers away from the epicenter. The types of rock and soil around the epicenter can affect where and how much the ground shakes. You will learn more about the effects of seismic waves in Section 3.

There are three categories of seismic waves: P waves, S waves, and surface waves. An earthquake sends out two types of waves from its focus: P waves and S waves. When these waves reach Earth's surface at the epicenter, surface waves develop.

Primary Waves The first waves to arrive are primary waves, or P waves. **P waves** are earthquake waves that compress and expand the ground like an accordion. P waves cause buildings to contract and expand. Look at Figure 12 to compare P waves and S waves.

Secondary Waves After P waves come secondary waves, or S waves. **S waves** are earthquake waves that vibrate from side to side as well as up and down. They shake the ground back and forth. When S waves reach the surface, they shake structures violently. Unlike P waves, which travel through both solids and liquids, S waves cannot move through liquids.

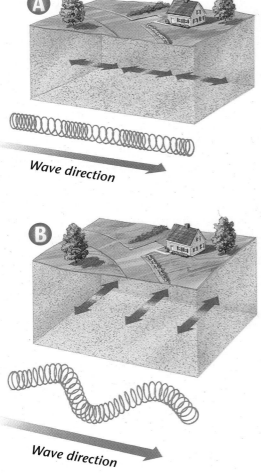

Figure 12 A. In P waves, the particles of the crust vibrate forward and back along the path of the wave. B. In S waves, the particles of the crust vibrate from side to side and up and down.

Surface Waves When P waves and S waves reach the surface, some of them are transformed into surface waves. **Surface waves** move more slowly than P waves and S waves, but they can produce severe ground movements. Some surface waves make the ground roll like ocean waves. Other surface waves shake buildings from side to side.

☑ *Checkpoint* *What are the three types of seismic waves?*

Detecting Seismic Waves

To record and measure the vibrations of seismic waves, geologists use instruments called seismographs. A **seismograph** (SYZ muh graf) records the ground movements caused by seismic waves as they move through the Earth.

Until recently, scientists used mechanical seismographs. As shown in Figure 13, a mechanical seismograph consists of a heavy weight attached to a frame by a spring or wire. A pen connected to the weight rests its point on a rotating drum. When the drum is still, the pen draws a straight line on paper wrapped around the drum. During an earthquake, seismic waves cause the drum to vibrate. Meanwhile, the pen stays in place and records the drum's vibrations. The height of the jagged lines drawn on the seismograph's drum is greater for a more severe earthquake.

Today, scientists use electronic seismographs that work according to the same principle as the mechanical seismograph. The electronic seismograph converts ground movements into a signal that can be recorded and printed.

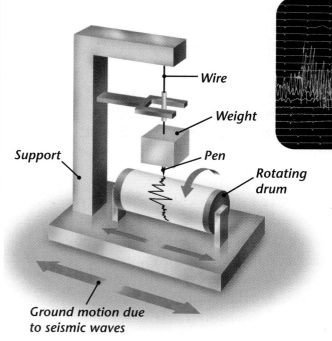

Figure 13 The mechanical seismograph records seismic waves. The record made by a seismograph shows the arrival times of different types of seismic waves.

The Mercalli Scale	
Earthquake Intensity	**Earthquake Effects**
I–II	Almost unnoticeable
III–IV	People notice vibrations like those from a passing truck. Unstable objects disturbed.
V–VI	Dishes and windows rattle. Books knocked off shelves. Slight damage.
VII–VIII	People run outdoors. Moderate to heavy damage.
IX–X	Buildings jolted off foundations or destroyed. Cracks appear in ground and landslides occur.
XI–XII	Severe damage. Wide cracks appear in ground. Waves seen on ground surface.

Figure 14 An earthquake in 1997 damaged the tower of this city hall in Foligno, Italy (left). The Mercalli scale (right) uses Roman numerals to rank earthquakes by how much damage they cause.
Applying Concepts How would you rate the damage to the Foligno city hall on the Mercalli scale?

Measuring Earthquakes

When geologists want to know the size of an earthquake, they must consider many factors. As a result, there are at least 20 different measures for rating earthquakes, each with its strengths and shortcomings. Three ways of measuring earthquakes, the Mercalli scale, the Richter scale, and the moment magnitude scale, are described here. **Magnitude** is a measurement of earthquake strength based on seismic waves and movement along faults.

The Mercalli Scale Early in the twentieth century, the **Mercalli scale** was developed to rate earthquakes according to their intensity. An earthquake's intensity is the strength of ground motion in a given place. The Mercalli scale is not a precise measurement. But the 12 steps of the Mercalli scale describe how earthquakes affect people, buildings, and the land surface. The same earthquake can have different Mercalli ratings because it causes different amounts of damage at different locations.

The Richter Scale The **Richter scale** is a rating of the size of seismic waves that was once measured by a type of mechanical seismograph. The Richter scale was developed in the 1930s. Geologists all over the world used this scale for about 50 years. Eventually, electronic seismographs replaced the mechanical seismographs used for the Richter scale. The Richter scale provides accurate measurements for small, nearby earthquakes. But the scale does not work well for large or distant earthquakes.

Earthquake Magnitudes	
Earthquake	**Moment Magnitude**
San Francisco, California, 1906	7.7
Southern Chile, 1960	9.5
Anchorage, Alaska, 1964	9.2
Loma Prieta, California, 1989	7.2
Northridge/ Los Angeles, California, 1994	6.7
Izmit, Turkey, 1999	7.4

Figure 15 The table lists the moment magnitudes for some of the twentieth century's biggest earthquakes.

The Moment Magnitude Scale Today, geologists use the **moment magnitude scale,** a rating system that estimates the total energy released by an earthquake. **The moment magnitude scale can be used to rate earthquakes of all sizes, near or far.** You may hear news reports that mention the Richter scale. But the magnitude number they quote is almost always the moment magnitude for that earthquake.

To rate an earthquake on the moment magnitude scale, geologists first study data from modern electronic seismographs. The data show what kinds of seismic waves the earthquake produced and how strong they were. The data also help geologists infer how much movement occurred along the fault and the strength of the rocks that broke when the fault slipped. Geologists combine all this information to rate the earthquake on the moment magnitude scale.

Earthquakes with a magnitude below 5.0 on the moment magnitude scale are small and cause little damage. Those with a magnitude above 5.0 can produce great destruction. A magnitude 6.0 quake releases 32 times as much energy as a magnitude 5.0 quake, and nearly 1,000 times as much as a magnitude 4.0 quake.

✓ *Checkpoint* *What are three scales for measuring earthquakes?*

Locating the Epicenter

Geologists use seismic waves to locate an earthquake's epicenter. Seismic waves travel at different speeds. P waves arrive first at a seismograph, with S waves following close behind. To tell how far the epicenter is from the seismograph, scientists measure the difference between the arrival times of the P waves and S waves.

Figure 16 In terms of magnitude, the 1906 San Francisco earthquake was not the strongest of the century. But it toppled buildings and caused fires that devastated the city.

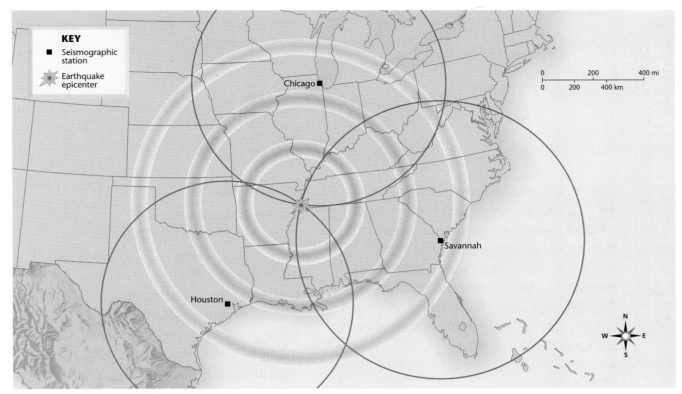

KEY
■ Seismographic station
✳ Earthquake epicenter

Chicago ■

0   200   400 mi
0   200   400 km

Savannah ■

Houston ■

N
W   E
S

The farther away an earthquake is, the greater the time between the arrival of the P waves and the S waves.

 INTEGRATING MATHEMATICS Geologists then draw at least three circles using data from different seismographs set up at stations all over the world. The center of each circle is a particular seismograph's location. The radius of each circle is the distance from the seismograph to the epicenter. The point where the three circles intersect is the location of the epicenter. If you look at Figure 17, you can see why two circles would not give enough information to pinpoint the epicenter.

Figure 17 The map shows how to find the epicenter of an earthquake using data from three seismographic stations. *Measuring Use the map scale to determine the distances from Savannah and Houston to the epicenter. Which is closer?*

Section 2 Review

1. How does the energy from an earthquake reach Earth's surface?
2. Describe the three types of seismic waves.
3. What system do geologists use today for rating the magnitude of an earthquake?
4. **Thinking Critically Relating Cause and Effect** Describe how energy released at an earthquake's focus, deep inside Earth, can cause damage on the surface many kilometers from the epicenter.

Check Your Progress

CHAPTER PROJECT

Now it is time to complete your design and construct your model. From what you have learned about earthquakes, what changes will you make in your design? Have a classmate review your model and make suggestions for improvements. When you have made the changes, test your model's ability to withstand an earthquake. Take notes on how well it withstands the quake.

Locating an Epicenter

Geologists who study earthquakes are called seismologists. If you were a seismologist, you would receive data from all across the country. Within minutes after an earthquake, seismographs located in Denver, Houston, and Miami would record the times of arrival of the P waves and S waves. You would use this data to zero in on the exact location of the earthquake's epicenter.

Problem

How can you locate an earthquake's epicenter?

Skills Focus

interpreting data, drawing conclusions

Materials

drawing compass with pencil
outline map of the United States

Procedure

1. Make a copy of the data table showing differences in earthquake arrival times.
2. The graph shows how the difference in arrival time between P waves and S waves depends on the distance from the epicenter of the earthquake. Find the difference in arrival time for Denver on the *y*-axis of the graph. Follow this line across to the point at which it crosses the curve. To find the distance to the epicenter, read down from this point to the *x*-axis of the graph. Enter this distance in the data table.

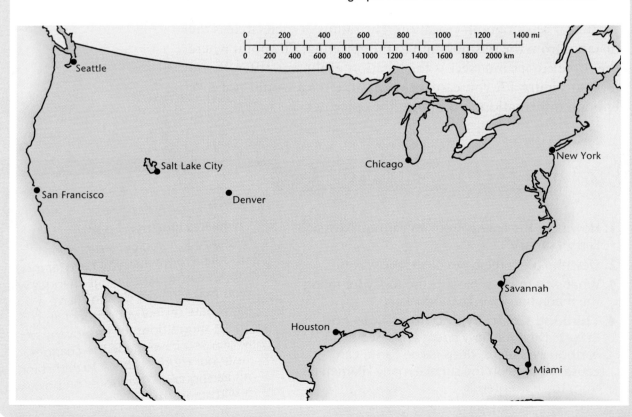

Data Table

City	Difference in P and S Wave Arrival Times	Distance to Epicenter
Denver, Colorado	2 min 10 s	
Houston, Texas	3 min 55 s	
Miami, Florida	5 min 40 s	

3. Repeat Step 2 for Houston and Miami.
4. Set your compass at a radius equal to the distance from Denver to the earthquake epicenter that you recorded in your data table.
5. Draw a circle with the radius determined in Step 4, using Denver as the center. Draw the circle on your copy of the map. (*Hint:* Draw your circles carefully. You may need to draw some parts of the circles off the map.)
6. Repeat Steps 4 and 5 for Houston and Miami.

Analyze and Conclude

1. Observe the three circles you have drawn to locate the earthquake's epicenter.
2. Which city on the map is closest to the earthquake epicenter? How far, in kilometers, is this city from the epicenter?
3. In which of the three cities listed in the data table would seismographs detect the earthquake first? Last?
4. When you are trying to locate an epicenter, why is it necessary to know the distance from the epicenter for at least three recording stations?
5. About how far is the epicenter that you found from San Francisco? What would the difference in arrival times of the P waves and S waves be for a recording station in San Francisco?
6. What happens to the difference in arrival times between P waves and S waves as the distance from the earthquake increases?
7. **Apply** Working as a seismologist, you find the epicenters of many earthquakes in a region. What features of Earth's crust would you expect to find in this region?

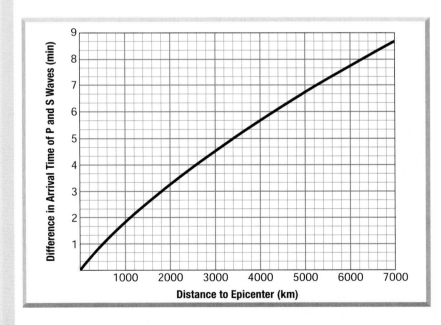

More to Explore

You have just located an earthquake's epicenter. Find this earthquake's location on the earthquake risk map on page 171. Judging from the map, was this earthquake a freak event? What is the risk of earthquakes in the area of this quake? Now look at the map of Earth's plates on page 133. What conclusions can you draw from this map about the cause of earthquakes in this area?

SECTION 3 Earthquake Hazards and Safety

DISCOVER ·· ACTIVITY

Can Bracing Prevent Building Collapse?

1. Tape four straws together to make a square frame. Hold the frame upright on a flat surface in front of you.

2. Hold the bottom straw down with one hand while you push the top straw to the left with the other. Push it as far as it will go without breaking the frame.

3. Tape a fifth straw horizontally across the middle of the frame. Repeat Step 2.

Think It Over

Predicting What effect did the fifth straw have? What effect would a piece of cardboard taped to the frame have? Based on your observations, how would an earthquake affect the frame of a house?

GUIDE FOR READING

◆ What kinds of damage does an earthquake cause?

◆ What can be done to reduce earthquake hazards?

Reading Tip Before you read preview the headings of the section. Then predict some of the ways that people can reduce earthquake hazards.

If you look closely at a globe, you can find a small sea that connects the Mediterranean Sea with the Black Sea. On the edge of this sea lies the city of Izmit, Turkey. On a normal day, people in Izmit would go to work in the city's many factories. But on August 17, 1999, a powerful earthquake destroyed much of the city. More than 14,000 people died.

Turkey has laws requiring buildings to be earthquake resistant. But many tall, cement apartment buildings collapsed during the Izmit quake. People in Turkey blamed poor construction for much of the damage. They demanded strict enforcement of the laws requiring earthquake-safe construction.

Figure 18 The Izmit earthquake destroyed many buildings, but left other buildings standing. The quake had a moment magnitude of 7.4.

162

Figure 19 An earthquake caused the soil beneath this house to liquefy. Liquefaction caused by seismic waves can change solid soil to liquid mud within seconds.
Posing Questions What are some questions people might ask before building a house in an area that is at risk for earthquakes?

How Earthquakes Cause Damage

When a major earthquake strikes, it can cause great damage. **The severe shaking produced by seismic waves can damage or destroy buildings and bridges, topple utility poles, and fracture gas and water mains.** S waves, with their side-to-side and up-and-down movement, can cause severe damage near the epicenter. As the twisting forces of S waves sweep through the ground, the S waves put enough stress on buildings to tear them apart. Earthquakes can also trigger landslides or avalanches. In coastal regions, giant waves pushed up by earthquakes can cause more damage.

Local Soil Conditions When seismic waves move from hard, dense rock to loosely packed soil, they transmit their energy to the soil. The loose soil shakes more violently than the surrounding rock. The thicker the layer of soil, the more violent the shaking will be. This means a house built on solid rock will shake less than a house built on sandy soil.

Liquefaction In 1964, when a powerful earthquake roared through Anchorage, Alaska, cracks opened in the ground. Some of the cracks were 9 meters wide. The cracks were created by liquefaction. **Liquefaction** (lik wih FAK shun) occurs when an earthquake's violent shaking suddenly turns loose, soft soil into liquid mud. Liquefaction is likely where the soil is full of moisture. As the ground gives way, buildings sink and pull apart.

Liquefaction can also trigger landslides. During the 1964 Anchorage earthquake, liquefaction caused a landslide that swept an entire housing development down a cliff and into the sea. Figure 19 shows the damage liquefaction can cause.

Aftershocks Sometimes, buildings weakened by an earthquake collapse during an aftershock. An **aftershock** is an earthquake that occurs after a larger earthquake in the same area. Aftershocks may strike hours, days, or even months later.

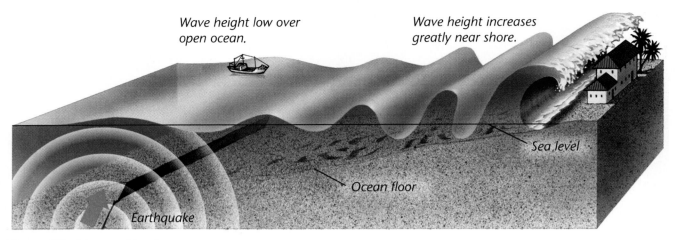

Wave height low over open ocean.

Wave height increases greatly near shore.

Sea level

Ocean floor

Earthquake

Figure 20 A tsunami begins as a low wave, but turns into a huge wave as it nears the shore.

Sharpen your Skills

Calculating ACTIVITY

The Tsunami Warning System alerts people who live near the Pacific Ocean. When geologists detect an earthquake on the ocean floor, they notify coastal areas.

An earthquake in the Gulf of Alaska occurs 3,600 kilometers from Hawaii. The quake's seismic waves travel about 560 kilometers per *minute*. The quake triggers a tsunami that travels at 640 kilometers per *hour*. The seismic waves arrive in Hawaii within minutes and are recorded on seismographs. The seismic waves' arrival warns of the dangerous tsunami that may follow. About how much advance warning will Hawaii have that a tsunami is on the way?

Tsunamis When an earthquake jolts the ocean floor, plate movement causes the ocean floor to rise slightly and push water out of its way. If the earthquake is strong enough, the water displaced by the quake forms large waves, called **tsunamis** (tsoo NAH meez). Figure 20 follows a tsunami from where it begins on the ocean floor.

A tsunami spreads out from an earthquake's epicenter and speeds across the ocean. In the open ocean, the distance between the waves of a tsunami is a very long—between 100 and 200 kilometers. But the height of the wave is low. Tsunamis rise only half a meter or so above the other waves. However, as they approach shallow water near a coastline, the waves become closer together. The tsunami grows into a mountain of water. Some are the height of a six-story building.

☑ *Checkpoint* *What are the major causes of earthquake damage?*

Making Buildings Safer

Most earthquake-related deaths and injuries result from damage to buildings or other structures. **To reduce earthquake damage, new buildings must be made stronger and more flexible. Older buildings must be modified to withstand stronger quakes.** A structure must be strong in order to resist violent shaking in a quake. It must also be flexible so it can twist and bend without breaking. *Exploring an Earthquake-Safe House* shows how a house can be made safer in an earthquake.

Choice of Location The location of a building affects the type of damage it may suffer during an earthquake. Steep slopes pose the danger of landslides. Filled land can shake violently. Therefore, people should avoid building on such sites. People should also avoid building structures near earthquake faults. As seismic waves pass through the earth, their strength decreases. So the farther a structure is from a fault, the less strong the shaking will be.

EXPLORING *an Earthquake-Safe House*

People can take a variety of steps to make their homes safer in an earthquake. Some steps strengthen the house itself. Others may help to keep objects from tipping or falling.

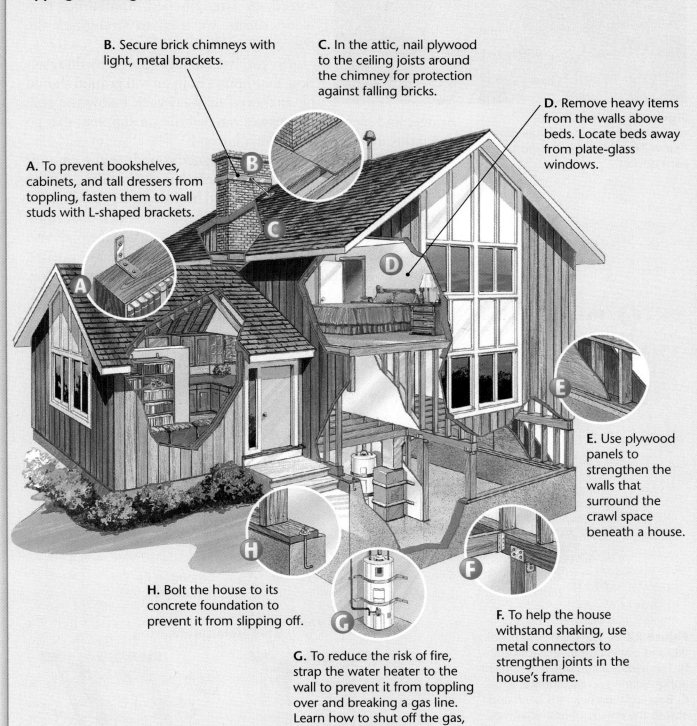

B. Secure brick chimneys with light, metal brackets.

C. In the attic, nail plywood to the ceiling joists around the chimney for protection against falling bricks.

D. Remove heavy items from the walls above beds. Locate beds away from plate-glass windows.

A. To prevent bookshelves, cabinets, and tall dressers from toppling, fasten them to wall studs with L-shaped brackets.

E. Use plywood panels to strengthen the walls that surround the crawl space beneath a house.

H. Bolt the house to its concrete foundation to prevent it from slipping off.

G. To reduce the risk of fire, strap the water heater to the wall to prevent it from toppling over and breaking a gas line. Learn how to shut off the gas, water, and electricity.

F. To help the house withstand shaking, use metal connectors to strengthen joints in the house's frame.

Figure 21 Architects and engineers work to design buildings that will be able to withstand earthquakes.

Construction Methods The way in which a building is constructed determines whether it can withstand an earthquake. During an earthquake, brick buildings as well as some wood-frame buildings may collapse if their walls have not been reinforced, or strengthened. Sometimes plywood sheets are used to strengthen the frames of wooden buildings.

To combat damage caused by liquefaction, new homes built on soft ground should be anchored to solid rock below the soil. Bridges and highway overpasses can be built on supports that go down through soft soil to firmer ground.

 **INTEGRATING TECHNOLOGY** A building designed to reduce the amount of energy that reaches the building during an earthquake is called a **base-isolated building.** As you can see in Figure 22, a base-isolated building rests on shock-absorbing rubber pads or springs. Like the suspension of a car, the pads and springs smooth out a bumpy ride. During a quake, a base-isolated building moves gently back and forth without any violent shaking.

A **Fixed-base building**

Foundation

Ground movement

Figure 22 **A.** The fixed-base building tilts and cracks during an earthquake. **B.** The base-isolated building remains upright during an earthquake. **C.** Base-isolation bearings bend and absorb the energy of seismic waves. *Inferring How does a base-isolation bearing absorb an earthquake's energy?*

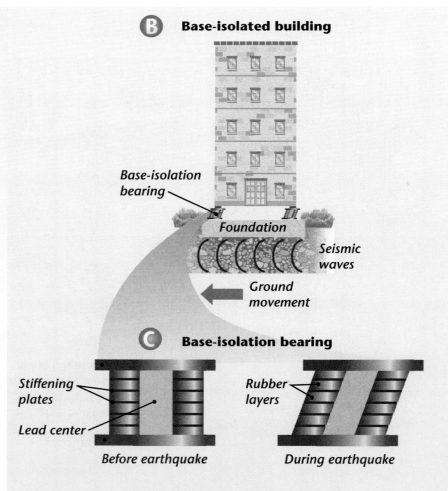

B **Base-isolated building**

Base-isolation bearing

Foundation

Seismic waves

Ground movement

C **Base-isolation bearing**

Stiffening plates

Lead center

Rubber layers

Before earthquake *During earthquake*

Much earthquake damage is not the direct result of shaking. Earthquakes indirectly cause fire and flooding when gas pipes and water mains break. Flexible joints can be installed in gas and water lines to keep them from breaking. Automatic shut-off valves also can be installed on these lines to cut off gas and water flow.

Protecting Yourself During an Earthquake

What should you do if an earthquake strikes? The main danger is from falling objects and flying glass. **The best way to protect yourself is to drop, cover, and hold.** This means you should crouch beneath a sturdy table or desk and hold on to it so it doesn't jiggle away during the shaking. The desk or table will provide a barrier against falling objects. If no desk or table is available, crouch against an inner wall, away from the outside of a building, and cover your head and neck with your arms. Avoid windows, mirrors, wall hangings, and furniture that might topple.

If you are outdoors, move to an open area such as a playground. Avoid vehicles, power lines, trees, and buildings, especially ones with brick walls or chimneys. Sit down to avoid being thrown down.

INTEGRATING HEALTH After a major earthquake, water and power supplies may fail, food stores may be closed, and travel may be difficult. People may have to wait several days for these services to be restored. To prepare for such an emergency, families living in a region at high risk for damaging quakes may want to put together an earthquake kit. The kit should contain canned food, water, and first aid supplies and should be stored where it is easy to reach.

Figure 23 Drop, cover, and hold to protect yourself indoors during an earthquake. **A.** If possible, crouch under a desk or table. **B.** Or, crouch against an interior wall and cover your head and neck with your hands.

Section 3 Review

1. Explain how liquefaction occurs and how it causes damage during an earthquake.
2. What can residents do to reduce the risk of earthquake damage to their homes?
3. Describe safety measures you can take to protect yourself during an earthquake.
4. **Thinking Critically Problem Solving** You are a builder planning a housing development where earthquakes are likely. What types of land would you avoid for your development? Where would it be safe to build?

Science at Home

Toppling Towers Show your family how an earthquake can affect two structures—one with more weight on top, the other with more weight on the bottom. Make a model of a fault by placing two small, folded towels side by side on a flat surface. Pile a stack of books on the fault by placing the light books on the bottom and the heaviest ones on top. Then, gently pull the towels in opposite directions until the pile topples. Repeat the process, but this time with the heavier books on the bottom. Discuss with your family which makes a more stable structure.

SECTION 4 Monitoring Faults

DISCOVER ·····························ACTIVITY···

Can Stress Be Measured?

1. Unfold a facial tissue and lay it flat on your desk.

2. Measure the length of the tissue with a ruler.

3. Grasping the ends of the tissue with both hands, gently pull it. As you are stretching it, hold the tissue against the ruler and measure its length again.

4. Stretch the tissue once more, but this time give it a hard tug.

Think It Over

Drawing Conclusions How is the tissue like the ground along a fault? How might measuring stress in the ground help predict an earthquake?

GUIDE FOR READING

◆ How do geologists monitor faults?

◆ How do geologists determine earthquake risk?

Reading Tip As you read, make a list of devices for monitoring earthquakes. Write a sentence about each.

The small town of Parkfield, California, lies on the San Andreas fault about halfway between Los Angeles and San Francisco. Geologists are fascinated by Parkfield because the town had a strong earthquake about every 22 years between 1857 and 1966. Scientists have not found any other place on Earth where the time from one earthquake to the next has been so regular.

In the early 1980s, geologists predicted that a strong earthquake was going to occur in Parkfield between 1985 and 1993. The geologists eagerly set up their instruments—and waited. They waited year after year for the predicted earthquake. But it didn't happen. Finally, several medium-sized earthquakes rumbled along the San Andreas fault near Parkfield in 1993–1994.

Did these quakes take the place of the larger earthquake that geologists had expected? Or had the San Andreas fault itself changed, breaking the pattern of 22 years between quakes? Geologists still don't know the answers to these questions. Nonetheless, geologists continue to monitor the San Andreas fault. Someday, they may find a way to predict when and where an earthquake will occur.

Figure 24 This laser beam detects movement along the San Andreas Fault in Parkfield, California.

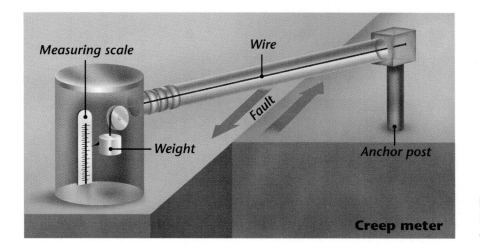

Figure 25 A creep meter can be used to measure movement along a strike-slip fault.

Devices that Monitor Faults

In trying to predict earthquakes, geologists have invented instruments to record the ground movements that occur along faults. **To observe these changes, geologists put in place instruments that measure stress and deformation in the crust.** Geologists hypothesize that such changes signal an approaching earthquake.

Unfortunately, earthquakes almost always strike without warning. The only clue may be a slight rise or fall in the elevation and tilt of the land. Instruments that geologists use to monitor these movements include creep meters, laser-ranging devices, tiltmeters, and satellites.

Creep Meters A creep meter uses a wire stretched across a fault to measure horizontal movement of the ground. On one side of the fault, the wire is anchored to a post. On the other side, the wire is attached to a weight that can slide if the fault moves. Geologists can measure the amount that the fault has moved by measuring how much the weight has moved against a measuring scale.

Laser-Ranging Devices A laser-ranging device uses a laser beam to detect even tiny fault movements. The device calculates any change in the time needed for the laser beam to travel to a reflector and bounce back. Thus, the device can detect any change in distance to the reflector.

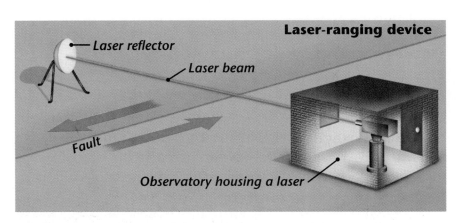

Figure 26 A laser-ranging device monitors fault movement by bouncing a laser beam off a reflector on the other side of the fault. *Comparing and Contrasting How are a laser-ranging device and a creep meter (shown above) similar? How are they different?*

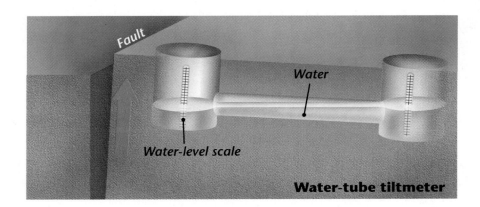

Figure 27 A tiltmeter monitors vertical movement along a fault.

Tiltmeters A tiltmeter measures tilting of the ground. If you have ever used a carpenter's level, you have used a type of tiltmeter. The tiltmeters used by seismologists consist of two bulbs that are filled with a liquid and connected by a hollow stem. Look at the drawing of a tiltmeter in Figure 27. Notice that if the land rises or falls even slightly, the liquid will flow from one bulb to the other. Each bulb contains a measuring scale to measure the depth of the liquid in that bulb. Geologists read the scales to measure the amount of tilt occurring along the fault.

Satellite Monitors Besides ground-based instruments, geologists use satellites equipped with radar to make images of faults. The satellite bounces radio waves off the ground. As the waves echo back into space, the satellite records them. The time it takes for the radio waves to make their round trip provides precise measurements of the distance to the ground. The distance from the ground to the satellite changes with every change in the ground surface. By comparing different images of the same area taken at different times, geologists detect small changes in elevation. These changes in elevation result when stress deforms the ground along a fault.

INTEGRATING SPACE SCIENCE

☑ *Checkpoint* *What do fault-monitoring instruments measure?*

Monitoring Risk in the United States

Even with data from many sources, geologists can't predict when and where a quake will strike. Usually, stress along a fault increases until an earthquake occurs. Yet sometimes stress builds up along a fault, but an earthquake fails to occur. Or, one or more earthquakes may relieve stress along another part of the fault. Exactly what will happen remains uncertain—that's why geologists cannot predict earthquakes.

Geologists do know that earthquakes are likely wherever plate movement stores energy in the rock along faults. **Geologists can determine earthquake risk by locating where faults are active and where past earthquakes have occurred.** In the United States, the risk is highest along the Pacific coast in the states of California,

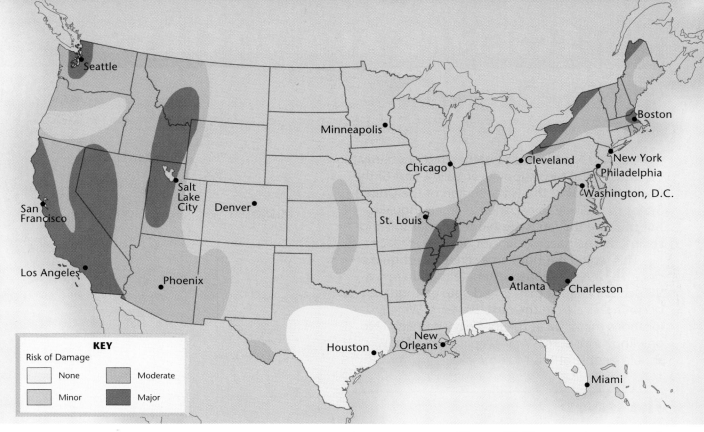

Figure 28 The map shows areas of the United States, excluding Alaska and Hawaii, where earthquakes are likely to occur and the relative damage they are likely to cause. *Interpreting Maps Where are damaging earthquakes least likely to occur? Most likely to occur?*

KEY

Risk of Damage

- None
- Minor
- Moderate
- Major

Washington, and Alaska. The risk of quakes is high because that's where the Pacific and North American plates meet.

Other regions of the United States also have some risk of earthquakes. Serious earthquakes are rare east of the Rockies. Nonetheless, the region has experienced some of the most powerful quakes in the nation's history. Scientists hypothesize that the plate forming most of North America is under stress. This stress could disturb faults that formed millions of years ago. Today, these faults lie hidden beneath thick layers of soil and rock. Find your state in Figure 28 to determine your area's risk of a damaging quake.

Section 4 Review

1. What equipment do geologists use to monitor the movement of faults?
2. What two factors do geologists consider when determining earthquake risk for a region?
3. Explain how satellites can be used to collect data on earthquake faults.
4. **Thinking Critically Making Generalizations** Why can't scientists predict the exact time and place an earthquake is going to occur?

Check Your Progress CHAPTER PROJECT

Use what you have learned about making buildings earthquake resistant to repair and improve your structure. Test your model again. Are your changes successful in preventing damage? Make additional repairs and improvements to your structure.

What's the Risk of an Earthquake?

The New Madrid fault system stretches beneath the central Mississippi River Valley. East of the Rocky Mountains, this is the region of the United States most likely to experience an earthquake. But because the faults are hidden under soil and sediment, the hazards are not obvious.

This region has not had a serious earthquake since 1812. Yet scientists estimate that there is a 90 percent chance that a moderate earthquake will occur in this area in the next 50 years. Which locations might be at risk for heavy damage? No one knows for sure. What preparations, if any, should people of this region make?

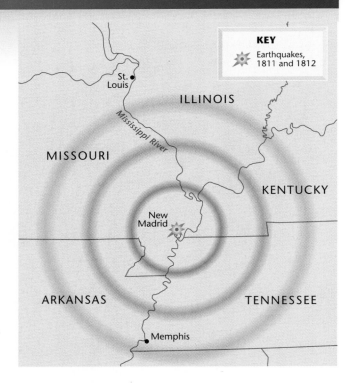

KEY
Earthquakes, 1811 and 1812

The Issues

How Much Money Should People Spend?
In areas where earthquakes are rare, such as the New Madrid fault region, communities face hard choices. Should they spend money for earthquake preparation now in order to cut costs later? Or should they save the money and risk the consequences?

Which Buildings Should Be Modified?
It's clear that the best way to save lives is to make buildings that can withstand severe shaking. Since damaged or collapsing buildings cause most injuries and deaths during earthquakes, modifying existing buildings could save lives. Unfortunately building renovations are costly.

Most new houses can withstand moderate earthquakes. But many older houses—especially brick or masonry houses—are not safe.

Unfortunately, few homeowners can afford the cost of making their houses safer. They might need financial aid or a tax break to help them make these changes.

What Other Structures Need Improvement?
Imagine what would happen if your community were without utility stations and lines for electricity, gas, and water, or without bridges, schools, and hospitals. Engineers who understand earthquake hazards have worked out design standards to reduce damage to these structures. Today, many cities follow these standards in their building codes. But not all structures can be made earthquake-safe. Furthermore, some structures are more crucial for public health and safety than others.

You Decide

1. Identify the Problem
Summarize the dilemma that communities face in regard to earthquake preparations. Which structures in a community are most important to make earthquake-resistant?

2. Analyze the Options
Consider what would happen if communities spent more money, less money, or nothing on earthquake preparations. In each case, who would benefit? Who might be harmed?

3. Find a Solution
Your community near the New Madrid fault system has received a large sum of money to spend on earthquake preparedness. Develop a plan for building and modifying structures. Explain and defend your use of funds.

SECTION 1 Earth's Crust in Motion

Key Ideas

◆ Stresses on Earth's crust produce compression, tension, and shearing in rock.
◆ Faults are cracks in Earth's crust that result from stress.
◆ Faulting and folding of the crust cause mountains and other features to form on the surface.

Key Terms

earthquake	hanging wall
stress	footwall
shearing	reverse fault
tension	fault-block mountain
compression	folds
deformation	anticline
fault	syncline
strike-slip fault	plateau
normal fault	

 SECTION 2 Measuring Earthquakes

Key Ideas

◆ As seismic waves travel through Earth, they carry the energy of an earthquake from the focus to the surface.
◆ Earthquakes produce two types of seismic waves, P waves and S waves, that travel out in all directions from the focus of an earthquake.
◆ Today, the moment magnitude scale is used to determine the magnitude of an earthquake. Other scales that geologists have used to rate earth-quakes include the Mercalli scale and the Richter scale.

Key Terms

focus	seismograph
epicenter	magnitude
seismic waves	Mercalli scale
P waves	Richter scale
S waves	moment magnitude scale
surface waves	

SECTION 3 Earthquake Hazards and Safety

Key Ideas

◆ Earthquakes can damage structures through tsunamis, landslides or avalanches, and shaking or liquefaction of the ground.
◆ New buildings can be designed to withstand earthquakes; old buildings can be modified to make them more earthquake-resistant.
◆ For personal safety indoors during an earthquake, drop, cover, and hold under a desk or table, or against an interior wall.

Key Terms

liquefaction	tsunamis
aftershock	base-isolated building

SECTION 4 Monitoring Faults

INTEGRATING TECHNOLOGY

Key Ideas

◆ Geologists use instruments to measure deformation and stress along faults.
◆ Scientists determine earthquake risk by monitoring active faults and by studying faults where past earthquakes have occurred.

Organizing Information

Concept Map Copy the concept map about stress on a separate piece of paper. Then complete it and add a title. (For more on concept maps, see the Skills Handbook.)

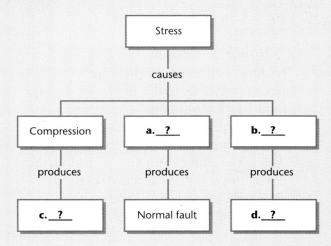

Reviewing Content

 For more review of key concepts, see the Interactive Student Tutorial CD-ROM.

Multiple Choice

Chose the letter of the answer that best completes each statement.

1. Shearing is the force in Earth's crust that
   a. squeezes the crust together.
   b. pushes the crust in opposite directions.
   c. forces the crust to bend and fold.
   d. stretches the crust apart.

2. When the hanging wall of a fault slips down with respect to the footwall, the result is a
   a. reverse fault.   b. syncline.
   c. normal fault.   d. strike-slip fault.

3. A seismograph measures
   a. the depth of an earthquake.
   b. friction forces along a fault.
   c. ground motion during an earthquake.
   d. movement along a fault.

4. Geologists use the difference in the arrival times of P waves and S waves at a seismograph to determine
   a. the magnitude of the earthquake.
   b. the depth of the earthquake's focus.
   c. the strength of the surface waves.
   d. the distance to the epicenter.

5. To monitor the upward movement along a fault, geologists would probably use a
   a. laser-ranging device.   b. tiltmeter.
   c. seismograph.   d. creep meter.

True or False

If the statement is true, write true. If it is false, change the underlined word or words to make the statement true.

6. Deformation is the breaking, tilting, and folding of rocks caused by <u>liquefaction</u>.

7. Rock uplifted by <u>strike-slip faults</u> creates fault-block mountains.

8. An earthquake's <u>epicenter</u> is located deep underground.

9. As <u>S waves</u> move through the ground, they cause it to compress and then expand.

10. <u>Tsunamis</u> are triggered by earthquakes originating beneath the ocean floor.

Checking Concepts

11. How does stress affect Earth's crust?

12. Explain the process that forms a fault-block mountain.

13. What type of stress in the crust results in the formation of folded mountains? Explain your answer.

14. What are plateaus and how do they form?

15. Describe what happens along a fault beneath Earth's surface when an earthquake occurs.

16. Explain how the moment magnitude and Richter scales of earthquake measurement are similar and how they are different.

17. When geologists monitor a fault, what kinds of data do they collect? Explain.

18. **Writing to Learn** You are a geologist studying earthquake risk in an eastern state. Your data show that a major earthquake might happen there within 10 years. Write a letter to the governor of your state explaining why there is an earthquake hazard there and recommending how your state should prepare for the earthquake.

Thinking Critically

19. **Classifying** How would you classify a fault in which the hanging wall has slid up and over the footwall?

20. **Comparing and Contrasting** Compare and contrast P waves and S waves.

21. **Predicting** A community has just built a street across a strike-slip fault that has frequent earthquakes. How will movement along the fault affect the street?

22. **Applying Concepts** If you were building a house in an earthquake-prone area, what steps would you take to limit potential damage in an earthquake?

23. **Making Generalizations** How can filled land and loose, soft soil affect the amount of damage caused by an earthquake? Explain.

24. **Relating Cause and Effect** A geologist is monitoring a fault using radar waves bounced off Earth's surface by a satellite. If the satellite detects a change in elevation near the fault, what does this indicate? Explain.

Applying Skills

The graph shows the seismograph record for an earthquake. The y-axis of the graph shows the up-and-down shaking in millimeters at the seismograph station. The x-axis shows time in minutes.

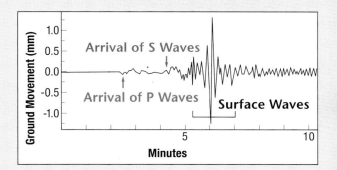

25. **Interpreting Diagrams** In what order do the seismic waves arrive at the seismograph station? Which type of seismic wave produces the largest ground movement?
26. **Interpreting Diagrams** What is the difference in arrival times for the P waves and S waves?

27. **Predicting** What would the seismograph record look like several hours after this earthquake? How would it change if an aftershock occurred?
28. **Drawing Conclusions** If the difference in arrival times for P waves and S waves is 5 minutes longer at a second seismograph station than at the first station, what can you conclude about the location of the second station?

Performance CHAPTER PROJECT Assessment

Present Your Project Before testing how your model withstands an earthquake, explain to your classmates how and why you changed your model. When your model is tested, make notes of how it withstands the earthquake.

Reflect and Record How would a real earthquake compare with the method used to test your model? If it were a real building, could your structure withstand an earthquake? How could you improve your model?

Test Preparation

Use these questions to prepare for standardized tests.

Use the diagram of a fault to answer Questions 29–33.

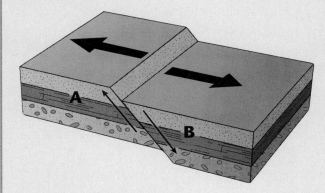

29. The rock on the side of the fault labeled B is the
    a. footwall.   b. shearing wall.
    c. hanging wall.   d. seismic wall.

30. The rock on the side of the fault labeled A is the
    a. hanging wall.   b. strike-slip wall.
    c. reverse wall   d. footwall.

31. The thick arrows in the diagram stand for forces in Earth's crust pulling apart the two slabs of rock. This force is called
    a. shearing.   b. compression.
    c. elevation.   d. tension.

32. In the fault shown, the footwall
    a. does not move.
    b. moves down relative to the hanging wall.
    c. moves up relative to the hanging wall.
    d. slides sideways along the hanging wall.

33. The fault in the diagram is a(n)
    a. normal fault.   b. strike-slip fault.
    c. reverse fault.   d. inactive fault.

CHAPTER

6 Volcanoes

176

Volcanoes and People

The frequent eruptions of Mount Kilauea can be spectacular. And they can be dangerous. Yet volcanoes and people have been closely connected throughout history, not only in Hawaii, but around the world. People often live near volcanoes because of the benefits they offer, from rich soil to minerals to hot springs. In your chapter project, you will research how volcanoes have affected the people living in a volcanic region.

Your Goal To make a documentary about life in a volcanic region.

Your project must
- describe the type of volcano you chose and give its history
- focus on one topic, such as how people have benefited from living near the volcano or how people show the volcano in their art and stories
- use a variety of media in your documentary presentation

Get Started Brainstorm with a group of other students which geographic area you would like to learn about. Your teacher may suggest some volcanic regions for you to check out. What research resources will your group need? Start planning what media you want to use to present your documentary. You might consider video, computer art, overhead transparencies, a rap song, a skit, or a mural. Be creative!

Check Your Progress You'll be working on this project as you study this chapter. To keep your project on track, look for Check Your Progress boxes at the following points.

Section 1 Review, page 181: Select the topic and region you will investigate and begin collecting information.
Section 3 Review, page 197: Use storyboards to organize your materials.
Section 4 Review, page 202: Prepare your visuals and narration.

Present Your Project At the end of the chapter (page 205), practice your presentation and then present your documentary to your class.

Kilauea volcano is on Hawaii, the largest of the Hawaiian Islands.

SECTION

4

Integrating Space Science

Volcanoes in the Solar System

Discover **What Forces Shaped the Surface of Io?**

SECTION

1 Volcanoes and Plate Tectonics

DISCOVER · ACTIVITY · · ·

Where Are Volcanoes Found on Earth's Surface?

1. Look at the map of Earth's volcanoes on page 179. What symbols are used to represent volcanoes? What other symbols are shown on the map?

2. Do the locations of the volcanoes form a pattern? Do the volcanoes seem related to any other features on Earth's surface?

Think About It

Developing Hypotheses Develop a hypothesis to explain where Earth's volcanoes are located. Are there any volcanoes on the map whose location cannot be explained by your hypothesis?

GUIDE FOR READING

◆ Where are Earth's volcanic regions found, and why are they found there?

Reading Tip Before you read, preview the headings in this section. Predict where volcanoes are likely to be located.

Before 1995, the island of Montserrat sat like a beautiful green gem in the Caribbean Sea. Some residents of the small island grew cotton, limes, and vegetables. Tourists flocked to the island to enjoy the scenery and tropical climate. What could possibly spoil this island paradise? A volcano named Soufrière (soo free EHR) Hills did. In 1995, Soufrière Hills began a series of eruptions that lasted more than two years. The volcano belched volcanic ash that fell like snow on roofs and gardens. Residents were evacuated as the volcano continued to erupt, and heavy falls of ash buried entire towns on the southern half of the island.

What Is a Volcano?

The eruption of a volcano is among the most dangerous and awe-inspiring events on Earth. A **volcano** is a weak spot in the crust where molten material, or magma, comes to the surface. **Magma** is a molten mixture of rock-forming substances, gases, and water vapor from the mantle. When magma reaches the surface, it is called **lava**. After lava has cooled, it forms solid rock. The lava released during volcanic activity builds up Earth's surface. Volcanic activity is a constructive force that adds new rock to existing land and forms new islands.

◀ **Soufrière Hills volcano**

Location of Volcanoes

There are about 600 active volcanoes on land. Many more lie beneath the sea. Figure 1 is a map that shows the location of Earth's volcanoes. Notice how volcanoes occur in belts that extend across continents and oceans. One major volcanic belt is the **Ring of Fire,** formed by the many volcanoes that rim the Pacific Ocean. Can you find other volcanic belts on the map?

Volcanic belts form along the boundaries of Earth's plates. At plate boundaries, huge pieces of the lithosphere diverge (pull apart) or converge (push together). Here, the lithosphere is weak and fractured, allowing magma to reach the surface. **Most volcanoes occur along diverging plate boundaries, such as the mid-ocean ridge, or in subduction zones around the edges of oceans.** But some volcanoes form at "hot spots" far from the boundaries of continental or oceanic plates.

Volcanoes at Diverging Plate Boundaries

Volcanoes form along the mid-ocean ridge, which marks a diverging plate boundary. Recall from Chapter 4 that the ridge is a long, underwater rift valley that winds through the oceans. Along the ridge, lava pours out of cracks in the ocean floor. Only in a few places, as in Iceland and the Azores Islands in the Atlantic Ocean, do the volcanoes of the mid-ocean ridge rise above the ocean's surface.

Language Arts
CONNECTION

The word *volcano* comes from the name of the Roman god of fire, Vulcan. According to Roman mythology, Vulcan lived beneath Mount Etna, a huge volcano on the island of Sicily in the Mediterranean Sea. Vulcan used the heat of Mount Etna to make metal armor and weapons for the ancient gods and heroes.

In Your Journal

Use the dictionary to find the definition of *plutonic* rock. Explain why the name of another Roman god was used for this term.

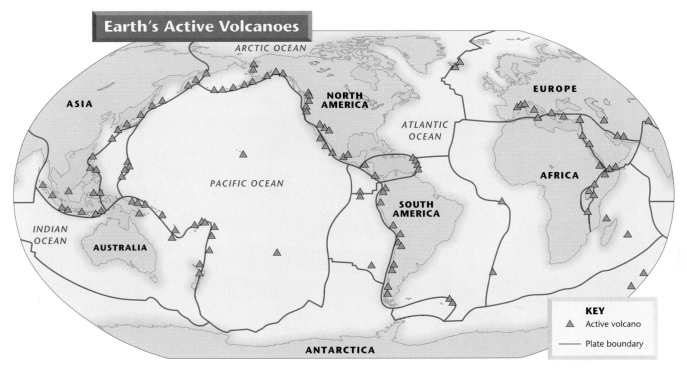

Earth's Active Volcanoes

KEY
△ Active volcano
— Plate boundary

Figure 1 Volcanoes dot Earth's land surface. *Observing What patterns can you see in the locations of the volcanoes on the map?*

Volcanoes at Converging Boundaries

Many volcanoes form near the plate boundaries where some oceanic crust returns to the mantle. Subduction causes slabs of oceanic crust to sink through a deep-ocean trench into the mantle. The crust melts and forms magma, which then rises back toward the surface. When the magma from the melted crust erupts as lava, volcanoes are formed. Figure 2 shows how converging plates produce volcanoes.

Many volcanoes occur on islands, near boundaries where two oceanic plates collide. The older, denser plate dives under the other plate, creating a deep-ocean trench. The lower plate sinks beneath the deep-ocean trench into the asthenosphere. There it begins to melt, forming magma. Because it is less dense than the surrounding rock, the magma seeps upward through cracks in the crust. Eventually, the magma breaks through the ocean floor, creating volcanoes.

The resulting volcanoes create a string of islands called an **island arc**. The curve of an island arc echoes the curve of its deep-ocean trench. Major island arcs include Japan, New Zealand, Indonesia, the Caribbean islands, the Philippines, and the Aleutians.

Subduction also occurs where the edge of a continental plate collides with an oceanic plate. Collisions between oceanic and continental plates produced both the volcanoes of the Andes mountains on the west coast of South America and the volcanoes of the Pacific Northwest in the United States.

☑ *Checkpoint* *How can oceanic crust eventually become magma?*

Figure 2 Converging plates often form volcanoes when two oceanic plates collide or when an oceanic plate collides with a continental plate. In both situations, oceanic crust sinks through a deep-ocean trench, melts to form magma, and then erupts to the surface as lava.

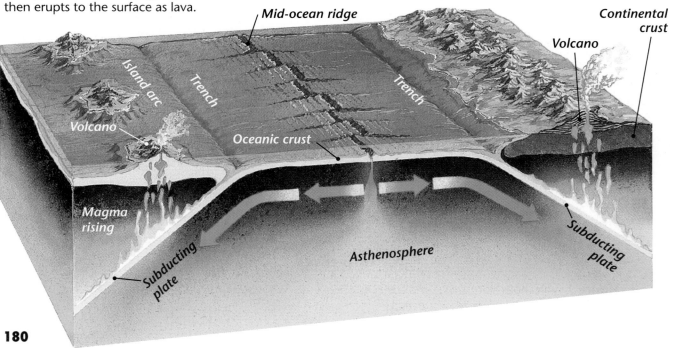

180

Kauai Oahu Maui

Pacific Ocean

Hawaiian Islands

Hawaii

Pacific plate

Hot spot

Figure 3 Hawaii sits on the moving Pacific plate. Beneath it is a powerful hot spot. Eventually, the plate's movement will carry the island of Hawaii away from the hot spot. *Inferring Which island on the map formed first?*

Hot Spot Volcanoes

Some volcanoes result from "hot spots" in Earth's mantle. A **hot spot** is an area where magma from deep within the mantle melts through the crust like a blow torch. Hot spots often lie in the middle of continental or oceanic plates far from any plate boundaries. Unlike the volcanoes in an island arc, the volcanoes at a hot spot do not result from subduction.

A hot spot volcano in the ocean floor can gradually form a series of volcanic mountains. For example, the Hawaiian Islands formed one by one over millions of years as the Pacific plate drifted over a hot spot.

Hot spots can also form under the continents. Yellowstone National Park in Wyoming marks a major hot spot under the North American plate. The last volcanic eruption in Yellowstone occurred about 75,000 years ago.

TRY THIS

Hot Spot in a Box

ACTIVITY

1. Fill a plastic box half full of cold water. This represents the ocean.

2. Mix red food coloring with hot water in a small, narrow-necked bottle to represent magma.

3. Hold your finger over the mouth of the bottle as you place the bottle in the center of the box. The mouth of the bottle must be under water.

4. Float a flat piece of plastic foam on the water to model a tectonic plate. Make sure the "plate" is floating above the bottle.

5. Take your finger off the bottle and observe what happens to the "magma."

Making Models Move the plastic foam slowly along. Where does the magma touch the "plate"? How does this model a hot spot volcano?

Section 1 Review

1. Where do most volcanoes occur on Earth's surface?

2. What process forms island arcs?

3. What causes hot spot volcanoes to form?

4. **Thinking Critically Predicting** What will eventually happen to the active volcano on the island of Hawaii, which is now over the hot spot?

Check Your Progress

CHAPTER PROJECT

Start by selecting the volcanic region you will study. Possible topics to investigate are myths and legends about volcanoes, the importance of volcanic soils, mineral resources from volcanoes, tourism, and geothermal power. Choose the topic that interests you the most. Begin your research and take notes on the information you collect.

Mapping Earthquakes and Volcanoes

In this lab, you will interpret data on the locations of earthquakes and volcanoes to find patterns.

Problem

Is there a pattern in the locations of earthquakes and volcanoes?

Materials

outline world map showing longitude and latitude
4 pencils of different colors

Procedure

1. Use the information in the table to mark the location of each earthquake on the world map. Use one of the colored pencils to draw a letter E inside a circle at each earthquake location.
2. Use a pencil of a second color to mark the locations of the volcanoes on the world map. Indicate each volcano with the letter V inside a circle.
3. Use a third pencil to lightly shade the areas in which earthquakes are found.
4. Use a fourth colored pencil to lightly shade the areas in which volcanoes are found.

Analyze and Conclude

1. How are earthquakes distributed on the map? Are they scattered evenly over Earth's surface? Are they concentrated in zones?
2. How are volcanoes distributed? Are they scattered evenly or concentrated in zones?
3. From your data, what can you infer about the relationship between earthquakes and volcanoes?

4. **Apply** Based on the data, which area of the North American continent would have the greatest risk of earthquake damage? Of volcano damage? Why would knowing this information be important to urban planners, engineers, and builders in this area?

More to Explore

On a map of the United States, locate active volcanoes and areas of earthquake activity. Determine the distance from your home to the nearest active volcano.

Earthquakes		Volcanoes	
Longitude	Latitude	Longitude	Latitude
120° W	40° N	150° W	60° N
110° E	5° S	70° W	35° S
77° W	4° S	120° W	45° N
88° E	23° N	61° W	15° N
121° E	14° S	105° W	20° N
34° E	7° N	75° W	0°
74° W	44° N	122° W	40° N
70° W	30° S	30° E	40° N
10° E	45° N	60° E	30° N
85° W	13° N	160° E	55° N
125° E	23° N	37° E	3° S
30° E	35° N	145° E	40° N
140° E	35° N	120° E	10° S
12° E	46° N	14° E	41° N
75° E	28° N	105° E	5° S
150° W	61° N	35° E	15° N
68° W	47° S	70° W	30° S
175° E	41° S	175° E	39° S
121° E	17° N	123° E	13° N

SECTION 2 Volcanic Activity

In Hawaii, there are many myths about Pele (PAY lay), the fire goddess of volcanoes. In these myths, Pele is the creator and the destroyer of the Hawaiian islands. She lives in the fiery depths of erupting volcanoes. According to legend, when Pele is angry, she releases the fires of Earth through openings on the mountainside. Evidence of her presence is "Pele's hair," a fine, threadlike rock formed by lava. Pele's hair forms when lava sprays out of the ground like water from a fountain. As it cools, the lava stretches and hardens into thin strands.

How Magma Reaches Earth's Surface

Where does this hot, molten lava come from? Lava begins as magma in the mantle. There, magma forms in the asthenosphere, which lies beneath the lithosphere. The materials of the asthenosphere are under great pressure.

Magma Rises Because liquid magma is less dense than the surrounding solid material, magma flows upward into any cracks in the rock above. Magma rises until it reaches the surface, or until it becomes trapped beneath layers of rock.

GUIDE FOR READING

◆ What happens when a volcano erupts?

◆ How do the two types of volcanic eruptions differ?

◆ What are some hazards of volcanoes?

Reading Tip Before you read, preview *Exploring a Volcano* on page 185. Write a list of any questions you have about how a volcano erupts.

Figure 4 Pele's hair is a type of rock formed from lava. Each strand is as fine as spun glass.

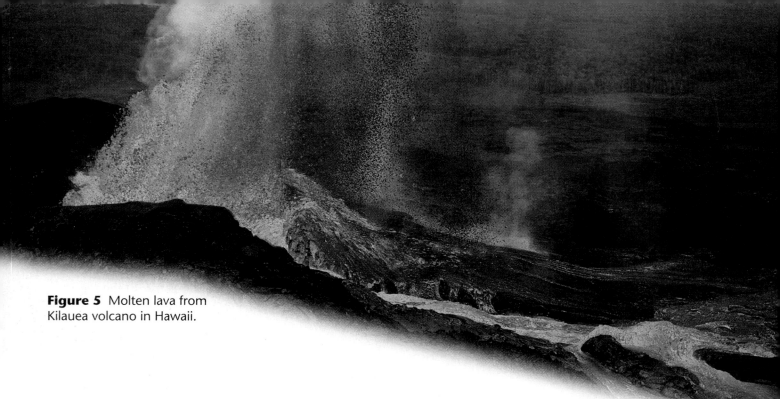

Figure 5 Molten lava from Kilauea volcano in Hawaii.

A Volcano Erupts Just like the carbon dioxide trapped in a bottle of soda pop, the dissolved gases trapped in magma are under tremendous pressure. You cannot see the carbon dioxide gas in a bottle of soda pop because it is dissolved in the liquid. But when you open the bottle, the pressure is released. The carbon dioxide forms bubbles, which rush to the surface.

As magma rises toward the surface, the pressure decreases. The dissolved gases begin to separate out, forming bubbles. A volcano erupts when an opening develops in weak rock on the surface. **During a volcanic eruption, the gases dissolved in magma rush out, carrying the magma with them.** Once magma reaches the surface and becomes lava, the gases bubble out.

Inside a Volcano

All volcanoes have a pocket of magma beneath the surface and one or more cracks through which the magma forces its way. You can see these features in *Exploring a Volcano*. Beneath a volcano, magma collects in a pocket called a **magma chamber.** The magma moves through a **pipe,** a long tube in the ground that connects the magma chamber to Earth's surface. Molten rock and gas leave the volcano through an opening called a **vent.** Often, there is one central vent at the top of a volcano. However, many volcanoes also have other vents that open on the volcano's sides. A **lava flow** is the area covered by lava as it pours out of a vent. A **crater** is a bowl-shaped area that may form at the top of a volcano around the volcano's central vent.

☑ *Checkpoint* *How does magma rise through the lithosphere?*

EXPLORING *a Volcano*

A volcano forms where magma breaks through Earth's crust and lava flows over the surface.

Scientists prepare the robot Dante II for its descent into the crater of a volcano in Alaska.

Crater
Lava collects in the crater, the bowl-shaped area that forms around the volcano's vent.

Vent
The point on the surface where magma leaves the volcano's pipe is called the vent.

Side vent
Sometimes magma forces its way out of a volcano through a side vent.

Lava
Magma that reaches the surface is called lava.

Lava flow
The river of lava that pours down a volcano and over the land is called a lava flow.

Pipe
A pipe is a narrow, almost vertical crack in the crust through which magma rises to the surface.

Magma
Magma is extremely hot, molten material that also contains dissolved gases including water vapor.

Magma chamber
As magma rises toward the surface, it forms a large underground pocket called a magma chamber.

Characteristics of Magma

The force of a volcanic eruption depends partly on the amount of gas dissolved in the magma. But gas content is not the only thing that affects an eruption. How thick or thin the magma is, its temperature, and its silica content are also important factors.

Some types of magma are thick and flow very slowly. Other types of magma are fluid and flow almost as easily as water. Magma's temperature partly determines whether it is thick or fluid. The hotter the magma, the more fluid it is.

The amount of silica in magma also helps to determine how easily the magma flows. **Silica,** which is a material that is formed from the elements oxygen and silicon, is one of the most abundant materials in Earth's crust and mantle. The more silica magma contains, the thicker it is.

Magma that is high in silica produces light-colored lava that is too sticky to flow very far. When this type of lava cools, it forms the rock rhyolite, which has the same composition as granite. Pumice and obsidian, which you observed if you did the Discover activity, also form from high-silica lava. Obsidian forms when lava cools very quickly, giving it a smooth, glossy surface. Pumice forms when gas bubbles are trapped in cooling lava, leaving spaces in the rock.

Magma that is low in silica flows readily and produces dark-colored lava. When this kind of lava cools, rocks such as basalt are formed.

Figure 6 Rhyolite (top) forms from high-silica lava. Basalt (bottom) forms from low-silica lava. When this type of lava cools, it sometimes forms six-sided columns like the ones in the picture.

Types of Volcanic Eruptions

A volcano's magma influences how the volcano erupts. **The silica content of magma helps to determine whether the volcanic eruption is quiet or explosive.**

Quiet Eruptions A volcano erupts quietly if its magma flows easily. In this case, the gas dissolved in the magma bubbles out gently. Thin, runny lava oozes quietly from the vent. The islands of Hawaii and Iceland were formed from quiet eruptions. On the Big Island of Hawaii, lava pours out of the crater near the top of Mount Kilauea (kee loo AY uh). Lava also flows out of long cracks on the volcano's sides. Quiet eruptions like the ones that regularly take place on Mount Kilauea have built up the Big Island over hundreds of thousands of years. In Iceland, lava usually emerges from gigantic fissures many kilometers long. The fluid lava from a quiet eruption can flow many kilometers from the volcano's vent.

Quiet eruptions produce two different types of lava: pahoehoe and aa. **Pahoehoe** (pah HOH ee hoh ee) is fast-moving, hot lava. The surface of a lava flow formed from pahoehoe looks like a solid mass of wrinkles, billows, and ropelike coils. Lava that is cooler and slower-moving is called **aa** (AH ah). When aa hardens, it forms a rough surface consisting of jagged lava chunks. Figure 7 shows how different these types of lava can be.

☑ *Checkpoint* *What types of lava are produced by quiet eruptions?*

Figure 7 Both pahoehoe and aa can come from the same volcano. **A.** Pahoehoe flows easily and hardens into a rippled surface. **B.** Aa hardens into rough chunks. *Inferring What accounts for the differences between these two types of lava?*

Figure 8 Mount St. Helens erupted at 8:30 A.M. on May 18, 1980. **A.** A large bulge that had formed on the north side of the mountain crashed downward.

B. As the mountainside collapsed, bottled up gas and magma inside began to escape.

Social Studies
CONNECTION

In A.D. 79, Mount Vesuvius in Italy erupted. A thick layer of ash from Vesuvius buried the Roman city of Pompeii, which lay between the volcano and the Mediterranean Sea. Beginning in the 1700s, about half of the buried city was dug out, and we now know the following: Pompeii was a walled city with shops, homes, paved streets, a forum (or public square), temples, and public baths. Perhaps 20,000 people lived there.

In Your Journal

Research Pompeii to find out what scientists have learned about daily life in the city. Write a paragraph summarizing your findings.

Explosive Eruptions If its magma is thick and sticky, a volcano erupts explosively. The thick magma does not flow out of the crater and down the mountain. Instead, it slowly builds up in the volcano's pipe, plugging it like a cork in a bottle. Dissolved gases cannot escape from the thick magma. The trapped gases build up pressure until they explode. The erupting gases push the magma out of the volcano with incredible force.

The explosion breaks the lava into fragments that quickly cool and harden into pieces of different sizes. The smallest pieces are volcanic ash—fine, rocky particles as small as a grain of sand. Cinders are pebble-sized particles. Larger pieces, called bombs, may range from the size of a baseball to the size of a car. A **pyroclastic flow** (py roh KLAS tik) occurs when an explosive eruption hurls out ash, cinders, and bombs as well as gases.

Look at Figure 8 to see the 1980 eruption of Mount St. Helens in the state of Washington. It was one of the most violent explosive eruptions that has ever occurred in the United States.

✓ *Checkpoint* *What causes an explosive eruption?*

Stages of a Volcano

The activity of a volcano may last from less than a decade to more than 10 million years. Most long-lived volcanoes, however, do not erupt continuously. Geologists often describe volcanoes with terms usually reserved for living things, such as sleeping, awakening, alive, and dead. An **active,** or live, volcano is one that is erupting or has shown signs that it may erupt in the near future. A **dormant,** or sleeping, volcano is like a sleeping bear. Scientists expect a dormant volcano to awaken in the future and become active. However, there may be thousands of years between eruptions. An **extinct,** or dead, volcano is unlikely to erupt again.

C. Shattered rock and pyroclastic flows blasted out sideways from the volcano.

D. The blast traveled outward, leveling the surrounding forest and causing mudflows that affected a wide area around the volcano.

Other Types of Volcanic Activity

Hot springs and geysers are two examples of volcanic activity that do not involve the eruption of lava. These features may occur in any volcanic area—even around an extinct volcano.

A **hot spring** forms when groundwater heated by a nearby body of magma rises to the surface and collects in a natural pool. (Groundwater is water that has seeped into the spaces among rocks deep beneath Earth's surface.) Water from hot springs may contain dissolved gases and other substances from deep within Earth.

Sometimes, rising hot water and steam become trapped underground in a narrow crack. Pressure builds until the mixture suddenly sprays above the surface as a geyser. A **geyser** (GY zur) is a fountain of water and steam that erupts from the ground.

![Integrating Technology icon] **INTEGRATING TECHNOLOGY** In volcanic areas, water heated by magma can provide a clean, reliable energy source called **geothermal energy.** The people of Reykjavik, Iceland, pipe this hot water directly into their homes for warmth. Geothermal energy is also a source of electricity in Iceland as well as northern California and New Zealand. Steam from deep underground is piped into turbines. Inside a turbine, the steam spins a wheel in the same way that blowing on a pinwheel makes the pinwheel turn. The moving wheel in the turbine turns a generator that changes the energy of motion into electrical energy.

Figure 9 Old Faithful, a geyser in Yellowstone National Park, erupts about every 33 to 93 minutes. That's how long it takes for the pressure to build up again after each eruption.

Monitoring Volcanoes

Geologists have been somewhat more successful in predicting volcanic eruptions than in predicting earthquakes. Changes in and around a volcano usually give warning a short time before the volcano erupts. Geologists use tiltmeters, laser-ranging devices, and other instruments to detect slight surface changes in elevation and tilt caused by magma moving underground. Geologists monitor the local magnetic field, water level in a volcano's crater lake, and any gases escaping from a volcano. They take the temperature of underground water to see if it is getting hotter—a sign that magma may be nearing the surface.

Geologists also monitor the many small earthquakes that occur in the area around a volcano before an eruption.

SCIENCE & History

The Power of Volcanoes

Within the last 150 years, major volcanic eruptions have greatly affected the land and people around them.

1883 Indonesia

The violent eruption of Krakatau volcano threw 18 cubic kilometers of ash skyward. The blast was heard 5,000 kilometers away.

1912 Alaska, U.S.A.

Today, a river in Alaska cuts through the thick layer of volcanic ash from the eruption of Mount Katmai. Mount Katmai blasted out almost as much ash as Krakatau.

1850   **1900**

1902 Martinique

Mount Pelée, a Caribbean volcano, erupted a burning cloud of hot gas and pyroclastic flows. Within two minutes of the eruption, the cloud had killed the 29,000 residents of St. Pierre, a city on the volcano's flank. Only two people survived.

The movement of magma into the magma chamber and through the volcano's pipe triggers these quakes.

All these data help geologists predict that an eruption is about to occur. But geologists cannot be certain about the type of eruption or how powerful it will be.

Volcano Hazards

The time between volcanic eruptions may span hundreds of years. So people living near a dormant volcano may be unaware of the danger. Before 1980, the people who lived, worked, and vacationed in the region around Mount St. Helens viewed it as a peaceful mountain. Few imagined the destruction the volcano would bring when it awakened from its 123-year slumber.

In Your Journal

People have written eye-witness accounts of famous volcanic eruptions. Research one of the eruptions in the time line. Then write a letter describing what someone observing the eruption might have seen.

1991 Philippines

Mount Pinatubo was dormant for hundreds of years before erupting in June 1991. Pinatubo spewed out huge quantities of ash that rose high into the atmosphere and also buried the surrounding countryside.

1950   2000

1980 Washington, U.S.A.

When Mount St. Helens exploded, it blasted one cubic kilometer of rock fragments and volcanic material skyward. The eruption was not unexpected. For months, geologists had monitored releases of ash, small earthquakes, and a bulge on the mountain caused by the buildup of magma inside.

1995 Montserrat

For more than two years, eruptions of volcanic ash from the Soufrière Hills volcano poured down on this small Caribbean island. Geologists anxiously waited for the eruption to run its course, not knowing whether it would end in a huge explosion.

Figure 10 A. Mudflows were one of the hazards of Mt. Pinatubo's 1991 eruption. B. People around Mt. Pinatubo wore masks to protect themselves from breathing volcanic ash.

Although quiet eruptions and explosive eruptions involve different volcano hazards, both types of eruption can cause damage far from the crater's rim. During a quiet eruption, lava flows pour from vents, setting fire to and then burying everything in their path. During an explosive eruption, a volcano can belch out hot, burning clouds of volcanic gases as well as cinders and bombs.

Volcanic ash can bury entire towns, damage crops, and clog car engines. If it becomes wet, the heavy ash can cause roofs to collapse. If a jet plane sucks ash into its engine, the engine may stall. Eruptions can also cause landslides and avalanches of mud, melted snow, and rock. Figure 10 shows some effects of mud and ash from Mount Pinatubo's eruption. When Mount St. Helens erupted, gigantic mudflows carried ash, trees, and rock fragments 29 kilometers down the nearby Toutle River.

Section 2 Review

1. What are the stages that lead up to a volcanic eruption?
2. Compare and contrast quiet and explosive eruptions.
3. Describe some of the hazards posed by volcanoes.
4. **Thinking Critically** Drawing Conclusions A geologist times a passing lava flow at 15 kilometers per hour. The geologist also sees that lava near the edge of the flow is forming smooth-looking ripples as it hardens. What type of lava is this? What type of magma produced it? Explain your conclusions.

Science at Home

Cooling Lava Place cold water in one cup and hot tap water in another. **CAUTION:** Handle the cup containing the hot water carefully to avoid spilling. Ask members of your family to predict what will happen when some melted candle wax drops into each cup of water. Have an adult family member drip melted wax from a candle into each cup. Explain how this models what happens when lava cools quickly or more slowly.

SECTION 3 Volcanic Landforms

DISCOVER

ACTIVITY

How Can Volcanic Activity Change Earth's Surface?

1. Use tape to secure the neck of a balloon over one end of a straw.

2. Place the balloon in the center of a box with the straw protruding.

3. Partially inflate the balloon.

4. Put damp sand on top of the balloon until it is covered.

5. Slowly inflate the balloon more. Observe what happens to the surface of the sand.

Think It Over

Making Models This activity models one of the ways in which volcanic activity can cause a mountain to form. What do you think the sand represents? What does the balloon represent?

Volcanoes have created some of Earth's most spectacular landforms. For example, the perfect volcanic cone of Mt. Fuji in Japan and the majestic profile of snow-capped Mt. Kilimanjaro rising above the grasslands of East Africa are famous around the world.

Some volcanic landforms arise when lava flows build up mountains and plateaus on Earth's surface. Other volcanic landforms are the result of the buildup of magma beneath the surface.

Landforms From Lava and Ash

Rock and other materials formed from lava create a variety of landforms including shield volcanoes, composite volcanoes, cinder cone volcanoes, and lava plateaus. Look at *Exploring Volcanic Mountains* on page 195 to see the similarities and differences among these features.

GUIDE FOR READING

◆ What landforms does lava create on Earth's surface?

◆ How does magma that hardens beneath the surface create landforms?

Reading Tip As you read, make a table comparing volcanic landforms. Include what formed each landform—lava, ash, or magma—as well as its characteristics.

◀ Mt. Fuji, Japan

Shield Volcanoes At some places on Earth's surface, thin layers of lava pour out of a vent and harden on top of previous layers. Such lava flows gradually build a wide, gently sloping mountain called a **shield volcano.** Shield volcanoes rising from a hot spot on the ocean floor created the Hawaiian Islands.

Cinder Cone Volcanoes A volcano can also be a **cinder cone,** a steep, cone-shaped hill or mountain. If a volcano's lava is thick and stiff, it may produce ash, cinders, and bombs. These materials pile up around the vent in a steep, cone-shaped pile. For example, Paricutín in Mexico erupted in 1943 in a farmer's cornfield. The volcano built up a cinder cone about 400 meters high.

Composite Volcanoes Sometimes, lava flows alternate with explosive eruptions of ash, cinder, and bombs. The result is a composite volcano. **Composite volcanoes** are tall, cone-shaped mountains in which layers of lava alternate with layers of ash. Examples of composite volcanoes include Mount Fuji in Japan and Mount St. Helens in Washington state.

Lava Plateaus Instead of forming mountains, some eruptions of lava form high, level areas called lava plateaus. First, lava flows out of several long cracks in an area. The thin, runny lava travels far before cooling and solidifying. Again and again, floods of lava flow on top of earlier floods. After millions of years, these layers of lava can form high plateaus. One example is the Columbia Plateau, which covers parts of Washington, Oregon, and Idaho.

Figure 11 Crater Lake in Oregon fills the caldera formed after an eruption that destroyed the top 2,000 meters of Mount Mazama nearly 7,000 years ago.
Developing Hypotheses Develop a hypothesis to explain the formation of Wizard Island, the small island in Crater Lake.

Calderas Enormous eruptions may empty the main vent and the magma chamber beneath a volcano. The mountain becomes a hollow shell. With nothing to support it, the top of the mountain collapses inward. The huge hole left by the collapse of a volcanic mountain is called a **caldera** (kal DAIR uh). The hole is filled with the pieces of the volcano that have fallen inward, as well as some lava and ash. In Figure 11 you can see one of the world's largest calderas.

☑ *Checkpoint What are the three types of volcanic mountains?*

EXPLORING *Volcanic Mountains*

Volcanic activity is responsible for building up much of Earth's surface. Lava from volcanoes cools and hardens into three types of mountains.

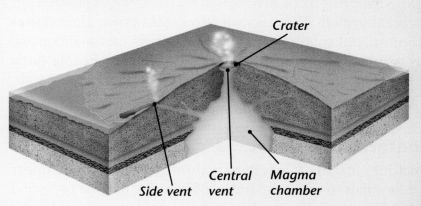

Crater

Side vent

Central vent

Magma chamber

▲ *Mauna Loa is one of the shield volcanoes that built the island Hawaii.*

Shield Volcano
Repeated lava flows during quiet eruptions gradually build up a broad, gently sloping volcanic mountain known as a shield volcano.

Cinder Cone Volcano
When cinders erupt explosively from a volcanic vent, they pile up around the vent, forming a cone-shaped hill called a cinder cone.

▲ *Sunset Crater is an extinct cinder cone in Arizona.*

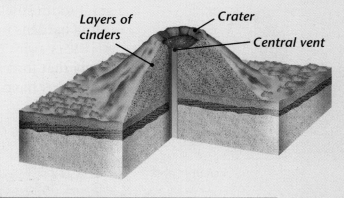

Layers of cinders

Crater

Central vent

Composite Volcano
Layers of lava alternate with layers of ash, cinders, and bombs in a composite volcano, which has both quiet and explosive eruptions.

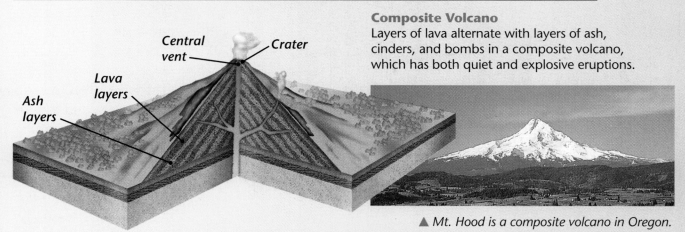

Central vent

Crater

Lava layers

Ash layers

▲ *Mt. Hood is a composite volcano in Oregon.*

Soils from Lava and Ash

 **INTEGRATING ENVIRONMENTAL SCIENCE** The lava, ash, and cinders that erupt from a volcano are initially barren. Over time, however, the hard surface of the lava flow breaks down to form soil. As soil develops, plants are able to grow. Some volcanic soils are among the richest soils in the world. Saying that soil is rich means that it's fertile, or able to support plant growth. Volcanic ash also breaks down and releases potassium, phosphorus, and other materials that plants need. Why would anyone live near an active volcano? People settle close to volcanoes to take advantage of the fertile volcanic soil.

☑ *Checkpoint* *How does volcanic soil form?*

Landforms from Magma

Sometimes magma forces its way through cracks in the upper crust, but fails to reach the surface. There the magma cools and hardens into rock. Eventually, the forces that wear away Earth's surface—such as flowing water, ice, or wind—may strip away the layers of rock above the magma and expose it. **Features formed by magma include volcanic necks, dikes, and sills, as well as batholiths and dome mountains.**

Volcanic Necks, Dikes, and Sills A volcanic neck looks like a giant tooth stuck in the ground. A **volcanic neck** forms when magma hardens in a volcano's pipe. The softer rock around the pipe wears away, exposing the hard rock of the volcanic neck. Magma that forces itself across rock layers hardens into a **dike.** On the other hand, when magma squeezes between layers of rock, it forms a **sill.**

Figure 12 Magma that hardens beneath the surface may form volcanic necks, dikes, and sills. *Compare and Contrast What is the difference between a dike and a sill?*

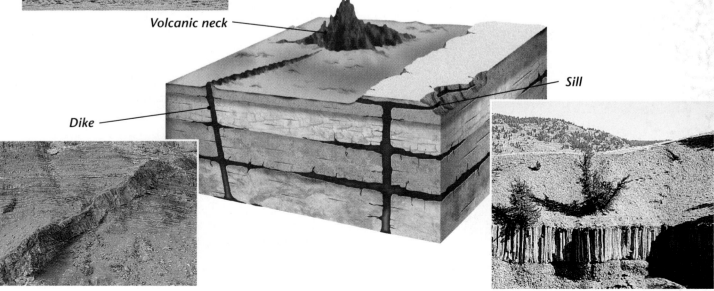

Volcanic neck

Dike

Sill

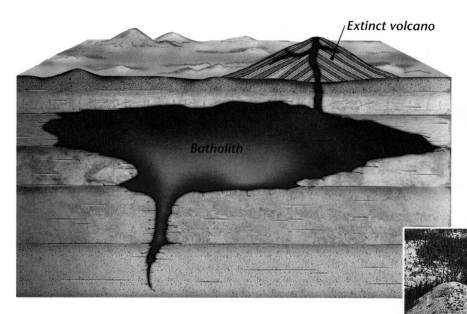

Extinct volcano

Batholith

Figure 13 A batholith forms when magma cools inside the crust. One of the largest batholiths in North America forms the core of the Sierra Nevada mountains in California. These mountains in Yosemite National Park are part of that granite batholith.

Batholiths Large rock masses called batholiths form the core of many mountain ranges. A **batholith** (BATH uh lith) is a mass of rock formed when a large body of magma cools inside the crust. The diagram in Figure 13 shows how a batholith looks when it forms. The photograph shows how it looks when the layers of rock above it have worn away.

Dome Mountains Other, smaller bodies of magma can create dome mountains. A dome mountain forms when rising magma is blocked by horizontal layers of rock. The magma forces the layers of rock to bend upward into a dome shape. Eventually, the rock above the dome mountain wears away, leaving it exposed. This process formed the Black Hills in South Dakota.

Section 3 Review

1. Describe five landforms formed from lava and ash.
2. Describe the process that creates a lava plateau.
3. What features form as a result of magma hardening beneath Earth's surface?
4. Describe how a dome mountain can eventually form out of magma that hardened beneath Earth's surface.
5. **Thinking Critically Relating Cause and Effect** Explain the formation of a volcanic landform that can result when a volcano uses up the magma in its magma chamber.

Check Your Progress

CHAPTER PROJECT

By now you should have collected information about what it's like to live in a volcanic region. Do you need to do more research? Now begin to plan your presentation. One way to plan a presentation is to prepare storyboards. In a storyboard, you sketch each major step in the presentation on a separate sheet of paper. Decide who in your group is presenting each portion.

Gelatin Volcanoes

Does the magma inside a volcano move along fractures, or through tubes or pipes? How does the eruption of magma create features such as dikes and sills? You can use a gelatin volcano model and red-colored liquid "magma" to find answers to these questions.

Problem

How does magma move inside a volcano?

Skills Focus

developing hypotheses, making models, observing

Materials

plastic cup
plastic knife
tray or shallow pan
aluminum pizza pan with holes punched
   at 2.5-cm intervals
unflavored gelatin mold in bowl
red food coloring and water
plastic syringe, 10 cc
3 small cardboard oatmeal boxes
rubber gloves
unlined paper

Procedure

1. Before magma erupts as lava, how does it travel up from underground magma chambers? Record your hypothesis.
2. Remove the gelatin from the refrigerator. Loosen the gelatin from its container by briefly placing the container of gelatin in a larger bowl of hot water.

3. Place the pizza pan over the gelatin so the mold is near the center of the pizza pan. While holding the pizza pan against the top of the mold, carefully turn the mold and the pizza pan upside down.
4. Place the pizza pan with the gelatin mold on top of the oatmeal boxes as shown in the photograph.
5. Carefully lift the bowl off the gelatin mold to create a gelatin volcano.
6. Fill the syringe with the red water ("magma"). Remove air bubbles from the syringe by holding it upright and squirting out a small amount of water.
7. Insert the tip of the syringe through a hole in the pizza pan near the center of the gelatin volcano. Inject the magma into the gelatin very slowly. It should take at least 30 seconds to empty the syringe. Observe what happens to the magma.
8. Repeat steps 6 and 7 as many times as possible. Observe the movement of the magma each time. Note any differences in the direction the magma takes when the syringe is inserted into different parts of the gelatin volcano. Record your observations.
9. Look down on your gelatin volcano from above. Make a sketch of the positions and shapes of the magma bodies. Label your drawing "Top View."
10. Carefully use a knife to cut your volcano in half. Separate the pieces and examine the cut surfaces for traces of the magma bodies.
11. Sketch the positions and shapes of the magma bodies on one of the cut faces. Label your drawing "Cross Section."

Analyze and Conclude

1. Describe how the magma moved through your model. Did the magma move straight up through the center of your model volcano or did it branch off in places? Explain why you think the magma moved in this way.
2. What knowledge or experience did you use to develop your hypothesis? How did the actual movement compare with your hypothesis?
3. Were there differences in the direction the magma flowed when the syringe was inserted in different parts of the gelatin volcano?
4. **Apply** How does what you observed in your model compare to the way magma moves through real volcanoes?

Plan to repeat the experiment using a mold made of two layers of gelatin. Before injecting the magma, predict what effect the layering will have on magma movement. Record your observations to determine if your hypothesis was correct. What volcanic feature is produced by this version of the model? Can you think of other volcanic features that you could model using gelatin layers?

SECTION 4 Volcanoes in the Solar System

DISCOVER

What Forces Shaped the Surface of Io?

Io is a moon of Jupiter. Pictures taken by the *Voyager* space probe as it passed by Io in 1979 show signs of unusual features and activity on Io.

1. Observe the blue cloud rising above the rim of Io in the top photo. What do you think it could be?

2. Look at the feature on Io's surface shown in the bottom photo. What do you think it looks like?

Think It Over

Posing Questions Is the volcanic activity on Io similar to that on Earth? State several questions that you would like to answer in order to find out.

GUIDE FOR READING

◆ How do volcanoes on Mars and Venus compare with volcanoes on Earth?

◆ What volcanic activity is found on the moons of Jupiter and Neptune?

Reading Tip Before you read, preview the headings in the section. Then predict where, besides Earth, volcanoes are found in the solar system.

Earth is not the only body in the solar system to show signs of volcanic activity. Pictures taken by space probes show evidence of past volcanic activity on Mercury, Venus, and Mars. These planets—like Earth and its moon—have rocky crusts. Scientists think these planets once had hot, molten cores. The heat caused volcanic activity. But because these planets are smaller than Earth, their cores have cooled, bringing volcanic activity to an end.

Geologists are eager for information about other planets and moons. By comparing other bodies in the solar system with Earth, geologists can learn more about the processes that have shaped Earth over billions of years.

Earth's Moon

If you looked at the full moon through a telescope you would notice that much of the moon's surface is pockmarked with light-colored craters. Other, darker areas on the moon's surface look unusually smooth. The craters mark where meteorites have smashed into the moon over billions of years. The smooth areas are where lava flowed onto the moon's surface more than three billion years ago.

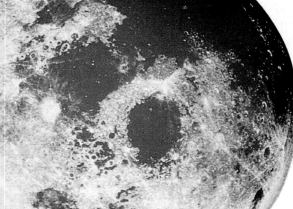

Figure 14 The dark areas on the moon's surface are flat plains made of basalt, a type of rock formed from lava.

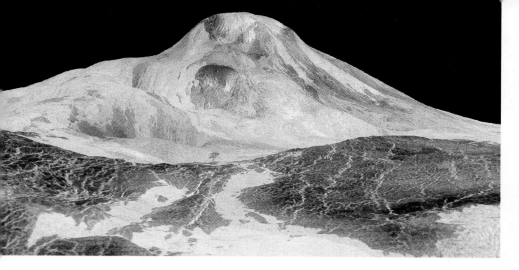

Figure 15 The space probe *Magellan* observed volcanoes on Venus, but no recent or ongoing eruptions.

Volcanoes on Venus

Geologists were excited about the results of the space probe *Magellan's* mission to Venus in 1990. Venus shows signs of widespread volcanic activity that lasted for billions of years. Venus has thousands of volcanoes. There are about 150 large volcanoes measuring between 100 and 600 kilometers across and about half a kilometer high. The largest volcano on Venus, Theia Mons, is 800 kilometers across and 4 kilometers high. Scientists are trying to find evidence that volcanoes on Venus are still active.

Like Earth, Venus has volcanic mountains and other features that are probably made of thin, runny lava. Such lava produces gently sloping shield volcanoes with broad bases, as well as long, riverlike lava flows. One of the lava flows on Venus is more than 6,800 kilometers long!

☑ *Checkpoint* *What type of volcano is most common on Venus?*

Volcanoes on Mars

Mars is a planet with a long history of volcanic activity. However, there are far fewer volcanoes on Mars than on Venus. Volcanoes are found in only a few regions of Mars' surface.

Mars has a variety of volcanic features. **On Mars there are large shield volcanoes similar to those on Venus and Earth, as well as cone-shaped volcanoes and lava flows.** Mars also has lava plains that resemble the lava flows on the moon.

The biggest volcano on Mars is the largest mountain in the solar system. This volcano, Olympus Mons, is a shield volcano similar to Mauna Loa on the island of Hawaii, but much, much bigger! Olympus Mons covers an area as large as Ohio. This huge volcano, shown in Figure 16, is over eight times taller than Theia Mons on Venus.

Figure 16 Scientists estimate that Olympus Mons on Mars is about one billion years old. Around most of the base of Olympus Mons is a huge cliff that in places is 10 kilometers high—more than 5 times the height of the Grand Canyon.

Figure 17 The surface of Neptune's moon Triton has areas covered by frozen "lava lakes" that show where liquid material erupted from inside Triton. *Posing Questions Imagine that you are observing Triton from a spacecraft. What questions would you want to answer about volcanic activity there?*

Scientists estimate that volcanic activity on Mars probably goes back about 3.5 billion years, to about the same time as the volcanic activity on the moon. Martian volcanoes don't seem to be active. Lava flows on Olympus Mons may be more than 100 million years old.

Volcanoes on Distant Moons

Besides Earth, there are only two other bodies in the solar system where volcanic eruptions have been observed: Io, a moon of the planet Jupiter, and Triton, a moon of the planet Neptune. *Voyager 1* photographed eruptions on these moons as it sped past them in 1979. Geologists on Earth were amazed when they saw these pictures. **Io and Triton have volcanic features very different from those on Earth, Mars, and Venus.** On Io, sulfur volcanoes erupt like fountains or spread out like umbrellas above the colorful surface.

The eruptions on Triton involve nitrogen. On Earth, nitrogen is a gas. Triton is so cold, however, that most of the nitrogen there is frozen solid. Scientists hypothesize that Triton's surface, which is made up of frozen water and other materials, absorbs heat from the sun. This heat melts some of the frozen nitrogen underneath Triton's surface. The liquid nitrogen then expands and erupts through the planet's icy crust.

Other moons of Jupiter, Saturn, and Neptune show signs of volcanic activity, but space probes have not observed any eruptions in progress on these moons.

Section 4 Review

1. Describe volcanic features found on Venus and Mars. Do volcanic features on these planets resemble volcanic features on Earth? Explain.

2. How is volcanic activity on the moons of Jupiter and Neptune different from volcanic activity on Earth?

3. What is the largest volcano in the solar system? What type of volcano is it?

4. **Thinking Critically Comparing and Contrasting** How do the volcanoes on Venus compare with the volcanoes on Mars?

Check Your Progress CHAPTER PROJECT
By this time, your group should have planned your documentary and know what materials you will need. Put the finishing touches on your presentation. Make sure any posters, overhead transparencies, or computer art will be easy for your audience to read. If you are using video or audio, make your recordings now. Revise and polish any narrative, rap, or skit. *(Hint: Check the length of your presentation.)*

SECTION 1 Volcanoes and Plate Tectonics

Key Ideas

◆ A volcano is an opening on Earth's surface where magma escapes from the interior. Magma that reaches Earth's surface is called lava.

◆ The constructive force of volcanoes adds new rock to existing land and forms new islands.

◆ Most volcanoes occur near the boundaries of Earth's plates and along the edges of continents, in island arcs, or along mid-ocean ridges.

Key Terms

volcano	lava	island arc
magma	Ring of Fire	hot spot

SECTION 2 Volcanic Activity

Key Ideas

◆ An eruption occurs when gases trapped in magma rush through an opening at the Earth's surface, carrying magma with them.

◆ Volcanoes can erupt quietly or explosively, depending on the amount of dissolved gases in the magma and on how thick or runny the magma is.

◆ When magma heats water underground, hot springs and geysers form.

◆ Volcano hazards include pyroclastic flows, avalanches of mud, damage from ash, lava flows, flooding, and deadly gases.

Key Terms

magma chamber	pyroclastic flow
pipe	active
vent	dormant
lava flow	extinct
crater	hot spring
silica	geyser
pahoehoe	geothermal energy
aa	

SECTION 3 Volcanic Landforms

Key Ideas

◆ Lava and other volcanic materials on the surface create shield volcanoes, cinder cones, composite volcanoes, and plateaus.

◆ Magma that hardens beneath the surface creates batholiths, dome mountains, dikes, and sills, which are eventually exposed when the covering rock wears away.

Key Terms

shield volcano	caldera	sill
cinder cone	volcanic neck	batholith
composite volcano	dike	

SECTION 4 Volcanoes in the Solar System

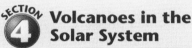 *INTEGRATING SPACE SCIENCE*

Key Ideas

◆ Venus and Mars both have extinct volcanoes similar to volcanoes on Earth.

◆ Spacecraft have photographed volcanic activity on moons of Jupiter and Neptune.

Organizing Information

Concept Map Copy the concept map about types of volcanic mountains onto a separate sheet of paper. Then complete it and add a title. (For more on concept maps, see the Skills Handbook.)

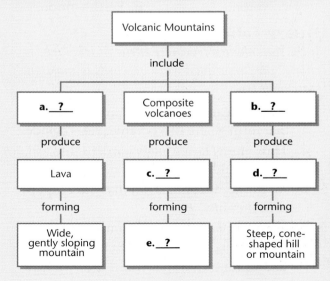

Reviewing Content

 For more review of key concepts, see the Interactive Student Tutorial CD-ROM.

Multiple Choice

Choose the letter of the best answer.

1. When two oceanic plates collide, the result may be
   a. volcanoes on the edge of a continent.
   b. a hot spot volcano.
   c. volcanoes in an island arc.
   d. a volcano along the mid-ocean ridge.
2. The force that causes magma to erupt at the surface is provided by
   a. heat.
   b. the shape of the pipe.
   c. geothermal energy.
   d. dissolved gases under pressure.
3. An eruption of thin, fluid lava would most likely be
   a. a cinder-cone eruption.
   b. an explosive eruption.
   c. a quiet eruption.
   d. a pyroclastic eruption.
4. Alternating layers of lava and volcanic ash are found in
   a. dome mountains.
   b. dikes and sills.
   c. shield volcanoes.
   d. composite volcanoes.
5. Which of the following has active volcanoes?
   a. Venus   b. Mars
   c. Triton   d. Earth's moon

True or False

If the statement is true, write true. If it is false, change the underlined word or words to make the statement true.

6. Many volcanoes are found in <u>island arcs</u> that form where two oceanic plates collide.
7. Thin, runny lava usually hardens into <u>ash, cinders, and bombs</u>.
8. An <u>extinct</u> volcano is not likely to erupt in your lifetime.
9. <u>Hot spots</u> form where a plume of magma rises through the crust from the mantle.
10. The volcano Olympus Mons is on <u>Venus</u>.

Checking Concepts

11. What is the Ring of Fire?
12. How does plate tectonics explain the volcanoes that form along the mid-ocean ridge?
13. Where are hot spot volcanoes located in relation to Earth's plates?
14. What effect does silica content have on the characteristics of magma?
15. Describe the three stages in the "life-cycle" of a volcano.
16. How do hot springs and geysers form?
17. While observing a lava flow from a recently active volcano, you notice an area of lava with a rough, chunky surface. What type of lava is this and how does it form?
18. How does a shield volcano form?
19. Why can earthquakes be a warning sign that an eruption is about to happen?
20. **Writing to Learn** Pretend you are a newspaper reporter in 1980. You have been assigned to report on the eruption of Mount St. Helens. Write a news story describing your observations.

Thinking Critically

21. **Applying Concepts** Is a volcanic eruption likely to occur on the east coast of the United States? Explain your answer.
22. **Comparing and Contrasting** Compare the way in which an island arc forms with the way in which a hot spot volcano forms.
23. **Making Generalizations** How might a volcanic eruption affect the area around a volcano, including its plant and animal life?
24. **Relating Cause and Effect** Why doesn't the type of eruption that produces a lava plateau produce a volcanic mountain instead?
25. **Making Generalizations** What is one major difference between volcanic activity on Earth and volcanic activity on Mars, Venus, and the moon? Explain.

Applying Skills

Refer to the diagram to answer Questions 26–29.

26. Classifying What is this volcano made of? How do geologists classify a volcano made of these materials?

27. Developing Hypotheses What is the feature labeled A in the diagram? What is the feature labeled B? How do these features form?

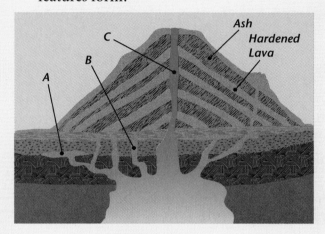

28. Inferring This volcano is located where oceanic crust is subducted under continental crust. Would the volcano erupt quietly or explosively? Give reasons for your answer.

29. Predicting What is the feature labeled C in the diagram? If this feature becomes plugged with hardened magma, what could happen to the volcano? Explain.

Test Preparation

Use these questions to prepare for standardized tests.

Read the passage. Then answer Questions 30–33.

Newsflash! At 8:30 A.M. today, May 8, 1980, Mount St. Helens in Washington State erupted. It blew away 400 meters of its top. A pyroclastic flow roared out of the volcano and burned leaves on trees 20 kilometers away. The volcano also blasted a cloud of ash 25 kilometers into the atmosphere. The cloud is drifting across several northwestern states, dumping a thick carpet of ash.

What led to this eruption? For 123 years, the snow-capped volcano had stood quietly. People thought it was dormant. But in March, the volcano began to rumble with small earthquakes. Scientists knew this meant magma was moving inside the volcano. In the weeks before the eruption, part of the mountain's northeastern slope also began to bulge. Then, in a moment, Mount St. Helens changed forever.

30. A good title for this passage is
 a. "Volcanoes of Washington State."
 b. "The Dramatic Eruption of Mount St. Helens."
 c. "The Danger of Volcanic Ash."
 d. "A Dormant Volcano."

31. The series of small earthquakes before the eruption of Mount St. Helens was the result of
 a. movement along nearby faults.
 b. water building up inside the volcano.
 c. movement of magma inside the volcano.
 d. the formation of a new caldera.

32. In the weeks before Mount St. Helens erupted, the volcano
 a. let off some steam. b. was very quiet.
 c. glowed at night. d. began to bulge.

33. Farm crops in nearby states would have been most affected by the volcano's
 a. ash. b. lava flows.
 c. cinders and bombs. d. pyroclastic flow.

FOCUS ON FAULTS

"When I was about fourteen, my family was living in Taiwan," Geologist Carol Prentice recalls. "One day I was playing pinball, and a little earthquake happened. It tilted my pinball machine."

Unlike most people experiencing their first quake, her reaction was not fright but fascination. "*What in the world is that?* I wondered. That was the first time I consciously remember thinking that earthquakes were something interesting." Later, she recalls, "When I was teaching earth science in high school, I realized that my favorite section to teach was on earthquakes and faults."

During an earthquake, forces from inside Earth fracture, or break, Earth's crust, producing a powerful jolt called an earthquake. As Earth's crust moves and breaks, it forms cracks called faults. Over the centuries, the faults may move again and again.

Geologist Carol Prentice climbs into these faults to study the soil and rocks. She hunts for clues about the history of a fault and estimates the risk of a serious earthquake in the future.

Carol Prentice studied geology at Humboldt State University and the California Institute of Technology. She is currently a Research Geologist for the United States Geological Survey in Menlo Park, California.

Finding Clues to Ancient Earthquakes

Today, Dr. Prentice is an expert in the field of paleoseismology. *Paleo* means "ancient" and *seismology* is "the study of earthquakes." So it's the study of ancient earthquakes. "Paleoseismologists search for evidence of earthquakes that happened hundreds or thousands of years ago," explains Dr. Prentice.

There are written records about earthquakes that happened years ago. But the real story of a quake is written in the rocks and soil. Years after an earthquake, wind, rain, and flowing water can wear the fault lines away from Earth's surface. Then the evidence of the quake is buried under layers of sediment. But the fault is still there.

The cracks of recent earthquakes, such as the Gobi-Altay fault shown here, are sometimes visible for hundreds of kilometers. Because this quake happened in the Mongolian desert, it is especially easy to see.

Choosing a Site

How do you pick a site to research? "First we study aerial photographs, geological maps, and satellite images of the fault line," Dr. Prentice explains. "We will have some sites in mind. Then, we go out and look at the sites and do some digging with a shovel to get samples."

"We look for places where sediments, such as sand and gravel, have been building up. If sediments have been depositing there for many thousands of years, you're likely to have a good record of prehistoric earthquakes at that site. When you dig, you're likely to see not only the most recent earthquake buried and preserved in the sediments, but also earlier earthquakes. That's a really good site." Once the site is established, the geological team begins digging a trench across the fault.

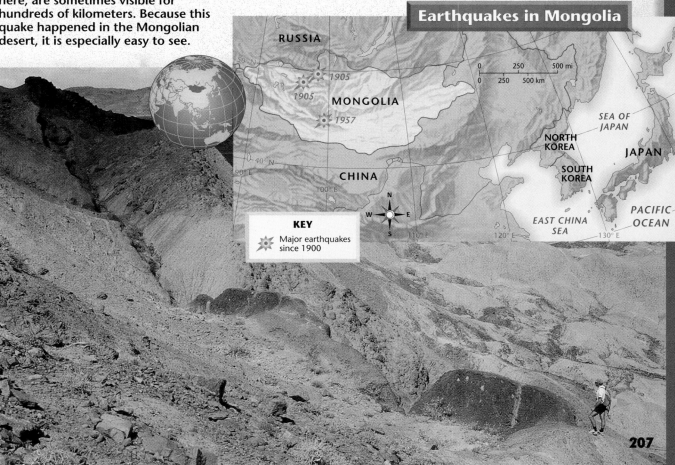

Earthquakes in Mongolia

RUSSIA

1905

1905

MONGOLIA

1957

CHINA

SEA OF JAPAN

NORTH KOREA

SOUTH KOREA

JAPAN

EAST CHINA SEA

PACIFIC OCEAN

0   250   500 mi
0   250   500 km

KEY

Major earthquakes since 1900

N W E S

40° N

90° E

100° E

110° E

120° E

130° E

Working in the Trenches

What's it like to work in a spot where Earth's surface ruptured? Does Carol Prentice ever think that an earthquake might occur when she is digging in the fault? "It's always in the back of your mind when you are working in the trench," she admits.

But, she says, "The trenches are dangerous, not so much because there might be an earthquake while you are working there but because the trench can cave in. If a trench is 4 to 5 meters deep, or just over your head, it needs shores—braces and supports— or it might cave in. When sediments are soft, and the trench is deep, it's more likely to cave in. That could happen in a place like Mongolia."

Carol (in back) and another geologist in a deep trench.

In Mongolia, in northeast Asia, it's difficult for geologists to find the right materials to support a deep trench. It could cave in while someone is in it. "That would be very frightening," she says.

Looking at the Gobi-Altay Quake

Carol Prentice travels to earthquake sites around the world—Dominican Republic, Thailand, Mongolia—as well as to the San Andreas fault in California. One of Dr. Prentice's most recent research expeditions was to the site of the monster Gobi-Altay earthquake of 1957 in the Mongolian desert. In earthquakes like this one, the faults are easy to see. "We're taking a look at this Gobi Altay earthquake and seeing whether the next-to-last earthquake had the same pattern," Dr. Prentice says.

The faults of the Gobi-Altay earthquake are similar in some ways to the San Andreas fault and to the faults of other earthquakes in the United States. That's one of the reasons the Gobi-Altay is so interesting to geologists.

Interpreting the Data

When Dr. Prentice finds evidence of several earthquakes in one spot, she takes measurements that tell her when the layers of rocks, sand, and gravel were deposited and when they split. From that she knows when and how frequently earthquakes have occurred there.

She also determines how fast the opposite sides of the fault are slipping past each other. "Those two pieces of information— the dates of prehistoric earthquakes and the slip rate—are very, very important in trying to

String grid lines are used to map out sections of the trench.

Shores support the trench walls.

An earthquake is caused by movement on a fault deep beneath Earth's surface. If this movement is large enough, it can cause cracks in the ground surface. Over the years, layers of sediment are deposited on top of the crack. The next earthquake causes a new crack in the surface, and new sediments are deposited. By studying evidence of the cracks in these layers of sediment, geologists learn about past earthquakes along the fault.

figure out how dangerous a particular fault is," Dr. Prentice explains.

Since faults don't move every year, but over thousands of years, you can figure out the average slip per year and make some predictions. The faster the fault is moving, the greater the danger. "We can look at the landforms around a fault.

> **" . . . the real story of a quake is written in the rocks and soil. "**

We can look at what our instruments record, and say: This is an active fault. Someday it might produce a big earthquake, but what we really want to know is when. Is that earthquake likely to happen in the next fifty years, in the next hundred years, or is it going to be a thousand years before the next big earthquake?"

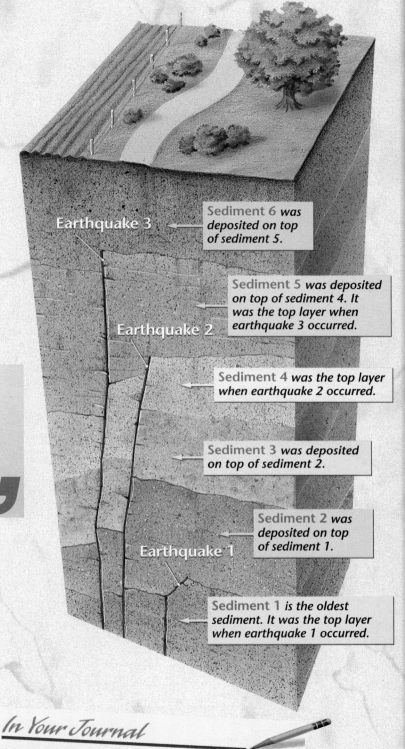

Earthquake 3

Sediment 6 *was deposited on top of sediment 5.*

Sediment 5 *was deposited on top of sediment 4. It was the top layer when earthquake 3 occurred.*

Earthquake 2

Sediment 4 *was the top layer when earthquake 2 occurred.*

Sediment 3 *was deposited on top of sediment 2.*

Sediment 2 *was deposited on top of sediment 1.*

Earthquake 1

Sediment 1 *is the oldest sediment. It was the top layer when earthquake 1 occurred.*

In Your Journal

Carol Prentice relies on close observation and making inferences in her study of earthquakes. Write a paragraph describing some of the other skills that Dr. Prentice needs to do her work as a paleoseismologist.

CHAPTER

7 Weathering and Soil Formation

WEB ACTIVITY www.phschool.com

Soils for Seeds

High above Paris, weathering attacks limestone statues that are hundreds of years old. The process of weathering affects all rocks exposed on Earth's surface. Weathering breaks rock down into smaller and smaller particles. When other ingredients, such as decayed plant and animal materials, mix with the rock particles, the mixture is called soil. In this chapter, you will test how soil and other growing materials affect the growth of plants.

Your Goal To determine how soil composition affects the growth of bean seeds.

To complete this project successfully, you must

◆ examine your different growing materials and compare their particle size, shape, and composition

◆ compare how bean seeds grow in several diffferent growing materials

◆ determine what type of soil or growing material is best for young bean plants

Get Started With your group, brainstorm what types of soil and other growing materials you will use in your experiment. Also consider these questions: What are the different variables that affect the growth of plants? How will you control these variables in your experiment? How will you measure the growth of your bean plants? Plan your experiment and obtain your teacher's approval.

Check Your Progress You will be working on this project as you study this chapter. To keep your project on track, look for Check Your Progress boxes at the following points.

Section 2 Review, page 227: Describe the different growing materials you have collected, and plant your bean seeds.

Section 3 Review, page 234: Observe and record the results of the growth of bean plants.

Present Your Project At the end of the chapter (page 243), you will present your results to the class. Your presentation will analyze how well bean plants grew in the different types of growing materials.

Integrating Environmental Science

SECTION 4

Waste Disposal and Recycling

Discover What's in the Trash?
Sharpen Your Skills Graphing
Try This It's In the Numbers
Science at Home Trash Weigh-In

These stone gargoyles on the cathedral of Notre Dame in Paris, France, are wearing away because of weathering.

SECTION 1 Rocks and Weathering

DISCOVER — ACTIVITY

How Fast Can It Fizz?

1.  Place a fizzing antacid tablet in a small beaker. Then grind up a second tablet and place it in another beaker. The whole tablet is a model of solid rock. The ground-up tablet is a model of rock fragments.

2. Add 100 mL of warm water to the beaker containing the whole tablet. Then stir with a stirring rod until the tablet dissolves completely. Use a stopwatch to time how long it takes.

3. Add 100 mL of warm water to the beaker containing the ground-up tablet. Then stir until all of the ground-up tablet dissolves. Time how long it takes.

Think It Over

Inferring Which dissolved faster, the whole antacid tablet or the ground-up tablet? What difference between the two affected how long it took them to dissolve?

GUIDE FOR READING

◆ What causes mechanical weathering?

◆ What causes chemical weathering?

◆ What determines how fast weathering occurs?

Reading Tip As you read, use the headings to make an outline about weathering.

Imagine a hike that lasts for months and covers hundreds of kilometers. Each year, many hikers go on such treks. They hike trails that run the length of America's great mountain ranges. For example, the John Muir Trail follows the Sierra Nevada mountains. The Sierras extend about 640 kilometers along the eastern side of California. In the east, the Appalachian Trail follows the Appalachian Mountains. The Appalachians stretch more than 2,000 kilometers from Alabama to Maine.

The two trails cross very different landscapes. The Sierras are rocky and steep, with many peaks rising 3,000 meters above sea level. The Appalachians are more rounded and gently sloping, and are covered with soil and plants. The highest peaks in the Appalachians are less than half the elevation of the highest peaks in the Sierras. Which mountain range do you think is older? The Appalachians formed more than 250 million years ago. The Sierras formed only within the last 10 million years. The forces that wear down rock on Earth's surface have had much longer to grind down the Appalachians.

The Effects of Weathering

The process of mountain building thrusts rock up to the Earth's surface. There, the rock becomes exposed to weathering. **Weathering** is the process that breaks down rock and other substances at Earth's surface. Heat, cold, water, and ice all contribute to weathering. So do the oxygen and carbon dioxide in the atmosphere. Repeated freezing

Figure 1 The jagged, rocky peaks of the Sierra Nevadas (left) show that the mountains are young. The more gently sloping Appalachians (right) have been exposed to weathering for 250 million years.

and thawing, for example, can crack rock apart into smaller pieces. Rainwater can dissolve minerals that bind rock together. You don't need to go to the mountains to see examples of weathering. The forces that wear down mountains also cause bicycles to rust, paint to peel, sidewalks to crack, and potholes to form.

The forces of weathering break rocks into smaller and smaller pieces. Then the forces of erosion carry the pieces away. **Erosion** (ee ROH zhun) is the movement of rock particles by wind, water, ice, or gravity. Weathering and erosion work together continuously to wear down and carry away the rocks at Earth's surface.

There are two kinds of weathering: mechanical weathering and chemical weathering. Both types of weathering act slowly, but over time they break down even the biggest, hardest rocks.

✓ *Checkpoint* *What is the difference between weathering and erosion?*

Mechanical Weathering

If you hit a rock hard enough with a hammer, the rock will break into pieces. Some forces of weathering can also break rock into pieces. The type of weathering in which rock is physically broken into smaller pieces is called **mechanical weathering.** These smaller pieces of rock have the same composition as the rock they came from. If you have seen rocks that are cracked or peeling in layers, then you have seen rocks that are undergoing mechanical weathering.

Mechanical weathering breaks rock into pieces by freezing and thawing, release of pressure, growth of plants, actions of animals, and abrasion. The term **abrasion** (uh BRAY zhun) refers to the grinding away of rock by rock particles carried by water, ice, wind, or gravity. Mechanical weathering works slowly. But over very long periods of time, it does more than wear down rocks. Mechanical weathering eventually wears away whole mountains.

In cool climates, the most important force of mechanical weathering is freezing and thawing of water. Water seeps into cracks in rocks and then freezes when the temperature drops. Water expands when it freezes. Ice therefore acts like a wedge, a simple machine that forces things apart. Wedges of ice in rocks widen and deepen cracks. This process is called **ice wedging.** When the ice melts, the water seeps deeper into the cracks. With repeated freezing and thawing, the cracks slowly expand until pieces of rock break off. *Exploring the Forces of Mechanical Weathering* shows how this process weathers rock.

✓ *Checkpoint* *How does ice wedging weather rock?*

EXPLORING the Forces of Mechanical Weathering

Mechanical weathering affects all the rock on Earth's surface. Given enough time, mechanical weathering can break down a massive mountain into tiny particles of sand.

Release of Pressure
As erosion removes material from the surface of a mass of rock, pressure on the rock below is reduced. This release of pressure causes the outside of the rock to crack and flake off like the layers of an onion.

Freezing and Thawing
When water freezes in a crack in a rock, it expands and makes the crack bigger. The process of ice wedging also widens cracks in sidewalks and causes potholes in streets.

Chemical Weathering

In addition to mechanical weathering, another type of weathering attacks rock. **Chemical weathering** is the process that breaks down rock through chemical changes. **The agents of chemical weathering include water, oxygen, carbon dioxide, living organisms, and acid rain.**

Chemical weathering produces rock particles that have a different mineral makeup from the rock they came from. Each rock is made up of one or more minerals. For example, granite is made up of several minerals, including feldspar, quartz, and mica. But chemical weathering of granite eventually changes the feldspar minerals to clay minerals.

Plant Growth
Roots of trees and other plants enter cracks in rocks. As the roots grow, they force the cracks farther apart. Over time, the roots of even small plants can pry apart cracked rocks.

Abrasion
Sand and other rock particles that are carried by wind, water, or ice can wear away exposed rock surfaces like sandpaper on wood. Wind-driven sand helped shape the rocks shown here.

Animal Actions
Animals that burrow in the ground—including moles, gophers, prairie dogs, and some insects—loosen and break apart rocks in the soil.

Figure 2 As weathering breaks apart rock, the surface area exposed to further weathering increases.

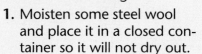

Chemical weathering creates holes or soft spots in rock, so the rock breaks apart more easily. Chemical and mechanical weathering often work together. As mechanical weathering breaks rock into pieces, more surface area becomes exposed to chemical weathering. The Discover activity in this section shows how increasing the surface area increases the rate of a chemical reaction.

Water Water is the most important agent of chemical weathering. Water weathers rock by dissolving it. When a rock or other substance dissolves in water, it mixes uniformly throughout the water to make a solution. Over time, many rocks will dissolve in water.

Oxygen The oxygen gas in air is an important cause of chemical weathering. If you have ever left a bicycle or metal tool outside in the rain, then you have seen how oxygen can weather iron. Iron combines with oxygen in the presence of water in a process called oxidation. The product of oxidation is rust. Rock that contains iron also oxidizes, or rusts. Rust makes rock soft and crumbly and gives it a red or brown color.

Carbon Dioxide Another gas found in air, carbon dioxide, also causes chemical weathering. Carbon dioxide becomes dissolved in rainwater and in water that sinks through air pockets in the soil. The result is a weak acid called carbonic acid. Carbonic acid easily weathers marble and limestone.

Living Organisms Imagine a seed landing on a rock face. As it sprouts, its roots push into cracks in the rock. As the plant's roots grow, they produce weak acids that slowly dissolve rock around the roots. Lichens—plantlike organisms that grow on rocks—also produce weak acids that chemically weather rock.

Acid Rain Over the past 150 years, people have been burning

INTEGRATING ENVIRONMENTAL SCIENCE large amounts of coal, oil, and gas for energy. Burning these fuels can pollute the air with sulfur, carbon, and nitrogen compounds. Such compounds react chemically with the water vapor in clouds, forming acids. These acids mix with raindrops and fall as acid rain. Acid rain causes very rapid chemical weathering.

Rate of Weathering

Visitors to New England's historic cemeteries may notice a surprising fact. Slate tombstones from the 1700s are less weathered and easier to read than marble gravestones from the 1800s. Why is this so? **The most important factors that determine the rate at which weathering occurs are type of rock and climate.**

Type of Rock Some kinds of rocks weather more rapidly than others. The minerals that make up the rock determine how fast it weathers. Rock made of minerals that do not dissolve easily in water weathers slowly. Rock made of minerals that dissolve easily in water weathers faster.

Some rock weathers easily because it is permeable. **Permeable** (PUR mee uh bul) means that a material is full of tiny, connected air spaces that allow water to seep through it. Permeable rock weathers chemically at a fast rate. Why? As water seeps through the spaces in the rock, it removes dissolved material formed by weathering.

Climate Climate refers to the average weather conditions in an area. Both chemical and mechanical weathering occur faster in wet climates. Rainfall provides the water needed for chemical changes as well as for freezing and thawing.

Chemical reactions occur faster at higher temperatures. That is why chemical weathering occurs more quickly where the climate is both hot and wet. Granite, for example, is a very hard rock that forms when molten material cools inside Earth. Granite weathers so slowly in cool climates that it is often used as a building stone. But in hot and wet climates, granite weathers faster and eventually crumbles apart.

Figure 3 The rate of weathering of these tombstones depends on the type of rock. Slate (top) resists weathering better than marble (bottom). *Inferring What type of weathering probably wore away the letters on the marble tombstone?*

Section 1 Review

1. What factors cause mechanical weathering?
2. Describe three causes of chemical weathering.
3. What factors affect the rate of weathering?
4. Explain why chemical weathering occurs faster in hot, wet climates than in cool, dry climates.
5. **Thinking Critically** **Predicting** Suppose you see a large boulder with several cracks in it. What would you expect to see if you could observe the boulder again in several hundred years? Explain.

Science at Home

Ice in a Straw Here's how to demonstrate one type of weathering for your family. Plug one end of a drinking straw with a small piece of clay. Fill the straw with water. Now plug the top of the straw with clay. Make sure that the clay plugs do not leak. Lay the straw flat in the freezer overnight. Remove the straw the next day. What happened to the clay plugs? What process produced this result? Be sure to dispose of the straw so that no one will use it for drinking.

Controlling Variables

ROCK SHAKE

Which do you think would weather faster, a rock attacked by plant acids or a rock in the rushing waters of a stream? Many factors affect the rate at which rock weathers. In this lab, you will compare the rates of weathering that take place under different conditions.

Problem

How will shaking and acid conditions affect the rate at which limestone weathers?

Materials

300 mL of water
balance
paper towels
masking tape
2 pieces of thin cloth
marking pen or pencil
300 mL of vinegar, an acid
plastic graduated cylinder, 250 mL
80 small pieces of water-soaked limestone
4 watertight plastic containers with
    screw-on caps, 500-mL

Procedure

Part 1—Day 1

1. Using masking tape, label the four 500-mL containers A, B, C, and D.
2. Separate the 80 pieces of limestone into four sets of 20.
3. Copy the data table in your notebook. Then place the first 20 pieces of limestone on the balance and record their mass in the data table. Place the rocks in Container A.
4. Repeat Step 3 for the other sets of rocks and place them in containers B, C, and D.
5. Pour 150 mL of water into container A and container B. Put caps on both containers.
6. Pour 150 mL of vinegar into container C and also into container D. Put caps on both containers.
7. Predict the effect of weathering on the mass of the limestone pieces. Which will weather more: the limestone in water or the limestone in vinegar? (*Hint:* Vinegar is an acid.) Also predict the effect of shaking on the limestone in containers B and D. Record your predictions in your notebook.
8. Allow the pieces to soak overnight.

Container	Total Mass Start	Total Mass Next Day	Change in Mass	Percent Change in Mass
A (water, no shaking)				
B (water, shaking)				
C (vinegar, no shaking)				
D (vinegar, shaking)				

Part 2—Day 2

9. Screw the caps tightly on containers B and D. Shake both containers for 10 to 15 minutes. Make sure that each container is shaken for exactly the same amount of time and at the same intensity. After shaking, set the containers aside. Do not shake containers A and C.

10. Open the top of container A. Place one piece of thin cloth over the opening of the container. Carefully pour all of the water out through the cloth into a waste container. Be careful not to let any of the pieces flow out with the water. Dry these pieces carefully and record their mass in your data table.

11. Next, determine how much limestone was lost through weathering in container A. (*Hint:* Subtract the mass of the limestone pieces remaining on Day 2 from the mass of the pieces on Day 1.)

12. Repeat Steps 10 and 11 for containers B, C, and D.

Analyze and Conclude

1. Calculate the percent change in mass of the 20 pieces for each container.

$$\% \text{ change} = \frac{\text{Change in mass} \times 100}{\text{Total mass start}}$$

Record the results in the data table.

2. Do your data show a change in mass of the 20 pieces in each of the four containers?

3. Is there a greater change in total mass for the pieces in one container than for the pieces in the other? Explain.

4. How correct were your predictions of how shaking and acid would affect the weathering of limestone? Explain.

5. If your data showed a greater change in the mass of the pieces in one of the containers, how might this change be explained?

6. **Think About It** Based on your data, which variable do you think was more responsible for breaking down the limestone: the vinegar or the shaking? Explain.

Design an Experiment

Would your results for this experiment change if you changed the variables? For example, you could soak or shake the pieces for a longer time, or test rocks other than limestone. You could also test whether adding more limestone pieces (30 rather than 20 in each set) would make a difference in the outcome. Design an experiment on the rate of weathering to test the effects of changing one of these variables. Have your teacher approve your experiment before you begin.

Preserving Stone Monuments

A statue with a human head and a lion's body crouches in the desert beside the pyramids of Egypt. This is the great Sphinx. It was carved out of limestone about 4,500 years ago. Thousands of years of weathering by water, wind, and sand have worn away much of the Sphinx's face. In the 1800s, sand that had protected the Sphinx's body was cleared away. Weathering attacked the newly exposed parts of the Sphinx. Flakes and even chunks of stone fell from the statue. Workers tried to repair the Sphinx with cement. But the repairs weakened the statue and changed its shape.

The Issues

Should Structures Be Restored?
Weathering threatens many ancient stone monuments throughout the world. Pollutants in air and rain make stone weather faster. But there are ways to slow the weathering of a monument without changing or damaging it. In 1998, workers in Egypt completed a new restoration of the Sphinx. They removed the added cement. They replaced the damaged stones with new, hand-cut limestone blocks of the same size and weight. The new stone will help protect what remains of the monument. Visitors to the Sphinx will now see only the original statue and repairs made with original materials. The new repairs preserve the statue's original shape.

Most people want the Sphinx and other monuments to be restored. But restoration is time-consuming and very expensive. And in some cases, repair work can damage or change the original structure.

Can New Technology Slow Weathering?
Advances in technology may provide some solutions. At the Sphinx, scientists measure wind direction, wind speed, and moisture in the air. This information helps scientists follow the weathering process and provides data that will help prevent more damage. Similar instruments are used at other monuments.

Other scientists are working on a way of coating stone with a chemical compound to strengthen and repair the surface. So far, they have found a compound that sticks well to sandstone, but not to marble or limestone.

What Else Can People Do? Repair and restoration are not the only options. Some say that ancient monuments should be buried again after being uncovered by archaeologists. Some people suggest that the Sphinx itself should be reburied in the sand that protected it for so many centuries. But scholars, archaeologists, and tourists disagree. Meanwhile, as people seek solutions, rain, wind, sun, and polluted air continue to take their toll.

You Decide

1. Identify the Problem
In your own words, explain the difficulties involved in preserving ancient monuments.

2. Analyze the Options
List methods for preserving ancient buildings and monuments. Note the advantages and disadvantages of repair work, technology, and other approaches.

3. Find a Solution
Make a plan to preserve a monument in your city. Write your recommendations in the form of a letter to a city mayor or town council.

② Soil Formation and Composition

DISCOVER ••••••••••••••••••••••••••••••••••••••ACTIVITY••••

What Is Soil?

1. Use a toothpick to separate a sample of soil into individual particles. With a hand lens, try to identify the different types of particles in the sample. Wash your hands when you are finished.

2. Write a "recipe" for the sample of soil, naming each of the "ingredients" that you think the soil contains. Include what percentage of each ingredient would be needed to create the soil.

3. Compare your recipe with those of your classmates.

Think It Over

Forming Operational Definitions Based on your observations, how would you define *soil*?

A bare rock surface does not look like a spot where a plant could grow. But look more closely. In that hard surface is a small crack. Over many years, mechanical and chemical weathering will slowly enlarge the crack. Rain and wind will bring bits of weathered rock, dust, and dry leaves. The wind also may carry tiny seeds. With enough moisture, a seed will sprout and take root. Then, when the plant blossoms a few months later, the rock itself will seem to have burst into flower.

Soil Formation

The crack in the rock seems to have little in common with a flower garden containing thick, rich soil. But soil is what the weathered rock and other materials in the crack have started to become. **Soil** is the loose, weathered material on Earth's surface in which plants can grow. **Soil forms as rock is broken down by weathering and mixes with other materials on the surface.**

Soil is constantly being formed wherever bedrock is exposed. **Bedrock** is the solid layer of rock beneath the soil. Once exposed at the surface, bedrock gradually weathers into smaller and smaller particles that are the basic material of soil.

GUIDE FOR READING

◆ How does soil form?

◆ What is soil made of?

◆ What is the role of plants and animals in soil formation?

Reading Tip Before you read, rewrite the headings as *how, what, where,* and *why* questions. Then look for answers as you read.

Figure 4 A crack between rocks holds just enough soil for this plant.

Composition of Loam

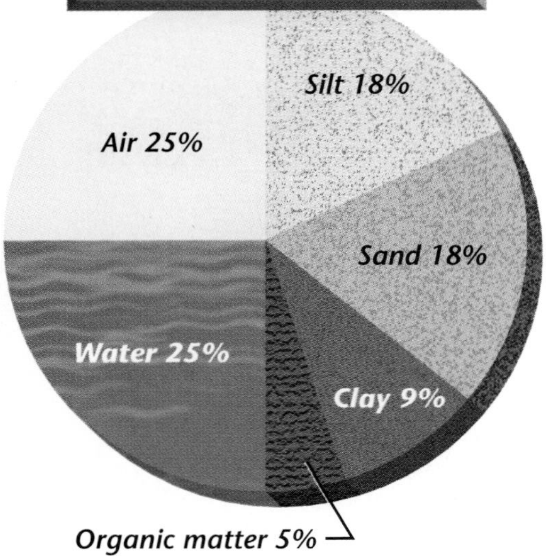

Silt 18%

Air 25%

Sand 18%

Water 25%

Clay 9%

Organic matter 5%

Figure 5 Loam, a type of soil, is made up of air, water, and organic matter as well as materials from weathered rock. The circle graph shows the composition of loam by volume. *Interpreting Graphs What two materials make up the major portion of this soil?*

Soil Composition

Soil is more than just particles of weathered bedrock. **Soil is a mixture of rock particles, minerals, decayed organic material, air, and water.**

The type of rock particles and minerals in any given soil depends on two factors: the bedrock that was weathered to form the soil and the type of weathering. Together, sand, silt, and clay make up the portion of soil that comes from weathered rock.

The decayed organic material in soil is humus. **Humus** (HYOO mus) is a dark-colored substance that forms as plant and animal remains decay. Humus helps create spaces in soil for the air and water that plants must have. Humus is also rich in the nitrogen, sulfur, phosphorus, and potassium that plants need to grow.

Soil Texture

Sand feels coarse and grainy, but clay feels smooth and silky. These differences are differences in texture. Soil texture depends on the size of individual soil particles.

The particles of rock in soil are classified by size. As you can see in Figure 6, the largest soil particles are gravel. Small pebbles and even large boulders are considered gravel. Next in size are particles of sand, followed by silt particles, which are smaller than sand. The smallest soil particles are clay. Clay particles are smaller than the period at the end of this sentence.

Soil texture is important for plant growth. Soil that is mostly clay has a dense, heavy texture. Some clay soils hold a lot of water, so plants grown in them may "drown" for lack of air. In contrast, sandy soil has a coarse texture. Water quickly drains through it, so plants may die for lack of water.

Soil that is made up of about equal parts of clay, sand, and silt is called **loam.** It has a crumbly texture that holds both air and water. Loam is best for growing most types of plants.

Figure 6 Soil particles range in size from gravel to clay particles too small to be seen by the unaided eye. The sand, silt, and clay shown here have been enlarged.

Gravel

2 mm and larger

Sand

less than 2 mm

Silt

less than $\frac{1}{16}$ mm

Clay

less than $\frac{1}{256}$ mm

Soil Horizons

Soil formation continues over a long period of time. Gradually, soil develops layers called horizons. A **soil horizon** is a layer of soil that differs in color and texture from the layers above or below it.

If you dug a hole in the ground about half a meter deep, you would see the different soil horizons. Figure 7 shows how soil scientists classify the soil into three horizons. The A horizon is made up of **topsoil,** a crumbly, dark brown soil that is a mixture of humus, clay, and other minerals. The B horizon, often called **subsoil,** usually consists of clay and other particles washed down from the A horizon, but little humus. The C horizon contains only partly weathered rock.

☑ *Checkpoint* **What are soil horizons?**

The Rate of Soil Formation

The rate at which soil forms depends on the climate and type of rock. Remember that weathering occurs most rapidly in areas with a warm, rainy climate. As a result, soil develops more quickly in these areas. In contrast, weathering and soil formation take place slowly in areas where the climate is cold and dry.

Some types of rock weather and form soil faster than others. For example, limestone weathers faster than granite. Thus, soil forms more quickly from limestone than from granite.

Sharpen your Skills

Predicting ACTIVITY

Gardeners often improve soil by adding materials to it. These added materials change the soil's composition. They make the soil more fertile or improve its ability to hold water. For example, a gardener might add compost (partly decayed leaves) to sandy soil. How would the compost change the sandy soil?

Figure 7 Soil horizons form in three steps.

1. The C horizon forms as bedrock weathers and rock breaks up into soil particles.

2. The A horizon develops from the C horizon when plant roots weather the rock mechanically and chemically. Plants also add organic material to the soil.

3. The B horizon develops as rainwater washes clay and minerals from the A horizon to the B horizon.

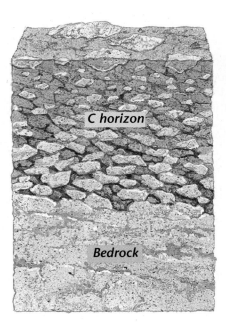

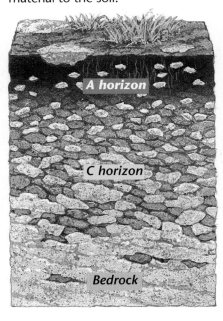

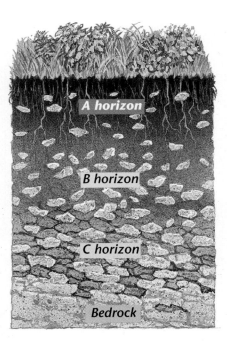

Life in Soil

INTEGRATING LIFE SCIENCE Soil is more than just bits of rock. If you look closely at some soil, you can see that it is teeming with living things. **Some soil organisms mix the soil and make spaces in it for air and water. Other soil organisms make humus, the material that makes soil fertile.** Fertile soil is rich in nutrients that plants need, such as nitrogen and phosphorus.

Plants contribute most of the organic remains that form humus. As plants shed leaves, they form a loose layer called **litter.**

EXPLORING Living Organisms in Soil

In every cubic meter of soil live billions of organisms. All organisms that live in soil enrich humus with their remains or wastes. Animals and plant roots break up the soil, opening spaces for air and water.

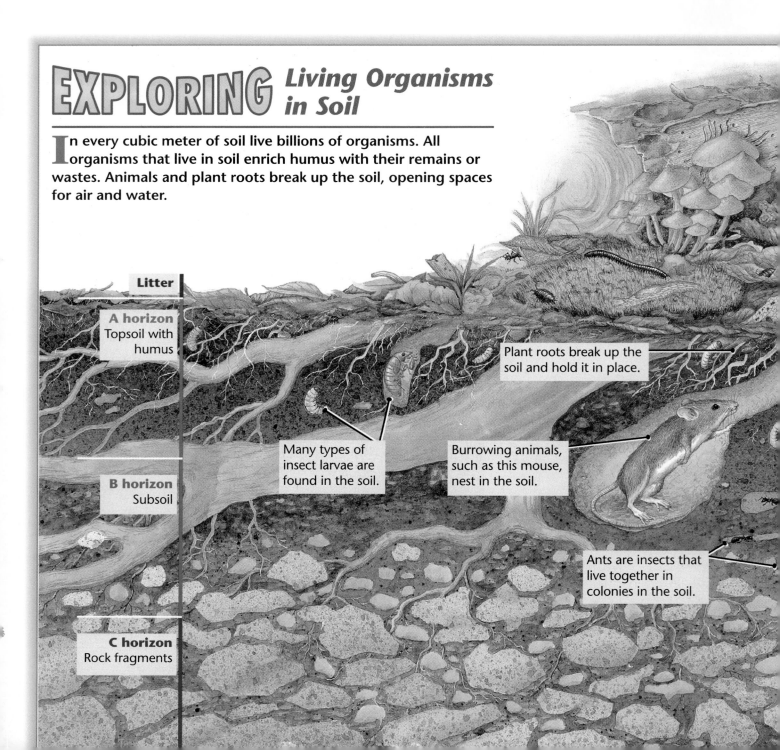

Litter

A horizon
Topsoil with humus

B horizon
Subsoil

C horizon
Rock fragments

Many types of insect larvae are found in the soil.

Plant roots break up the soil and hold it in place.

Burrowing animals, such as this mouse, nest in the soil.

Ants are insects that live together in colonies in the soil.

When plants die, their remains fall to the ground and become part of the litter. Plant roots also die and begin to decay underground. Although plant remains are full of stored nutrients, they are not yet humus.

Humus forms in a process called decomposition. As decomposition occurs, organisms that live in soil turn dead organic material into humus. These organisms are called decomposers. **Decomposers** are the organisms that break the remains of dead organisms into smaller pieces and digest them with chemicals.

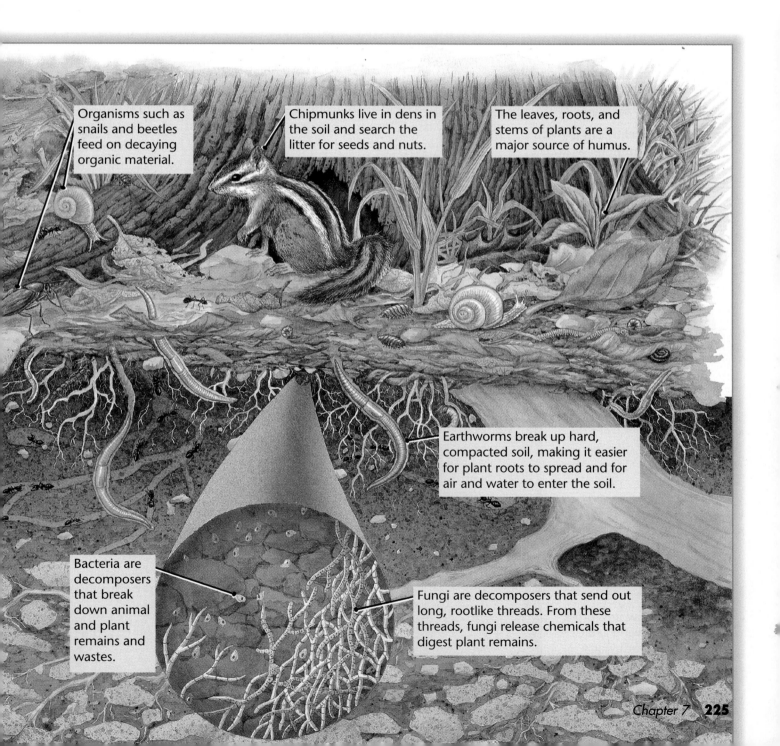

Organisms such as snails and beetles feed on decaying organic material.

Chipmunks live in dens in the soil and search the litter for seeds and nuts.

The leaves, roots, and stems of plants are a major source of humus.

Earthworms break up hard, compacted soil, making it easier for plant roots to spread and for air and water to enter the soil.

Bacteria are decomposers that break down animal and plant remains and wastes.

Fungi are decomposers that send out long, rootlike threads. From these threads, fungi release chemicals that digest plant remains.

TRY THIS

A Square Meter of Soil

ACTIVITY

1. Outdoors, measure an area of one square meter. Mark your square with string.

2. Observe the color and texture of the surface soil. Is it dry or moist? Does it contain sand, clay, or gravel? Are there plants, animals, or humus?

3. Use a trowel to dig down several centimeters into the soil. What is the soil's color and texture there?

4. When you finish, leave the soil as you found it. Wash your hands.

Drawing Conclusions What can you conclude about the soil's fertility? What evidence supports your conclusions?

Fungi, protists, bacteria, and worms are the main soil decomposers. Fungi are organisms such as molds and mushrooms. Fungi grow on, and digest, plant remains. Bacteria are microscopic decomposers that cause decay. Bacteria attack dead organisms and their wastes in soil. Other very small animals, such as mites and worms, also decompose dead organic material and mix it with the soil.

Earthworms do most of the work of mixing humus with other materials in soil. As earthworms eat their way through soil, they carry humus down to the subsoil and subsoil up to the surface. Earthworms also pass out the soil they eat as waste. The waste soil is enriched with substances that plants need to grow, such as nitrogen.

Many burrowing mammals such as mice, moles, prairie dogs, and gophers break up hard, compacted soil and mix humus through it. These animals also add nitrogen to the soil when they excrete waste. They add organic material when they die and decay.

Earthworms and burrowing animals also help to aerate, or mix air into, the soil. Plant roots need the oxygen that this process adds to the soil.

✓ *Checkpoint* *How do decomposers contribute to the formation of soil?*

Soil Types in the United States

If you were traveling across the hills of north-central Georgia, you would see soils that seem to be made of red clay. In other parts of the country, soils can be black, brown, yellow, or gray. In the United States alone, differences in climate and local bedrock have led to the formation of thousands of different types of soil.

Figure 8 Earthworms break up the soil, allowing in air and water. An earthworm eats its own weight in soil every day.

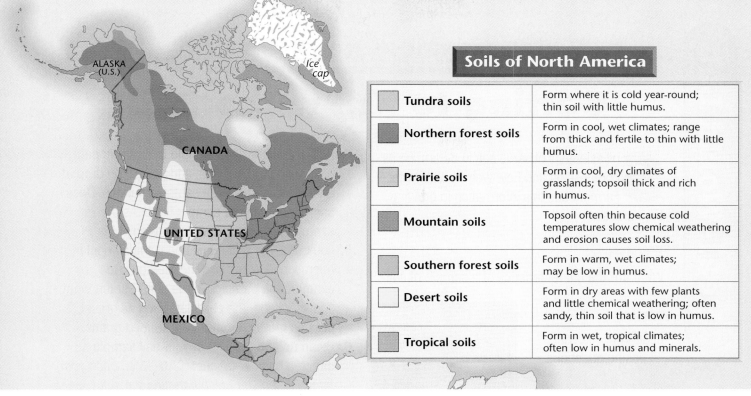

Soils of North America

	Tundra soils	Form where it is cold year-round; thin soil with little humus.
	Northern forest soils	Form in cool, wet climates; range from thick and fertile to thin with little humus.
	Prairie soils	Form in cool, dry climates of grasslands; topsoil thick and rich in humus.
	Mountain soils	Topsoil often thin because cold temperatures slow chemical weathering and erosion causes soil loss.
	Southern forest soils	Form in warm, wet climates; may be low in humus.
	Desert soils	Form in dry areas with few plants and little chemical weathering; often sandy, thin soil that is low in humus.
	Tropical soils	Form in wet, tropical climates; often low in humus and minerals.

Figure 9 An area's climate and plant life help to determine what type of soil forms from bedrock. *Interpreting Maps Recall that soil forms more rapidly in warm, wet areas than in cold, dry areas. Which types of soil on the map would you expect to form most slowly?*

Scientists classify the different types of soil into groups. These groups are based partly on the climate in a region. The most common plants found in a region are also used to help classify the soil. In addition, scientists classify soil by its composition—whether it is rocky, sandy, or rich in clay. Major soil types found in North America include forest, prairie, desert, mountain, tundra, and tropical soils. Look at Figure 9 to see where each of the major soil types is found. Which soil type is found in your part of the country?

Section 2 Review

1. What role does weathering play in the formation of soil?
2. What are the different materials that make up soil?
3. How do plants and animals affect the formation and composition of soil?
4. How do forest soils differ from prairie soils?
5. **Thinking Critically Relating Cause and Effect** Earthworms breathe by absorbing air in the soil through their skin. Why do you think earthworms crawl to the surface when it rains? Explain.

CHAPTER PROJECT

Check Your Progress
Obtain samples of the soil and growing materials you will use to grow your bean seeds. Choices include sand, vermiculite, gravel, potting soil, and local topsoil. **CAUTION:** *Avoid collecting soil near animal droppings. Wash your hands after handling the soil.* Make notes describing each sample. Predict which soil or mixture will be best for the growth of bean seeds. Design a method for recording the growth of your bean plants. Plant the bean seeds in the growing materials.

Getting to Know the Soil

Soil scientists observe soil to determine its composition and how well it holds water. Farmers use this information in growing their crops.

Problem

What are the characteristics of a sample of soil?

Skills Focus

observing, inferring, posing questions

Materials

20–30 grams of soil
plastic spoon
plastic dropper
toothpick
water
binocular microscope
graph paper ruled
    with 1- or 2-mm
    spacing
plastic petri dish or jar lid

Procedure

1. Your teacher will give you a dry sample of soil. As you observe the sample, record your observations in your lab notebook.
2. Spread half of the sample on the graph paper. Spread the soil thinly so that you can see the lines on the paper through the soil. Using graph paper as a background, estimate the sizes of the particles that make up the soil.
3. Place the rest of the sample in the palm of your hand, rub it between your fingers, and squeeze it. Is it soft or gritty? Does it clump together or crumble when you squeeze it?

4. Place about half the sample in a plastic petri dish. Using the dropper, add water one drop at a time. Watch how the sample changes. Does any material in the sample float? As the sample gets wet, do you notice any odor?
5. Look at some of the soil under the binocular microscope. (*Hint:* Use the toothpick to examine the particles in the soil.) Sketch what you see. Label the particles, such as gravel, organic matter, or strangely shaped grains.
6. Clean up and dispose of your soil sample as directed by your teacher. **CAUTION:** *Wash your hands when you finish handling the soil.*

Analyze and Conclude

1. What did you notice about the appearance of the soil sample when you first obtained it?
2. What can you infer about the composition of the soil from the different sizes of its particles? From your observations of its texture? From how the sample changed when water was added? What surprised you the most about the composition of your sample?
3. Based on the composition of your soil sample, can you determine the type of environment from which it was taken?
4. **Apply** List several questions that a soil scientist would need to answer to determine whether a soil sample was good for growing flowers or vegetables. Did your observations answer these questions for your soil sample?

More to Explore

Repeat the procedure using a soil sample from a different location. How does it compare with the first soil sample you tested?

SECTION
3 Conserving Land and Soil

DISCOVER ·························· ACTIVITY

How Can You Keep Soil From Washing Away?

1. Pour about 500 mL of soil into a pie plate, forming a pile.

2. Devise a way to keep the soil from washing away when water is poured over it. To protect the pile of soil, you may use craft sticks, paper clips, pebbles, modeling clay, strips of paper, or other materials approved by your teacher.

3. After arranging your materials to protect the soil, hold a container containing 200 mL of water about 20 cm above the center of the soil. Slowly pour the water in a stream onto the pile of soil.

4. Compare your pan of soil with those of your classmates.

Think It Over

Observing Based on your observations, what do you think is the best way to prevent soil on a slope from washing away?

Less than a quarter of Earth's surface is dry land. Except for the small amount added when volcanoes erupt, new land cannot be created. All the people on Earth must share this limited amount of land to produce their food, build shelter, and obtain other resources. Land is a precious resource. As the American author Mark Twain once said about land, "They don't make it anymore."

Types of Land Use

People use land in many ways. **Three uses that change the land are agriculture, development, and mining.** There are many other types of land use. Figure 10 shows what percentage of land in the United States is devoted to several major land uses.

Agriculture Since land is the source of most food, agriculture is an important land use. Crops such as wheat require large areas of fertile land. New farmland must be created by clearing forests, draining wetlands, and irrigating deserts. Other land serves as pasture or rangeland for grazing animals.

GUIDE FOR READING

◆ How do people use land?

◆ Why is soil one of Earth's most valuable resources?

◆ What are some ways that soil can be conserved?

Reading Tip As you read, make a list of activities that can harm the soil and a list of activities that can help save the soil.

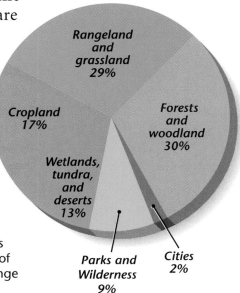

Figure 10 Land in the United States is used in many ways. *Classifying* Which of these land uses cause the greatest change in the land's natural appearance?

Rangeland and grassland 29%

Forests and woodland 30%

Cropland 17%

Wetlands, tundra, and deserts 13%

Parks and Wilderness 9%

Cities 2%

Figure 11 Agriculture, mining, and development are land uses that affect the soil.

Development A type of land use that changes the land even more than agriculture is development. **Development** is the construction of homes, stores, office buildings, roads, bridges, and other structures. Development begins when people first settle in an area. The process continues as population grows, and settlements become towns and cities.

In the United States, about a million hectares of farmland (an area half the size of New Jersey) are developed each year. Development not only reduces the amount of farmland, but can also destroy wildlife habitats.

Mining Mining changes the land as mineral resources such as iron, copper, and coal are removed. Recall from Chapter 2 that there are three main kinds of mining: strip mining, underground mining, and open-pit mining. Once land has been mined, it is often difficult to use the land for another purpose.

☑ *Checkpoint* *What are three main kinds of land use?*

The Value of Soil

Soil is one of Earth's most valuable resources because everything that lives on land depends directly or indirectly on soil. Plants depend directly on the soil to live and grow. Animals depend on plants—or on other animals that depend on plants—for food. Soil is a renewable resource that can be found wherever weathering occurs. But soil formation takes a long time. It can take hundreds of years for just a few centimeters of soil to form. The thick, fertile soil may take thousands of years to develop.

Fertile soil is valuable because there is a limited supply. Less than one eighth of the land on Earth has soils that are well suited for farming. In many areas, farming is difficult and little food is produced. The reasons for this include low soil fertility, lack of water, steep slopes, or a short growing season.

Soil Damage and Loss

Soil is one of Earth's most important resources. But soil can be lost or damaged. For example, soil can become exhausted, or lose its fertility. This occurred in large parts of the South in the late 1800s. Soils in which only cotton had been grown were exhausted. Many farmers abandoned their farms. Early in the 1900s in Alabama, a scientist named George Washington Carver developed new crops and farming methods that helped to restore soil fertility in the South. Peanuts were one crop that helped make the soil fertile again.

Soil can be lost to erosion by water and wind. Water erosion can occur wherever soil is not protected by plant cover. Plants break the force of falling rain, and plant roots hold the soil together. Wind erosion is another cause of soil loss.

In parts of the world that receive little rain, desertification is an important cause of soil loss. **Desertification** is the advance of desertlike conditions into areas that previously were fertile. In the past 50 years, desertification has occurred on about five billion hectares of land. Figure 13 shows regions where desertification is a threat.

One cause of desertification is climate. During periods of drought, crops fail. Without plant cover, the exposed soil easily blows away. Overgrazing of grasslands by cattle and sheep also exposes the soil. Cutting down trees for firewood can also cause desertification.

Desertification is a very serious problem. People cannot grow crops and graze livestock where desertification has occurred. Parts of the United States were severely affected by desertification during the 1930s. Wind erosion and farming methods not suited to dry conditions created a "Dust Bowl" on the Great Plains.

Figure 12 George Washington Carver (1864–1943) taught new methods of soil conservation to farmers in the South.

Figure 13 Large areas of the world are at risk of desertification. One cause is overgrazing. Without grass to hold the soil in place, the Senegal plain is becoming a barren desert. *Interpreting Maps Which continents are most threatened by desertification?*

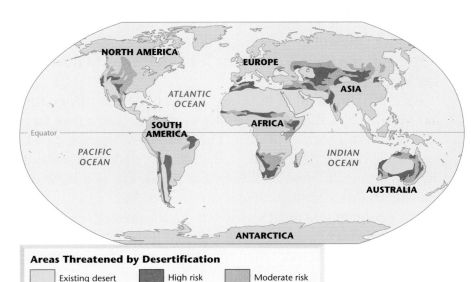

NORTH AMERICA
EUROPE
ASIA
ATLANTIC OCEAN
SOUTH AMERICA
AFRICA
Equator
PACIFIC OCEAN
INDIAN OCEAN
AUSTRALIA
ANTARCTICA

Areas Threatened by Desertification

Existing desert   High risk   Moderate risk

Figure 14 The Dust Bowl included western Oklahoma and parts of the surrounding states. Wind blew dry particles of soil into great clouds of dust that traveled thousands of kilometers.

KEY
■ Dust Bowl
□ Other areas affected by dust storms

MONTANA, NORTH DAKOTA, WYOMING, SOUTH DAKOTA, ROCKY MOUNTAINS, NEBRASKA, IOWA, COLORADO, KANSAS, MISSOURI, NEW MEXICO, OKLAHOMA, Mississippi River, TEXAS

Language Arts
CONNECTION

Woody Guthrie wrote and sang folk songs. Guthrie lived in Oklahoma and Texas at the time of the Dust Bowl and wrote a series of songs called "Dust Bowl Ballads." (A ballad is a song that tells a story.) One of the ballads describes how

We saw outside our window
Where wheat fields they had
* grown*
Was now a rippling ocean
Of dust the wind had blown.

In Your Journal

Write the words for a ballad that tells the story of a problem in your community and how you think the problem should be solved.

The Dust Bowl

Toward the end of the 1800s, new settlers moved on to the Great Plains. This region sweeps eastward from the base of the Rocky Mountains across the western parts of North and South Dakota, Nebraska, Kansas, Oklahoma, and Texas.

The soil of the Great Plains is fertile. Before the settlers arrived, the soil was covered with short grass that required little moisture. The **sod**—a thick mass of tough roots at the surface of the soil—kept the soil in place and held the moisture. As the settlers plowed the soil to grow crops, the soil was exposed. In times of drought, the topsoil quickly dried out, turned to dust, and blew away.

By 1930, almost all of the Great Plains had been turned into farms or ranches. But after several very dry years in a row, large areas of the soil turned to dust. The wind blew the soil east in great, black clouds. The clouds turned the sky dark as far away as Chicago and even New York City. Eventually the soil blew out over the Atlantic Ocean, where it was lost forever.

The problem was most serious in the southern Plains states. There, the drought and topsoil loss lasted until 1938. This area, shown in Figure 14, was called the **Dust Bowl.** Many people in the Dust Bowl states abandoned their farms and moved away.

Soil Conservation

After the Dust Bowl, farmers in the United States began to take better care of their land. They adopted methods of farming that helped save the soil. **Soil conservation** is the management of soil to prevent its destruction. **Ways that soil can be conserved include contour plowing, conservation plowing, leaving the soil to lie fallow, and crop rotation.** You can read about some of these methods in *Exploring Soil Conservation*.

Contour plowing is the practice of plowing fields along the curves of a slope. This helps slow the runoff of excess rainfall and prevents it from washing the soil away.

Conservation plowing disturbs the soil and its plant cover as little as possible. Dead weeds and stalks of the previous year's crop are left in the ground to help return soil nutrients, retain moisture, and hold soil in place.

EXPLORING *Soil Conservation*

These farming practices can help reduce soil erosion.

◄ Strip cropping and contour plowing
Farmers alternate strips of tall crops, such as corn, with short crops, such as squash. The short crops prevent soil from washing out of the tall crop rows, which are less protected. Crops are planted in curving rows that follow the slope, or contour, of the land. Contour plowing can reduce soil erosion as much as 50 percent on gently sloping land.

▲ Windbreaks
Rows of trees are planted along the edges of fields. These windbreaks block the wind and also trap eroding soil. Using fruit or nut trees as windbreaks provides an extra benefit for the farmer and wildlife.

Conservation plowing ▼
Rather than plowing fields and leaving them bare, farmers use machines that break up only the subsoil. This method leaves the dead stalks and weeds from the previous year's crop in the ground to hold the topsoil in place.

Terracing ►
Steep hillsides are built up into a series of flat "terraces." The ridges of soil at the edges of the terraces slow down runoff and catch eroding soil.

Figure 15 When the mining operation (at left) was completed, the mine operators smoothed out the sides of the mining cuts. Then they carefully replaced the subsoil and topsoil that was removed before mining. Finally, they planted grass. The former mine is now agricultural land (at right).

To restore fertility to soil, farmers periodically leave fields **fallow,** or unplanted with crops. A method that helps preserve the soil's fertility is **crop rotation.** In crop rotation, a farmer plants different crops in a field each year. Some crops use less nutrients than others. Certain crops, such as peanuts and other legumes, actually improve soil fertility.

Restoring the Land

It is often possible to restore land damaged by erosion or mining. The process of restoring an area of land to a more natural, productive state is called **land reclamation.** In addition to restoring lands for agriculture, land reclamation can restore habitats for wildlife. Many different types of land reclamation projects are currently underway all over the world. But it is generally more difficult and expensive to restore damaged land and soil than it is to protect them in the first place. Figure 15 shows an example of land reclamation.

Section 3 Review

1. Explain how one of the major kinds of land use can change Earth's surface.
2. Explain the importance of soil as one of Earth's resources.
3. What are some techniques that farmers use to conserve soil?
4. **Thinking Critically Problem Solving** If you had to plant corn on a steep hillside, how would you do it so that rain would not wash the soil away?

CHAPTER PROJECT

Check Your Progress
Check your bean seeds daily and water them as needed. Count and record the number of seeds that sprout. You can also measure the height of each plant, count the number of leaves, and note the leaf color. After about 14 days, you should be able to make comparisons. What differences did you observe in the bean plants grown in the different materials? When did these differences appear? Based on your data, what conclusions can you draw about which material is best for growing bean plants?

SECTION 4 Waste Disposal and Recycling

DISCOVER ·················· ACTIVITY····

What's in the Trash?

Your teacher will give you a trash bag. The items in the bag represent the most common categories of household waste in the United States.

1. Before you open the bag, predict what the two most common categories are.

2. Put on some plastic gloves. Open the bag and sort the trash items into categories based on what they are made of.

3. Count the number of trash items in each category. Construct a bar graph showing the number of pieces of trash in each category.

Think It Over

Interpreting Data Based on your graph, what are the two most common types of household waste? Was your prediction correct?

Every year, people in the United States throw away enough white paper to build a wall 4 meters high from coast to coast. People also throw away 1.6 billion pens, 2.9 million tons of paper towels, and 220 million automobile tires. Disposable products can be convenient, but they have created a big problem—what to do with all the trash.

The Problem of Waste Disposal

In their daily activities, people generate many types of waste, including used paper, empty packages, and food scraps. **Municipal solid waste** includes all the waste materials produced in homes, businesses, and other places in a community. **Three methods of handling solid waste are to bury it, to burn it, or to recycle it.** Each method has advantages and disadvantages.

Landfills Until fairly recently, people usually disposed of waste in open holes in the ground. But these open dumps were dangerous. Rainwater falling on the wastes dissolved chemicals from the waste, forming a polluted liquid called **leachate.** Leachate could run off into streams and lakes, or trickle down into the groundwater.

GUIDE FOR READING

◆ What can be done with solid waste?

◆ What are the "three R's"?

◆ What techniques can be used to manage hazardous waste?

Reading Tip Before you read, preview *Exploring a Landfill* on page 236. Make a list of any unfamiliar words in the diagram. Look for the meanings of these words as you read.

In 1976, the government banned open dumps. Now much solid waste is buried in landfills that are constructed to hold the wastes more safely. A **sanitary landfill** holds municipal solid waste, construction debris, and some types of agricultural and industrial waste. *Exploring a Landfill* shows the parts of a well-designed sanitary landfill. Once a landfill is full, it is covered with a clay cap to keep rainwater out.

Even well-designed landfills can pollute groundwater. And while capped landfills can be reused for some purposes, such as parks, they cannot be used for housing or agriculture.

EXPLORING *a Landfill*

A well-designed sanitary landfill contains the waste and prevents it from polluting the surrounding land and water.

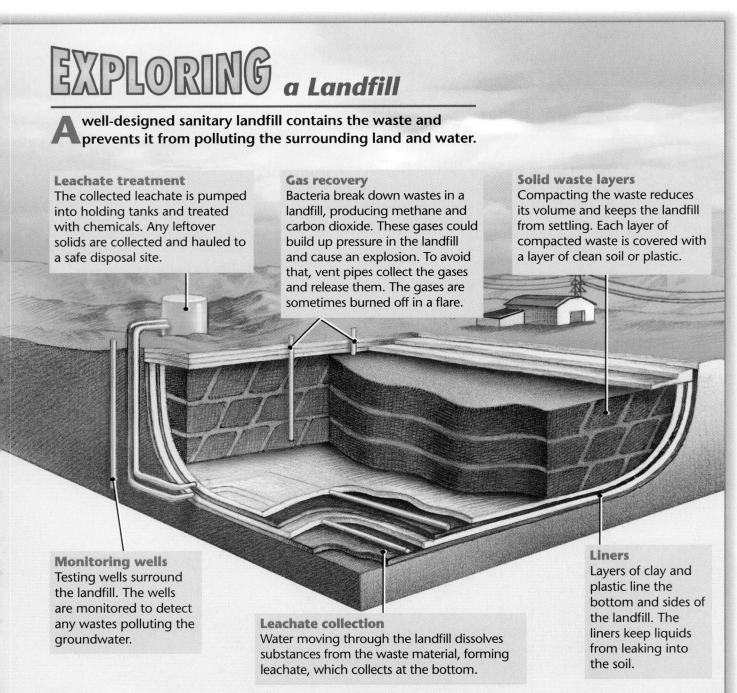

Leachate treatment
The collected leachate is pumped into holding tanks and treated with chemicals. Any leftover solids are collected and hauled to a safe disposal site.

Gas recovery
Bacteria break down wastes in a landfill, producing methane and carbon dioxide. These gases could build up pressure in the landfill and cause an explosion. To avoid that, vent pipes collect the gases and release them. The gases are sometimes burned off in a flare.

Solid waste layers
Compacting the waste reduces its volume and keeps the landfill from settling. Each layer of compacted waste is covered with a layer of clean soil or plastic.

Monitoring wells
Testing wells surround the landfill. The wells are monitored to detect any wastes polluting the groundwater.

Leachate collection
Water moving through the landfill dissolves substances from the waste material, forming leachate, which collects at the bottom.

Liners
Layers of clay and plastic line the bottom and sides of the landfill. The liners keep liquids from leaking into the soil.

Incineration The burning of solid waste is called **incineration** (in sin ur ay shun). Incineration has some advantages over landfills. Incinerators do not take up as much space. They do not pollute groundwater. The heat produced by burning solid waste can be used to generate electricity in "waste-to-energy" plants.

Unfortunately, incinerators have drawbacks. Incinerators release some pollution into the air. And although incinerators reduce the volume of waste by as much as 90 percent, some waste still remains. This waste needs to be disposed of somewhere. Incinerators also cost much more to build than sanitary landfills.

☑ *Checkpoint* *What is a waste-to-energy plant?*

Recycling

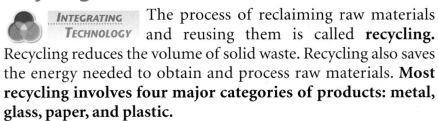 **INTEGRATING TECHNOLOGY** The process of reclaiming raw materials and reusing them is called **recycling.** Recycling reduces the volume of solid waste. Recycling also saves the energy needed to obtain and process raw materials. **Most recycling involves four major categories of products: metal, glass, paper, and plastic.**

Metal Common metals such as iron and aluminum can be melted and reused. The aluminum in soda cans, for example, can be recycled. Recycling metal saves money and causes less pollution than making new metal. With recycling, no ore needs to be mined, transported to factories, or processed. Recycling metals also helps conserve these nonrenewable resources.

Glass Recycling glass is easy and inexpensive. The glass pieces can be melted down over and over to make new glass containers. The recycled pieces melt at a lower temperature than the raw materials. Therefore less energy is required. Recycling glass also reduces the environmental damage caused by mining the raw materials used to make glass.

Graphing

What happens to trash? Use the data in the table below to construct a circle graph of methods of municipal solid waste disposal in the United States. Give your circle graph a title. (For help making a circle graph, see the Skills Handbook.)

Method of Disposal	Percentage of Waste
Landfills	56%
Recycling	27%
Incineration	17%

It's in the Numbers

Plastic bottles and other plastic products usually have numbers inside a triangle indicating the type of plastic they are made of. Plastics must be sorted by type before they can be recycled.

Sort pieces of plastic products into groups by their recycling numbers. Compare and contrast the pieces in each group with each other and with those in other groups.

Classifying Write a sentence describing characteristics of the plastics in each group.

Paper About 17 trees are needed to make one metric ton of paper. Paper mills turn wood into a thick liquid called pulp. Pulp is spread out and dried to produce paper. Pulp can also be made from used paper such as old newspapers. Most paper products can only be recycled a few times. Recycled paper is not as smooth or strong as paper made from wood pulp. Each time paper is recycled, the new paper is rougher, weaker, and darker.

Plastic When oil is refined to make gasoline and other petroleum products, solid materials called resins are left over. Resins can be heated, stretched, and molded into plastic products. Common products made from plastic include milk jugs, detergent containers, and soda bottles. When they are recycled, they can take on very different forms: as carpeting, park benches, fiber filling for jackets, and many other things!

Is Recycling Worthwhile? Recycling is not a complete answer to the solid waste problem. Some materials cannot be recycled. There are not enough uses for some recycled products, such as low-quality newspaper. Finally, all recycling processes require energy and create some pollution.

✓ *Checkpoint* *What are some advantages and disadvantages of recycling?*

What Can You Do?

There are lots of actions individuals can take to help control the solid waste problem. **These actions are sometimes called the "three R's"—reduce, reuse, and recycle.** Reduce means creating less waste in the first place. For example, you can use a cloth shopping bag instead of a disposable paper or plastic bag. Reuse means finding another use for an object instead of discarding it. For example, you could refill plastic drink bottles with drinking water or juice you mix instead of buying drinks in new bottles. Recycle means reclaiming raw materials to create new products. You can make sure you recycle at home, and you can also encourage others to recycle. How about starting a used paper collection and recycling program at your school?

Figure 17 Composting is a form of recycling in which natural processes break down waste such as leaves, grass clippings, and vegetable scraps. Many communities have neighborhood compost bins like this one in Brooklyn, in New York City.

Hazardous Wastes

Many people picture hazardous wastes as bubbling chemicals, thick fumes, or oozing slime. But even some harmless-looking, common materials such as window cleaner, radio batteries, and nail polish remover can become hazardous wastes. **Hazardous waste** is any material that can be harmful to human health or the environment if it is not properly disposed of.

Hazardous wastes are created during the manufacture of many household products. Many more are produced by agriculture and industry.

Types of Hazardous Wastes There are four categories of hazardous waste: toxic, explosive, flammable, and corrosive. Toxic, or poisonous, wastes can damage the health of humans and other organisms. Explosive wastes react very quickly when exposed to air or water, or explode when they are dropped. Flammable wastes catch fire easily. Corrosive wastes dissolve or eat through many materials.

Other wastes that require special disposal are radioactive wastes. Radioactive wastes contain unstable atoms. These unstable atoms give off radiation that can cause cancer and other diseases. Radioactive waste can remain dangerous for thousands of years.

Health Effects of Hazardous Wastes A person can be exposed

INTEGRATING HEALTH to hazardous wastes by breathing, eating, drinking, or touching them. Many factors determine the effects of a hazardous substance on a person. One factor is how harmful the substance is. Another factor is how much of the substance a person is exposed to. A third factor is how long the exposure lasts. A person may be exposed for only a short time or for many years. Finally, a person's age, weight, and health all influence how a substance affects that person.

Figure 18 Vehicles transporting dangerous materials must use signs like these to alert people of the potential dangers of their loads.

Category: Radioactive
Examples: Uranium, plutonium

Category: Flammable
Example: Kerosene

Category: Toxic
Examples: Chlorine, PCBs, mercury

Category: Explosive
Example: Nitroglycerin

Category: Corrosive
Examples: Hydrochloric acid, sodium hydroxide

In general, short-term exposure to hazardous wastes may cause irritation or more severe health problems. These health problems can include breathing difficulties, internal bleeding, paralysis, coma, and even death. Long-term exposure to hazardous wastes may cause diseases such as cancer, and may damage body organs, including the brain, liver, kidneys, and lungs. These effects may eventually be life threatening.

Disposal of Hazardous Wastes It is hard to safely dispose of hazardous wastes. Burying them can pollute the soil or groundwater. Releasing wastes into lakes or rivers can pollute surface water. Burning hazardous wastes can pollute the air. You can feel, smell, and see the problem!

Methods of hazardous waste disposal include burial in landfills, incineration, and breakdown by living organisms. Liquid wastes can be stored in deep rock layers. Hazardous wastes are most often disposed of in carefully designed landfills. These landfills are lined with clay and plastic to keep chemicals from leaking into the soil and groundwater. A clay and plastic cover prevents rainwater from seeping into the wastes.

Scientists are still researching methods that will provide safe, permanent disposal of radioactive wastes. Some radioactive wastes are currently stored in vaults dug hundreds of meters underground or in concrete and steel containers above ground.

Reducing Hazardous Wastes The best way to manage hazardous wastes is to produce less of them in the first place. Industries are eager to develop safe alternatives to harmful chemicals. At home, you can find substitutes for some hazardous household chemicals.

Figure 19 Hazardous wastes can pollute the soil, water, and air. Environmental scientists in protective gear test the contents of an old storage tank.

Section 4 Review

1. What happens to most solid waste in the United States?
2. Name and define the "three R's" of solid waste management.
3. What are hazardous wastes?
4. Describe one method used to dispose of hazardous waste.
5. **Thinking Critically Comparing and Contrasting** Compare the recycling of metal and paper. How are they similar? How are they different?
6. **Thinking Critically Inferring** Why must the workers who clean up hazardous wastes wear protective clothing? Explain.

Science at Home

Trash Weigh-In For one week, have your family collect their household trash in large bags. Do not include food waste. At the end of the week, hold a trash weigh-in. Multiply the total amount by 52 to show how much trash your family produces in a year. Together, can you suggest any ways to reduce your family trash load?

1 Rocks and Weathering

Key Ideas

◆ Rock weathers, or wears down, when it is exposed to air, water, weather, and living things at Earth's surface.

◆ Mechanical weathering breaks rock into smaller pieces. The agents of mechanical weathering include freezing and thawing, release of pressure, growth of plants, actions of animals, and abrasion.

◆ Chemical weathering changes the mineral content of rock. The agents of chemical weathering are water, oxygen, carbon dioxide, living organisms, and acid rain.

◆ Climate and rock type determine how fast weathering occurs.

Key Terms

weathering   ice wedging
erosion   chemical weathering
mechanical weathering   permeable
abrasion

2 Soil Formation and Composition

Key Ideas

◆ Soil is made of small particles of rock mixed with the decaying remains of organisms.

◆ Soil forms in layers called horizons as bedrock weathers and organic materials build up.

◆ The three soil horizons are the A horizon, the B horizon, and the C horizon. The A horizon is made up of topsoil, which is rich in humus. The B horizon consists of clay and other particles washed down from the A horizon, but little humus. The C horizon is made up of partly weathered rock without clay or humus.

◆ Plants and animals break up and mix the soil, and also add the organic materials that form humus.

Key Terms

soil   loam   subsoil
bedrock   soil horizon litter
humus   topsoil   decomposers

3 Soil Conservation

Key Ideas

◆ Land is a limited resource. All the people on Earth must share land for agriculture, development, mining, and other uses.

◆ Soil can be eroded away and its fertility can be decreased by improper farming practices.

◆ Soil can be conserved and its fertility can be maintained by using various methods of soil conservation.

Key Terms

development   contour plowing
desertification   conservation plowing
sod   fallow
Dust Bowl   crop rotation
soil conservation land reclamation

4 Waste Disposal and Recycling

INTEGRATING ENVIRONMENTAL SCIENCE

Key Ideas

◆ Three ways of handling solid waste are to bury it, burn it, or recycle it.

◆ One way to reduce solid waste is to practice the "three R's"—reduce, reuse, and recycle.

◆ Hazardous wastes are materials that can threaten human health and safety or harm the environment if not properly disposed of.

Key Terms

municipal solid waste   incineration
leachate   recycling
sanitary landfill   hazardous waste

Organizing Information

Compare/Contrast Table On a separate piece of paper, make a table of ways to dispose of municipal solid waste. Your table should compare landfills and incinerators with regard to cost, pollution, attractiveness, and usefulness to a community. Then complete your table and add a title. For tips on compare/contrast tables, see the Skills Handbook.)

Reviewing Content

 For more review of key concepts, see the Interactive Student Tutorial CD-ROM.

Multiple Choice
Choose the letter of the best answer.

1. The most important force of mechanical weathering in cool climates is
   a. oxidation.
   b. freezing and thawing.
   c. animal activity.
   d. abrasion.
2. Most chemical weathering is caused by
   a. acid rain.
   b. water.
   c. oxygen.
   d. carbon dioxide.
3. The B horizon consists of
   a. subsoil.   b. topsoil.
   c. rock particles.   d. bedrock.
4. The loss of so much topsoil that plants can no longer grow in an area is called
   a. desertification.
   b. crop rotation.
   c. conservation plowing.
   d. land reclamation.
5. Hazardous wastes that contain unstable atoms are
   a. toxic.   b. flammable.
   c. corrosive.   d. radioactive.

True or False
If the statement is true, write true. If it is false, change the underlined word or words to make the statement true.

6. <u>Mechanical weathering</u> is the movement of rock particles by wind, water, or ice.
7. Weathering occurs faster in a <u>wet</u> climate.
8. The decayed organic material in soil is called <u>loam</u>.
9. Three types of land use that change Earth's surface are agriculture, <u>recycling</u>, and mining.
10. The bottom of a sanitary landfill is lined with clay and plastic to prevent <u>leachate</u> from polluting groundwater.

Checking Concepts

11. Where is mechanical weathering likely to occur more quickly: where the winter temperature usually stays below freezing, or where it more often shifts back and forth around the freezing point? Explain.
12. Briefly describe how soil is formed.
13. Which contains more humus, topsoil or subsoil?
14. Explain how plants can act as agents of both mechanical and chemical weathering.
15. How does conservation plowing contribute to soil conservation?
16. Explain how individuals can help control the solid waste problem by practicing the "three R's."
17. **Writing to Learn** Write a description of your life as an earthworm. What would it be like to live in the soil? What would you see? What would you eat? How would you move through the soil? How would you change it?

Thinking Critically

18. **Predicting** Suppose mechanical weathering breaks a rock into pieces. How would this affect the rate at which the rock weathers chemically?
19. **Classifying** Classify the following examples as either mechanical weathering or chemical weathering:
    a. Cracks appear in a sidewalk next to a large tree.
    b. A piece of limestone develops holes like Swiss cheese.
    c. A rock exposed at the surface slowly turns reddish brown.
20. **Relating Cause and Effect** Two rocks, each in a different location, have been weathering for the same amount of time. Mature soil has formed from one rock but only immature soil from the other. What factors might have caused this difference in rate of soil formation?
21. **Applying Concepts** Why is it unsafe to bury or incinerate radioactive waste?

Applying Skills

Use the following information to answer Questions 23–25. You have two samples of soil. One is mostly sand and one is mostly clay.

22. **Developing Hypotheses** Which soil sample do you think would lose water more quickly? Why?

23. **Designing Experiments** Design an experiment to test how quickly water passes through each soil sample.

24. **Posing Questions** Suppose you are a farmer who wants to grow soybeans in one of these two soils. What questions would you need to answer before choosing where to plant your soybeans?

Performance   **Assessment**

Present Your Project You are ready to present your conclusions about what type of material is best for growing bean plants. Decide how to display the data you collected on the different materials. How did your group's results compare with those of the other groups in your class?

Reflect and Record In your journal, describe how well the results of your experiment matched your predictions. What have you learned from this project about soil characteristics that help plants to grow? What improvements could you make to your experiment?

Test Preparation

Use these questions to prepare for standardized tests.

Use the diagram of soil horizons to answer Questions 25–29.

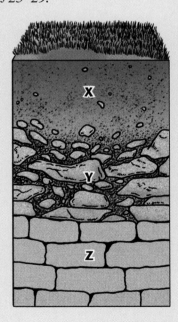

25. Layer X in the diagram consists of a mixture of humus, clay, and other minerals called
    - **a.** litter.
    - **b.** gravel.
    - **c.** subsoil.
    - **d.** topsoil.

26. Layer Y is made up of partly weathered rock called the
    - **a.** C horizon.
    - **b.** B horizon.
    - **c.** A horizon.
    - **d.** humus horizon.

27. One soil horizon, made up of clay and other particles but little humus, has not yet developed in this soil. The missing soil horizon is the
    - **a.** A horizon.
    - **b.** B horizon.
    - **c.** C horizon.
    - **d.** bedrock horizon.

28. The missing soil horizon will develop
    - **a.** above layer X.
    - **b.** below layer Z.
    - **c.** between layers X and Y.
    - **d.** between layers Y and Z.

29. In which layer or layers would you expect to find the most plant roots, insects, and other soil organisms?
    - **a.** layers Y and Z
    - **b.** layer Z
    - **c.** layer Y
    - **d.** layer X

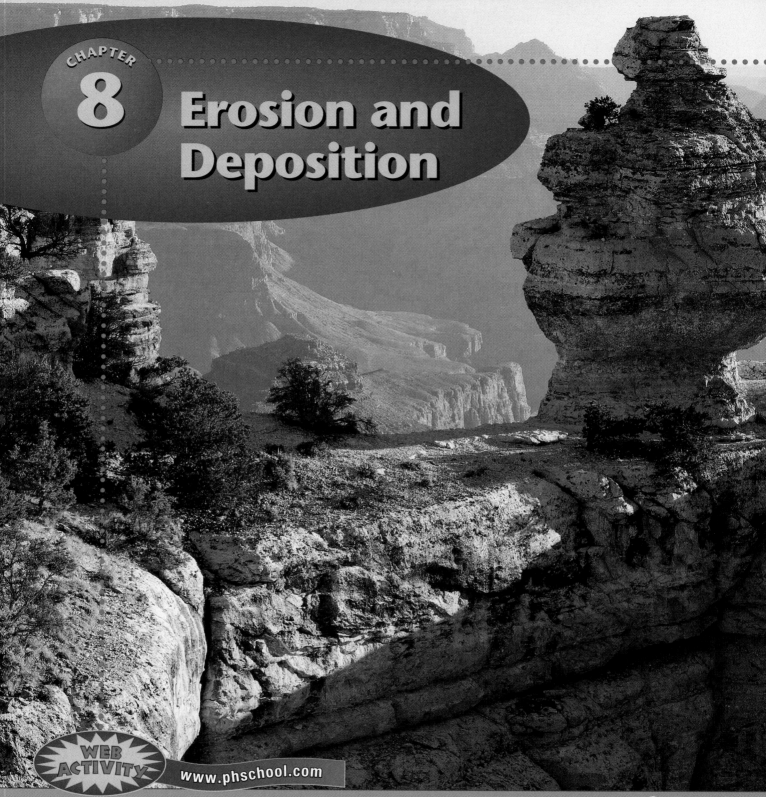

CHAPTER

8 Erosion and Deposition

WEB ACTIVITY
www.phschool.com

CHAPTER 8 PROJECT

Changes In the Land

The view from the South Rim of the Grand Canyon in Arizona is one of Earth's most memorable sights.

The walls of the Grand Canyon reveal the colorful rock layers that make up the Colorado Plateau. What force shaped such a vast canyon? For about 6 million years the Colorado River has been cutting and grinding through the plateau. The river also carries away the broken particles of rock.

In this chapter you will explore the forces that change Earth's surface. Flowing water, frozen glaciers, waves, and wind all wear down and build up landforms. Throughout the chapter, you will build models showing how erosion shapes a landscape.

Your Goal To make three-dimensional models that show how the forces of erosion and deposition can change a landscape over millions of years.

To complete this project, you must
- make a three-dimensional model of a landscape
- predict how the model would be affected by erosion
- construct a second model showing how your landscape might look after erosion has continued for millions of years

Get Started Begin by sketching a mountainous or hilly landscape. Include sharp peaks, deep valleys, a river, and a coastline.

Check Your Progress You will be working on this project as you study this chapter. To keep your project on track, look for Check Your Progress boxes at the following points.
Section 3 Review, page 268: Draw and make your first model.
Section 4 Review, page 273: Begin to make your second model, showing how water and glaciers cause erosion.
Section 5 Review, page 277: Add the effects of wave erosion to the model.

Present Your Project At the end of the chapter (page 283), you will present your models to the class. In your presentation, you will explain how the landscape changed and predict how it might change in the future.

SECTION 4 Glaciers

Discover How Do Glaciers Change the Land?

SECTION 5 Waves

Discover What Can Be Learned From Beach Sand?
Sharpen Your Skills Calculating

SECTION 6 Wind

Discover How Does Moving Air Affect Sediment?
Science at Home Modeling Desert Pavement

SECTION
1 Changing Earth's Surface

DISCOVER ······································ ACTIVITY

How Does Gravity Affect Materials on a Slope?

1. Place a small board flat on your desk. Place a marble on the board and slowly tip the board up slightly at one end. Observe what happens.

2. Place a block of wood on the board. Slowly lift one end of the board and observe the result.

3. Next, cover the board and the wood block with sandpaper and repeat Step 2.

Think It Over

Developing Hypotheses How do the results of each step compare? Develop a hypothesis to explain the differences in your observations.

GUIDE FOR READING

◆ What processes wear down and build up Earth's surface?

◆ What force pulls rock and soil down slopes?

◆ What are the different types of mass movement?

Reading Tip As you read, make a list of main ideas and supporting details about erosion, deposition, and mass movement.

Madison River Canyon is a quiet wilderness area in the Rocky Mountains of Montana. In 1959, something happened to change the canyon forever. When a strong earthquake jolted nearby Yellowstone National Park, a mountainside along the canyon gave way. In a few seconds, nearly 30 million cubic meters of rock, soil, and trees slid into the canyon. If this much material were in the shape of a cube, then each side of the cube would be three times longer than a football field. Rock and soil from the landslide dammed the Madison River, forming a new lake.

Figure 1 During a landslide, loose rock and soil on the side of a mountain suddenly slide away from underlying bedrock. This landslide in Madison River Canyon, Montana, buried a highway and campground.

246

Wearing Down and Building Up

A landslide like the one in Madison River Canyon is a spectacular example of erosion. **Erosion** is the process by which natural forces move weathered rock and soil from one place to another. A landslide is a very rapid type of erosion. Other types of erosion move soil and rock more slowly. Gravity, running water, glaciers, waves, and wind can all cause erosion. You may have seen water carrying soil and gravel down a driveway after it rains. That's an example of erosion. Erosion also caused the damage to the road in Figure 2.

The material moved by erosion is **sediment.** Both weathering and erosion produce sediment. **Deposition** occurs where the agents of erosion lay down sediment. Deposition changes the shape of the land. You may have watched a playing child who picked up several toys and then carried them across a room and put them down. This child was acting something like an agent of erosion and deposition.

Weathering, erosion, and deposition act together in a cycle that wears down and builds up Earth's surface. Erosion and deposition are at work everywhere on Earth. Sometimes they work slowly. At other times, they work more quickly, such as during a thunderstorm. Then, heavy rain soaks into rock and soil. These water-soaked materials may then come loose suddenly and slide down a mountain. But as a mountain wears down in one place, new landforms build up in other places. Erosion and deposition are never-ending.

Figure 2 Heavy winter rains washed out this California highway. *Relating Cause and Effect What caused the erosion that you can see in the photograph?*

☑ *Checkpoint* *What happens to sediment as a result of erosion and deposition?*

Mass Movement

Imagine that you are sitting on a bicycle at the top of a hill. With only a slight push, you can coast down the hill. If the slope of the hill is very steep, you will reach a high speed before reaching the bottom. The force that pulls you and your bicycle downward is gravity. Gravity pulls everything toward the center of Earth.

Gravity is the force that moves rock and other materials downhill. Gravity causes **mass movement,** any one of several processes that move sediment downhill. Mass movement can be rapid or slow. **The different types of mass movement include landslides, mudslides, slump, and creep.**

Landslides The most destructive kind of mass movement is a landslide, which occurs when rock and soil slide quickly down a steep slope. Some landslides may contain huge masses of rock. But many landslides contain only a small amount of rock and soil. Such mass movement is common where road builders have cut highways through hills or mountains.

Figure 3 A mudflow caused by heavy rains raced through the streets of this town in Italy. *Relating Cause and Effect What characteristic of soil can contribute to a mudflow?*

Mudflows A mudflow is the rapid downhill movement of a mixture of water, rock, and soil. The amount of water in a mudflow can be as high as 60 percent. Mudflows often occur after heavy rains in a normally dry area. In clay soils with a high water content, mudflows may occur even on very gentle slopes. Under certain conditions, clay soils suddenly turn to liquid and begin to flow. For example, an earthquake can trigger both mudflows and landslides. Mudflows like the one in Figure 3 can be very dangerous.

Slump If you slump your shoulders, the entire upper part of your body drops down. In the type of mass movement known as slump, a mass of rock and soil suddenly slips down a slope. Unlike a landslide, the material in slump moves down in one large mass. It looks as if someone pulled the bottom out from under part of the slope. Figure 4 shows an example of slump. Slump often occurs when water soaks the base of a mass of soil that is rich in clay.

Figure 4 Slump can look as if a giant spoon has started to scoop a mass of soil out from a hillside.

Creep Landscapes affected by creep may have the eerie, out-of-kilter look of a funhouse in an amusement park. Creep is the very slow downhill movement of rock and soil. It can even occur on gentle slopes. Like the movement of an hour hand on a clock, creep is so slow you can barely notice it. But you can see the effects of creep in objects such as telephone poles, gravestones, and fenceposts. Creep may tilt these objects at spooky angles. Creep often results from the freezing and thawing of water in cracked layers of rock beneath the soil. How have the trees in Figure 5 been affected by creep?

Figure 5 Creep has slowly tilted these trees downhill, causing their trunks to grow in a curve. *Predicting If creep continues, how might it affect the road, the fence, and the electric power lines?*

 Section 1 Review | **Science at Home**

1. Explain the difference between erosion and deposition.
2. What force causes erosion?
3. What are four types of mass movement?
4. **Thinking Critically** **Relating Cause and Effect** Why would a landslide be more likely on a steep mountain than on a gently sloping hill?

Science at Home

Evidence of Erosion After a rainstorm, take a walk with an adult family member around your neighborhood. Look for evidence of erosion. Try to find areas where there is loose soil, sand, gravel, or rock. (**CAUTION:** *Stay away from any large pile of loose sand or soil—it may slide without warning.*) Which areas have the most erosion? The least erosion? How does the slope of the ground affect the amount of erosion? Sketch or take photographs of the areas showing evidence of erosion.

Sand Hills

In this lab, you will develop and test a hypothesis about how mass movement affects the size and shape of a sand hill.

Problem

What is the relationship between the height and width of a sand hill?

Materials

dry sand, 500 mL
cardboard toilet paper tube
tray (about 15 cm × 45 cm × 60 cm)
wooden barbecue skewer   masking tape
spoon   ruler   pencil or crayon
several sheets of white paper

Procedure

1. Begin by observing how gravity causes mass movement in sand. To start, place the cardboard tube vertically in the center of the tray.

2. Using the spoon, fill the cardboard tube with the dry sand. Take care not to spill the sand around the outside of the tube.

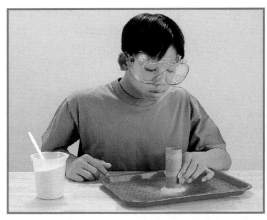

3. Carefully lift the sand-filled tube straight up so that all the sand flows out. As you lift the tube, observe the sand's movement.

4. Develop a hypothesis about how the height and width of the pile will change as you add more sand. Be sure to write your hypothesis as an "If ... then ..." statement.

5. Plan a method for testing your hypothesis. To test your hypothesis, you will need a method of measuring a sand hill (see instructions below).

6. Empty the sand in the tray back into a container. Then set up your system for measuring the sand hill.

7. Copy the data table into your lab notebook.

How to Measure a Sand Hill

1. Cover the bottom of the tray with unlined white paper and tape it firmly in place.

2. Mark off points 0.5 cm apart along one side of the paper in the tray.

3. Carefully draw the sand hill's outline on the paper. The line should go completely around the base of the hill.

4. Now measure the width of the hill against the marks you made along the edge of the paper.

5. Measure the sand hill's height by inserting a barbecue skewer through its center. Make a mark on the skewer at the top of the hill.

6. Remove the skewer and use the ruler to measure how much of the skewer was buried in the hill. Try not to disturb the sand.

DATA TABLE

Test	1	2	3	4	5
Height					
Width					

8. Following Steps 1 through 3, make a new sand hill.

9. Measure and record the sand hill's height and width for Test 1.

10. Now test what happens when you add more sand to the sand hill. Place your cardboard tube vertically at the center of the sand hill. Be careful not to push the tube down into the sand hill! Using the spoon, fill the tube with sand as before.

11. Carefully raise the tube and observe the results of the sand's movement.

12. Measure and record the sand hill's height and width for Test 2.

13. Repeat Steps 10 through 12 at least three more times. After each test, record your results. Be sure to number each test.

Analyze and Conclude

1. Make a graph showing how the sand hill's height and width changed with each test. (*Hint:* Use the *x*-axis of the graph for height. Use the *y*-axis of the graph for width.)

2. What does your graph show about the relationship between the sand hill's height and width?

3. Does your graph support your hypothesis about the sand hill's height and width? Why or why not?

4. How would you revise your original hypothesis after examining your data? Give reasons for your answer.

5. **Think About It** Predict what would happen if you continued the experiment for five more tests. Extend your graph with a dashed line to show your prediction. How could you test your prediction?

Design an Experiment

Do you think the use of different materials, such as wet sand or gravel, would produce different results from dry sand? Make a new hypothesis about the relationship between slope and width in hills made of materials other than dry sand. Design an experiment in which you test how these different materials form hills. Obtain your teacher's approval before you try the experiment.

How Does Moving Water Wear Away Rocks?

1. Obtain two bars of soap that are the same size and brand.

2. Open a faucet just enough to let the water drip out very slowly. How many drops of water does the faucet release per minute?

3. Place one bar of soap in a dry place. Place the other bar of soap under the faucet. Predict the effect of the dripping water droplets on the soap.

4. Let the faucet drip for 10 minutes.

5. Turn off the faucet and observe both bars of soap. What difference do you observe between them?

Think It Over

Predicting What would the bar of soap under the dripping faucet look like if you left it there for another 10 minutes? For an hour? How could you speed up the process? Slow it down?

GUIDE FOR READING

◆ What process is mainly responsible for shaping Earth's land surface?

◆ What features are formed by water erosion?

◆ What features are formed when rivers and streams deposit sediment?

Reading Tip Before you read, use the headings to make an outline on water erosion and deposition.

Walking in the woods in summer, you can hear the racing water of a stream before you see the stream itself. The water roars as it foams over rock ledges and boulders. When you reach the stream, you see water rushing by. Sand and pebbles tumble along the bottom of the stream. As it swirls downstream, it also carries twigs, leaves, and bits of soil. In sheltered pools, insects such as water striders silently skim the water's calm surface. Beneath the surface, you see a rainbow trout hovering in the clear water.

If you visit the stream at other times of year, it will be very different. In winter, the stream freezes. Chunks of ice scrape and grind away at the stream's bed and banks. In spring, the stream floods. Then the flow of water may be strong enough to move large rocks. But throughout the year, the stream continues to erode its small part of Earth's surface.

A woodland stream ▼

Figure 6 A falling raindrop starts the process of erosion. Water flowing across the surface runs together in small rills. Rills combine to form larger gullies. *Predicting What will happen to the land between the gully and the side gully as the two gullies grow wider?*

Runoff and Erosion

Running water creates many landforms. **Moving water is the major agent of the erosion that has shaped Earth's land surface.**

Erosion by water begins with the splash of rain, as you can see in Figure 6. Some rainfall sinks into the ground. Some evaporates or is taken up by plants. The force of a falling raindrop can loosen and pick up soil particles. As water moves over the land, it carries these particles with it. This moving water is called runoff. **Runoff** is all the remaining water that moves over Earth's surface. When runoff flows in a thin layer over the land, it may cause a type of erosion called sheet erosion.

Rills and Gullies Because of gravity, runoff and the material it contains move downhill. As runoff travels, it forms tiny grooves in the soil called **rills.** As the rills flow into one another, they grow larger, forming gullies. A **gully** is a large groove, or channel, in the soil that carries runoff after a rainstorm. As water flows through gullies, it moves soil and rocks with it, thus enlarging the gullies through erosion. Gullies flow only after it rains.

Figure 7 As water erodes gullies, soil can be lost.

Streams and Rivers Gullies join together to form a larger channel called a stream. A **stream** is a channel along which water is continually flowing down a slope. Unlike gullies, streams rarely dry up. Small streams are also called creeks or brooks. As streams flow together, they form larger and larger bodies of flowing water. A large stream is often called a **river.**

Amount of Runoff The amount of runoff in an area depends on five main factors. The first factor is the amount of rain an area receives. A second factor is vegetation. Grasses, shrubs, and trees reduce runoff by absorbing water and holding soil in place. A third factor is the type of soil. Some types of soils absorb more water than others. A fourth factor is the shape of the land. Land that is steeply sloped has more runoff than flatter land. Finally, a fifth factor is how people use the land. For instance, a paved parking lot absorbs no water, so all the rain that falls on it becomes runoff. Runoff also increases when a farmer cuts down crops, since this removes vegetation from the land.

Generally, more runoff means more erosion. In contrast, things that reduce runoff, such as plant leaves and roots, will reduce erosion. Even though deserts have little rainfall, they often have high runoff and erosion. This is because deserts usually have few plants. In wet areas, runoff and erosion may be low because there are more plants to protect the soil.

Checkpoint What factors affect the amount of runoff in a region?

River Systems

A stream grows into a larger stream or river by receiving water from tributaries. A **tributary** is a stream that flows into a larger stream. A small creek that flows into a large river is a tributary to that river. So too is a large river that adds its water to another large river. For instance, the Missouri River becomes a tributary of the Mississippi River near the city of St. Louis, even though both rivers are about the same size there.

Look at Figure 8. Notice all the tributaries to the Ohio River. Together, all these streams—from tiny rills to great rivers—form a system that drains a large part of eastern North America. A **drainage basin** is the land area from which a river and its tributaries collect their water.

If you were to follow a river upstream all the way to its source, you would finally reach a divide. A **divide** is the high ground between two drainage basins. The most famous divide within the United States is the Continental Divide, which follows the high ground of the Rocky Mountains. The Continental Divide separates streams that flow into the Gulf of Mexico from streams that flow into the Great Basin or the Pacific Ocean.

Ohio River Drainage Basin

KEY
— Boundary of drainage basin

Figure 8 The drainage basin of the Ohio River drains much of eastern North America. *Interpreting Maps* What are the tributaries of the Ohio River? Could a tributary come from outside the drainage basin?

Erosion by Rivers

Scientists classify rivers by identifying certain features that form as a result of erosion. **Through erosion, a river creates valleys, waterfalls, flood plains, meanders, and oxbow lakes.**

Rivers often form on steep mountain slopes. Near its source, a river is often fast-flowing and generally follows a straight, narrow course. The steep slopes along the river erode rapidly. The result is a deep, V-shaped valley.

Waterfalls may occur where a river meets an area of rock that is very hard and erodes slowly. The river flows over this rock and then flows over softer rock downstream. The softer rock wears away faster than the harder rock. Eventually a waterfall develops where the softer rock was removed. This process formed Niagara Falls, shown in Figure 9. Areas of rough water called rapids also occur where a river tumbles over hard rock.

Figure 9 Niagara Falls formed on the Niagara River, which connects Lake Erie and Lake Ontario. A flat layer of tough rock lies over a layer of softer rock that erodes easily. When the softer rock erodes, pieces of the harder rock above break off, creating the waterfall's sharp drop.

Harder rock layer

Softer rock layers

Figure 10 The oxbow lake (above) was formerly a part of the channel of the Kasanak River in Alaska. These meanders (right) were formed by a river in Australia.

Lower down on its course, a river usually flows over more gently sloping land. The river spreads out and erodes the land, forming a wide river valley. The flat, wide area of land along a river is a **flood plain.** A river often covers its flood plain when it overflows its banks during floods. On a wide flood plain, the valley walls may be kilometers away from the river itself.

A river often develops meanders where it flows through easily eroded rock or sediment. A **meander** is a looplike bend in the course of a river. As the river widens from side to side, it tends to erode the outer bank and deposit sediment on the inner bank of a bend. Over time, the bend—or meander—becomes more and more curved.

When the gently sloping part of a river flows through an area of sediment or soft rock, it can erode a very wide flood plain. Along this part of a river's course, its channel is deep and wide. Meanders are common along this part of a river. The southern stretch of the Mississippi River is one example of a river that meanders on a wide, gently sloping flood plain.

Sometimes a meandering river forms a feature called an oxbow lake. An **oxbow lake** is a meander that has been cut off from the river. An oxbow lake may form when a river floods. During the flood, high water finds a straighter route downstream. As the flood waters fall, sediments dam up the ends of a meander. The meander has become an oxbow lake.

✓ *Checkpoint* **How does an oxbow lake form?**

Deposits by Rivers

As water moves, it carries sediments with it. Any time moving water slows down, it drops, or deposits, some of the sediment. As the water slows down, fine particles fall to the river's bed. Larger stones quit rolling and sliding. **Deposition creates landforms such as alluvial fans and deltas. It can also add soil to a river's flood plain.** In *Exploring the Course of a River* on pages 258–259, you can see these and other features shaped by rivers and streams.

Alluvial Fans Where a stream flows out of a steep, narrow mountain valley, the stream suddenly becomes wider and shallower. The water slows down. Here sediments are deposited in an alluvial fan. An **alluvial fan** is a wide, sloping deposit of sediment formed where a stream leaves a mountain range. As its name suggests, this deposit is shaped like a fan.

Deltas A river ends its journey when it flows into a still body of water, such as an ocean or a lake. Because the river water is no longer flowing downhill, the water slows down. At this point, the sediment in the water drops to the bottom. Sediment deposited where a river flows into an ocean or lake builds up a landform called a **delta.** Deltas can be a variety of shapes: some are arc-shaped, others are triangle-shaped. The delta of the Mississippi River is an example of a type of delta called a "bird's foot" delta.

Soil on Flood Plains Deposition also occurs during floods.

![INTEGRATING LIFE SCIENCE] Then heavy rains or melting snow cause a river to rise above its banks and spread out over its flood plain. When the flood water finally retreats, it deposits sediment as new soil. Deposition of new soil over a flood plain is what makes a river valley fertile. Dense forests can grow in the rich soil of a flood plain. The soil is also perfect for growing crops.

Figure 11 This alluvial fan in Death Valley, California, was formed from deposits by streams from the mountains.

Figure 12 This satellite image shows part of the Mississippi River delta, which is always growing and changing. *Observing What happens to the Mississippi River as it flows through its delta? Can you find the river's main channel?*

EXPLORING *the Course of a River*

The slope and size of a river, as well as the land through which it flows, determine how a river shapes the land.

Tributary A river receives water and sediment from a tributary—a smaller river or stream that flows into it.

Oxbow lakes An oxbow lake is a meander cut off from a river by deposition of sediment.

Valley widening As a river approaches sea level, it may meander more and develop a wider valley and a broader flood plain.

Delta Where a river flows into the ocean, the river deposits sediment, forming a delta.

Waterfalls and rapids Waterfalls and rapids are common where the river passes over harder rock.

V-shaped valley Near its source, a river often flows through a deep, V-shaped valley. As the river flows, it cuts a deeper valley.

Meanders Where a river flows across easily eroded sediment, its channel bends from side to side in a series of meanders.

Oxbow lake

Flood plain A flood plain forms when a river's power of erosion widens its valley rather than deepening it.

Beaches Sand carried downstream by rivers spreads along the coast to form beaches.

Groundwater Erosion and Deposition

When rain falls and snow melts, not all of the water evaporates or becomes runoff. Some water soaks into the ground. There it fills the openings in the soil and trickles into cracks and spaces in layers of rock. **Groundwater** is the term geologists use for this underground water. Like running water on the surface, groundwater affects the shape of the land.

INTEGRATING CHEMISTRY Groundwater can cause erosion through a process of chemical weathering. When water sinks into the ground, it combines with carbon dioxide to form a weak acid, called carbonic acid. Carbonic acid can break down limestone. Groundwater containing carbonic acid flows into cracks in the limestone. Then some of the limestone changes chemically and is carried away in a solution of water. This gradually hollows out pockets in the rock. Over time, these pockets develop into large holes underground, called caves or caverns.

The action of carbonic acid on limestone can also result in deposition. Inside limestone caves, deposits called stalactites and stalagmites often form. Water containing carbonic acid and calcium from limestone drips from a cave's roof. As the water

Figure 13 Over millions of years, chemical weathering of limestone and groundwater erosion created the beautiful shapes in Carlsbad Caverns in New Mexico.
Interpreting Photos What evidence of deposition do you see in the photo of Carlsbad Caverns?

Figure 14 A sinkhole, such as this one in Florida, is a characteristic feature of karst topography. Sinkholes can pose a hazard for people who live in a karst region.

evaporates, a deposit of calcite forms. A deposit that hangs like an icicle from the roof of a cave is called a **stalactite** (stuh LAK tyt). Slow dripping builds up a cone-shaped **stalagmite** (stuh LAG myt) from the cave floor.

In rainy regions where there is a layer of limestone near the surface, groundwater erosion can significantly change the shape of the land. Surface streams are rare, because water sinks easily down into the weathered limestone. Deep valleys and caverns are common. If the roof of a cave collapses because of the erosion of the underlying limestone, the result is a depression called a sinkhole. This type of landscape is called **karst topography** after a region in Eastern Europe. In the United States, there are regions of karst topography in Florida, Kentucky, and Indiana.

Section 2 Review

1. What is the major cause of erosion on Earth's surface?
2. Briefly describe five features formed by rivers and streams as they erode the land.
3. What are the results of deposition along the course of a stream or river?
4. How can groundwater contribute to erosion?
5. **Thinking Critically Comparing and Contrasting** How is an alluvial fan similar to a delta? How is it different?

Science at Home

Erosion Cube In a small dish, build a cube out of 27 small sugar cubes. Your cube should be three sugar cubes on a side. Fold a square piece of paper towel to fit the top of the cube. Wet the paper towel, place it on the cube, and let it stand for 15 or 20 minutes. Every few minutes, sprinkle a few drops of water on the paper towel to keep it wet. Then remove the paper towel. What happened to your cube? How is the effect of water on a sugar cube similar to groundwater eroding limestone? How is it different?

Streams in Action

Erosion can form gullies, wash away topsoil, and pollute rivers with sediment. You can observe the effects of erosion using a stream table.

Problem

How do rivers and streams erode the land?

Skills Focus

making models, observing, predicting

Materials

plastic tub at least 27 cm × 40 cm × 10 cm
diatomaceous earth   plastic measuring cup
spray bottle   hand lens
watch or clock   water
1 metal spoon   plastic foam cup
blue food coloring   liquid detergent
scissors
2 wood blocks about 2.5 cm thick
bucket to hold 2–3 L of water or a source of
    tap water
plastic stirrers, 10–12 cm long, with two
    small holes each
wire 13–15 cm long, 20 gauge

Procedure

Part A Creating Streams Over Time

1. Your teacher will give you a plastic tub containing diatomaceous earth that has been soaked with water. Place the tub on a level surface. **CAUTION:** *Dry diatomaceous earth produces dust that may be irritating if inhaled. To keep the diatomaceous earth from drying out, spray it lightly with water.*

Making the Dripper

1. Insert the wire into one of the two holes in a plastic stirrer. The ends of the wire should protrude from the stirrer.

2. Gently bend the stirrer into a U shape. Be careful not to make any sharp bends. This is the dripper.

3. With scissors, carefully cut two small notches on opposite sides of the top of the foam cup.

4. Fill the cup to just below the notches with water colored with two drops of blue food coloring. Add more food coloring later as you add more water to the cup.

5. Add one drop of detergent to keep air bubbles out of the dripper and increase flow.

6. To start the dripper, fill it with water. Then quickly tip it and place it in one of the notches in the cup, as shown above.

7. Adjust the flow rate of the dripper to about 2 drips per 1 second. (*Hint:* Bend the dripper into more of a U shape to increase flow. Lessen the curve to reduce flow.)

2. One end of the tub will contain more diatomaceous earth. Use the block of wood to raise this end of the tub 2.5 cm.

3. Place the cup at the upper end of the slope with the notches pointing to the left and right.

4. Press the cup firmly down into the earth to secure its position.

5. Start the dripper (see Step 6 in the box above). Allow the water to drip to the right onto the diatomaceous earth.

6. Allow the dripper to drip for 5 minutes. (*Hint:* When you need to add more water, be careful not to disturb the dripper.)

7. Observe the flow of water and the changes it makes. Use the hand lens to look closely at the stream bed.

8. After 5 minutes, remove the dripper.

9. In your lab notebook, draw a picture of the resulting stream and label it "5 minutes."

10. Now switch the dripper to the left side of the cup. Restart the dripper and allow it to drip for 10 minutes. Then remove the dripper.

11. Draw a picture and label it "10 minutes."

Part B Changing the Angle of Slope

1. Remove the cup from the stream table.

2. Save the stream bed on the right side of the tub. Using the bowl of the spoon, smooth out the diatomaceous earth on the left side.

3. To increase the angle of slope of your stream table, raise the end of the tub another 2.5 cm.

4. In your lab notebook, predict the effects of increasing the angle of slope.

5. Replace the cup and restart the dripper, placing it in the notch on the left side of the cup. Allow the dripper to drip for 5 minutes. Notice any changes in the new stream bed.

6. At the end of 5 minutes, remove the dripper.

7. Draw a picture of the new stream bed in your lab notebook. Label it "Increased Angle."

8. Follow your teacher's instructions for clean-up after this activity. Wash your hands when you have finished.

Analyze and Conclude

1. Compare the 5-minute stream with the 10-minute stream. How did the length of time that the water flowed affect erosion along the stream bed?

2. Were your predictions about the effects of increasing the angle of slope correct? Explain your answer.

3. What eventually happened to the eroded material that was carried downstream?

4. What other variables besides time and angle of slope might affect the way rivers and streams erode the land?

5. **Apply** Have you ever seen water flowing down a hillside or street after a heavy rain? If so, how much did the land slope in that area? Did you notice anything about the color of the water? Explain.

Design an Experiment

Design a stream table experiment to measure how the amount of sediment carried by a river changes as the volume of flow of the river increases. Obtain your teacher's approval before you try the experiment.

Protecting Homes in Flood Plains

At least ten million American households are located in flood plains. Living near a river is tempting. Riverside land is often flat and easy to build on. Because so many people now live in flood plains, the cost of flood damage has been growing. Communities along rivers want to limit the cost of flooding. They want to know how they can protect the people and buildings already in flood plains. They also want to know how to discourage more people from moving into flood plains.

The Issues

Should the Government Insure People Against Flood Damage? The United States government offers insurance to households in flood plains. The insurance pays part of the cost of repairs after a flood. Insurance helps people, but it is very expensive. Only 17 percent of people who live in flood plains buy the government insurance. Government flood insurance is available only in places that take steps to reduce flood damage. Cities must allow new building only on high ground. The insurance will not pay to rebuild homes that are badly damaged by floodwater. Instead, these people must use the money to find a home somewhere else.

Critics say that insurance just encourages people to move back into areas that flood. Supporters say it rewards towns and cities that make rules to control building on flood plains.

How Much of the Flood Plain Should Be Protected? Government flood insurance is available only in areas where scientists expect flooding about once in 100 years, or once in 500 years. Such figures are just estimates. Three floods occurred in only 12 years in a government flood-insurance area near Sacramento, California.

Should the Government Tell People Where They Can Live? Some programs of flood control forbid all new building. Other programs may also encourage people to move to safer areas. The 1997 flood on the Red River in Grand Forks, North Dakota, is one example. After the flood, the city of Grand Forks offered to buy all the damaged buildings near the river. The city wants to build high walls of earth to protect the rest of the town.

The Grand Forks plan might prevent future damage, but is it fair? Supporters say that since the government has to pay for flood damage, it has the right to make people leave flood plains. Critics of such plans say that people should be free to live where they want, even in risky areas.

Who should decide in which neighborhood no new houses can be built? Who decides which people should be asked to move away from a flood plain? Experts disagree over whether local, state, or United States government officials should decide which areas to include. Some believe scientists should make the decision.

You Decide

1. Identify the Problem
In your own words, describe the controversy surrounding flood plains and housing.

2. Analyze the Options
List several steps that could be taken to reduce the damage done to buildings in flood plains. For each step, include who would benefit from the step, and who would pay the costs.

3. Find a Solution
Your town has to decide what to do about a neighborhood damaged by the worst flood in 50 years. Write a speech that argues for your solution.

SECTION 3 The Force of Moving Water

How Are Sediments Deposited?

1. Put on your goggles.

2. Obtain a clear plastic jar or bottle with a top. Fill the jar about two-thirds full with water.

3. Fill a plastic beaker with 200 mL of fine and coarse sand, soil, clay, and small pebbles.

4. Pour the mixture into the jar of water. Screw on the top tightly and shake for two minutes. Be sure to hold onto the jar firmly.

5. Set the jar down and observe it for 10 to 15 minutes.

Think It Over

Inferring In what order are the sediments in the jar deposited? What do you think causes this pattern?

The Merrimack River in New Hampshire and Massachusetts is only 180 kilometers long. But the Merrimack does a great deal of work as it runs from the mountains to the sea. The river's waters fall 82 meters through many rapids and waterfalls. During the 1800s, people harnessed this falling water to run machines. These machines could spin thread and weave cloth very quickly and cheaply. Thanks to water power, the towns along the river grew quickly into cities.

Work and Energy

The waters of the Merrimack River could drive machines because a river's water has energy. **Energy** is the ability to do work or cause change. There are two kinds of energy. **Potential energy** is energy that is stored and waiting to be used later. The Merrimack's waters begin with potential energy due to their position above sea level. **Kinetic energy** is the energy an object has due to its motion. **As gravity pulls water down a slope, the water's potential energy changes to kinetic energy that can do work.**

◆ What enables water to do work?

◆ How does sediment enter rivers and streams?

◆ What factors affect a river's ability to erode and carry sediment?

Reading Tip Before you read, rewrite the headings of the section as *how, why,* or *what* questions. As you read, look for answers to these questions.

Figure 15 Dams like this one on the Merrimack River in Lowell, Massachusetts, help to harness the power of flowing water.

The cotton mills in Lowell, Massachusetts, were built in the 1820s. The mills employed young women from the farms and small towns of New England. At that time, it was unusual for women to work outside the home. The hours of work at a mill were long and pay was low. But mill work helped these women to earn and save their own money. Most later returned to their hometowns.

In Your Journal

Use library references to find out more about the daily life of the mill workers. Write a diary entry describing a worker's typical day.

When energy does work, the energy is transferred from one object to another. At the textile mills along the Merrimack River, the kinetic energy of the moving water was transferred to the spinning machines. It became mechanical energy harnessed for a human purpose—making cloth. But all along a river, kinetic energy does other work. A river is always moving sediment from the mountains to the sea. At the same time, a river is also eroding its banks and valley.

☑ *Checkpoint* What are potential energy and kinetic energy?

How Water Erodes and Carries Sediment

Gravity causes the movement of water across Earth's land surface. But how does water cause erosion? In the process of water erosion, water picks up and moves sediment. Sediment includes soil, rock, clay, and sand. Sediment can enter rivers and streams in a number of ways. **Most sediment washes or falls into the river as a result of mass movement and runoff. Other sediment erodes from the bottom or sides of the river.** Wind may also drop sediment into the water.

Abrasion is another process by which a river obtains sediment. **Abrasion** is the wearing away of rock by a grinding action. Abrasion occurs when particles of sediment in flowing water bump into the streambed again and again. Abrasion grinds down sediment particles. For example, boulders become smaller as they are moved down a streambed. Sediments also grind and chip away at the rock of the streambed, deepening and widening the stream's channel.

The amount of sediment that a river carries is its **load.** Gravity and the force of the moving water cause the sediment load to move downstream. Most large sediment falls to the bottom and moves by rolling and sliding. Fast-moving water actually lifts sand and other, smaller, sediment and carries it downstream. Water dissolves some sediment completely. The river carries these dissolved sediments in solution. If you look at Figure 16, you can observe the different ways in which water can carry sediment. Notice for example, how grains of sand or small stones can move by bouncing.

Figure 16 Rivers and streams carry sediment in several ways. *Predicting What will eventually happen to a boulder on the bottom of a river?*

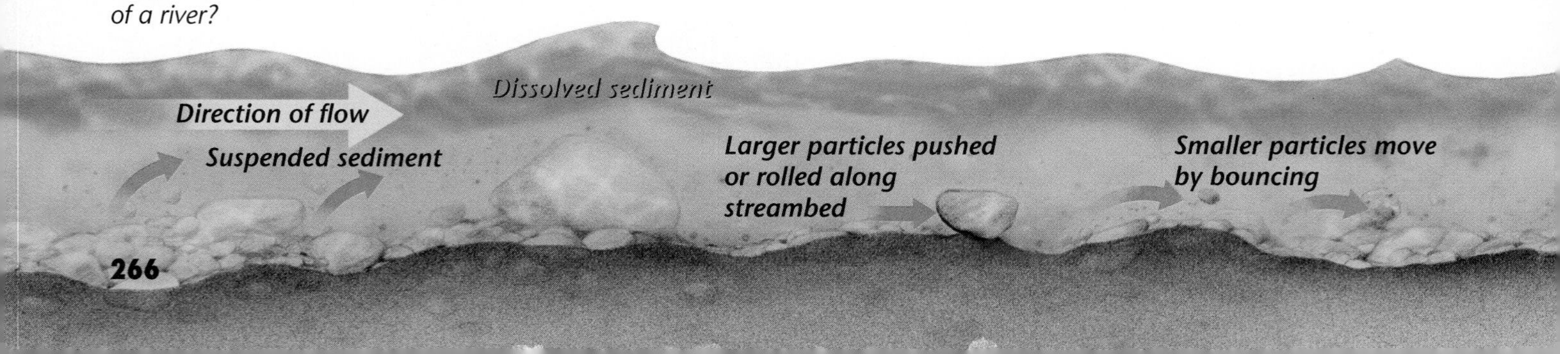

Direction of flow

Suspended sediment

Dissolved sediment

Larger particles pushed or rolled along streambed

Smaller particles move by bouncing

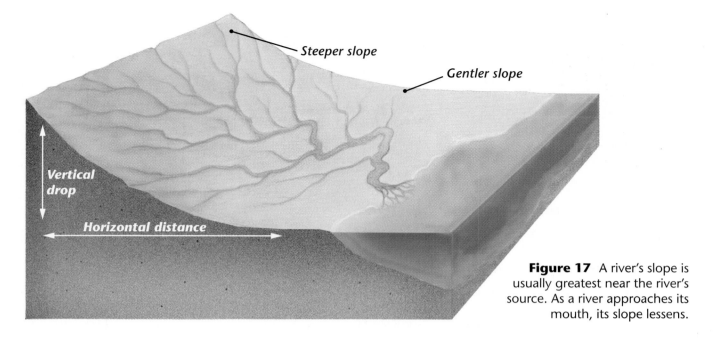

Steeper slope

Gentler slope

Vertical drop

Horizontal distance

Figure 17 A river's slope is usually greatest near the river's source. As a river approaches its mouth, its slope lessens.

Erosion and Sediment Load

The power of a river to cause erosion and carry sediment depends on several factors. **A river's slope, volume of flow, and the shape of its streambed all affect how fast the river flows and how much sediment it can erode.**

A fast-flowing river carries more and larger particles of sediment. When a river slows down, its sediment load is deposited. The larger particles of sediment are deposited first.

Slope Generally, if a river's slope increases, the water's speed also increases. A river's slope is the amount the river drops toward sea level over a given distance. If a river's speed increases, its sediment load and power to erode may increase. But other factors are also important in determining how much sediment the river erodes and carries.

Volume of Flow A river's flow is the volume of water that moves past a point on the river in a given time. As more water flows through a river, its speed increases. During a flood, the increased volume of water helps the river to cut more deeply into its banks and bed. A flooding river may have hundreds of times more eroding power than the river has at other times. A flooding river can carry huge amounts of sand, soil, and other sediments. It may move giant boulders as if they were pebbles.

Streambed Shape A streambed's shape affects the amount of friction between the water and the streambed. **Friction** is the force that opposes the motion of one surface as it moves across another surface. Friction, in turn, affects a river's speed. Where a river is deep, only a small fraction of the water comes in contact with the

Sharpen your Skills

Developing Hypotheses

ACTIVITY

A geologist is comparing alluvial fans. One alluvial fan is composed of gravel and small boulders. The other fan is composed of sand and silt. Propose a hypothesis to explain the difference in the size of the particles in the two fans. (*Hint:* Think of the characteristics of the streams that formed each alluvial fan.)

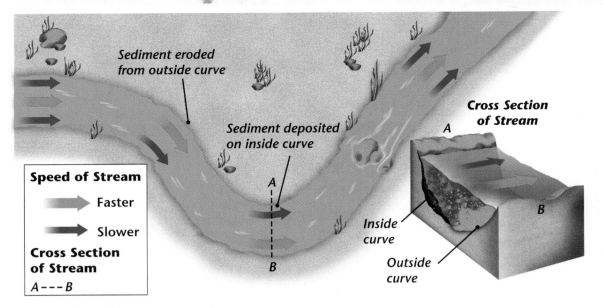

Speed of Stream

→ Faster

→ Slower

Cross Section of Stream
A - - - B

Sediment eroded from outside curve

Sediment deposited on inside curve

Cross Section of Stream

A

B

Inside curve

Outside curve

Figure 18 A river erodes sediment from its banks on the outside curve and deposits its sediment on the inside curve.
Relating Cause and Effect Why does a river deposit sediment on the inside of a curve?

streambed. This reduces friction and allows the river to flow faster. In a shallow river, much of the water comes in contact with the streambed. Therefore friction increases, reducing the river's speed.

A streambed is often full of boulders and other obstacles. This roughness prevents the water from flowing smoothly. Roughness thus increases friction and reduces the river's speed. Instead of moving downstream, the water moves every which way in a type of movement called **turbulence.** For example, a stream on a steep slope may flow at a lower speed than a large river on a gentle slope. Friction and turbulence slow the stream's flow. But a turbulent stream or river may have great power to erode.

The shape of a river affects the way it deposits sediment. Where a river flows in a straight line, the water flows faster near the center of the river than along its sides. Deposition occurs along the sides of the river, where the water moves more slowly.

If a river curves, the water moves fastest along the outside of the curve. There, the river tends to cut into its bank. Sediment is deposited on the inside curve, where the water speed is slowest. You can see this process in Figure 18.

Section 3 Review

1. How can moving water on Earth's surface do work?
2. How does a river collect sediment?
3. What are three factors that affect a river's sediment load?
4. Describe three ways that sediment moves in a river.
5. **Thinking Critically** **Relating Cause and Effect** What effect does increased slope have on a river's speed and sediment load? Explain.

Check Your Progress

CHAPTER PROJECT

Make a drawing of the landscape that you plan to model. This landscape will show the land before erosion. What kinds of landforms will you show in the model? Be sure to include a high mountain and a coastline. Make a list of materials that you will use to build your model. Once your teacher has approved your drawing and your list of materials, you may build your first model.

DISCOVER ••ACTIVITY••••

How Do Glaciers Change the Land?

1. Put some sand in a small plastic container.

2. Fill the container with water and place the container in a freezer until the water turns to ice.

3. Remove the block of ice from the container.

4. Holding the ice with paper towels, rub the ice, sand side down, over a bar of soap. Observe what happens to the surface of the soap.

Think It Over

Inferring Based on your observations, how do you think moving ice could change the surface of the land?

Y ou are on a boat trip near the coast of Alaska. You sail by vast evergreen forests and snow-capped mountains. Then, as your boat rounds a point of land, you see an amazing sight. A great mass of ice winds like a river between rows of mountains. Suddenly you hear a noise like thunder. Where the ice meets the sea, a giant chunk of ice breaks off and plunges into the water. Carefully, you pilot your boat around the iceberg and toward the mass of ice. It towers over your boat. You see that it is made up of solid ice that is deep blue and green as well as white. What is this river of ice?

GUIDE FOR READING

◆ What are the two kinds of glaciers?

◆ How do glaciers cause erosion and deposition?

Reading Tip Before you read, preview the headings and key terms in the section. Predict some characteristics of glaciers.

Kinds of Glaciers

Geologists define a **glacier** as any large mass of ice that moves slowly over land. **There are two kinds of glaciers—valley glaciers and continental glaciers.**

A **valley glacier** is a long, narrow glacier that forms when snow and ice build up high in a mountain valley. The sides of mountains keep these glaciers from spreading out in all directions. Instead, they usually move down valleys that have already been cut by rivers. Valley glaciers are found on many high mountains.

A **continental glacier** is a glacier that covers much of a continent or large island. Continental glaciers are much larger than

Figure 19 The Mendenhall Glacier in Alaska winds downhill between high mountains.

The Ice Age in North America

KEY
Area covered by continental glacier

Figure 20 The continental glacier of the last ice age covered most of Canada and Alaska as well as much of the northern United States. The ice age lasted about 70,000 years and ended about 10,000 years ago.

valley glaciers. They spread out over large areas of the land. Today, continental glaciers cover about 10 percent of Earth's land. They cover Antarctica and most of Greenland. The glacier covering Antarctica spreads out over 14 million square kilometers and is over 2 kilometers thick.

Ice Ages

Many times in the past, continental glaciers have covered large parts of Earth's surface. These times are known as **ice ages.** For example, about 9 million years ago, continental glaciers began to form in North America, Europe, and Asia. These glaciers slowly grew and advanced southward. By about 2.5 million years ago, they covered about a third of Earth's land. The glaciers advanced and retreated, or melted back, several times. Figure 20 shows how far south the glaciers came on the North American continent during the most recent ice age. They finally retreated about 10,000 years ago.

How Glaciers Form and Move

Glaciers can form only in an area where more snow falls than melts. High in mountain valleys, temperatures seldom rise above freezing. Snow builds up year after year. The pressure of the weight of more and more snow compacts the snow at the bottom into ice. Once the depth of snow and ice reaches more than 30 to 40 meters, gravity begins to pull the glacier downhill.

Valley glaciers flow at a rate of a few centimeters to a few meters per day. But sometimes a valley glacier slides down more quickly in what is called a surge. A surging glacier can flow as much as 6 kilometers a year. Unlike valley glaciers, continental glaciers can flow in all directions. Continental glaciers spread out much as pancake batter spreads out in a frying pan.

✓ *Checkpoint* How do glaciers form?

Glacial Erosion

The movement of a glacier changes the land beneath it. Although glaciers work slowly, they are a major force of erosion. **The two processes by which glaciers erode the land are plucking and abrasion.**

As a glacier flows over the land, it picks up rocks in a process called **plucking.** Beneath a glacier, the weight of the ice can break rocks apart. These rock fragments freeze to the bottom of the glacier. When the glacier moves, it carries the rocks with it. Figure 21 shows plucking by a glacier. Plucking can move even huge boulders.

Many rocks remain on the bottom of the glacier, and the glacier drags them across the land. This process, called abrasion, gouges and scratches the bedrock. You can see the results of erosion by glaciers in *Exploring Glacial Landforms* on pages 272–273.

Direction of ice flow

Ice in cracks

Bedrock

Figure 21 As a glacier moves downhill, the ice plucks pieces of bedrock from the ground. *Predicting What evidence of plucking might you find after a glacier melts?*

Glacial Deposition

A glacier gathers a huge amount of rock and soil as it erodes the land in its path. **When a glacier melts, it deposits the sediment it eroded from the land, creating various landforms.** These landforms remain for thousands of years after the glacier has melted.

The mixture of sediments that a glacier deposits directly on the surface is called **till.** Till is made up of particles of many different sizes. Clay, silt, sand, gravel, and boulders can all be found in till.

The till deposited at the edges of a glacier forms a ridge called a **moraine.** A terminal moraine is the ridge of till at the farthest point reached by a glacier. Long Island in New York is a terminal moraine from the continental glaciers of the last ice age.

INTEGRATING LIFE SCIENCE Other features left in glacial sediments are prairie potholes. These potholes are shallow depressions in till that were formed by flowing water as the continental glacier melted. Today, prairie potholes contain water for only part of the year. Each prairie pothole is a small oasis for living things. Grasses and moisture-loving plants grow thickly in and around the potholes. In the spring, the potholes brim with water from melting snow or rain. Thousands of migrating ducks and other birds stop off at the potholes to feed and rest on their way north. Some stay to build nests and raise their young.

Figure 22 This prairie pothole in Wisconsin is surrounded by farmland. Prairie potholes were left in till deposited by glaciers.

EXPLORING Glacial Landforms

As glaciers advance and retreat, they sculpt the landscape by erosion and deposition.

Horn When glaciers carve away the sides of a mountain, the result is a horn, a sharpened peak.

Cirque A cirque is a bowl-shaped hollow eroded by a glacier.

Arête An arête is a sharp ridge separating two cirques.

Fiord A fiord forms when the level of the sea rises, filling a valley once cut by a glacier in a coastal region.

Retreating glaciers also create features called kettles. A **kettle** is a small depression that forms when a chunk of ice is left in glacial till. When the ice melts, the kettle remains. The continental glacier of the last ice age left behind many kettles. Kettles often fill with water, forming small ponds or lakes called kettle lakes. Such lakes are common in areas that were covered with ice.

The continental glacier of the last ice age also formed the Great Lakes. Before the ice age, there were large river valleys in the area now occupied by the lakes. As the ice advanced over these valleys, it scooped out loose sediment and soft rock, forming broad, deep basins. The Great Lakes formed over thousands of years as the glaciers melted and these basins filled with water.

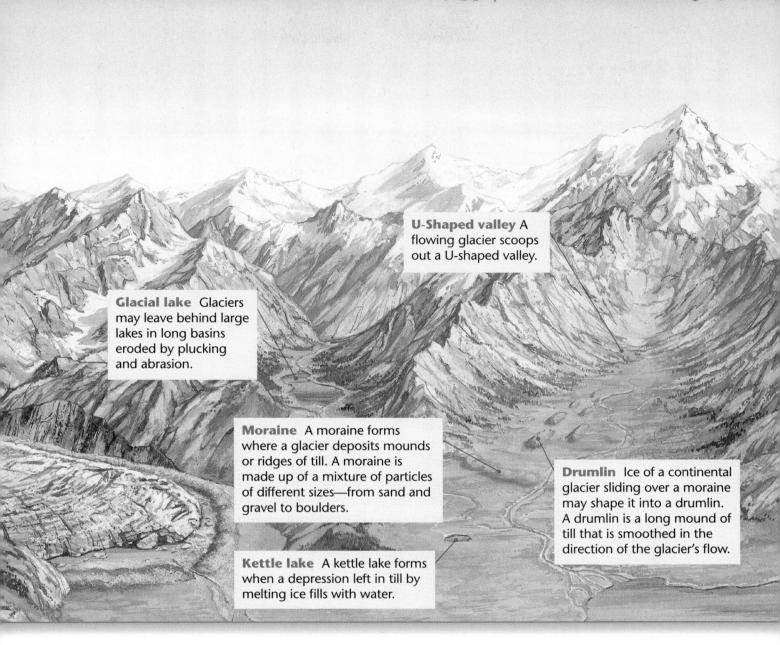

U-Shaped valley A flowing glacier scoops out a U-shaped valley.

Glacial lake Glaciers may leave behind large lakes in long basins eroded by plucking and abrasion.

Moraine A moraine forms where a glacier deposits mounds or ridges of till. A moraine is made up of a mixture of particles of different sizes—from sand and gravel to boulders.

Drumlin Ice of a continental glacier sliding over a moraine may shape it into a drumlin. A drumlin is a long mound of till that is smoothed in the direction of the glacier's flow.

Kettle lake A kettle lake forms when a depression left in till by melting ice fills with water.

Section 4 Review

1. How are valley glaciers and continental glaciers different?
2. What are two types of glacial erosion?
3. Describe three features formed by glacial deposition.
4. **Thinking Critically** **Relating Cause and Effect** Driving through the countryside in Michigan, you and your family come upon a series of small, round lakes. Explain the process that formed these features.

Check Your Progress CHAPTER PROJECT

Now you are ready to begin building your second model. Pattern the model after your drawing that predicts the effects of erosion and deposition. The model will show how gravity, water, and glaciers have changed your model landscape. Where on your model would glaciers be likely to form?

SECTION
5 Waves

DISCOVER ••• ACTIVITY

What Can Be Learned From Beach Sand?

1. Collect a spoonful of sand from each of two different beaches. The two samples also may come from different parts of the same beach.

2. Examine the first sample of beach sand with a hand lens.

3. Record the properties of the sand grains, for example, color and shape. Are the grains smooth and rounded or angular and rough? Are all the grains in the sample the same shape and color?

4. Examine the second sample and repeat Step 3. How do the two samples compare?

Think It Over
Posing Questions What questions do you need to answer to understand beach sand? Use what you know about erosion and deposition to help you think of questions.

GUIDE FOR READING

◆ What gives waves their energy?

◆ How do waves shape a coast?

Reading Tip As you read, make a concept map showing features formed by wave erosion and deposition.

Ocean waves contain energy—sometimes a great deal of energy. The waves that sweep onto the Pacific coast are especially powerful. Created by ocean winds, they carry energy vast distances across the Pacific Ocean. Acting like drills or buzzsaws, the waves erode the solid rock of the coast into cliffs and caves. Waves also carry sediment that forms features such as beaches. But these features do not last long. More waves follow to change the shoreline yet again.

How Waves Form

The energy in waves comes from wind that blows across the water's surface. As the wind makes contact with the water, some of its energy transfers to the water. Large ocean waves are the result of powerful storms far out at sea. But ordinary breezes can produce waves in lakes or small ponds.

The energy that water picks up from the wind causes water particles to move up and down as the wave goes by. But the water particles themselves don't move forward. Only the form of the wave moves. Have you ever watched a wave in a field of tall grass? Each blade of grass moves back and forth but doesn't move from its place. But the energy of the wave moves across the field.

Waves on the Oregon coast ▼

274

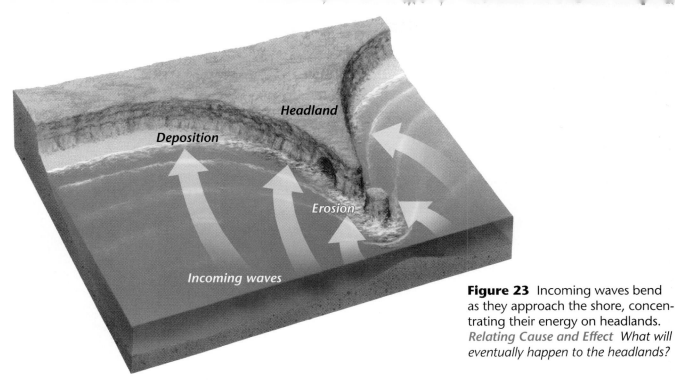

Headland

Deposition

Erosion

Incoming waves

Figure 23 Incoming waves bend as they approach the shore, concentrating their energy on headlands. *Relating Cause and Effect* What will eventually happen to the headlands?

A wave changes as it approaches land. In deep water, a wave only affects the water near the surface. But as the wave approaches shallow water, the wave begins to drag the bottom. The friction between the wave and the bottom causes the wave to slow down. Now the water actually does move forward with the wave. This forward-moving water provides the force that shapes the land along the shoreline.

Erosion by Waves

Waves are the major force of erosion along coasts. One way waves erode the land is by impact. Large waves can hit rocks along the shore with great force. This energy in waves can break apart rocks. Over time, waves can make small cracks larger. Eventually, the waves cause pieces of rock to break off.

Waves also erode land by abrasion. As a wave approaches shallow water, it picks up sediment, including sand and gravel. This sediment is carried forward by the wave. When the wave hits land, the sediment wears away rock like sandpaper wearing away wood.

Waves coming to shore gradually change direction. The change in direction occurs as different parts of a wave begin to drag on the bottom. Notice how the waves in Figure 23 change direction as they approach the shore. The energy of these waves is concentrated on headlands. A headland is a part of the shore that sticks out into the ocean. Headlands stand out from the coast because they are made of harder rock that resists the waves. But, over time, waves erode the headlands and even out the shoreline.

✓ *Checkpoint* *What are two of the processes by which waves can cause erosion?*

Sharpen your Skills

Calculating
ACTIVITY

A sandy coast erodes at a rate of 1.25 meters per year. But a severe storm can erode an additional 3.75 meters from the shore. If 12 severe storms occur during a 50-year period, how much will the coast erode? If you wish, you may use an electronic calculator to find the answer.

Figure 24 Waves cut these cliffs on the coast of Australia. The blocks of rock offshore are sea stacks.
Developing Hypotheses Develop a hypothesis to explain how these sea stacks formed.

Landforms Created by Wave Erosion

When waves hit a steep, rocky coast, they strike the area again and again. Think of an ax striking the trunk of a tree. The cut gets bigger and deeper with each strike of the blade. Finally the tree falls. In a similar way, ocean waves erode the base of the land along a steep coast. Where the rock is softer, the waves erode the land faster. Over time the waves may erode a hollow area in the rock called a sea cave.

Eventually, waves may erode the base of a cliff so much that the rock above collapses. The result is a wave-cut cliff. You can see an example of such a cliff in Figure 24.

Another feature created by wave erosion is a sea arch. A sea arch forms when waves erode a layer of softer rock that underlies a layer of harder rock. If an arch collapses, the result might be a sea stack, a pillar of rock rising above the water.

✓ *Checkpoint* *How can waves produce a cliff on a rocky coast?*

Deposits by Waves

Waves not only erode the land, they also deposit sediment. **Waves shape the coast through both erosion and deposition.** Deposition occurs when waves slow down and the water drops its sediment. This process is similar to the deposition that occurs on a river delta when the river slows down and drops its sediment load.

276

As waves reach the shore, they drop the sediment they carry, forming a beach. A **beach** is an area of wave-washed sediment along a coast. The sediment deposited on beaches is usually sand. Most sand comes from rivers that carry eroded particles of rock into the ocean. But not all beaches are made of sand carried by rivers. Some beaches are made of small fragments of coral or sea shells piled up by wave action. Florida has many such beaches.

The sediment on a beach usually moves down the beach after it has been deposited. Waves usually hit the beach at an angle instead of straight on. These angled waves create a current that runs parallel to the coastline. As repeated waves hit the beach, some of the beach sediment moves down the beach with the current, in a process called **longshore drift.**

One result of longshore drift is the formation of a spit. A **spit** is a beach that projects like a finger out into the water. Spits form as a result of deposition by longshore drift. Spits occur where a headland or other obstacle interrupts longshore drift, or where the coast turns abruptly. Incoming waves carrying sand may build up sandbars, long ridges of sand parallel to the shore.

 INTEGRATING ENVIRONMENTAL SCIENCE A barrier beach is similar to a sandbar, but a barrier beach forms when storm waves pile up sand above sea level. Barrier beaches are found in many places along the Atlantic coast of the United States, such as the Outer Banks of North Carolina. People have built homes on many of these barrier beaches. But the storm waves that build up the beaches can also wash them away. Barrier beach communities must be prepared for the damage that hurricanes and other storms can bring.

Figure 25 This satellite image of Cape Cod in Massachusetts shows how longshore drift can carry sand and deposit it to form a spit. *Observing How many spits can you find in this image?*

Section 5 Review

1. How do ocean waves form?
2. Describe two landforms created by wave erosion and two landforms created by wave deposition.
3. Why are headlands eroded faster than the land at the ends of inlets and bays?
4. **Thinking Critically** **Predicting** You visit a rocky headland by the ocean that has a sea arch and several sea stacks. How might this area change in the next 500 years?

Check Your Progress

CHAPTER PROJECT

Now you are ready to add the effects of wave erosion to your model. What landforms will wave erosion produce along the coastline on your model? What materials will you use to model these landforms? When you have finished your second model, make labels for the landforms on your models.

SECTION 6 Wind

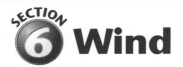

DISCOVER ACTIVITY

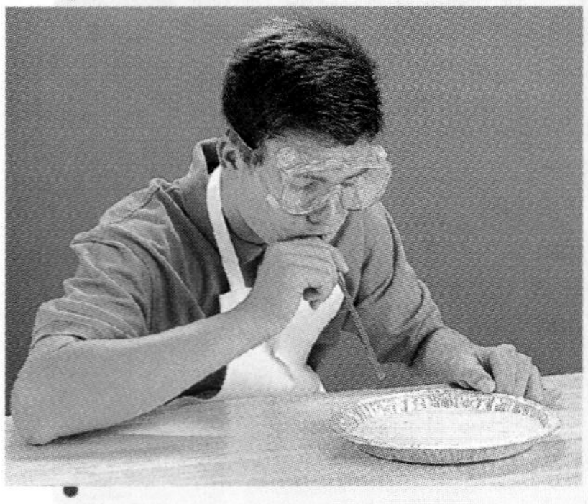

How Does Moving Air Affect Sediment?

1. Cover the bottom of a pan with a flat layer of cornmeal 1–2 centimeters deep.
2. Gently blow over the layer of cornmeal using a straw to direct your breath. Observe what happens.

CAUTION: *Do not blow the cornmeal in the direction of another student.*

Think It Over

Observing What changes did the wind you created make in the flat layer of cornmeal?

GUIDE FOR READING

- **How does wind cause erosion?**
- **What features result from deposition by wind?**

Reading Tip **Before you read, preview Figure 27. Predict some characteristics of wind erosion.**

Imagine a landscape made almost entirely of sand. One such place is the Namib Desert. The desert stretches for about 1,900 kilometers along the coast of Namibia in Africa. In the southern half of the Namib are long rows of giant sand dunes. A **sand dune** is a deposit of wind-blown sand. Some sand dunes in the Namib are more than 200 meters high and 15 kilometers long. Much of the sand in the dunes originally came from the nearby Orange River. Over thousands of years, wind has swept the sand across the desert, piling up huge, ever-changing dunes.

How Wind Causes Erosion

Wind by itself is the weakest agent of erosion. Water, waves, moving ice, and even mass movement have more effect on the land. Yet wind can be a powerful force in shaping the land in areas where there are few plants to hold the soil in place. As you might guess, wind is very effective in causing erosion in deserts. There few plants can grow, and wind can easily move the grains of dry, light sand.

Figure 26 Wind erosion continues to shape the giant sand dunes in the Namib Desert along Africa's southwestern coast.

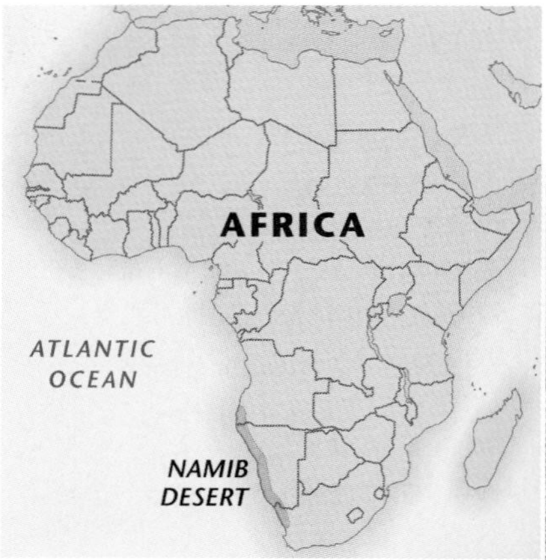
AFRICA
ATLANTIC OCEAN
NAMIB DESERT

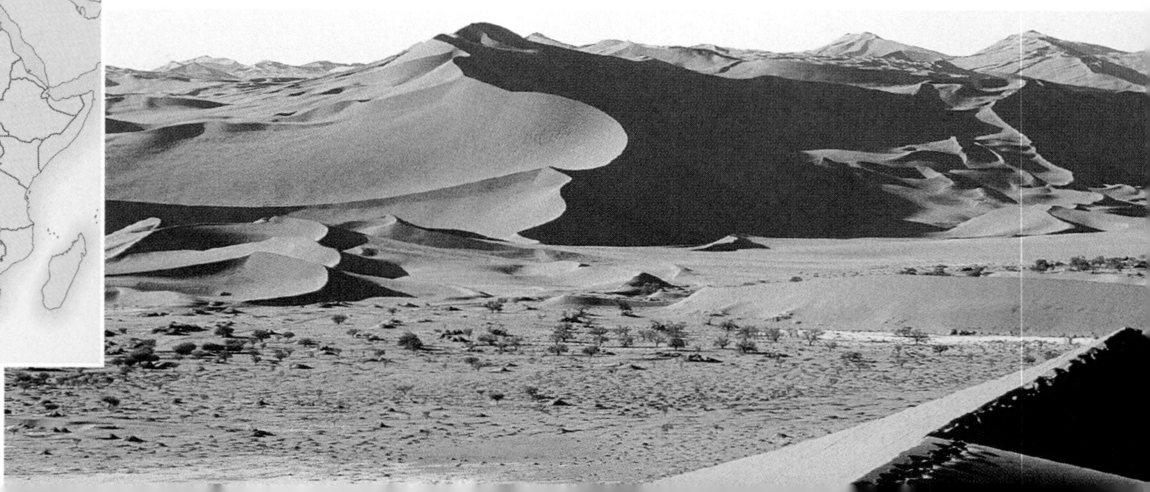

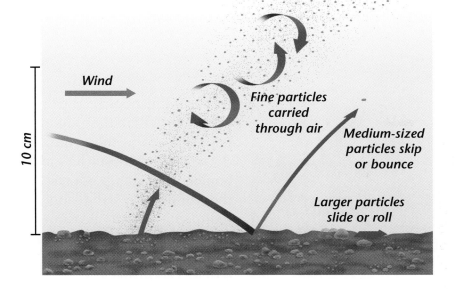

Wind

10 cm

Fine particles carried through air

Medium-sized particles skip or bounce

Larger particles slide or roll

Figure 27 Wind erosion moves sediment particles of different sizes in the three ways shown above. *Comparing and Contrasting Compare the movement of sediment by wind with the movement of sediment by water in Figure 16 on page 86. How are the processes similar? How are they different?*

The main way that wind causes erosion is by deflation. Geologists define **deflation** as the process by which wind removes surface materials. When wind blows over the land, it picks up the smallest particles of sediment. This sediment is made of bits of clay and silt. The stronger the wind, the larger the particles that it can pick up and move through the air. Slightly heavier particles, such as sand, might skip or bounce for a short distance. But sand soon falls back to the ground. Strong winds can even roll heavier sediment particles over the ground. Figure 27 shows how wind erodes by deflation.

Deflation does not usually have a great effect on the land. However, in parts of the Great Plains in the 1930s, deflation caused the loss of about 1 meter of topsoil in just a few years. In deserts, deflation can sometimes create an area of rock fragments called desert pavement. You can see an area of desert pavement in Figure 28. There, wind has blown away the smaller sediment. All that remains are rocky materials that are too large and heavy to be moved. Where there is already a slight depression in the ground, deflation can produce a bowl-shaped hollow called a blowout.

Abrasion by wind-carried sand can polish rock, but it causes little erosion. At one time, geologists thought that the sediment carried by wind cut the stone shapes seen in deserts. But now evidence shows that most desert landforms are the result of weathering and water erosion.

Figure 28 Wind erosion formed this desert pavement in the Arizona desert. Wind-driven sand may polish and shape individual stones.

✓ *Checkpoint Where would you be most likely to see evidence of wind erosion?*

Figure 29 Wind carrying fine particles of silt built up this loess deposit near Natchez, Mississippi.

Deposits Resulting From Wind Erosion

All the sediment picked up by wind eventually falls to the ground. This happens when the wind slows down or some obstacle, such as a boulder or a clump of grass, traps the windblown sand and other sediment. **Wind erosion and deposition may form sand dunes and loess deposits.** When the wind strikes an obstacle, the result is usually a sand dune. Sand dunes can be seen on beaches and in deserts where wind-blown sediment has built up.

Sand dunes come in many shapes and sizes. Some are long, with parallel ridges, while others are U-shaped. They can also be very small or very large—some sand dunes in China have grown to heights of 500 meters. Sand dunes move over time. Little by little, the sand shifts with the wind from one side of the dune to the other. Sometimes plants begin growing on a dune. Plant roots can help to anchor the dune in one place.

Sand dunes are most often made of the coarser sediments carried by wind. The finer sediments, including particles of clay and silt, are sometimes deposited in layers far from their source. This fine, wind-deposited sediment is **loess** (LES). Large loess deposits are found in central China and in such states as Nebraska, South Dakota, Iowa, Missouri, and Illinois. Loess helps to form fertile soil. Many areas with thick loess deposits are valuable farmlands.

Section 6 Review

1. Describe how wind erodes the land.
2. How do sand dunes and loess deposits form?
3. What is a blowout and what is the process that produces one?
4. **Thinking Critically Predicting** You visit a beach that has sand dunes covered with dune grass. But where people take a shortcut over one dune, the grass has been worn away. What may eventually happen to the dune if people keep taking this path?

Science at Home

Modeling Desert Pavement Here's how to make a model of desert pavement. Put a few coins in a shallow pan about 1 centimeter deep. Sprinkle enough flour over the coins to bury them beneath a thin layer of flour. Then blow air gently through a straw across the surface of the flour. Be careful not to draw in any flour through the straw. Be certain the blown flour will not get in your or anyone else's eyes. Ask your family to predict what the surface of the pan would look like if the "wind" continued to blow for a long time.

SECTION 1 Changing Earth's Surface

Key Ideas

◆ Weathering, erosion, and deposition act to wear down and build up Earth's surface.

◆ Gravity pulls sediment downhill in the process of mass movement. There are four main types of mass movement: landslides, mudslides, slump, and creep.

Key Terms

erosion   deposition
sediment   mass movement

SECTION 2 Water Erosion

Key Ideas

◆ Moving water is the major force of erosion that has shaped Earth's land surface.

◆ A river may form V-shaped valleys, waterfalls, meanders, oxbow lakes, and flood plains.

◆ When a river slows down, it deposits some of the sediment load it carries, forming features such as alluvial fans and deltas.

Key Terms

runoff	drainage basin	delta
rill	divide	groundwater
gully	flood plain	stalactite
stream	meander	stalagmite
river	oxbow lake	karst topography
tributary	alluvial fan	

SECTION 3 The Force of Moving Water

INTEGRATING PHYSICS

Key Ideas

◆ When gravity pulls water down a slope, water's potential energy changes to kinetic energy, and it does work.

◆ Most sediment washes or falls into streams, or is eroded from the streambed by abrasion.

◆ The greater a river's slope or volume of flow, the more sediment it can erode.

Key Terms

energy   abrasion   friction
potential energy   load   turbulence
kinetic energy

SECTION 4 Glaciers

Key Ideas

◆ The two kinds of glaciers are valley glaciers and continental glaciers.

◆ Glaciers erode the land through plucking and abrasion. Melting glaciers deposit sediment.

Key Terms

glacier	ice age	moraine
valley glacier	plucking	kettle
continental glacier	till	

SECTION 5 Waves

Key Ideas

◆ The energy of ocean waves comes from wind blowing across the water's surface and transferring energy to the water.

◆ Ocean waves hitting land cause erosion through impact and abrasion. Waves also move and deposit sediment along the shore.

Key Terms

beach   longshore drift   spit

SECTION 6 Wind Erosion

Key Ideas

◆ Wind causes erosion mainly through deflation, the blowing of surface materials.

◆ Landforms created by wind deposition include sand dunes and loess deposits.

Key Terms

sand dune   deflation   loess

Organizing Information

Flowchart Make a flowchart showing how a stream forms. Your flowchart should include the following terms in the correct order: rills, runoff, gullies, stream, raindrops. Give your flowchart a title. (For tips on making a flowchart, see the Skills Handbook.)

Reviewing Content

 For more review of key concepts, see the Interactive Student Tutorial CD-ROM.

Multiple Choice

Choose the answer that best completes the sentence.

1. The eroded materials carried by water or wind are called
   a. stalactites.
   b. desert pavement.
   c. sediment.
   d. moraines.

2. The downhill movement of eroded materials is known as
   a. mass movement.
   b. abrasion.
   c. deposition.
   d. deflation.

3. A mass of rock and soil deposited directly by a glacier is called
   a. load.   b. till.
   c. loess.   d. erosion.

4. When waves strike a shoreline, they concentrate their energy on
   a. beaches.
   b. cirques.
   c. sand dunes.
   d. headlands.

5. The erosion of sediment by wind is
   a. deposition.   b. deflation.
   c. plucking.   d. glaciation.

True or False

If the statement is true, write true. If it is false, change the underlined word or words to make the statement true.

6. The process by which sediment in water settles in new locations is <u>mass movement</u>.

7. An area of <u>alluvial fans</u> may be found where groundwater erodes limestone to form valleys, sinkholes, and caverns.

8. Because it is moving, flowing water has a type of energy called <u>kinetic energy</u>.

9. A looplike bend in the course of a river is a <u>meander</u>.

10. The sediment deposited at the edge of a glacier forms a ridge called a <u>kettle</u>.

Checking Concepts

11. What agents of erosion are in part caused by the force of gravity?

12. How do a river's slope and volume of flow affect the river's sediment load?

13. Describe how the speed of flowing water changes where a river bends. How does this affect a river's deposition of sediment?

14. Why does a delta develop when a river flows into a larger body of water?

15. Describe the process by which groundwater can cause erosion and deposition in limestone beneath Earth's surface.

16. What are ice ages?

17. **Writing to Learn** You go on a rafting journey that takes you down a river from the mountains to the sea. Write a letter to a friend describing the features created by erosion and deposition that you see as you travel down the river. Include features near the river's source, along the middle of its course, and where it reaches the ocean.

Thinking Critically

18. **Applying Concepts** Under what conditions would you expect abrasion to cause the most erosion of a riverbed?

19. **Relating Cause and Effect** In a desert, you see an area that looks as if it were paved with rock fragments. Explain how this situation occurred naturally.

20. **Problem Solving** Suppose you are a geologist studying a valley glacier. What method could you use to tell if it is advancing or retreating?

21. **Making Judgments** A salesperson offers to sell your family a new house right on a riverbank for very little money. Why might your family hesitate to buy this house?

22. **Inferring** You see a sandy beach along a coastline. What can you infer about where the sand came from?

23. **Comparing and Contrasting** How are landslides similar to mudflows? How are they different?

Applying Skills

The table below shows how a river's volume of flow and sediment load change over six months. Use the table to answer Questions 24–26.

Month	Volume of Flow (cubic meters/second)	Sediment Load (metric tons/day)
January	1.5	200
February	1.7	320
March	2.6	725
April	4.0	1600
May	3.2	1100
June	2.8	900

24. **Graphing** Make one graph with the month on the *x*-axis and the volume of flow on the *y*-axis. Make a second graph with the sediment load on the *y*-axis. Compare your two graphs. When were the river's volume of flow and load the greatest? The lowest?

25. **Developing Hypotheses** What can you infer from your graphs about the relationship between volume of flow and sediment load?

26. **Relating Cause and Effect** What may have occurred in the river's drainage basin in April to cause the changes in volume of flow and sediment load? Explain.

Performance CHAPTER PROJECT Assessment

Present Your Project Now you are ready to explain your models of erosion to your class. Label your models to indicate the features that changed during erosion.

Reflect and Record In your journal, write about the easiest and hardest parts of this project. How would you do each model differently if you did the project again?

Test Preparation

Use these questions to prepare for standardized tests.

Read the passage. Then answer Questions 27–30.

This is the story of a great river. The Missouri River is America's second longest river after the Mississippi River. Its vast drainage basin covers parts of 10 states and 2 Canadian provinces. Early settlers called the Missouri the "Big Muddy" because its waters carry a heavy sediment load.

The Missouri River begins in the Rocky Mountains near Three Forks, Montana, where three small streams join. The upper Missouri flows through a deep valley called the Gates of the Mountains. Then at Great Falls, Montana, it plunges down a series of waterfalls and rapids.

Leaving the mountains, the middle Missouri flows across the Great Plains. Major tributaries, such as the Yellowstone and Platte rivers, flow into it. The Missouri has eroded a wide valley as it winds through the plains. Steep ridges called bluffs sometimes form the edges of the valley.

The Missouri ends just north of St. Louis, Missouri, where it flows into the Mississippi.

27. A good title for this passage is
   a. The Rivers of America.
   b. Following the Missouri River.
   c. Tributaries of the Missouri River.
   d. Sedimental Journey.

28. A deep valley, waterfalls, and rapids can be found
   a. where the Missouri crosses the Plains.
   b. nowhere along the Missouri.
   c. on the upper Missouri.
   d. on the lower Missouri.

29. Along the middle Missouri's valley are features called
   a. gullies.   **b.** drainage basins.
   c. gates.   **d.** bluffs.

30. The nickname "Big Muddy" refers to the Missouri's
   a. sediment load.
   b. source.
   c. meanders.
   d. tributaries.

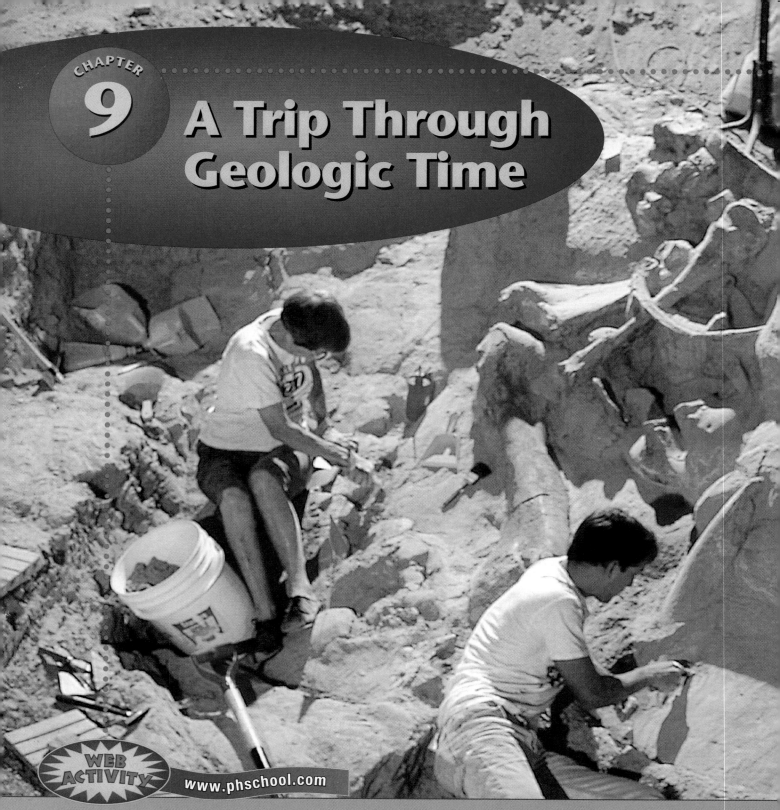

WEB ACTIVITY
www.phschool.com

At a site in South Dakota, scientists uncover mammoth bones that are 26,000 years old. Mammoths were relatives of modern elephants.

A Journey Back in Time

With great care, scientists remove soil covering the bones of a mammoth. At this site, they have unearthed fossils of more than 30 other animals. These animals lived on the Great Plains during the last Ice Age. From such fossils, scientists can develop a picture of life in the distant past.

This chapter will take you back on a journey through geologic time. You will learn how fossils reveal the history of life on Earth. To guide you on your journey, you and your classmates will make a time line showing the many periods of geologic time.

Your Goal To become an expert on one geologic time period and assist in constructing a time line.

To complete this project, you must
◆ research a geologic time period of your choice
◆ create a travel brochure that shows what life was like in this time period
◆ illustrate your time period for the time line

Get Started Begin by previewing *Exploring Geologic History* on pages 312–315. Select a time period you would like to investigate. Check with your teacher to be sure that all the time periods will be covered by members of your class.

Check Your Progress You will be working on this project as you study this chapter. To keep your project on track, look for Check Your Progress boxes at the following points.

Section 2 Review, page 297: Collect information on the animals, plants, and environment of your time period.

Section 4 Review, page 305: Write a travel brochure about the animals, plants, and environment of your selected time period.

Section 5 Review, page 320: Create illustrations that depict your time period and complete your travel brochure.

Present Your Project At the end of the chapter (page 323), place your illustrations on the time line. Use the travel brochure to present your geologic time period to your classmates.

 SECTION 4 The Geologic Time Scale

Discover This Is Your Life!
Skills Lab As Time Goes By

 SECTION 5 Earth's History

Discover What Do Fossils Reveal About Earth's History?
Try This Life and Times

SECTION 1 Fossils

GUIDE FOR READING

◆ How do fossils form?

◆ What are the different kinds of fossils?

◆ What do fossils tell about how organisms have changed over time?

Reading Tip As you read, use the headings to make an outline showing what fossils are, how they form, and why they are important.

You are a geologist at work in the high mountains of western Canada. You carefully split apart a piece of soft rock. Pressed into the rock is the shape of a tiny animal about the size of your thumb. The animal looks like no creature you have ever seen.

The rock is from a layer of rocks called the Burgess shale. The Burgess shale is famous because it contains evidence of life on Earth more than 500 million years ago. The creatures in the Burgess shale are tiny, soft-bodied animals without backbones. Some look like present-day crabs or worms. These animals lived on the bottom of a shallow sea. Scientists hypothesize that a mudslide suddenly buried the animals. Over millions of years, the mud turned to shale. The remains of the animals also became solid rock.

Evidence of Ancient Life

Fossils are the preserved remains or traces of living things. Fossils provide evidence of how life has changed over time. Fossils also help scientists infer how Earth's surface has changed. Fossils are clues to what past environments were like.

Most fossils form when living things die and are buried by sediments. The sediments slowly harden into rock and preserve the shapes of the organisms. Scientists who study fossils are called **paleontologists** (pay lee un TAHL uh jists). Fossils are usually found in sedimentary rock.

Figure 1 Paleontologists chip out the fossil-bearing rock of the Burgess shale.

Figure 2 A fossil may form when sediment quickly covers an animal's body.
Predicting What would happen to the fossil if erosion continued after Step D?

A. An animal dies and sinks into shallow water.

B. Sediment covers the animal.

C. The sediment becomes rock, preserving parts of the animal.

D. Mountain building, weathering, and erosion eventually expose the fossil at the surface.

Sedimentary rock is the type of rock that is made of hardened sediment. Most fossils form from animals or plants that once lived in or near quiet water such as swamps, lakes, or shallow seas where sediments build up. In Figure 2, you can see how a fossil might form.

When an organism dies, its soft parts often decay quickly or are eaten by animals. Thus, generally only hard parts leave fossils. These hard parts include bones, shells, teeth, seeds, and woody stems. It is rare for the soft parts of an organism to become a fossil.

Figure 3 Although they look as if they were just cut down, these petrified tree trunks were formed 200 million years ago. These fossils can be seen in the Petrified Forest National Park in Arizona.

Kinds of Fossils

For a fossil to form, the remains or traces of an organism must be protected from decay. Then one of several processes may cause a fossil to form. **Fossils found in rock include petrified fossils, molds and casts, carbon films, and trace fossils. Other fossils form when the remains of organisms are preserved in substances such as tar, amber, or ice.**

Petrified Fossils A fossil may form when the remains of an organism become petrified. The term *petrified* means "turning into stone." **Petrified fossils** are fossils in which minerals replace all or part of an organism. The fossil tree trunks shown in Figure 3 are examples of petrified wood. These fossils formed after sediment covered the wood. Then water rich in dissolved minerals seeped into spaces in the plant's cells. Over time, the water evaporated, leaving the hardened minerals behind. Some of the original wood remains, but the minerals have hardened and preserved it.

Petrified fossils may also form by replacement. In replacement, the minerals in water make a copy of the organism. For example, water containing dissolved minerals may slowly dissolve a clamshell buried in sediment. At the same time, the minerals in the water harden to form rock. The result is a copy of the clamshell made of rock.

Molds and Casts The most common fossils are molds and casts. Both copy the shape of ancient organisms. A **mold** is a hollow area in sediment in the shape of an organism or part of an organism. A mold forms when the hard part of the organism, such as a shell, is buried in sediment.

Later, water carrying dissolved minerals and sediment may seep into the empty space of a mold. If the water deposits the minerals and sediment there, the result is a cast. A **cast** is a copy of the shape of an organism. Figure 4 shows a mold (top) that became filled with minerals to form a cast (bottom). As you can see, a cast is the opposite of its mold. Also notice how the mold and cast have preserved details of the animal's structure.

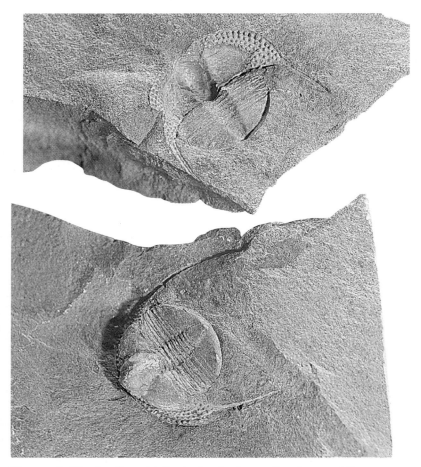

Figure 4 The fossil mold (top) clearly shows the shape of the animal called *Cryptolithus*. So does the fossil cast (bottom). *Cryptolithus* lived in the oceans about 450 million years ago.

Carbon Films Another type of fossil is a **carbon film,** an extremely thin coating of carbon on rock. How does a carbon film form? Remember that all living things contain carbon. When sediment buries an organism, some of the materials that make up the organism can become gases. These gases escape from the sediment, leaving carbon behind. Eventually, only a thin film of carbon remains. This process can preserve the delicate parts of plant leaves and insects.

INTEGRATING CHEMISTRY

Figure 5 This carbon film fossil of insects is between 5 million and 23 million years old.

Trace Fossils Most types of fossils preserve the shapes of ancient animals and plants. In contrast, **trace fossils** provide evidence of the activities of ancient organisms. A fossilized footprint is one example of a trace fossil. A dinosaur made the fossil footprint shown in Figure 6. The mud or sand that the animal stepped into eventually was buried by layers of sediment. Slowly the sediment became solid rock, preserving the footprints for millions of years.

Fossil footprints provide clues about an animal's size and behavior. How fast could the animal move? Did it walk on two or four legs? Did it live alone or with others of its kind? A scientist can infer the answers to such questions by looking at fossil footprints.

Other examples of trace fossils include the trails that animals followed or the burrows that they lived in. A trail or burrow can give clues about the size and shape of the organism, where it lived, and how it obtained food.

☑ *Checkpoint* *What can a trace fossil reveal about an early animal?*

Preserved Remains Some processes preserve the remains of organisms with little or no change. For example, some remains are preserved when organisms become trapped in tar. Tar is sticky oil that seeps from Earth's surface. Many fossils preserved in tar have been found at the Rancho La Brea tar pits in Los Angeles, California. Thousands of years ago, animals came to drink the water that covered these pits. Somehow, they became stuck in the tar

Figure 6 These dinosaur footprints are in the Painted Desert in Arizona.
Inferring What can you infer about this dinosaur from its footprints?

Figure 7 A fossil preserved in amber provides a window into the history of past life on Earth. Body parts, including the hairlike bristles on an insect's legs, its antennae, and its delicate wings, are often perfectly preserved.

and then died. The tar soaked into their bones, preserving the bones from decay.

Ancient organisms also have been preserved in amber. Amber is the hardened resin, or sap, of evergreen trees. First, an insect is trapped on sticky resin. After the insect dies, more resin covers it, sealing it from air and protecting its body from decay.

Freezing is another way in which remains can be preserved. The frozen remains of relatives of elephants called woolly mammoths have been found in very cold regions of Siberia and Alaska. Freezing has preserved even the mammoths' hair and skin.

☑ *Checkpoint* *What are three ways in which the remains of an organism can be preserved?*

Change Over Time

Paleontologists collect fossils from sedimentary rocks all over the world. They use this information to determine what past life forms were like. They want to learn what these organisms ate, what ate them, and in what environment they lived.

Paleontologists also classify organisms. They group similar organisms together. They arrange organisms in the order in which they lived, from earliest to latest. Together, all the information that paleontologists have gathered about past life is called the fossil record. **The fossil record provides evidence about the history of life on Earth. The fossil record also shows that different groups of organisms have changed over time.**

The fossil record reveals a surprising fact: Fossils occur in a particular order. Older rocks contain fossils of simpler organisms. Younger rocks contain fossils of more complex organisms. In other words, the fossil record shows that life on Earth has evolved, or changed. Simple, one-celled organisms have given rise to complex plants and animals.

The fossil record provides evidence to support the theory of evolution. A **scientific theory** is a well-tested concept that explains a wide range of observations. **Evolution** is the gradual change in living things over long periods of time. You can trace the evolution of one group of animals in *Exploring the Evolution of Elephants*.

The fossil record shows that millions of types of organisms have evolved. But many others have become extinct. A type of organism is **extinct** if it no longer exists and will never again live on Earth.

EXPLORING the Evolution of Elephants

Here are some members of the elephant family. Modern elephants, mammoths, and mastodons all evolved from a common ancestor that lived about 34 million years ago.

Asian Elephant
present day
Asian elephants live in India and Southeast Asia. They can be trained to move objects with their trunks and to carry heavy loads on their backs.

African Elephant
present day
About 4 meters high at the shoulder, the African elephant is larger than the Asian elephant. African elephants are fierce and difficult to tame.

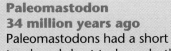

Woolly Mammoth
2 million years ago
The woolly mammoth lived during the last Ice Age. Hunting by humans may have led to their extinction about 10,000 years ago.

Mastodon
25–30 million years ago
Mastodons developed long, flexible trunks and long tusks. Later mastodons looked similar to mammoths, but were smaller and stockier. Mastodons became extinct about 10,000 years ago.

Gomphotherium
23 million years ago
Gomphotherium stood over 2 meters at the shoulder. It had a small trunk, two tusks on the upper jaw, and two tusks on the lower jaw.

Moeritherium
36 million years ago
A pig-sized relative of modern elephants, *Moeritherium* had long front teeth—primitive tusks—and a long upper lip.

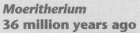

Paleomastodon
34 million years ago
Paleomastodons had a short trunk and short tusks on both upper and lower jaws. The paleomastodon was an ancestor of later elephantlike animals.

Figure 8 These are fossils of brachiopods and crinoids that lived more than 435 million years ago. Similar organisms still live in the oceans today. From these fossils, scientists know that the environment where they were found was once a shallow sea.

Fossils and Past Environments

Paleontologists use fossils to build up a picture of Earth's environments in the past. The fossils found in an area tell whether the area was a shallow bay, an ocean bottom, or a fresh-water swamp.

Fossils also provide evidence of Earth's climate in the past. For example, coal has been found in Antarctica. But coal only forms from the remains of plants that grow in warm, swampy regions. As you probably know, thick layers of ice and snow now cover Antarctica. The presence of coal shows that the climate of Antarctica was once much warmer than it is today.

Scientists can use fossils to learn about changes in Earth's surface. For example, corals are organisms that thrive in warm, shallow seas. Yet fossil corals are often found in many areas of the midwestern United States. From this fact, scientists infer that shallow seas once covered those areas.

Section 1 Review

1. Describe the process by which most fossils are formed in rock.
2. What are the five types of fossils that can be found in rock?
3. How does the fossil record support the theory of evolution?
4. Describe one way in which the remains of an organism can be preserved.
5. **Thinking Critically** **Inferring** Fossil seashells have been found in rock beds on land. What can you infer about how the area has changed?

Science at Home

Fossil Object A fossil is something old that has been preserved. Why is it that some old things are preserved, while others are destroyed? With your parents' permission, look around your house for the oldest object you can find. Interview family members to determine how old the object is, why it has been preserved, and how it may have changed since it was new. Make a drawing of the object and bring it to class. Tell your class the story of this "fossil."

② Finding the Relative Age of Rocks

DISCOVER ··· ACTIVITY

In What Order Are Sediments Deposited?

1. Make a stack of different-colored layers of clay. Each layer should be about the size and thickness of a pancake. If these flat layers are sediments, which layer of sediment was deposited first? (*Hint:* This is the oldest layer.)

2. Now form the stack into a dome by pressing it over a small rounded object, such as a small bowl. With a cheese-slicer or plastic knife, carefully cut off the top of the dome. Look at the layers that you have exposed. Which layer is the oldest?

Think It Over

Inferring If you press the stack into a small bowl and trim away the clay that sticks above the edge, where will you find the oldest layer?

Have you ever seen rock layers exposed on a cliff beside a road? Often the rock layers differ in color or texture. What are these layers, and how did they form?

The sediment that forms sedimentary rocks is deposited in flat layers one on top of the other. Over years, the sediment becomes deeply buried. Then it hardens and changes into sedimentary rock. At the same time, remains of organisms in the sediment may become fossils. Over time, many layers of sediment become different layers of rock. These rock layers provide a record of Earth's geologic history.

Relative and Absolute Ages

When you look at a rock containing a fossil, your first question may be, "How old is it?" The **relative age** of a rock is its age compared to the ages of other rocks. You have probably used the idea of relative age when comparing your age with someone else's age. For example, if you say that you are older than your brother but younger than your sister, you are describing your relative age.

The relative age of a rock does not provide its absolute age. The **absolute age** of a rock is the number of years since the rock formed. It may be impossible to know a rock's absolute age exactly. But sometimes geologists can determine a rock's absolute age to within a certain number of years.

GUIDE FOR READING

◆ How do geologists determine the relative age of rocks?

◆ How are index fossils useful to geologists?

Reading Tip Before you read, rewrite the headings in the section as *how, why,* or *what* questions. As you read, look for answers to these questions.

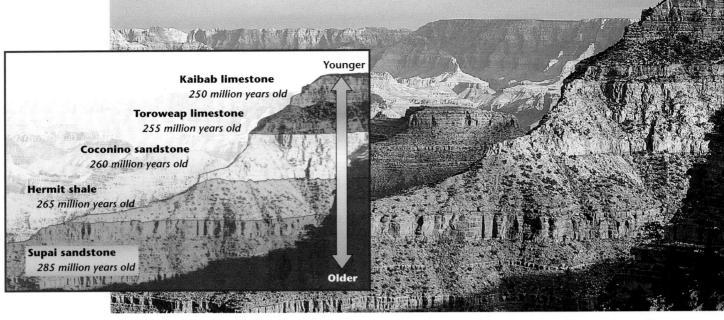

Younger

Kaibab limestone
250 million years old

Toroweap limestone
255 million years old

Coconino sandstone
260 million years old

Hermit shale
265 million years old

Supai sandstone
285 million years old

Older

Figure 9 More than a dozen rock layers make up the walls of the Grand Canyon. You can see five layers clearly in the photograph. *Applying Concepts In which of the labeled layers in the diagram would you find the oldest fossils? Explain.*

Sampling a Sandwich

Your teacher will give you a sandwich that represents rock layers in Earth's crust.

1. Use a round, hollow, uncooked noodle as a coring tool. Push the noodle through the layers of the sandwich.

2. Pull the noodle out of the sandwich. Break the noodle gently to remove your core sample.

3. Draw a picture coloring and labeling what you see in each layer of the core.

Observing If this were a real sample of rock layers, which layer would be the oldest? The youngest? Why do you think scientists study core samples?

The Position of Rock Layers

It can be difficult to determine the absolute age of a rock. So geologists use a method to find a rock's relative age. Geologists use the **law of superposition** to determine the relative ages of sedimentary rock layers. **According to the law of superposition, in horizontal sedimentary rock layers the oldest layer is at the bottom. Each higher layer is younger than the layers below it.** If you did the Discover activity at the beginning of this section, you have already used the law of superposition.

The walls of the Grand Canyon in Arizona illustrate the law of superposition. The sedimentary rock layers in the canyon walls represent 2 billion years of Earth's history. You can see some of the rock layers found in the Grand Canyon in Figure 9. Scientists have given names to all the layers of rock exposed on the walls of the Grand Canyon. By using the law of superposition, you should be able to determine the relative ages of these layers.

If you were to start at the top of the Grand Canyon, you would see Kaibab limestone. Because it is on top, it is the youngest layer. As you began your descent into the canyon, you would pass by Toroweap limestone. Next, you would see Coconino sandstone. The deeper you traveled into the canyon, the older the rocks would become. Your trip into the canyon is like a trip into Earth's history. The deeper you go, the older the rocks.

✓ *Checkpoint How would a geologist find the relative age of a rock?*

Other Clues to Relative Age

There are other clues to the relative ages of rocks. Geologists find some of these clues by studying extrusions and intrusions of igneous rock and faults.

Clues From Igneous Rock Igneous rock forms when magma or lava hardens. Magma is molten material beneath Earth's surface. Magma that flows onto the surface is called lava.

Lava that hardens on the surface is called an **extrusion.** The rock layers below an extrusion are always older than the extrusion.

Beneath the surface, magma may push into bodies of rock. There, the magma cools and hardens into a mass of igneous rock called an **intrusion.** An intrusion is always younger than the rock layers around and beneath it. Figure 10A shows an intrusion. Geologists study where intrusions and extrusions formed in relation to other rock layers. This helps geologists understand the relative ages of the different types of rock.

Clues From Faults More clues come from the study of faults. A **fault** is a break in Earth's crust. Forces inside Earth cause movement of the rock on opposite sides of a fault.

A fault is always younger than the rock it cuts through. To determine the relative age of a fault, geologists find the the relative age of the most recent rock layer through which the fault slices.

Movements along faults can make it harder for geologists to determine the relative ages of rock layers. In Figure 10B you can see how the rock layers no longer line up because of movement along the fault.

Music CONNECTION

The Grand Canyon provides one of Earth's best views of the geologic record. The American composer Ferde Grofé composed his *Grand Canyon Suite* for orchestra in 1931. The music paints a picture of desert scenery and a trip on muleback into the Grand Canyon.

In Your Journal

Listen to a recording of the *Grand Canyon Suite.* How does Grofé's music express what it's like to visit the Grand Canyon? What words would you use to describe what you heard?

Figure 10 Intrusions and faults give clues to the relative ages of rocks. In 10A, an intrusion cuts through rock layers. In 10B, rock layers are broken and shifted along a fault. *Inferring Which is older, the intrusion in 10A or the rock layers it crosses?*

1. Sedimentary rocks form in horizontal layers.

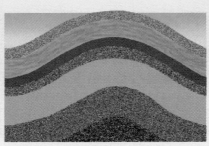

2. Folding tilts the rock layers.

Figure 11 An unconformity occurs where erosion wears away layers of sedimentary rock and other rock layers then form on top of the eroded surface.

3. The surface is eroded.

Unconformity

4. New sediment is deposited, forming rock layers above the unconformity.

Gaps in the Geologic Record

The geologic record of sedimentary rock layers is not always complete. Deposition slowly builds layer upon layer of sedimentary rock. But some of these layers may erode away, exposing an older rock surface. Then deposition begins again, building new rock layers.

The surface where new rock layers meet a much older rock surface beneath them is called an unconformity. An **unconformity** is a gap in the geologic record. An unconformity shows where some rock layers have been lost because of erosion. Figure 11 shows how an unconformity forms.

Using Fossils to Date Rocks

To date rock layers, geologists first give a relative age to a layer of rock at one location. Then they can give the same age to matching layers of rock at other locations.

Certain fossils, called index fossils, help geologists match rock layers. To be useful as an **index fossil,** a fossil must be widely distributed and represent a type of organism that existed only briefly. A fossil is considered widely distributed if it occurs in many different areas. Geologists look for index fossils in layers of rock. **Index fossils are useful because they tell the relative ages of the rock layers in which they occur.**

Geologists use particular types of organisms as index fossils— for example, certain types of trilobites. Trilobites (TRY luh byts) were a group of hard-shelled animals whose bodies had three

Figure 12 Trilobite fossils are widely distributed. Some types of trilobites serve as index fossils.

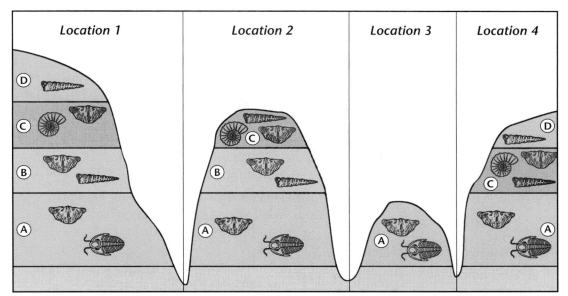

Location 1	Location 2	Location 3	Location 4

Figure 13 Scientists use index fossils to match up rock layers at locations that may be far apart. The trilobites in Layer A are index fossils. *Interpreting Diagrams Can you find another index fossil in the diagram?* (*Hint:* Look for a fossil that occurs in only one time period, but in several different locations.)

distinct parts. Trilobites evolved in shallow seas more than 500 million years ago. Over time, many different types of trilobites appeared. They became extinct about 245 million years ago. Trilobite fossils have been found in many different places.

To serve as an index fossil, a type of trilobite must be different in some way from other trilobites. One example is a type of trilobite with large eyes. These large-eyed trilobites survived for a time after other trilobites became extinct. Suppose a geologist finds large-eyed trilobites in a rock layer. The geologist can infer that those rocks are younger than rocks containing other types of trilobites.

You can use index fossils to match rock layers. Look at Figure 13, which shows rock layers from four different locations. Notice that two of the fossils are found in only one of these rock layers. These are the index fossils.

Section 2 Review

1. What is the law of superposition?
2. What characteristics are necessary for a fossil to be considered an index fossil?
3. What do unconformities show?
4. **Thinking Critically** **Applying Concepts** Horseshoe crabs are common in the ocean along the east coast of North America. They have existed with very little change for about 200 million years. Would horseshoe crabs be useful as an index fossil? Explain why or why not.

Check Your Progress
Locate reference materials you will need to research your chosen geologic time period. Possible sources include library books, magazines, encyclopedias, and Internet articles. Also keep a list of the resources you used. As you do your research, keep in mind the pictures and facts you will need for the class time line and travel brochure. Be sure to include the organisms and environment of the time period.

CHAPTER PROJECT

You Be the Detective

Finding Clues to ROCK LAYERS

Fossil clues give geologists a good idea of what life on Earth was like millions or even billions of years ago.

Problem

How can you use fossils and geologic features to interpret the relative ages of rock layers?

Skills Focus

interpreting data, drawing conclusions

Procedure

1. Study the rock layers at Sites 1 and 2. Write down the similarities and differences between the layers at the two sites.
2. List the kinds of fossils that are found in each rock layer of Sites 1 and 2.

Analyze and Conclude

Site 1

1. What "fossil clues" in layers A and B indicate the kind of environment that existed when these rock layers were formed? How did the environment change in layer D?
2. Which layer is the oldest? How do you know?

3. Which of the layers formed most recently? How do you know?
4. Why are there no fossils in layers C and E?
5. What kind of fossils occurred in layer F?

Site 2

6. Which layer at Site 1 might have formed at the same time as layer W at Site 2?
7. What clues show an unconformity or gap in the horizontal rock layers? Which rock layers are missing? What might have happened to these rock layers?
8. Which is older, intrusion V or layer Y? How do you know?
9. **Think About It** Working as a geologist, you find a rock containing fossils. What information would you need in order to determine this rock's age relative to one of the rock layers at Site 1?

More to Explore

Draw a sketch similar to Site 2 and include a fault that cuts across the intrusion. Have a partner then identify the relative age of the fault, the intrusion, and the layers cut by the fault.

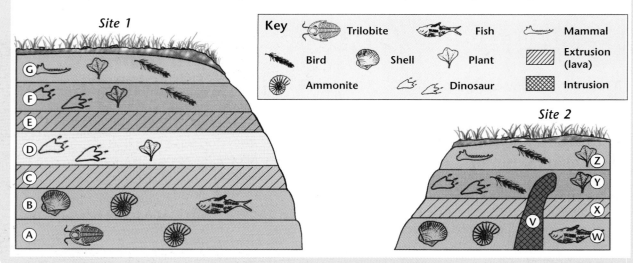

Site 1

Key — Trilobite, Fish, Mammal, Bird, Shell, Plant, Extrusion (lava), Ammonite, Dinosaur, Intrusion

Site 2

SECTION 3 Radioactive Dating

I n Australia, scientists have found sedimentary rocks that contain some of the world's oldest fossils—stromatolites (stroh MAT uh lyts). Stromatolites are the remains of reefs built by organisms similar to present-day bacteria. The bacteria grew together in dense mats shaped like stacks of pancakes. The mats formed reefs in shallow water near the shores of ancient oceans. Sediment eventually covered these reefs. As the sediments changed to rock, so did the reefs.

Paleontologists have determined that some stromatolites are more than 3 billion years old. But how did scientists determine the age of these fossils? To understand the methods of absolute dating, you need to learn more about the chemistry of rocks.

Changing From One Element to Another

What do you, the air you breathe, a lemon, and a puddle of water have in common? All are kinds of matter. In fact, everything around you is made of matter. Although different kinds of matter look, feel, or smell different, all the matter you see is made of tiny particles called **atoms.** When all the atoms in a particular type of matter are the same, the matter is an **element.** Carbon, oxygen, iron, lead, and potassium are just a few of the 109 currently known elements.

Figure 14 Stromatolites were formed by clumps of one-celled organisms that lived in shallow seas more than 3 billion years ago. Similar organisms grow in the ocean near Australia today.

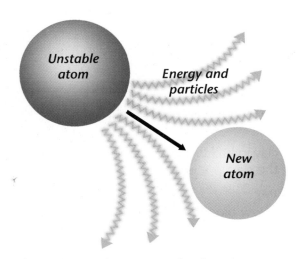

Figure 15 In the process of radioactive decay, an atom releases energy.

Most elements are stable. They do not change under normal conditions. But some elements exist in forms that are unstable. Over time, these elements break down, or decay, by releasing particles and energy in a process called **radioactive decay.** These unstable elements are said to be radioactive. **During radioactive decay, the atoms of one element break down to form atoms of another element.** Radioactive elements occur naturally in igneous rocks. Scientists use the rate at which these elements decay to calculate the rock's age.

The Rate of Radioactive Decay

You have a birthday, a specific day from which you calculate your age. What's the "birthday" of a rock? For an igneous rock, that "birthday" is when it first hardens to become rock. (Recall that igneous rocks form from molten magma and lava.) As a radioactive element within the igneous rock decays, it changes into another element. So the composition of the rock changes slowly over time. The amount of the radioactive element goes down. But the amount of the new element goes up.

The rate of decay of each radioactive element is constant—it never changes. This rate of decay is the element's half-life. The **half-life** of a radioactive element is the time it takes for half of the radioactive atoms to decay. You can see in Figure 16 how a radioactive element decays over time.

Figure 16 The half-life of a radioactive element is the amount of time it takes for half of the radioactive atoms to decay. *Calculating After three half-lives, how much of the radioactive element remains?*

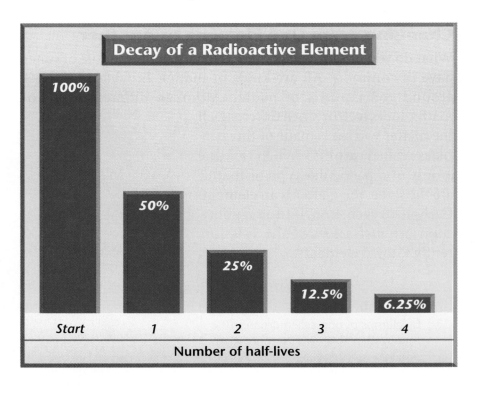

Elements Used in Radioactive Dating		
Radioactive Element	Half-life (years)	Dating Range (years)
Carbon-14	5,730	500–50,000
Potassium-40	1.3 billion	50,000–4.6 billion
Rubidium-87	47 billion	10 million–4.6 billion
Thorium-232	14.1 billion	10 million–4.6 billion
Uranium-235	713 million	10 million–4.6 billion
Uranium-238	4.5 billion	10 million–4.6 billion

Figure 17 The half-lives of different radioactive elements vary greatly. This scientist is testing a sample of material to determine how much carbon-14 it contains.

Absolute Ages From Radioactive Dating

Geologists use radioactive dating to determine the absolute ages of rocks. In radioactive dating, scientists first determine the amount of a radioactive element in a rock. Then they compare that amount with the amount of the stable element into which the radioactive element decays. Figure 17 lists several common radioactive elements and their half-lives.

Potassium–Argon Dating Scientists often date rocks using potassium-40. This form of potassium decays to stable argon-40 and has a half-life of 1.3 billion years. Potassium-40 is useful in dating the most ancient rocks because of its long half-life.

Carbon-14 Dating A radioactive form of carbon is carbon-14. All plants and animals contain carbon, including some carbon-14. As plants and animals grow, carbon atoms are added to their tissues. After an organism dies, no more carbon is added. But the carbon-14 in the organism's body decays. It changes to stable nitrogen-14. To determine the age of a sample, scientists measure the amount of carbon-14 that is left in the organism's remains. From this amount, they can determine its absolute age. Carbon-14 has been used to date fossils such as frozen mammoths, as well as pieces of wood and bone. Carbon-14 even has been used to date the skeletons of prehistoric humans.

Carbon-14 is very useful in dating materials from plants and animals that lived up to about 50,000 years ago. Carbon-14 has a half-life of only 5,730 years. For this reason, it can't be used to date really ancient fossils or rocks. The amount of carbon-14 left would be too small to measure accurately.

☑ *Checkpoint* *What are two types of radioactive dating?*

Sharpen your Skills

Calculating ACTIVITY
You have 3 grams of the radioactive element potassium-40. Calculate the mass of the remaining potassium-40 after 4 half-lives. Now calculate how much time has gone by. (*Hint:* One half-life of potassium-40 takes 1.3 billion years.) What would happen to the amount of potassium-40 if you continued through several more half-lives?

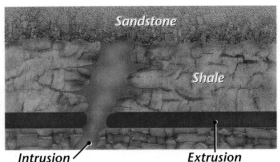

Sandstone

Shale

Intrusion
120 million years old

Extrusion
150 million years old

Figure 18 Radioactive dating has been used to determine the absolute ages of the intrusion and extrusion in the diagram. The shale lies above the extrusion and is crossed by the intrusion. Therefore the shale is younger than the extrusion, but older than the intrusion—between 150 million years old and 120 million years old. *Inferring What can you infer about the age of the sandstone?*

Radioactive Dating of Rock Layers

Radioactive dating cannot usually be used for dating rocks other than igneous rocks. As you recall, sedimentary rocks form as sediments are deposited by water or wind. The rock particles in sedimentary rocks are from other rocks, all of different ages. Radioactive dating would provide the age of the particles. It would not provide the age of the sedimentary rock.

How, then, do scientists date sedimentary rock layers? They date the igneous intrusions and extrusions near the sedimentary rock layers. Look at Figure 18. As you can see, sedimentary rock above an igneous intrusion must be younger than that intrusion.

How Old is Earth?

Radioactive dating has been used to calculate the age of Earth. The oldest rocks ever found on Earth have been dated at about 4.0 billion years old. But scientists think Earth formed even earlier than that. According to one theory, Earth and the moon are about the same age. When Earth was very young, a large object from space collided with Earth. This collision threw a large amount of material from both bodies into orbit around Earth. This material combined to form the moon. Scientists have dated moon rocks brought to Earth by astronauts during the 1970s. **Radioactive dating shows that the oldest moon rocks are about 4.6 billion years old. Scientists infer that Earth is only a little older than those moon rocks—roughly 4.6 billion years old.**

Section 3 Review

1. Describe the process of radioactive decay.
2. What is a half-life? How is it used to determine the absolute age of a rock?
3. When do scientists use both radioactive dating and relative dating to find the age of a rock?
4. How were moon rocks used to determine the age of Earth?
5. **Thinking Critically Applying Concepts** Which of the following types of fossils can be dated using carbon-14: molds and casts, trace fossils, frozen remains, remains preserved in tar? Explain your answer.

Science at Home

How Old Is It? Collect 10 items out of a drawer that is full of odds and ends such as keys, coins, receipts, photographs, and souvenirs. Have your family members put them in order from oldest to newest. What clues will you use to determine their relative ages? Do you remember when certain items were bought or a photograph was taken? How can you determine the oldest object of all? Make a list of the ten items in order by relative age. Are there any items for which you know the absolute age?

SECTION 4 The Geologic Time Scale

Imagine squeezing Earth's 4.6-billion-year history into a 24-hour day. Earth forms at midnight. About seven hours later, the earliest one-celled organisms appear. Over the next 14 hours, simple, soft-bodied organisms such as jellyfish and worms develop. A little after 9:00 P.M.—21 hours later—larger, more complex organisms evolve in the oceans. Reptiles and insects first appear about an hour after that. Dinosaurs arrive just before 11:00 P.M., but are extinct by 11:30 P.M. Modern humans don't appear until less than a second before midnight!

The Geologic Time Scale

Months, years, or even centuries aren't very helpful for thinking about Earth's long history. **Because the time span of Earth's past is so great, geologists use the geologic time scale to show Earth's history.** The **geologic time scale** is a record of the life forms and geologic events in Earth's history. You can see this time scale in Figure 19.

Scientists first developed the geologic time scale by studying rock layers and index fossils worldwide. With this information, scientists placed Earth's rocks in order by relative age. Later, radioactive dating helped determine the absolute age of the divisions in the geologic time scale. As geologists studied the fossil record, they found major changes in life forms at different times. They used these changes to mark where one unit of geologic time ends and the next begins. Therefore the divisions of the geologic time scale depend on events in the history of life on Earth.

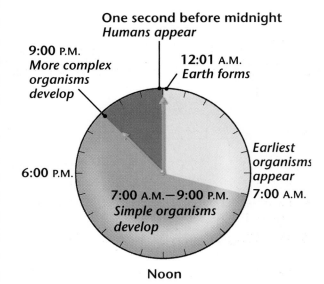

Figure 19 If geologic time went by in a single day, all of human history would take place in less than the last second!

Geologic Time Scale

Era	Period	Millions of Years Ago	Duration (millions of years)
Cenozoic	Quaternary	— 1.6 —	1.6 to present
Cenozoic	Tertiary		65
		— 66.4 —	
Mesozoic	Cretaceous		78
		— 144 —	
Mesozoic	Jurassic		64
		— 208 —	
Mesozoic	Triassic		37
		— 245 —	
Paleozoic	Permian		41
		— 286 —	
Paleozoic	Carboniferous		74
		— 360 —	
Paleozoic	Devonian		48
		— 408 —	
Paleozoic	Silurian		30
		— 438 —	
Paleozoic	Ordovician		67
		— 505 —	
Paleozoic	Cambrian		39
		— 544 —	
Precambrian			544 million years ago– 4.6 billion years ago

Figure 20 The eras and periods of the geologic time scale are used to date the events in Earth's long history. *Interpreting Diagrams How long ago did the Paleozoic Era end?*

Divisions of Geologic Time

When speaking of the past, what names do you use for different spans of time? You probably use such names as *century, decade, year, month, week,* and *day.* You know that a month is longer than a week but shorter than a year. Scientists use similar divisions for the geologic time scale.

Geologic time begins with a long span of time called Precambrian Time (pree KAM bree un). Precambrian Time, which covers about 88 percent of Earth's history, ended 544 million years ago. **After Precambrian Time, the basic units of the geologic time scale are eras, periods, and epochs.**

☑ *Checkpoint* How much of Earth's history is included in Precambrian Time?

Eras, Periods, and Epochs

Geologists divide the time between Precambrian Time and the present into three long units of time called **eras.** They are the Paleozoic Era, the Mesozoic Era, and the Cenozoic Era.

Eras The Paleozoic (pay lee uh ZOH ik) began about 544 million years ago and lasted for 300 million years. The word part *paleo-* means "ancient" or "early," and *-zoic* means "life." Many animals that lived during the Paleozoic were animals without backbones, or **invertebrates.**

The Mesozoic (mez uh ZOH ik) began about 245 million years ago and lasted about 180 million years. The word part *meso-* means "middle." People often call the Mesozoic the Age of Dinosaurs. Yet dinosaurs were only one of the many groups of organisms that lived during this era. For example, mammals began to evolve during the Mesozoic Era.

Earth's most recent era is the Cenozoic (sen uh ZOH ik). It began about 65 million years ago and continues to the present day. The word part *ceno-* means "recent." The Cenozoic is sometimes called the Age of Mammals, because mammals became common during this time.

Periods Eras are subdivided into units of geologic time called **periods.** Geologic periods range in length from tens of millions of years to less than two million years. You can see in Figure 20 that the Mesozoic Era includes three periods: the Triassic Period, the Jurassic Period, and the Cretaceous Period.

You may wonder where the names of the geologic periods come from. Many come from places around the world where geologists first described the rocks and fossils of that period. The name Cambrian, for example, refers to Cambria, the old Roman name for Wales. Jurassic refers to the Jura Mountains in France.

The Carboniferous Period is named for the large coal deposits that formed during that period. *Carboniferous* means "carbon bearing." Geologists in the United States often divide the Carboniferous Period into the Mississippian Period (320–360 million years ago) and the Pennsylvanian Period (286–320 million years ago.)

Epochs Geologists further subdivide the periods of the Cenozoic Era into **epochs.** Why are epochs used in the time scale? The fossil record in the Cenozoic is much more complete than the fossil record of earlier eras. There are a lot more events to place in sequence, and using epochs makes this task easier.

Figure 21 The sedimentary rock layers (top) were laid down during the Ordovician period. The fossil of the plant (bottom) formed during the Carboniferous period.

Section 4 Review

1. What is the geologic time scale?
2. What are geologic periods?
3. What method of dating did geologists first use when they developed the geologic time scale? How is the scale different today?
4. **Thinking Critically Interpreting Diagrams** Which period in the Paleozoic was the longest? If you could travel back in time 100 million years, what period would you be in? What era would you be in?

Check Your Progress *CHAPTER PROJECT*
Make a list of illustrations for the time line and travel brochure. Before creating the illustrations, think about what they will look like and the materials you will need to complete them. Will they be three-dimensional? Will they be drawn using a computer? Begin to plan how you will use illustrations in your travel brochure. Space in a brochure is limited, so focus on the highlights of your geologic period.

Making Models

As Time Goes By

Earth's history goes back 4.6 billion years. How can people grasp the vast scale of geologic time? In this lab, you will make a model to represent Earth's history.

Problem

How can you make a model of geologic time?

Materials

worksheet with 2,000 asterisks
one ream of paper

Procedure

Part 1 Table A

1. Copy Table A into your lab notebook. Figure how long ago these historic events happened and write the answers on your chart.

2. Obtain a worksheet with 2,000 asterisks printed on it. Each asterisk represents one year. The first asterisk at the top represents one year ago.

3. Starting from this asterisk, circle the asterisk that represents how many years ago each event in Table A occurred.

4. Label each circled asterisk to indicate the event.

5. Obtain a ream of copy paper. There are 500 sheets in a ream. If each sheet had 2,000 asterisks on it, there would be a total of 1 million asterisks. Therefore, each ream would represent 1 million years.

Part 2 Fill in Chart B

6. Copy Table B into your lab notebook. Determine how much paper in reams or sheets would be needed to represent the events in geologic time found in Table B. (*Hint:* Recall that each ream represents 1 million years.)

Table A Historic Events		
Event	Date	Number of Years Ago
You are born		
One of your parents is born		
Space shuttle *Challenger* explodes	1986	
Neil Armstrong first walks on the moon	1969	
World War I ends	1918	
Civil War ends	1865	
Declaration of Independence signed	1776	
Columbus crosses Atlantic	1492	
Leif Ericson visits North America	1000	

Table B Geologic Events			
Event	Number of Years Ago	Reams or Sheets of Paper	Thickness of Paper
End of the last Ice Age	10,000		
Whales evolve	50 million		
Pangaea begins to break up	225 million		
First vertebrates develop	530 million		
Multicellular organisms develop (algae)	1 billion		
First life (bacteria)	3.5 billion		
Oldest known rocks form	4.0 billion		
Age of Earth	4.6 billion		

7. Measure the thickness of a ream of paper. Use this thickness to calculate how thick a stack of paper would need to be to represent how long ago each geologic event occurred. (*Hint:* Use a calculator to multiply the thickness of the ream of paper by the number of reams.) Enter your results in Table B.

Analyze and Conclude

1. Measure the height of your classroom. How many reams of paper would you need to reach the ceiling? How many years would the height of the ceiling represent? Which geologic events listed in Table B would fall on a ream of paper inside your classroom?

2. At this scale, how many classrooms would have to be stacked on top of each other to represent the age of Earth? The time when vertebrates appeared?

3. How many times higher would the thickness of the stack be for the age of Earth than for the breakup of Pangaea?

4. On your model, how could you distinguish one era or period from another? How could you show when particular organisms evolved and when they became extinct?

5. Think About It Is the scale of your model practical? What would be the advantages and disadvantages of a model that fit geologic time on a time line 1 meter long?

More to Explore

This model represents geologic time as a straight line. Can you think of other ways of representing geologic time graphically? Using colored pencils, draw your own version of the geologic time scale so that it fits on a single typing paper. (*Hint:* You could represent geologic time as a wheel, a ribbon, or a spiral.)

SECTION 5 Earth's History

DISCOVER · ACTIVITY · · ·

What Do Fossils Reveal About Earth's History?

1. Compare the two fossils in photos A and B. How did these organisms become fossils?

2. Work with one or two other students to study the organisms in the two photos. Think about how these organisms may have lived. Then make sketches showing what each of these organisms may have looked like.

Think It Over
Posing Questions If you were a paleontologist, what questions would you want to ask about these organisms?

GUIDE FOR READING

◆ What were the major events in Earth's geologic history?

◆ What were the major events in the development of life on Earth?

Reading Tip Preview *Exploring Geologic History* on pages 312–315. Make a list of questions you have about Earth's history. Then look for answers as you read.

Your science class is going on a field trip, but this trip is a little out of the ordinary. You're going to travel back billions of years to the earliest days on Earth. Then you will move forward through time to the present. Enter the time machine and strap yourself in. Take a deep breath—you're off!

A dial on the dashboard shows the number of years before the present. You stare at the dial—it reads 4.6 billion years. You peer out the window as the time machine flies above the planet. Earth looks a little strange. Where are the oceans? Where are the continents? How will Earth change over the next billions of years? You'll answer these and other questions about Earth's history as you take this extraordinary trip.

Precambrian Time

Your journey through the first part of Earth's history will need to be very fast. Remember, Precambrian time includes most of Earth's history!

Precambrian Earth **Earth formed from a mass of dust and gas about 4.6 billion years ago.** Gravity pulled this mass together. Over time, Earth's interior became very hot and molten. Hundreds of millions of years passed. Then lava flowed over the surface, building the first continents. An atmosphere formed, and the world was covered with an ocean.

The Earliest Forms of Life Scientists cannot pinpoint when or where life began on Earth. But scientists have found fossils of single-celled organisms in rocks that formed about 3.5 billion years ago. These earliest life forms were probably similar to present-day bacteria. All other forms of life on Earth evolved from these simple organisms.

About 2.5 billion years ago, organisms first began using energy from the sun to make their own food. This process is called photosynthesis. One waste product of photosynthesis is oxygen. As oxygen was released into the air, the amount of oxygen in the atmosphere slowly increased. Over time, organisms evolved that could use oxygen to produce energy from food. These organisms included animals that are like today's sponges and worms. Because they all had soft bodies, these animals left few fossils. However, the evolution of these organisms set the stage for great changes during the Paleozoic Era. You can trace the development of life in *Exploring Geologic History* on pages 312–315.

The Paleozoic Era

Your time machine slows. You watch in fascination as you observe the "explosion" of life that began the Paleozoic Era.

Life Explodes During the Cambrian Period life took a big leap forward. **At the beginning of the Paleozoic Era, a great number of different kinds of organisms evolved.** Paleontologists call this event the Cambrian Explosion because so many new life forms appeared within a relatively short time. For the first time, many organisms had hard parts, including shells and outer skeletons.

At this time, all animals lived in the sea. Invertebrates such as jellyfish, worms, and sponges drifted through the water, crawled along the sandy bottom, or attached themselves to the ocean floors. Recall that invertebrates are animals without backbones.

Figure 22 During the early Cambrian period, Earth's oceans were home to many strange organisms unlike any animals that are alive today. The fossil above is an organism of the middle Cambrian called *Burgessia bella* from the Burgess shale.

Brachiopods and trilobites were common in the Cambrian seas. Brachiopods were small ocean animals with two shells. They resembled modern clams. Clams, however, are only distantly related to them.

During the Ordovician (awr duh VISH ee un) and Silurian (sih LOOR ee un) periods, the ancestors of the modern octopus and squid appeared. Some of these organisms, called cephalopods, grew to a length of almost 10 meters. **During this time, jawless fishes evolved. Jawless fishes were the first vertebrates.** A **vertebrate** is an animal with a backbone. These fishes had suckerlike mouths, and they soon became common in the seas.

Life Reaches Land Until the Silurian Period, only one-celled organisms lived on the land. But during the Silurian Period, plants began to grow on land. These first, simple plants grew low to the ground in damp areas. But by the Devonian Period (dih VOH nee un), plants that could grow in drier areas had evolved. Among these plants were the earliest ferns. The first insects also appeared during the Silurian Period.

Both invertebrates and vertebrates lived in the Devonian seas. Even though the invertebrates were more numerous, the Devonian Period is often called the Age of Fishes. This is because every main group of fishes was present in the oceans at this time. Most fishes now had jaws, bony skeletons, and scales on their bodies. Sharks appeared in the late Devonian Period.

During the Devonian Period, animals began to invade the land. The first vertebrates to crawl onto land were lungfish with strong, muscular fins. The first amphibians evolved from these fishes. An **amphibian** (am FIB ee un) is an animal that lives part of its life on land and part of its life in water. *Ichthyostega,* shown in Figure 23, was one of the first amphibians.

Throughout the rest of the Paleozoic Era, life expanded over Earth's continents. Other groups of

Figure 23 One of the first amphibians, *Icthyostega* (center), was about 1 meter long. It lived during the late Devonian Period. Another, more fishlike amphibian, *Acanthostega* (bottom), lived at about the same time.

Figure 24 Forests flourished during the Carboniferous Period. Insects such as dragonflies were common. *Predicting What types of fossils would you expect to find from the Carboniferous Period?*

Figure 25 *Dimetrodon,* which lived during the Permian Period, was one of the first reptiles. This meat-eater was about 3.5 meters long.

vertebrates evolved from the amphibians. For example, small reptiles developed during the Carboniferous Period. **Reptiles** have scaly skin and lay eggs with tough, leathery shells. Some types of reptiles became very large during the later Paleozoic.

During the Carboniferous Period, winged insects evolved into many forms, including huge dragonflies and cockroaches. Giant ferns and cone-bearing plants and trees formed vast swampy forests called "coal forests." How did the coal forest get its name? The remains of the coal forest plants formed thick deposits of sediment that changed into coal over millions of years.

Mass Extinction Ends the Paleozoic At the end of the Paleozoic Era, many kinds of organisms died out. This was a **mass extinction,** in which many types of living things became extinct at the same time. **The mass extinction at the end of the Paleozoic affected both plants and animals, on land and in the seas. Scientists do not know what caused the mass extinction, but as much as 95 percent of the life in the oceans disappeared.** For example, trilobites, which had existed since early in the Paleozoic, suddenly became extinct. Many amphibians also became extinct. But not all organisms disappeared. The mass extinction did not affect fishes. Many reptiles also survived.

☑ *Checkpoint* *What were three major events in the development of life during the Paleozoic Era?*

EXPLORING Geologic History

Using the fossil record, paleontologists have created a picture of the different types of common organisms in each geologic period.

PRECAMBRIAN TIME
4.6 billion–544 million years ago

PALEOZOIC ERA
544–245 million years ago

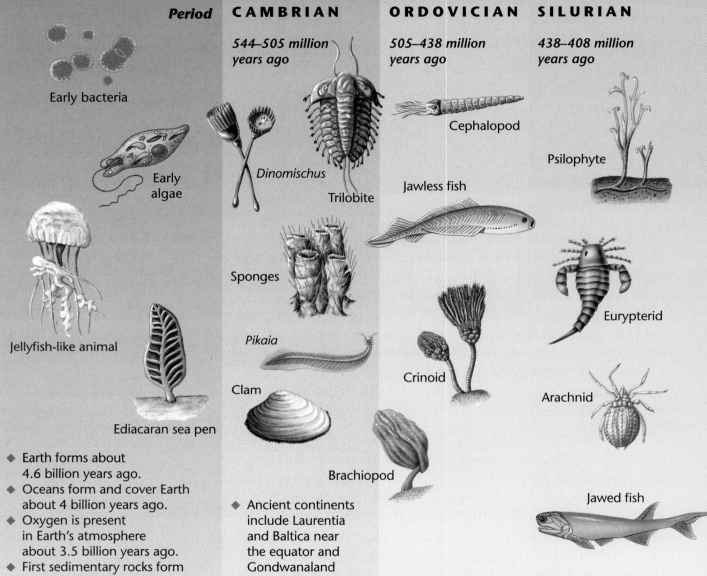

Period

CAMBRIAN
544–505 million years ago

ORDOVICIAN
505–438 million years ago

SILURIAN
438–408 million years ago

Early bacteria

Early algae

Jellyfish-like animal

Ediacaran sea pen

Dinomischus

Trilobite

Sponges

Pikaia

Clam

Brachiopod

Cephalopod

Jawless fish

Crinoid

Psilophyte

Eurypterid

Arachnid

Jawed fish

- Earth forms about 4.6 billion years ago.
- Oceans form and cover Earth about 4 billion years ago.
- Oxygen is present in Earth's atmosphere about 3.5 billion years ago.
- First sedimentary rocks form about 3.5 billion years ago.
- Bacteria appear about 3.5 billion years ago.
- Earth's first ice age occurs about 2.3 billion years ago.
- Soft-bodied, multicellular organisms develop late in the Precambrian.
- First mass extinction probably occurs near the end of the Precambrian.

- Ancient continents include Laurentia and Baltica near the equator and Gondwanaland near the South Pole.
- Shallow seas cover much of the land.
- Great "explosion" of invertebrate life occurs in seas.
- Invertebrates with shells appear, including trilobites, mollusks, and brachiopods.

- Warm, shallow seas cover much of Earth.
- Ice cap covers what is now North Africa.
- Invertebrates dominate the oceans.
- Early vertebrates— jawless fish— become common.

- Early continents Laurentia and Baltica collide.
- Coral reefs develop.
- Fish with jaws develop.
- Land plants appear.
- Insects and spiders appear.

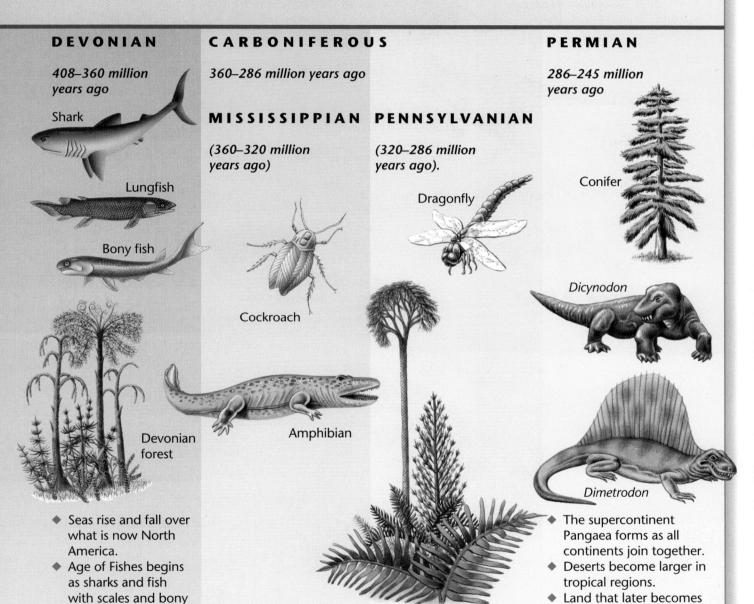

DEVONIAN

408–360 million years ago

Shark

Lungfish

Bony fish

Devonian forest

- Seas rise and fall over what is now North America.
- Age of Fishes begins as sharks and fish with scales and bony skeletons become common.
- Trilobites, corals, brachiopods, and other invertebrates flourish in the oceans.
- Lungfish develop.
- First amphibians reach land.
- Forests grow in swampy areas.

CARBONIFEROUS

360–286 million years ago

MISSISSIPPIAN

(360–320 million years ago)

Cockroach

Amphibian

- Appalachian Mountains begin to form.
- North America and Northern Europe lie in warm, tropical region.
- Cold conditions are present in what is now South America and Africa.

PENNSYLVANIAN

(320–286 million years ago).

Dragonfly

Coal forest

- Great swamp forests of huge, woody trees cover eastern North America and parts of Europe.
- First true reptiles appear.
- Insects become abundant.
- Winged insects appear.

PERMIAN

286–245 million years ago

Conifer

Dicynodon

Dimetrodon

- The supercontinent Pangaea forms as all continents join together.
- Deserts become larger in tropical regions.
- Land that later becomes present-day southern continents is in an ice age.
- Reptiles become dominant on land.
- Warm-blooded reptiles appear.
- Mass extinction causes many marine invertebrates, including trilobites, to disappear.

MESOZOIC ERA
245–65 million years ago

Period TRIASSIC

245–208 million years ago

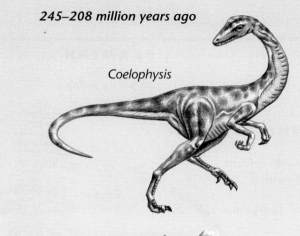

Coelophysis

Morganucodon

Cycad

JURASSIC

208–144 million years ago

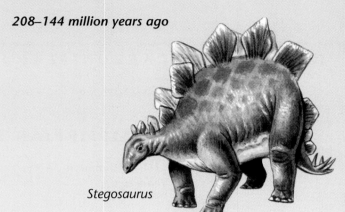

Stegosaurus

Megazostrodon

Archaeopteryx

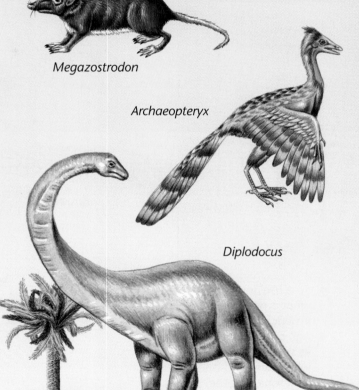

Diplodocus

- ◆ Pangaea holds together for much of the Triassic.
- ◆ Hot, dry conditions dominate center of Pangaea.
- ◆ Age of Reptiles begins.
- ◆ First dinosaurs appear.
- ◆ First mammals, which evolve from warm-blooded reptiles, appear.
- ◆ First turtles and crocodiles appear.
- ◆ Conifers, palmlike trees, and ginkgo trees dominate forests.

- ◆ Pangaea continues to break apart as North America separates from Africa and South America.
- ◆ Sea levels rise in many parts of the world.
- ◆ Largest dinosaurs thrive, including *Stegosaurus, Diplodocus,* and *Apatosaurus.*
- ◆ First birds appear.
- ◆ First flying reptiles, pterosaurs, appear.

CENOZOIC ERA
65 million years ago to the present

CRETACEOUS

144–65 million years ago

Magnolia

Tyrannosaurus rex

Creodonts

Triceratops

- Continents move toward their present-day positions, as South America splits from Africa.
- Widespread volcanic activity occurs.
- First flowering plants appear.
- Dinosaurs dominate, including *Tyrannosaurus rex*.
- First snakes appear.
- Mass extinction at end causes disappearance of many land and marine life forms, including dinosaurs.

TERTIARY

65–1.6 million years ago

Uintatherium

Hyracotherium

Plesiadapis

- The Rocky Mountains, Alps, Andes, and Himalayas form.
- Continents move into present-day positions.
- Continental glacier covers Antarctica about 25 million years ago.
- Flowering plants thrive.
- First grasses appear.
- Age of Mammals begins.
- Modern groups such as horses, elephants, bears, rodents, and primates appear.
- Mammals return to the seas in the forms of whales and dolphins.
- Ancestors of humans evolve.
- Continental glaciers repeatedly cover part of North America beginning about 2.5 million years ago.

QUATERNARY

1.6 million years ago to the present

Saber-toothed cat

Megatherium

Homo sapiens

- Thick glaciers advance and retreat over much of North America and Europe, parts of South America and Asia, and all of Antarctica.
- The Great Lakes form.
- Giant mammals flourish in parts of North America and Eurasia not covered by ice. But they become extinct when the Ice Age ends about 10,000 years ago.
- Mammals, flowering plants, and insects dominate land.
- Modern humans evolve in Africa about 100,000 years ago.

260 million years ago

Figure 26 The supercontinent Pangaea began to break apart about 225 million years ago. *Observing How have North America and South America moved in relation to Africa and Europe?*

Present

The Supercontinent Pangaea

Scientists aren't sure what caused the mass extinction at the end of the Paleozoic. One theory is that Earth's climate changed. But what caused this climate change? Scientists hypothesize that it may have been caused by the slow movement of the continents.

During the Permian period, about 260 million years ago, Earth's continents moved together to form a great landmass, or "supercontinent," called Pangaea (pan JEE uh). The formation of Pangaea caused deserts to expand in the tropics. At the same time, sheets of ice covered land closer to the South Pole. Many organisms could not survive the new climate. After Pangaea formed, it broke apart again. Figure 26 shows how the continents moved toward their present-day positions. They moved very slowly—only a few centimeters per year.

The movement of continents is sometimes called continental drift. But the continents don't really "drift." The continents move slowly over Earth's surface because of forces inside Earth.

☑ *Checkpoint* What was Pangaea?

The Mesozoic Era

Millions of years flash by. Your time machine cruises above Pangaea and the landmasses that formed when it broke apart. Watch out—there's a dinosaur! You're observing an era that you've read about in books and seen in movies.

The Triassic Period Some living things survived the Permian mass extinction. These organisms became the main forms of life early in the Triassic Period (try AS ik). Plants and animals that survived included fish, insects, reptiles, and cone-bearing plants called conifers. **Reptiles were so successful during the Mesozoic Era that this time is often called the Age of Reptiles.**

About 225 million years ago, the first dinosaurs appeared. One of the earliest dinosaurs, *Coelophysis,* was a meat eater that had light, hollow bones and ran swiftly on its hind legs. It was about 2.5 meters long.

Mammals also first appeared during the Triassic Period. A **mammal** is a warm-blooded vertebrate that feeds its young milk. Mammals probably evolved from warm-blooded reptiles. The mammals of the Triassic Period were very small, about the size of a mouse or shrew. From these first small mammals, all mammals that live today evolved.

The Jurassic Period During the Jurassic Period (joo RAS ik), dinosaurs became the dominant animal on land. Scientists have identified several hundred different kinds of dinosaurs. Some were plant eaters, while others were meat eaters. Dinosaurs "ruled" Earth for about 150 million years, but different types lived at different times. At 20 meters long, *Dicraeosaurus* was one of the larger dinosaurs of the Jurassic Period. The smallest known dinosaur, *Compsognathus,* was only about 50 centimeters long when fully grown.

Figure 27 *Dicraeosaurus* was a plant-eating dinosaur that lived during the late Jurassic Period.

One of the first birds, called *Archaeopteryx*, appeared during the Jurassic Period. The name *Archaeopteryx* means "ancient wing thing." Many paleontologists now think that birds evolved from dinosaurs. During the 1990s, scientists discovered fossils in China with the skulls and teeth of dinosaurs. But these creatures had birdlike bodies and feathers.

Figure 28 From a fossil (above right), paleontologists can tell that *Archaeopteryx* was about 30 centimeters long, had feathers and teeth, and also had claws on its wings. The artist of the illustration (above) has given *Archaeopteryx* colorful feathers.

The Cretaceous Period Reptiles were still the dominant vertebrates throughout the Cretaceous Period (krih TAY shus). Dinosaurs, such as the meat-eating *Tyrannosaurus rex*, ruled the land. But mammals continued to evolve. Flying reptiles and birds competed for places in the sky. The hollow bones and feathers of birds made them better adapted to their environment than the flying reptiles, which became extinct during the Cretaceous Period. In the seas, reptiles such as turtles and crocodiles swam among fishes and marine invertebrates.

The Cretaceous Period also brought new forms of life. Flowering plants evolved. These included leafy trees, shrubs, and small flowering plants like the ones you see today. Unlike the conifers, flowering plants produce seeds that are inside a fruit. The fruit helps the seeds survive.

Another Mass Extinction About 65 million years ago, at the close of the Cretaceous Period, another mass extinction occurred. Some scientists hypothesize that this mass extinction occurred when an object from space struck Earth. This object was probably an asteroid. Asteroids are rocky masses that orbit the sun between Mars and Jupiter. On rare occasions, the orbits of certain asteroids come dangerously close to Earth. Once in many millions of years, an impact may occur.

INTEGRATING SPACE SCIENCE

When the asteroid hit Earth, the impact threw huge amounts of dust and water vapor into the atmosphere. Many organisms on land and in the oceans died immediately. Dust and heavy clouds blocked sunlight around the world for years. Without sunlight, plants died, and plant-eating animals starved. This mass extinction wiped out over half of all plant and animal groups. No dinosaurs survived. Many other kinds of reptiles also became extinct.

Not all scientists agree that an asteroid impact caused the mass extinction. Some scientists think that climate changes caused by increased volcanic activity were responsible.

☑ *Checkpoint* *What major groups of organisms developed during the Mesozoic Era?*

The Cenozoic Era

Your voyage through time continues through the Cenozoic Era toward the present. Paleontologists often call the Cenozoic Era the Age of Mammals. During the Mesozoic Era, mammals had a hard time competing with dinosaurs for food and places to live. **The extinction of dinosaurs created an opportunity for mammals. During the Cenozoic Era, mammals evolved adaptations that allowed them to live in many different environments—on land, in water, and even in the air.**

The Tertiary Period During the Tertiary Period, Earth's climates were generally warm and mild. In the oceans, many types of mollusks appeared. Marine mammals such as whales and dolphins evolved. On land, flowering plants, insects, and mammals flourished. When grasses evolved, they provided a food source for grazing mammals. These were the ancestors of today's cattle, deer, sheep, and other grass-eating mammals. Some mammals became very large, as did some birds.

Figure 29 Scientists hypothesize that during the Cretaceous an asteroid hit Earth near the present-day Yucatán Peninsula, in southeastern Mexico.
Relating Cause and Effect How did the asteroid impact affect life on Earth?

Figure 30 This extinct mammal was related to present-day horses. The fossil formed during the Tertiary Period between 36 and 57 million years ago.

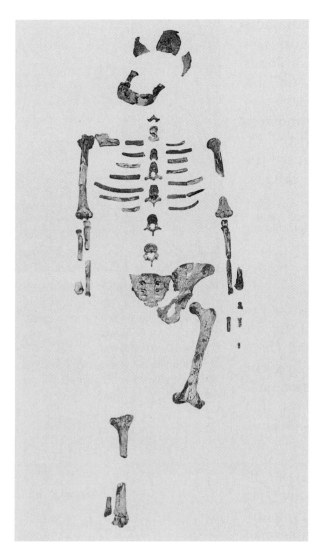

Figure 31 Scientists nicknamed this fossil skeleton Lucy. An early ancestor of modern humans, Lucy lived about 3.3 million years ago.

The Quaternary Period The mammals that had evolved during the Tertiary Period eventually faced a changing environment. **Earth's climate cooled, causing a series of ice ages during the Quaternary Period.** Repeatedly, thick continental glaciers advanced and retreated over parts of Europe and North America.

So much of Earth's water was frozen in continental glaciers that the level of the oceans fell by more than 100 meters. Then, about 20,000 years ago, Earth's climate began to warm. Over thousands of years, the continental glaciers melted. This caused sea level to rise again.

In the oceans, algae, coral, mollusks, fish, and mammals thrived. Insects and birds shared the skies. On land, flowering plants and mammals such as bats, cats, dogs, cattle, and humans—just to name a few—became common.

The fossil record suggests that human ancestors appeared about 3.5 million years ago. Modern humans, or *Homo sapiens,* may have evolved as early as 100,000 years ago. By about 12,000 to 15,000 years ago, humans had migrated around the world to every continent except Antarctica.

Your time machine has now arrived back in the present. You and all organisms on Earth are living in the Quaternary Period of the Cenozoic Era. Is this the end of evolution and the changing of Earth's surface? No, these processes will continue as long as Earth exists. But you'll have to take your time machine into the future to see just what happens!

Section 5 Review

1. What is the "Cambrian explosion"? Why is it important to the history of life on Earth?
2. What was Pangaea? When did it form?
3. How did the extinction of dinosaurs affect the evolution of mammals?
4. What do scientists think was the source of the oxygen in Earth's atmosphere?
5. **Thinking Critically Making Generalizations** How do you think mass extinctions have affected evolution?

Check Your Progress   CHAPTER PROJECT
Create illustrations of your portion of the time line. How will you show animals, plants, and environments of that time? When you have finished your illustrations, place them on the time line. Then make a rough draft of your travel brochure. Have a classmate or teacher edit your rough draft before you write the final draft. Do you have all the information about your geologic period that will make a person want to travel there?

SECTION 1 Fossils

Key Ideas

◆ Most fossils form when living things die and are quickly buried by sediment, which eventually hardens and preserves parts of the organisms.
◆ The major kinds of fossils include petrified remains, molds, casts, carbon films, trace fossils, and preserved remains.
◆ The fossil record shows that many different organisms have lived on Earth at different times and that groups of organisms have changed over time.

Key Terms

fossil	mold	scientific
paleontologist	cast	theory
sedimentary rock	carbon film	evolution
petrified fossil	trace fossil	extinct

 SECTION 2 Finding the Relative Age of Rocks

Key Ideas

◆ The law of superposition can be used to determine the relative ages of rock layers.
◆ Scientists also study faults, intrusions, and extrusions to find the relative ages of rock layers.
◆ Index fossils are useful in dating rock layers.

Key Terms

relative age	fault
absolute age	intrusion
law of superposition	extrusion
unconformity	index fossil

 SECTION 3 Radioactive Dating

INTEGRATING CHEMISTRY

Key Ideas

◆ During radioactive decay, the atoms of one element decay into atoms of another element.
◆ Scientists use radioactive dating to determine the absolute ages of rocks.

Key Terms

atom	radioactive decay
element	half-life

 SECTION 4 The Geologic Time Scale

Key Ideas

◆ The basic divisions of the geologic time scale are eras, periods, and epochs.

Key Terms

geologic time scale	invertebrate	epoch
era	period	

SECTION 5 Earth's History

Key Ideas

◆ A great number of different kinds of living things evolved during the "Cambrian explosion" at the beginning of the Paleozoic Era.
◆ During the Permian Period, the continents joined to form the supercontinent Pangaea.

Key Terms

vertebrate	reptile	mammal
amphibian	mass extinction	

Organizing Information

Concept Map Copy the concept map about fossils onto a piece of paper. Then complete it and add a title. (For more on concept maps, see the Skills Handbook.)

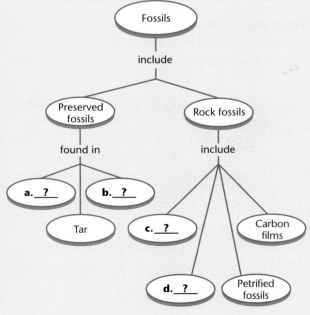

Reviewing Content

 For more review of key concepts, see the Interactive Student Tutorial CD-ROM.

Multiple Choice

Choose the answer that best completes each sentence.

1. A hollow area in sediment in the shape of all or part of an organism is called a
   - **a.** mold.
   - **b.** cast.
   - **c.** trace fossil.
   - **d.** carbon film.

2. A gap in the geologic record formed when sedimentary rocks cover an erosion surface is called a(n)
   - **a.** intrusion.
   - **b.** unconformity.
   - **c.** fault.
   - **d.** extrusion.

3. When a radioactive element decays, it releases
   - **a.** atoms.
   - **b.** potassium-40.
   - **c.** particles and energy.
   - **d.** carbon-14.

4. Eras of geologic time are subdivided into
   - **a.** epochs.
   - **b.** centuries.
   - **c.** decades.
   - **d.** periods.

5. What is an animal that doesn't have a backbone called?
   - **a.** vertebrate
   - **b.** mammal
   - **c.** invertebrate
   - **d.** amphibian

True or False

If the statement is true, write true. If it is false, change the underlined word or words to make the statement true.

6. A dinosaur footprint in rock is an example of a <u>trace fossil</u>.

7. A <u>carbon film</u> is a fossil in which minerals have replaced all or part of an organism.

8. The <u>relative age</u> of something is the exact number of years since an event has occurred.

9. A <u>period</u> is the time required for half of the atoms of a radioactive element to decay.

10. The <u>Paleozoic Era</u> is often called the Age of Reptiles.

Checking Concepts

11. How does a petrified fossil form?

12. Which organism has a better chance of leaving a fossil: a jellyfish or a bony fish? Explain.

13. Describe a process that could cause an unconformity.

14. What evidence would a scientist use to determine the absolute age of a fossil found in a sedimentary rock?

15. What era is often called the Age of Mammals? Why is this appropriate?

16. **Writing to Learn** Imagine that your time machine comes to a halt just as a big event occurs at the end of the Mesozoic Era. Describe what you see, and then describe how this event affects the life you see on Earth.

Thinking Critically

17. **Applying Concepts** Suppose that paleontologists found a certain kind of trilobite in a rock layer at the top of a hill in South America. Then they found the same kind of trilobite in a rock layer at the bottom of a cliff in Africa. What could the paleontologists conclude about the two rock layers?

18. **Making Judgments** If you see a movie in which early humans fight giant dinosaurs, how would you judge the scientific accuracy of that movie? Give reasons for your judgment.

19. **Relating Cause and Effect** When Pangaea formed, the climate changed and the land on Earth became drier. Why do you think that this climate change favored reptiles over amphibians?

20. **Problem Solving** Carbon-14 has a half-life of 5,730 years, while uranium-235 has a half-life of 713 million years. Which would be better to use in dating a fossil from Precambrian time? Explain.

Applying Skills

Use the diagram of rock layers below to answer Questions 21–24.

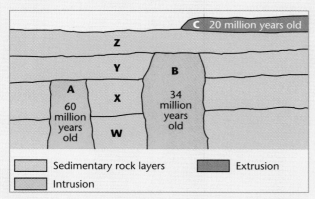

Sedimentary rock layers   Extrusion

Intrusion

21. **Inferring** Which is the oldest layer of sedimentary rock? Which is the youngest? How do you know?

22. **Measuring** What method did a scientist use to determine the age of the intrusion and extrusion?

23. **Interpreting Data** What is the relative age of layer Y (*Hint:* With what absolute ages can you compare it?)

24. **Interpreting Data** What is the relative age of layer Z?

Performance ▼ Assessment

Present Your Project You have completed your illustrations for the time line and travel brochure. Now you are ready to present the story of the geologic time period you researched. Be sure to include the wonderful and awesome things people will see when they travel to this time period. Don't forget to warn them of any dangers that await them.

Reflect and Record In your journal, reflect on what you have learned about Earth's history. What were the most interesting things you found out? If you could travel back in time, how far back would you go?

Test Preparation

Use these questions to prepare for standardized tests.

The diagrams show the index fossils found in rock layers at two different locations. Use the diagrams to answer Questions 25–28.

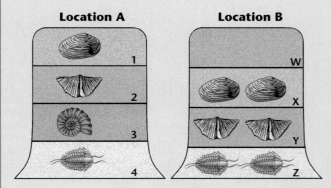

25. According to the law of superposition, the oldest rock layers at Locations A and B are Layers
    a. 2 and Y.   b. 3 and Y.
    c. 4 and Z   d. 1 and W.

26. The youngest rock layer at either location is Layer
    a. 1.   b. X.
    c. 3.   d. W.

27. The index fossil for the Cambrian period is the
    a. ammonite.   b. clam.
    c. trilobite.   d. brachiopod.

28. Layer 1 at Location A and Layer X at Location B both contain fossil clams. These index fossils indicate that both layers formed during the
    a. Devonian Period.
    b. Silurian Period.
    c. Ordovician Period.
    d. Cambrian Period.

PANK OF AMERICA

818

WEB ACTIVITY
www.phschool.com

Energy Audit

The Los Angeles skyline comes alive with electric lights as the sun goes down. It takes a lot of energy to keep a city running. Energy keeps the people of Los Angeles cool, provides them with electricity, and helps them move from place to place. Energy is also needed to make the products that clothe, feed, inform, and entertain them.

How much energy does it take to keep your school running? Throughout the chapter, you will work in a group to study energy use in your school.

Your Goal To write a report on a type of energy use in your school including your suggestions for saving energy.

To complete the project, you must
- Survey the types and amount of energy used in the area
- Identify ways to conserve energy in that area
- Prepare a written report summarizing your observations and proposing your suggestions

Get Started With your group, select an area of the school to study, such as a classroom, the cafeteria, or the school grounds. You could also consider the school's heating or cooling system or transportation to and from school. Brainstorm a list of the ways in which you think energy is used in and around your school.

Check Your Progress You'll be working on this project as you study this chapter. To keep your project on track, look for Check Your Progress boxes at the following points.

Section 1 Review, page 332: Observe the area and record the types of energy used.

Section 2 Review, page 338: Collect data on the amount of energy used and look for ways to reduce it.

Section 3 Review, page 345: Write a draft of your report.

Present Your Project At the end of the chapter (page 353), you will present your group's proposal to make your school more energy-efficient.

Electricity makes downtown Los Angeles sparkle at dusk.

SECTION

4 Energy Conservation

Discover Which Bulb Is More Efficient?
Skills Lab Keeping Comfortable
Science at Home Saving Energy

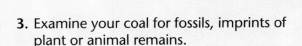

DISCOVER ● ACTIVITY ● ● ● ●

What's in a Piece of Coal?

1. Observe a chunk of coal. Record your observations in as much detail as possible, including color, texture, and shape.

2. Now use a hand lens to observe the coal more closely.

3. Examine your coal for fossils, imprints of plant or animal remains.

Think It Over
Observing What did you notice when you used the hand lens compared to your first observations? What do you think coal is made of?

GUIDE FOR READING

◆ How do fuels provide energy?

◆ What are the three fossil fuels?

◆ Why are fossil fuels considered nonrenewable resources?

Reading Tip As you read, make a table comparing coal, oil, and natural gas. Describe each fuel and note how it is obtained and used.

The blackout happened on a November afternoon in 1965, just as evening rush hour was beginning. One small part in one power plant stopped working. To replace the lost power, the automatic controls shifted electricity from another source. This overloaded another part of the system, causing it to shut down. The problem kept growing. Within minutes, much of the Northeast was without electricity! Lights went out, plunging buildings into darkness. Thousands of people were trapped in dark elevators. Traffic signals stopped working, causing huge traffic jams. Electric stoves, radios, clocks—nothing worked. It took 13 hours to restore the power. During that time, more than 30 million people were reminded just how much their lives depended on electricity.

Producing electricity is an important use of energy resources. Other uses include transportation and heating. As you read about Earth's energy resources, think about how each is used to meet people's energy needs.

Fuels and Energy

INTEGRATING PHYSICS How did you travel to school today? Whether you traveled in a car or a bus, walked, or rode your bike, you used some form of energy. The source of that energy was a fuel. **A fuel is a substance that provides a form of energy— such as heat, light, electricity, or motion— as the result of a chemical change.**

◀ Electric power lines stretch against the evening sky.

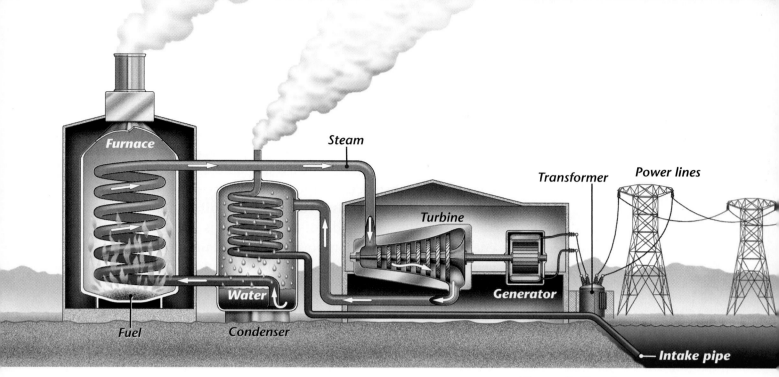

Furnace

Steam

Transformer Power lines

Turbine

Generator

Fuel Condenser

Water

Intake pipe

Figure 1 Electric power plants generate electricity by converting energy from one form to another. In the furnace, fuel is burned, releasing thermal energy. This energy is used to boil water and make steam. The mechanical energy of the moving steam turns the blades of a turbine. The turbine turns the shaft of the generator, producing an electric current.

Energy can be converted from one form to another. To see how, rub your hands together quickly for several seconds. Did you feel them become warmer? When you moved your hands, they had mechanical energy, the energy of motion. The friction of your hands rubbing together converted some of this mechanical energy to thermal energy, which you felt as heat.

Combustion Fuels contain stored chemical energy, which can be released by burning. The process of burning a fuel is called **combustion.** For example, the fuel used by most cars is gasoline. When gasoline is burned in a car engine, it undergoes a chemical change. The gasoline combines with oxygen, producing carbon dioxide and water. The combustion of gasoline also converts some of the stored chemical energy into thermal energy. This thermal energy is converted to mechanical energy that moves the car.

Production of Electricity The energy stored in fuels can be used to generate electricty. In most power plants, the thermal energy produced by burning fuel is used to boil water, making steam, as shown in Figure 1. The mechanical energy of the steam turns the blades of a turbine. The shaft of the turbine is connected to a generator. The generator consists of powerful magnets surrounded by coils of copper wire. As the shaft rotates, the magnets turn inside the wire coil, producing an electric current. The electric current flows through power lines to homes and industries.

☑ *Checkpoint* *What are three energy conversions that might occur in a power plant?*

Graphing ACTIVITY

Use the data in the table below to make a circle graph showing the uses of energy in the United States. (To review circle graphs, see the Skills Handbook.)

End Use of Energy	Percent of Total Energy
Transportation	26.5
Industry	38.1
Homes and businesses	35.4

Figure 2 In the photo, a farmer in Ireland turns over blocks of soft peat. Peat is formed from the remains of plants in the early stages of coal formation. As these remains are more and more deeply buried, peat changes to lignite, then to bituminous coal, and then to anthracite.

What Are Fossil Fuels?

Most of the energy used today comes from organisms that lived hundreds of millions of years ago. As these plants, animals, and other organisms died, their remains piled up. Layers of sand, rock, and mud buried the dead organisms. Over time, heat and pressure changed the material into other substances. **Fossil fuels** are the energy-rich substances formed from the remains of once-living organisms. **The three fossil fuels are coal, oil, and natural gas.**

Fossil fuels are made of hydrocarbons. **Hydrocarbons** are energy-rich chemical compounds that contain carbon and hydrogen atoms. During combustion, the carbon and hydrogen combine with oxygen in the air to form carbon dioxide and water. This process releases energy in the forms of heat and light.

Fossil fuels have more hydrocarbons per kilogram than most other fuels. For this reason, they are an excellent source of energy. Combustion of one kilogram of coal, for example, provides twice as much heat as burning one kilogram of wood. Oil and natural gas provide three times the energy of wood.

☑ *Checkpoint* Why do fossil fuels yield more energy than other fuels?

Coal

Coal is a solid fossil fuel formed from plant remains. People have burned coal to produce heat for thousands of years. But coal was only a minor source of energy compared to wood until the 1800s. As Europe and the United States entered the Industrial Revolution, the need for fuel increased rapidly. As forests were cut down, firewood became more expensive.

Peat
A. Layers of dead plant material build up to form peat.

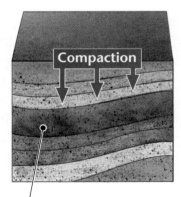

Compaction

Lignite
B. Lignite is soft brown coal, a sedimentary rock.

It became worthwhile to find, mine, and transport coal. Coal fueled the huge steam engines that powered trains, ships, and factories during the Industrial Revolution.

Today, coal provides 23 percent of the energy used in the United States. The major use of coal is to fuel electric power plants.

Coal Mining Before it can be used to produce energy, coal has to be removed from the ground, or mined. Some coal is located very deep underground or is mixed with other materials, making it too difficult to obtain. Known deposits of coal (and other fossil fuels) that can be obtained using current technology are called **reserves.**

INTEGRATING TECHNOLOGY

A century ago, miners had to break the coal apart with hand tools. Today they use machines to chop the coal into chunks and lift it to the surface. The coal is then cleaned to remove rocks, sand, and other materials that do not burn. Removing them also makes the coal lighter, reducing the cost of transporting it.

Coal as an Energy Source Coal is the most plentiful fossil fuel in the United States. It is fairly easy to transport, and provides a lot of energy when burned. But coal also has some disadvantages. Coal mining can increase erosion. Runoff from mines can cause water pollution. Finally, burning most types of coal results in more air pollution than other fossil fuels.

In addition, coal mining can be a dangerous job. Thousands of miners have been killed or injured in accidents in the mines. Many more suffer from "black lung," a disease caused by years of breathing coal dust. Fortunately, the mining industry has been working hard to improve conditions. New safety procedures and better equipment, including robots and drills that produce less coal dust, have made coal mining safer.

Figure 3 A miner obtains hard coal from a shaft deep underground.

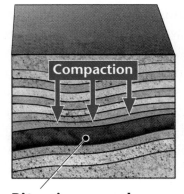

Bituminous coal

C. Bituminous coal is also a sedimentary rock.

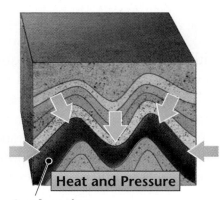

Anthracite

D. Heat and pressure deep beneath the surface produce anthracite, hard coal which is a metamorphic rock.

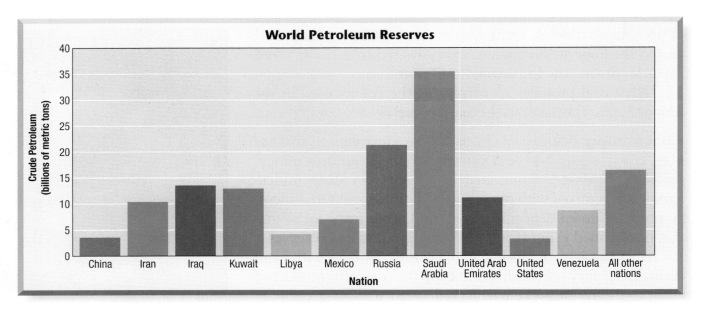

World Petroleum Reserves

Crude Petroleum (billions of metric tons) vs. *Nation*

Figure 4 Known petroleum deposits, called reserves, are located in many parts of the world. *Interpreting Graphs Which two nations have the largest reserves?*

Oil

Oil is a thick, black, liquid fossil fuel. It formed from the remains of small animals, algae, and protists that lived in oceans and shallow inland seas hundreds of millions of years ago. **Petroleum** is another name for oil, from the Latin words *petra* (rock) and *oleum* (oil). Most oil deposits are located underground in tiny holes in sandstone or limestone. The oil fills the holes somewhat like water trapped in the holes of a sponge.

Petroleum accounts for more than one third of the energy produced in the world. Fuel for most cars, airplanes, trains, and ships comes from petroleum. Many homes are heated by oil.

The United States consumes about one third of all the oil produced in the world. But only three percent of the world's supply is located in this country. The difference must be purchased from countries with large oil supplies.

Locating Oil Deposits Because it is usually located deep below the surface, finding oil is difficult. Scientists *INTEGRATING TECHNOLOGY* can use sound waves to test an area for oil without drilling. This technique relies on the fact that sound waves bounce off objects and return as echoes. Scientists send pulses of sound down into the rocks below ground. Then they measure how long it takes the echoes to return. The amount of time depends on whether the sound waves must travel through solid rock or liquid oils. This information can indicate the most likely places to find oil. However, only about one out of every six wells drilled produces a usable amount of oil.

Figure 5 An oil rig bobs up and down as it pumps oil from a Texas oil field.

Refining Oil When oil is first pumped out of the ground, it is called crude oil. Crude oil can be a runny or a thick liquid. In order to be made into useful products, crude oil must undergo a process called refining. A factory where crude oil is separated into fuels and other products by heating is called a **refinery.**

In addition to gasoline and heating oil, many products you use every day are made from crude oil. **Petrochemicals** are compounds that are made from oil. Petrochemicals are used in plastics, paints, medicines, and cosmetics.

☑️ *Checkpoint* *How is petroleum used?*

Natural Gas

The third fossil fuel is natural gas, a mixture of methane and other gases. Natural gas forms from the same organisms as petroleum. Because it is less dense than oil, natural gas often rises above an oil deposit, forming a pocket of gas in the rock.

Pipelines transport the gas from its source to the places where it is used. If all the gas pipelines in the United States were connected, they would reach to the moon and back—twice! Natural gas can also be compressed into a liquid and stored in tanks as fuel for trucks and buses.

Natural gas has several advantages. It produces large amounts of energy, but lower levels of many air pollutants than coal or oil. It is also easy to transport once the network of pipelines is built. One disadvantage of natural gas is that it is highly flammable. A gas leak can cause a violent explosion and fire.

Gas companies help to prevent dangerous explosions from leaks. If you use natural gas in your home, you probably are familiar with the "gas" smell that alerts you whenever there is unburned gas in the air. You may be surprised to learn that natural gas actually has no odor at all. What causes the strong smell? The gas companies add a chemical with a distinct smell to the gas before it is piped to homes and businesses so that any leaks will be noticed.

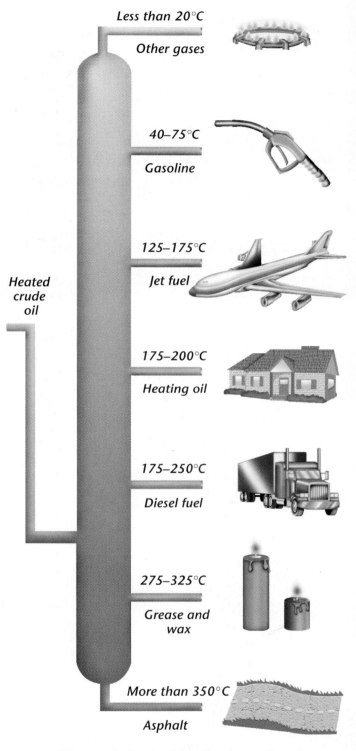

Less than 20°C
Other gases

40–75°C
Gasoline

125–175°C
Jet fuel

Heated crude oil

175–200°C
Heating oil

175–250°C
Diesel fuel

275–325°C
Grease and wax

More than 350°C
Asphalt

Figure 6 Crude oil is refined to make many different products. In the refining process, heat causes the different molecules in crude oil to separate. Different substances vaporize at specific temperatures.

Figure 7 During the gasoline crisis, people frequently had to wait in long lines to buy gas. This shortage reminded Americans of their dependence on oil imported from other nations.
Relating Cause and Effect What caused the gasoline shortage?

Fuel Supply and Demand

The many advantages of using fossil fuels as an energy source have made them essential to modern life. **But remember that fossil fuels take hundreds of millions of years to form. For this reason, fossil fuels are considered a nonrenewable resource.** Earth's **nonrenewable resources** are natural resources that are not replaced as they are used. For example, Earth's known oil reserves took 500 million years to form. One fourth of this oil has already been used. If fossil fuels continue to be used more rapidly than they are formed, the reserves will eventually be used up.

Many of the nations that consume large amounts of fuel have very limited reserves of their own. They have to buy oil, natural gas, and coal from the regions that have large supplies. The uneven distribution of fossil fuel reserves has often been a cause of political problems in the world. For example, in the 1970s, a group of oil-exporting nations decided to reduce their oil exports to the United States. As the supply of gasoline fell, prices rose very rapidly. People sometimes waited in line for hours to buy gasoline.

New sources of energy are needed to replace the decreasing fossil fuel reserves. The rest of this chapter will describe some other sources of energy, as well as ways to make current fuel resources last longer.

 Section 1 Review

1. Explain how fuels provide energy.
2. Name the three fossil fuels and briefly describe each.
3. Explain why fossil fuels are classified as nonrenewable resources.
4. List two advantages and one disadvantage of natural gas as an energy source.
5. **Thinking Critically** **Applying Concepts** Why is it impossible to know exactly how large the world's oil reserves are?

Check Your Progress **CHAPTER PROJECT**

With your team, observe your selected area of the school. Determine which types of energy use take place in this area: heating, cooling, lighting, mechanical devices, electronic equipment, or moving vehicles. Record the specific types and amounts of energy use in a data table. To find the amounts, you will need to collect data from electric meters or fuel gauges. (*Hint:* Observe your area at several different times of the day, since the pattern of energy use may vary.)

SECTION
② Renewable Sources of Energy

DISCOVER · ACTIVITY · · · ·

Can You Capture Solar Energy?

1. Pour 250 milliliters of water into each of two sealable, clear plastic bags.

2. Measure and record the water temperature in each bag. Seal the bags.

3. Put one bag in a dark or shady place. Put the other bag in a place where it will receive direct sunlight.

4. Predict what the temperature of the water in each bag will be after 30 minutes.

5. Measure and record the ending temperatures.

Think It Over

Developing Hypotheses How did the water temperature in each bag change? What could account for these results?

As the sun rises over the rim of the canyon where your family is camping, you feel its warmth on your face. The night's chill disappears quickly. A breeze stirs, carrying with it the smell of the campfire. Maybe you'll take a morning dip in the warm water of a nearby hot spring.

This relaxing scene is far from the city, with its bustling cars and trucks, factories and power plants. But there are energy resources all around you here, too. The sun warms the air, the wind blows, and heat from inside Earth warms the waters of the spring. These sources of energy are all **renewable resources**—that is, they are constantly being supplied. Renewable resources, such as sunlight, wind, and trees, are naturally replaced in a short period of time. As you read about each source of renewable energy, think about how it could help meet people's energy needs.

Energy From the Sun

The warmth you feel on a sunny day is **solar energy,** energy from the sun. **The sun constantly gives off energy in the form of light and heat.** Solar energy is the source, directly or indirectly, of most other renewable energy resources. In one day, Earth receives enough solar energy to meet the energy needs of the entire world for 40 years. Solar energy does not cause pollution, and it will not run out for billions of years.

So why hasn't solar energy replaced fossil fuels? One reason is that solar energy is available only when the sun is shining. A backup energy source must be available on cloudy days and at night. Another problem is that

GUIDE FOR READING

◆ How does the sun provide energy?

◆ What are some renewable sources of energy?

Reading Tip Before you read, preview the headings in this section. Predict some sources of energy that are renewable.

Figure 8 Aimed at the sun, these mirrors provide power to an electric plant in New South Wales, Australia. *Inferring How does the shape of these mirrors make them more effective?*

although Earth receives a lot of energy from the sun every day, this energy is very spread out. To obtain enough power, it is necessary to collect this energy from a huge area.

Solar Technologies

INTEGRATING TECHNOLOGY Improving technologies to capture and use solar energy will help meet future energy needs. Some current solar technologies are described below.

Solar Plants One way to capture the sun's energy involves using giant mirrors. In a solar plant, rows of mirrors focus the sun's rays to heat a tank of water. The water boils, making steam that can be used to generate electricity.

Solar Cells Solar energy can be converted directly into electricity in a solar cell. A solar cell consists of a "sandwich" of very thin layers of the element silicon and other materials. The upper and lower parts of the sandwich have a negative and a positive terminal, like a battery. When light hits the cell, electrons move across the layers, producing an electric current.

The amount of electricity produced by solar cells depends on the area of the cell and the amount of light available. Solar cells are used to power calculators, lights, telephones, and other small devices. However, it would take more than 5,000 solar cells the size of your palm to produce enough electricity for a typical American home. Building solar cells on a large scale is very expensive. As a result, solar cells are used mostly in areas where fossil fuels are difficult to transport.

Checkpoint *What are solar cells made of and how do they work?*

Solar Heating Systems Solar energy can be used to heat buildings. As shown in *Exploring a Solar House,* there are two types of solar heating systems: passive and active.

A **passive solar system** converts sunlight into thermal energy without using pumps or fans. If you have ever stepped into a car on a sunny day, you have experienced passive solar heating. Solar energy passes through the car's windows as light. The sun's rays heat the seats and other parts of the car, which then transfer heat to the air. The heated air is trapped inside, so the car gets warmer. The same principle can be used to heat a home.

An **active solar system** captures the sun's energy, then uses fans and pumps to distribute the heat. Light strikes the black metal surface of a solar collector. There, it is converted to thermal energy. Water is pumped through pipes in the solar collector to absorb the thermal energy. The heated water flows to a storage tank. Pumps and fans distribute the heat throughout the building.

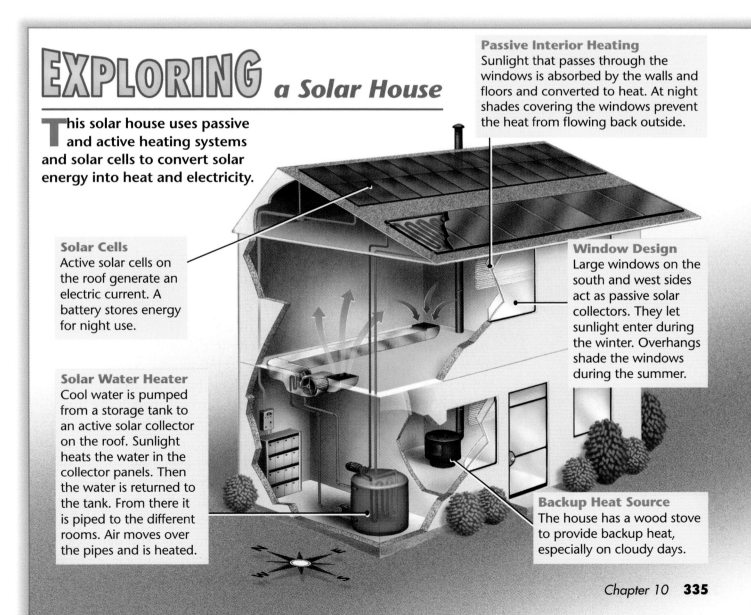

EXPLORING *a Solar House*

This solar house uses passive and active heating systems and solar cells to convert solar energy into heat and electricity.

Passive Interior Heating
Sunlight that passes through the windows is absorbed by the walls and floors and converted to heat. At night shades covering the windows prevent the heat from flowing back outside.

Solar Cells
Active solar cells on the roof generate an electric current. A battery stores energy for night use.

Window Design
Large windows on the south and west sides act as passive solar collectors. They let sunlight enter during the winter. Overhangs shade the windows during the summer.

Solar Water Heater
Cool water is pumped from a storage tank to an active solar collector on the roof. Sunlight heats the water in the collector panels. Then the water is returned to the tank. From there it is piped to the different rooms. Air moves over the pipes and is heated.

Backup Heat Source
The house has a wood stove to provide backup heat, especially on cloudy days.

Figure 9 This wind farm in the Mojave Desert is one of many in the state of California.
Making Generalizations What are some advantages of wind power?

Other Sources of Renewable Energy

The sun is one source of renewable energy. Other renewable energy sources include wind, water, biomass materials, Earth's interior, and hydrogen.

Wind Wind can be used to turn a turbine and generate electricity. Wind power plants or "wind farms" consist of many windmills. Together, the windmills generate large amounts of electric power.

Although wind now provides less than one percent of the world's electricity, it is the fastest-growing energy source. Wind energy is free and does not cause pollution.

Wind energy is not ideal for all locations. Few places have winds that blow steadily enough to be a worthwhile energy source. But as fossil fuels become more scarce and expensive, wind generators will become more important.

Flowing Water As water flows over the land into lakes and oceans, it provides another source of energy. Flowing water can turn a turbine and generate electricity in the same way as steam or wind. A dam across a river blocks the flow of water, creating an artificial lake called a reservoir. Water flows through tunnels at the bottom of the dam. As the water moves through the tunnels, it turns turbines connected to a generator.

Hydroelectric power is electricity produced by flowing water. This type of power is the most widely used source of renewable energy in the world today. Hydroelectric power is inexpensive and does not create air pollution. But hydroelectric power does have drawbacks. In the United States, for example, most suitable rivers have already been dammed. And dams can have negative effects on the environment.

Biomass Fuels Wood is one of a group of fuels, called **biomass fuels,** which are fuels made from things that were once alive. Other biomass fuels include leaves, food wastes, and even manure. Burning breaks down complicated molecules in these fuels, releasing energy.

Biomass materials also can be converted into other fuels. For example, corn, sugar cane, and other crops can be used to make alcohol. Adding the alcohol to gasoline forms a mixture called gasohol. Gasohol can be used as fuel for cars and trucks. When bacteria decompose waste materials, they convert the waste into methane gas. The methane produced in some landfills is used for heating buildings.

Biomass fuels are not widely used today. Producing alcohol and methane in large quantities can be expensive. And although wood is renewable, it takes time for new trees to grow. But in the future, biomass fuels may play a larger role in meeting energy needs.

✓ *Checkpoint* *What are the advantages and disadvantages of biomass fuels?*

Geothermal Energy In certain regions, such as Iceland and New Zealand, magma heats underground water to the boiling point. The hot water and steam are valuable sources of **geothermal energy.** In Reykjavik, Iceland, 90 percent of homes are heated by water warmed underground in this way. Geothermal energy can also be used to generate electricity.

Geothermal energy is an unlimited source of cheap energy. Unfortunately, there are only a few places where magma comes close to Earth's surface. Elsewhere, very expensive, deep wells must be drilled to tap this energy. Although it can be costly, geothermal energy is likely to play a part in meeting energy needs in the future.

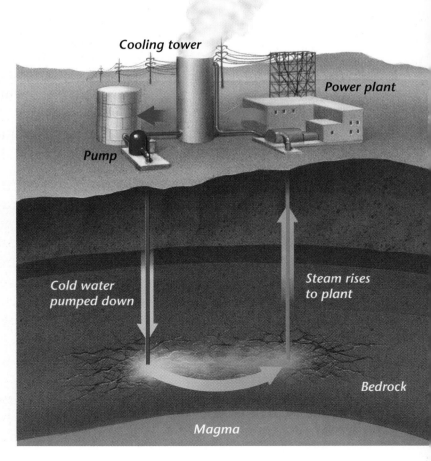

Figure 10 A geothermal power plant uses heat from Earth's interior as an energy source. Cold water is piped deep into the ground, where it is heated by magma. The resulting steam can be used for heat or to generate electricity.

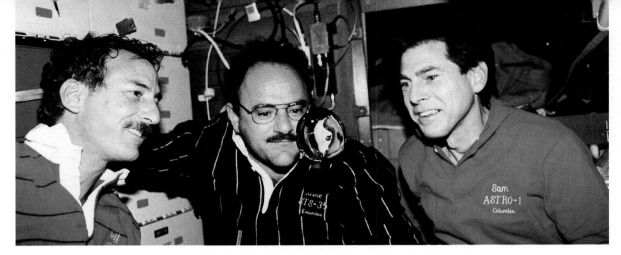

Figure 11 The object fascinating these three astronauts is a bubble of water—the harmless by-product of the hydrogen fuel cells used on the space shuttle.

Hydrogen Power

Now that you have read about so many energy sources, consider a fuel with this description: It burns cleanly, forming only water as a by-product. It creates no smoke, smog, or acid rain. It can be handled and transported through pipelines, much like natural gas. This fuel exists on Earth in large supply.

This ideal-sounding fuel is real—it's hydrogen. However, there is an obstacle. Almost all the hydrogen on Earth is combined with oxygen in the form of water. Pure hydrogen can be obtained by passing an electric current through water. But it takes more energy to obtain the hydrogen than is produced by burning it again.

Scientists aren't ruling out hydrogen as a good fuel for the future. At present, hydroelectric plants decrease their activity when the demand for electricity is low. Instead, they could run at full power all the time, using the excess electricity to produce hydrogen. Similarly, solar power plants often generate more electricity than is needed during the day. This extra electricity could be used to produce hydrogen. If a way can be found to produce hydrogen cheaply, it could someday be an important source of energy.

Section 2 Review

1. What is solar energy?
2. What are some advantages and disadvantages of solar energy?
3. How are active and passive solar heating systems different?
4. List three examples of biomass fuels.
5. What limits the use of geothermal energy?
6. **Thinking Critically** **Predicting** Which of the renewable sources of energy do you think is most likely to be used in your community in 100 years? Give reasons to support your answer.

Check Your Progress
CHAPTER PROJECT

Continue to collect data on how much energy is used in your group's area of the school. Begin to brainstorm ideas for reducing energy usage in this area. For example, is there a way to use some electrical devices for shorter periods of time? (*Hint:* Interviewing some adults who are responsible for the operation of the school building may give you some good ideas. Be sure to check with your teacher before interviewing anyone.)

Cooking With Sunshine

In the future, will you cook your meals with sunshine instead of electricity? That's certainly a possibility. In this lab, you'll investigate how solar energy can be used to cook food.

Problem

What is the best shape for a solar cooker?

Skills Focus

predicting, designing experiments, forming operational definitions

Suggested Materials

scissors	glue	3 thermometers
3 dowels	tape	marshmallows
3 sheets of aluminum foil		clock or watch
3 sheets of oaktag paper		

Procedure

Part 1 Capturing Solar Energy

1. Read over the entire lab. Then predict which shape will produce the largest temperature increase when placed in the sun.
2. Glue a sheet of aluminum foil, shiny side up, to each sheet of oaktag paper. Before the glue dries, gently smooth out any wrinkles in the foil.
3. Bend one sheet into a V shape. Bend another sheet into a U shape. Leave the last sheet flat.
4. Place the aluminum sheets in direct sunlight, using wood blocks or books to hold the U- and V-shapes in position.
5. Tape a dowel to each thermometer. Record the starting temperature on each thermometer.
6. Use the dowels to hold the thermometer bulbs in the center of the aluminum shapes. After 15 minutes, record the final temperature on each thermometer.

Part 2 Designing a Solar Cooker

7. Use the results from Step 6 to design a solar cooker that can toast a marshmallow. Prepare a written description of your plan for your teacher's approval. Include an operational definition of a "well-toasted" marshmallow.
8. After your teacher has approved your plan, test your design by placing a marshmallow on a wooden dowel. Record the time it takes to toast the marshmallow.

Analyze and Conclude

1. What was the role of the aluminum foil in this investigation? What other materials could you have used instead? Explain.
2. Which of the three shapes—V, U, or flat— produced the largest increase in temperature? Propose an explanation for this result.
3. What other variables might have affected your results? Explain.
4. **Apply** What are some possible advantages of a solar cooker based on this design? What are some possible disadvantages?

More to Explore

Try adapting your design to heat water. Show your new design to your teacher before trying it.

Hydroelectric Dams: Are They All Here to Stay?

There are hundreds of hydroelectric dams on United States rivers. These dams provide electricity for millions of people. Hydroelectric dams provide clean, inexpensive, and renewable energy. They are a good source of power.

Recently, however, people have learned that dams can have negative effects on river ecosystems. Some people have even suggested removing certain dams. But is this wise? When do the benefits of dams outweigh the problems?

The Issues

How Do Dams Affect the Environment? Because dams change water depth and flow, they can alter the temperature of a river. The water may become too cold or too warm for fish that normally live there. A change in temperature can also reduce the number of algae in a river. This affects other organisms in the river food web.

Some species of fish, such as salmon, herring, and menhaden, hatch in rivers but then travel to the ocean. To breed, they must return to the river. Dams can block the movement of these fish populations. For example, the Columbia River Basin, which has more than 50 dams, once contained more than 10 million salmon. Today it is home to only 2 million salmon.

What Are the Effects of Removing Dams? Some people say that the only way to restore ecosystems is to remove dams. However, these dams supply a small but important part of the nation's electricity. Removing them could force the United States to use more nonrenewable fossil fuels. Fossil fuels also produce more pollution than hydroelectric plants.

The reservoirs behind hydroelectric dams supply water for irrigation and drinking. These supplies would be difficult to replace. In addition, a series of dams on a river can reduce flooding downstream during heavy rains.

What Can People Do? Removing dams might restore some river ecosystems. For example, Edwards Dam on the Kennebec River in Maine was removed in 1999 to allow several threatened fish species to spawn. Edwards Dam provided only a small percent of Maine's electric power. This small amount was easier to replace than the power provided by a much larger dam.

There are other ways to protect migrating fish. Fish ladders, for example, are step-like waterways that help fish pass over dams. Fish can even be carried around dams in trucks. Still, these methods are costly and not always successful.

The government issues licenses for hydroelectric dams. In considering license renewals, officials examine environmental impact as well as energy production.

You Decide

1. Identify the Problem
In your own words, explain some of the major issues surrounding hydroelectric dams.

2. Analyze the Options
Examine the pros and cons of removing dams. What are the benefits? What are the costs? Who will be affected by the change?

3. Find a Solution
The license of a nearby dam is up for review. The dam provides electricity, but also blocks the migration of fish. What do you recommend? Explain.

SECTION 3 Nuclear Energy

Wouldn't it be great if people could use the same method as the sun to produce energy? In a way, they can! The kind of reactions that power the sun involve the central cores of atoms. The central core of an atom that contains the protons and neutrons is called the **nucleus** (plural nuclei). The reactions that involve nuclei, called nuclear reactions, involve tremendous amounts of energy. Two types of nuclear reactions are fission and fusion.

Fission Reactions and Energy

Nuclear reactions convert matter into energy. In 1905, Albert Einstein developed a formula that described the relationship between energy and matter. You have probably seen this famous equation, $E = mc^2$. In the equation, the E represents energy and the m represents mass. The c, which represents the speed of light, is a very large number. This equation states that when matter is changed into energy, an enormous amount of energy is released.

Nuclear fission is the splitting of an atom's nucleus into two smaller nuclei. The fuel for the reaction is a large atom that has an unstable nucleus, such as uranium-235 (U-235). A neutron is shot at the U-235 atom at high speed. **When the neutron hits the U-235 nucleus, the nucleus splits apart into two smaller nuclei and two or more neutrons.** The total mass of all these particles is a bit less than the mass of the original nucleus. The small amount of mass that makes up the difference has been converted into energy—a lot of energy, as described by Einstein's equation.

GUIDE FOR READING

◆ What happens during fission and fusion reactions?

◆ How does a nuclear power plant produce electricity?

Reading Tip As you read, create a Venn diagram to compare and contrast nuclear fission and nuclear fusion.

Figure 12 Albert Einstein, shown here in 1930, described the relationship between energy and matter.

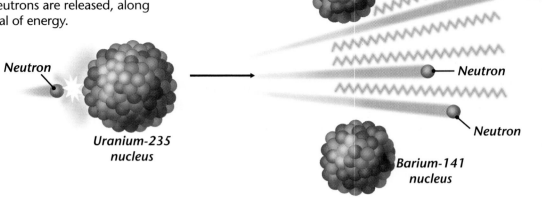

Figure 13 In a nuclear fission reaction, a neutron "bullet" strikes a U-235 nucleus. As a result, the nucleus splits into two smaller nuclei. More neutrons are released, along with a great deal of energy.

Neutron

Uranium-235 nucleus

Krypton-92 nucleus

Neutron

Neutron

Neutron

Barium-141 nucleus

Meanwhile, the fission reaction has produced three more neutrons. If any of these neutrons strikes another nucleus, the fission reaction is repeated. More neutrons and more energy are released. If there are enough nuclei nearby, the process continues over and over in a chain reaction, just like a row of dominoes falling. In a nuclear chain reaction, the amount of energy released increases rapidly with each step in the chain.

What happens to all the energy released by these fission reactions? If a nuclear chain reaction is not controlled, the released energy causes a huge explosion. The explosion of an atomic bomb is an uncontrolled nuclear reaction. A few kilograms of matter explode with more force than several thousand tons of a nonnuclear explosive such as dynamite. However, if the chain reaction is controlled, the energy is released as heat, which can be used to generate electricity.

Nuclear Power Plants

Controlled nuclear fission reactions take place inside nuclear power plants. **In a nuclear power plant, the heat released from the reactions is used to change water into steam. As in other types of power plants, the steam then turns the blades of a turbine to generate electricity.** Look at the diagram of a nuclear power plant in Figure 14. In addition to the generator, it has two main parts: the reactor vessel and the heat exchanger.

Reactor Vessel The **reactor vessel** is the section of a nuclear reactor where nuclear fission occurs. The reactor contains rods of U-235, called **fuel rods.** When several fuel rods are placed close together, a series of fission reactions occurs. The reactions are controlled by placing **control rods** made of the metal cadmium between the fuel rods. The cadmium absorbs the neutrons

Shoot the Nucleus

ACTIVITY

In an open area of your classroom, make a model of a nuclear fission reaction. Place a handful of marbles on the floor in a tight cluster, so that they touch one another. Step back about a half-meter from the marbles. Shoot another marble at the cluster.

Making Models What does the marble you shot at the cluster represent? What effect did the marble have on the cluster? How is this similar to a nuclear fission reaction?

released during the fission reactions. As the cadmium control rods are removed, the fission reactions speed up. If the reactor vessel starts to get too hot, the control rods are moved back in place to slow the chain reaction.

Heat Exchanger Heat is removed from the reactor vessel by water or another fluid that is pumped through the reactor. This fluid passes through a heat exchanger. There, the fluid boils water to produce steam, which runs the electrical generator. The steam is condensed again and pumped back to the heat exchanger.

☑️ *Checkpoint* *How are fission reactions controlled?*

The Risks of Nuclear Fission

When it was first demonstrated, people thought that nuclear fission would provide an almost unlimited source of clean, safe energy. Today nuclear power plants generate much of the world's electricity—about 20 percent in the United States and more than 70 percent in France. But these plants have some problems.

In 1986, in Chernobyl, Ukraine, the reactor vessel in a nuclear power plant overheated. The fuel rods generated so much heat that they started to melt, a condition called a **meltdown.** The excess heat increased the steam pressure in the generator. A series of explosions blew parts of the roof off and injured or killed dozens of plant workers and firefighters. Radioactive materials escaped into the environment. Today, the soil in an area the size of Florida remains contaminated with radioactive waste.

Sharpen your Skills

Calculating

ACTIVITY

A single pellet of U-235 the size of a breath mint can produce as much energy as 615 liters of fuel oil. An average home uses 5,000 liters of oil a year. How many U-235 pellets would be needed to supply the same amount of energy?

Figure 14 In a nuclear plant, uranium fuel undergoes fission, producing heat. The heat boils water, and the resulting steam drives the turbines that generate electricity. *Interpreting Diagrams From which part of the power plant is heat released to the environment?*

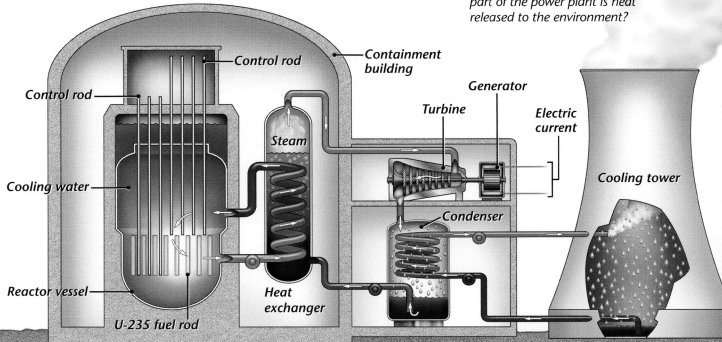

Control rod
Control rod
Containment building
Generator
Turbine
Electric current
Steam
Cooling water
Cooling tower
Condenser
Reactor vessel
Heat exchanger
U-235 fuel rod

Figure 15 One problem with nuclear power is disposal of the used radioactive fuel rods. In this plant in France, the fuel rods are stored in a deep pool of water.

Chernobyl and less serious accidents at other nuclear power plants have led to public concerns about nuclear plant safety.

The danger of a meltdown is a serious concern. However, a meltdown can be avoided by careful planning. A more difficult problem is the disposal of radioactive wastes produced by power plants. Radioactive wastes remain dangerous for many thousands of years. Scientists must find a way to safely store these wastes for a long period of time. Finally, nuclear power has turned out to be a much more costly source of power than was originally expected. The safety features required for nuclear plants make the plants very expensive.

☑ *Checkpoint* *What are three problems with using nuclear fission as an energy source?*

The Quest to Control Fusion

A second type of nuclear reaction is fusion. **Nuclear fusion** is the combining of two atomic nuclei to produce a single larger nucleus. **As shown in Figure 16, two kinds of hydrogen nuclei are forced together in a fusion reaction.** One kind (hydrogen-2) has one proton and one neutron, and the other kind (hydrogen-3) has one proton and two neutrons. The tremendous heat and pressure

Figure 16 In a nuclear fusion reaction, two nuclei combine to form a single larger nucleus. *Interpreting Diagrams What is released during a fusion reaction?*

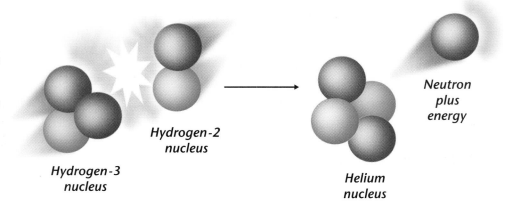

Hydrogen-2
nucleus

Hydrogen-3
nucleus

Neutron
plus
energy

Helium
nucleus

cause them to combine and create a helium nucleus with two protons and two neutrons. This helium nucleus has slightly less mass than the total mass of the two hydrogen nuclei. The difference is converted to energy.

Nuclear fusion would have many advantages as an energy source. Fusion can produce much more energy per atom than nuclear fission. The fuel for a nuclear fusion reactor is also readily available. Water, which is plentiful in Earth's oceans, contains one of the kinds of hydrogen needed for fusion. Fusion should be safer and less polluting than nuclear fission. You can see why scientists are eager to find a way to build a nuclear fusion reactor!

Although some fusion bombs have been exploded, scientists have not yet been able to control a large-scale fusion reaction. The biggest problem is temperature. In the sun, nuclear fusion occurs at 15 million degrees Celsius. Such conditions are almost impossible to control on Earth. No material has been found that can serve as a reactor vessel under the high temperature and pressure of a nuclear fusion reaction. Extremely powerful magnetic fields can contain a fusion reaction. However, it takes more energy to generate these fields than the fusion reaction produces.

Although many more years of research are expected, some scientists believe that they will eventually be able to control fusion reactions. If they succeed, the quest for a clean, cheap energy source may be over at last.

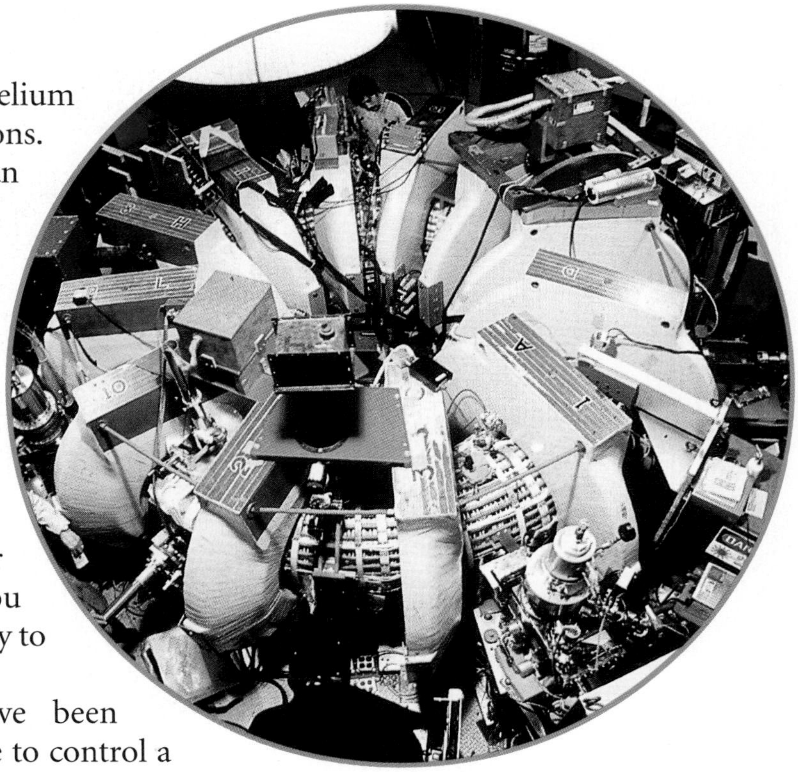

Figure 17 Researchers at Los Alamos National Laboratory in New Mexico are studying fusion as an energy source. This machine creates strong magnetic fields that allow fusion to occur for short periods of time.

Section 3 Review

1. Draw and label a simple diagram of a nuclear fission reaction. Include the following labels: U-235 nucleus, neutrons, smaller nuclei, and energy.
2. How can the energy released in a fission reaction be used to produce electricity?
3. Explain the purpose of control rods.
4. Give two reasons that people have not been able to use nuclear fusion as an energy source.
5. **Thinking Critically Classifying** Is nuclear fission a renewable or nonrenewable energy source? Is nuclear fusion renewable or nonrenewable? Explain.

Check Your Progress   CHAPTER PROJECT
By now you should begin preparing the written report of your findings about energy use in your group's area of the school. Your report should include the major ways energy is used in your chosen area. You should also include recommendations on how energy use might be reduced.

Keeping Comfortable

Two ways to use less energy are to keep heat out of your home when the weather is hot, and to keep heat in when the weather is cold. In this lab, you will design an experiment to compare how well different materials do this.

Problem

How well do different materials stop heat transfer?

Suggested Materials

thermometers	ice water	hot water
watch or clock	beakers	

containers and lids made of paper, plastic foam, plastic, glass, and metal

Design a Plan

Part 1 Measuring Temperature Changes

1. Use a pencil to poke a hole in the lid of a paper cup. Fill the cup about halfway with cold water.
2. Put the lid on the cup. Insert a thermometer into the water through the hole. When the temperature stops dropping, place the cup in a beaker. Add hot water to the beaker until the water level is about 1 cm below the lid.
3. Record the water temperature once every minute until it has increased by 5°C. Use the time it takes for the temperature to increase 1°C as a measure of the effectiveness of the paper cup in preventing heat transfer.

Part 2 Comparing Materials

4. Use the ideas from Part 1 to design a controlled experiment to rank the effectiveness of different materials in preventing heat transfer.

5. Use these questions to help you plan your experiment:
   - ◆ What hypothesis will you test?
   - ◆ Which materials do you predict will be the best and worst at preventing heat transfer? How will you define these terms?
   - ◆ What will your manipulated variable be? What will your responding variable be?
   - ◆ What variables do you need to control? How will you control them?
   - ◆ What step-by-step procedures will you use?
   - ◆ What kind of data table will you use?
6. After your teacher has reviewed your plans, make any necessary changes in your design. Then perform your experiment.

Analyze and Conclude

1. In Part 1, what was the starting temperature of the hot water? What was the starting temperature of the cold water? In which direction did the heat flow? How do you know?
2. If the materials in Part 1 are used to represent your home in very hot weather, which material would represent the rooms in your home? Which would represent the outdoor weather? Which would represent the walls of the building?
3. Which material was most effective at preventing the transfer of heat? Which was the least effective? Explain.
4. **Think About It** Would experiments similar to this one provide you with enough information to choose materials to build a home? Explain.

Design an Experiment

Design an experiment to compare how well the materials would work if the hot water were inside the cup and the cold water were outside. With your teacher's permission, carry out your experiment.

SECTION 4 Energy Conservation

Imagine what would happen if the world ran out of fossil fuels today. Much of the electric power that people depend on would disappear. Most buildings would lose their heating and cooling. Forests would disappear as people began to burn wood for heat and cooking. Almost all transportation would stop. Cars, buses, trains, airplanes, and ships would be stranded wherever they ran out of fuel. Since radios, televisions, computers, and telephones depend on electricity, communication would be greatly reduced.

Although fossil fuels won't run out immediately, they also won't last forever. Most people think that it makes sense to start planning now to avoid a fuel shortage in the future. **One approach to the problem is to find new sources of energy. The second way is to make the fuels that are available now last as long as possible while other solutions are being developed.**

Conservation and Efficiency

Reducing energy use is called **energy conservation.** For example, if you walk to the store instead of getting a ride, you are conserving the gasoline needed to drive to the store. Reducing energy use is a solution to energy problems that will help no matter what form of energy is used in the future.

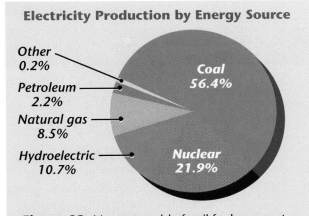

Electricity Production by Energy Source

Other 0.2%
Petroleum 2.2%
Natural gas 8.5%
Hydroelectric 10.7%
Coal 56.4%
Nuclear 21.9%

Figure 18 Nonrenewable fossil fuels generate over two thirds of the nation's electricity.

A way to get as much work as possible out of fuels is to use them efficiently. **Efficiency** is the percentage of energy that is actually used to perform work. The rest of the energy is "lost" to the surroundings, usually as heat. People have developed many ways to increase energy efficiency.

Lighting Lights can use as much as 10 percent of the electricity in your home, but much of that electricity is wasted. An incandescent light bulb converts less than 10 percent of the electricity it uses into light. The rest is given off as heat. You can prove this to yourself by holding your hand close to an incandescent light bulb. But don't touch it! Compact fluorescent bulbs, on the other hand, use only about one fourth as much energy to provide the same amount of light.

☑ *Checkpoint* Which type of light bulb is more energy-efficient?

SCIENCE & History

Energy-Efficient Devices

Scientists and engineers have developed many technologies that improve energy efficiency and reduce energy use.

1932
Fiberglass Insulation

Long strands of glass fibers trap air and keep buildings from losing heat. Less fuel is used for heating.

1958
Solar Cells

More than 150 years ago, scientists discovered that silicon can convert light into electricity. The first useful application of solar cells was to power the radio on a satellite. Now solar cells are even used on experimental cars like the one below.

1930   1940   1950

1936
Fluorescent Lighting

Fluorescent bulbs were introduced to the public at the 100th anniversary celebration of the United States Patent Office. Because these bulbs use less energy than incandescent bulbs, most offices and schools use fluorescent lights.

348

Heating and Cooling One method of increasing the efficiency of heating and cooling systems is insulation. **Insulation** is a layer of material that helps block the transfer of heat between the air inside and outside a building. You have probably seen insulation made of fiberglass, which looks like fluffy pink cotton candy. The mat of thin glass fibers trap air. **This layer of trapped air helps keep the building from losing or gaining heat from the outside.** A layer of fiberglass 15 centimeters thick insulates a room as well as a brick wall 2 meters thick or a stone wall almost 6 meters thick!

Buildings lose a lot of heat around the windows. Look at the windows in your school or home. Was the building built after 1980? Have the windows been replaced recently? If so, you will most likely see two panes of glass with space between them. The air between the panes of glass acts as insulation.

In Your Journal

Design an advertisement for one of the energy-saving inventions described in this time line. The advertisement may be a print, radio, or television ad. Be sure that your advertisement clearly explains the benefits of the invention.

1967
Microwave Ovens

The first countertop microwave oven for the home was introduced. Microwaves cook food by heating the water the food contains. The microwave oven heats only the food, not the air, racks, and oven walls as in a conventional oven. Preheating is also not required, saving even more energy.

1997
Smart Roads

The Department of Transportation demonstrated that cars can be controlled by computers. Sensors built into the road control all the cars, making traffic flow more smoothly. This uses less energy.

1970	1980	1990	2000

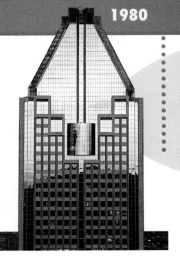

1981
High-Efficiency Window Coatings

Materials that reflect sunlight were first used to coat windows in the early 1980s. This coating reduces the air conditioning needed to keep the inside of the building cool.

Figure 19 A single city bus can transport dozens of people, reducing the number of cars on the roads and saving energy.
Applying Concepts How does riding a bus conserve energy?

Transportation Engineers have improved the energy efficiency of cars by designing better engines and tires. Another way to save energy is to reduce the number of cars on the road. In many communities, public transit systems provide an alternative to driving. Other cities encourage carpooling. If four people travel together in one car, they use much less energy than they would by driving separately. Many cities now set aside lanes for cars containing two or more people.

In the future, cars that run on electricity may provide the most energy savings of all. Electric power plants can convert fuel into electricity more efficiently than a car engine converts gasoline into motion. Therefore, a car that runs on electricity is more energy-efficient than one that runs directly on fuel.

What You Can Do

You can reduce your personal energy use by changing your behavior in some simple ways.

◆ Keep your home cooler in winter and warmer in summer. Instead of turning up the heat, put on a sweater. Use fans instead of air conditioners.

◆ Use natural lighting instead of electric lights when possible.

◆ Turn off the lights or television when you leave a room.

◆ Walk or ride a bike for short trips. Ride buses and trains.

◆ Recycle, especially metal products. Recycling an aluminum can uses only 5 percent of the energy making a new can uses!

The items in this list are small things, but multiplied by millions of people they add up to a lot of energy saved for the future.

Section 4 Review

1. What are two ways to make energy resources last longer?
2. Explain how putting insulation in a building conserves energy.
3. How does carpooling conserve energy?
4. **Thinking Critically** **Predicting** An office building contains only incandescent lights. The building next door contains fluorescent lights. Predict which building has higher energy bills. Explain your answer.

Science at Home

Saving Energy With an adult family member, conduct an energy audit of your home. Look for places where energy is being lost, such as cracks around windows and doors. Also look for ways to reduce energy use, such as running the dishwasher only when it is full. Together, create a list of energy-saving suggestions for your family. Post the list where everyone can see it.

SECTION 1 Fossil Fuels

Key Ideas

◆ A fuel is a substance that provides a form of energy as a result of a chemical change.

◆ Energy can be converted from one form to another.

◆ The three major fossil fuels are coal, oil, and natural gas. These fuels release more energy when they are burned than most other substances do.

◆ Because fossil fuels take hundreds of millions of years to form, they are considered nonrenewable resources.

Key Terms

combustion	petroleum
fossil fuels	refinery
hydrocarbons	petrochemicals
reserves	nonrenewable resources

SECTION 2 Renewable Sources of Energy

Key Ideas

◆ Solar energy is plentiful and renewable, and does not cause pollution. However, a backup energy source is needed.

◆ Because the sun causes winds and drives the water cycle, wind power and water power are considered indirect forms of solar energy.

◆ Biomass fuels, geothermal energy, and hydrogen power are other renewable energy sources that are currently in limited use.

Key Terms

solar energy	biomass fuels
passive solar system	gasohol
active solar system	geothermal energy
hydroelectric power	

SECTION 3 Nuclear Energy

INTEGRATING CHEMISTRY

Key Ideas

◆ Nuclear reactions include fission reactions and fusion reactions.

◆ In a fission reaction, the impact of a neutron splits an atom's nucleus into two smaller nuclei and two or more neutrons. A large amount of energy is released in the process.

◆ In a nuclear power plant, the thermal energy released from controlled fission reactions is used to generate electricity.

◆ Disadvantages of nuclear power include the risk of a meltdown and radioactive waste.

Key Terms

nucleus	fuel rods	meltdown
nuclear fission	control rods	nuclear fusion
reactor vessel		

SECTION 4 Energy Conservation

Key Ideas

◆ To avoid an energy shortage in the future, people must find new sources of energy and conserve the fuels that are available now.

◆ Insulation keeps a building from losing heat to, or gaining heat from, the outside.

◆ Ways to conserve energy use in transportation include making more efficient vehicles, carpooling, and using public transit.

Key Terms

energy conservation	insulation	efficiency

Organizing Information

Compare/Contrast Table Make a table listing an advantage and a disadvantage for each of the following types of energy: coal, petroleum, solar, wind, water, geothermal, nuclear. For example, advantages of coal include the fact that it produces a large amount of energy and is easy to transport. Can you recall any disadvantages of using coal as an energy source? (For tips on making compare/contrast tables see the Skills Handbook.)

Reviewing Content

 For more review of key concepts, see the Interactive Student Tutorial CD-ROM.

Multiple Choice

Choose the letter of the best answer.

1. Which of the following is *not* a fossil fuel?
   a. coal
   b. wood
   c. oil
   d. natural gas
2. Wind and water energy are both indirect forms of
   a. nuclear energy.
   b. electrical energy.
   c. solar energy.
   d. geothermal energy.
3. Which of the following is *not* a biomass fuel?
   a. methane
   b. gasohol
   c. hydrogen
   d. sugar-cane wastes
4. The particle used to start a nuclear fission reaction is a(n)
   a. neutron.
   b. nucleus.
   c. proton.
   d. atom.
5. A part of a nuclear power plant that undergoes a fission reaction is called a
   a. turbine.
   b. control rod.
   c. heat exchanger.
   d. fuel rod.

True or False

If the statement is true, write true. If it is false, change the underlined word or words to make the statement true.

6. Products made from petroleum are called <u>hydrocarbons</u>.
7. The process of burning a fuel for energy is <u>combustion</u>.
8. Geothermal energy is an example of a <u>nonrenewable</u> energy source.
9. Solar energy is harnessed to run calculators using <u>solar satellites</u>.
10. Most of the energy used in the United States today comes from <u>fossil fuels</u>.

Checking Concepts

11. Explain why coal mining is a difficult task.
12. Describe how coal forms.
13. What are some advantages and disadvantages of natural gas as an energy source?
14. Describe three features of a solar home. (Your answer may include passive or active solar systems.)
15. Explain how wind can be used to generate electricity.
16. What factors limit the use of biomass fuels as an energy source?
17. Describe the advantages and disadvantages that hydrogen power would have as a source of energy.
18. How is a nuclear fission reaction controlled in a nuclear power plant?
19. Define *energy efficiency*. Give three examples of inventions that increase energy efficiency.
20. **Writing to Learn** Suppose you had no electricity. Write a journal entry describing a typical weekday, including your meals, classes, and after-school activities. Explain how you might get things done without electricity.

Critical Thinking

21. **Comparing and Contrasting** Discuss how the three fossil fuels are alike and how they are different.
22. **Classifying** State whether each of the following energy sources is renewable or nonrenewable: coal, solar power, methane, hydrogen. Give a reason for each answer.
23. **Making Judgments** Write a short paragraph explaining why you agree or disagree with the following statement: "The United States should build more nuclear power plants to prepare for the future shortage of fossil fuels."
24. **Relating Cause and Effect** Explain the steps in which an electric power plant generates electricity by burning a fossil fuel.

Applying Skills

The table below shows how the world's energy production changed between 1973 and 1995. Use the information in the table to answer Questions 25–28.

Source of Energy	Energy Units Produced 1973	Energy Units Produced 1995
Coal	1,498	2,179
Gas	964	1,775
Hydroelectric	107	242
Nuclear	54	646
Oil	2,730	3,228
TOTAL Energy Units	5,353	8,070

25. **Interpreting Data** How did total energy production change from 1973 to 1995?
26. **Calculating** What percentage of total world energy production did nuclear power provide in 1973? In 1995?
27. **Classifying** Classify the different types of energy as renewable or nonrenewable. How important was renewable energy in 1995?
28. **Drawing Conclusions** Which energy source was the most important in 1995?

Performance ▼ Assessment

CHAPTER PROJECT

Present Your Project Have another group review your report for clarity, organization, and detail. Make revisions based on feedback from the other group. As a class, discuss each group's findings. Make a list of suggestions for conserving energy in your school.

Reflect and Record In your project notebook, explain what types of energy use were the hardest to measure. What other information would you have liked to have when making your recommendations? Record your overall opinion of energy efficiency in your school.

Test Preparation

Use these questions to prepare for standardized tests.

Read the passage. Then answer Questions 29–33.

Tides are a source of renewable energy. Along some coasts, great amounts of water move into bays at high tide and flow out to sea again as the tide falls.

A few tidal power plants have been built to take advantage of this regular motion. A low dam across the entrance to a shallow bay holds water in the bay at high tide. As the tide goes out, water flowing past turbines in the dam generates electricity, as in a hydroelectric power plant.

Tidal power will probably never become a major source of energy because only a few coastal areas in the world are suitable for building tidal power plants. Also, a dam across a bay blocks boats and fish from traveling up the river.

29. How many tidal power plants are now in use?
   a. only a few
   b. several dozen
   c. zero
   d. several hundred

30. Tides are an energy source that is
   a. widely used throughout the world.
   b. renewable.
   c. nonrenewable.
   d. impossible to use in generating power.

31. Tidal power plants most resemble
   a. geothermal power plants.
   b. windmills.
   c. hydroelectric power plants.
   d. water-cooled nuclear power plants.

32. The selection concludes that tidal power
   a. will replace other types of power.
   b. already produces too much energy.
   c. can be developed wherever the tide rises.
   d. won't become a major source of energy.

33. A good title for this reading selection would be
   a. The Limitless Power of Tides.
   b. Tidal Power Blocks Boats.
   c. A Minor Source of Renewable Energy.
   d. A Major Source of Energy.

Mammals of the JURASSIC PERIOD

Spending half your summer alone in a tiny trailer in a deserted part of Wyoming may not sound like fun. But for Kelli Trujillo, a graduate student in paleontology (pay lee un TAHL uh jee), it's a dream come true. As a paleontologist, she studies the remains of ancient living things.

Kelli Trujillo is working near Como Bluff, Wyoming, one of the most famous dinosaur graveyards in the United States. But she is not searching for dinosaur bones. Kelli is looking for the remains of mammals that lived during the late Jurassic Period, about 150 million years ago.

During the Jurassic Period, southeast Wyoming was flat and dotted with lakes and streams. The Rocky Mountains had not yet formed. Small animals lived in the shadows of the dinosaurs. Among these small animals were some of the earliest mammals: mouselike and shrewlike creatures. Very little is known about these mammals. Their bones are tiny, so finding them is difficult. "If I find a mammal tooth, that's a big deal, because those discoveries are still really rare," says Kelli.

Apatosaurus **and small mammals lived in the same period.**

Kelli Trujillo, 31, is a graduate student in vertebrate paleontology at the University of Wyoming. During the summer, she splits her time between several fossil digs. Kelli is a musician as well as an outdoor enthusiast. She plays guitar, flute, and piano.

Talking with Kelli Trujillo

Q *How did you get interested in science?*

A My dad was a history teacher, but he had a passion for geology, so we always had rocks around the house. We spent a lot of time outside, camping and hiking and looking at rocks. I knew what quartz and mica were before I even went to school.

Q *How did you choose geology?*

A In high school I took a geology class with a really great teacher who helped develop my interest, especially in fossils. But I didn't think I could be a geologist because you have to take algebra. Algebra was difficult for me. It scared me. So I got a degree in veterinary technology, which didn't require any math. I worked in that field for three years, but I just didn't like it. So I decided to go back to college and take the math classes I needed for a science degree.

Q *Why did you specialize in paleontology?*

A I got started as a volunteer on some fossil digs. The first was a student project near Gunnison, Colorado. A couple of students there had dug up more than 900 bone fragments from an *Apatosaurus,* a large four-legged dinosaur. Later, I helped a friend dig out an *Allosaurus,* a big meat-eating dinosaur, near Medicine Bow, Wyoming.

Q *What have you found at your fossil sites so far?*

A There are a lot of turtle shell fragments, about four or five square centimeters in size, with bumps and ridges in them. I've got lots of crocodile teeth and some lungfish teeth. I also have some salamander vertebrae—spinal column bones— and several vertebrae and jaw fragments from a small lizard called *Cteniogenys.* I've found twenty mammal teeth.

Q *How did those fragments happen to be preserved?*

A The animals probably lived in or near a small lake. When they died, their bodies got buried in sediments—layers of soil—at the bottom of the lake. The remains of these animals stayed buried for 150 million years.

Q *What can you infer about an organism from teeth or bone fragments?*

A You can usually tell a lot about animals from their teeth. That's because animals with different diets have different types of teeth. For instance, meat-eaters don't need grinding teeth like those that plant-eaters have. Crocodile and lizard teeth are pretty easy to identify. Mammal teeth are very specialized. In fact, these

KEY   Dinosaur sites ■   Cities •

▲ Kelli looks for mammal fragments at this site in Wyoming (above). Kelli and a co-worker examine a fossil from the Jurassic Period (right).

◄ Kelli worked at some of the mammal and dinosaur sites located on this map.

specialized teeth are one of the things that separate mammals from other animals.

With bones, it really depends. If you have the entire bone, you can usually make a good guess about what type of animal it came from. But often you just find unidentifiable fragments.

Q *How does the rock where the fossil is found provide clues to the age of the fossil?*

A It's difficult to get an absolute age on sedimentary rocks. Often we just go by the rule that younger rocks are on top of older rocks. If we're really lucky, there will be a volcanic ash layer in the rocks, or certain crystals or iron minerals that we know how to date. In Wyoming, I'm working in a layer of rocks known as the Morrison Formation, which has been dated to the late Jurassic Period.

Q *How do scientists know where to dig for fossils?*

A Usually you see something on the surface, some scraps of bone sticking out from the rock. Bone has a different shape and texture and is often a different color. So if you know what you're looking for, a bone catches your eye.

Q *What tools do you use?*

A One of my most useful tools is a broom. I use it to clean the rocks so I can see their surfaces clearly. When you're digging out big bones, you use everything from picks and shovels to power tools like jackhammers and air drills. For small or delicate pieces, you need hand tools, like rock hammers and chisels, and a screen box. A screen box is basically a wooden box with a screen bottom. You put a couple of handfuls of rock in it and put the box

Dinosaur and Mammal Teeth

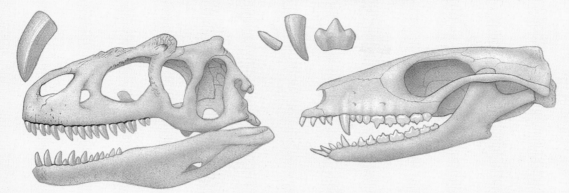

The strong jaws and long pointed teeth of *Allosaurus* (above) worked like a saw to tear apart smaller dinosaurs. *Allosaurus* was a large, meat-eating dinosaur of the Jurassic Period.

Mammal teeth are different from dinosaur teeth. The teeth of Jurassic mammals (above) are specialized for different functions. The combination of canines, incisors, and molars allowed the mammal to tear, shred, and grind.

⟵ **Actual size of early mammal tooth**

Actual size of *Allosaurus* tooth

In her lab, Kelli uses her microscope to examine tiny mammal teeth.

in a big trough of water. You let the water wash the rock off the fossil. If you have the right kind of rock, it will wash away. But some rock never dissolves, and you're just out of luck.

Q *How do you recover the small mammal fossils?*

A I collect a couple of bags of rocks and bring them back to the lab. Then I wash them in the screen box, dry what's left, and search through it. The fossils are very small—some of them fit on the head of a pin! So you have to look at everything under a microscope, grain by grain, to see if you've got any fossils mixed in with the rock. It takes an awful lot of patience.

Q *What do you hope to find?*

A Usually teeth are all that's left of early mammals, but I'm hopeful this site will yield skulls and other bones, like arms or legs or vertebrae. I was

pretty excited when I found those twenty mammal teeth.

Q *Do you ever get discouraged or lonely out in the field?*

A When I'm out working at the site, the time goes so fast I don't even think about it. Being outside all day is wonderful. The bugs and wind aren't so good, but I'm in the middle of nowhere, and it's absolutely beautiful.

In Your Journal

Kelli Trujillo's work as a paleontologist involves a number of different steps. At each step, from searching a site for fossils to drawing conclusions in the lab, Kelli uses a wide range of skills. Make a two-column list. In one column list the steps Kelli follows. In the second column describe the skills Kelli uses at each step.

CHAPTER
11 Fresh Water

WEB ACTIVITY
www.phschool.com

Every Drop Counts

With an almost deafening roar, water rushes over this waterfall and plunges into the rocky pool below. Every day, hundreds of thousands of liters of water flow over the falls. How do you think this amount compares with the amount of water that flows out of your faucets at home each day?

In this chapter, you will explore the many ways that living things depend on Earth's water. To learn how water is used in your own home and community, you will design a method for tracking water use over a one-week period.

Your Goal To monitor water use in your home and in another building in your community for one week.

To complete the project you will
◆ track your personal water use at home
◆ determine the total amount of water used in your home
◆ find out how much water is used by a business, school, hospital, or other building in your community

Get Started Begin now by brainstorming the ways you use water at home. Use this list to create a data table in which you will record each time you perform these activities during the week.

Check Your Progress You'll be working on this project as you study this chapter. To keep your project on track, look for Check Your Progress boxes at the following points.

Section 1 Review, page 366: Calculate your total water use.
Section 3 Review, page 381: Investigate water use at another building in your community.

Present Your Project At the end of the chapter (page 391), you will graph your household water-use data and share the information with your classmates.

Hikers in California's Yosemite National Park are awed by its thundering waterfalls.

SECTION 4 *Integrating Life Science*
Wetlands Environments

Discover Wet or Dry?
Science at Home Model Wetland

SECTION 1 The Water Cycle

DISCOVER ·**ACTIVITY**· · ·

Where Does the Water Come From?

1. Fill a glass with ice cubes and water, being careful not to spill any water. Set the glass aside for 5 minutes.

2. Observe the outside of the glass and the surface it was sitting on.

Think It Over

Inferring Where did the water on the outside of the glass come from? How do you think it got there?

◆ How is Earth's water distributed among saltwater and freshwater sources?

◆ How does Earth's water move through the water cycle?

◆ How do people and other living things use water?

Reading Tip As you read, use the headings to make an outline showing how water is important and where it is found.

Why do you think Earth is often called the "water planet"? Perhaps an astronaut suggested this name. From space, an astronaut can see that there is much more water than land on planet Earth. Oceans cover nearly 71 percent of Earth's surface.

Water on Earth

Figure 1 shows how Earth's water is distributed. **Most of Earth's water — roughly 97 percent — is salt water that is found in the oceans. Only 3 percent is fresh water.** Of that 3 percent, about three quarters is found in the huge masses of ice near the North and South Poles. A fraction more is found in the atmosphere. Most water in the atmosphere is invisible **water vapor,** the gaseous form of water. Less than 1 percent of the water on Earth is fresh water that is available for humans to use.

Oceans To explore where Earth's water is found, you can take an imaginary boat trip around the world. Your journey starts in Miami, Florida. From here, you can sail completely around the world without ever going ashore. Although people have given names to regions of the ocean, these regions are all connected, forming a single world ocean.

First you sail southeast across the Atlantic Ocean toward Africa. Swinging around the continent's southern tip, you enter the smaller but deeper Indian Ocean. Next, you head east across the Pacific Ocean, the longest part of your trip. This vast ocean, dotted with islands, covers an area greater than all the land on Earth put together.

360

Ice How can you get back to Miami? You could sail all the way around South America. But watch out for icebergs! These floating chunks of ice are made of fresh water. Icebergs in the southern Pacific and Atlantic oceans have broken off the massive sheets of ice that cover most of Antarctica. You would also find icebergs in the Arctic Ocean around the North Pole.

Rivers and Lakes To see examples of fresh water in rivers and lakes, you'll have to make a side trip inland. Sail north past Nova Scotia, Canada, to the beginning of the St. Lawrence Seaway. Navigate through the series of locks along the St. Lawrence River. Suddenly the river widens and you enter Lake Ontario, one of North America's five Great Lakes. Together, the Great Lakes contain nearly 20 percent of all the water in the world's freshwater lakes.

Below Earth's Surface When rain or snow falls, some of the water soaks into the ground. This water trickles down through spaces between the particles of soil and rock. Eventually the water reaches a layer that it cannot move through. Water that fills the cracks and spaces in underground soil and rock layers is called **groundwater.** Far more fresh water is located underground than in all Earth's rivers and lakes. You will learn more about groundwater in section 3.

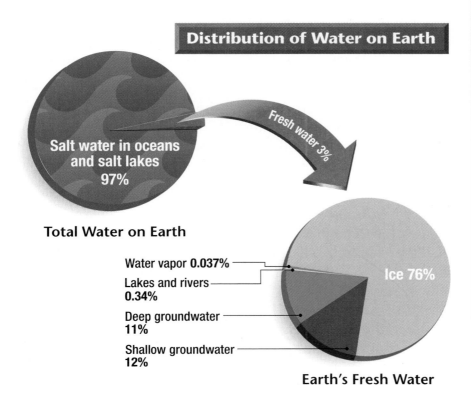

Distribution of Water on Earth

Salt water in oceans and salt lakes 97%

Fresh water 3%

Total Water on Earth

Water vapor **0.037%**

Lakes and rivers **0.34%**

Deep groundwater **11%**

Shallow groundwater **12%**

Ice 76%

Earth's Fresh Water

Figure 1 Most of Earth's water is salt water. Of the freshwater sources shown in the bottom circle graph, only the water in lakes, rivers, and shallow groundwater is available for human use.

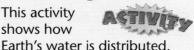

Tabletop Water Cycle

In this activity you will build a model of the water cycle.

ACTIVITY

1. Put on your goggles. Pour enough water into a flat-bottomed bowl to cover the bottom. Fill a small jar with sand and place it in the bowl.

2. Loosely cover the top of the bowl with plastic wrap. Secure with a rubber band.

3. Place a rock on top of the plastic, directly over the jar.

4. Place the bowl in direct sunlight or under a lamp. After one hour, observe the bowl and plastic wrap.

Making a Model What features of the water cycle are represented in your model?

The Water Cycle

Water is naturally recycled through the water cycle. The **water cycle** is the continuous process by which water moves through the living and nonliving parts of the environment. **In the water cycle, water moves from bodies of water, land, and living things on Earth's surface to the atmosphere and back to Earth's surface.** The sun is the source of energy that drives the water cycle.

Water Evaporates Water moves continuously through the water cycle. The cycle has no real beginning or end. You can follow a water molecule through one complete cycle in *Exploring the Water Cycle* on the facing page.

Think about a molecule of water floating near the surface of an ocean. The sun is shining and the air is warm. Soon, the molecule has absorbed enough heat energy to change state. It evaporates and becomes water vapor. **Evaporation** is the process by which molecules at the surface of a liquid absorb enough energy to change to the gaseous state. Although the water comes from the salty ocean, it becomes fresh through the process of evaporation. The salt remains in the ocean.

Large amounts of water evaporate constantly from the surfaces of oceans and large lakes. In addition, small amounts evaporate from the soil, puddles, and even from your skin. A significant amount of water is given off by plants. Plants draw in water from the soil through their roots. Eventually the water is given off through the leaves as water vapor in a process called **transpiration.**

Clouds Form Once a water molecule has found its way into the atmosphere, warm air carries it upward. Higher up, the air tends to become much colder. Cold air holds less water vapor than warm air. Some of the water vapor cools and condenses into liquid water. Condensed droplets of water clump together around tiny dust particles in the air, forming clouds.

Water Falls as Precipitation As more water vapor condenses, the water droplets in a cloud eventually become so heavy that they fall back to Earth. Water that falls to Earth as rain, snow, hail, or sleet is called **precipitation.** Most water molecules probably spend only about 10 days in the atmosphere before falling back to Earth. Most precipitation falls directly into the oceans. Water in the ocean may stay there for many years before evaporating, thus continuing the cycle.

When precipitation falls on land, some of the water evaporates again immediately. Some runs off the surface of the land into rivers and lakes. From there, it may eventually evaporate or flow back into the ocean. Some water trickles down into the ground and forms groundwater. Groundwater may move underground until it reaches a river, lake, or ocean. Once groundwater reaches the surface, it can continue through the cycle by evaporating again.

Precipitation is the source of all fresh water on and below Earth's surface. The water cycle renews the usable supply of fresh water on Earth. For millions of years, the total amount of water on Earth has remained fairly constant. In the world as a whole, the rates of evaporation and precipitation are balanced.

☑ *Checkpoint* *List three places from which water evaporates.*

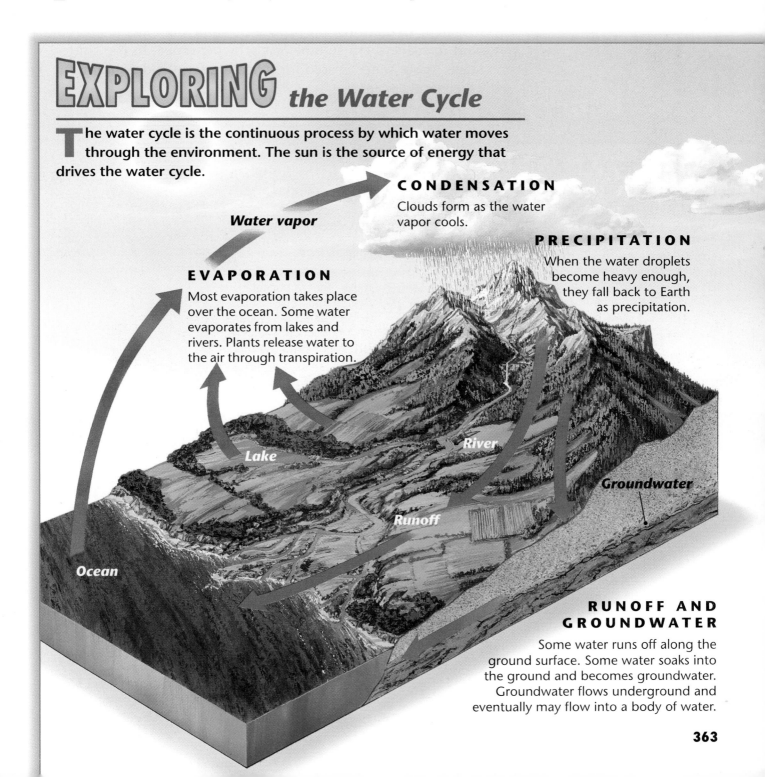

EXPLORING *the Water Cycle*

The water cycle is the continuous process by which water moves through the environment. The sun is the source of energy that drives the water cycle.

Water vapor

CONDENSATION
Clouds form as the water vapor cools.

PRECIPITATION
When the water droplets become heavy enough, they fall back to Earth as precipitation.

EVAPORATION
Most evaporation takes place over the ocean. Some water evaporates from lakes and rivers. Plants release water to the air through transpiration.

Lake

River

Groundwater

Runoff

Ocean

RUNOFF AND GROUNDWATER
Some water runs off along the ground surface. Some water soaks into the ground and becomes groundwater. Groundwater flows underground and eventually may flow into a body of water.

How Do People Use Water?

The water people use at home is just a small percentage of all the water used in the United States. **In addition to household purposes, people use water for agriculture, industry, transportation, and recreation.**

Agriculture Has your family ever had a garden? If so, you know that growing fruits and vegetables requires water. On a large farm, a constant supply of fresh water is essential.

However, some parts of the United States don't receive enough regular rainfall for agriculture. In such areas, farmland must be irrigated. **Irrigation** is the process of supplying water to areas of land to make them suitable for growing crops. In the United States, more water is used for irrigating farmland than for any other single purpose.

SCIENCE & History

Water and Agriculture

Plants require a steady supply of water to grow. How have farmers throughout history provided their crops with water? This time line shows some methods developed in different parts of the world.

2000 B.C. Egypt

Egyptian farmers invented a way to raise water from the Nile River. The device, called a *shaduf*, acted as a lever to make lifting a bucket of water easier. The farmers then emptied the water into a network of canals to irrigate their fields. The *shaduf* is still in use in Egypt, India, and other countries.

3000 B.C.	2000 B.C.	1000 B.C.

3000 B.C. China

One of the oldest known methods of irrigation was developed for growing rice. Farmers built paddies, or artificial ponds with raised edges. The farmers flooded the paddies with water from a nearby stream. This ancient technique is still widely used throughout Southeast Asia.

700 B.C. Assyria

Sennacherib, king of the ancient nation Assyria, surrounded the capital city of Nineveh with fruit trees, cotton, and exotic plants. To help irrigate the plantations, he built a 10-kilometer canal and a stone aqueduct to transport water from the nearby hills.

Industry Think about the objects in a typical school locker. Did you know that water is needed to produce all these objects? Even though water is not part of the final products, it plays a role in the industrial processes that created them.

Industries use water in many other ways. For example, power plants and steel mills both need huge volumes of water to cool down hot machinery. Water that is used for cooling can often be recycled, or used again for another purpose.

Transportation Oceans and rivers have been used for transporting people and goods since ancient times. If you look at a map of the United States, you will notice that many large cities are located on the coasts. Ocean travel led to the growth of such port cities. In early America, rivers also served as natural highways.

In Your Journal

Find out more about one of these agricultural techniques. Imagine that you are a farmer seeing the method in action for the first time. Write a letter to a friend describing the new technique. What problem will it solve? How will it improve your farming?

A.D. 1870 United States

When homesteaders arrived on the dry Great Plains of the central United States, they had to rely on water stored underground. Windmills provided the energy to pump the groundwater to the surface. The farmers dug ditches to carry the water to irrigate their fields.

| A.D. 1 | A.D. 1000 | A.D. 2000 |

A.D. 500 Mexico

To grow crops in areas covered by swampy lakes, the Aztecs built raised plots of farmland called *chinampas*. They grew maize on fertile soil scooped from the lake bottom. A grid of canals kept the crops wet and allowed the farmers to navigate boats between the *chinampas*.

Present Israel

Irrigation is the key to survival in desert regions. Today, methods such as drip irrigation ensure that very little water is wasted when crops are watered. Holes in the pipe allow water to drip directly onto the soil around the roots of each plant.

Water Used in the Home	
Task	Water Used (liters)
Showering for 5 minutes	95
Brushing teeth	10
Washing hands	7.5
Flushing standard toilet	23
Flushing "low-flow" toilet	6
Washing one load of laundry	151
Running dishwasher	19
Washing dishes by hand	114

Figure 2 Many common household activities involve water.

Recreation Do you like to swim in a neighborhood pool? Catch fish from a rowboat in the middle of a lake? Walk along a beach collecting seashells? Or maybe just sit on the edge of a dock and dangle your feet in the water? Then you know some ways that water is used for recreation. And if you brave the winter cold to ski, snowboard, or skate, you are enjoying water in its frozen form.

☑ *Checkpoint* List an agricultural use, an industrial use, and a household use of water that you relied on today.

Water and Living Things

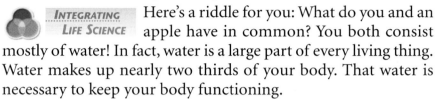
INTEGRATING LIFE SCIENCE Here's a riddle for you: What do you and an apple have in common? You both consist mostly of water! In fact, water is a large part of every living thing. Water makes up nearly two thirds of your body. That water is necessary to keep your body functioning.

Water is essential for living things to grow, reproduce, and carry out other important processes. For example, plants use water, plus carbon dioxide and energy from the sun, to make food in a process called **photosynthesis** (foh toh SIN thuh sis). Animals and many other living things depend on the food made by plants. They may eat the plants directly or eat other organisms that eat plants.

Another way that living things use water is as a home. An organism's **habitat** is the place where it lives and that provides the things it needs to survive. Both fresh water and salt water provide habitats for many different types of living things.

Section 1 Review

1. Where is most of the fresh water on Earth found?
2. Describe the general path of water as it moves through the water cycle.
3. How does the water cycle renew Earth's supply of fresh water?
4. What are five major ways that people in the United States use water?
5. **Thinking Critically Relating Cause and Effect** How might cutting down trees affect the amount of evaporation in an area?

CHAPTER PROJECT

Check Your Progress
Complete your water-use data table by calculating the total amount of water you used during the week. Use Figure 2 to estimate the water used for some common activities. Then determine how much water your family used during the week. You can do this by reading your water meter, estimating based on your personal water use, or having your family members record their usage. (Hint: Convert all amounts to liters.)

You and Your Environment

Water From Trees

Trees play many important roles in the environment—they keep the soil from washing away, remove carbon dioxide from the air, and produce oxygen. Trees are also a vital part of the water cycle. In this lab you will discover how trees help to keep water moving through the cycle.

Problem

How much water do the leaves on a tree give off in a 24-hour period?

Skills Focus

observing, calculating, inferring

Materials

3 plastic sandwich bags   balance
3 small pebbles   3 twist ties

Procedure

1. Copy the data table into your notebook.
2. Place the sandwich bags, twist ties, and pebbles on a balance. Determine their total mass to the nearest tenth of a gram.
3. Select an outdoor tree or shrub with leaves that are within your reach.
4. Put one pebble into a sandwich bag and place the bag over one of the tree's leaves as shown. Fasten the twist tie around the bag, forming a tight seal around the stem of the leaf.
5. Repeat Step 4 with the other plastic bags on two more leaves. Leave the bags in place on the leaves for 24 hours.
6. The following day, examine the bags and record your observations in your notebook.

DATA TABLE

Starting mass of bags, ties, and pebbles	
Mass of bags, ties, and pebbles after 24 hours	
Difference in mass	

7. Carefully remove the bags from the leaves and refasten each twist tie around its bag so that the bag is closed tightly.
8. Place the three bags, including pebbles and twist ties, on the balance. Determine their total mass to the nearest tenth of a gram.
9. Subtract the original mass of the bags, ties, and pebbles that you found in Step 2 from the mass you found in Step 8.

Analyze and Conclude

1. Based on your observations, how can you account for the difference in mass?
2. What is the name of the process that caused the results you observed? Explain the role of that process in the water cycle.
3. A single birch tree may transpire as much as 260 liters of water in a day. How much water would a grove of 1,000 birch trees return to the atmosphere in a year?
4. **Apply** Based on what you learned from this investigation, what is one reason that people may be concerned about the destruction of forests around the world?

More to Explore

Find another type of tree and repeat this experiment. What might account for any differences in the amount of water the two trees transpire?

DISCOVER • ACTIVITY • • •

What's in Pond Water?

1. Using a hand lens, observe a sample of pond water.

2. Make a list of everything you see in the water. If you don't know the name of something, write a short description or draw a picture.

3. Your teacher has set up a microscope with a slide of pond water. Observe the slide and add any new items to your list. Wash your hands with soap when you are done.

Think It Over

Classifying Use one of these systems to divide the items on your list into two groups: moving/still, living/nonliving, or microscopic/visible without a microscope. What does your classification system tell you about pond water?

GUIDE FOR READING

◆ What is a river system?

◆ What conditions can cause a flood?

◆ How do ponds and lakes form?

Reading Tip Before you read, use the section headings to make an outline. Leave space to take notes as you read.

Standing on a bridge in Albuquerque, New Mexico, you look through your binoculars at the waters of the Rio Grande—the "Big River." The name fits this broad, deep stretch of water. But 700 kilometers upstream, the Rio Grande looks very different. The river begins as trickles of melting snow high in the San Juan Mountains in Colorado. As more water joins the river, it carves deep, narrow canyons out of the rock.

By the time it reaches Albuquerque the river has grown wider. It continues into Texas, winding back and forth across the dusty desert valley. In places, the river is so shallow that it may even dry up during the summer. When the Rio Grande finally empties into the Gulf of Mexico, it is sluggish and heavy with mud.

River Systems

If you were hiking in the San Juan Mountains, you could observe the path of the runoff from melting snow. As you followed one small stream downhill, you would notice that the stream reached a larger stream and joined it. You could then continue along this stream until it flowed into a small river. Eventually this path would lead you to the Rio Grande itself.

Tributaries are the smaller streams and rivers that feed into a main river. **A river and all its tributaries together make up a river system.** The tributaries flow toward the main river following a downhill path due to the pull of gravity.

Watersheds Just as all the water in a bathtub flows toward the drain, all the water in a river system drains into the main river. The land area that supplies water to a river system is called a **watershed.** Watersheds are also called drainage basins.

A river can flow into another, larger river. When rivers join another river system, the areas they drain become part of the largest river's watershed. You can identify a river's watershed on a map by drawing an imaginary line around the region drained by all its tributaries. Some watersheds are very small. By contrast, the watershed of the Mississippi River covers more than 3 million square kilometers!

Divides One watershed is separated from another by a ridge of land called a **divide.** Streams on each side of the divide flow in different directions. The Continental Divide, the longest divide in North America, follows the line of the Rocky Mountains. West of the Continental Divide, water either flows toward the Pacific Ocean or into the dry Great Basin. Between the Rocky Mountains and the Appalachian Mountains, water flows toward the Mississippi River or directly into the Gulf of Mexico.

✓ *Checkpoint* *Into what ocean do rivers east of the Appalachian Mountains flow?*

The Knuckle Divide

Make your hand into a fist and put it on a paper towel, knuckles facing up. With your other hand, dribble water from a spoon so that it falls onto your knuckles. Observe how the water flows over your hand.

Making a Model How are your knuckles similar to a mountain range on land? What parts of your hand represent a watershed?

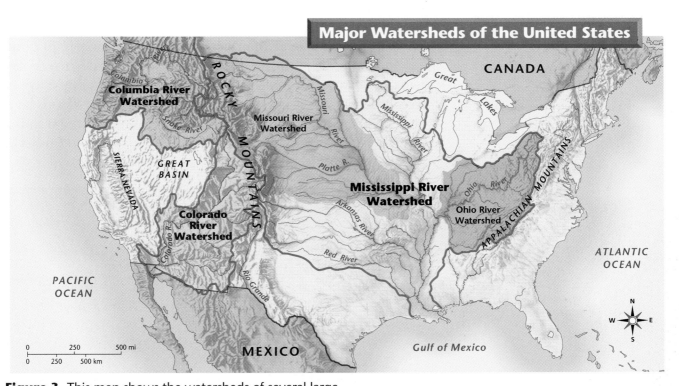

Figure 3 This map shows the watersheds of several large rivers in the United States.
Interpreting Maps Name four tributaries of the Mississippi River. Which tributary has the largest watershed?

Rivers and Floods

Spring floods occur frequently on rivers in the Midwest, but the floods of 1997 were far worse than usual. The residents of Fargo, North Dakota, had already used a million sandbags, and the Red River of the North was still rising! As the flood waters rose, people piled the sandbags higher around their houses, hoping no water would break through. People moved their belongings to their attics, then watched as water flowed through their homes.

The Red River floods went on for weeks, fed by rain and melting snow. A spring blizzard added more snow. Other nearby rivers also flooded. Parts of North Dakota, South Dakota, and Minnesota were declared a disaster area. Weary residents just waited for the waters to recede so they could start to repair the damage.

What caused the Red River to flood so badly? **A flood occurs when the volume of water in a river increases so much that the river overflows its channel.** As rain and melting snow added more and more water, the river gained in speed and strength. Recall that as the speed of a river increases, so does the amount of energy it has. A flooding river can uproot trees and pluck boulders from the ground. As it overflows onto its floodplain, the powerful water can even wash away bridges and houses.

Throughout history, people have both feared and welcomed floods. Ancient Egyptians, for instance, called their fertile cropland "the gift of the Nile." Deposition from regular floods left a layer of rich soil on each side of the river, creating a green strip of good land in the middle of the desert. But floods can also destroy farms, towns, and crops. In the United States, 20 million people live in places where flooding is likely. Even in the last century, floods have killed millions of people around the world, many of them in the heavily populated flood plains of China, Bangladesh, and India.

Figure 4 A flood can be disastrous for nearby residents, such as the owners of this house. *Making Generalizations Explain how floods can be both harmful and helpful to people.*

Can Floods Be Controlled?

INTEGRATING TECHNOLOGY For as long as people have lived on flood plains, they have tried to control floods. Building dams is one method of flood control. A dam is a barrier across a river that may redirect the flow of a river to other channels or store the water in an artificial lake. Engineers can open the dam's flood-gates to release water in dry seasons. Dams work fairly well to control small floods. During severe floods, however, powerful flood waters can wash over the top of a dam or break through it.

Sediment deposits actually build a natural defense against floods. As a river overflows onto its flood plain, it slows down, depositing the heavier sediments alongside the channel. Over time, these deposits build up into long ridges called **levees.** These natural levees help keep the river inside its banks. People sometimes build up the natural levees with sandbags or stone and concrete to provide further protection against floods.

But building up levees can sometimes backfire. These walls prevent the natural channel-widening process that rivers normally undergo as their volume increases. As a result, during a flood, the water has nowhere to go except downstream. Although built-up levees can work well to prevent small floods, they often make heavy flooding worse for areas farther downstream. The full power of the surge of flood water is passed on to flood the downstream areas.

Figure 5 These people are working together to protect their community during a flood. *Applying Concepts How do sandbags help control flooding?*

Bodies of Fresh Water

While water in streams and rivers is always on the move, the water in lakes and ponds is still, or standing, water. Although there is no definite rule to determine whether a body of water is called a pond or a lake, ponds are generally smaller and shallower than lakes. Sunlight usually reaches to the bottom of all parts of a pond. Most lakes have parts where the water is too deep for sunlight to reach all the way to the bottom.

Ponds and lakes form when water collects in hollows and low-lying areas of land. Rainfall, melting snow and ice, and runoff supply water to ponds and lakes. Others are fed by rivers or groundwater. Eventually, water may flow out of a pond or lake into a river, or evaporate from its surface.

EXPLORING a Pond

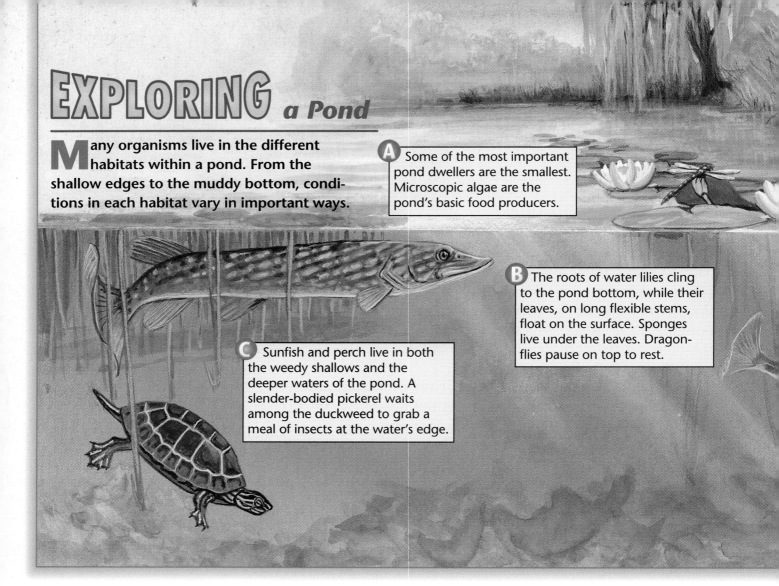

Many organisms live in the different habitats within a pond. From the shallow edges to the muddy bottom, conditions in each habitat vary in important ways.

A Some of the most important pond dwellers are the smallest. Microscopic algae are the pond's basic food producers.

B The roots of water lilies cling to the pond bottom, while their leaves, on long flexible stems, float on the surface. Sponges live under the leaves. Dragonflies pause on top to rest.

C Sunfish and perch live in both the weedy shallows and the deeper waters of the pond. A slender-bodied pickerel waits among the duckweed to grab a meal of insects at the water's edge.

Ponds

INTEGRATING LIFE SCIENCE Compared to a tumbling mountain stream, a pond seems still and peaceful at first glance. Silvery minnows glide smoothly below the surface. A dragonfly touches the water, then whirs away. Lily pads with broad, green leaves and waxy, white blossoms float on the surface. This quiet pond is actually a thriving habitat, supporting a wide diversity of living things.

If you have ever waded in a pond, you know that the muddy bottom is often covered with weeds. Because the water is shallow enough for sunlight to reach the bottom, plants grow throughout a pond. Plantlike organisms called algae also live in the pond. As the plants and algae use sunlight to make food through photosynthesis, they also produce oxygen. Animals in the pond use the oxygen and food provided by plants and algae. You can see some common pond organisms in *Exploring a Pond.*

D The shore is edged with grasses and trees that require a lot of water, such as willows and maples. These plants provide shelter and nesting places for redwing blackbirds and other birds.

E Frogs lay eggs in the shallow water near shore. They hatch in the water as tadpoles and move to the land as adults.

F Snails find food on the soft bottom of the pond. Crayfish lie buried in the mud, waiting for bits of food to drift down.

Not all ponds exist year-round. For example, some ponds in the northern and western United States appear only in the spring, when runoff from spring rains and melting snow collects in low areas. The ponds dry up by midsummer as the shallow water quickly evaporates in the heat.

Ponds in colder climates often freeze over during the winter. As you learned in Chapter 1, ice floats because it is less dense than liquid water. As a result, ice forms on the surface of the pond, while the living things survive in the liquid water below.

☑ *Checkpoint* *Why can plants grow throughout a pond?*

Lakes

Suppose you suddenly found yourself on a sandy beach. Waves break on the shore. The water stretches as far as your eye can see. Gulls screech overhead. Where are you? Although you might think you're at the ocean, this immense body of water could

Figure 6 Standing water is found in lakes and ponds. **A.** The cold waters of Crater Lake in Oregon fill the hollow of an ancient volcano. **B.** Water lilies float in a Colorado pond. *Interpreting Photographs In which of these bodies of water does sunlight reach the bottom? Give evidence to support your answer.*

actually be a lake! You could be on a beach in Indiana, on the shore of Lake Michigan.

Although most lakes are not as large as Lake Michigan, they are generally bigger and deeper than ponds. Most lakes are deep enough that sunlight does not reach all the way to the bottom. A lake bottom may consist of sand, pebbles, or rock. The bottom of a pond is usually covered with mud and algae.

Lake Formation Lakes form in many ways. For example, a cut-off river meander may become an oxbow lake. Ice sheets that melted at the end of the Ice Age created depressions that became lakes. Some lakes were created by movements of Earth's crust. Such movements created the deep valleys in central Africa that lie below Lake Tanganyika and Lake Victoria. Other lakes are the result of volcanoes. An erupting volcano can cause a flow of lava or mud that blocks a river and forms a lake. Some lakes, like the one in Figure 6, form in the empty craters of volcanoes.

People can also create a lake by building a dam across a river. The lake may be used for supplying drinking water, for irrigating fields, and for boating and fishing. A lake that stores water for human use is called a **reservoir.** One of the largest reservoirs in the United States is Lake Mead in Nevada, behind Hoover Dam on the Colorado River.

Lake Habitats Like a pond, a lake provides habitats for many

INTEGRATING LIFE SCIENCE organisms. In the shallow water near shore, the wildlife is similar to that in a pond. Water beetles scurry over the slippery, moss-covered rocks. Loons and kingfishers pluck fish from the open water. But unlike a pond, sunlight does not reach the bottom at the center of a lake. Without sunlight, plants cannot live in the deep water. As a result, fewer other organisms live in the chilly, dark depths of the lake. A few worms and mollusks do live on the bottom. They feed on food particles that drift down from the surface. The deep waters of lakes are also the home of large, bony fish such as pike and sturgeon. These fish eat the tiny bottom dwellers. They also swim to the surface to feed on fish and even small birds.

☑ *Checkpoint* *List four possible ways a lake might form.*

Changes in a Lake

Particularly in cool, northern areas of North America, many lakes undergo changes with the seasons. In the summer, the sun warms the upper layer of water in the lake. The warm water floats on top of the cooler, denser lower layer. But in the fall, the top layer cools off, too. As the water cools, it becomes denser and sinks. This causes the lake waters to mix together. **As the water mixes, minerals, plant matter, and other nutrients rise from the lake bottom to the surface. Called lake turnover, this seasonal change refreshes the supply of nutrients throughout the lake.**

A second type of change that occurs in a lake happens over a long period of time. The organisms in a lake constantly release waste products into the water. The wastes and the remains of dead organisms contain nutrients such as nitrates and phosphates. Algae feed on these nutrients. Over many years, the nutrients build up in the lake in a process called **eutrophication** (you troh fih KAY shuhn). As eutrophication causes more algae to grow, a thick, green scum forms on the surface of the water.

Figure 7 This island floating on Lake Titicaca is woven from totora reeds.

Social Studies CONNECTION

Imagine living on a floating island in the middle of a deep, cold lake. The island is a mat made of thick reeds you have woven tightly together. During a storm, you must anchor your island or it could be swept away. If you were a member of a group of Native Americans who live on Lake Titicaca in South America, such an island might be your home.

Lake Titicaca lies high in the Andes Mountains. Around the edges of the lake grows a hollow reed called totora. The people weave totora reeds together to form "islands" that are strong enough to hold homes and livestock. They also make ropes, boats, tea, and even medicine from the totora reeds.

In Your Journal

How would living on a totora reed island on Lake Titicaca affect your daily routine? Write a journal entry describing what a typical day might be like if you lived on a floating island.

A. The process begins as algae and other organisms add nutrients to the lake. These nutrients support more plant growth.

B. Soil, fallen leaves, and decaying matter pile up on the lake bottom. The lake becomes shallower and marshy.

C. Eventually, the plants completely fill the lake, creating a grassy meadow.

Figure 8 A lake environment gradually changes over time. *Predicting Would you expect the water temperature in the lake to be higher in A or B?*

When the algae layer becomes so thick that it begins to block out the sunlight, plants in the lake cannot carry out photosynthesis. They stop producing food and oxygen and die. As dead organisms in the lake decay, the amount of oxygen in the water decreases. The lake environment changes. Many of the fish and other animals no longer have enough oxygen to live. Material from decaying plants and animals piles up on the bottom, and the lake becomes shallower. The sun warms the water to a higher temperature. Now many plants take root in the rich mud on the lake bottom. Eventually, the lake becomes completely filled with plants. The remaining water evaporates, and a grassy meadow takes the place of the former lake.

Icebergs

It was a dark night in the spring of 1912. The gleaming new ocean liner *Titanic* sailed through the North Atlantic on its first voyage, from Southampton, England, to New York City. Suddenly a huge white wall loomed out of the darkness in front of the ship! It was an iceberg, the terror of ships at sea. Underwater, the jagged ice tore a

Figure 9 The *Titanic* sank on its first voyage when it hit an iceberg in the North Atlantic Ocean.

series of cuts in the *Titanic's* side. As the ship sank to the bottom of the ocean, more than 1,500 people died.

Recall from Chapter 8 that a glacier is a mass of ice and snow that moves slowly over land. When a glacier reaches the seacoast, icebergs form. With a loud roar, large chunks break off, or calve, and float away. Although icebergs are found in the salty ocean, remember that they consist of fresh water.

In the North Atlantic and Arctic oceans, about 10,000 new icebergs form every year. Many of these icebergs calve from Greenland's continental glacier. As they drift south, the icebergs break into chunks as big as houses. They begin to melt in the warmer water.

The ocean around Antarctica is filled with even larger icebergs. Flat-topped pieces calve from the edges of the glaciers along the coast. In 1995, a giant iceberg broke off Antarctica's Larsen Ice Shelf. Scientists flying over the new iceberg reported that it was about 70 kilometers long and 25 kilometers wide—more than half the size of the state of Rhode Island!

The thought of a chunk of floating ice that big is scary enough, but it's more frightening to realize that only about 10 percent of an iceberg is visible above the water. **About 90 percent of an iceberg lies below the surface. The underwater part is a hazard to ships because it is often much wider than the visible part of the iceberg.**

After the *Titanic* disaster, countries involved in Atlantic shipping set up the International Ice Patrol. The Patrol, which is managed by the United States Coast Guard, uses ships, planes, and satellites to track icebergs. The Patrol's warnings have saved many people from disasters like the *Titanic*.

Figure 10 If you could see an entire iceberg at once, how would it look? An artist created this composite photograph to reveal the hidden part of the iceberg. *Applying Concepts What percentage of the ice is underwater?*

Section 2 Review

1. What bodies of water make up a river system?
2. Explain how ponds and lakes form.
3. Give three examples of typical pond organisms. Describe where in a pond each is found.
4. Where do icebergs form?
5. **Thinking Critically** **Relating Cause and Effect** How is the depth of the water in the middle of a lake related to the variety of living things there?

Science at Home

Home-made Iceberg With a family member, make a model iceberg. Fill the cut-off bottom of a milk or juice carton with water and freeze. When the water has frozen, peel the carton away from the iceberg. Add salt to a large bowl of water to create an "ocean." Float the iceberg in the bowl. Help your family member use a ruler to measure how much of the iceberg's thickness is above the surface of the water and how much is below. Use these measurements to explain why icebergs can be dangerous to ships.

SECTION
3 Water Underground

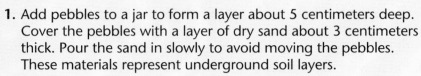

DISCOVER · ACTIVITY · · ·

Where Does the Water Go?

1. Add pebbles to a jar to form a layer about 5 centimeters deep. Cover the pebbles with a layer of dry sand about 3 centimeters thick. Pour the sand in slowly to avoid moving the pebbles. These materials represent underground soil layers.

2. Sprinkle water onto the sand to simulate rainfall.

3. Looking through the side of the jar, observe the path of the water as it soaks through the layers. Wash your hands when you are finished with this activity.

Think It Over

Observing Describe what happens when the water reaches the bottom of the jar.

GUIDE FOR READING

◆ How does water move through underground layers of soil and rock?

◆ How do people obtain water from an aquifer?

Reading Tip As you read, create a flowchart that shows one possible path of water from a rainstorm to a well.

When you were younger, did you ever dig a hole in the ground hoping to find a buried treasure? Though you probably never found a trunk full of gold, you could have found a different kind of treasure without even realizing it. If you continued to dig deeper, past tangled grass roots and small stones, you would have noticed the soil begin to feel heavier and wetter. If you dug deep enough, the bottom of your hole would have started to fill up with water. You would have "struck groundwater!" In the days before pipes and public water systems, such a discovery was like finding a treasure. A usable source of fresh water enabled people to build a house or farm and settle on that land. Today, many people still rely on the water underground to meet their water needs.

Underground Layers

Where does this underground water come from? Like the water in rivers, lakes, and glaciers, it comes from precipitation. Recall what can happen to precipitation when it falls. It can evaporate right away, run off the surface, or soak into the ground. The water that soaks in trickles downward, following the pull of gravity.

If you pour water into a glass full of pebbles, the water trickles down around the pebbles until it reaches the bottom of the glass. Then the water begins to fill up the spaces between the pebbles. **In the same way, water underground trickles down between particles of soil and through cracks and spaces in layers of rock.**

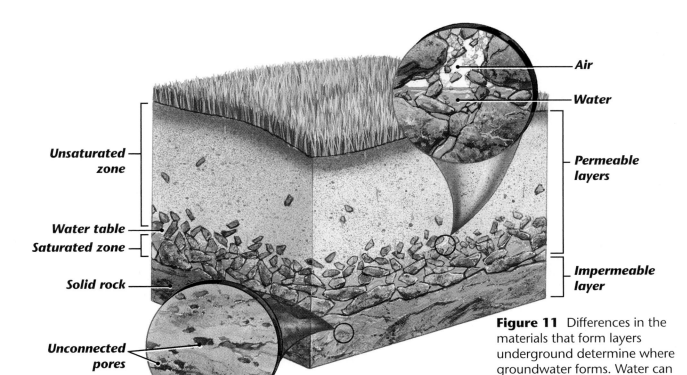

Unsaturated zone

Water table

Saturated zone

Solid rock

Unconnected pores

Air

Water

Permeable layers

Impermeable layer

Figure 11 Differences in the materials that form layers underground determine where groundwater forms. Water can move through the pores of permeable layers, but not through impermeable layers. *Interpreting Diagrams What is the difference between the saturated and unsaturated zone?*

Different types of rock and soil have different-sized spaces, or **pores,** between their particles. How easily water moves through the material depends not only on the size of the pores, but also on whether the pores are connected to each other. Materials that allow water to easily pass through, or permeate, are called **permeable.** Sand and gravel are permeable materials.

As water soaks down through permeable rock, it eventually reaches layers of material that it cannot pass through. These materials have few or no pores or cracks for the water to flow through. Materials that water cannot pass through easily are called **impermeable.** Clay and granite are impermeable materials.

Once water reaches an impermeable layer, it is trapped. It can't soak any deeper. Instead, the water begins to fill up the spaces above the impermeable material. The area of permeable rock or soil that is totally filled, or saturated, with water is called the **saturated zone.** The top of the saturated zone is the **water table.** Knowing the depth of the water table in an area tells you how deep you must dig to reach groundwater.

Soil and rock layers above the water table contain some moisture, too. But here the pores contain air as well as water. They are not saturated with water. Therefore, the layer of rocks and soil above the water table is called the **unsaturated zone.**

☑ *Checkpoint* *Give an example of a permeable material other than sand or gravel.*

Sharpen your Skills

Drawing Conclusions

You have just bought some land and need to dig a well. By drilling a number of holes on your property, you learn that there is a layer of impermeable granite rock located approximately 12 meters underground. If the saturated zone is 3 meters thick, how deep should you dig your well? (*Hint:* Drawing a diagram may be helpful.)

An Artesian Well

In this activity you will build **ACTIVITY** a model of an artesian well. Before you start, cover your desk or table with newspaper.

1. Cover the bottom of a loaf pan with clay. Pile the clay higher at one end.

2. Cover the clay with about 4 cm of moist sand.

3. Cover the sand with a thin sheet of clay. Seal the edges of the clay tightly against the sides of the pan.

4. Push a funnel into the high end so that the bottom of the funnel is in the sand.

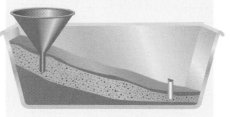

5. Insert a short piece of plastic straw through the clay and into the sand layer at the low end. Remove the straw, discard it, and then insert a new piece of straw in the same hole.

6. Slowly pour water into the funnel. Do not let the water overflow the funnel.

7. Observe the level of water in the straw. Wash your hands after this activity.

Making a Model What real-world feature does each part of your model represent? How is your model like a real artesian well? How is it different?

Aquifers

Any underground layer of rock or sediment that holds water is called an **aquifer.** Aquifers can range in size from a small underground patch of permeable material to an area the size of several states. The huge Ogallala aquifer lies beneath the plains of the midwest, stretching from South Dakota to Texas. Millions of people obtain their drinking water from this underground storehouse. The Ogallala aquifer also provides water for crops and livestock.

Maybe you picture groundwater as a large, still pool beneath Earth's surface. In fact, the water is actually in motion, seeping through the layers of rock. How fast it moves depends largely on how steeply the aquifer slopes and how permeable the rocks are. Groundwater in some aquifers moves only a few centimeters a day. At that rate, the water moves about 10 meters a year—less than the length of a typical classroom. Groundwater may travel hundreds of kilometers and stay in an aquifer for thousands of years before coming to the surface again.

✓ *Checkpoint* *What factors affect how fast water moves in an aquifer?*

Bringing Groundwater to the Surface

Look at Figure 12 and notice how the level of the water table generally follows the shape of the underground rock layers. The depth of the water table can vary greatly even over a small area of land. Heavy rain or lots of melting snow raise the level of the water table. The level falls in dry weather.

Where the water table meets the ground surface, groundwater bubbles or flows out of cracks in the rock in places called **springs.** The groundwater may feed a stream or pond, or form a wetland. People can also bring groundwater to the surface.

Wells Since ancient times, people have brought groundwater to the surface for drinking and other everyday uses. **People can obtain groundwater from an aquifer by drilling a well below the water table.** Locate the well near the center of Figure 12. Because the bottom of the well is in the saturated zone, the well contains water. Notice the level of the bottom of the dry well in the diagram. Because this well does not reach below the water table, water cannot be obtained from it.

Long ago, people dug wells by hand. They lined the sides of the well with brick or stone to keep the walls from collapsing. To bring up water, they lowered and raised a bucket. Today, most wells are dug with well-drilling equipment. Pumps bring up the groundwater.

Pumping water out of an aquifer lowers the water level near the well. If too much water is pumped out too fast, the well may

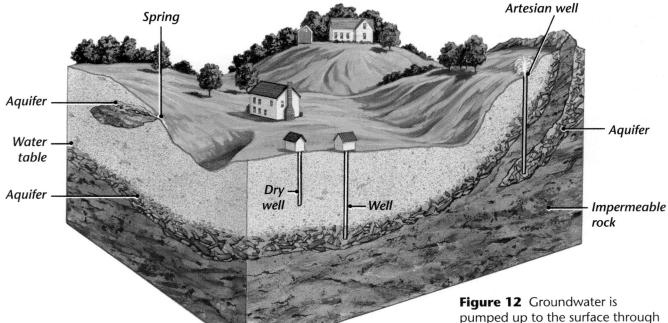

Spring

Artesian well

Aquifer

Water table

Aquifer

Dry well

Well

Aquifer

Impermeable rock

Figure 12 Groundwater is pumped up to the surface through wells like the one near the center of the diagram. At the right, pressure causes water to spurt from an artesian well. Where an aquifer meets the ground surface, at the left, a spring may form.
Interpreting Diagrams Why does the dry well not contain any water?

run dry. It will be necessary either to dig deeper to reach the lowered water table, or to wait for rainfall to refill the aquifer. New water that enters the aquifer from the surface is called **recharge.**

Artesian Wells In some aquifers, groundwater is trapped between two layers of impermeable rock or sediment. This water is under great pressure from the weight of the water above it. If the top layer of rock is punctured, the pressure sends water spurting up through the hole. Water flows without pumping from a well dug in such an aquifer. A well in which water rises because of pressure within the aquifer is called an **artesian well** (ahr TEEZH uhn well).

Section 3 Review

1. Describe what happens to water that soaks into the ground.
2. Why is it important to know the depth of an aquifer before drilling a well?
3. Draw a cross section of the ground that includes the following labeled features: permeable layer, saturated zone, unsaturated zone, impermeable layer, and water table.
4. **Thinking Critically Inferring** During the winter, a small spring flows on your property. Every summer, the spring dries up. What might be the reason for the change?

Check Your Progress CHAPTER PROJECT

By now you should have chosen a building in your community to monitor. How will you determine the amount and type of water usage there? Be sure to check with your teacher before contacting anyone at the site. (*Hint:* A building manager or facilities manager often has information about water use. You may find it helpful to write down your questions before you interview the person.)

SOIL TESTING

In what type of soil is it best to site a well? This is a question that hydrologists, scientists who study groundwater, need to answer before new houses or other buildings can be constructed. In this lab, you will compare different soil types to learn more about their water-holding properties.

HELP WANTED

Hydrologists to conduct soil tests for new housing development. Homes will have private wells. Engineers must test soil permeability to select best locations. Please send resumé and references to

Problem

How fast does water move through sand, clay, and pebbles?

Skills Focus

observing, measuring, drawing conclusions

Materials (per group)

hand lens   3 100-mL beakers
sand, 100 mL   water, 300 mL
stopwatch   pebbles, 100 mL
3 rubber bands
powdered potter's clay, 100 mL
3 squares of cheesecloth
3 large funnels or cut-off plastic soda bottle tops

Procedure

1. Copy the data table into your notebook.

2. Use a hand lens to observe each of the three material samples closely. Record your observations in your data table.

3. Place a piece of cheesecloth over the bottom of each funnel or bottle top and secure it with a rubber band.

4. Place the sand in one funnel, the pebbles in another, and the clay in another. Be sure that there is at least 5 cm of space above the material in each funnel.

5. Place each funnel on top of a beaker.

6. Slowly pour 100 mL of water into the funnel containing the sand. Do not let the water overflow the funnel.

7. Start the stopwatch when the water begins to flow or drip out of the bottom of the funnel.

DATA TABLE		
Material	Observations	Time for Water to Stop Dripping
Sand		
Clay		
Pebbles		

8. Stop the stopwatch when the water stops dripping out of the funnel or after 5 minutes. Record the time to the nearest second in your data table.

9. Repeat Steps 6 through 8 with the pebbles and then with the clay. When you are finished with this activity, dispose of your materials according to your teacher's instructions. Wash your hands thoroughly with soap.

Analyze and Conclude

1. Through which material did water move the fastest? The slowest?
2. What can you conclude about the permeability of the three materials?

3. Based on your observations of each sample, suggest an explanation for the differences in their permeability.
4. Based on the results of this lab, would you expect to get more water from a well dug in sand, pebbles, or clay? Explain.
5. **Apply** Why might gardeners and landscapers need to know about the permeability of different soil types?

More to Explore

Which of the soil samples that you tested do you think the soil of the grounds at your school most resembles? Design an experiment to test your hypothesis. With your teacher's permission, carry out your experiment.

SECTION 4 Wetland Environments

Wet or Dry?

1. Hold a kitchen sponge under water until it is soaked. Then squeeze out the water until the sponge is just damp.

2. Place the damp sponge next to a dry sponge in a pan. The sponges represent areas of wet and dry land.

3. Pour water into two paper cups until each is half full.

4. Hold one cup in each hand so that the cups are about 10 centimeters above the pan. Pour the water onto both sponges at the same time.

Think It Over

Observing Which of the sponges absorbs water faster? How are your observations related to what might happen in areas of wet and dry land?

GUIDE FOR READING

◆ What features of wetlands make them good habitats for living things?

◆ How do wetlands help control flooding?

Reading Tip Before you read, write a short description of what you think a wetland is. As you read, add details and examples to your description.

A wetland is an area of land that is covered with a shallow layer of water during some or all of the year. Wetlands form in places where water is trapped in low areas or where groundwater seeps onto the surface of the land. They can range in size from a water-filled roadside ditch to an area covering thousands of square kilometers. Some wetlands fill up during spring rains and dry up over the summer. Others are covered with water year-round.

Marshes, swamps, and bogs are three common types of freshwater wetlands. Marshes generally are grassy areas covered by a shallow layer or stream of water. They contain cattails, rushes, tule, and other tall grass-like plants. Swamps look more like flooded forests, with trees and shrubs growing in the water. In the United States, many swamps are located in the South, where trees grow quickly in the warm, humid climate. Bogs, which are more common in cooler northern states, often form in depressions left by melting ice sheets thousands of years ago. The water in bogs tends to be acidic. Many types of mosses thrive in the conditions found in bogs.

Wetlands along coasts usually contain both fresh and salt water. Coastal wetlands include salt marshes and mangrove forests. Salt marshes are found along both coasts of the United States. They often contain tall, strong grasses growing in a rich, muddy bottom. Mangrove forests, which are found along the central and southern coasts of Florida, consist of short trees with a thick tangle of roots. The tough roots anchor the mangroves against tropical winds and storms.

☑ *Checkpoint* *Name three types of freshwater wetlands.*

Wetland Habitats

If you've ever enjoyed tart cranberry sauce or crunchy wild rice, you've eaten plants that grow in wetlands. The layer of water covering a wetland can range from several centimeters to a few meters deep. Dead leaves and other plant and animal material serve as natural fertilizer, adding nitrogen, phosphates, and other nutrients to the water and soil. **Because of their sheltered waters and rich supply of nutrients, wetlands provide habitats for many living things.**

Many year-round residents of wetlands are similar to those in other freshwater habitats. As in a pond, frogs, salamanders, turtles, raccoons, muskrats, and many types of insects find food and shelter among the wetland plants. Birds nest in and around the wetlands, feeding on the plants and insects there.

Wetlands also have many temporary residents. Many ducks, geese, and other waterfowl travel from Alaska and Canada to their winter homes in the South along a "flyway." These birds depend on the millions of small, shallow marshes called prairie potholes along their route. Birds stop there to rest, feed, and mate. In the spring, thousands of birds build their nests in the prairie pothole region.

Figure 13 Freshwater wetlands come in many forms. **A.** In Montana, colorful flowers dot a bed of velvety moss in an alpine bog. **B.** Water flows slowly through a marsh in Oregon's Willamette Valley. **C.** Curtains of Spanish moss hang from cypress trees in a Louisiana swamp. *Comparing and Contrasting How are these three environments similar? How are they different?*

The Importance of Wetlands

Imagine coming home from a long trip, only to find that your house is gone and in its place is a parking lot! That happened to thousands of migrating birds before people began to understand the importance of wetlands. Farmers and builders once considered the soggy soil of wetlands to be "wasteland." This land could not be used unless it was drained and filled in. Thousands of square kilometers of wetlands were developed for farmland or for building homes and businesses. Beginning in the 1970s, however, the government enacted laws to protect wetland habitats.

Wetlands serve important functions for people as well as for wildlife. For example, wetlands provide natural water filtration. As water moves slowly through a wetland, waste materials settle out. The thick network of plant roots traps silt and mud. **Wetlands also help control floods by absorbing extra runoff from heavy rains.** They act like giant sponges, storing water and gradually releasing it as it drains or evaporates. When wetlands are drained or paved over, the water cannot be absorbed. Instead, it runs off the land quickly and can cause floods.

Figure 14 Many unusual species live in the freshwater wetland habitats of the Everglades.

Roseate spoonbills

Great egret

Snowy egret

Little blue heron

Sawgrass

Anhinga

Florida panther

The Everglades: A Unique Environment

Walking down a path in Florida's Everglades National Park, you would feel the ground squish under your feet. Water is the key to the Everglades, a unique region of wetlands. A shallow layer of water moves slowly over the gently sloping land from Lake Okeechobee south to Florida Bay. Tall, sharp-edged blades of sawgrass grow in the water. The thick growth of sawgrass gave this region its Native American name, *Pahay-okee*, which means "river of grass." Low islands called hammocks are scattered throughout the sawgrass marsh. Trees like gumbo limbos and palms grow on the hammocks.

Everglades Wildlife As in other wetlands, water means life for many Everglades creatures. Fish and snakes gobble up tiny organisms in the warm, muddy water. Wading birds in a rainbow of colors—pink flamingoes, white egrets, and purple gallinules—stand on skinny legs in the water. A raccoon digs for alligator eggs, unaware of the alligator lying low in the sawgrass nearby.

The Everglades provide habitats for many rare or endangered species. The endangered Florida panther lives deep in the wilderness portions of the Everglades. Many species of birds, such as the wood stork and the roseate spoonbill (named for the unusual

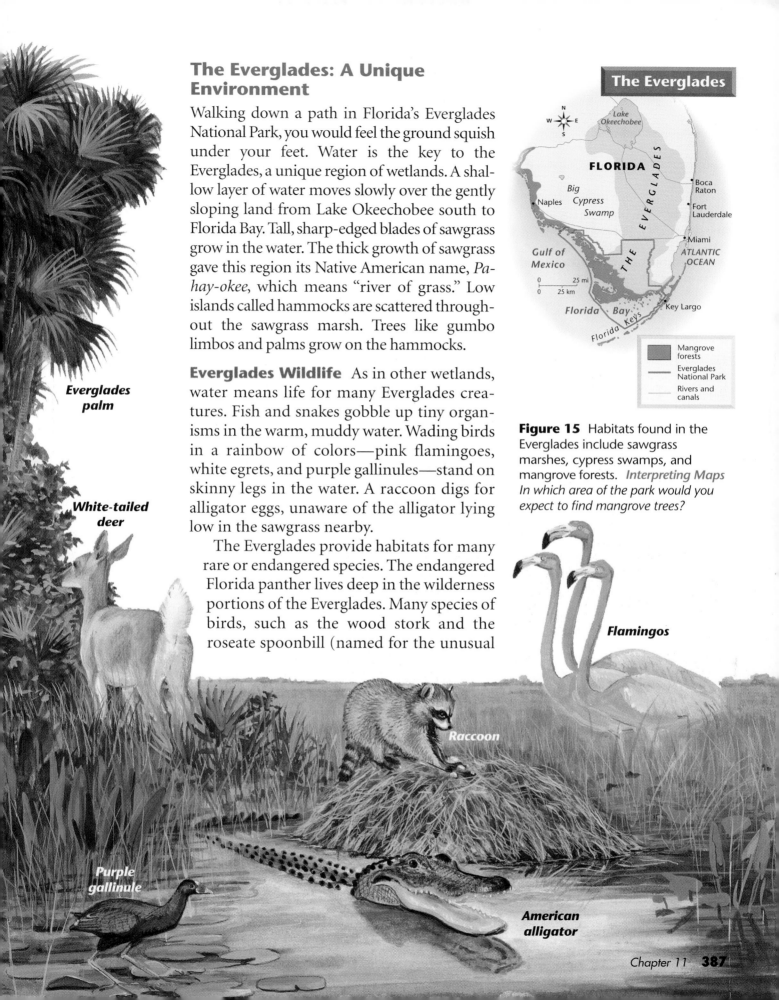

Everglades palm

White-tailed deer

The Everglades

Figure 15 Habitats found in the Everglades include sawgrass marshes, cypress swamps, and mangrove forests. *Interpreting Maps In which area of the park would you expect to find mangrove trees?*

Flamingos

Purple gallinule

Raccoon

American alligator

shape of its beak), depend on the Everglades as a nesting area. The awkward-looking manatee, or sea cow, lives in the mangrove forests along the coast. Because manatees swim so slowly, they are easily injured by the propellers of powerboats. They have become an endangered species as a result of increased boating.

Threats to the Everglades The Everglades are a fragile environment. Nearby farming has introduced new chemicals into the slow-moving water of the marsh, upsetting the balance of nutrients. Outside the protected limits of the national park, developers have filled in areas of wetland to build new homes and roads. New organisms brought into the area accidentally or for pest control compete with other organisms for space and food.

Water that once flowed into the Everglades from Lake Okeechobee has been diverted for farming. New canals and levees built to provide drinking water and to control flooding have changed the flow of water into and out of the Everglades. Some areas are drying up, while others are flooded.

Preserving the Everglades Scientists and government officials have been trying for many years to develop a plan to preserve the Everglades and save its endangered wildlife. One plan involves building an elaborate system of pipes and canals to refill some drained areas with fresh water. The National Park Service, the State of Florida, and the U.S. Army Corps of Engineers are working together to manage the supply of water to areas around and within the Everglades.

Figure 16 A manatee floats in the warm waters of Florida Bay. This species is threatened by the increased use of coastal waters around the Everglades.

Section 4 Review

1. How are wetlands important to wildlife?
2. Explain how wetlands help control floods.
3. How are the Everglades unusual?
4. **Thinking Critically Making Judgments** Some of the plans to restore the Everglades will require millions of dollars and will negatively affect local farmers. What information would you want to have to help decide what plan of action to take to save the Everglades?

Science at Home

Model Wetland With a family member, make a model of a wetland using a loaf pan, sponge, soil, and water. In one end of the loaf pan, build a sloping hill of damp soil. Add water to the other end of the pan to form a model lake. Use a watering can to sprinkle water onto the hill to simulate rain. Observe what happens to the hill and the lake. Next, empty the water out of the pan and rebuild the hill. Push a sponge into the soil across the bottom of the hill to model a wetland. Then repeat the above steps for adding water and sprinkling "rain." Observe the result. What happened to the soil with and without the wetland? How did the lake look in each case?

The Water Cycle

Section 1 — The Water Cycle

Key Ideas

◆ About 97 percent of Earth's water is salt water stored in the oceans. Less than 1 percent is usable fresh water.

◆ In the water cycle, water evaporates from Earth's surface into the atmosphere. The water forms clouds, then falls back to Earth as precipitation. Energy from the sun drives the water cycle.

◆ The water cycle renews Earth's supply of fresh water. In the world as a whole, the rates of evaporation and precipitation balance each other.

◆ People use water for many purposes, including household use, industry, agriculture, transportation, and recreation.

◆ All living things need water to carry out their life processes.

Key Terms

water vapor   precipitation
groundwater   irrigation
water cycle   photosynthesis
evaporation   habitat
transpiration

 Water on the Surface

Key Ideas

◆ Runoff from precipitation forms streams, which flow together to form rivers. The area drained by a river system is its watershed.

◆ Floods occur when a river overflows its channel and spreads out over its floodplain.

◆ Ponds and lakes are bodies of standing water that form when fresh water collects in depressions in the land.

Key Terms

tributary   levee
watershed   reservoir
divide   eutrophication

 Water Underground

Section 3 — Water Underground

Key Ideas

◆ As water soaks into the ground, it moves through the pores between particles of soil and rock. Water moves easily through permeable materials, but does not move easily through impermeable materials.

◆ People dig wells to obtain groundwater from aquifers.

Key Terms

pore   water table   spring
permeable   unsaturated zone   recharge
impermeable   aquifer   artesian well
saturated zone

Section 4 — Wetland Environments

Wetland Environments

INTEGRATING LIFE SCIENCE

Key Ideas

◆ Wetlands are covered with a shallow layer of water for all or part of the year.

◆ Wetlands provide nesting and feeding areas for birds and other wildlife. Wetlands also filter water and help control floods.

Key Term

wetland

Organizing Information

Cycle Diagram Copy the cycle diagram about the water cycle onto a separate piece of paper and complete it. (For more on cycle diagrams, see the Skills Handbook.)

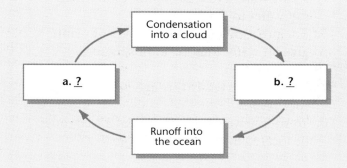

Reviewing Content

 For more review of key concepts, see the Interactive Student Tutorial CD-ROM.

Multiple Choice

Choose the letter of the best answer.

1. More than 97 percent of Earth's total water supply is found in
   a. ice sheets.
   b. the atmosphere.
   c. the oceans.
   d. groundwater.
2. The energy that drives the water cycle comes from the
   a. Earth.   b. sun.
   c. rain.   d. ocean.
3. Rain that falls on a steep, paved street during a thunderstorm will most likely become
   a. groundwater.   b. runoff.
   c. a spring.   d. a reservoir.
4. More than two thirds of Earth's fresh water is found in
   a. rivers and streams.
   b. ponds and lakes.
   c. wetlands.
   d. glaciers and icebergs.
5. Groundwater is stored in
   a. wetlands.   b. water tables.
   c. aquifers.   d. impermeable layers.

True or False

If the statement is true, write true. If it is false, change the underlined word or words to make the statement true.

6. Most of Earth's liquid fresh water is found in the form of <u>lakes</u>.
7. In the water cycle, precipitation returns <u>salt</u> water to Earth.
8. The process by which the leaves of plants give off water into the atmosphere is <u>condensation</u>.
9. Water moves easily through <u>permeable</u> rock layers.
10. To supply water, the bottom of a well must be located in the <u>saturated zone</u>.

Checking Concepts

11. Explain why Earth is called the "water planet."
12. Describe two changes of state that occur during the water cycle.
13. Explain why so little of Earth's water is available for human use.
14. How is the water supplied to plants important for many other living things on Earth?
15. Describe how temperature changes in the fall and spring can help distribute nutrients throughout a lake.
16. Explain how wetlands are important to migrating birds.
17. **Writing to Learn** As the information officer aboard a starship, you are assigned to write a handbook describing Earth's waters to visitors from other galaxies. Write a description in which you explain how water is important to living things on Earth.

Thinking Critically

18. **Making Generalizations** Explain why towns and cities are often located along bodies of water.
19. **Comparing and Contrasting** How is the variety of organisms you would find in the center of a pond different from those you would find in deep water at the center of a lake?
20. **Classifying** Determine which of the following materials are permeable and which are impermeable: aluminum foil, cotton, plastic wrap, glass, paper towel, and bread.
21. **Relating Cause and Effect** A molecule of water is likely to evaporate more quickly from the Caribbean Sea near the equator than from the Arctic Ocean. Explain why this statement is true.

Applying Skills

Use the diagram of underground layers to answer Questions 22–24.

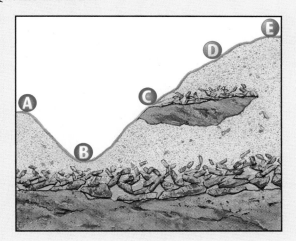

22. **Drawing Conclusions** Would point D or point E be a better location to dig a well? Explain your reasoning.

23. **Inferring** At which location could you obtain groundwater without having to pump it up? What is such a place called?

24. **Predicting** Draw a simple diagram showing how this area might look during a very rainy season.

Performance ▼ CHAPTER PROJECT **Assessment**

Present Your Project Now you are ready to share the data you have collected. Make a graph of your household water-use data. As a class, discuss any surprising results. How do your findings compare to those of your classmates?

Reflect and Record In your project notebook, reflect on the data collection process. What part of the project was the most difficult? How might you approach this task differently? Write a paragraph summarizing what your class discovered about how water is used in your community. Do you notice any similarities among buildings where a lot of water is used, or among those where little water is used?

Test Preparation

Use these questions to prepare for standardized tests.

Study the circle graph. Then answer Questions 25–28.

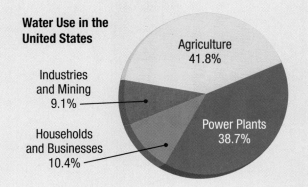

Water Use in the United States
- Agriculture 41.8%
- Industries and Mining 9.1%
- Households and Businesses 10.4%
- Power Plants 38.7%

25. Together the two largest categories of water users represent about what percentage of the total water used in the United States?
   a. 19.5 percent
   b. 49.9 percent
   c. 51.1 percent
   d. 80.5 percent

26. Which of the four categories of water users shown in the graph represents the largest use of water in the United States?
   a. agriculture
   b. households and businesses
   c. industries and mining
   d. power plants

27. If the total daily usage of water in the United States is 1,280 billion liters, about how many liters are used each day by power plants?
   a. 38.7 billion
   b. 387 billion
   c. 495 billion
   d. 49,500 billion

28. If farmers were able to reduce their water use by 10 percent, by about how much would total water use decrease in the United States?
   a. 1.5 percent
   b. 4.2 percent
   c. 10 percent
   d. 41.8 percent

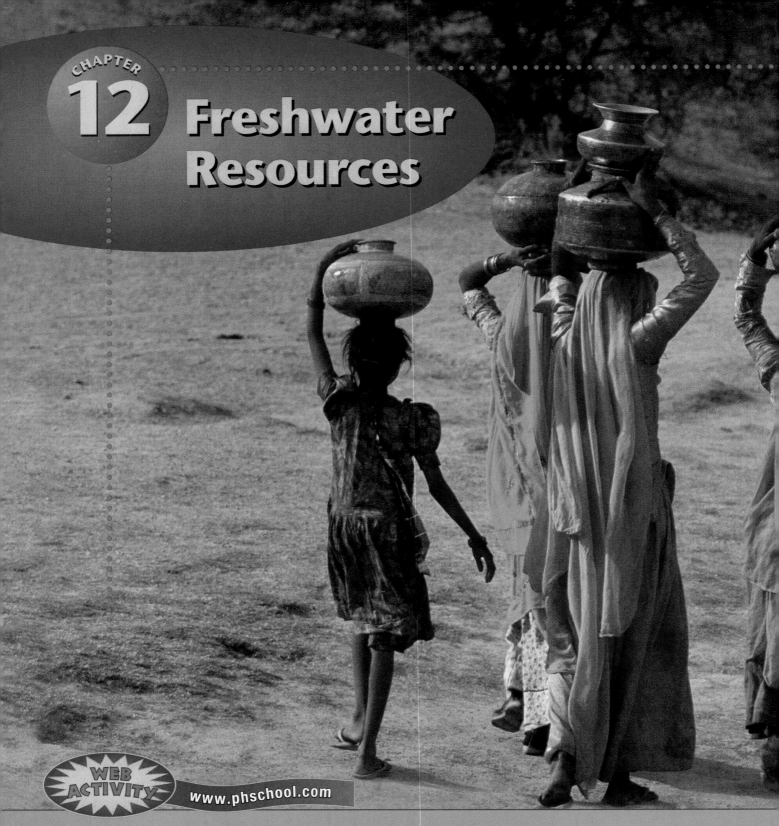

WEB ACTIVITY
www.phschool.com

A Precious Resource

If you lived in Rajasthan, India, you might walk two kilometers every morning to collect a heavy bucket of water from a spring-fed oasis. Your family would use this water for breakfast, washing dishes, and laundry. When you came home from school, you would fetch more water for the evening meal and bathing.

In this chapter, you will explore water as a resource. You will discover what happens when water is scarce, and how water can become polluted. You will also learn how people can use freshwater resources more wisely, and how water pollution can be prevented or cleaned up. Throughout the chapter, you will be building your own model water treatment system.

Your Goal To design and build a water treatment system to clean one liter of dirty water.

Your treatment system should

◆ consist of at least two treatment steps
◆ be made from materials that have been approved by your teacher
◆ recover as much of one liter of clean water as possible
◆ be built following the safety guidelines in Appendix A

Get Started Your teacher will give you a sample of dirty water. Begin now by using your senses to observe your sample. Make a list of all your observations. Think about what types of substances might be present in this water. **CAUTION:** *Never taste or drink the water samples before or after treatment.*

Check Your Progress You'll be working on this project as you study this chapter. To keep your project on track, look for Check Your Progress boxes at the following points.

Section 1 Review, page 403: Plan the steps of your system.
Section 3 Review, page 418: Assemble your treatment system.
Section 4 Review, page 422: Test and modify your system.

Present Your Project At the end of the chapter (page 425), you will demonstrate how well your system cleans up the dirty water sample.

SECTION 4

Integrating Physics
Water as an Energy Resource

Discover Can Water Do Work?
Try This Making a Water Wheel

These residents of Rajasthan, India, balance steel and brass containers of water on their heads for the walk home from the oasis.

① Water to Drink

DISCOVER ···································· ACTIVITY ···

How Hard Is It to Move Water?

1. Line two large trash barrels with heavy plastic bags. Fill one barrel with about 100 liters of water. This is about how much water a person uses during a five-minute shower.

2. Form a line of students between the barrels. Your goal is to transfer all the water from the first barrel to the second barrel. Avoid spilling the water. Be careful of slippery floors if you are doing this activity indoors.

3. The first person in line should fill a large plastic pitcher with water, put the cover on, and hand it to the next person.

4. Pass the pitcher to the end of the line, where the last person should empty it into the second barrel. Hand the empty pitcher back down the line to the first person.

5. Repeat Steps 3 and 4 until all the water has been transferred to the second barrel. How many times did you pass the pitcher down the line?

Think It Over

Calculating Suppose a person uses an average of 250 liters of water a day. How many times would you have to pass the pitcher to move the amount of water this person would use in a day? In a year?

GUIDE FOR READING

◆ What is the goal of drinking-water treatment?

◆ What happens to wastewater in most large communities?

Reading Tip Before you read, rewrite the section headings as how, why, or what questions. As you read, find answers to these questions.

At first, doctors in Milwaukee, Wisconsin, thought that 1993 was just a bad year for the flu. Patient after patient complained of nausea, fever, and other flulike symptoms. Within just a few weeks, about 400,000 people came down with symptoms of the disease. Public health officials began looking for another explanation for the epidemic.

The investigators discovered that all the victims had drunk water from the same water treatment plant. Tests revealed that the water contained a tiny parasite, a protist called *Cryptosporidium*. One sip of water could contain enough *Cryptosporidium* to make a person ill! This parasite had not been killed by the chemicals used to treat water at the plant. The scientists hypothesized that the *Cryptosporidium* might have come from runoff from fields where cows grazed. Although most of the victims recovered after a few weeks, about 100 deaths were blamed on the contamination.

Figure 1 An aqueduct carries water from one place to another. This aqueduct, the Pont du Gard in France, was built by the Romans more than 2,000 years ago. *Inferring Why do you think the Romans found it necessary to construct aqueducts?*

Milwaukee's experience was a reminder of the importance of a safe, clean water supply. In this section, you will follow drinking water on its journey to and from homes, schools, and businesses.

Sources of Drinking Water

Where does the water in your kitchen faucet come from? The first step in tracing the path of your water supply is to identify its source. Recall that Earth's liquid fresh water is found on the surface in rivers, lakes, and reservoirs, and underground in rock layers called aquifers. Most people in the United States get their drinking water from one of these sources.

If you live near a large lake or river, your water may come from that source. A distant lake or reservoir could also supply your drinking water. For instance, the city of Los Angeles draws much of its water from the Sierra Nevada Mountains, halfway across California. Or you may rely on groundwater as a source of drinking water. About half the people in the United States, including most people in rural areas, pump drinking water from aquifers.

Your drinking water comes from either a public or private water supply. Most large communities maintain public water supplies. These communities collect, treat, and distribute water to residents. In smaller communities and rural areas, people rely on private wells that supply water for individual families.

☑ *Checkpoint* *List three possible sources of drinking water.*

Treating Drinking Water

After you have identified the source of your drinking water, what is the next step in its journey to your faucet? **Water from both public and private supplies often needs some treatment to ensure that the water is safe and appealing to drink.** Treatment can range from a simple filter on a household well to complex processes at public treatment plants.

Appearance and Taste Picture a glass of water. What observations would affect whether or not you were willing to take a sip? What if the water were cloudy, or had a funny smell? What if the water were rust-colored? Cloudiness, odor, and color are three factors that affect water quality. **Water quality** is a measurement of the substances in water besides water molecules. Some substances, such as iron, can affect the taste or color of water but are harmless unless present at very high levels. Other

You, the Consumer

Testing the Waters

How does the bottled water sold in supermarkets differ from the water that comes out of your kitchen faucet? In this lab, you will discover some differences among various types of water.

Problem

How do distilled water, spring water, and mineral water differ from tap water?

Skills Focus

observing, inferring, drawing conclusions

Materials

hot plate   liquid soap
ruler   wax pencil
tap water, 200 mL distilled water, 200 mL
spring water, 200 mL mineral water, 200 mL
4 200-mL beakers   4 test tubes and stoppers
4 pieces of pH paper pH indicator chart
25-mL graduated cylinder
4 paper cups per person

Procedure

1. Copy the data table into your notebook.

2. Label the beakers A, B, C, and D. Pour 100 mL of tap water into beaker A. Pour 100 mL of the other water samples into the correct beaker (refer to the data table).

3. Heat each water sample on a hot plate until about 20 mL remains. Do not allow the water to boil completely away. **CAUTION:** *Do not touch the hot plate or beakers.*

4. After the water samples have cooled, look for solids that make the water cloudy. Rank the samples from 1 to 4, where 1 has the fewest visible solids and 4 has the most visible solids. Record your rankings in the data table.

5. Label the test tubes A, B, C, and D. Pour 10 mL of each water sample from the source bottle into the correct test tube.

6. Dip a piece of pH paper into test tube A to measure its acidity. Match the color of the pH paper to a number on the pH indicator chart. Record the pH (0–14) in your data table.

substances, such as certain chemicals and microorganisms, can be harmful to your health.

Acidity The **pH** of water is a measurement of how acidic or basic it is, on a scale of 0 to 14. Pure water is neutral, meaning it is neither an acid or a base, and has a pH of 7. The lower the pH, the more acidic the water. Acidic water can cause problems by dissolving lead or other metals from the pipes it passes through. The higher the pH, the more basic the water.

DATA TABLE

Water Sample	Visible Solids (1–4)	pH (0–14)	Soapsud Height (cm)	Taste
A - Tap water				
B - Distilled water				
C - Spring water				
D - Mineral water				

7. Repeat Step 6 for the other samples.
8. Add 0.5 mL of liquid soap to test tube A. Put a stopper in the test tube and shake it 30 times. With the ruler, measure the height of the soapsuds in the test tube. Record the measurement in your data table.
9. Repeat Step 8 for the other samples.
10. Label the four cups A, B, C, and D. Write your name on each cup.
11. Pour a little tap water into cup A directly from the original source bottle. Taste the tap water. In your data table, describe the taste using one or more of these words: salty, flat, bitter, metallic, refreshing, tasteless.
    CAUTION: *Do not conduct the taste test in a lab room. Use a clean cup for each sample and discard it after use.*
12. Repeat Step 11 with the other samples.

Analyze and Conclude

1. Review your data table. Compare each of the bottled water samples to the tap water sample. What similarities and differences did you detect?
2. Rank the samples from the one with the fewest soapsuds to the one with the most. Compare this ranking to the one for visible solids. What pattern do you see? What do both of these tests have to do with the hardness of water?
3. What other information about the water samples might you need before deciding which one to drink regularly? Explain.
4. **Apply** Based on your results, which sample would you most want to use for (a) drinking, (b) boiling in a kettle, and (c) washing laundry? Which sample would you least want to use for each purpose? Explain.

Getting Involved

Conduct a survey to find out what percentage of people buy bottled mineral water, distilled water, and spring water. Why do they buy each type of water and how do they use it in their homes?

Math TOOLBOX

Parts per . . .

Concentrations are often measured in parts per million (ppm) or parts per billion (ppb). What do these units mean? If you own one compact disc by your favorite band, and the disc sells one million copies, your disc is one of the one million sold, or one part per million. When you see a concentration written in this form, you can rewrite it as a fraction:

1. Suppose the concentration of iron in a water sample is 500 parts per million.

2. Write this concentration as a fraction by putting the number of parts on top, and the "whole" on the bottom:

500 parts per million =

$$\frac{500}{1,000,000}$$

Hardness The level of two minerals—calcium and magnesium—in water is referred to as **hardness.** Hard water contains high levels of these minerals. The minerals come from rocks such as limestone that water flows through. For most people, the main drawback of hard water is that it does not form suds well when mixed with soap. That means that it takes more soap or detergent to get laundry clean in hard water. The minerals in hard water also form deposits that can clog pipes and machinery. Soft water, on the other hand, contains lower levels of calcium and magnesium. Soft water leaves fewer deposits and forms better soapsuds than hard water.

Disease-Causing Organisms Another factor affecting water quality is the presence of disease-causing organisms. The coliform count measures the number of *Escherichia coli* bacteria. Since these bacteria are found in human and animal wastes, their presence in the water shows that it contains waste material. A high coliform count is an indicator, or sign, that the water may also contain other disease-causing organisms.

Standards of Quality The Environmental Protection Agency (EPA), which is responsible for protecting the quality of water and other natural resources in the United States, has developed water-quality standards for drinking water. These standards set concentration limits for certain chemicals, minerals, and bacteria in drinking water. A **concentration** is the amount of one substance in a certain volume of another substance. For example, the concentration of letters in alphabet soup might be written as the number of letters per liter of soup. Figure 2 shows the standards for some different substances.

☑ *Checkpoint* *List five factors that affect water quality.*

Figure 2 The EPA has set standards for the amounts of various substances in drinking water. *Interpreting Data Based on this table, is a concentration of 0.09 ppm of arsenic in drinking water acceptable? Is a concentration of 0.05 ppm of cyanide acceptable?*

Selected Water-Quality Standards	
Substance	**Limit**
Arsenic	0.05 parts per million (ppm)
Carbon tetrachloride	0.005 ppm
Copper	1.3 ppm
Cyanide	0.2 ppm
Lead	0.015 ppm
Coliform count	No more than 5% of samples taken in a month can be positive.
pH	6.5–8.5

Source: U.S. Environmental Protection Agency, National Primary and Secondary Drinking-Water Standards.

A Typical Treatment Plant

Follow the water from river to faucet in *Exploring Drinking-Water Treatment* to see what happens in a typical water treatment plant.

The first step in treating water from a lake or river is usually filtration. **Filtration** is the process of passing water through a series of screens that allows the water through, but not larger solid particles. During this first step, trash, leaves, branches, and other large objects are removed from the water.

In the second step, a chemical such as alum is added to cause sticky globs, called **flocs,** to form. Other particles in the water stick to the flocs, a process called **coagulation.** The heavy clumps sink to the bottom in the settling basins. The water is then filtered again.

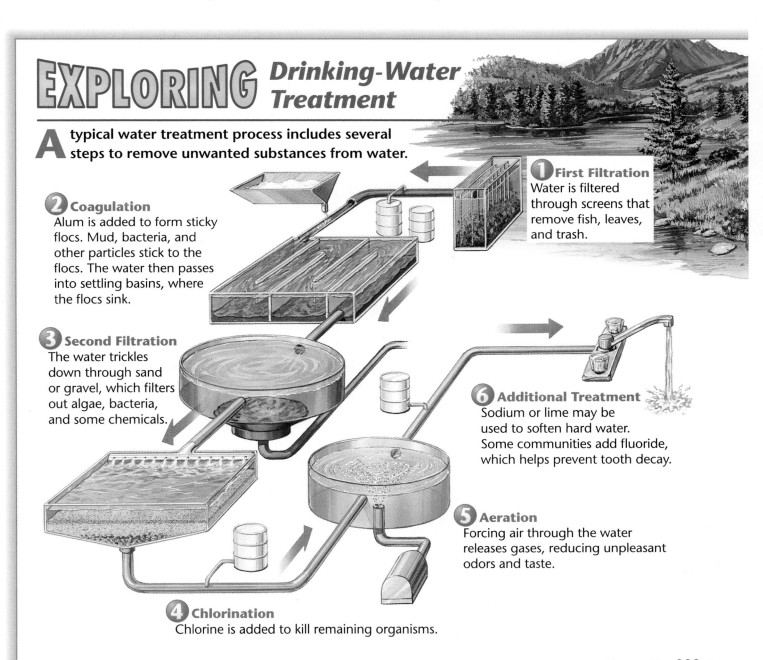

EXPLORING Drinking-Water Treatment

A typical water treatment process includes several steps to remove unwanted substances from water.

① First Filtration
Water is filtered through screens that remove fish, leaves, and trash.

② Coagulation
Alum is added to form sticky flocs. Mud, bacteria, and other particles stick to the flocs. The water then passes into settling basins, where the flocs sink.

③ Second Filtration
The water trickles down through sand or gravel, which filters out algae, bacteria, and some chemicals.

④ Chlorination
Chlorine is added to kill remaining organisms.

⑤ Aeration
Forcing air through the water releases gases, reducing unpleasant odors and taste.

⑥ Additional Treatment
Sodium or lime may be used to soften hard water. Some communities add fluoride, which helps prevent tooth decay.

Moving Water Uphill

In this activity
you will see
how a device called a siphon
can be used to move water.

1. Pile a stack of books on a table. Place one bowl on top of the books and another bowl on the table. Pour water into the higher bowl until it is about half full.

2. Submerge a piece of plastic tubing in the water in the upper bowl. When the tubing is full of water, put a finger over each end.

3. Keeping one end of the tubing underwater, place the other end in the lower, empty bowl. Release both fingers and watch what happens.

Observing In what direction does the water first have to travel to get out of the higher bowl? Can you explain this movement?

The next step is to chlorinate the water. If you have ever been to a public swimming pool, you are familiar with the smell of chlorine. Chlorine is added to drinking water for the same reason it is added to swimming pools—to kill disease-causing microorganisms. At this point, the water is usually ready to be distributed to homes. Sometimes other chemicals are added to kill specific organisms, such as the *Cryptosporidium* you read about earlier.

Water from an aquifer may require less treatment than water from a lake or river. Flowing through the rocks or sand naturally filters and purifies the water. However, most public water supplies that use a groundwater source still add chlorine to kill disease-causing organisms.

Public health officials regularly test samples from water treatment plants to assess water quality. They test for the substances covered by the drinking-water standards, including chemicals, dissolved solids, pH, hardness, and disease-causing organisms. Private well owners should also test their water regularly to make sure no treatment is needed.

☑ *Checkpoint* *What is the goal of most drinking-water treatment systems?*

Water Distribution

 INTEGRATING PHYSICS Once it has been treated, the water is ready to be distributed to homes and businesses. From a treatment plant, water goes to a central pumping station. There the water is pumped into an underground network of steel or concrete pipes called water mains. The water mains branch off to smaller pipes. These feed into smaller copper or plastic pipes that carry water into houses and other buildings.

Water pressure causes the water to move through this system of pipes. Whenever water is in an enclosed space, it exerts pressure in all directions. For example, water pressure pushes water through a garden hose. If the hose springs a leak, a jet of water sprays out of the hole into the air. The pressure pushes the water out through the hole.

Pumping stations are designed to keep water pressure steady throughout the system. If there is a leak in one of the pipes, water escapes—just as it did from the garden hose—and the pressure drops. A typical distribution system can push water up against the downward force of gravity about five or six stories. High-rise buildings must use additional pumps to raise the water to higher floors.

Rather than use a central pumping station, some communities store their water high in the air! No, not as clouds or water vapor, but in a water tower or tank on top of a hill. Treated

water is pumped up into the water tower. When the water is released, the weight of the water supplies additional pressure that sends the water rushing downward, filling the town's water mains and pipes.

Treating Wastewater

Finally, after a long journey, the water reaches your house. You take a shower, flush the toilet, or wash a load of laundry. What happens now to the used water that goes down the drain? That wastewater and the different kinds of wastes in it are called **sewage.** You might be surprised to learn that this water could someday return as part of your drinking water! No need to worry, however. The wastewater goes through many changes to make this possible.

In many communities, a network of pipes called sanitary sewers carries sewage away from homes. Sanitary sewers are separated from storm sewers, which drain rainwater and runoff from sidewalks, lawns, and parking lots.

Cities and towns have had sanitary sewer systems for only about the last 200 years. Before then, wastewater was often dumped into open gutters and allowed to run directly back into rivers or oceans. Although people eventually realized that this practice helped spread disease, it still occurs in some places, both in the United States and the rest of the world. Coastal cities, in particular, sometimes still pump untreated sewage into the oceans.

Most communities treat their wastewater to make it safe to return to the environment. Different communities may use different treatment processes.

Figure 4 If your community has a sanitary sewer system, you may have seen a sewer cover like this one in the street. Sanitary sewers carry wastewater away from homes and businesses.

You can follow one typical wastewater treatment process, called a trickling filter system, in *Exploring Wastewater Treatment*.

During primary treatment, deposits of fine solids called **sludge** settle out from the wastewater. Despite its unappetizing name, sludge is a useful material. It can be treated with heat and chemicals and used as fertilizer. Sludge can also be reused in secondary treatment. In one method, bacteria are added to the sludge to create "activated sludge." The activated sludge is mixed into the wastewater. The bacteria then break down the remaining sewage in the water.

If necessary, additional treatment may remove other substances from the water, such as metals and industrial chemicals. Once wastewater has gone through an effective treatment process, it is safe to return to the environment. It may be released

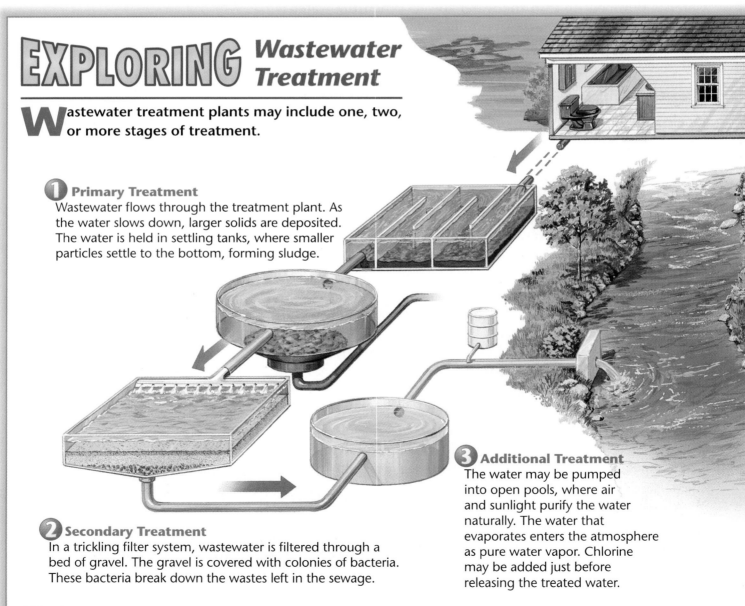

EXPLORING Wastewater Treatment

Wastewater treatment plants may include one, two, or more stages of treatment.

1 Primary Treatment
Wastewater flows through the treatment plant. As the water slows down, larger solids are deposited. The water is held in settling tanks, where smaller particles settle to the bottom, forming sludge.

2 Secondary Treatment
In a trickling filter system, wastewater is filtered through a bed of gravel. The gravel is covered with colonies of bacteria. These bacteria break down the wastes left in the sewage.

3 Additional Treatment
The water may be pumped into open pools, where air and sunlight purify the water naturally. The water that evaporates enters the atmosphere as pure water vapor. Chlorine may be added just before releasing the treated water.

back into lakes, rivers, and oceans or pumped back into the ground. The water rejoins the water cycle. Eventually, it could return to the same reservoir or aquifer that is the source of your water supply.

Treated wastewater that is not quite clean enough for drinking can still be used in other ways. For instance, some communities use this "gray water" to water the grass on golf courses or public parks. Gray water can also be used for irrigation or as cooling water in factories.

Septic Systems

Just as some people rely on private wells rather than public water supplies, many people are not connected to public sanitary sewer systems. They use other methods to dispose of sewage, such as a septic system. A septic system like the one in Figure 5 includes a **septic tank,** an underground tank containing bacteria that treat wastewater as it passes through. Sludge settles to the bottom of the tank and must be cleaned out regularly so it does not fill up the tank. The remaining water filters out through holes in the septic tank into the ground around it. The area around the septic tank that the water filters through is called a **leach field.** Over time, the remaining wastes break down naturally in the soil of the leach field.

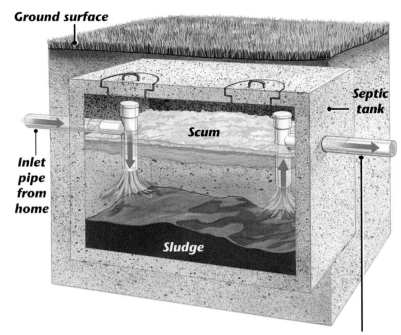

Figure 5 Sewage flows into a septic tank, where bacteria break down the waste material. Cleaner water leaves the tank and flows into a leach field. There, the water slowly releases the remaining dissolved minerals into the soil.

Section 1 Review

1. How does drinking-water treatment improve water quality?
2. What is the goal of wastewater treatment?
3. List the main sources of drinking water. Classify each source as surface water or groundwater.
4. Describe how drinking water is delivered to homes and businesses in a community.
5. **Thinking Critically** **Inferring** Explain why it is important to know the depth and location of drinking-water wells before deciding where to build a septic tank.

Check Your Progress

CHAPTER PROJECT

Now you are ready to plan the steps of your water treatment system. What will each step accomplish? What materials will you use to perform each step? Draw a diagram of your system and a flow-chart showing how it will work. Check your plans with your teacher. (Hint: Be sure to consider how your treatment unit will be constructed. How will you hold the pieces in place?)

2 Balancing Water Needs

DISCOVER

Can You Reach a Balance?

1. Fill a large measuring cup with water to represent a reservoir. Record the level of the water. One partner, the water supplier, should have a plastic dropper and a small bowl of water. The other partner, the water user, should have a spoon and an empty bowl.

2. Start a stopwatch. For two minutes, the water supplier should add water to the measuring cup one dropperful at a time. Each time the water supplier adds a dropperful of water, the water user should remove one spoonful of water from the reservoir.

3. At the end of two minutes, record the level of water in the cup.

4. Now increase the rate of water use by removing two spoonfuls of water for every dropperful added.

5. After another two minutes, record the level of water in the cup again.

Think It Over

Predicting What changes will you need to make so that the water level in the reservoir stays constant?

GUIDE FOR READING

◆ What conditions can result in a water shortage?

◆ What are some ways industries can conserve water?

Reading Tip Before you read, write an explanation of what you think water conservation means. As you read, add to your explanation.

Has this ever happened to you? You're eating dinner with your family and you ask someone to pass the rolls. As the basket makes its way around the table, each person takes a roll. By the time it gets to you, there's nothing left in the basket but crumbs!

This scenario is an example of a limited resource, the rolls, being used by many people. The same thing can happen to a river! For example, the Colorado River holds a resource that is precious in the Southwest—water. In this desert region there is little precipitation to provide water for people's needs. As the river flows through seven states and into Mexico, it is tapped again and again to provide water for drinking, irrigation, and other uses. The river's mouth at the Gulf of California is now often only a dry riverbed.

Figure 6 Cracks appear in the dry soil of an empty riverbed.

Water Supply and Demand

States along a river such as the Colorado have to decide how much water each one can take from the river. The deserts of Nevada and Arizona are home to some of the fastest-growing cities in the country. As more people move to Las Vegas, Phoenix, and Tucson, these cities need more water. They increase their demand on already scarce water supplies. Meanwhile, farmers claim a large share to irrigate their fields. Mining companies use water to cool down machinery and flush out the mines they dig. The cities, farms, and mines compete for water rights—the legal right to take water from a particular source.

The Southwest is just one of many places in the world where there doesn't seem to be enough water to go around. As you know, the water cycle ensures that water is a renewable resource. However, the water supply in a specific area is only renewed when there is enough time for rainfall to replace what has been used. **A water shortage occurs when there is too little water or too great a demand in an area—or both.**

Figure 7 Farmers require large amounts of water to irrigate crops in the dry desert. *Relating Cause and Effect* What are two factors that might result in a shortage of water available for irrigation?

Drought Places that normally get enough precipitation may experience a few years of scarce rainfall, a condition known as a **drought.** A drought affects the supply of groundwater as well as surface water. Without precipitation to recharge the aquifer, the amount of groundwater in the aquifer decreases. What happens to a well as the level of the water table falls? Imagine trying to drink from a tall glass of milk through a straw the length of a toothpick. When the level of the milk falls below the bottom of the straw, you can no longer reach it to drink. In the same way, when the water table falls below the bottom of a well, the well runs dry.

Aquifer Overuse Even without droughts, the demands of growing populations can result in overuse of aquifers. When water is used up faster than the aquifer can be recharged, the aquifer is depleted, or emptied.

INTEGRATING TECHNOLOGY

When too much water is pumped out of an aquifer, the ground above the aquifer can sink or collapse. The ground is no longer supported by the pressure of the water inside it. To

Laws regarding the use of water are a very old concept. Nearly 4,000 years ago in ancient Mesopotamia, now modern-day Iraq, a ruler named Hammurabi wrote in his code of laws:

"If a man neglects the canal so that water floods a neighboring field, he shall repay the loss with his own grain."

In Your Journal

A river carries 10,000 liters of water a day through your village. Imagine that you are a member of the village council. Propose a fair way to assign water rights to the following people. (*Hint:* Think about which uses will return water to the river and which will not.)

- Grain farmer, wants 4,000 liters a day for watering crops
- Livestock owner, wants 600 liters a day for washing animals and 500 liters a day for animals to drink
- Fisherman, needs to keep the river at least half full for the fish to survive
- Miller, needs 3,500 liters a day to turn waterwheel

prevent collapse, engineers can artificially recharge an aquifer. One method is to pump water from wastewater treatment plants or industrial cooling water into shallow ponds that feed the aquifer. Another method is to inject water down wells directly into the saturated zone. However, because these techniques require expensive equipment and additional water, it is a better solution not to overuse the aquifer.

☑ *Checkpoint* **How can a drought cause a well to run dry?**

Conserving Water

During a water shortage, people often pay more attention to how they use water. They look for ways to avoid wasting water both at home and at work. Using a resource wisely so that it will not be used up is called **conservation.**

In the Home Most people in the United States have access to as much clean, safe water as they want. As a result, it is often easy to use more water than needed without thinking much about it. But as Figure 8 shows, there are some simple things you can do to help conserve water around your home.

Can these suggestions really make a difference? Figure it out. How long do you stand under the shower? For every minute, you use about 18 liters of water. If you stand under the shower for 10 minutes, that's about 180 liters. But if you showered for 5 minutes instead, you would use only 90 liters. And if each student in a class of 25 showered for 5 minutes instead of 10, they would save a total of 2,250 liters of water— enough to fill 22 trash barrels! As you can see, small efforts by many individuals can add up to a lot of water savings.

In Agriculture As you learned in Chapter 1, the biggest use of water in the United States is for agriculture. In the last few decades, farmers have found new ways to use less water. When water is carried into fields in open canals or ditches, much of it is lost through evaporation. Using pipes to carry water reduces the time that water is exposed to the air. Two such methods are sprinkler irrigation and drip irrigation. Sprinkler irrigation sprays water onto crops from overhead pipes. Drip irrigation distributes water through pipes with tiny holes. The water drips directly onto the soil near the plants' roots so that very little is wasted.

In Industry Paper mills, oil refineries, chemical factories, and other industries have made changes in manufacturing processes to use less water. For example, in the 1950s it took about 227,000 liters of water to make 1,000 kilograms of writing paper. By the 1980s, paper mills needed only half that much water to produce the same amount of paper.

New water-saving techniques help industries save money in water costs and meet the requirements of environmental laws. **Reducing water use, recycling water, and reusing water are three major forms of water conservation by industries.** These approaches conserve water while also reducing the amount of wastewater that plants release. For example, some factories that use water to cool machinery are building lagoons on their property. The heated water cools off in the lagoons and then can be used again. Other factories are replacing water-cooling systems with cooling systems that use air. Another change is to use high-pressure water sprays to clean products and equipment instead of dipping the objects in large tanks of water.

Fresh Water for the Future

As the number of people in the world increases, so does the need for water. Where can people find new sources of water for the future? One obvious place would seem to be the other 97 percent of water on Earth—the salt water in the oceans. For thousands

Sharpen your Skills

Predicting

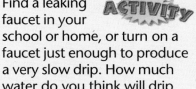

Find a leaking faucet in your school or home, or turn on a faucet just enough to produce a very slow drip. How much water do you think will drip from the faucet in half an hour? Write down your prediction. Place a large measuring cup under the faucet. After half an hour, check the cup. How does the result compare with your prediction? How much water would you save per day if you fixed the leaking faucet?

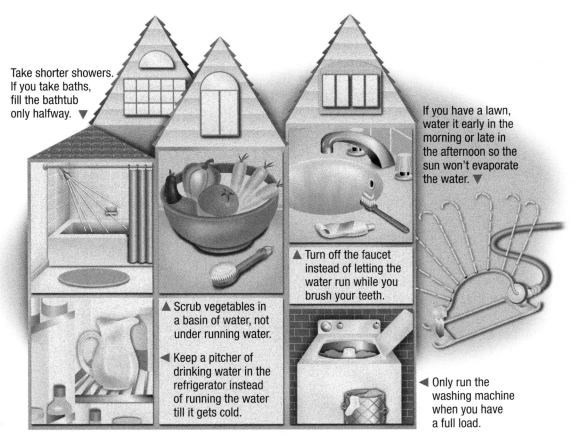

Take shorter showers. If you take baths, fill the bathtub only halfway. ▼

If you have a lawn, water it early in the morning or late in the afternoon so the sun won't evaporate the water. ▼

▲ Turn off the faucet instead of letting the water run while you brush your teeth.

▲ Scrub vegetables in a basin of water, not under running water.

◄ Keep a pitcher of drinking water in the refrigerator instead of running the water till it gets cold.

◄ Only run the washing machine when you have a full load.

Figure 8 There are many simple ways to conserve water around the home. *Developing Hypotheses Which of these ideas do you think would save the most water per day in your home? How could you test your hypothesis?*

of years, people have tried different methods to make salty ocean water drinkable.

Desalination The process of obtaining fresh water from salt water is called **desalination.** One method of desalination, called distillation, is to boil water so that it evaporates, leaving the salt behind. The water vapor is then condensed to produce liquid fresh water. Another method involves freezing the water, which also leaves the salt behind. Still another method is to pump water at high pressure through a very fine filter. The filter separates out pure water and returns saltier water to the ocean.

Desalination is very expensive because of the energy and equipment it requires. In spite of the cost, however, Saudi Arabia, Kuwait, Israel, and other nations in the dry Middle East depend on this technology. A few cities in the United States, such as Santa Barbara, California, have also built desalination plants.

Icebergs Some people think that icebergs are another possible source of fresh water for dry regions. Tugboats could tow a wrapped iceberg from Antarctica to a coastal area of Africa or South America. An iceberg would provide millions of liters of pure water that could be piped to shore as the iceberg melted. However, such plans raise environmental questions: How would a huge mass of ice offshore affect local weather? What would happen to living things as the ice cooled the water around it? These questions need to be answered before icebergs can be seen as a solution to Earth's future water needs.

Figure 9 The ocean is one possible source of drinking water for the future.
Applying Concepts How can ocean water be made suitable for drinking?

Section 2 Review

1. Describe a situation that could lead to a water shortage in a community.
2. Name three ways that industries can conserve water.
3. Describe the possible effects overpumping might have on an aquifer.
4. Explain how an iceberg might provide drinking water in the future.
5. **Thinking Critically Making Judgments** Do you think communities should be able to limit how often people water their lawns or wash their cars? Why or why not?

Science at Home

Water Use for Brushing Place a stopper over the drain in a sink. Ask a family member to brush his or her teeth over the sink, allowing the water to run until he or she is done. Mark the level of the water in the sink with a small piece of tape. Remove the stopper and let the water drain. Replace the stopper and have the person repeat the brushing, this time turning the water on only when needed. Mark the water level with another piece of tape. Point out the difference in the amount of water used in each case.

GETTING THE SALT OUT

Desalination plants use many methods to produce fresh water from ocean water. In this lab, you will make a model of a desalination plant using the method of distillation.

Problem

How can distillation be used to obtain fresh water from salt water?

Materials

hot plate	aluminum foil	250-mL beaker
plastic spoon	water, 100 mL	shallow pan
ice	plastic tube	500-mL flask
stirring rod	rubber stopper	salt
rubber tubing, 50 cm		

Procedure

1. Pour 100 mL of water into the flask.
2. Add one spoonful of salt to the water in the flask and stir until dissolved. The solution should not be cloudy.
3. Gently insert the plastic tube through the hole of the rubber stopper. Do not force the tube into the hole; ask your teacher for help if you are having difficulty.
4. Insert one end of the plastic tube into the rubber tubing.
5. Put the rubber stopper in the flask. The bottom of the plastic tube should be above the surface of the solution.
6. Cover the beaker with aluminum foil. Press the edges of the foil against the beaker.
7. Push the free end of the rubber tubing through the center of the aluminum foil covering the top of the beaker.
8. Place the beaker in the pan, surrounded by ice.
9. Put the flask on the hot plate, keeping it away from the pan of ice. Turn the hot plate

on. Bring the solution to a boil. **CAUTION:** *Do not touch the hot plate or flask. Do not allow the solution to boil completely away.*
10. Observe what happens in the flask and the beaker. Continue heating the solution until a liquid has accumulated in the beaker.
11. Turn off the hot plate and allow the flask and the beaker to cool. What is left behind in the flask? Record your observations.

Analyze and Conclude

1. What happened to the water in the flask during the boiling process? What happened inside the beaker?
2. How does the liquid collected in the beaker differ from the liquid in the flask?
3. What is the purpose of the ice in this activity?
4. **Think About It** Imagine building a desalination plant that uses the method of distillation to produce water for a city. What difficulties might you encounter in using this process on such a large scale?

More to Explore

How could you change the setup and procedure to recover fresh water from salt water without using the hot plate? Design an experiment to accomplish this goal. Obtain your teacher's permission before carrying out your experiment.

SCIENCE AND SOCIETY

The Ogallala Aquifer

The Ogallala Aquifer lies beneath eight states of the Great Plains. It contains about 4 quadrillion liters of groundwater—about the amount of water in Lake Huron. Rainfall is scarce on the Great Plains. But by pumping water out of the aquifer, farmers can grow cotton, wheat, sorghum, and corn to feed cattle. More than one third of the nation's livestock are raised in this area.

Water in the Ogallala was trapped there during the last Ice Age, about 12,000 years ago. Now, due to the demands of irrigation, water levels are dropping much faster than the aquifer can recharge. In certain parts of the aquifer, water levels have fallen as much as 12 meters since 1980. Farmers recognize that the Ogallala cannot withstand this heavy use for long. However, not all agree on what should be done.

The Issues

Should Water Use Be Regulated? One way to reduce water use might be to charge people for water. But who owns the water and who would determine the cost? In most of the Great Plains, water has been free to anyone who dug a well on their land. To charge for water, local governments would need to construct a public water system as in most cities. This would be a very complex and costly task. Both farmers and consumers would be affected by the charge. Higher costs for growing crops would result in higher supermarket prices for grains and meat.

Should Farmers Change Their Practices? Farmers could switch to crops such as sunflowers and grains that need less water. These crops, how-ever, are less valuable than others for producing food and for feeding livestock. As a result, they would be less profitable than traditional crops. Farmers could use water-saving methods of irrigation. Such methods are expensive to install but eventually save both water and money.

Another possibility is "dryland farming," a method that was used by pioneer farmers. This method involves keeping the soil moist using only rainwater. Because dryland farming depends on the amount of rainfall, it is unpredictable. It may not produce large harvests.

Should Current Use Continue? Many residents of the Great Plains depend on the aquifer for a living. Some people feel that farmers there must continue their present water use in order to compete with farmers elsewhere in the nation and around the world. They feel that people today should not have to suffer in order to preserve the aquifer for future generations. New sources of water may be discovered, or better methods of transporting water to the Great Plains may be developed. Better irrigation techniques that use less water may also be invented. But other people feel that since these possibilities are not certain, water use must be greatly reduced now to save the aquifer.

You Decide

1. Identify the Problem
In your own words, explain the problem facing the farmers on the Great Plains.

2. Analyze the Options
Make a chart of the solutions mentioned. List advantages and drawbacks of each. Who would benefit from each solution? Who would suffer?

3. Find a Solution
As a resident of the Great Plains, write a letter to the newspaper proposing a solution to the Ogallala problem.

SECTION 3 Freshwater Pollution

DISCOVER ·····································ACTIVITY

Will the Pollution Reach Your Wells?

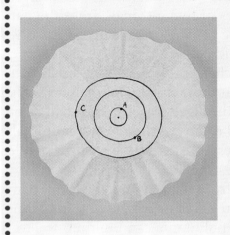

1. With a permanent marker, draw three rings on a coffee filter as shown in the picture. Draw three dots and label them A, B, and C as shown. These dots represent the locations of drinking-water supply wells.

2. Place the coffee filter on a paper plate. Moisten the coffee filter with a wet sponge. The damp coffee filter represents an aquifer.

3. Squirt five drops of food coloring onto the center of the damp coffee filter. Observe how the "pollution" travels.

Think It Over

Observing Which wells are affected by the pollution? Describe the pattern the pollution forms.

The newspaper headlines told an amazing story: "River in Flames!" "Bridges Burn As River Catches Fire!" This really happened to the Cuyahoga River in Cleveland, Ohio, in the summer of 1969. Are you wondering how a river could catch fire? What was in the Cuyahoga that allowed it to burn?

The Cuyahoga flows through a large industrial region on its way to Lake Erie. Factories along its banks used to dump their wastes into the river. Freighters spilled oil and gasoline into the water. Over time, the river became so full of chemicals and sewage that the pollution floating in it could actually burn.

Alarmed by the fire and the destruction it caused, people in Ohio began a massive campaign to clean up the Cuyahoga. Today it is safe to use for boating and fishing. The Cuyahoga River is a dramatic example of how serious water pollution can become—and of how people can work together to undo its damage.

What Is Pollution?

If you turned on your faucet and a stream of bright green water came out, you'd be fairly sure that the water contained something it shouldn't. But many things that can make water unsafe to drink don't change its color, taste, or smell. The addition of any substance that has a negative effect on water or the living things that depend on the water is called **water pollution.** Water pollution can affect surface water, groundwater, and even rain. It can result from both natural causes and human activities.

GUIDE FOR READING

◆ What are some sources of water pollution?

◆ How does agricultural runoff affect ponds and streams?

◆ How can living things help clean up polluted water?

Reading Tip As you read, make a list of sources of freshwater pollution. Write one sentence about each source.

WARNING
Fish Contaminated
DO NOT EAT

The substances that cause water pollution are called pollutants. Disease-causing organisms such as the *Cryptosporidium* you read about in Section 1 are one form of pollutant. As Figure 10 shows, other types of pollutants include toxic, or poisonous, chemicals and metals, as well as radioactive substances.

INTEGRATING LIFE SCIENCE Some types of pollutants can build up in the bodies of living things. Trace the path of one such pollutant in Figure 11. The pesticide DDT dissolves in water and is absorbed by microscopic algae. The algae, which contain only low levels of the chemical, are eaten by small water animals. When frogs or fish eat these smaller animals, they also consume the chemicals from the algae these animals had eaten. The frogs and fish are in turn eaten by birds or other animals. Each larger organism consumes a greater number of the smaller organisms, and therefore more of the DDT.

When humans eat the fish from such a pond, the toxic chemicals build up in their bodies in the same way. Over a long time, even tiny amounts of certain pollutants can build up to levels that can cause birth defects or illnesses such as cancer. Drinking impure water or eating contaminated fish are not the only ways that pollutants can affect humans. Bathing or swimming in polluted water can irritate the skin or cause more serious problems.

Point and Nonpoint Sources

To clean up a polluted body of water like the Cuyahoga River, people first need to identify the source of the pollution to prevent further damage. **The major sources of water pollution are human wastes, industrial wastes, agricultural chemicals, and runoff from roads.**

Figure 10 This table lists some examples of the different types of freshwater pollutants. *Relating Cause and Effect Why might it be helpful to know the source of a particular pollutant detected in a body of water?*

Freshwater Pollutants		
Kind of Pollutant	**Examples**	**Sources**
Disease-causing organisms	*Giardia, Cryptosporidium,* bacteria	Human wastes, runoff from livestock pens
Pesticides and fertilizers	DDT, nitrates, phosphates	Runoff from farm fields, golf courses
Industrial chemicals	PCBs, carbon tetrachloride, dioxin	Factories, industrial waste disposal sites
Metals	Lead, mercury, copper	Factories, waste disposal sites
Radioactive wastes	Uranium, carbon-14	Medical and scientific disposal sites, nuclear power plants
Petroleum products	Oil, gasoline	Road runoff, leaking underground storage tanks

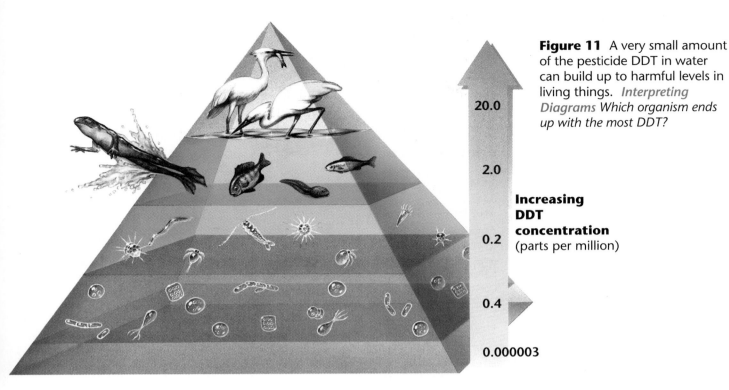

Figure 11 A very small amount of the pesticide DDT in water can build up to harmful levels in living things. *Interpreting Diagrams Which organism ends up with the most DDT?*

20.0

2.0

Increasing DDT concentration (parts per million)

0.2

0.4

0.000003

Each of these sources of pollution can be a point source or a nonpoint source, depending on how the pollution enters a body of water. For example, suppose you notice a pipe gushing white sudsy water into a river. The pipe is a **point source,** a specific source of pollution that can be identified. More often, though, the source of pollution is less obvious. Pollutants may be carried along in runoff from a farm field, a street, or a construction site. The chemicals, sewage, or radioactive materials eventually flow into a lake or river or seep into groundwater and are carried far away. It's hard to trace the exact source of this pollution. A widely spread source of pollution that can't be tied to a specific point of origin is called a **nonpoint source.**

☑ *Checkpoint* Why are nonpoint sources difficult to identify?

Human Wastes

Today it seems obvious that dumping human wastes into drinking water can spread disease. But scientists have only understood this connection for the last 150 years.

Dr. Snow's Discovery Cholera is a disease caused by bacteria

 INTEGRATING HEALTH

that live in human wastes. Cholera causes people to become very dehydrated and can be fatal. In 1854, an English doctor named John Snow discovered the cause of a cholera outbreak in London. In the poorer sections of the city, people carried water home in buckets from public wells. After 500 people in one neighborhood died in just ten days, Dr. Snow traced the cholera to a well near a pipe carrying sewage. He ended the epidemic by removing the pump handle so no one could get water from that source. Dr. Snow's work showed the danger of releasing untreated sewage into bodies of water that might be used for drinking water.

Sewage in Cities As you know, today wastewater is usually treated before being released to the environment. However, while water treatment usually kills bacteria, some viruses and parasites are able to resist chlorine and other water treatment processes. Most of these organisms come from human or animal wastes that get into the water supply.

During heavy rains and floods, sanitary sewers sometimes overflow and run into storm sewers. Since the storm sewers generally lead directly into surface water, the sewage from the sanitary sewers can pollute the water. For this reason, people are often told to boil water for drinking and cooking after a flood. The boiling kills many disease-causing organisms.

Figure 12 This engraving from the late 1800s shows people in Hamburg, Germany, getting water from a cart during a cholera epidemic. The city wells were closed, and water was brought in from the countryside.

Sewage in Rural Areas Disposing of human waste is not just a problem in big cities. In rural areas, people must be careful where they locate septic tanks. If a tank is too near a stream or on a hill, wastewater can leak into the stream or flow into the area of a well downhill.

Wastes from cattle, pigs, and chickens can also be a problem in rural areas. They contribute disease-causing bacteria and other kinds of pollution to water that runs off from pastures and barnyards.

✓ *Checkpoint* *Why should drinking water and sewage be kept separate?*

Industrial Wastes

Most cities and towns in the United States have wastewater treatment systems that handle sewage effectively. For this reason, water pollution by factories and mines is a more serious problem than sewage in most areas of the country. Chemicals, smoke, and heated water are three types of industrial pollutants.

Chemicals Many factory processes, especially those for making dyes and plastics or treating metals, involve toxic chemicals and strong acids. Other toxic wastes are produced as by-products, or side effects, of manufacturing and mining. Although laws now limit and control chemical pollution, some factories still release toxic chemicals directly into nearby rivers and lakes.

Another problem is leftover wastes. In the past, many industries stored toxic wastes in barrels or other containers buried underground. Over the years, however, many of these containers rusted or broke. The chemicals leaked out, polluting both the soil and the groundwater.

Figure 13 Many lakes and rivers have been polluted by wastes from nearby industries. These environmental scientists are collecting water samples from a pond for testing.

Smoke and Exhaust Many power plants and factories burn

INTEGRATING CHEMISTRY coal or oil to fuel their processes. The engines of millions of cars, trucks, and buses burn gasoline. Every day, smoke and exhaust from these sources pour into the air, especially around large cities. When coal, oil, and gasoline are burned, molecules of the gases sulfur dioxide and nitrogen oxide are released into the atmosphere. There the sulfur and nitrogen react with water, forming sulfuric and nitric acids. The result is rain or other forms of precipitation that are more acidic than normal, called **acid rain.** When acid rain falls on lakes and ponds, the water can become so acidic that fish and other wildlife cannot survive. Acid rain also eats away the stone of buildings and statues.

Heat Pollution Think about how hot a metal slide gets on a sunny day. Imagine borrowing enough water from a swimming pool to cool the slide, and then returning the water to the pool. How would this change the swimming pool? Would you still want to jump in to cool off? The warm water would probably not be very refreshing.

Figure 14 A noisy jumble of taxis, cars, and buses crowds a city street. *Relating Cause and Effect How are these vehicles related to water pollution?*

Much of the water in factories is used to cool machinery or metal objects. Even if it contains no chemicals, the warm water alone can act as a pollutant. Many water organisms can live in only a narrow range of temperatures. Warm water released by a factory into a nearby river or pond raises the temperature of the water, sometimes enough to harm the living things there.

Agricultural Chemicals

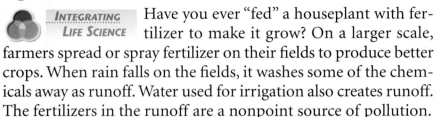

INTEGRATING LIFE SCIENCE Have you ever "fed" a houseplant with fertilizer to make it grow? On a larger scale, farmers spread or spray fertilizer on their fields to produce better crops. When rain falls on the fields, it washes some of the chemicals away as runoff. Water used for irrigation also creates runoff. The fertilizers in the runoff are a nonpoint source of pollution.

The rich supply of nutrients from fertilizers encourages the growth of plants and algae in and around nearby bodies of water. As you learned in Chapter 11, ponds and lakes naturally change over time due to the process of eutrophication. As more plants grow in the water, dead plant material piles up on the bottom, making the water shallower and warmer. As the plant matter decays, the amount of oxygen in the water decreases. With the addition of fertilizers, this natural process speeds up. A thick, soupy scum of algae forms on top of the water. The scum blocks the sunlight and chokes the flow of water, changing the living conditions for other organisms.

Runoff and irrigation water also carry away other pollutants from farm fields. **Pesticides** are chemicals intended to kill insects and other organisms that damage crops. Pesticides may be sprayed on crops and then run off. Sometimes they are sprayed directly on ponds to kill mosquitoes. But at the same time, these chemicals can harm other insects or the animals that eat them.

✓ *Checkpoint* How can chemicals used in agriculture reach streams, ponds, and lakes?

Runoff from Roads

Have you ever noticed an oily sheen on a puddle in a parking lot after a rain shower? The sheen was probably caused by gasoline and motor oil that leaked from cars. When it rains, these oily substances are washed off along with the runoff. During cold winter weather, runoff also picks up the salt that is sprinkled on roads and sidewalks to melt ice. This runoff is a nonpoint source of pollution. Gasoline, oil, and salt pollute rivers and lakes that the runoff enters. These substances can also seep down into groundwater and pollute wells or even an entire aquifer.

Figure 15 A thick layer of red algae tints a pond the color of tomato soup. *Inferring What might be the cause of the algae growth in this pond?*

Cleaning Up Polluted Water

Many pollutants are eventually removed from freshwater bodies through natural cleaning processes. **Living things in lakes, streams, and wetlands filter out and break down waste materials.** For example, plant roots filter larger particles from the water. Some plants, such as water hyacinths and duckweed, can absorb metals and chemicals. And just as certain bacteria are used in purifying wastewater, some are also useful in cleaning up toxic chemicals. Bacteria that consume oil have been used to help clean up oil spills. Waste-eating bacteria may also prove to be useful in breaking down toxic chemicals in rivers and lakes.

Pollution clean-up programs can be based on such natural treatment processes. For example, both natural and artificial wetlands are being used to clean up water pollution. Wetlands have been built near coal mines to treat acidic mining runoff before it returns to the environment.

Not only living things can help clean up polluted water. Passing through the sand or rock of an aquifer naturally filters and purifies groundwater. But natural filtering cannot remove or destroy many pollutants, such as metals or manufactured chemicals. Cleaning up this kind of pollution in groundwater is very difficult. One method involves pumping polluted groundwater to the surface, sending it through a treatment plant, and returning it to a nearby lake.

Figure 16 These purple water hyacinths can be an attractive part of a cleanup program. The plants absorb certain metals and chemicals from polluted water.

Preventing Pollution

Despite the successes in cleaning up some water pollution, most pollutants are very difficult to remove. It is often easier to avoid causing the pollution in the first place. In the late 1960s, as

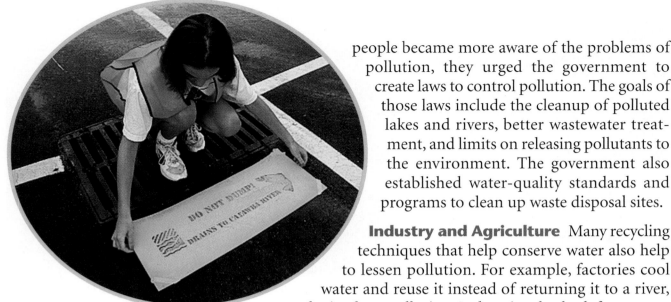

Figure 17 One way you can help prevent water pollution is to educate others about its causes. This student is stenciling a storm drain to remind people of its connection to a nearby river.

people became more aware of the problems of pollution, they urged the government to create laws to control pollution. The goals of those laws include the cleanup of polluted lakes and rivers, better wastewater treatment, and limits on releasing pollutants to the environment. The government also established water-quality standards and programs to clean up waste disposal sites.

Industry and Agriculture Many recycling techniques that help conserve water also help to lessen pollution. For example, factories cool water and reuse it instead of returning it to a river, reducing heat pollution. Industries also look for ways to replace toxic materials with less harmful ones. Printing inks, for instance, can be made with water instead of chemical solvents.

Farmers are trying to reduce the problem of runoff from pastures and barnyards. Some collect and reuse this water for irrigation. Other farmers plant fields of coarse grasses that filter out pollutants before the water reaches a river or pond.

What Can You Do? You can also help keep pollutants from entering the environment. Dispose of toxic substances carefully. For example, chemicals like paint and motor oil should never be poured down the drain, but instead be taken to sites that collect hazardous waste. Avoid overfertilizing lawns or gardens. Form a group of students to educate others in your community about the causes and effects of freshwater pollution. Because many kinds of water pollution are so difficult to clean up, the most important place to stop pollution is at its source.

Section 3 Review

1. List four sources of water pollution.
2. How can fertilizers cause water pollution?
3. Explain why people are often instructed to boil drinking water after a flood.
4. **Thinking Critically Making Judgments** To prevent water pollution, a factory proposes pumping its wastes into the ground instead of into a river. Would you support this change? Why or why not?

Check Your Progress
CHAPTER PROJECT
At this point, you should be ready to assemble your model treatment system. Does the system include at least two treatment steps? Be sure to ask an adult to help you cut materials or assemble them if necessary. (Hint: Test your treatment setup for leaks using clean tap water.)

INTEGRATING PHYSICS

SECTION 4 Water as an Energy Resource

DISCOVER •••••••••••••••••••••••••••••••••••• ACTIVITY ••••

Can Water Do Work?

1. Spread out a large plastic trash bag on the ground. On top of the bag, place several cylindrical objects such as corks, spools, marbles, balls, and empty cans.

2. Fill a plant sprayer with water. Then turn the nozzle to produce a fine mist of water. Try to move the objects with the spray of water. **CAUTION:** *Be careful of slippery wet floors if you are doing this activity indoors.*

3. Now turn the sprayer nozzle to produce a narrower stream of water. Try again to move the objects. Be sure to wipe up any spilled water when you are done.

Think It Over

Observing How does changing the nozzle opening affect the stream of water? At which setting did the objects move more easily? Why?

Picture a curving wall of concrete swooping up nearly 170 meters—taller than a 40-story building. On one side of the wall is a deep reservoir. On the other side, only a narrow river trickles between rocky canyon walls. This is Grand Coulee Dam on the Columbia River in Washington. Completed in 1942, it is still one of the largest dams in the world. Behind Grand Coulee, the water in the reservoir pushes on the concrete dam. The dam's floodgates control that awesome energy. When the gates open to release the water, the water's energy is transformed into enough electricity to light thousands of homes and businesses.

For centuries, people have used the energy of moving water to turn water wheels and run machinery. Today that energy is also a source of electrical power in many parts of the world.

Power from Moving Water

Have you ever seen a fast-moving river propel a kayaker along? If so, you know how much energy moving water can have. It can move boats, carve out canyons, and sweep away cars in a flood. The energy that sends the kayak through the rapids is kinetic

GUIDE FOR READING

◆ How does moving water produce electricity?

◆ In what ways is hydroelectric power a good source of energy?

Reading Tip Before you read the section, preview *Exploring a Hydroelectric Power Plant.* Write a list of questions you have about hydroelectric power.

Making a Water Wheel

In this activity you will see how the kinetic energy of water can do work.

1. Put on your goggles.

2. ✂ Cut an aluminum pie plate into four squares about 5 cm on a side. **CAUTION:** *Be careful not to cut yourself on the sharp edges of the pie plate.*

3. Push the sides of the aluminum squares into a foam ball as shown. Insert two toothpicks into the sides of the ball.

4. Rest the toothpicks on top of your fingers and place the blades under a stream of slowly running water.

Developing Hypotheses How would increasing the volume of water affect the speed of the water wheel? Test your hypothesis. Describe what happens to the speed of the water wheel.

energy. **Kinetic energy** is the form of energy that an object has when it is moving.

Energy can change from one form to another. If the water's movement is stopped, all of its energy becomes potential energy. **Potential energy** is energy that is stored and waiting to be used. To think about potential energy in another way, imagine that you're holding a baseball bat at the top of your swing. The bat at that point has potential energy. As you swing at a ball, the bat's energy becomes kinetic energy. If you hit the ball, the energy is transferred again, becoming the kinetic energy of the ball.

Hydroelectric power is electricity produced by the kinetic energy of water moving over a waterfall or a dam. To generate hydroelectric power (or "hydropower"), engineers build a dam across a river. Water backs up behind the dam, floods the valley, and creates a reservoir. Water stored behind a dam has potential energy, which is changed to kinetic energy when the water is released. **Hydroelectric power plants capture the kinetic energy of moving water and change it into electrical energy.**

How is the kinetic energy of moving water changed into the energy that lights your house and runs your computer? Follow the path of the water in *Exploring a Hydroelectric Power Plant* on the next page to see how these energy changes take place.

☑ *Checkpoint* *What type of energy does a diver have while standing at the edge of a diving board?*

The Impact of Dams

In some ways, hydroelectric power seems like an ideal way to produce electricity. **Hydroelectric power is clean, safe, and efficient. Although building a dam is expensive, the water is free and is naturally renewed by the water cycle.** Unlike power plants that burn coal or oil, hydroelectric plants do not contribute to air pollution. In the United States, hydroelectric power accounts for about 8 or 9 percent of electricity produced, while worldwide it generates about 20 percent. Some countries, such as Norway and Brazil, produce almost all their electrical energy through hydropower.

Hydroelectric plants do have limitations, however. Only certain locations are suitable for building a dam. A fast-moving river is necessary, as is an area that can be flooded to create a reservoir.

Dams and the Environment Dams affect all living things in the area around them. Flooding the land behind a dam can destroy wildlife habitats as well as farms and towns. What was once a fast-moving river becomes the still, deep waters of a reservoir. Some organisms

INTEGRATING LIFE SCIENCE

EXPLORING *a Hydroelectric Power Plant*

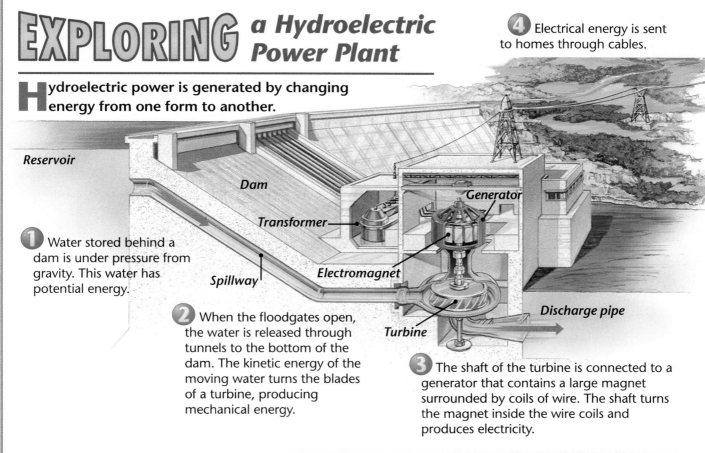

Hydroelectric power is generated by changing energy from one form to another.

4 Electrical energy is sent to homes through cables.

Reservoir

Dam

Transformer

Generator

Electromagnet

Spillway

Turbine

Discharge pipe

1 Water stored behind a dam is under pressure from gravity. This water has potential energy.

2 When the floodgates open, the water is released through tunnels to the bottom of the dam. The kinetic energy of the moving water turns the blades of a turbine, producing mechanical energy.

3 The shaft of the turbine is connected to a generator that contains a large magnet surrounded by coils of wire. The shaft turns the magnet inside the wire coils and produces electricity.

Figure 18 This photograph shows the Theodore Roosevelt Dam in Arizona. *Interpreting Photographs What natural feature of the river made this a good location to build a dam?*

cannot survive the change. In addition, the dam is a barrier across the river. It may prevent fish from traveling to the parts of a river where they usually lay their eggs and young fish are hatched. Dams like Grand Coulee on the Columbia River, for instance, have greatly reduced the population of salmon in the river.

As a river slows down, it deposits some of the sediments it carries. These deposits can build up behind a dam instead of being carried downstream to enrich the flood plain near the river's mouth. Since the Aswan Dam was built in Egypt, for example, farmlands near the mouth of the Nile River no longer receive the rich load of nutrients the river once brought.

Displaced by a Dam How would you feel if you discovered that your riverside home would soon be dozens of meters under the water of a lake? People whose homes or farms are located

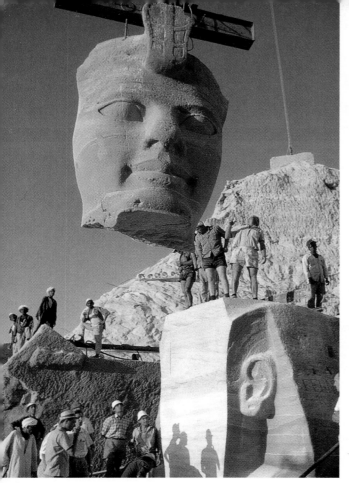

Figure 19 Building the Aswan Dam meant flooding the valley that housed these statues of ancient Egyptian rulers. Piece by piece, workers carefully dismantled the great monuments and moved them to higher ground.

where a dam's reservoir is planned have had to face this issue. Large dams flood hundreds or thousands of square kilometers, covering towns and valleys with water. When the Aswan High Dam was built on the Nile, about 80,000 people had to relocate. The ancient monuments of Abu Simbel had to be moved as the water in Lake Nasser rose higher and higher.

One of the largest dams ever built is now under construction on the Yangzi River in China. The Three Gorges Dam, due to be completed in 2009, could displace more than 1.5 million people.

Benefits of Dams For countries that want to build up their industries, hydroelectric power often seems the best way to provide the electricity they need. Water power is the least expensive and least polluting large-scale energy source. Besides electricity, dams can supply water for irrigation and help in flood control.

In some places, people have suggested building small dams to supply power to a local area. Smaller dams uproot fewer people and do less harm to the environment, while still providing energy for a region to grow. However, since dams are expensive to build, small dams may not produce enough power to be worthwhile. Large dams, on the other hand, produce great amounts of power, but they also have a major effect on the land around them.

 Section 4 Review

1. How does a hydroelectric plant use moving water to generate electric power?
2. Name two advantages of hydroelectric power.
3. Give one positive example and one negative example of how building a dam could affect wildlife in the area.
4. **Thinking Critically** **Problem Solving** Suppose you were assigned to choose a site to build a new hydroelectric plant. What features would you look for to find a good site? Be sure to consider the impact on living things as well as the physical characteristics of the site.

Check Your Progress   **CHAPTER PROJECT**
Now you are ready to test your model system, using the dirty water sample your teacher has provided. Does your treatment unit clean up the water? Measure how much of the original one liter of water is recovered. Based on your results, decide whether you need to redesign any part of your treatment system. (*Hint:* To modify your system, consider changing materials as well as adding more steps.)

SECTION 1 — Water to Drink

Key Ideas
- Sources of drinking water include rivers, lakes, reservoirs, and groundwater.
- Many communities maintain public water supplies to collect, treat, and distribute water to residents. Some homes have private wells.
- Most drinking water is treated to ensure that it is safe and appealing to drink.
- Pumps and gravity are used to increase water pressure and move water through a system of pipes.
- Wastewater and sewage are treated to prevent contamination of drinking water.

Key Terms
water quality	filtration	sludge
pH	flocs	septic tank
hardness	coagulation	leach field
concentration	sewage	

SECTION 2 — Balancing Water Needs

Key Ideas
- Water is scarce in many places, leading to competition for limited supplies.
- Water shortage can occur when there is too little water or too much demand in an area.
- Industries can conserve water by reducing water use, recycling water, and reusing water.
- Desalination of ocean water and icebergs are two possible future sources of fresh water.

Key Terms
drought   conservation   desalination

SECTION 3 — Freshwater Pollution

Key Ideas
- Sources of water pollution include human and animal wastes, industrial and agricultural chemicals, and runoff from roads.
- Acid rain is caused by sulfur and nitrogen from smokestacks and car exhausts.

Key Terms
water pollution	nonpoint source	pesticide
point source	acid rain	

SECTION 4 — Water As an Energy Resource

INTEGRATING PHYSICS

Key Ideas
- Hydroelectric power plants capture the kinetic energy of moving water and change it into electrical energy.

Key Terms
kinetic energy	hydroelectric power
potential energy	

Organizing Information

Concept Map Copy the concept map about freshwater pollution onto a separate sheet of paper. Complete it and add a title.

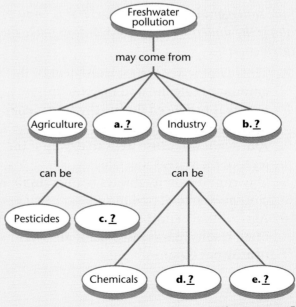

Reviewing Content

 For more review of key concepts, see the Interactive Student Tutorial CD-ROM.

Multiple Choice
Choose the letter of the best answer.

1. Chlorine is added during water treatment in order to
   a. make particles form flocs.
   b. kill disease-causing organisms.
   c. improve the taste of the water.
   d. remove objects such as fish and trash.
2. Primary treatment of wastewater typically involves
   a. adding chlorine.
   b. filtering out solids.
   c. adding sludge.
   d. adding waste-eating bacteria.
3. One process used to obtain fresh water from salt water is
   a. coagulation.   b. filtration.
   c. recharge.   d. desalination.
4. The main source of acid precipitation is
   a. smoke from coal-burning factories.
   b. pesticides sprayed in the air.
   c. runoff from farm fields.
   d. toxic chemicals buried underground.
5. Water flowing swiftly possesses
   a. mechanical energy. b. electrical energy.
   c. potential energy.   d. kinetic energy.

True or False
If the statement is true, write true. If it is false, change the underlined word or words to make the statement true.

6. The <u>pH</u> of water is a measurement of the amount of calcium and magnesium.
7. Sludge is produced during the treatment of <u>drinking water</u>.
8. A drought can cause wells to dry up if the level of the water table <u>falls</u>.
9. Oily runoff from highways is an example of a <u>point</u> source of pollution.
10. Agricultural runoff containing <u>pesticides</u> often results in increased plant growth in nearby ponds and streams.

Checking Concepts

11. Describe one possible path of drinking water from its source to a home.
12. Explain how a septic system works.
13. Why are water rights an important issue in dry areas?
14. Describe one way that farmers can reduce the amount of water lost during irrigation.
15. Why isn't most of the water on Earth's surface available for people to use?
16. Explain how low levels of a pollutant in a stream can have harmful effects on wildlife in and around the stream.
17. How does acid rain form?
18. How might building a dam affect people living nearby?
19. **Writing to Learn** You have been hired as a public relations specialist for the city water department. Your first assignment is to prepare a brief fact sheet for city residents about the importance of conserving water. The fact sheet should also include some simple suggestions of ways to conserve water at home.

Thinking Critically

20. **Relating Cause and Effect** How can increased demand for water cause the ground above an aquifer to collapse?
21. **Comparing and Contrasting** How is the process of desalination similar to the water cycle? How is it different?
22. **Problem Solving** Explain why finding the source of water pollution can be difficult.
23. **Making Judgments** Do you think that the benefits of hydroelectric power outweigh the disadvantages? Give reasons to support your answer.

Applying Skills

A family had their drinking-water well tested to check the water quality. The test results are shown in the table below. Use the data in the table to answer Questions 24–27.

Drinking Water Sample Test Results

Lead	0.2 parts per million
Copper	0.006 parts per million
pH	5.0
Coliform count	5 out of 5 samples positive

24. **Inferring** The family suspects that their septic tank is polluting the well. What evidence exists to support this conclusion?
25. **Designing Experiments** What might be the source of the lead in the water? How could you test your answer?
26. **Developing Hypotheses** How might the low pH of the water be related to the lead contamination?

27. **Predicting** The family noticed that their water does not form suds well when mixed with soap. Predict what other substances may be present in high levels in the water.

Performance CHAPTER PROJECT **Assessment**

Present Your Project It's time to put your treatment system to the test! Use your system to clean up the dirty water sample. Measure the volume of water recovered by your system. How can you evaluate your results?

Reflect and Record In your journal, reflect on what you have learned as you built your water treatment system. Explain how the different materials used in your classmates' projects affected their results. How could you improve your process to recover more water or make the water cleaner? What else would you want to know about the treated water before you would consider it drinkable?

Test Preparation

Use these questions to prepare for standardized tests.

A family conducted a survey of their current water use. Study the bar graph below, which shows their average use for one day. Then answer Questions 28–31.

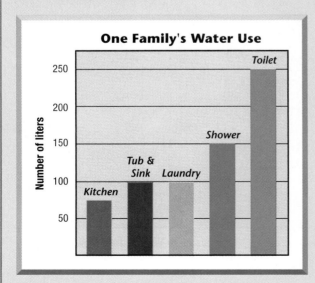

One Family's Water Use

28. Which of the categories represents the family's largest water use?
    a. laundry   **b.** shower
    c. kitchen   **d.** toilet
29. If everyone in the family agreed to take 5-minute showers instead of 10-minute showers, about how many liters of water would be saved each day?
    a. 5   **b.** 11   **c.** 75   **d.** 150
30. The family found that they used about 675 liters of water per day on average. About what percentage of this is used for the laundry?
    a. 10   **b.** 15   **c.** 37   **d.** 100
31. The family decided to try to reduce their water use. Which of the following measures could help them save water?
    a. run washing machines only when full
    b. repair leaky faucets
    c. turn off the tap when brushing their teeth
    d. all of the above

  WEB ACTIVITY

www.phschool.com

Integrating Space Science

Protecting a Shoreline

The world's oceans are always in motion. Waves, tides, and currents each move Earth's waters in different ways. In this chapter you will study these movements and their power to change the land. You will build your own model of a shoreline with a lighthouse and use the model to demonstrate how some ocean motions can affect the land along the coast.

Your Goal To design and build a model ocean beach and test possible methods for preventing shoreline erosion.

To complete this project successfully, you must
- ◆ build a model beach and use it to demonstrate the effects of wave erosion
- ◆ test methods of protecting the lighthouse from damage
- ◆ follow the safety guidelines outlined in Appendix A

Get Started Begin now by previewing Figure 4 on page 432. Start thinking about how you will build a model of an ocean beach like the one in the diagram. Brainstorm a list of materials that you could use to build your model.

Check Your Progress You'll be working on this project as you study this chapter. To keep your project on track, look for Check Your Progress boxes at the following points.

Section 1 Review, page 433: Design your model beach.
Section 2 Review, page 438: Construct your model and test it.
Section 4 Review, page 452: Improve your model and test it again.

Present Your Project At the end of the chapter (page 455), you will show how well your design keeps the lighthouse from toppling into the surf.

SECTION 4 Currents and Climate

Discover Which Is More Dense?
Sharpen Your Skills Drawing Conclusions
Real-World Lab Modeling Ocean Currents

Waves crash against the rocky Maine coast. Sweeping its beacon of light across the water, the Portland Head Lighthouse warns ships of the treacherous rocks.

SECTION
1 Wave Action

How Do Waves Change a Beach?

1. In one end of an aluminum pan, build a "beach" of sand and pebbles. Put a book under that end of the pan to raise it about 5 centimeters.

2. Pour water slowly into the other end of the pan until it covers the edge of the sand, just as water touches the edge of a beach.

3. Place a wooden tongue depressor in the water. Move it back and forth gently in a regular rhythm to make waves in the pan. Continue for about 2 minutes.

4. Once the water has stopped moving, observe what has happened to the beach. Wash your hands when you are finished with this activity.

Think It Over

Observing How has the motion of the water changed the edge of the beach?

GUIDE FOR READING

◆ How does a wave form?

◆ How do waves change near the shore?

◆ How do waves affect beaches and coastlines?

Reading Tip Before you read, preview the diagrams and photographs in the section to see different types of wave action. Make a list of questions you have about wave motion.

Stretched flat on his surfboard, the surfer paddles out into the clear turquoise water. The surfboard bobs up and down as he awaits the perfect surfing wave. After a few minutes, he spots the telltale signs in an approaching wave. At the last possible moment before the wave crashes over him, the surfer jumps into a standing position. He balances skillfully as the energy of the wave sends the surfboard skimming down the smooth front of the curling wave.

If you've ever seen a video of surfers "catching a wave" along a Pacific beach, you know that they make this difficult sport look almost easy. But even experienced surfers can seldom predict when the next good wave will roll into shore. As you will read in this section, many different forces influence the size, shape, and timing of waves.

How Waves Form

When you watch the surfer's wave crash onto the beach, you are seeing the last step in the process of the wave's development. The process begins with wind. Without the energy of wind, the surface of the ocean would be as smooth as a mirror. **Most waves form when winds blowing across the water's surface transmit their energy to the water.** A **wave** is the movement of energy through a body of water.

Waves start in the open ocean. The size of the wave depends on the strength of the wind and on the length of time it blows. A gentle breeze creates small ripples on the surface of the water. Stronger winds create larger waves.

The size of the wave also depends on the distance over which the wind blows. Winds blowing across longer distances build up bigger waves. In the wide Pacific Ocean, a wave might travel a third of the way around the world before reaching the California coast.

Although waves may appear to carry water toward shore, the water does not actually move forward in deep water. If it did, ocean water would eventually pile up on the coasts of every continent! The energy of the wave moves toward shore, but the water itself remains where it was. You can test this for yourself by floating a piece of wood or a cork in a bowl of water. Use a spoon to make a wave in the bowl. As the wave passes, the object lurches forward a little, then bobs backward. It ends up in almost the same spot where it started.

Figure 1 A surfer cruises along the smooth front of this cresting wave. The wave's energy moves along, but the water mostly stays where it is. *Applying Concepts In which direction is the energy of this wave moving?*

Wave Motion

This activity shows how waves formed at the surface affect deeper water.

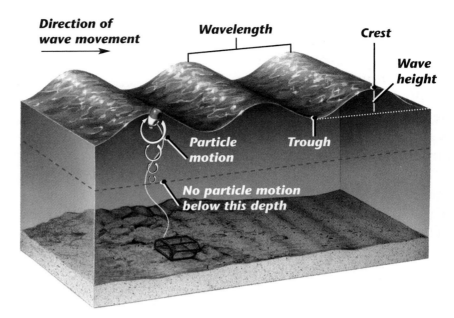

Figure 2 As a wave passes by, the water particles move in a circular motion. The buoy on the surface swings down into the trough of one wave, then back up to the crest of the next wave. Below the surface, the water particles move in smaller circles. At a depth equal to about one half the wavelength, the water particles are not affected by the surface wave.

1. Fill an aquarium about three-quarters full of water.

2. Tie enough metal washers to a cork so that the cork floats about 3 cm from the bottom of the tank.

3. Repeat Step 2 with more corks so that they float 9 cm from the bottom, 15 cm from the bottom, and so on until the last cork floats on the surface.

4. Make small, steady waves in the tank by moving your hand up and down in the water. Note what happens to each cork.

5. Repeat Step 4, increasing the height of the waves by moving your hand faster.

Observing How does increasing the wave height affect the motion of each cork?

Figure 2 shows what happens to the water as a wave travels along. As the wave passes, water particles move in a circular path. They swing forward and down with the energy of the wave, then back up to their original position.

Notice that the deeper water particles in Figure 2 move in smaller circles than those near the surface. The wind affects the water at the surface more than the deep water. Below a certain depth, the water does not move at all as the wave passes. If you were inside a submarine in deep water, you would not be able to tell whether the water above you was rough or smooth.

Describing Waves

If you ask a sailor to describe a wave, you might hear some unfamiliar terms. To a sailor, "a following sea" refers to waves traveling in the same direction as the boat. "Combers" are large, cresting waves. And "spindrift" is ocean spray torn by the wind from the surface of the waves.

Scientists have their own vocabulary of terms to describe the size and strength of waves. The name for the highest part of a wave is the **crest.** The horizontal distance between crests is the **wavelength.** Long, rolling waves with lots of space between crests have long wavelengths. Short, choppy waves have shorter wavelengths. Waves are also measured by their **frequency,** the number of waves that pass a point in a certain amount of time.

The name for the lowest part of a wave is the **trough.** The vertical distance from the crest to the trough is the **wave height.** The energy and strength of a wave depend mainly on its wave height. In the open ocean, most waves are between 2 and 5 meters high. During storms, the waves can grow much higher and more powerful.

☑ *Checkpoint* *Do waves that are close together have a longer or shorter wavelength than waves that are far apart?*

How Waves Change Near Shore

In deep water, waves usually travel as long, low waves called swells. As the waves approach the shore, the water becomes shallower. Follow the waves in Figure 3 as they enter the shallow water. The bottoms of the waves begin to touch the sloping ocean floor. Friction between the ocean floor and the water causes the waves to slow down. As the speed of the waves decrease, their shapes change. **Near shore, the wave height increases and the wavelength decreases.** When the wave reaches a certain height, the crest of the wave topples. The wave breaks onto the shore, forming surf.

At first, the energy of the breaking wave, or breaker, causes the water to surge up the beach. But the force of gravity pulling down on the rising water soon causes it to lose its energy. The water that moves up the beach flows back into the sea. Have you ever stood at the water's edge and felt the pull of the water rushing back out to the ocean? This pull, often called an undertow, carries shells, seaweed, and sand away from the beach. A strong undertow can be dangerous to swimmers.

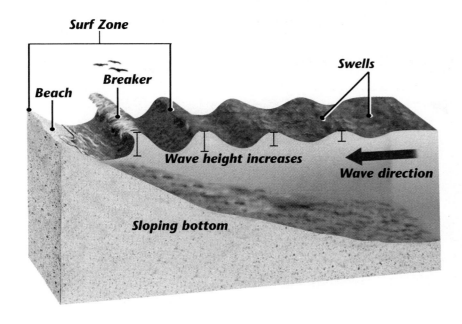

Figure 3 Friction with the ocean floor causes waves to slow down in the shallow water near shore. The wave height increases until the waves break, forming surf. *Interpreting Diagrams What happens to the wavelength as the waves approach shore?*

How Waves Affect the Shore

What happens on shore as waves pound the beach? The diagram in Figure 4 shows some of their effects. Since wave direction at sea is determined by the wind, waves usually roll toward shore at an angle. But as they touch bottom, the shallower water slows the shoreward side of the wave first. The rows of waves gradually turn and become more nearly parallel to the shore.

Longshore Drift As the waves come into shore, water washes up the beach at an angle, carrying sand grains with it. The water and sand then run straight back down the beach. This movement of sand along the beach is called **longshore drift.** As the waves slow down, they deposit the sand they are carrying on the shallow, underwater slope in a long ridge called a **sandbar.**

Rip Currents As a sandbar grows, it can trap the water flowing along the shore. In some places, water breaks through the sandbar and begins to flow back down the sloping ocean bottom. This process creates a **rip current,** a rush of water that flows rapidly back to sea through a narrow opening. Rip currents can carry a swimmer out into deep water. Because rip currents are narrow, a strong swimmer can usually escape by swimming across the current, parallel to the beach.

☑ *Checkpoint* In what direction does a rip current pull a swimmer?

Figure 4 Waves approach the shore at an angle. This results in a gradual movement of sand along the beach. *Interpreting Diagrams In which direction is longshore drift moving the sand along this beach?*

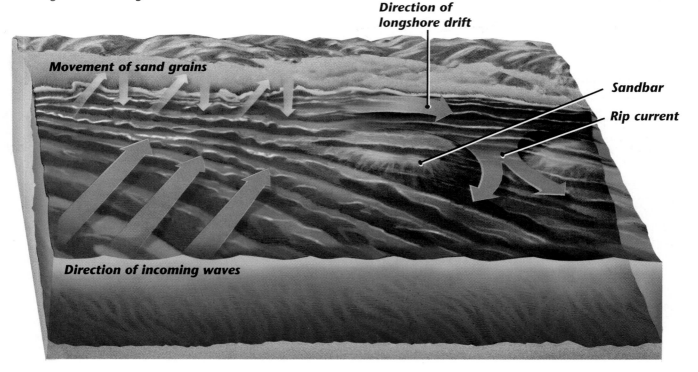

Direction of longshore drift

Movement of sand grains

Sandbar

Rip current

Direction of incoming waves

Figure 5 "The Breaking Wave off Kanagawa" is a wood-block print by the Japanese artist Hokusai.

Visual Arts
CONNECTION

The Japanese artist Hokusai (1760–1849) is well known for his land and ocean scenes. His print at the left shows a cresting wave with the snow-capped Mt. Fuji in the background.

As a teenager, Hokusai was apprenticed to a wood-block engraver. A wood-block print is made by engraving a separate block of wood for each color ink used in the picture. How many blocks do you think Hokusai needed for this print?

In Your Journal

Imagine you are writing a catalog for a museum exhibit of ocean scenes. Write a brief description of Hokusai's print for the catalog.

Reducing Beach Erosion

Many people like to live near the ocean. But over time, erosion can wear away the beach. This threatens the homes and other buildings. To avoid losing their property, people look for ways to reduce the effect of erosion.

One method of reducing erosion along a stretch of beach is to build a wall of rocks or concrete, called a **groin,** outward from the beach. The sand carried by the water piles up against the groins instead of moving along the shore. However, the groins increase the amount of erosion farther down the beach.

Section 1 Review

1. Describe how ocean waves form.
2. How do wavelength and wave height change as a wave enters shallow water?
3. How do water particles move within a wave?
4. **Thinking Critically** **Relating Cause and Effect** Explain how building a groin affects the beach on each side of the groin.

Check Your Progress

CHAPTER PROJECT

You are ready to design your model ocean beach. Sketch your design. Be sure to consider what materials you will use for your shoreline and lighthouse. How will you make waves? When your design is finished, you are ready to gather your materials and construct your model. (*Hint:* Design your model, including the lighthouse, to scale.)

SECTION 2 Tides

DISCOVER ••••••••••••••••••••••••••••••••••••• ACTIVITY

When Is High Tide?

Twice a day, the ocean rises and falls on the New England coast. These daily changes in water level are called tides. The map shows the times of the two high tides in each city on a particular day.

1. Calculate the length of time between the two high tides for each city. Remember to consider both hours and minutes.

2. Look at the times of the high tides in Bar Harbor and in Portsmouth. Is there a pattern in the times of the high tides?

Think It Over

Predicting Notice that the high tides for Portland are not shown. Based on the times of the other high tides on the map, predict when the high tides will occur in Portland.

GUIDE FOR READING

◆ What causes tides?

◆ How are tides a source of energy?

Reading Tip As you read, use the headings to make an outline about tides.

You're standing on a riverbank in the town of Saint John, Canada. In the distance there's a loud roaring sound, like a train approaching. Suddenly a wall of water twice your height thunders past. The surge of water rushes up the river channel so fast that it almost looks as if the river is flowing backward!

This thundering wall of water is an everyday event at Saint John. The town is located where the Saint John River enters the Bay of Fundy, an arm of the Atlantic Ocean. The Bay of Fundy is famous for its dramatic daily tides. When the tide comes in, fishing boats float on the water near the piers. But once the tide goes out, so much water flows back to sea that the boats are stranded on the muddy harbor bottom.

Figure 6 The Bay of Fundy in Canada is noted for its great differences in water level at high and low tide. **A.** Near the mouth of the bay, boats float in the Saint John River at high tide. **B.** At low tide, the boats are grounded.

What Causes Tides?

The daily rise and fall of Earth's waters on its coastlines are called **tides.** As the tide comes in, the level of the water on the beach rises gradually. When the water reaches its highest point, it is high tide. Then the tide goes out, flowing back toward the sea. When the water reaches its lowest point, it is low tide. Unlike the surface waves you read about in Section 1, tides happen regularly no matter how the wind blows. Tides occur in all bodies of water, but they are most noticeable in the ocean and large lakes.

Tides are caused by the interaction of Earth, the moon, and the sun. How can distant objects like the moon and sun influence water on Earth? The answer is gravity. Gravity is the force exerted by an object that pulls other objects toward it. Gravity keeps you and everything around you on Earth's surface. As the distance between objects increases, however, gravity's pull grows weaker.

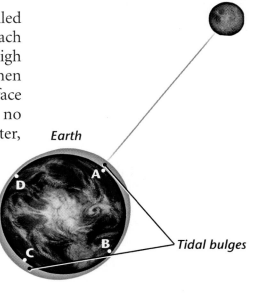

Figure 7 shows the effect of the moon's gravity on the water on Earth's surface. The moon pulls on the water on the side closest to it (point A) more strongly than it pulls on the center of the Earth. This pull creates a bulge of water, called a tidal bulge, on the side of Earth facing the moon. The water at point C is pulled toward the moon less strongly than is Earth as a whole. This water is "left behind," forming a second bulge.

Figure 7 The moon's pull on Earth's water causes tidal bulges to form on the side closest to the moon and the side farthest from the moon. *Comparing and Contrasting Where is the level of the water higher, at point C or point D?*

In the places in Figure 7 where there are tidal bulges (points A and C), high tide is occurring along the coastlines. In the places between the bulges (points B and D), low tide is occurring. As Earth rotates, different places on the planet's surface pass through the areas of the tidal bulges and experience the change in water levels.

✓ *Checkpoint* *What force causes the tides to occur on Earth's surface?*

The Daily Tide Cycle

As Earth turns completely around once each day, people on or near the shore observe the rise and fall of the tides as they reach the area of each tidal bulge. The high tides occur about 12 hours and 25 minutes apart in each location. As Earth rotates, easternmost points pass through the area of the tidal bulge before points farther to the west. Therefore, high tide occurs later the farther west you go along a coastline.

In some places, the two high tides and two low tides are easy to observe each day. But in other places, the range between the water levels is less dramatic. One set of tides may even be so minimal that there appears to be only one high tide and one low tide per day. This situation is common along the coasts of Texas and western Florida, due to the gradual slope of the ocean floor in the Gulf of Mexico.

Several factors affect the height of the tide in any particular location. For example, high tide on a certain day in southern California is not necessarily the same height as high tide farther up the Pacific coast in Oregon. Landforms such as capes, peninsulas, and islands interrupt the water's movements. A basin at the mouth of a river can also increase the range of tides. As you read in Chapter 11, the speed and depth of moving water increases when it flows into a narrower channel. That is what causes the dramatic tides in the mouth of the Saint John River you read about earlier.

☑ *Checkpoint* *Describe one factor that affects the height of the tides in a particular area.*

The Monthly Tide Cycle

Even though the sun is 150 million kilometers from Earth, it is so massive that its gravity also affects the tides. The sun pulls the water on Earth's surface toward it. In Figure 8 on the facing page, you can follow the positions of the Earth, moon, and sun at different times during a month. Notice that sometimes the moon and sun pull together on Earth's waters. At other times, they pull in different directions. Changes in the positions of Earth, the moon, and the sun affect the height of the tides during a month.

Spring Tides Twice a month, at the new moon and the full moon, the sun and moon are lined up. Their combined gravitational pull produces the greatest range between high and low tide, called a **spring tide.** These tides get their name not because they occur during the spring season, but from an Old English word, *springen,* which means "to jump."

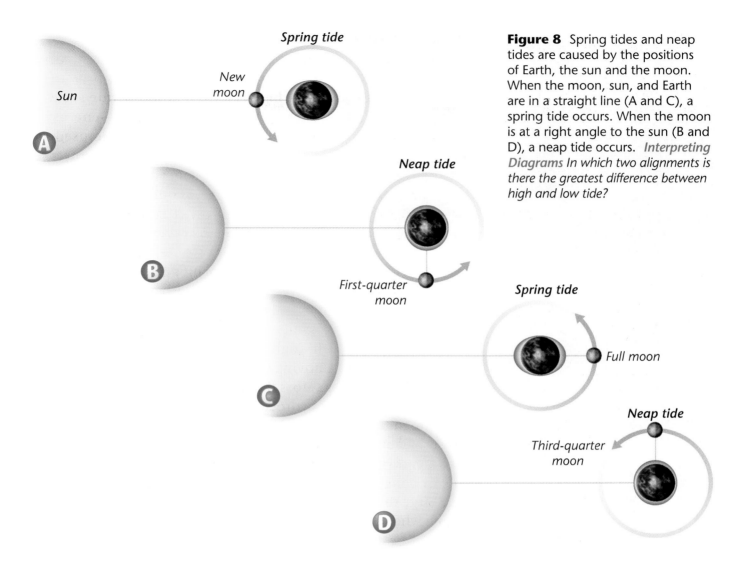

Figure 8 Spring tides and neap tides are caused by the positions of Earth, the sun and the moon. When the moon, sun, and Earth are in a straight line (A and C), a spring tide occurs. When the moon is at a right angle to the sun (B and D), a neap tide occurs. *Interpreting Diagrams In which two alignments is there the greatest difference between high and low tide?*

Labels in figure: Spring tide, Sun, New moon, A, Neap tide, B, First-quarter moon, Spring tide, C, Full moon, Neap tide, Third-quarter moon, D

Neap Tides In between spring tides, at the first and third quarters of the moon, the sun and moon pull at right angles to each other. This line-up produces a **neap tide,** a tide with the least difference between low and high tide. During a neap tide, the sun's gravity pulls some of the water away from the tidal bulge facing the moon. This acts to "even out" the water level over Earth's surface, reducing the difference between high and low tides.

Monthly Tide Tables Despite the complex factors affecting the tides, scientists can predict tides quite accurately for various locations. They combine knowledge of the movements of the moon and Earth with information about the shape of the coastline and other local conditions. If you live near the coast, your local newspaper probably publishes a tide table. Knowing the times and heights of tides is important to sailors, marine scientists, people who fish, and others who live along a coast.

Energy From Tides

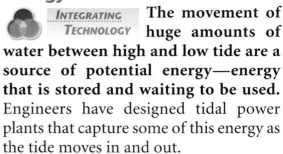 **The movement of huge amounts of water between high and low tide are a source of potential energy—energy that is stored and waiting to be used.** Engineers have designed tidal power plants that capture some of this energy as the tide moves in and out.

The first large-scale tidal power plant was built in 1967 on the Rance River in northwestern France. As high tide swirls up the river, the plant's gates open so that the water flows into a basin. As the tide retreats, the gates shut to trap the water. Gravity pulls the water back to sea through tunnels. The energy of the water moving through the tunnels powers generators that produce electricity, just as in a hydroelectric dam on a river.

Figure 9 Pulled by the tide, water rushes through this tidal power plant in France.
Making Generalizations Why are very few locations suitable for building tidal power plants?

Although tidal energy is a clean, renewable source of energy, it has several limitations. Harnessing tidal power is practical only where there is a large difference between high and low tides—at least 4 or 5 meters. There are very few places in the world where such a large difference occurs. Daily tides also may not occur at the time when there is a demand for electricity. However, tidal power can be a useful part of an overall plan to generate electricity that also includes other power sources between tides.

Section 2 Review

1. Explain how the moon causes a tidal bulge to form on the side of Earth closest to it.
2. How can tides be used to generate electricity?
3. Describe the positions of the sun and the moon in relation to Earth when spring tides occur.
4. **Thinking Critically Applying Concepts** Imagine that you are the captain of a fishing boat. Why would it be helpful to know the times of the tides?

Check Your Progress CHAPTER PROJECT
Now that you have built your model, plan an experiment to observe the effects of wave erosion on the shoreline. How will you measure the amount of wave action needed to topple the lighthouse? Once you have observed how waves cause shoreline erosion, repair the beach and design a way to reduce the erosion. Test your method by sending more waves against the shore. (*Hint:* For both tests, place toothpicks at regular intervals on the beach to measure erosion.)

SECTION
3 Ocean Water Chemistry

Will the Eggs Sink or Float?

1. Fill two beakers or jars with tap water.

2. Add three teaspoons of salt to one beaker. Stir until it dissolves.

3. Place a whole, uncooked egg in each jar. Handle the eggs gently to avoid breakage. Observe what happens to each egg.

4. Wash your hands when you are finished with this activity.

Think It Over

Observing Compare what happens to the two eggs. What does this tell you about the difference between salt water and fresh water?

If you've ever been swimming in the ocean and swallowed some water, you know that it is salty. Why? According to an old Swedish legend, it's all because of a magic mill. This mill could grind out anything its owner wanted, such as herring, porridge, or even gold. A greedy sea captain once stole the mill and took it away on his ship, but without finding out how to use it. He asked the mill to grind some salt but then could not stop it. The mill ground more and more salt, until the captain's ship sank from its weight. According to the tale, the mill is still at the bottom of the sea, grinding out salt!

Probably no one ever took this tale seriously, even when it was first told. The scientific explanation for the ocean's saltiness begins with the early stages of Earth's formation, when the ocean covered much of the surface of the planet. Undersea volcanoes erupted, spewing chemicals into the water. Gradually, the lava from these volcanic eruptions built up areas of land. Rain fell on the bare land, washing more chemicals from the rocks into the ocean. Over time, these dissolved substances built up to the levels present in the ocean today.

GUIDE FOR READING

◆ How salty is ocean water?

◆ How do conditions in the ocean change with depth?

Reading Tip Before you read, preview the headings in the section. Then write some predictions about the characteristics of ocean water.

The Salty Ocean

Just how salty is the ocean? If you boiled a kilogram of seawater in a pot until the water was all gone, there would be about 35 grams of salts left in the bottom of the pot. **On average, one kilogram of ocean water contains about 35 grams of salts—that is, 35 parts per thousand.** The total amount of dissolved salts in water is called **salinity.**

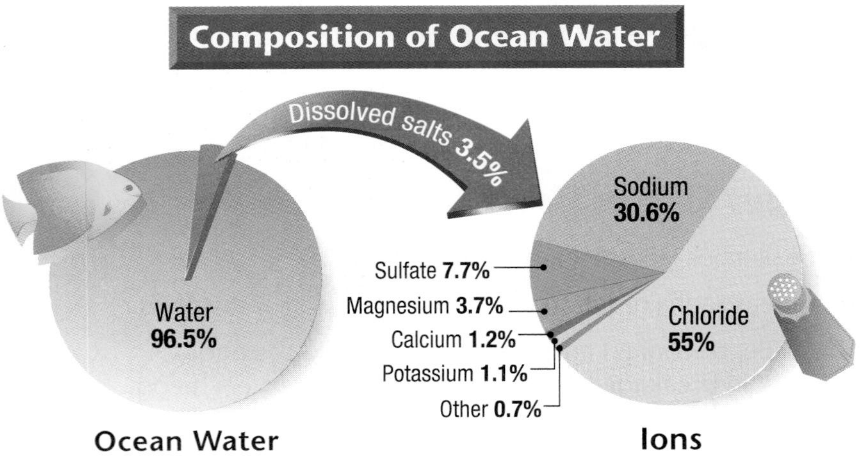

Composition of Ocean Water

Dissolved salts 3.5%

Water 96.5%

Ocean Water

Sulfate **7.7%**
Magnesium **3.7%**
Calcium **1.2%**
Potassium **1.1%**
Other **0.7%**

Sodium **30.6%**

Chloride **55%**

Ions

Figure 10 Ocean water contains many different dissolved salts. When salts dissolve, they separate into particles called ions. *Interpreting Graphs Which ion is most common in ocean water?*

The substance you know as table salt—sodium chloride—is the salt present in the greatest amount in ocean water. When sodium chloride dissolves in water, it separates into sodium and chloride particles called ions. Other salts, such as magnesium chloride, form ions in water in the same way. Together, chloride and sodium make up almost 86 percent of the ions dissolved in ocean water, as shown in Figure 10. Ocean water also contains smaller amounts of about a dozen other ions, including magnesium and calcium, and other substances that organisms need, such as nitrogen and phosphorus.

Variations in Salinity In most parts of the ocean, the salinity is between 34 and 37 parts per thousand. But near the surface, rain, snow, and melting ice add fresh water to the ocean, lowering the salinity there. Salinity is also lower near the mouths of large rivers such as the Amazon or Mississippi. These rivers empty great amounts of fresh water into the ocean. Evaporation, on the other hand, increases salinity, since the salt is left behind as the water evaporates. For example, in the Red Sea, where the climate is hot and dry, the salinity can be as high as 41 parts per thousand. Salinity can also be higher near the poles. As the surface water freezes into ice, the salt is left behind in the remaining water.

Figure 11 These people are relaxing with the paper while floating in the water! The Dead Sea in Israel is so salty that people float easily on its surface. *Relating Cause and Effect How is Israel's hot, dry climate related to the Dead Sea's high salinity?*

Effects of Salinity Salinity affects several properties of ocean water. For instance, ocean water does not **INTEGRATING CHEMISTRY** freeze until the temperature drops to about −1.9°C. The salt acts as a kind of antifreeze by interfering with the formation of ice crystals. Salt water also has a higher density than fresh water. That means that the mass of one liter of salt water is greater than the mass of one liter of fresh water. Because its density is greater, seawater has greater buoyancy. It lifts, or buoys up, less dense objects floating in it. This is why an egg floats higher in salt water than in fresh water.

Gases in Ocean Water

Just as land organisms use oxygen and other gases in the air, marine organisms use gases dissolved in ocean water. Two gases found in ocean water that are necessary for living things are oxygen and carbon dioxide.

Oxygen in seawater comes from the atmosphere and from algae in the ocean. Algae use sunlight to carry out photosynthesis, releasing oxygen into the water in the process. Oxygen is scarcer in seawater than in air and is most plentiful near the surface. Carbon dioxide, on the other hand, is about 60 times as plentiful in the oceans as in the atmosphere. Algae need carbon dioxide for photosynthesis. Animals such as corals also use carbon dioxide, which provides the carbon to build their hard skeletons.

✓ *Checkpoint* *What are two sources of the oxygen in ocean water?*

The Temperature of Ocean Water

In New England, the news reports on New Year's Day often feature the shivering members of a "Polar Bear Club" taking a dip in the icy Atlantic Ocean. Yet on the same day, people enjoy the warm waters of a Puerto Rico beach. Like temperatures on land, temperatures at the surface of the ocean vary with location and the seasons.

The broad surface of the ocean absorbs energy from the sun. Because warm water is less dense than cold water, this warm water stays as a layer on the surface. Near the equator, surface temperatures often reach 25°C, about room temperature. The temperature drops as you travel away from the equator.

The temperature of water affects the amount of dissolved oxygen it can hold. The cold waters in the polar regions contain more dissolved oxygen than warm, tropical waters. But there is still enough oxygen in tropical seas to support a variety of organisms, such as those shown in Figure 12.

Math TOOLBOX

Calculating Density

To calculate the density of a substance, divide the mass of the substance by its volume.

$$\text{density} = \frac{\text{mass}}{\text{volume}}$$

For example, one liter (L) of ocean water has a mass of 1.03 kilograms (kg). Therefore, its density is

$$\frac{1.03 \text{ kg}}{1.00 \text{ L}} = 1.03 \text{ kg/L}$$

Five liters of one type of crude oil has a mass of 4.10 kg. What is its density?

$$\frac{4.10 \text{ kg}}{5.00 \text{ L}} = 0.82 \text{ kg/L}$$

If this oil spilled on the ocean's surface, would it sink or float? Explain your answer in terms of density.

Figure 12 Both this neon-pink basslet and the lacy green sponge depend on the dissolved gases in ocean water.

EXPLORING the Water Column

Conditions change as you descend from the surface to the ocean floor.

▼ A scuba diver can descend to about 40 meters.

Surface Zone
Extends from surface to about 200 meters. Average temperature worldwide is 17.5°C.

The submersible *Alvin* can descend to about 4 kilometers. ▼

Transition Zone
Extends from bottom of surface zone to about 1 kilometer. Temperature rapidly drops to 4°C.

Deep Zone
Extends from about 1 kilometer to ocean floor. Average temperature is 3.5°C.

DEPTH

0.5 km

1.0 km

1.5 km

2.0 km

2.5 km

3.0 km

3.5 km

3.8 km — Average ocean depth

4.0 km

PRESSURE INCREASES

▼ In 1960, the submersible *Trieste* dived to a record depth of 11 kilometers.

Color and Light
Sunlight penetrates the surface of the ocean. It appears first yellowish, then blue-green, as the water absorbs the red light. No light reaches below about 200 meters.

Temperature
Near the surface, temperature is affected by the weather above. In the transition zone, the temperature drops rapidly. In the deep zone, the water is always extremely cold.

Salinity
Rainfall decreases salinity near the surface, while evaporation increases salinity in warm, dry areas. Below the surface zone, salinity remains fairly constant throughout the water column.

Density
The density of seawater depends on temperature and salinity. The ocean is generally least dense in the surface zone, where it is warmest. However, higher salinity also increases density. The most dense water is found in the cold deep zone.

Pressure
Pressure increases at the rate of 10 times the air pressure at sea level per 100 meters of depth.

Changes with Depth

Gazing down into the blue-green water from the deck of a ship, you might think that the vast volume of water beneath you is all the same. But in fact, conditions change dramatically from the surface to the depths. If you could descend from the surface to the ocean floor, you would pass through a vertical section of the ocean referred to as the water column. *Exploring the Water Column* shows some of the changes you would observe.

Temperature Decreases If you took temperature readings at different depths, you would observe a pattern. **Temperature decreases as you descend through the water column.** There are three temperature zones in the water column. The first zone, the surface zone, typically extends from the surface to between 100 and 500 meters. Next is the transition zone, which extends from the bottom of the surface zone to about one kilometer. The temperature drops very quickly in the transition zone, to about 4°C. Below the transition zone is the deep zone. The temperature in the deep zone is a constant 3.5°C or colder in most of the ocean.

Pressure Increases Pressure is the force exerted by the weight of water above pressing down. **Pressure increases continuously from the surface to the deepest part of the ocean.** The average depth of the ocean floor is 3.8 kilometers. There the pressure is about 400 times greater than air pressure at Earth's surface.

 INTEGRATING TECHNOLOGY Pressure is one obstacle facing scientists who want to study the ocean. A diver can descend safely only to about 40 meters. To survive in deeper water, scientists must use a submersible. A **submersible** is an underwater vehicle built of strong materials to resist pressure. In a submersible, scientists can directly observe the ocean floor, collect samples, and study deep ocean water chemistry.

Section 3 Review

1. What is the salinity of ocean water?
2. How do temperature and pressure change as you descend from the surface to the ocean floor?
3. Describe one factor that increases the salinity of seawater and one factor that decreases salinity.
4. **Thinking Critically** **Inferring** Would you expect the seawater just below the floating ice in the Arctic Ocean to be higher or lower in salinity than the water in the deep zone there? Explain.

Science at Home

Water Pressure Use a ballpoint pen to poke two holes in a milk carton—one about one third of the way from the bottom and one about two thirds of the way from the bottom. Cover the holes with tape and fill the carton with water. Holding the carton a meter above a sink, remove the tape and observe the streams of water. Explain that increased pressure causes the water to flow out of the bottom hole more quickly. How does this model conditions in the ocean?

Investigating Changes in Density

In this lab, you will practice the skill of designing experiments as you learn more about density.

Problem

How do various factors affect the density of ocean water?

Materials

thumbtacks	beaker, 250 mL	water
thermometer	ice	hot plate
table salt	balance	spoon
metric ruler	sharpened pencil	
unsharpened pencil with eraser		
graduated cylinders, 100 mL and 250 mL		

Procedure

1. Work with your group to brainstorm a list of variables that affect the density of ocean water. Some variables to consider are water temperature and salinity. As a group, choose one variable to test in this investigation.
2. One way to measure density is with a tool called a *hydrometer.* To make a hydrometer, follow the instructions on the facing page.
3. Design an experimental plan to determine how the variable you chose affects density. For example, if you have chosen temperature as your variable, you might choose to start with salt water at 0°C, then heat it to 10°C, 20°C, and 30°C. If salinity is your variable, you might start with 100 mL of tap (fresh) water and add 10 g of salt, then add another 10 g to make 20 g, then add 10 g more to make 30 g. Write out your experimental plan.

DATA TABLE

Manipulated Variable: _____

Condition Tested	Hydrometer Reading

4. List all the variables you will need to keep constant during your experiment. Revise your experimental plan and add steps to ensure that all other variables remain constant.
5. Review your plan. Make sure it includes the materials you will use and their amounts. Also make sure you have addressed all safety issues. Then check the plan with your teacher.
6. Copy the data table into your notebook.
7. Perform your experiment using the pencil hydrometer.

Analyze and Conclude

1. In your experimental plan, which variable was the manipulated variable, and which was the responding variable? Explain. (Refer to the Skills Handbook if you need more information about these types of variables.)
2. Make a graph of the data you collected in the experiment. Graph the manipulated variable on the horizontal axis. Graph the responding variable on the vertical axis.
3. How do changes in the hydrometer reading relate to density?

Making a Hydrometer

A. Begin with an unsharpened pencil. Starting 1 cm from the unsharpened end, use a second, sharpened pencil to make marks every 0.5 cm along the side of the pencil. Continue making marks until you reach the 4-cm mark.

B. Label each mark, starting at the unsharpened end of the pencil with the label 0.5.

C. Insert 3 thumbtacks as weights into the eraser end of the pencil. **CAUTION:** *Be careful not to cut yourself on the sharp points of the thumbtacks.*

D. Fill the 250-mL graduated cylinder with water at room temperature. Place the pencil in the water, eraser down.

E. Add or remove thumbtacks and adjust their placement in the eraser until the pencil floats upright, with about 2 cm sticking up above the surface of the water.

F. In your notebook, record the number next to the mark that is closest to the point where the pencil hydrometer projects from the water. As the density of the water increases, the hydrometer will float above the point you have just marked. If the water becomes less dense, the hydrometer will float below that point.

4. Use the graph to describe the relationship between the manipulated variable you tested and density.
5. Where in Earth's oceans would you find conditions like the ones that you tested?
6. **Think About It** Why is it important to make sure that all conditions other than the manipulated variable are kept constant in an experiment? How well were you able to keep the other variables constant?

More To Explore

In this experiment you observed how manipulating a particular variable affects the density of ocean water. Now conduct a second experiment, this time manipulating a different variable. As you design this experiment, make sure to control all variables except the one you are testing. Be sure to check your experimental plan with your teacher before you begin.

Currents and Climate

Which Is More Dense?

1. Fill a plastic container three-quarters full with warm water. Wait for the water to stop moving.

2. Add several drops of food coloring to a cup of ice water and stir.

3. Gently dribble colored water down the inside of the container. Observe.

Think It Over

Inferring Describe what happened to the cold water. Which is more dense, warm water or cold water? Explain.

GUIDE FOR READING

◆ What forces cause surface currents and deep currents?

◆ How do surface currents affect climate on land?

Reading Tip As you read, make a list of the kinds of ocean currents. Write a sentence describing the causes of each.

People strolling along a Washington beach one May day in 1990 could hardly believe their eyes. Hundreds of sneakers, in all colors and sizes, were washing ashore from the Pacific Ocean. Puzzled, people gathered up the soggy shoes and took them home, wondering where the sneakers had come from. Eventually, the sneaker spill was traced to a cargo ship from South Korea. Containers had washed overboard in a storm and broken open, spilling thousands of shoes into the water.

The sneakers were a ready-made experiment for oceanographers, scientists who study the oceans. From the shoes' drifting, oceanographers could infer both the path and the speed of water movements in the Pacific. Using what they already knew about these movements, scientists made a computer model predicting when and where more sneakers would come ashore. Right on schedule, sneakers washed up in Oregon and British Columbia, Canada. The model also predicted that the shoes would turn back westward across the Pacific. Again it was correct, as some sneakers arrived in Hawaii. The shoes that did not sink could have traveled all the way back to South Korea!

Earlier in this chapter you learned how the oceans move as a result of wave action and tides. A third type of water movement is currents. A **current** is a large stream of moving water that flows through the oceans. Unlike waves, which do not actually transport water from one place to another, currents carry water great distances. Some currents move water at the surface of the ocean, while other currents move the deep water.

Surface Currents

Figure 16 shows the major surface currents in Earth's oceans. **Surface currents, which affect water to a depth of several hundred meters, are driven mainly by winds.** Following the major wind patterns of the globe, surface currents move in circular patterns in the five major ocean basins. Trace these currents on the map. Notice that most of the currents flow east or west, then double back to complete the circle.

Why do the currents move in these circular patterns? If Earth were standing still, winds and currents would flow in straight lines between the poles and the equator. But as Earth rotates, the paths of the winds and currents curve in relation to Earth's surface. This effect of Earth's rotation on the direction of winds and currents is called the **Coriolis effect** (kawr ee OH lis effect). In the Northern Hemisphere, the Coriolis effect causes the currents to curve to the right. In the Southern Hemisphere, the Coriolis effect causes the currents to curve to the left. You can see the impact of the Coriolis effect by comparing the directions of the currents in the two hemispheres on Figure 13.

Figure 13 Large surface currents generally move in circular patterns in Earth's oceans. *Interpreting Maps Name four currents that flow along the coasts of North America. State whether each current is warm or cold.*

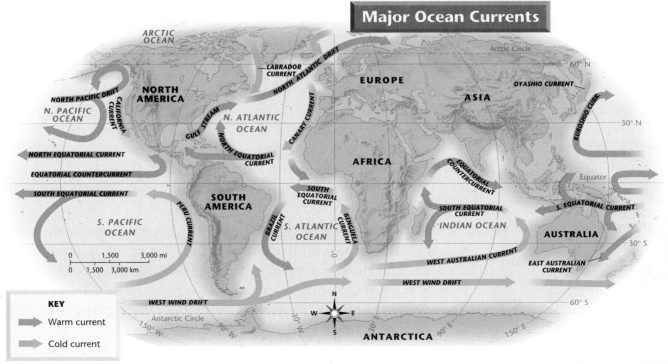

Major Ocean Currents

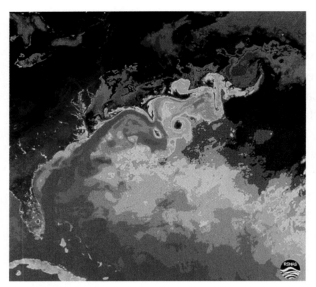

The largest and most powerful surface current in the North Atlantic Ocean, the Gulf Stream, is caused by strong winds from the west. The Gulf Stream resembles a fast-moving, deep-blue river within the ocean. It is more than 30 kilometers wide and 300 meters deep, and it carries a volume of water 100 times greater than the Mississippi River. The Gulf Stream carries warm water from the Gulf of Mexico to the Caribbean Sea, then northward along the coast of the United States. Near Cape Hatteras, North Carolina, it curves eastward across the Atlantic, as a result of the Coriolis effect.

✓ *Checkpoint* *Why doesn't the Gulf Stream travel in a straight line?*

Figure 14 This satellite image of the Atlantic Ocean has been enhanced with colors that show water temperature. Red and orange indicate warmer water, while green and blue indicate colder water. The warm Gulf Stream flows around Florida as you can see in the lower left corner of the image.

How Surface Currents Affect Climate

The Gulf Stream and North Atlantic Drift are very important to people in the city of Trondheim, Norway. Trondheim is located along Norway's western coast. Although it is very close to the Arctic Circle, winter there is fairly mild. Snow melts soon after it falls. And fortunately for the fishing boats, the local harbors are free of ice most of the winter. The two warm currents bring this area of Norway its mild climate. **Climate** is the pattern of temperature and precipitation typical of an area over a long period of time.

Currents affect climate by moving cold and warm water around the globe. In general, currents carry warm water from the tropics toward the poles and bring cold water back toward the equator. **A surface current warms or cools the air above it, influencing the climate of the land near the coast.**

Winds pick up moisture as they blow across warm-water currents. For example, the warm Kuroshio Current brings mild, rainy weather to the southern islands of Japan. In contrast, cold-water currents cool the air above them. Since cold air holds less moisture than warm air, these currents tend to bring cool, dry weather to the land areas in their path.

Sharpen your Skills

Drawing Conclusions

ACTIVITY

Locate the Benguela Current on Figure 13 on the previous page. Near the southern tip of Africa, the winds blow from west to east. Using what you have learned about surface currents and climate, what can you conclude about the impact of this current on the climate of the southwestern coast of Africa?

Deep Currents

So far you have been reading about currents that move the water in the top few hundred meters of the ocean. Deeper below the surface, another type of current causes the chilly waters at the bottom of the ocean to creep slowly across the ocean floor. **These deep currents are caused by differences in density rather than surface winds.**

As you read in Section 3, the density of water depends on its temperature and its salinity. When a warm-water surface current moves from the equator toward the poles, its water gradually cools off. As ice forms near the poles, the salinity of the water increases from the salt left behind during freezing. As its temperature decreases and salinity increases, the water becomes denser and sinks. Then, the cold water flows back along the ocean floor as a deep current. Deep currents follow the hills and valleys of the ocean floor. Deep ocean currents are also affected by the Coriolis effect, which causes them to curve.

Deep ocean currents move and mix water around the world. They carry cold water from the poles back toward the equator. Deep ocean currents flow much more slowly than surface currents. They may take as long as 1,000 years to make the round trip from the pole to the equator and back again!

Upwelling

In most parts of the ocean, the surface waters do not usually mix with the deep ocean waters. However, some mixing does occur in the polar regions when the surface waters cool, sink, and form deep currents. Mixing also occurs when winds cause upwelling. **Upwelling** is the upward movement of cold water from the ocean depths. As winds blow away the warm surface water, cold water rises to replace it, as shown in Figure 15.

Upwelling brings up tiny ocean organisms, minerals, and other nutrients from the deeper layers of the water. Without this

Figure 15 As cold water rises from the deep ocean, it brings a new supply of nutrients to the surface. The nutrients feed enormous schools of fish such as these anchovies. *Relating Cause and Effect What causes cold water to rise during upwelling?*

Wind

Warm surface water

Upwelling

motion, the surface waters of the open ocean would be very scarce in nutrients. Because of the increased supply of nutrients, zones of upwelling are usually home to enormous schools of fish.

One major area of upwelling lies in the Pacific Ocean off the west coast of South America. Here, upwelling occurs when strong winds from the Andes Mountains sweep across the ocean. Huge schools of silvery anchovies thrive on the nutrients that are brought to the surface. This rich fishing area is important to millions of people who depend on it for food and jobs.

How Things Work

Modeling Ocean Currents

Why is the climate in Dublin, Ireland, so different from the climate in St. John's in Newfoundland, Canada? Since both cities are located at the same latitude, you might expect similar climate conditions in the two locations. But when it's 8°C in Dublin in January, it's usually below 0°C in St. John's. This investigation will help you understand why.

Problem

How can you model the movement of ocean water due to surface currents?

Skills Focus

making models, observing, inferring

Materials

rectangular baking tray   chalk
modeling clay, 3 sticks   ruler
permanent marker   hole puncher
newspaper
construction paper, blue and red
jointed drinking straws, one per student
light-reflecting rheoscopic fluid, 400 mL
   (or water and food coloring)

Procedure

1. Cover your work area with newspaper. Place the baking tray on top of the newspaper.
2. Using the map on the facing page as a guide, draw a chalk outline of the eastern coast of North and South America on the left side of the tray. Draw the outline of the western coast of Europe and Africa on the right side of the tray.
3. Use modeling clay to create the continents, roughly following the chalk outlines you have drawn. Build the continents to a depth of about 3 cm. Press the clay tightly to the pan to form a watertight seal.
4. Fill the ocean area of your model with rheoscopic fluid (or water and food coloring) to a depth of 1 cm.
5. Place 10 blue paper punches in the ocean area marked with a blue X on the map. Place 10 red paper punches in the area marked with a red X.
6. Select a drinking straw and bend it at the joint. Write your initials on the short end of the straw with the marker.

El Niño

Changes in winds and currents can greatly impact the oceans and the neighboring land. One example is **El Niño,** an abnormal climate event that occurs every 2 to 7 years in the Pacific Ocean. El Niño begins when an unusual pattern of winds forms over the western Pacific. This causes a vast sheet of warm water to move eastward toward the South American coast. El Niño conditions can last for one to two years before the usual winds and currents return.

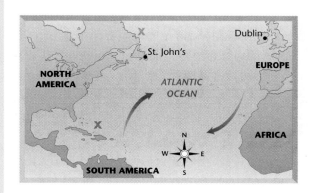

7. With a partner, simulate the pattern of winds that blow in this region of the world. One partner should position his or her straw across the westernmost bulge of Africa and blow toward the west (see arrow on map). The other partner should position his or her straw across the northern end of South America and blow toward the northeast (see arrow on map). Make sure that the straws are bent and that the short ends are parallel to the ocean surface. Both partners should begin blowing gently through the straws at the same time. Try to blow as continuously as possible for one to two minutes.

8. Observe the motion of the fluid and paper punches over the surface of the ocean. Notice what happens when the fluid and punches flow around landmasses.

Analyze and Conclude

1. Draw a map that shows the pattern of ocean currents that was produced in your model. Use red arrows to show the flow of warm water moving north from the equator. Use blue arrows to show the flow of cold water southward from the polar regions.
2. Use Figure 13 to add names to the currents you drew on your map. Which currents are warm-water currents? Which are cold-water currents?
3. Use your model to describe the relationship between winds and surface currents in the ocean.
4. Use your knowledge of ocean currents to explain why the climate in St. John's is different from the climate in Dublin.
5. **Apply** Suppose you wanted to sail to Europe from the east coast of the United States. What two natural factors could help speed up your trip? Explain your answer.

More to Explore

Use your model to simulate an upwelling off the coast of Africa. What conditions cause upwellings to occur? What are the results?

Figure 16 Heavy rains caused by El Niño washed out this road in La Honda, California, forcing homes to be evacuated. El Niño can result in severe weather all around the world.

El Niño's Impact El Niño can have disastrous consequences. For example, the arrival of El Niño's warm surface water prevents upwelling off the western coast of South America. Without the nutrients brought by upwelling, fish die or go elsewhere to find food, ruining the fishing catch that season. Seabirds, with no fish to eat, also must leave the area or starve.

El Niño has serious effects on land, too. It causes shifts in weather patterns around the world, bringing unusual and often severe conditions to different areas. For example, El Niño of 1997 and 1998 caused an unusually warm winter in the northeastern United States. However, it was also responsible for heavy rains, flooding, and mudslides in California, as well as a string of deadly tornadoes in Florida.

Forecasting El Niño Although scientists do not fully understand the conditions that create El Niño, they have been able to predict its occurrence using computer models of world climate. Knowing when El Niño will occur can reduce its impact. Scientists and public officials can plan emergency procedures and make changes to protect people and wildlife.

Section 4 Review

1. Describe how surface currents form and travel in the ocean.
2. How is heat transferred from Earth's oceans to land areas?
3. Explain how deep currents form and move in the ocean.
4. **Thinking Critically Comparing and Contrasting** Describe the similarities and differences in the movement of surface currents in the Northern Hemisphere and Southern Hemisphere.

Check Your Progress   CHAPTER PROJECT
This is the time to make final changes to your method of shoreline protection to further decrease erosion. Test your improved method. How much additional wave action does the lighthouse withstand? (*Hint:* Try using a combination of methods to protect the shoreline and lighthouse.)

SECTION 1 Wave Action

Key Ideas
◆ Most waves are caused by winds blowing across the surface of the water.
◆ When waves enter shallow water, the wavelength shortens and wave height increases. The wave becomes unstable and breaks on the shore.
◆ Waves erode shorelines, carving cliffs and breaking up rocks into pebbles and sand.

Key Terms
wave   crest   wavelength
frequency   trough   wave height
longshore drift sandbar   rip current
groin

SECTION 2 Tides
INTEGRATING SPACE SCIENCE

Key Ideas
◆ Tides are caused by the interaction of Earth, the moon, and the sun.
◆ There are two high tides and two low tides each day in most places.
◆ The height of tides during a month varies with changes in the positions of Earth, the moon, and the sun.

Key Terms
tide   spring tide   neap tide

SECTION 3 Ocean Water Chemistry

Key Ideas
◆ Chloride and sodium are the most abundant ions in ocean water.
◆ Salinity varies throughout the ocean, depending on the amount of evaporation or freezing, as well as the addition of fresh water from rivers or precipitation.
◆ Below the ocean surface, the water is divided into layers by temperature, with uniformly cold temperatures in deep water.
◆ Pressure increases greatly with increasing depth in the ocean.

Key Terms
salinity   submersible

SECTION 4 Currents and Climate

Key Ideas
◆ Currents are formed by Earth's rotation, winds, and differences in water temperature.
◆ The movement of warm-water and cold-water surface currents carries water around the world and influences coastal climates.
◆ Density differences between warm and cold water cause many deep-water currents in the ocean.
◆ El Niño changes the pattern of winds and currents and affects Earth's weather.

Key Terms
current   Coriolis effect   climate
upwelling   El Niño

Organizing Information

Flowchart Complete a flowchart about the movement of a wave by putting the following five steps in the correct sequence: *wave travels as low swell; wind creates ripple on ocean surface; wave breaks on shore; wavelength decreases and wave height increases; wave touches bottom in shallow water.* Add a title. (For more on flowcharts, see the Skills Handbook.)

Reviewing Content

For more review of key concepts, see the Interactive Student Tutorial CD-ROM.

Multiple Choice

Choose the letter of the best answer.

1. Rolling waves with a large distance between crests have a long
   a. wave height. **b.** wavelength.
   c. frequency. **d.** trough.

2. Groins are built to reduce the effect of
   a. tsunamis.
   b. longshore drift.
   c. rip currents.
   d. deep currents.

3. At the full moon, the combined gravitational pulls of the sun and moon produce the biggest difference between low and high tide, called a
   a. surface current. **b.** neap tide.
   c. spring tide. **d.** rip current.

4. Ocean water is more dense than fresh water at the same temperature because of
   a. pressure.
   b. the Coriolis effect.
   c. upwelling.
   d. salinity.

5. Winds and currents move in curved paths because of
   a. the Coriolis effect. **b.** longshore drift.
   c. wave height. **d.** tides.

True or False

If the statement is true, write true. If it is false, change the underlined word or words to make the statement true.

6. Sand is gradually carried down the beach by <u>upwelling</u>.

7. The most common ions dissolved in ocean water are sodium and <u>potassium</u>.

8. Two gases dissolved in ocean water that are important to living things are oxygen and <u>carbon dioxide</u>.

9. As you descend deeper into the ocean, the water gets colder and pressure <u>decreases</u>.

10. <u>Currents</u> carry cold and warm ocean water around the world.

Checking Concepts

11. What factors influence the size of a wave?

12. Explain why the height of a wave changes as it approaches the shore.

13. Explain how a rip current forms.

14. Why are there two high tides a day in most places?

15. What is a spring tide? How does it differ from a neap tide?

16. How do warm-water currents affect climate?

17. What is the Coriolis effect? How does it influence ocean currents?

18. Describe the causes and result of upwelling.

19. What is El Niño? What are some of its effects?

20. **Writing to Learn** Imagine a beach or seashore that you have visited or would like to visit. Using what you know about wave action, write a description of the shape of the beach, sand drift, cliffs, dunes, and other features.

Thinking Critically

21. **Classifying** Classify these different movements of ocean water by whether each is caused by winds or not caused by winds: waves, tides, surface currents, deep currents, upwelling.

22. **Applying Concepts** Would you expect salinity to be high or low in a rainy ocean region near the mouth of a river? Why?

23. **Comparing and Contrasting** In what ways is the ocean at 1,000 meters deep different from the ocean at the surface in the same location?

24. **Relating Cause and Effect** How does the movement of ocean currents explain the fact that much of western Europe has a mild, wet climate?

Applying Skills

The temperature readings in the table were obtained in the Atlantic Ocean near Bermuda. Use the data to answer Questions 25–27.

Depth (m)	Temp. (°C)	Depth (m)	Temp. (°C)
0	19	1,000	9
200	18	1,200	5
400	18	1,400	5
600	16	1,600	4
800	12	1,800	4

25. Graphing Construct a line graph using the data in the table. Plot depth readings on the horizontal axis and temperature readings on the vertical axis.

26. Drawing Conclusions Use your graph to identify the temperature range in the transition zone.

27. Predicting Predict how the ocean temperature at depths of 0 meters and at 1,400 meters would change with the seasons in this location. Explain your reasoning.

Performance ▽ CHAPTER PROJECT Assessment

Present Your Project Use your model to demonstrate your improved method of shoreline protection to the class. If you need to make any final changes to the model, do so before your presentation. Explain to your classmates why you chose this particular method to protect the lighthouse.

Reflect and Record In your project notebook, record the results of your trials. How effective was your method of shoreline protection? How could you improve your model? How well do you think it would perform in the real world?

Test Preparation
Use these questions to prepare for standardized tests.

Read the passage. Then answer Questions 28–30.

Tsunamis are large waves caused by earthquakes on the ocean floor. They are most common in the Pacific Ocean.

Despite the tremendous amount of energy a tsunami carries, people on a ship at sea may not even realize a tsunami is passing! A tsunami in deep water may have a wavelength of 200 kilometers or more, but a wave height of less than a meter. But when the tsunami reaches shallow water near the coast, friction with the ocean floor causes the tsunami to become a towering wall of water up to 20 meters in height. Tsunamis are capable of causing great damage.

Some nations have developed ways to warn coastal residents and decrease damage from tsunamis, such as barriers designed to break up large waves. Scientists also monitor the ocean floor for earthquakes that may produce tsunamis and issue tsunami alerts when necessary.

28. Tsunamis are caused by
  a. huge walls of water.
  b. ocean currents.
  c. hurricanes.
  d. earthquakes.

29. Tsunamis often cause great damage to
  a. ships at sea.
  b. coastal areas along the Pacific Ocean.
  c. the ocean floor.
  d. coral reefs in the Atlantic Ocean.

30. One can conclude from the passage that
  a. there is no way to reduce the damage caused by tsunamis.
  b. given enough warning, the loss of life from tsunamis can be reduced.
  c. more damage is caused by hurricanes than tsunamis.
  d. an earthquake is just as likely to occur underwater as on land.

CHAPTER
14 Ocean Zones

WEB ACTIVITY
www.phschool.com

At Home in the Sea

A coral reef is a beautiful home for the organisms who dart, crawl, and hide within its lacy structure. But the reef is also a fragile place. Slight changes in water temperature and other conditions can threaten the delicate coral and the other organisms that inhabit the reef.

A coral reef is one of many different ocean habitats. From sandy tropical beaches to the cold depths of the ocean floor, organisms are able to thrive in all of them. In this chapter you will learn about the conditions in different parts of the ocean and the organisms that live there. Throughout the chapter you will work in a group to create your own model of one of the habitats.

Your Goal To build a three-dimensional model of a marine habitat and include some of the organisms that live there.

To complete the project successfully, you will need to
◆ include the significant physical features of the habitat
◆ create a life-size model of one organism that lives in the habitat
◆ write an explanation of how the organism is adapted to its habitat
◆ follow the safety guidelines in Appendix A

Get Started Begin now by previewing the visuals in the chapter to identify different ocean habitats. With your group, discuss which habitat you would like to learn more about. Begin a list of questions you have about the habitat. Also start to think about the materials you will need to build your model.

Check Your Progress You'll be working on this project as you study this chapter. To keep your project on track, look for Check Your Progress boxes at the following points.
Section 2 Review, page 471: Draw a scale diagram of your model.
Section 3 Review, page 478: Research your organism and build your model.

Present Your Project At the end of the chapter (page 489), you will display your model organism in its habitat.

The many residents of this New Guinea coral reef include golden fairy basslets, a red gorgonian sea fan, and a vibrant blue sea star.

SECTION
1 Exploring the Ocean

DISCOVER • ACTIVITY • • • •

What Can You Learn Without Seeing?

1. Your teacher will provide your group with ten plastic drinking straws and a covered box containing a mystery object. The top of the box has several holes punched in it. Using the straws as probes, try to determine the size, shape, and location of the object inside the box.

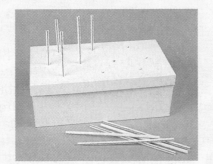

2. Based on the information you gathered, describe your object. What can you say about its length, shape, and position? Write down your hypothesis about the identity of the object.

3. Remove the box top to reveal the object.

Think It Over

Inferring Explain how you used the method of indirect observation in this activity to learn about the object.

GUIDE FOR READING

◆ What factors make ocean-floor research difficult?

◆ What are some features of the ocean floor?

Reading Tip As you read, make a list of features found on the ocean floor. Write one sentence about each feature.

Figure 1 This engraving shows HMS *Challenger* in the Indian Ocean in 1874, two years into its journey around the world.

Imagine going on a voyage around the world lasting three and a half years. Your assignment: to investigate "everything about the sea." Your vessel: a former warship, powered by sails and a steam engine. Its guns have been removed to make room for scientific gear. On board there are thermometers for measuring the temperature of ocean water and hundreds of kilometers of cable for lowering dredges to the bottom of the ocean. With the dredges, you scrape sand, muck, and rock from the ocean floor. You drag trawl nets behind the ship to collect ocean organisms.

The crew of a British ship, HMS *Challenger,* began such a voyage in 1872. By the end of the journey, the scientists had gathered enough data to fill 50 volumes and had collected more than 4,000 new organisms! It took 23 years to publish all the information they learned about oceanwater chemistry, currents, ocean life, and the shape of the ocean floor. The voyage of the *Challenger* was so successful that it became the model for many later ocean expeditions.

Voyages of Discovery

For thousands of years before the *Challenger* expedition, people explored the ocean. Knowledge of the ocean has always been important to the people living along its coasts. The ocean has provided food and served as a route for trade and travel to new settlements.

The Phoenicians, who lived along the Mediterranean Sea, were one of the earliest cultures to explore the oceans. By 1200 B.C., they had established sea routes for trade with the other nations around the Mediterranean. After the Phoenicians, people of many European, African, and Asian cultures sailed along the coasts to trade with distant lands.

In the Pacific Ocean around 2,000 years ago, the Polynesians left the safety of the coastline and boldly sailed into the open ocean. Their knowledge of winds and currents enabled the Polynesians to settle the scattered islands of Hawaii, Tahiti, and New Zealand.

As modern science developed and trade increased, ocean exploration changed. Nations needed accurate maps of the oceans and lands bordering them. Governments also wanted their countries to be known for new scientific discoveries. For example, in the late 1700s, the British government hired Captain James Cook to lead three voyages of exploration. Cook's crew included scientists who studied the stars and collected new species of plants and animals.

Within a century of Cook's voyages, almost all of Earth's coastlines had been mapped. Scientists then turned to the study of the ocean's waters and invented methods to explore its unknown depths. The *Challenger* expedition marked the beginning of the modern science of oceanography.

☑ *Checkpoint* What are two reasons why people have explored the oceans?

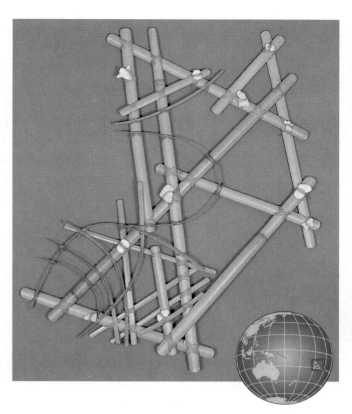

Figure 2 Polynesian sailors used stick charts to navigate the Pacific Ocean. The curved sticks represent currents and winds. The pieces of coral might represent rocks or small islands. *Interpreting Maps Use the map to explain why navigation tools were important to the Polynesians.*

Exploring the Ocean Floor

![Integrating Technology] **INTEGRATING TECHNOLOGY** Following the *Challenger*'s example, governments and universities sponsored many other major ocean research expeditions. Until recently, however, the ocean floor was unexplored, and much of the life in the oceans was unknown. Why did it take so long to reach this part of the ocean? Studying the ocean floor is difficult because the

ocean is so deep—3.8 kilometers deep on average, more than twice as deep as the Grand Canyon. As you learned in Chapter 4, conditions are very harsh at such depths. First, because sunlight does not penetrate far below the surface, the deep ocean is in total darkness. Second, the water is very cold—only a few degrees above freezing. Finally, there is tremendous pressure due to the mass of water pushing down from above.

Because of the darkness, cold, and extreme pressure, scientists have had to develop new technology to enable them to study the deep ocean floor. Since humans cannot survive these conditions, many of the inventions have involved indirect methods of gathering information. One of the simplest methods, used by the *Challenger*'s crew, was to lower a weight on a long line into the water until the weight touched the bottom. The length of line

Technology and Ocean Exploration

The time line includes several inventions that have helped scientists overcome the challenges of studying the ocean world.

1943 SCUBA

Jacques Cousteau and Emile Gagnan invented SCUBA, which stands for "**s**elf-**c**ontained **u**nderwater **b**reathing **a**pparatus." A tank containing compressed air is strapped to the diver's back and connected by a tube to a mouthpiece. SCUBA enables divers to explore to a depth of 40 meters.

| 1915 | 1930 | 1945 | 1960 |

1925 Sonar

Scientists aboard the German ship *Meteor* used sonar to map the ocean floor. They used a device called an echo sounder to produce pulses of sound. The ship's crew then timed the return of the echoes.

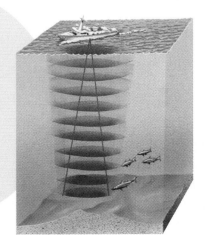

1960 Submersibles

Vehicles with very thick metal hulls protect explorers from extreme pressure and temperature, while enabling them to directly observe the ocean depths.

that got wet was approximately equal to the water's depth at that location. This method was slow and often inaccurate, as the line would descend at an angle. Nevertheless, these depth readings produced the first rough maps of the floor of the North Atlantic.

A major advance in ocean-floor mapping was sonar, a technology invented during World War I to detect submarines. **Sonar**, which stands for **so**und **na**vigation and **r**anging, is a system that uses sound waves to calculate the distance to an object. The sonar equipment on a ship sends out pulses of sound that bounce off the ocean floor. The equipment then measures how quickly the sound waves return to the ship. Sound waves return quickly if the ocean floor is close. Sound waves take longer to return if the ocean floor is farther away.

☑ *Checkpoint* **How is sonar an indirect way of gathering data?**

In Your Journal

Each of the inventions shown on these two pages helped solve a problem of ocean exploration. Find out more about one of these inventions. Write a short newspaper article telling the story of its development. Include details about the people who invented it and how it added to people's knowledge of the oceans.

1986

Remote Underwater Manipulator

The Remote Underwater Manipulator, or RUM III, is about the size of a small car. It is controlled by a computer aboard a ship at the surface. Without a crew, the RUM III can collect samples, take photographs, and map the ocean floor.

| 1975 | 1990 | 2005 | 2020 |

1978 Satellites

Seasat A was the first satellite in Earth's orbit to study the oceans. Since satellites make millions of observations a day, they provide data on rapidly changing and widespread ocean conditions. Such data include temperatures, algae growth patterns, and even the movement of large schools of fish.

1995

Gravity Mapping

The United States Navy used advanced satellite data to create a new map of the ocean floor. The satellite detected slight changes in gravity related to the shape of the ocean floor, providing accurate measurements within a few centimeters.

Features of the Ocean Floor

Once scientists were able to map the ocean floor, they discovered something surprising. The bottom of the ocean was not a flat, sandy plain. The deep waters hid mountain ranges and deep canyons.

If you could take a submarine voyage along the ocean floor, what would you see? **Features of the ocean floor include the continental shelf, continental slope, seamounts, abyssal plains, and the mid-ocean ridge.** Trace your journey from the edge of one continent to another in *Exploring the Ocean Floor.*

As you leave the harbor, your submarine first passes over the **continental shelf,** a gently sloping, shallow area of the ocean floor that extends outward from the edge of a continent. At a depth of about 130 meters, the ocean floor begins to slope more steeply. This incline at the edge of the continental shelf is called the **continental slope.** The continental slope marks the true edge of a continent, where the rock that makes up the continent stops and the rock of the ocean floor begins.

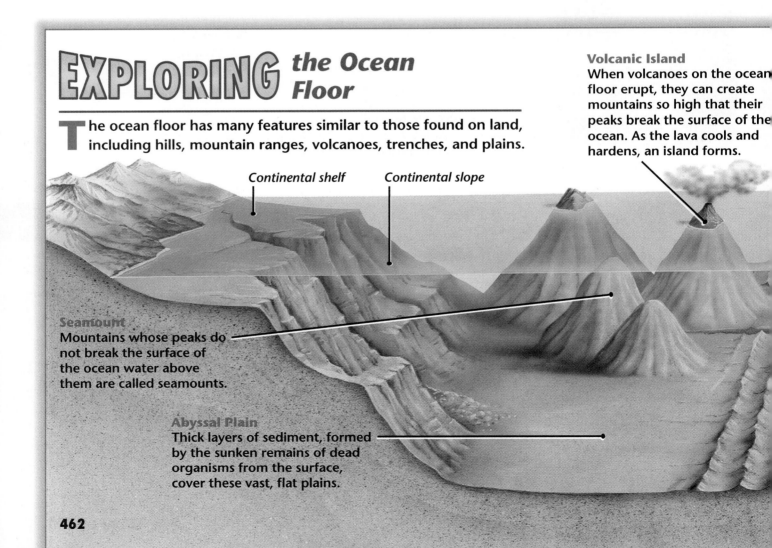

EXPLORING *the Ocean Floor*

The ocean floor has many features similar to those found on land, including hills, mountain ranges, volcanoes, trenches, and plains.

Volcanic Island
When volcanoes on the ocean floor erupt, they can create mountains so high that their peaks break the surface of the ocean. As the lava cools and hardens, an island forms.

Continental shelf

Continental slope

Seamount
Mountains whose peaks do not break the surface of the ocean water above them are called seamounts.

Abyssal Plain
Thick layers of sediment, formed by the sunken remains of dead organisms from the surface, cover these vast, flat plains.

Your submarine descends more gradually now, following the ocean floor as it slopes toward the deep ocean. After some distance, you encounter a group of mountains. Some are tall enough to break the ocean's surface, forming islands. Others, called **seamounts,** are mountains that are completely underwater. Some seamounts have flat tops because their peaks have eroded away.

Next you cross a broad area covered with thick layers of mud and silt. This smooth, nearly flat region of the ocean floor is called the **abyssal plain** (uh BIHS uhl plain). After gliding over the abyssal plain for many kilometers, you need to steer the submarine sharply upward to avoid a mountain range ahead. The **mid-ocean ridge** is a continuous range of mountains that winds around Earth, much as a line of stitches winds around a baseball. The mid-ocean ridge passes through all of Earth's oceans. Nearly 80,000 kilometers long, it is the longest mountain range on Earth.

At the top of the mid-ocean ridge, your submarine is about two kilometers above the abyssal plain, but you are still at least one kilometer below the surface. From this vantage you can see

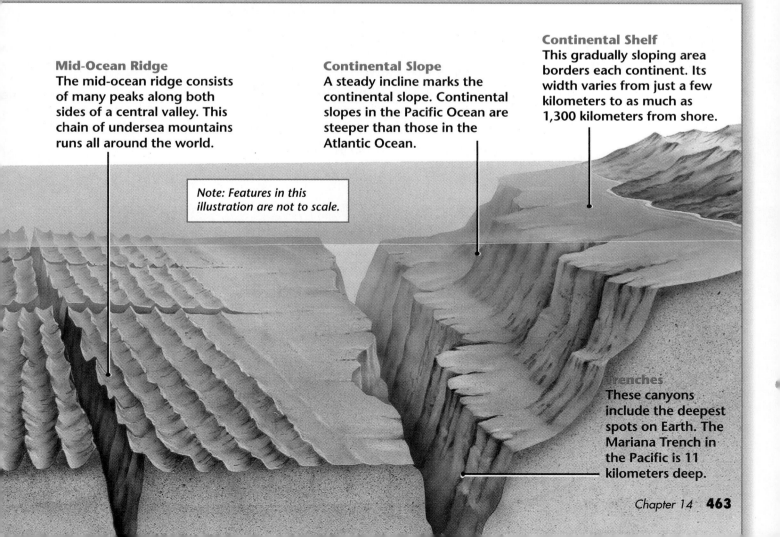

Mid-Ocean Ridge
The mid-ocean ridge consists of many peaks along both sides of a central valley. This chain of undersea mountains runs all around the world.

Note: Features in this illustration are not to scale.

Continental Slope
A steady incline marks the continental slope. Continental slopes in the Pacific Ocean are steeper than those in the Atlantic Ocean.

Continental Shelf
This gradually sloping area borders each continent. Its width varies from just a few kilometers to as much as 1,300 kilometers from shore.

Trenches
These canyons include the deepest spots on Earth. The Mariana Trench in the Pacific is 11 kilometers deep.

Interpreting Data

ACTIVITY

What is Earth's largest mountain? Use the following data to answer the question. Mauna Kea projects about 4,200 meters above sea level. Its base is on the floor of the Pacific Ocean, approximately 9,600 meters deep. Mt. Everest rises 8,850 meters from base to summit. Its base is located 100 meters above sea level. (*Hint:* Drawing a diagram may be helpful. Start with a line that represents sea level.)

Figure 3 When an undersea volcano reaches above the surface of the water, it forms an island. This peak is Mauna Kea in Hawaii.

that the mid-ocean ridge actually consists of two parallel chains of mountains separated by a central valley.

You descend from the mid-ocean ridge to another abyssal plain. Soon your submarine's lights reveal a dark gash in the ocean floor ahead of you. As you pass over it, you look down into a steep-sided canyon in the ocean floor called a **trench**. The trench is so deep you cannot see the bottom.

Your journey is nearly over as your submarine slowly climbs the continental slope. Finally you cross the continental shelf and maneuver the submarine into harbor.

Section 1 Review

1. List three factors that make exploring the deep ocean difficult.
2. Explain how sonar can be used to determine the depth of the ocean.
3. Describe one technique or expedition that has added to people's knowledge of the oceans.
4. Which ocean floor feature makes up the deepest parts of the ocean?
5. **Thinking Critically** **Inferring** Newly formed volcanic islands have a rich supply of minerals. Explain why this is so.

Science at Home

Make a "Room-Floor" Map With a family member, choose a room in your house and make a "room-floor" map based on depth readings. Imagine that the ceiling is the ocean surface and the floor is the bottom of the ocean. Follow a straight path across the middle of the room from one wall to another. At regular intervals, use a carpenter's measuring tape to take a depth reading from the ceiling to the floor or to the top of any furniture in that spot. Plot the depths on a graph. Then challenge another family member to identify the room by looking at the graph.

THE SHAPE OF THE OCEAN FLOOR

Imagine you are an oceanographer traveling across the Atlantic along the 45° N latitude line marked on the map. You and your crew are using sonar to gather data on the depth of the ocean between Nova Scotia, Canada, and the town of Soulac on the coast of France. In this lab, you will interpret the data to create a profile of the ocean floor.

Problem

How can you use data about ocean depths to determine the shape of the ocean floor?

Materials

pencil   graph paper

Procedure

1. Draw the axes of a graph. Label the horizontal axis Longitude. Mark from 65° W to 0° from left to right. Label the vertical axis Ocean Depth. Mark 0 meters at the top of the vertical axis to represent sea level. Mark −5000 meters at the bottom to represent the depth of 5000 meters below sea level. Mark depths at equal intervals along the vertical axis.

2. Examine the data in the table. The numbers in the Longitude column give the ship's location at 19 points in the Atlantic Ocean. Location 1 is Nova Scotia, and Location 19 is Soulac. The numbers in the Ocean Depth column give the depth measurements recorded at each location. Plot each measurement on your graph. Remember that the depths are represented on your graph as numbers below 0, or sea level.

3. Connect the points you have plotted with a line to create a profile of the ocean floor.

Analyze and Conclude

1. On your graph, identify and label the continental shelf and continental slope.
2. Label the abyssal plain on your graph. How would you expect the ocean floor to look there?
3. Label the mid-ocean ridge on your graph. Describe the process that is occurring there.
4. What might the feature at 10° W be? Explain.
5. **Think About It** How is it helpful to organize data into a data table or graph?

More to Explore

Use the depth measurements in the table to calculate the average depth of the Atlantic Ocean between Nova Scotia and France.

Ocean Depth Sonar Data	
Longitude	**Ocean Depth** (m)
1. 64° W	0
2. 60° W	91
3. 55° W	132
4. 50° W	73
5. 48° W	3512
6. 45° W	4024
7. 40° W	3805
8. 35° W	4171
9. 33° W	3439
10. 30° W	3073
11. 28° W	1756
12. 27° W	2195
13. 25° W	3146
14. 20° W	4244
15. 15° W	4610
16. 10° W	4976
17. 05° W	4317
18. 04° W	146
19. 01° W	0

SECTION 2 Life at the Ocean's Edge

DISCOVER ·····························ACTIVITY·····

Can Your Animal Hold On?

1. Your teacher will give you a ping-pong ball, a rock, and a box containing some materials. The ping-pong ball represents an ocean animal. Use some of the materials to design a way for the animal to cling to the rock.

2. Attach the ping-pong ball to the rock.

3. Place the rock in a sink or deep pan. Run water over the rock from a faucet or pitcher. Observe how well your animal stays in place on the rock.

Think About It

Inferring How might the ability to "hold on" be important to an animal that lives on the shore?

GUIDE FOR READING

◆ What factors affect where ocean organisms live?

◆ What conditions must organisms in the rocky intertidal zone overcome?

◆ What are the major types of coastal wetlands?

Reading Tip As you read, make a list of the habitats described in this section. Write a sentence or two describing each habitat.

At first glance, a sandy ocean beach may seem lifeless. As you walk along the water's edge in the soft, wet sand, you may notice some dark, tangled seaweed that has washed up on the shore. A crab scuttles away from the pile as you walk by. Seagulls screech and swoop overhead. But for the most part, the beach appears deserted.

If you look more closely at the wet sand, you will see evidence of living things right beneath your feet. Tiny, round holes are signs of burrowing clams. These clams dig down into the sand for protection and to prevent being washed away in the waves. If you wade into the water, you may be able to spot a sand crab taking advantage of the surf to feed. The bottom half of its body buried in the sand, the crab waits for the waves to carry in a fresh supply of food for its next meal.

The organisms on this beach are well suited to the conditions there. In this section, you will learn how marine organisms have adapted to other areas where the land and ocean meet.

Living Conditions

A sandy beach is one type of marine, or ocean, habitat. Remember that an organism's habitat provides the things the organism needs to survive. An organism also must be suited to the physical conditions of the environment it lives in. **Some physical factors that determine where marine organisms can live include salinity, water temperature, light, dissolved gases, nutrients, and wave action.**

As you learned in Chapter 13, these conditions vary in different parts of the ocean. For example, salinity is lower where rivers flow into the ocean, bringing a stream of fresh

water. Salinity is higher in shallow, warm seas, where more evaporation takes place. Because cold water holds more dissolved gas than warm water, cold ocean waters contain more oxygen than tropical waters. Different organisms are suited to live in these different conditions. As a result, the same organisms do not live in every part of the ocean.

On land, most organisms live on or near the surface. The ocean, on the other hand, is a three-dimensional environment. It is inhabited by organisms at every depth. Scientists classify marine organisms according to where they live and how they move.

Plankton are tiny algae and animals that float in the water and are carried by waves and currents. Algae plankton include geometrically shaped diatoms like those shown in Figure 4. Animal plankton include microscopic crustaceans and fish larvae. **Nekton** are free-swimming animals that can move throughout the water column. Octopus and squid, most fishes, and marine mammals such as whales and dolphins are nekton. **Benthos** are organisms that inhabit the ocean floor. Some benthos, like crabs, sea stars, and lobsters, move from place to place. Others, like sponges and sea anemones, stay in one location.

Plankton, nekton, and benthos are all found in most marine habitats. Many plankton and benthos are algae which, like plants, use sunlight to produce their own food through photosynthesis. Other plankton and benthos, as well as all nekton, are consumers. They eat either the algae or other consumers. Finally, some organisms, including many benthos, are decomposers. They break down wastes and remains of other organisms. These feeding relationships in a habitat make up a **food web**.

Figure 4 Marine organisms can be classified as plankton, nekton, or benthos. **A.** Intricate diatoms, one type of algae plankton, float on the ocean surface. **B.** These microscopic crustaceans, called copepods, are animal plankton. **C.** Free-swimming animals, such as this school of sweetlip fish, are nekton. **D.** Benthos live on the ocean floor. The sea stars and sea anemones in this colorful array are benthos.

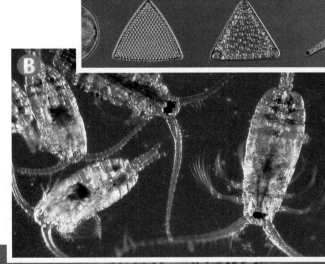

The first group of ocean habitats you will learn about are those found at the very edge of the ocean. The sandy beach you read about earlier is one example. Two habitats with a richer variety of life are rocky shores and salt marshes. As you read, think about how conditions in these habitats are similar, and how they are different.

☑ *Checkpoint* *Are sharks plankton, nekton, or benthos? Why?*

Rocky Shores

Imagine if your home had no walls or roof. Twice a day, a huge storm passes through, bringing a drenching downpour and winds so strong you can hardly keep your balance. At other times, the hot sun beats down, leaving you parched and dry. This is what life is like for organisms that live on rocky shores in the intertidal zone. The **intertidal zone** stretches from the highest high-tide line on land out to the point on the continental shelf exposed by the lowest low tide.

Organisms that live in the rocky intertidal zone must be able to tolerate the pounding of the waves and changes in salinity and temperature. They must also withstand periods of being underwater and periods of being exposed to the air. They must avoid drying out, hide from predators, and find food in this harsh setting. How are organisms able to survive?

Along the Rocks Rocky shores are found along much of both coasts of the United States. Figure 5 shows some of the colorful organisms that typically live along the rocky California coast.

The highest rocks, above the highest high-tide line, make up the spray zone. The spray zone is never completely covered with water, but it gets wet as the waves break against the rocks. A stripe of black algae indicates the highest high-tide line. The rocks below this level are encrusted with barnacles. Barnacles can close up their hard shells, trapping a drop of water inside to carry

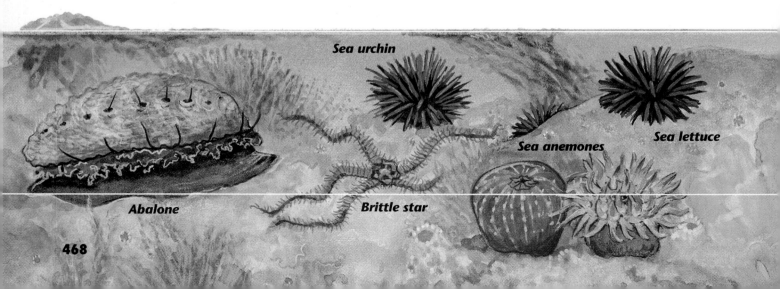

Sea urchin

Sea anemones

Sea lettuce

Abalone

Brittle star

them through the dry period until the next high tide. Lower down, clumps of blue and black mussels stick out amidst the algae. The mussels produce sticky threads that harden on contact with the water, attaching the mussels to the rock. The threads are so strong that scientists are studying them as a model for new glues. The rocks are also home to flat mollusks called limpets. Limpets have a large, muscular foot to hold on tightly. They secrete drops of mucus around the edges of their shells to form a tight seal.

Algae that live in the intertidal zone are also adapted to withstand the physical conditions. Rootlike structures anchor the strands of algae firmly to the rocks. Some algae are covered with a thick layer of slime. The slime keeps the algae from drying out during low tide.

In Tide Pools When the tide goes out, some water remains in depressions among the rocks called tide pools. As the water in a tide pool is warmed by the sun, it begins to evaporate. The remaining water becomes saltier. If it rains, however, the salinity quickly decreases. Organisms in the tide pool must be able to withstand these changes in temperature and salinity, as well as the force of the waves when the tide comes in again.

Sea stars cling to the rocks with rows of tiny suction cups on their undersides. Spiny purple sea urchins crawl slowly along the bottom of the tide pool. If the bottom is sandy, sea urchins can use their spines to dig a hole in which to bury themselves during heavy surf. Under shady rock ledges, sponges and sea anemones wait for the incoming tide to bring a fresh supply of plankton and other food particles. A sea anemone may look delicate, but some can survive out of water for over two weeks. When out of the water, the anemone pulls its tentacles inside. It folds up into a round blob, resembling a rolled-up sock.

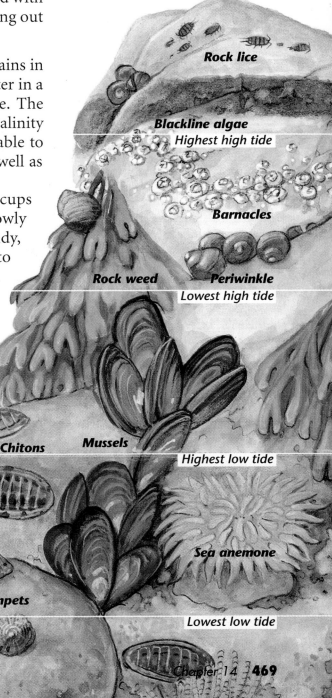

Figure 5 The constantly changing water level in the intertidal zone creates different habitats along a rocky coast. *Comparing and Contrasting* How are conditions different for organisms near the top of the rocks compared to organisms at the bottom?

Rock lice

Blackline algae
Highest high tide

Barnacles

Rock weed — Periwinkle
Lowest high tide

Chitons — Mussels
Highest low tide

Sea star

Sea anemone

Limpets
Lowest low tide

Hermit crab

Where River Meets Ocean

Other important environments along the ocean's edge are estuaries. **Estuaries** are coastal inlets or bays where fresh water from rivers mixes with the salty ocean water. Water that is partly salty and partly fresh is **brackish.**

Coastal wetlands are habitats found in and around estuaries. **Along the United States coasts, most coastal wetlands are either salt marshes or mangrove forests.** Salt marshes are especially abundant along the east coast from Massachusetts to Florida. Mangrove forests are found in the tropical waters along the southern coast of Florida and the Gulf of Mexico.

Salt Marshes A salt marsh oozes with smelly mud. Mosquitoes swarm over the water as it flows slowly through the tall, green grasses. The fresh water and tides contribute sediments, animal and plant matter, and other nutrients to the salt marsh, forming a soft, rich mud bottom.

A single plant, cordgrass, dominates the marsh. Unlike most plants, cordgrass can survive in salt water. The plant releases salt through small openings in its long, narrow leaves. The cordgrass that is not eaten by animals breaks down and is decomposed by bacteria and fungi in the water. The decomposed material supplies nutrients to organisms in the marsh.

Tidal channels run through the cordgrass. Waves break up as they enter the channels, so that organisms in the marsh are protected from the surf. Within the shelter of the marsh, fish, crabs, shrimp, and oysters hatch and feed before entering the harsher ocean environment offshore. As the tide retreats, mud flats are exposed. Hordes of crabs search for food in the rich mud. Herons, stilts, and egrets stalk across the mud to prey on the crabs and other benthos exposed by the low tide.

Mangrove Forests Mangroves—short, gnarled trees that grow well in brackish water—fringe the coastline of southern Florida. The mangroves'

Figure 6 Salt marshes and mangrove forests are two types of coastal wetlands. **A.** Salt water flows through tidal channels in a salt marsh. **B.** Arching prop roots anchor these black mangrove trees firmly in the soft, sandy soil around Florida Bay. *Making Generalizations How does the plant life in each of these habitats provide shelter for marine organisms?*

prop roots anchor the trees to the land. Mangroves can withstand all but the strongest hurricane winds. Without the mangroves to break the action of winds and waves, the coastline would change dramatically each hurricane season. The prop roots also trap sediment from the land. They create a protected nursery rich in nutrients for many young animals.

Protecting Estuaries The rivers that flow into estuaries can carry harmful substances as well as nutrients. When pollutants such as pesticides, sewage, and industrial waste get into the river water, they end up in the estuary. The pollutants change the water quality in the estuary. In turn, organisms that live in the estuary are affected. It can take many years for ocean tides to flush a heavy load of pollutants out of an estuary.

For example, Chesapeake Bay is a huge estuary located on the mid-Atlantic coast. It has been a rich source of oysters, clams, and blue crabs. However, pollutants from inland sources accumulated in the bay for many years. Their effect was to greatly reduce the number and kinds of organisms in the Chesapeake. When people realized the threat to the estuary, they took action. The water quality of rivers that empty into Chesapeake Bay is now regulated by law. Cleanup efforts have reduced much of the pollution in the bay. Today, organisms like the blue crab are making a comeback.

Figure 7 A crabber in Chesapeake Bay pulls up the last trap of the day. As the health of the estuary improves, the blue crab population is growing again.

Section 2 Review

1. Name five physical factors that affect organisms in marine habitats.
2. Describe conditions in the rocky intertidal zone.
3. List two ways that salt marshes and mangrove forests are alike and two ways they are different.
4. **Thinking Critically Making Judgments** A builder has proposed filling in a salt marsh to create a seaside resort. What positive and negative impacts might this proposal have on wildlife, local residents, and tourists? Would you support the proposal? Why or why not?

Check Your Progress   CHAPTER PROJECT
Your group should now select the marine environment you will create. Measure the space where you will build your model. Make a list of the physical features you will need to represent. Draw a scale diagram of your model and show it to your teacher. Label the different features and note the materials you will use. (*Hint:* Draw your sketch on graph paper to plan its size to fit the space.)

SECTION 3 The Neritic Zone and Open Ocean

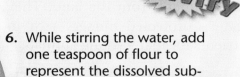

DISCOVER ·············· ACTIVITY

How Deep Can You See?

1. With a permanent marker, divide a white plastic lid into four quarters. Shade in two quarters as shown.

2. ✂ Use a pair of scissors to carefully poke a small hole in the center of the lid.

3. Tie a piece of string to a paper clip. Place the clip underneath the lid and thread the string up through the hole.

4. Tape the string tightly to a meterstick so that the lid presses against the bottom of the meterstick.

5. Fill a large, deep bucket with tap water.

6. While stirring the water, add one teaspoon of flour to represent the dissolved substances in seawater. The water should be slightly cloudy.

7. Lower the lid into the water so that it is 5 cm below the surface. Note whether the lid is still visible in the water.

8. Lower the lid 10 cm below the surface, then 15 cm, and so on until the lid is no longer visible.

Think It Over

Observing At what depth could you no longer see the lid? Based on your results, how do you think visibility changes with depth in the ocean?

GUIDE FOR READING

◆ What conditions in the neritic zone support organisms?

◆ Where do algae live in the open ocean?

◆ How do hydrothermal vents support organisms?

Reading Tip Before you read, preview Figure 8 on the facing page. Write some predictions about how the neritic zone and open ocean are similar and how they are different.

Floating mats of golden-brown, leaflike fronds on the ocean surface mark the location of a kelp forest. Diving below the surface, you find yourself surrounded by tall, swaying stalks of giant kelp. Sunlight filters through the water, producing a greenish light. As you pull yourself hand over hand down one of the kelp strands, you notice small bulbs at the base of each frond. You pinch one of the bulbs, and a bubble of gas escapes. These bulbs keep the heavy kelp fronds upright in the water.

The kelp forest is full of life. Bright-orange sheephead fish dart past you. Young sea lions chase one another around the kelp stalks. A sea otter, surrounded by a stream of bubbles, dives past you, down to the rocky bottom. When it rises, the otter is clutching a sea star between its paws. On the surface again, you watch the sea otter as it rolls on to its back among the kelp. The otter deftly uses its paws to scoop out the meat from the soft underside of the sea star.

◄ **Sea otter eating a sea star**

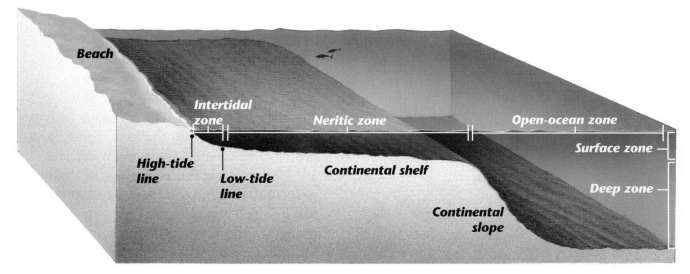

Beach

Intertidal zone

Neritic zone

Open-ocean zone

Surface zone

High-tide line

Low-tide line

Continental shelf

Deep zone

Continental slope

A kelp forest is one habitat found in the neritic zone. The **neritic zone** is the part of the ocean that extends from the low-tide line out to the edge of the continental shelf. Beyond the edge of the continental shelf lies the **open-ocean zone.** Locate the neritic and open-ocean zones in Figure 8. In this section you will learn how organisms are adapted to the conditions in these zones, from the sunlit surface waters to the coldest depths.

Conditions in the Neritic Zone

A huge variety of organisms are found in the neritic zone, more than in any other area of the ocean. Most of the world's major fishing grounds are found in this zone. What makes the neritic zone home to so many living things? The answer has to do with its location over the continental shelf. **The shallow water over the continental shelf receives sunlight and a steady supply of nutrients washed from the land into the ocean.** The light and nutrients enable large plantlike algae, such as the giant kelp, to grow. These algae serve as a food source and shelter for other organisms.

In many parts of the neritic zone, upwelling currents bring additional nutrients from the bottom to the surface. These nutrients support large numbers of plankton, which form the base of ocean food webs. Schools of fish such as sardines and anchovies feed on the plankton. Major fisheries in upwelling areas include Monterey Canyon off the California coast, Newfoundland's Grand Banks, and Georges Bank off the New England coast.

Two diverse habitats typically found within the neritic zone are kelp forests and coral reefs. As you read about each, think about how they are similar and how they are different.

☑ *Checkpoint* *What are two ways that nutrients may be supplied to the neritic zone?*

Figure 8 The ocean zone closest to land is the intertidal zone, which is bounded by the high-tide and low-tide lines. Next is the neritic zone, followed by the open-ocean zone, which makes up most of the world's oceans. The open ocean is divided by depth into the surface zone and the deep zone.
Interpreting Diagrams Which zones lie over the continental shelf?

Figure 9 Light streams through a forest of giant kelp and shadowy rockfish near Monterey, California. The closeup shows the gas-filled bulbs that keep the kelp upright in the water.

Life in a Kelp Forest

Kelp forests grow in cold neritic waters, such as those along the Pacific coast from Alaska to Mexico. These large, heavy algae require a solid, rocky bottom to anchor their stalks. A bundle of rootlike strands called a **holdfast** attaches the algae to the rocks. A stalk of giant kelp can grow to 30 meters in length. The gas-filled bulbs shown in the closeup to the left keep the heavy kelp stalk upright in the water.

The kelp use the sunlight and dissolved gases in the neritic zone to produce their own food. The kelp also provide a habitat for many other organisms. The curtains of kelp hide young gray whales from predators while their mothers are feeding. Sea slugs and snails live amid the tangle of the holdfasts.

Sea otters play a particularly important role in the kelp forest. In addition to eating abalone, sea otters feed on sea urchins, which eat the kelp. In areas where sea otters have disappeared, armies of sea urchins have devoured the kelp. The once-thriving forest has become a barren rocky zone.

Coral Reefs

Although a coral reef may look as if it is made of rock, it is actually made of living things. Coral reefs are created by colonies of tiny coral animals, each of which is not much larger than a pencil eraser. The coral animals produce a hard structure that surrounds their soft bodies. After the coral dies, the empty structure remains. New coral animals attach and grow on top of it. Over many years, a reef is built. Most of the coral reefs that exist today were begun about 5,000 to 10,000 years ago.

Microscopic algae live within the bodies of the coral animals and provide food for them. Because the algae require warm temperatures and sunlight, coral reefs can only form in shallow, tropical ocean waters. The reefs grow above continental shelves or around volcanic islands, where the water is shallow.

In areas where the seafloor is sinking, a reef may develop over time into an atoll. An **atoll** is a ring-shaped reef surrounding a shallow lagoon. Figure 10 shows the development of an atoll. It begins as a fringing reef that closely surrounds the edges of the island. As the reef grows upward, the island sinks, and a barrier reef forms. Water separates the top of the barrier reef from the land. The island continues to sink until it is eventually underwater, forming the atoll.

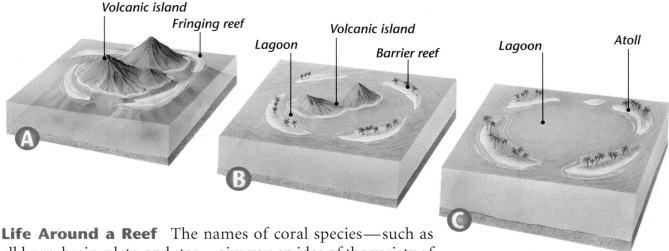

A

B

C

Volcanic island
Fringing reef

Volcanic island
Lagoon
Barrier reef

Lagoon
Atoll

Life Around a Reef The names of coral species—such as elkhorn, brain, plate, and star—give you an idea of the variety of shapes coral can form. Many animals live in and around the crevices of the reef, including octopuses, spiny lobsters, shrimp, toothy moray eels, and fish in all colors and sizes. Parrotfish like the one in Figure 11 scrape coral off the reef to eat. The parrotfish grind up the broken coral inside their bodies, producing the fine, soft sand commonly found around the reef.

Coral Reefs and Humans Coral reefs are natural aquarium exhibits, displaying a colorful diversity of life to be enjoyed and studied. Reefs also protect coastlines during violent storms. The reefs break up the surf, preventing waves from severely eroding the land. However, human activities can harm the fragile reefs. Boat anchors dragging across a reef can damage it. Divers can accidentally break off pieces of the reef. Even brushing against the reef can harm some of the coral animals. Because coral only grows a few millimeters a year, a reef cannot quickly recover.

Changes in water temperature and clarity also affect coral reefs. For example, if the water becomes too warm, the corals release the algae that live inside them. Cloudy water endangers the algae by reducing the amount of light that reaches them. If sediments produced by storms or human activities bury a reef, the algae in the living coral cannot survive. Without the algae, the coral animals do not grow well and eventually die.

Today many people understand the importance of coral reefs and try to protect them. Many reef areas have been designated as marine sanctuaries, which limits the amount of diving and other activity allowed near the reef. Scientists worldwide are also studying the effects of temperature change and pollution on the reefs to better protect them.

☑ *Checkpoint* *How can human activities impact a coral reef?*

Figure 10 An atoll develops in stages. **A.** A fringing reef closely surrounds an island. **B.** As the island sinks, a lagoon forms inside the barrier reef. **C.** Finally, the island sinks below the surface, leaving a ring-shaped atoll. *Interpreting Diagrams In which stage is the reef the youngest?*

Figure 11 A parrotfish delicately nibbles away at a coral reef in the Red Sea. Reefs provide a habitat for many fish and other marine organisms.

Sharpen your Skills

Inferring

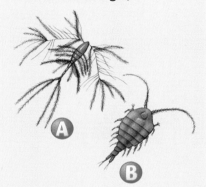

To keep from sinking, many plankton rely on the friction between their bodies and the surrounding water. More friction is needed to stay afloat in warm water than in denser cold water. One of the copepods below is found in tropical ocean waters, while the other is found near the poles. Which do you think is which? Explain your reasoning. (*Hint:* More streamlined shapes create less friction with their surroundings.)

Conditions in the Open Ocean

The open ocean begins where the neritic zone ends, at the edge of the continental shelf. Diving into the open ocean is like descending a long staircase with a light only at the very top. Light from the sun only penetrates a short distance into the water, typically to a depth of less than 200 meters. If the water is cloudy with sediment, sunlight does not reach as deep. In clear tropical waters, on the other hand, some light may reach as deep as a few hundred meters.

The fact that only a small portion of the open ocean receives sunlight is one way it differs from the neritic zone. Another difference is the amount of dissolved nutrients in the water. While the neritic zone receives a constant supply of nutrients from shore, dissolved nutrients are less abundant in the open ocean. As a result, the open ocean zone supports fewer organisms.

The Surface Zone The surface zone extends as far as sunlight reaches below the surface. **The surface zone is the only part of the open ocean that receives enough sunlight to support the growth of algae.** These microscopic algae are the base of open-ocean food webs. Animal plankton that feed on algae include tiny crustaceans called copepods, shrimp-like krill, and the young of many ocean animals such as crabs, mollusks, and fishes.

Figure 13 on the facing page shows an Arctic food web. Each organism in this food web depends either directly or indirectly on the plankton. Throughout the ocean, plankton are a source of food for other organisms of all sizes. If you think of sharks as sharp-toothed, meat-eating hunters, you might be surprised to learn that the biggest sharks of all feed entirely on tiny plankton! Whale sharks, which can grow to more than 10 meters long, strain plankton from the water. Many whales feed only on plankton as well, including Earth's largest animal, the blue whale.

The Deep Zone When you explored the water column in Chapter 13, you observed that the ocean became darker and colder as you descended. Because of its harsh conditions, the deep ocean is often compared to a desert. Compared to other land and ocean environments, few organisms live in the deep zone. But unlike a desert baking under the bright sun, the deep ocean is cold, dark, and wet.

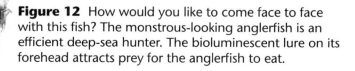

Figure 12 How would you like to come face to face with this fish? The monstrous-looking anglerfish is an efficient deep-sea hunter. The bioluminescent lure on its forehead attracts prey for the anglerfish to eat.

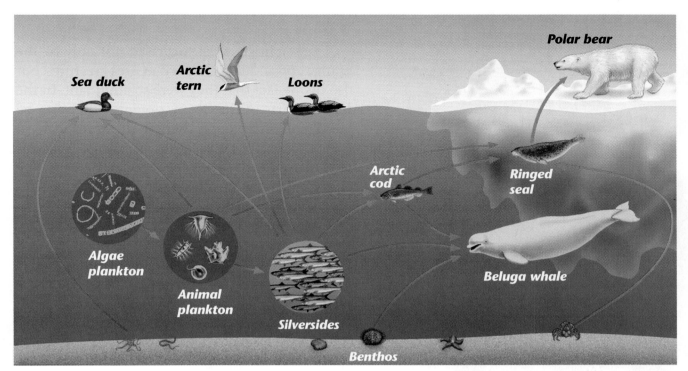

Figure 13 This marine food web includes typical organisms found in the Arctic Ocean. The arrows indicate what each organism eats. *Interpreting Diagrams Which organisms feed directly on the Arctic cod? Which organisms depend indirectly on the cod?*

Finding food in the darkness is a challenge. Many deep-sea fishes produce their own light. The production of light by living things is called **bioluminescence.** Some fishes use chemical reactions to produce their own light, like fireflies on land. Other fishes have colonies of bioluminescent bacteria living in pockets on their bodies. Still others have light-producing organs. The anglerfish, for example, has a light organ on its head. The fish lurks in the shadows below the pool of light. Shrimp and fishes that are attracted to the light become the anglerfish's prey.

Because the food supply in most of the deep ocean is much more limited than in shallower water, animals in this zone must be good hunters to survive. The gaping mouths of many deep-sea fishes are filled with fang-like teeth. Rows of sharp teeth stick out at angles, ensuring that any animal it bites cannot escape.

✓ *Checkpoint* *Why do very few organisms live in the deep zone?*

Hydrothermal Vents

As the submersible *Alvin* descended to a depth of 2,500 meters into the Galápagos Rift in the Pacific Ocean one day in 1977, the scientists aboard could hardly believe their eyes. Outside the submersible, the headlights revealed a bizarre scene. Clouds of black water billowed up from chimney-shaped structures on the ocean floor. Meter-long tubes with gaping, lipstick-red ends swayed in the water. White crabs scuttled over the rocks, crawling around clams as big as dinner plates.

Figure 14 Giant tube worms cluster around a hydrothermal vent on the deep ocean floor.

The scientists were surprised not only by the strange appearance of these deep-sea creatures, but also by the fact that they were so abundant. In the deepest parts of the ocean, organisms tend to be very small and slow-moving because food is so rare. The number, size, and variety of organisms were unusually large for such a deep part of the ocean. What could these organisms find to eat so far from sunlight?

The strange community the scientists in *Alvin* observed was located around a hydrothermal vent. A **hydrothermal vent** is an area where ocean water sinks through cracks in the ocean floor, is heated by the underlying magma, and rises again through the cracks. These vents are located along ocean ridges, where the plates are moving apart and new ocean floor is forming.

The heated water coming from a vent carries gases and minerals from Earth's interior. **The chemical nutrients in the heated water support the unique group of organisms that are found around hydrothermal vents.** Bacteria feed directly on the chemical nutrients that are spewed out of the vents. Like the algae in the surface zone that use sunlight to produce food, these bacteria use the chemicals to produce food. They form the base of the food web at a hydrothermal vent.

Other organisms, like the giant clams, feed on the bacteria. The red-tipped tube worms are supplied with food by bacteria living within their tissues. Meanwhile, the scuttling crabs feed on the remains of the other inhabitants in their unusual habitat.

Section 3 Review

1. Describe the physical conditions in the neritic zone.
2. What factor limits where algae are found in the open ocean?
3. What is the source of nutrients for organisms around a hydrothermal vent?
4. Explain how bioluminescence is important to some fish that live in the deep ocean.
5. **Thinking Critically** **Relating Cause and Effect** When forests on a tropical island are cut down, the soil is more easily eroded. Explain how this could affect a coral reef near the island.

Check Your Progress

CHAPTER PROJECT

By now you should have selected an organism to model. Research your organism to determine its size and other physical characteristics. How does the organism survive in its marine habitat? Check your plan for constructing the organism with your teacher. Your group should also begin building your model habitat. Make sure you have collected all the necessary materials before you begin building.

4 Resources From the Ocean

Is It From the Ocean?

1. Your teacher will give you some labels from common house-hold products. Read the ingredient information on each label.

2. Divide the products into two piles—those you think include substances that come from the ocean and those that do not.

Think It Over

Classifying For each product that you classified as coming from the ocean, name the item from the ocean that is used to produce it. In what ocean zone is it found?

When European explorers began sailing to North America, they were astounded by the huge number of codfish that lived off its eastern coast. One traveler reported that this area was so "swarming with fish that they could be taken not only with a net but in baskets let down and weighted with a stone." Others reported sailing through schools of cod so thick they slowed the boats down!

This cod fishery stretched from Newfoundland to a hook of land appropriately named Cape Cod. For more than 400 years, the seemingly endless supply of "King Cod" supported a thriving fishing industry. But beginning in the early 1900s, fishing crews had to work harder to catch the same amount of cod. As the fishing grew more difficult each year, it became clear that the cod were disappearing. With the price of cod rising, there was more competition to catch the fewer fish available. In 1992, the Canadian government had to declare the fishery closed.

No one knows for sure how long it will take the cod population to fully recover. Scientists are studying cod and other fisheries to learn how to preserve them for future generations.

Living Resources

Cod are just one example of a living resource from the ocean. How many other kinds of seafood

◆ How does the supply of fish in a fishery change from year to year?

◆ Who controls and protects ocean resources?

Reading Tip Before you read, rewrite the headings in the section as how, why, or what questions. As you read, look for answers to those questions.

Figure 15 Big catches of cod like this one from Georges Bank, off the New England coast, have become less common since the early 1900s.

have you tasted: tuna, shrimp, flounder, lobster, clams, squid, oysters, seaweed, or mussels? These foods and the many others that come from the ocean make up about five percent of the world's total food supply.

Harvesting Fish   Just six species make up the majority of fishes harvested for eating: herring, sardine, anchovy, cod, pollock, and mackerel. Locate the world's major fisheries in Figure 16. You can see that they are all located close to coasts. Nearly all fishes caught are harvested from coastal waters or areas of upwelling. These waters contain nutrients and plankton on which they feed.

If used wisely, fisheries naturally renew themselves each year. **New fish are born, replacing those that are caught, but only as long as the fishery is not overfished. Overfishing causes the supply of fish to decrease.** Overfishing has become a problem as better technology has enabled people to catch large numbers of fish very quickly. For example, some fishing fleets have electronic equipment that allows them to locate schools of fish precisely. They can be caught faster than they can reproduce. Once this occurs, it begins a cycle that leads to fewer and fewer fish each season. Eventually, the fishery may be depleted, like the cod fishery you read about earlier.

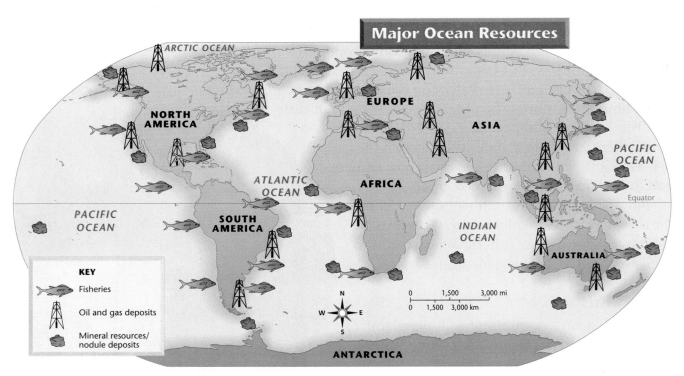

Figure 16 All over the world, the oceans are an important source of food, oil and gas, and minerals. *Interpreting Maps Where are Africa's major fisheries located?*

Aquaculture As fish stocks become depleted, **aquaculture,** the

 INTEGRATING TECHNOLOGY farming of saltwater and freshwater organisms, is likely to become more common. Aquaculture has been practiced in some Asian countries for centuries. This process involves creating an environment for the organisms and controlling nutrient levels, water temperature, light, and other factors to help them thrive. Oysters, abalone, and shrimp have successfully been farmed in artificial saltwater ponds and protected bays. Even landlocked regions can produce seafood using aquaculture. For example, salmon are now being raised in Nebraska fields that once were cattle ranches.

Other Ocean Products People harvest ocean organisms for many purposes besides food. For example, algae is an ingredient in many household products. Its gelatin-like texture makes it an ideal base for detergents, shampoos, cosmetics, paints, and even ice cream! Sediments containing the hard fragments of diatoms are used for abrasives and polishes. Many researchers believe that other marine organisms may be important sources of chemicals for medicines in the future.

☑ *Checkpoint* *How are fisheries naturally renewed each year?*

Mineral Resources

In addition to living organisms, the ocean contains valuable nonliving resources. Some of these are found within ocean water itself. Chapter 12 described how fresh water can be extracted from ocean water in the process of desalination. Desalination provides fresh water for many dry areas and islands. When the fresh water is removed from ocean water, the salts that are left behind are also a valuable resource. Over half of the world's supply of magnesium, a strong, light metal, is obtained from seawater in this way.

A second source of nonliving resources is the ocean floor. From the layer of sediments covering the continental shelves, gravel and sand are mined for use in building construction. In some areas of the world diamonds and gold are mined from sand deposits. Metals such as manganese also accumulate on the ocean floor. The metals concentrate around pieces of shell, forming black lumps called **nodules** (NAHJ oolz). Because they sometimes occur in waters as deep as 5,000 meters, recovering the nodules is a difficult process. The technology to gather them is still being developed.

Not all nations have agreed on who owns the rights to nodules and other resources on the deep ocean floor. Some feel the

Seaweed Candy

Make this Asian dessert **ACTIVITY** to discover one way to eat algae. Remember to prepare food only in a non-science classroom. Be sure to get permission before using a stove.

2 blocks of agar (one 0.5-ounce package)
1 cup sugar
4 cups guava juice or other fruit juice
food coloring

1. Rinse the agar, a substance obtained from algae.

2. Break agar into cubes and place them in a saucepan.

3. 🧤 Put on your goggles. Add the sugar and juice to the pan. Bring the mixture to a boil. Turn down the heat and cook, stirring, until the agar dissolves.

4. Remove pan from heat and stir in a few drops of food coloring. Pour the mixture into a shallow pan. Let cool.

5. Refrigerate candy until firm.

6. Cut into blocks and serve.

Inferring What purpose does the agar serve in this recipe? What purposes do the sugar and juice serve?

Figure 17 Lit up like a city at night, this Norwegian oil-drilling platform rises above the icy waters of the North Sea. Hundreds of people may live and work aboard such an oil rig.

nations who find and recover the minerals should own them. Others feel that this is unfair to nations that cannot yet afford the technology to obtain a share of these resources.

Fuels From the Ocean Floor

Another type of nonliving resource forms from the remains of dead marine organisms. These remains sink to the bottom of the ocean, where they are buried by sediments. As more sediments accumulate, the buried remains decompose. Over hundreds of thousands of years, the heat and pressure from the overlying layers gradually transform the remains into oil and natural gas.

As you know, many organisms live in the part of the ocean above the continental shelf. The thick sediments on the continental shelves bury the remains of living things. As a result, the richest deposits of oil and gas are often located on the continental shelves.

Oil rigs like the one in Figure 17 drill the rocky ocean floor as much as 300 meters below the surface. Imagine trying to dig a hole in the concrete bottom of a swimming pool, while standing on a raft floating on the surface of the water. You can see why drilling the ocean floor is very difficult! Ocean drilling is made even harder by strong currents, winds, and violent storms.

✓ *Checkpoint* *What is the source of the oil and gas deposits on the ocean floor?*

Ocean Pollution

It was once thought that the ocean was so vast that people could not damage it by throwing wastes into it. This is partially true—the ocean is a self-cleaning system that can absorb some wastes without permanent damage. But dumping large amounts of wastes into the ocean threatens many marine organisms.

Sharpen your Skills

Observing

ACTIVITY

Refer back to the map of ocean resources in Figure 16. Which resources are located close to land? Which are located throughout the ocean? Can you suggest an explanation for any patterns you observe?

Recall that water pollution is the addition of any substance that has a negative effect on the living things that depend on the water. Most ocean pollution comes from the land. Although some is the result of natural occurrences, most pollution is related to human activities.

Natural Sources Some pollution is the result of weather. For example, heavy rains wash fresh water into estuaries and out into the water offshore. This surge of fresh water pollutes the ocean by lowering its salinity. A sudden change in salinity may kill ocean animals that are unable to adjust to it.

Human Sources Pollutants related to human activities include sewage, chemicals, and trash dumped into coastal waters. Chemicals that run off fields and roads often end up in the ocean. These substances can harm ocean organisms directly. The pollutants can also build up in their bodies and poison other animals, including people, that feed on them. Trash can cause serious problems, too. Seals, otters, and other marine mammals that need to breathe air can get tangled in old fishing lines or nets and drown. Other animals are harmed when they swallow plastic bags that block their stomachs.

Oil Spills One major threat to ocean life is oil pollution. When an oil tanker or drilling platform is damaged, oil leaks into the surrounding ocean. Oil is harmful to many organisms. It coats the bodies of marine mammals and birds. This destroys their natural insulation and affects their ability to float. The oil is also harmful to animals that swallow it.

Figure 18 Removing oil from a beach is a difficult, messy chore. This cleanup worker is using absorbent mops to remove oil from the sand. In the closeup, two more workers try to clean oil from a bird's beak and feathers. *Inferring What might have caused this oil pollution?*

Figure 19 Flags fly outside the United Nations headquarters in New York City. The United Nations develops policies on the use of the oceans by countries. *Applying Concepts Why can't each nation make its own laws regarding ocean resources?*

Interestingly, there is a natural cleaning process that slowly takes place after oil spills. Certain bacteria that live in the ocean feed on the oil and multiply. It takes many years, but eventually an oil-covered beach can become clean again. This has happened even in the portions of the Prince William Sound in Alaska that were blanketed with oil from the 1989 wreck of the oil tanker *Exxon Valdez.*

Protecting Earth's Oceans

Who owns the ocean and its resources? Who has the responsibility of protecting them? These are questions that nations have been struggling to answer for hundreds of years. **Because the world ocean is a continuous body of water that has no boundaries, it is difficult to determine who, if anyone, should control portions of it. Nations must cooperate to manage and protect the oceans.**

The United Nations has established different boundaries in the oceans. According to one treaty, a nation now controls the first 22 kilometers out from its coasts. The nation also controls resources in the waters or on the continental shelf within 370 kilometers of shore. This treaty leaves approximately half of the ocean's surface waters as "high seas," owned by no nation. Ownership of the ocean floor beneath the high seas is still under debate.

Other international efforts have resulted in cooperation aimed at reducing ocean pollution. Examples include the establishment of marine refuges and regulations for building safer oil tankers.

Section 4 Review

1. How can overfishing affect a fishery?
2. Explain why international cooperation is necessary to solve many problems related to ocean resources.
3. Name a nonliving resource found in the ocean. Where is it located? How is it obtained and used?
4. **Thinking Critically Making Judgments** Should mineral resources on the ocean floor belong to whoever finds them, or to the closest nation? Consider each position and write a short paragraph stating your opinion.

Science at Home

Ocean Escape Have a family member hook one end of a rubber band around his or her wrist. Stretch the rubber band across the back of the hand and hook the free end over three fingers as shown. Now ask the person to try to remove the rubber band without using the other hand. Explain that this shows how difficult it is for seals or dolphins to free themselves from a plastic beverage ring or piece of net. Can you propose any ways to reduce this threat to marine mammals?

Shrimp Farms—At What Cost to the Environment?

About one quarter of the world's shrimp are raised on shrimp farms. Many shrimp farms are created by clearing trees from mangrove forests and digging shallow, fenced-in ponds. Farmers then fill the ponds with ocean water and shrimp larvae. After about six months, when the shrimp are big enough to sell, the farmers drain the pond water back into the ocean.

To grow healthy shrimp, farmers often add fertilizers, medicines, and pesticides to the ponds. When the pond water is released to the ocean, these chemicals can harm other animals. The United Nations has estimated that 25 percent of the world's mangrove forests have been destroyed as a result of shrimp farming. As awareness of the environmental impact of shrimp farms has grown, the industry has come under attack.

▲ Shrimp farmer in Malaysia

The Issues

How Important Is Shrimp Farming? For many people in the world, shrimp is more than luxury food: It is a staple of their diet and their main source of animal protein. The demand for shrimp currently is greater than the natural supply in Earth's oceans. To meet the demand, many countries, including the United States, have turned to shrimp farming. Shrimp farms provide needed food and jobs that some people believe are worth a certain amount of damage to the environment. They feel it is not possible to have shrimp farms that are both highly productive and environmentally safe.

Can the Pollution Be Reduced? Shrimp farmers are exploring ways to reduce the impact of their farms on the coastal environment. Better pond construction can help stop chemicals from leaking into the surrounding waters. Some governments recognize the importance of mangrove forests in providing a habitat for many species and in protecting the shoreline. These governments have passed laws regulating where shrimp farms may be built. Farmers must investigate the impact their ponds will have on nearby mangrove forests and get approval before choosing a location. These methods of reducing environmental damage, however, are expensive and time-consuming for the shrimp farmers.

Should Farmers Use Alternative Methods? In some parts of Asia, a less destructive method of shrimp farming has been practiced for centuries. Raising shrimp in ditches dug around clusters of mangroves provides the young shrimp with a natural nutrient supply that includes debris from the trees. A gate keeps the shrimp from escaping into the ocean and also allows the motion of the tides to replenish the water in the ditches. The disadvantage of this method is that it is much less profitable than the constructed shrimp ponds. Many shrimp farmers could not afford to switch to this method. If they did, the price of shrimp worldwide would rise.

You Decide

1. Identify the Problem

In your own words, summarize the problem facing shrimp farmers.

2. Analyze the Options

Make a list of the solutions mentioned. List the advantages and drawbacks of each. Who would benefit from each plan? Who might suffer?

3. Find a Solution

Write a brochure or pamphlet for shrimp farmers that states your proposed solution to their problem. After you have written the text, illustrate your brochure.

CLEANING UP AN OIL SPILL

Oil Spill in Bay

An oil tanker hit a reef yesterday, spilling thousands of barrels of crude oil into the water. Cleanup efforts will begin today. Workers must race against time to save birds and sea otters. With stormy weather forecasted, however, scientists expect considerable damage. Volunteers are needed to help clean up.

Imagine that you are a volunteer helping to clean up an oil spill. In this activity, you will use a variety of materials to remove as much oil as possible from the water and to keep oil from reaching the beach. You will also see how oil affects animals that are exposed to a spill.

Problem

How can an oil spill be cleaned up?

Skills Focus

making models, forming operational definitions

Materials

water	shallow pan	vegetable oil
feather	paper cup	plastic dropper
paper towels	cotton balls	wooden sticks
marking pen	graduated cylinder, 100 mL	

Procedure

1. Place a pan on a table or desk covered with newspaper. Label one end of the pan "Beach" and the other end "Open Ocean."
2. Pour water into the pan to a depth of 2 cm.
3. Gently pour 20 mL of vegetable oil into the center of the pan. Record your observations.
4. Dip a feather and your finger into the oil. Observe how each is affected by the oil.

5. Try to wipe oil off the feather and your finger using paper towels. Record whether any oil is left on the feather or your skin.
6. Now try to clean up the spill. Record your observations with each step. First, using the wooden sticks, try to keep the oil from reaching the "beach." Next, gently blow across the surface of the water from the "open ocean" side to simulate wind and waves. Then use the cotton balls, paper towels, and dropper to recover as much of the oil as possible.
7. When you are finished, dispose of the oil and used items in the paper cup. Wash your hands.

Analyze and Conclude

1. How successful were you in cleaning up the oil? Is the water as clean as it was at the start?
2. How well were you able to keep the oil from reaching the beach? Describe how useful the different materials were in cleaning up the oil.
3. Describe what happened when you cleaned the feather and your finger. What might happen to fish, birds, and other animals if they were coated with oil as a result of an oil spill?
4. Predict how storms with strong winds and waves would affect the cleanup of an oil spill.
5. **Apply** Look at the used cleanup materials in the paper cup. What additional problems for cleanup crews does this suggest?

Getting Involved

One way to reduce the threat of oil spills is to transport less oil across the oceans. To make that possible, people would need to use less oil in their daily lives. Oil is used to heat homes, to produce gasoline, and to make products such as plastics and textiles. List at least three ways to reduce the amount of oil you and your family use.

SECTION 1 Exploring the Ocean

Key Ideas

◆ Technology such as sonar enables scientists to study the deep ocean floor despite the darkness, cold, and extreme pressure there.

◆ The ocean floor has features similar to those found on the continents, including plains, mountain ranges, volcanoes, and trenches.

Key Terms

sonar	continental shelf	continental slope
seamount	abyssal plain	mid-ocean ridge
trench		

SECTION 2 Life at the Ocean's Edge
INTEGRATING LIFE SCIENCE

Key Ideas

◆ Physical factors that affect marine organisms include salinity, water temperature, light, dissolved gases, nutrients, and wave action.

◆ Organisms in the rocky intertidal zone must be able to tolerate the pounding of the waves, as well as being both underwater and exposed to the air for long periods of time.

◆ Coastal wetlands include salt marshes and mangrove forests.

Key Terms

plankton	nekton	benthos
food web	intertidal zone	estuary
brackish		

SECTION 3 The Neritic Zone and Open Ocean
INTEGRATING LIFE SCIENCE

Key Ideas

◆ The neritic zone receives sunlight and nutrients washed from the land. Habitats in this zone include kelp forests and coral reefs.

◆ The thin layer of sunlit water at the surface is the only part of the open ocean that can support algae, which need the sunlight to produce food. Other marine organisms depend on the food made by algae.

◆ The chemical nutrients in the hot water around a hydrothermal vent support the organisms that live around the vent.

Key Terms

neritic zone	open-ocean zone
holdfast	atoll
bioluminescence	hydrothermal vent

SECTION 4 Resources From the Ocean

Key Ideas

◆ If used wisely, fisheries are a renewable resource. New fish will replace those that are caught, but only if overfishing does not reduce the population too severely.

◆ Nonliving resources from the ocean include dissolved substances in seawater and minerals and fuels from the ocean floor.

Key Terms

aquaculture	nodules

Organizing Information

Compare/Contrast Table Make a table about ocean habitats on a separate sheet of paper. Include rows for the following habitats: tide pool, coral reef, surface zone, and hydrothermal vent. For each habitat, fill in the ocean zone where it is found, the conditions (such as sunlight, pressure, and temperature) that exist there, and the types of organisms typically found there. (See the Skills Handbook for more on compare/contrast tables.)

Reviewing Content

 For more review of key concepts, see the Interactive Student Tutorial CD-ROM.

Multiple Choice

Choose the letter of the best answer.

1. A smooth, nearly flat region of the ocean floor is called a(n)
   a. trench.   b. mid-ocean ridge.
   c. abyssal plain. d. sea mount.

2. An area where rivers flow into the ocean and fresh water and salt water mix is a(n)
   a. tide pool.
   b. hydrothermal vent.
   c. estuary.
   d. kelp forest.

3. A tropical ocean community made by tiny animals that have algae growing in their tissues is a(n)
   a. mangrove forest.   b. salt marsh.
   c. intertidal zone.   d. coral reef.

4. In the open-ocean zone, organisms depend directly or indirectly on food that is made by
   a. marine mammals.
   b. nekton in the water column.
   c. plants growing on the deep ocean floor.
   d. algae near the surface.

5. Most ocean pollutants come from
   a. marine organisms. b. the land.
   c. the atmosphere.   d. Earth's core.

True or False

If the statement is true, write true. If it is false, change the underlined word or words to make the statement true.

6. <u>Benthos</u> are free-swimming animals that can move throughout the water column.

7. The area between the high and low tide lines is the <u>neritic</u> zone.

8. Water that is partly salty and partly fresh is <u>brackish</u>.

9. A ring-shaped coral reef surrounding a lagoon is called a(n) <u>seamount</u>.

10. Many deep-sea fishes use their <u>bioluminescence</u> to attract prey.

Checking Concepts

11. Describe one method that has been used to study the ocean floor.

12. How can sonar be used to measure the depth of the ocean?

13. Describe a typical marine food web.

14. Describe three physical factors that organisms in the rocky intertidal zone must overcome.

15. Explain why estuaries are especially vulnerable to pollution.

16. What is an atoll? How is it formed?

17. Explain why scientists were surprised to discover the variety of organisms living around hydrothermal vents.

18. **Writing to Learn** Imagine that you are an "aquanaut" on a voyage of discovery across the ocean floor. Write a logbook entry that summarizes your observations as you travel from one continent to another. Include details about the shape of the ocean floor, as well as some organisms you encounter along your journey.

Thinking Critically

19. **Classifying** Classify each of the following organisms as plankton, nekton, or benthos: squid, sea stars, microscopic algae, whales, sea otters, anglerfish, and giant clams.

20. **Making Generalizations** Explain why many of the world's fisheries are located in the neritic zone.

21. **Predicting** Suppose the number of plankton in the ocean suddenly decreased to half their current number. Predict how this would affect other marine organisms.

22. **Relating Cause and Effect** How might fertilizers used on farmland result in ocean pollution near shore?

Applying Skills

Use the diagram of a portion of the ocean floor to answer Questions 23–25.

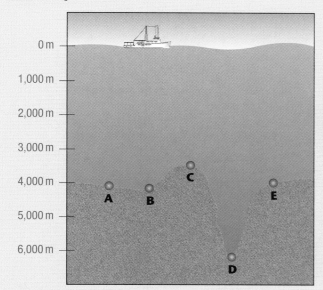

23. Interpreting Diagrams What is the approximate depth of the ocean floor at point A? At point C?

24. Inferring What might the feature between locations A and B be? The feature at point D?

25. Posing Questions What other information would help you determine whether point A or point E is closer to the mid-ocean ridge? Explain.

Performance   CHAPTER PROJECT   Assessment

Present Your Project With your group, rehearse the guided tour of the environment you will give. As you rehearse, check to see that your marine environment is complete. Make any final changes now.

Reflect and Record In your notebook, write a paragraph summarizing how each organism your group modeled belongs in the habitat you built. What was the most difficult element of the environment to model?

Test Preparation

Use these questions to prepare for standardized tests.

Study the diagram. Then answer Questions 26–29.

26. Which part of the ocean supports the greatest variety of organisms?
 a. neritic zone
 b. intertidal zone
 c. open-ocean deep zone
 d. open-ocean surface zone

27. Which part of the ocean is in constant darkness and cold, with few organisms?
 a. neritic zone
 b. intertidal zone
 c. open-ocean deep zone
 d. open-ocean surface zone

28. Organisms in this area must be able to survive severe changes in salinity, temperature, and exposure to air.
 a. neritic zone
 b. intertidal zone
 c. open-ocean surface zone
 d. open-ocean deep zone

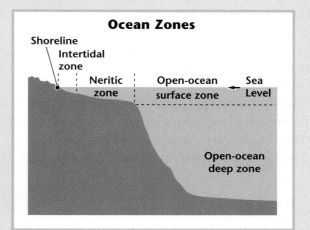

29. The edge of the continental shelf forms the boundary between which parts of the ocean?
 a. high tide and low tide lines
 b. intertidal zone and neritic zone
 c. neritic zone and open ocean
 d. open-ocean deep zone and hydrothermal vents

THE MISSISSIPPI

What would you name a river that—

- *carries about 420 million metric tons of cargo a year,*
- *drains 31 states and 2 Canadian provinces,*
- *looks like a tree that has a thin top trunk and 2 strong branches,*
- *flows at about 18,100 cubic meters of water per second?*

Native Americans called the river *misi sipi*, an Algonquin word meaning "big water," or "father of waters."

Have you ever traveled on a river or lake that feeds into the mighty Mississippi River? Perhaps you have but did not realize it. The map below shows the watershed of this great river. From the west, the Missouri River — the "Big Muddy"— carries soft silt eroded from the Great Plains. The Missouri joins the Mississippi near St. Louis, turning the river's clear water to muddy brown. From the east, the Ohio River flows in from the rocky Appalachian plateau, nearly doubling the volume of water in the river. In all, the huge Mississippi watershed drains about 40 percent of the United States.

The Mississippi River starts at Lake Itasca and flows through 10 states to the Gulf of Mexico. The river is a drainage point for hundreds of tributaries in the vast Mississippi watershed. ▶

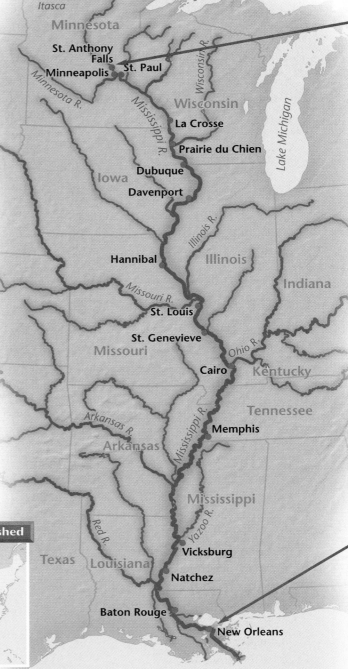

The Mississippi River Watershed

A National Trade Route

Since Native Americans settled in villages along the Mississippi around 1,200 years ago, the river has served as a water highway for trade and travel.

▲ St. Anthony Falls is the northernmost point of navigation on the Mississippi.

In the late 1600s, French explorers, fur traders, and soldiers arrived in the Mississippi Valley. They chose strategic sites for forts and fur-trading posts — Prairie du Chien, St. Louis, and St. Genevieve. At first, traders used canoes, rafts, and flatboats to carry goods downstream. But traveling up the river was difficult. Crews had to use long poles to push narrow keelboats upstream against the current.

In 1811, the arrival of *The New Orleans*, the first steamboat on the Mississippi River, changed the river forever. Within 40 years, there were hundreds more steamboats and many new river towns. On the upper Mississippi, the city of Minneapolis grew up around flour mills near the falls. Farther downstream, Memphis became a center for transporting cotton. Later, it was a stopping point for showboats and musicians. New Orleans quickly became a world port. It received cotton, tobacco, and sugar cane from southern plantations and exported corn, wheat and indigo to Europe. Imported luxury items, such as soap, coffee, shoes, and textiles, traveled upstream from the port of New Orleans. Up and down the river townspeople eagerly waited for the cry, "Steamboat comin'!"

▲ Crews in flatboats rode the river currents, steering with long oars.

▲ New Orleans has been a major trading port since its founding in 1718.

Social Studies Activity

Use the map to choose a city on the Mississippi River to learn about. Imagine that you are an early settler in the city. Write a letter to persuade relatives to move to your city. Before writing, learn about the history, founding, and trade of the city. Look for answers to the following questions:

◆ Who founded the city? When was the city founded? Why did settlers decide to move there? Where did they come from?

◆ What part did the Mississippi River play in the city's founding?

◆ What other physical features were important to the city?

◆ Where did the city's name come from?

◆ What products were grown, bought, or sold there?

Taming the River

Navigating the sandbars, shallow water, and rocky rapids on the upper Mississippi River was treacherous for captains of ships and barges in the 1800s. To make traveling easier, engineers in the early 1900s built a "water staircase," a series of 29 locks and dams between Minneapolis, Minnesota, and Alton, Illinois, above St. Louis. A lock is an enclosed basin, with gates at each end. Locks allow engineers to raise or lower the water level in a certain area of the river. Between the locks on the upper Mississippi, the river forms wide pools of quiet water, maintaining a channel deep enough for large boats.

Use the diagrams to trace how a boat "locks through" as it travels upstream. This technology allowed boats to travel to cities on the upper Mississippi. ▶

1 The lock gate opens. Your boat moves in and you tie up to the wall.

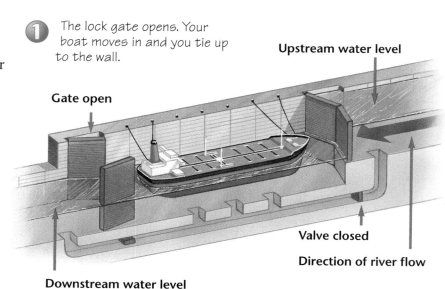

Gate open

Upstream water level

Valve closed

Direction of river flow

Downstream water level

Gate closed

Upstream water level

Valve open

Downstream water level

Science Activity

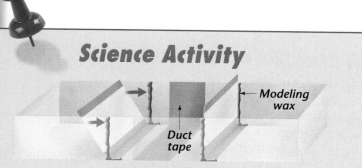

Modeling wax

Duct tape

Cut-out side view

Use a cardboard milk container to build a working model of a lock. Set up your lock following the illustration. Then demonstrate how your lock works, using a cork or pen cap as your ship and sailing it through the lock.

2 The gate closes, and water pours in. As water fills the lock—like a bathtub filling—it lifts the boat a meter or more. When the water in the lock is even with the water level upstream, the gates at the upstream end open. You untie your boat and move out into the river.

If you were going downstream, you would "lock through" in reverse. The water would empty out of the lock, lowering the water level to match the level downstream.

All Aboard

The whistle blows. The gleaming white steamboat pulls away from the dock just below Fort Snelling, Minnesota. You head downstream toward New Orleans. As you watch the paddlewheel splashing in the water, you think of the old-time steamboats that carried passengers up and down the Mississippi River in the 1800s.

Today you are cruising at a speed of 11.3 kilometers per hour. You want to stay awake until you enter Lock 3 at Red Wing, Minnesota. It's 4:30 P.M. on Monday now. You know that it's about 78.8 kilometers to Red Wing. It should take about 7 hours to reach the lock. So you'll be there at 11:30 P.M. and through the lock by midnight.

As your boat travels along the river, it will follow the schedule you see on this page. The highlight of your trip will be Mark Twain's hometown of Hannibal, Missouri. You will arrive there on Friday.

Look at the Upper Mississippi River schedule to answer the questions below. Distances are given from Fort Snelling.

◆ What is your average speed between Dubuque and Hannibal? Use the following equation:

$$speed = \frac{distance}{time}$$

Round to the nearest tenth.

◆ How long will you spend in Prairie du Chien?

◆ About how long does it take to travel from Prairie du Chien to Dubuque?

MISSISSIPPI RIVERBOAT
SCHEDULE
MAY to SEPTEMBER

UPPER MISSISSIPPI RIVERBOAT SCHEDULE

Port	Arrival Time	Departure Time	Distance From Fort Snelling
Fort Snelling, MN		4:30 P.M. Mon.	0 km
Lock 3, Red Wing, MN	11:30 P.M. Mon.	12:00 midnight	78.8 km
Prairie du Chien, WI	11:00 P.M. Tues.	10:30 A.M. Wed.	337.8 km
Dubuque, IA	6:30 P.M. Wed.	7:00 P.M. Wed.	426.3 km
Hannibal, MO	1:00 A.M. Fri.	——	863.9 km

LOWER MISSISSIPPI RIVERBOAT SCHEDULE

Port	Arrival Time	Departure Time	Distance From Fort Snelling
Hannibal, MO		6 P.M. Fri.	863.9 km
Lock 26 at Alton, IL	a. ?	b. ?	1033 km
St. Louis, MO	c. ?	d. ?	1070.7 km
Cape Girardeau, MO	6:30 A.M. Sun.	——	e. ?

Math Activity

Now complete the riverboat schedule for the Lower Mississippi. Your boat will leave Hannibal at 6 P.M. Friday and will travel at a speed of 14.7 kilometers per hour for the rest of the journey.

◆ When will you arrive at Lock 26?

◆ You spend 34 minutes in the lock. When will you depart from Lock 26? Your boat travels on. When will it arrive in St. Louis?

◆ The boat will spend 4 hours in St. Louis and head to Cape Girardeau, arriving at 6:30 A.M. Sunday. How far is it from St. Louis to Cape Girardeau?

Mark Three! Mark Twain!

To steer a boat on the Mississippi, early riverboat pilots had to memorize landmarks at every bend and curve of the river, going both upstream and down. They had to know where the channel was deep enough for the boat, where the current was strong, where there were sandbars or sunken logs.

When Samuel Clemens was growing up in the small river town of Hannibal, Missouri, his ambition was to become a Mississippi River steamboat pilot. He was a pilot for a while. Later he became one of America's most famous writers, using the pen name Mark Twain. In the passage below from his book *Life on the Mississippi*, Twain describes a lesson he learned from an experienced pilot, Mr. Bixby.

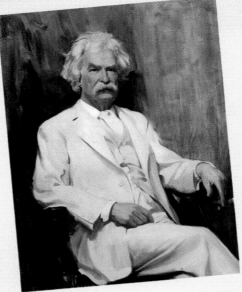

What's in a Name?

Mark Twain's name comes from a term that steamboat crews used to measure the depth of river water. *Twain* means "two." Dropping a weighted line, they would call out the depth: "Mark twain!"—2 fathoms deep; "Mark three!"—3 fathoms deep. (Note: One fathom equals 1.8 meters.)

"My boy," [Bixby said] "you've got to know the shape of the river perfectly. It is all there is left to steer by on a very dark night. Everything else is blotted out and gone. But mind you, it hasn't the same shape in the night that it has in the daytime."

"How on earth am I ever going to learn it, then?"

"How do you follow a hall at home in the dark? Because you know the shape of it. You can't see it."

"Do you mean to say that I've got to know all the million trifling variations of shape in the banks of this interminable [endless] river as well as I know the shape of the front hall at home?"

"On my honor, you've got to know them better than any man ever did know the shapes of the halls in his own house."

"I wish I was dead!"

"Now I don't want to discourage you, but —. . . . You see, this has got to be learned; there isn't any getting around it. . . .

The river is a very different shape on a pitch-dark night from what it is on a starlight night. All shores seem to be straight lines, then, and mighty dim ones, too; and you'd run them for straight lines, only you know better. . . . Then there's your gray mist. You take a night when there's one of these grisly, drizzly gray mists, and then there isn't any particular shape to a shore. A gray mist would tangle the head of the oldest man that ever lived. Well, then, different kinds of moonlight change the shape of the river in different ways. You see —"

"Oh, don't say any more, please! Have I got to learn the shape of the river according to all these five hundred thousand different ways? If I tried to carry all that cargo in my head, it would make me stoop-shouldered."

"No! You only learn the shape of the river; and you learn it with such absolute certainty that you can always steer by the shape that's in your head, and never mind the one that's before your eyes."

Language Arts Activity

Read the excerpt, focusing on what the dialogue tells you about the characters of Mark Twain and Mr. Bixby.

◆ What lesson does Mark Twain learn?

◆ How does Mr. Bixby feel about the Mississippi River? How can you tell?

Now, use dialogue to write an ending to this riverboat excerpt. Before you begin writing, think carefully about the characters, setting, and your conclusion.

Riverboat captains were licensed to navigate the river. ▶

Tie It Together

Celebrate the River

Plan a class fair featuring cities on the Mississippi River today, such as St. Louis (above). Set up a booth for each city and create a travel brochure to persuade people to visit.

As a team, choose a city to represent. Then divide up tasks so different members find information on the following topics:

◆ Interesting attractions and events that your city offers—zoos, museums, parks, sports events, music festivals, and so on.

◆ Influences of different groups on the city's food, customs, music, and architecture.

◆ Physical features of the area around the city.

◆ Famous people—writers, political figures, entertainers—who lived there.

◆ Historic places to visit, such as monuments, houses, battlefields, and statues.

◆ Illustrations and pictures of special attractions.

◆ Maps of walking tours and historic areas.

◆ Native plants and animals in the area.

Before starting your brochure, decide which attractions to highlight. Think of a slogan for your travel campaign. If you wish, make a poster. Celebrate life on the river today.

CHAPTER 15 The Atmosphere

  www.phschool.com

Integrating Environmental Science

SECTION 1 The Air Around You

Discover How Long Will the Candle Burn?
Try This Breathe In, Breathe Out
Real-World Lab How Clean Is the Air?

SECTION 2 Air Quality

Discover What's On the Jar?
Sharpen Your Skills Predicting
Science at Home Air Particles

SECTION 3 Air Pressure

Discover Does Air Have Mass?
Try This Soda-Bottle Barometer
Skills Lab Working Under Pressure
Science at Home Under Pressure

Watching the Weather

The air is cool and clear—just perfect for a trip in a hot-air balloon. As you rise, a fresh breeze begins to move you along. Where will it take you? Hot-air balloon pilots need to know about the weather to plot their course.

In this chapter, you will learn about the air around you. As you learn about the atmosphere, you will use your senses to collect information about weather conditions. Even without scientific instruments it is possible to make many accurate observations about the weather.

Your Goal To observe weather conditions without using instruments and to look for hints about tomorrow's weather in the weather conditions today.

Your completed project must
◆ include a plan for observing and describing a variety of weather conditions over a period of two to three weeks
◆ show your observations in a daily weather log
◆ display your findings about weather conditions

Get Started Begin by discussing what weather conditions you can observe. Brainstorm how to use your senses to describe the weather. For example, can you describe the wind speed by observing the school flag? Can you describe the temperature based on what clothes you need to wear outside? Be creative.

Check Your Progress You'll be working on this project as you study this chapter. To keep your project on track, look for Check Your Progress boxes at the following points.

Section 1 Review, page 501: Collect and record observations.
Section 4 Review, page 520: Look for patterns in your data.

Present Your Project At the end of the chapter (page 523), use your weather observations to prepare a display for the class.

Hot-air balloons soar into the atmosphere at a balloon festival in Snowmass, Colorado.

1 The Air Around You

DISCOVER

ACTIVITY

How Long Will the Candle Burn?

1. Put on your goggles.

2. 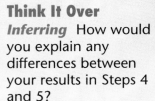 Stick a small piece of modeling clay onto an aluminum pie pan. Push a short candle into the clay. Carefully light the candle.

3. Hold a small glass jar by the bottom. Lower the mouth of the jar over the candle until the jar rests on the pie pan. As you do this, start a stopwatch or note where the second hand is on a clock.

4. Watch the candle carefully. How long does the flame burn?

5. Wearing an oven mitt, remove the jar. Relight the candle and then repeat Steps 3 and 4 with a larger jar.

Think It Over

Inferring How would you explain any differences between your results in Steps 4 and 5?

GUIDE FOR READING

◆ How is the atmosphere important to living things?

◆ What gases are present in Earth's atmosphere?

Reading Tip Before you read, preview Figure 2. As you read, write a sentence about each of the major gases in the atmosphere.

As you walk home from school, the air is warm and still. The sky is full of thick, dark clouds. In the distance you see a bright flash. A few seconds later, you hear a crack of thunder. As you turn the corner onto your street, raindrops start to fall. You begin to run and reach your home just as the downpour begins. That was close! From the shelter of the entrance you pause to catch your breath and watch the storm.

Importance of the Atmosphere

Does the weather where you live change frequently, or is it fairly constant from day to day? **Weather** is the condition of Earth's atmosphere at a particular time and place. But what is the atmosphere? Earth's **atmosphere** (AT muh sfeer) is the layer of gases that surrounds the planet. To understand the relative size of the atmosphere, imagine that the planet Earth is the size of an apple.

Figure 1 When seen from space, Earth's atmosphere appears as a thin layer near the horizon. The atmosphere makes life on Earth possible.

If you breathe on the apple, a thin film of water will form on its surface. Earth's atmosphere is like that water on the apple—a thin layer of gases on Earth's surface.

Earth's atmosphere makes conditions on Earth suitable for living things. The atmosphere contains oxygen and other gases that you and other living things need to live. In turn, living things affect the atmosphere. The atmosphere is constantly changing, with atoms and molecules of gases moving around the globe and in and out of living things, the land, and the water.

Living things also need warmth and liquid water. By trapping energy from the sun, the atmosphere keeps most of Earth's surface warm enough for water to exist as a liquid. In addition, Earth's atmosphere protects living things from dangerous radiation from the sun. It also prevents Earth's surface from being hit by most meteoroids, or chunks of rock from outer space.

☑ *Checkpoint* *What would conditions on Earth be like without the atmosphere?*

Composition of the Atmosphere

The atmosphere is made up of a mixture of atoms and molecules of different kinds of gases. An atom is the smallest unit of a chemical element that can exist by itself. Molecules are made up of two or more atoms. **Earth's atmosphere is made up of nitrogen, oxygen, carbon dioxide, water vapor, and many other gases, as well as particles of liquids and solids.**

Nitrogen As you can see in Figure 2, nitrogen is the most abundant gas in the atmosphere. It makes up a little more than three fourths of the air we breathe. Each nitrogen molecule consists of two nitrogen atoms.

Language Arts
CONNECTION

The word *atmosphere* comes from two Greek words: *atmos*, meaning "vapor," and *sphaira*, meaning "ball," or "globe." So the atmosphere is the vapors or gases surrounding a globe—in this case, Earth.

In Your Journal

As you read this chapter, write down all the words that end in -*sphere*. Look up the roots of each word in a dictionary. How does knowing the roots of each word help you understand its meaning?

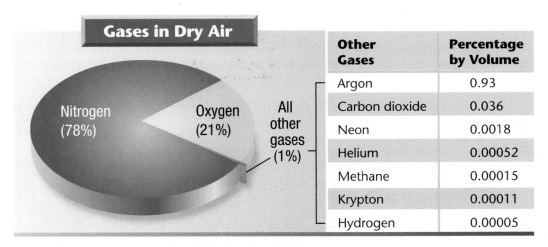

Gases in Dry Air

Nitrogen (78%)

Oxygen (21%)

All other gases (1%)

Other Gases	Percentage by Volume
Argon	0.93
Carbon dioxide	0.036
Neon	0.0018
Helium	0.00052
Methane	0.00015
Krypton	0.00011
Hydrogen	0.00005

Figure 2 Dry air in the lower atmosphere always has the same composition of gases. *Interpreting Data What two gases make up most of the air?*

Breathe In, Breathe Out ACTIVITY

How can you detect carbon dioxide in the air you exhale?

1. Put on your goggles.
2. Fill a glass or beaker halfway with limewater.

3. ☠ Using a straw, slowly blow air through the limewater for about a minute. **CAUTION:** *Do not suck on the straw or drink the limewater.*
4. What happens to the limewater?

Developing Hypotheses What do you think would happen if you did the same experiment after jogging for 10 minutes? If you tried this, what might the results tell you about exercise and carbon dioxide?

INTEGRATING LIFE SCIENCE Nitrogen is essential to living things. Proteins and other complex chemical substances in living things contain nitrogen. You and all other organisms must have nitrogen in order to grow and to repair body cells.

Most living things cannot obtain nitrogen directly from the air. Instead, some bacteria convert nitrogen into substances called nitrates. Plants then absorb the nitrates from the soil and use them to make proteins. To obtain proteins, animals must eat plants or other animals.

Oxygen Most oxygen molecules have two oxygen atoms. Even though oxygen is the second-most abundant gas in the atmosphere, it makes up less than one fourth of the volume. Plants and animals take oxygen directly from the air and use it to release energy from food in a usable form.

Oxygen is also involved in other important processes. Any fuel you can think of, from the gasoline in a car to the candles on a birthday cake, uses oxygen as it burns. Without oxygen, a fire will go out. Burning uses oxygen rapidly. During other processes, oxygen is used slowly. For example, steel in cars and other objects reacts slowly with oxygen to form iron oxide, or rust.

Have you ever noticed a pungent smell in the air after a thunderstorm? This is the odor of ozone, which forms when lightning interacts with oxygen in the air. **Ozone** is a form of oxygen that has three oxygen atoms in each molecule instead of the usual two.

Carbon Dioxide Each molecule of carbon dioxide has one atom of carbon and two atoms of oxygen. Even though the atmosphere contains only a small amount of carbon dioxide, it is essential to life. Plants must have carbon dioxide to produce food. Animals, on the other hand, give off carbon dioxide as a waste product.

When fuels such as coal and gasoline are burned, they release carbon dioxide. Burning these fuels increases the amount of carbon dioxide in the atmosphere. Rising carbon dioxide levels may be raising Earth's temperature. The issue of Earth's rising temperature, or global warming, is discussed in Chapter 18.

Figure 3 To burn, these candles need oxygen, one of the gases in the atmosphere. *Predicting What would happen if the candles used up all of the oxygen around them?*

Other Gases Oxygen and nitrogen together make up 99 percent of dry air. Carbon dioxide and argon make up most of the other one percent. The remaining gases are called trace gases because only small amounts of them are present.

Water Vapor The composition of the air discussed so far has been for dry air. In reality, air is not dry because it contains water vapor. **Water vapor** is water in the form of a gas. Water vapor is invisible—it is not the same thing as steam, which is made up of tiny droplets of liquid water. Each water molecule contains two atoms of hydrogen and one atom of oxygen.

The amount of water vapor in the air varies greatly from place to place and from time to time. Air above a desert or polar ice sheet may contain almost no water vapor. In tropical rain forests, on the other hand, as much as five percent of the air may be water vapor.

Water vapor plays an important role in Earth's weather. Clouds form when water vapor condenses out of the air to form tiny droplets of liquid water or crystals of ice. If these droplets or crystals become large enough, they can fall as rain or snow.

Figure 4 This lush vegetation grows in a rain forest in Costa Rica. The percentage of water vapor in the air in a rain forest may be as high as five percent.

Particles Pure air contains only gases. But pure air exists only in laboratories. In the real world, air also contains tiny solid and liquid particles of dust, smoke, salt, and other chemicals. Sometimes you can see particles in the air around you, but most of them are too small to see.

Section 1 Review

1. Describe two ways in which the atmosphere is important to life on Earth.
2. What are the four most common gases in dry air?
3. Why are the amounts of gases in the atmosphere usually shown as percentages of dry air?
4. **Thinking Critically** Applying Concepts How would the amount of carbon dioxide in the atmosphere change if there were no plants? If there were no animals?

Check Your Progress
Have you determined *how, where,* and *when,* you will make your observations? Organize a notebook to record them. Think of ways to compare weather conditions from day to day. Make your observations without weather instruments or TV weather reports. (*Hint:* You can estimate how much of the sky is covered by clouds.) For your own safety, do not try to make observations during storms.

CHAPTER PROJECT

How Clean Is the Air?

Sometimes you can actually see the atmosphere! How? Since air is normally transparent, it can only be visible because it contains particles. In this activity, you will use a vacuum cleaner to gather particles from the air.

Problem

How do weather factors affect the number of particles in the air?

Skills Focus

measuring, interpreting data

Materials

coffee filters
rubber band
thermometer
low-power microscope
vacuum cleaner with
   intake hose (1 per class)

Procedure

1. Predict what factors will affect the number of particles you collect. How might different weather factors affect your results?
2. In your notebook, make a data table like the one below.

3. Place the coffee filter over the nozzle of the vacuum cleaner hose. Fasten the coffee filter securely to the hose with a rubber band. Make sure the air passes through the coffee filter before entering the vacuum cleaner.
4. You will take air samples in the same place each day for five days. If possible, find a place outdoors. Otherwise, you can run the vacuum cleaner out a classroom window. **CAUTION:** *Do not use the vacuum cleaner outdoors on wet or rainy days.* If it is wet or rainy, collect the sample as soon as possible after it stops raining.
5. Hold the vacuum nozzle at least one meter above the ground each time you use the vacuum. Turn on the vacuum. Run the vacuum for 30 minutes. Shut off the vacuum.

DATA TABLE

Date and Time	Temperature	Amount of Precipitation	Wind Direction	Wind Speed	Number of Particles

6. While the vacuum is running, observe the weather conditions. Measure the temperature. Estimate the amount of precipitation, if any, since the previous observation. Note the direction from which the wind, if any, is blowing. Also note whether the wind is heavy, light, or calm. Record your observations.

7. Remove the coffee filter from the nozzle. Label the filter with the place, time, and date. Draw a circle on the filter to show the area that was over the vacuum nozzle.

8. Place the coffee filter on the stage of a microscope (40 power). Be sure that the part of the filter that was over the vacuum nozzle is directly under the microscope lens. Without moving the coffee filter, count all the particles you see. Record the number in your data table.

9. Repeat Steps 3–8 each clear day.

Analyze and Conclude

1. Was there a day of the week when you collected more particles?

2. What factors changed during the week that could have caused changes in the particle count?

3. Did the weather have any effect on your day-to-day results? If so, which weather factor do you think was most important?

4. Make a list of some possible sources of the particles you collected. Are these sources natural, or did the particles come from manufactured products?

5. How could you improve your method to get more particles out of the air?

6. **Apply** Identify areas in or around your school where there may be high levels of dust and other particles. What can people do to protect themselves in these areas?

Design an Experiment

Do you think time of day will affect the number of particles you collect? Develop a hypothesis and a plan for testing it. Could you work with other classes to get data at different times of the day? Before carrying out your plan, get your teacher's approval.

SECTION 2 Air Quality

DISCOVER

ACTIVITY

What's On the Jar?

1. Put on your goggles.
2. Put a small piece of modeling clay on a piece of aluminum foil. Push a candle into the clay. Light the candle.
3. Wearing an oven mitt, hold a glass jar by the rim so that the bottom of the jar is just above the flame.

Think It Over

Observing What do you see on the jar? Where did it come from?

GUIDE FOR READING

◆ What are the main sources of air pollution?

◆ How do photochemical smog and acid rain form?

Reading Tip As you read, look for evidence to support this statement: Most air pollution is caused by human activities. What facts support this statement? What facts do not support it?

One hundred years ago, the city of London, England, was dark and dirty. Factories burned coal, and most houses were heated by coal. The air was full of soot. In 1905, the term *smog* was created by combining the words *sm*oke and f*og* to describe this type of air pollution. Today, people in London burn much less coal. As a result, the air in London now is much cleaner than it was 100 years ago.

Air Pollution

As you are reading this, you are breathing without even thinking about it. Breathing brings air into your lungs, where the oxygen you need is taken into your body. You may also breathe in tiny particles or even a small amount of harmful gases. In fact, these particles and gases are a concern to people everywhere.

If you live in a large city, you probably already know what air pollution is. You may have noticed a brown haze or an unpleasant smell in the air. Even if you live far from a city, the air around you may be polluted. Harmful substances in the air, water, or soil are known as **pollutants**. Figure 5 shows some of the effects of air pollution on human health.

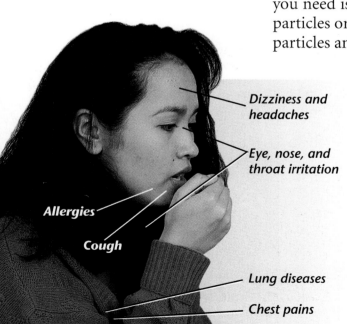

Dizziness and headaches

Eye, nose, and throat irritation

Allergies

Cough

Lung diseases

Chest pains

Figure 5 Air pollution can cause many different problems. Some air pollutants are natural, but most are caused by human activities. *Interpreting Photographs* What parts of the body are most affected by air pollution?

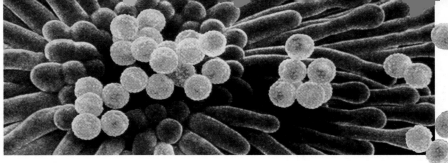

Figure 6 These pollen grains from a ragweed flower have been greatly magnified to show detail. Pollen can cause people who are allergic to it to sneeze.

Some air pollution occurs naturally, but much of it is caused by human activities. **Most air pollution is the result of burning fossil fuels such as coal, oil, gasoline, and diesel fuel.** Almost half of the air pollution from human activities comes from cars and other motor vehicles. A little more than one fourth comes from factories and power plants that burn coal and oil. Burning fossil fuels produces a number of air pollutants, including particles and gases that can form smog and acid rain.

☑ *Checkpoint* *What are two sources of air pollution that you see every day?*

Particles

As you know, air contains particles along with gases. When you draw these particles deep into your lungs, the particles can be harmful. Particles in the air come from both natural sources and human activities.

Natural Sources Many natural processes add particles to the atmosphere. When ocean waves splash salt water against rocks, some of the water sprays into the air and evaporates. Tiny salt particles stay in the air. The wind blows particles of molds and plant pollen. Forest fires, soil erosion, and dust storms add particles to the atmosphere. Erupting volcanoes spew out clouds of dust and ashes along with poisonous gases.

 INTEGRATING HEALTH Even fairly clean air usually contains particles of dust and pollen. Figure 6 shows pollen, a fine, powdery material produced by many plants. The wind carries pollen not only to other plants, but also to people. One type of allergy, popularly called "hay fever," is caused by pollen from plants such as ragweed. Symptoms of hay fever include sneezing, a runny nose, red and itchy eyes, and headaches. Weather reports often include a "pollen count," which is the average number of pollen grains in a cubic meter of air.

Human Activities When people burn fuels such as wood and coal, particles made mostly of carbon enter the air. These particles of soot are what gives smoke its dark color. Farming and construction also release large amounts of soil particles into the air.

Figure 7 These people in Pontianak, Indonesia, are being given dust masks to protect them from smoke caused by widespread forest fires. *Inferring What effects do you think this smoke might have had on the people who live in this area?*

Sharpen your Skills

Smog

London-type smog forms when particles in coal smoke combine with water droplets in humid air. Fortunately, London-type smog is no longer common in the United States. Today sunny cities like Los Angeles often have another type of smog. The brown haze that forms in cities is called **photochemical smog**. The *photo-* in photochemical means "light." Photochemical smog is caused by the action of sunlight on chemicals.

 INTEGRATING CHEMISTRY Photochemical smog is formed by a complex process. All fossil fuels contain hydrocarbons, which are substances composed of carbon and hydrogen. When fossil fuels are burned, some hydrocarbons are not burned completely and escape into the air. At the same time, the high temperatures that accompany burning cause some of the nitrogen in the air to react with oxygen to form nitrogen oxides. **The nitrogen oxides, hydrocarbons, and other air pollutants then react with one another in the presence of sunlight to form a mix of ozone and other chemicals called photochemical smog.** The ozone in photochemical smog irritates breathing passages, harms plants, and damages rubber, paint, and some plastics.

Temperature Inversion

Normally, air close to the ground is heated by Earth's surface. As the air warms, it rises into the cooler air above it. Pollutants are carried higher into the atmosphere where they blow away. But certain weather conditions cause a condition known as a temperature inversion. During a **temperature inversion,** a layer of warm air prevents the rising air from escaping. The polluted air is trapped and held close to Earth's surface. The smog becomes more concentrated and dangerous.

☑ *Checkpoint* *What happens during a temperature inversion?*

Figure 8 Normally, pollutants rise high in the air and blow away (left). But during a temperature inversion, a layer of warm air traps pollutants close to the ground (right).

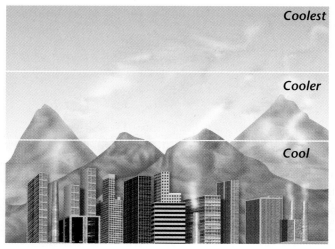

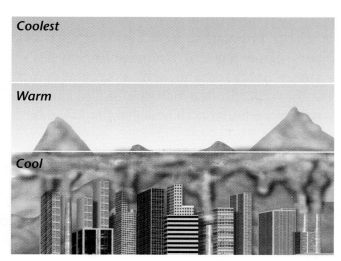

Acid Rain

One result of air pollution is acid rain. The burning of coal that contains a lot of sulfur produces substances composed of oxygen and sulfur called sulfur oxides. **Acid rain forms when nitrogen oxides and sulfur oxides combine with water in the air to form nitric acid and sulfuric acid.**

Rain, sleet, snow, fog, and even dry particles carry these two acids from the air to trees, lakes, and buildings. Rain is naturally slightly acidic, but rain that contains more acid than normal is known as **acid rain.** Acid rain is sometimes strong enough to damage the surfaces of buildings and statues.

As Figure 9 shows, needle-leafed trees such as pines and spruce are especially sensitive to acid rain. It also harms lakes and ponds. Acid rain can make water so acidic that plants, amphibians, fish, and insects can no longer survive in it.

Figure 9 This scientist is studying trees damaged by acid rain. Acid rain may make tree needles turn brown or fall off.

Improving Air Quality

The federal and state governments have passed a number of laws and regulations to reduce air pollution. For example, pollution-control devices are required equipment on cars. Factories and power plants must install filters in smokestacks to remove pollutants from smoke before they are released into the atmosphere.

Air quality in this country has improved over the past 30 years. The amounts of most major air pollutants have decreased. Newer cars cause less pollution than older models. Recently built power plants are less polluting than older power plants.

However, there are now more cars on the road and more power plants burning fossil fuels than in the past. Unfortunately, the air in many cities is still polluted. Many people think that stricter regulations are needed to control air pollution. Others argue that reducing air pollution is expensive.

Section 2 Review

1. How is most air pollution produced?
2. Name two natural and two artificial sources of particles in the atmosphere.
3. How is photochemical smog formed? What kinds of harm does it cause?
4. What substances combine to form acid rain?
5. **Thinking Critically Inferring** Do you think that photochemical smog levels are higher during the winter or during the summer? Explain.

Science at Home

Air Particles It's easy to see particles in the air. Gather your family members in a dark room. Open a window shade or blind slightly, or turn on a flashlight. Can they see tiny particles suspended in the beam of light? Discuss with your family where the particles came from. What might be some natural sources? What might be some human sources?

Cars and Clean Air

New technology and strict laws have brought cleaner air to many American cities. But in some places the air is still polluted. Cars and trucks still cause about half the air pollution in cities. And there are more cars on the road every year!

Worldwide, there are about 500 million cars. More cars will mean more pollution and more traffic jams. Unfortunately, cars stuck in traffic produce three times as much pollution as cars on the open road. What can people do to reduce air pollution by cars?

The Issues

Can Cars Be Made To Pollute Less?

In the past 20 years, cars have become more fuel-efficient and pollution levels have been lowered. Now engineers are running out of ways to make cars run more efficiently and produce less pollution. But technology does offer other answers.

Some vehicles use fuels other than gasoline. For instance, natural gas can power cars and trucks. Burning natural gas produces less pollution than burning gasoline.

Battery-powered electric cars produce no air pollution. However, the electricity to charge the batteries often comes from power plants that burn oil or coal. So electric cars still produce some pollution indirectly. Car makers have produced a few electric cars, but they are expensive and can make only fairly short trips.

Should People Drive Less? Many car trips are shorter than a mile—an easy distance for most people to walk. For longer trips, people might consider riding a bicycle. Many cars on the road carry just one person. Some people might consider riding with others in car pools or taking buses or subways.

Are Stricter Standards or Taxes the Answer? Some state governments have led efforts to reduce pollution. The state of California, for example, has strict anti-pollution laws. These laws set standards for gradually reducing pollutants released by cars. Stricter laws might make some old cars illegal.

Another approach is to make driving more expensive so that people use their cars less. That might mean higher gasoline taxes or fees for using the roads at busy times.

You Decide

1. Identify the Problem
In your own words, explain why automobiles make it hard to improve air quality. What kinds of pollution are caused by automobiles?

2. Analyze the Options
What are some ways to reduce the pollution caused by cars? Should these actions be voluntary, or should governments require them?

3. Find a Solution
How would you encourage people to try to reduce the pollution from cars? Create a visual essay from newspaper and magazine clippings. Write captions to explain your solution.

SECTION 3 Air Pressure

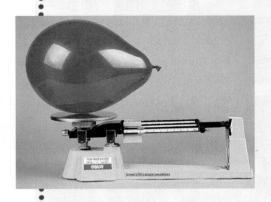
One of the best parts of eating roasted peanuts is opening the jar. When a jar of peanuts is "vacuum packed," most of the air is pumped out, creating low pressure inside. When you break the seal, the "whoosh" you hear is air from the outside rushing into the jar. The "whoosh" is the result of a difference in pressure between the outside of the jar and the inside.

Properties of Air

It may seem to you that air has no mass. However, air consists of atoms and molecules, which have mass. So air must have mass. **Because air has mass, it also has other properties, including density and pressure.**

Density The amount of mass in a given volume of air is its **density**. You can calculate density by dividing mass by volume.

$$Density = \frac{Mass}{Volume}$$

If there are more molecules in a given volume of air, the density is higher. If there are fewer molecules, the density is lower.

Pressure The force pushing on an area or surface is known as **pressure**. A denser substance has more mass per unit volume than a less dense one. So denser air exerts more pressure than less dense air.

To understand pressure, think of carrying a heavy backpack. The weight presses the straps into your shoulders just as the pack does to the hiker in the photo.

509

When you take off a backpack, it feels as if all the pressure has been taken off your shoulders. But has it? The weight of the column of air above you remains, as shown in Figure 10.

Air pressure is the result of the weight of a column of air pushing down on an area. The weight of the column of air above your desk is about the same as the weight of a large school bus! So why doesn't air pressure crush your desk? The reason is that the molecules in air push in all directions—down, up, and sideways. So the air pushing down on the top of your desk is balanced by the air pushing up on the bottom of the desk.

Measuring Air Pressure

Have you ever heard a weather report say that the air pressure is falling? Falling air pressure usually indicates that a storm is approaching. Rising air pressure usually means that the weather is clearing. A **barometer** (buh RAHM uh tur) is an instrument that is used to measure changes in air pressure. **There are two kinds of barometers: mercury barometers and aneroid barometers.**

Mercury Barometers The first barometers invented were mercury barometers. Figure 11 shows how a mercury barometer works. A **mercury barometer** consists of a glass tube open at the bottom end and partially filled with mercury. The space in the tube above the mercury is almost a vacuum—it contains no air. The open end of the tube rests in a dish of mercury. The air pressure pushing down on the surface of the mercury in the dish is equal to the

Figure 10 There is a column of air above you all the time. The weight of the air in the atmosphere causes air pressure.

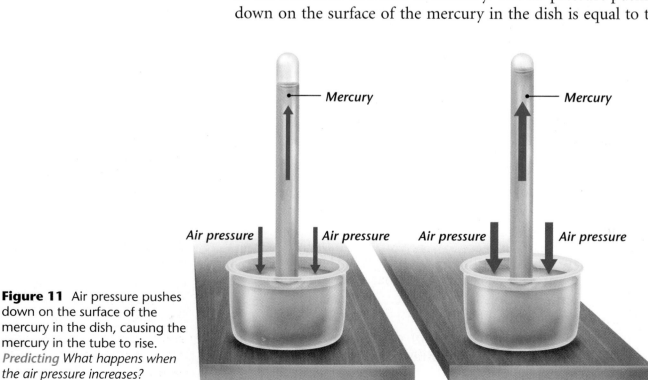

Figure 11 Air pressure pushes down on the surface of the mercury in the dish, causing the mercury in the tube to rise. *Predicting What happens when the air pressure increases?*

Mercury

Mercury

Air pressure   Air pressure   Air pressure   Air pressure

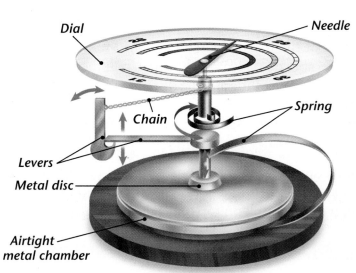

Dial

Needle

Chain

Spring

Levers

Metal disc

Airtight
metal chamber

Figure 12 Changes in air pressure cause the walls of the airtight metal chamber to flex in and out. The needle on the dial indicates the air pressure.

weight of the column of mercury in the tube. At sea level the mercury column is about 76 centimeters high, on average.

When the air pressure increases, it presses down more on the surface of the mercury. Greater air pressure forces the column of mercury higher. What will happen to the column of mercury if the air pressure decreases? The column will fall.

Aneroid Barometers If you have a barometer on a desk or wall at home, it is probably an aneroid barometer. The word *aneroid* means "without liquid." An **aneroid barometer** (AN uh royd) has an airtight metal chamber, as shown in Figure 12. The metal chamber is sensitive to changes in air pressure. When air pressure increases, the thin walls of the chamber are pushed in. When the pressure drops, the walls bulge out. The chamber is connected to a dial by a series of springs and levers. As the shape of the chamber changes, the needle on the dial moves.

Aneroid barometers are smaller than mercury barometers and don't contain a liquid. Therefore, they are portable and often more practical for uses such as airplane instrument panels.

Units of Air Pressure Weather reports use several different units for air pressure. Most weather reports for the general public use inches of mercury. For example, if the column of mercury in a mercury barometer is 30 inches high, the air pressure is "30 inches of mercury" or just "30 inches."

National Weather Service maps indicate air pressure in millibars. One inch of mercury equals approximately 33.87 millibars, so 30 inches of mercury is approximately equal to 1,016 millibars.

✓ *Checkpoint* *Name two common units used to measure air pressure.*

Soda-Bottle Barometer

Here's how to build a device that shows changes in air pressure.

1. Fill a 2-liter soda bottle one-half full with water.

2. Lower a long straw into the bottle so that the end of the straw is in the water. Seal the mouth of the bottle around the straw with modeling clay.

3. Squeeze the sides of the bottle. What happens to the level of the water in the straw?

4. Let go of the sides of the bottle. Watch the level of the water in the straw.

Inferring Explain your results in terms of air pressure.

Increasing Altitude

The air pressure at the top of Alaska's Mount McKinley—more than 6 kilometers above sea level—is less than half the air pressure at sea level. **Altitude,** or elevation, is the distance above sea level, the average level of the surface of the oceans. **Air pressure decreases as altitude increases. As air pressure decreases, so does density.**

Altitude Affects Air Pressure Imagine a stack of ten books. Which book has more weight on it, the second book from the top or the book at the bottom? The second book from the top has only the weight of one book on top of it. The book at the bottom

Working Under Pressure

Air pressure changes are related to changing weather conditions. In this lab, you will build and use your own barometer to measure air pressure.

Problem

How can a barometer detect changes in air pressure?

Materials

modeling clay   scissors
white glue   tape
pencil   wide-mouthed glass jar
metric ruler   rubber band
large rubber balloon
drinking straw, 12–15 cm long
cardboard strip, 10 cm x 25 cm

Procedure

1. Cut off the narrow opening of the balloon.
2. Fold the edges of the balloon outward. Carefully stretch the balloon over the open end of the glass jar. Use a rubber band to hold the balloon on the rim of the glass jar.

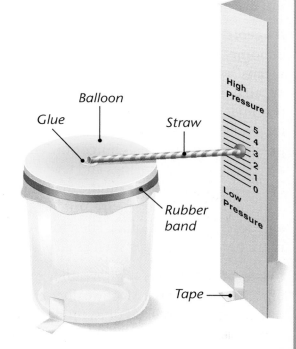

3. Place a small amount of glue on the center of the balloon top. Attach one end of the straw to the glue. Allow the other end to extend several centimeters beyond the edge of the glass jar. This is your pointer.

of the stack has the weight of all the other books pressing on it.

Air at sea level is like the bottom book. Recall that air pressure is the weight of the column of air pushing down on an area. Sea-level air has the weight of the whole atmosphere pressing on it. So air pressure is greatest at sea level. Air near the top of the atmosphere is like the second book from the top. There, the air has less weight pressing on it, and thus has lower air pressure.

DATA TABLE

Date and Time	Air Pressure	Weather Conditions

4. While the glue dries, fold the cardboard strip lengthwise and draw a scale along the edge with marks 0.5 cm apart. Write "High pressure" at the top of your scale and "Low pressure" at the bottom.
5. After the glue dries, add a pea-sized piece of modeling clay to the end of the pointer. Place your barometer and its scale in a location that is as free from temperature changes as possible. Arrange the scale and the barometer as shown in the diagram. Note that the pointer of the straw must just reach the cardboard strip.
6. Tape both the scale and the barometer to a surface so they do not move during your experiment.

7. In your notebook, make a data table like the one at the left. Record the date and time. Note the level of the straw on the cardboard strip.
8. Check the barometer twice a day. Record your observations in your data table.
9. Record the weather conditions for each day.

Analyze and Conclude

1. What change in atmospheric conditions must occur to cause the free end of the straw to rise? What change must occur for it to fall?
2. According to your observations, what kind of weather is usually associated with high air pressure? With low air pressure?
3. If the balloon had a tiny hole in it, what would happen to the accuracy of your barometer?
4. **Think About It** What effect, if any, would a great temperature change have on the accuracy of your barometer?

More to Explore

Compare changes in air pressure shown by your barometer with high and low air pressure readings shown on newspaper weather maps during the same time period. How do your readings compare with the readings in the newspapers?

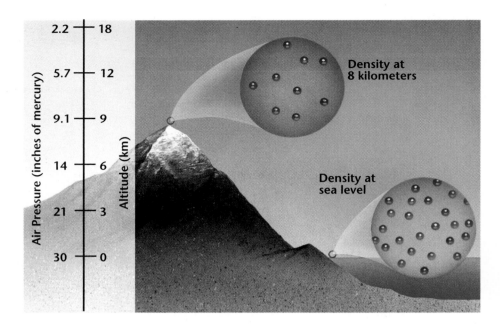

Air Pressure (inches of mercury) | Altitude (km)

2.2	18
5.7	12
9.1	9
14	6
21	3
30	0

Density at 8 kilometers

Density at sea level

Figure 13 The density of air decreases as altitude increases. Air at sea level has more gas molecules in each cubic meter than air at the top of a mountain.

Altitude Also Affects Density

INTEGRATING LIFE SCIENCE If you were near the top of Mount McKinley and tried to run, you would get out of breath quickly. Why would you have difficulty breathing at high altitudes?

As you go up through the atmosphere, the air pressure decreases. As air pressure decreases, the density of the air decreases. So density decreases as altitude increases, as shown in Figure 13.

Whether air is at sea level or at 6 kilometers above sea level, the air still contains 21 percent oxygen. However, since the air is less dense at a high altitude, there are fewer oxygen molecules to breathe in each cubic meter of air than there are at sea level. You are taking in less oxygen with each breath. That is why you get out of breath quickly.

Section 3 Review

1. How does increasing the density of a gas affect its pressure?
2. Describe how a mercury barometer measures air pressure.
3. Why is the air at the top of a mountain hard to breathe?
4. **Thinking Critically** **Predicting** What changes in air pressure would you expect to see if you carried a barometer down a mine shaft? Explain.

Science at Home

Under Pressure Here's how you can show your family that air has pressure. Fill a glass to the brim with water. Place a piece of heavy cardboard over the top of the glass. Hold the cardboard in place with one hand as you turn the glass upside down. **CAUTION:** Be sure the cardboard does not bend. Now remove your hand from the cardboard. What happens? Explain to your family that the cardboard doesn't fall because the air pressure pushing up on it is greater than the weight of the water pushing down.

SECTION 4 Layers of the Atmosphere

Imagine taking a trip upward into the atmosphere in a hot-air balloon. You begin on a warm beach near the ocean, at an altitude of 0 kilometers.

You hear a roar as the balloon's pilot turns up the burner to heat the air in the balloon. The balloon begins to rise, and Earth's surface gets farther and farther away. As the balloon rises to an altitude of 3 kilometers, you realize that the air is getting colder. As you continue to rise, the air gets colder and colder. At 6 kilometers you begin to have trouble breathing. The air is becoming less dense. It's time to go back down.

What if you could have continued your balloon ride up through the atmosphere? As you rose farther up through the atmosphere, the air pressure and temperature would change dramatically. **The four main layers of the atmosphere are classified according to changes in temperature. These layers are the troposphere, the stratosphere, the mesosphere, and the thermosphere.**

The Troposphere

You live in the inner, or lowest, layer of Earth's atmosphere, the **troposphere** (TROH puh sfeer). *Tropo-* means "turning" or "changing"; conditions in the troposphere are more variable than in the other layers. The troposphere is where Earth's weather occurs.

Figure 14 This weather balloon will carry a package of instruments to measure weather conditions high in the atmosphere.
Applying Concepts Which is the first layer of the atmosphere the balloon passes through on its way up?

Although hot-air balloons cannot travel very high into the troposphere, other types of balloons can. To measure weather conditions, scientists launch weather balloons that carry instruments up into the atmosphere. The balloons are not fully inflated before they are launched. Recall that air pressure decreases as you rise through the atmosphere. Leaving the balloon only partly inflated gives the gas inside the balloon room to expand as the air pressure outside the balloon decreases.

The depth of the troposphere varies from more than 16 kilometers above the equator to less than 9 kilometers above the North and South Poles. Even though it is the shallowest layer of the atmosphere, the troposphere contains almost all of the mass of the atmosphere.

As altitude increases in the troposphere, the temperature decreases. On average, for every 1-kilometer increase in altitude the air gets about 6.5 Celsius degrees cooler. At the top of the troposphere, the temperature stops decreasing and stays constant at about −60°C. Water here forms thin, feathery clouds of ice.

☑ *Checkpoint* **Why are clouds at the top of the troposphere made of ice crystals instead of drops of water?**

The Stratosphere

The **stratosphere** extends from the top of the troposphere to about 50 kilometers above Earth's surface. *Strato-* is similar to *stratum,* which means "layer" or "spreading out."

The lower stratosphere is cold, about −60°C. You might be surprised to learn that the upper stratosphere is warmer than the lower stratosphere. The upper stratosphere contains a layer of ozone, the three-atom form of oxygen. When the ozone absorbs energy from the sun, the energy is converted into heat, warming the air.

As a weather balloon rises through the stratosphere, the air pressure outside the balloon continues to decrease. The volume of the balloon increases. Finally, the balloon bursts, and the instrument package falls back to Earth's surface.

The Mesosphere

Above the stratosphere, a drop in temperature marks the beginning of the next layer, the **mesosphere.** *Meso-* means "middle," so the mesosphere is the middle layer of the atmosphere. The mesosphere begins 50 kilometers above Earth's surface and ends at 80 kilometers. The outer mesosphere is the coldest part of the atmosphere, with temperatures near −90°C.

EXPLORING Layers of the Atmosphere

The atmosphere is divided into four layers: the troposphere, the stratosphere, the mesosphere, and the thermosphere. The thermosphere is further divided into the ionosphere and the exosphere.

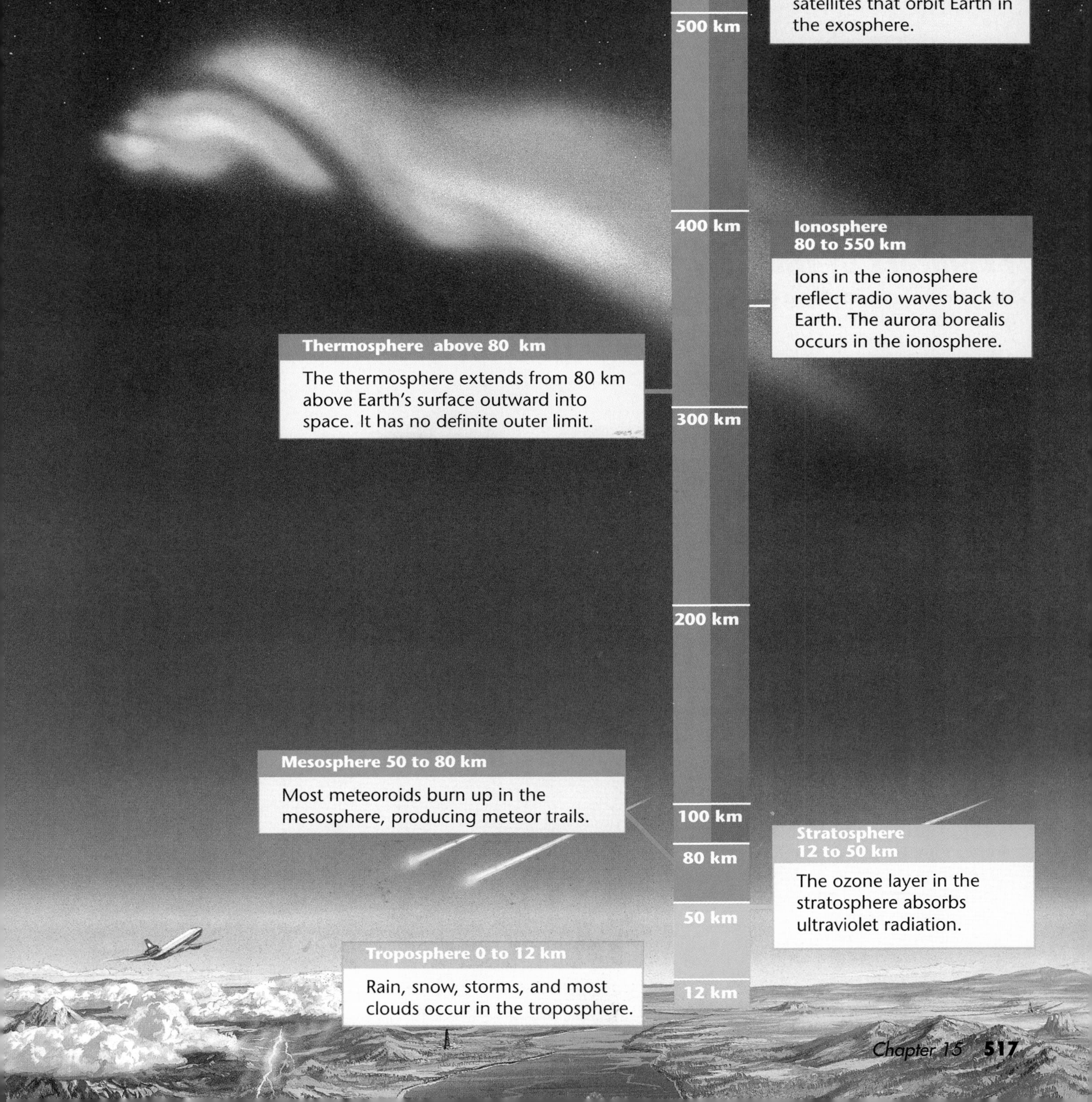

Exosphere above 550 km

Phone calls and television pictures often reach you by way of communications satellites that orbit Earth in the exosphere.

Ionosphere 80 to 550 km

Ions in the ionosphere reflect radio waves back to Earth. The aurora borealis occurs in the ionosphere.

Thermosphere above 80 km

The thermosphere extends from 80 km above Earth's surface outward into space. It has no definite outer limit.

Mesosphere 50 to 80 km

Most meteoroids burn up in the mesosphere, producing meteor trails.

Stratosphere 12 to 50 km

The ozone layer in the stratosphere absorbs ultraviolet radiation.

Troposphere 0 to 12 km

Rain, snow, storms, and most clouds occur in the troposphere.

550 km
500 km
400 km
300 km
200 km
100 km
80 km
50 km
12 km

If you watch a shooting star streak across the night sky, you are seeing a meteoroid burn up as it enters the mesosphere. The mesosphere protects Earth's surface from being hit by most meteoroids, which are chunks of stone and metal from space. What you see as a shooting star, or meteor, is the trail of hot, glowing gases the burning meteoroid leaves behind.

☑ *Checkpoint* **What is the depth of the mesosphere?**

The Thermosphere

Near the top of the atmosphere, the air is very thin. The air 80 kilometers above Earth's surface is only about 0.001 percent as dense as the air at sea level. It's as though you took a cubic

SCIENCE & History

Explorers of the Atmosphere

The atmosphere has been explored from the ground and from space.

1746
Franklin's Experiment with Electricity

American statesman and inventor Benjamin Franklin and some friends in Philadelphia experimented with electricity in the atmosphere. To demonstrate that lightning is a form of electricity, Franklin flew a kite in a thunderstorm. However, Franklin did not hold the kite string in his hand, as this historical print shows.

1600	1700	1800

1643
Torricelli Invents the Barometer

Italian physicist and mathematician Evangelista Torricelli improved existing scientific instruments and invented some new ones. In 1643 he invented the barometer, using a column of mercury 1.2 meters high.

1804
Gay-Lussac Studies the Upper Troposphere

French chemist Joseph-Louis Gay-Lussac ascended to a height of about 7 kilometers in a hydrogen balloon to study the upper troposphere. Gay-Lussac studied pressure, temperature, and humidity.

meter of air at sea level and expanded it into 100,000 cubic meters at the top of the mesosphere. The outermost layer of the atmosphere, the **thermosphere**, extends from 80 kilometers above Earth's surface outward into space. It has no definite outer limit. The atmosphere does not end suddenly at the outer edge of the thermosphere. Gas atoms and molecules there are so far apart that the air blends gradually with outer space.

The *thermo-* in thermosphere means "heat." Even though the air in the thermosphere is thin, it is very hot, up to 1,800°C. The temperature in the thermosphere is actually higher than the temperature in a furnace used to make steel! But why is the thermosphere so hot? Energy coming from the sun strikes the thermosphere first. Nitrogen and oxygen molecules convert energy from the sun into heat.

In Your Journal

Imagine you were one of the first people to go up into the atmosphere in a balloon. What would you need to take? Find out what the early explorers took with them in their balloons. Write at least two paragraphs about what you would take, and why.

1931

Piccard Explores the Stratosphere

Swiss-Belgian physicist Auguste Piccard made the first ascent into the stratosphere. He reached a height of about 16 kilometers in an airtight cabin attached to a huge hydrogen balloon. Piccard is shown here with the cabin.

1900

2000

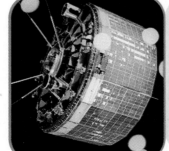

1960

First Weather Satellite Launched

TIROS-1, the first weather satellite equipped with a camera to send data back to Earth, was put into orbit by the United States. As later weather satellites circled Earth, they observed cloud cover and recorded temperatures and air pressures in the atmosphere.

1994

Space Shuttle Investigates the Atmosphere

The NASA space shuttle *Atlantis* traveled to a height of 300 kilometers in the thermosphere. *Atlantis* carried the ATLAS–3 research program, which observed the sun's influence on the atmosphere.

Figure 15 The aurora borealis, seen from Fairbanks, Alaska, creates a spectacular display in the night sky.

Despite the high temperature, however, you would not feel warm in the thermosphere. An ordinary thermometer would show a temperature well below 0°C. Why is that? Temperature is the average amount of energy of motion of each molecule of a substance. The gas molecules in the thermosphere move very rapidly, so the temperature is very high. However, the molecules are spaced far apart in the thin air. And there are not enough of them to collide with a thermometer and warm it very much. So an ordinary thermometer would not detect the molecules' energy.

The Ionosphere The thermosphere is divided into two layers. The lower layer of the thermosphere, called the **ionosphere** (eye AHN uh sfeer), begins 80 kilometers above the surface and ends at 550 kilometers. Energy from the sun causes gas molecules in the ionosphere to become electrically charged particles called ions. Radio waves bounce off ions in the ionosphere and then bounce back to Earth's surface.

The brilliant light displays of the **aurora borealis**—the Northern Lights—also occur in the ionosphere. The aurora borealis is caused by particles from the sun that enter the ionosphere near the North Pole. These particles strike oxygen and nitrogen atoms in the ionosphere, causing them to glow.

The Exosphere *Exo-* means "outer," so the **exosphere** is the
INTEGRATING TECHNOLOGY outer layer of the thermosphere. The exosphere extends from 550 kilometers outward for thousands of kilometers. When you make a long-distance phone call or watch television, the signal may have traveled up to a satellite orbiting in the exosphere and then back down to your home. Satellites are also used for watching the world's weather and carrying telescopes that look deep into space.

Section 4 Review

1. Describe one characteristic of each of the four main layers of the atmosphere.
2. What is a shooting star? In which layer of the atmosphere would you see it?
3. What is the aurora borealis? In which layer of the atmosphere does it occur?
4. **Thinking Critically** **Drawing Conclusions** Why is the mesosphere the coldest part of the atmosphere?

CHAPTER PROJECT

Check Your Progress
At this point, review your weather log. What do you notice about the weather on one day that might allow you to predict the next day's weather? What weather conditions changed the most from day to day? Continue to record your observations and start thinking about how you will present them.

SECTION 1 The Air Around You

Key Ideas
- Earth's atmosphere makes conditions on Earth suitable for living things.
- Earth's atmosphere is made up of molecules of nitrogen, oxygen, carbon dioxide, and water vapor, as well as some other gases and particles of liquids and solids.

Key Terms
weather   ozone
atmosphere   water vapor

SECTION 2 Air Quality

INTEGRATING ENVIRONMENTAL SCIENCE

Key Ideas
- Most air pollution results from the burning of fossil fuels such as coal and oil.
- Nitrogen oxides, hydrocarbons, and other air pollutants react with one another in the presence of sunlight to form a mix of ozone and other chemicals called photochemical smog.
- Acid rain forms when nitrogen oxides and sulfur oxides combine with water in the air to form nitric acid and sulfuric acid.

Key Terms
pollutant   temperature inversion
photochemical smog   acid rain

SECTION 3 Air Pressure

Key Ideas
- Properties of air include mass, density, and pressure.
- Air pressure is the result of the weight of a column of air pushing down on an area.
- Air pressure is measured with mercury barometers and aneroid barometers.
- Air pressure decreases as altitude increases. As air pressure decreases, so does density.

Key Terms
density   barometer   altitude
pressure   mercury barometer
air pressure   aneroid barometer

SECTION 4 Layers of the Atmosphere

Key Ideas
- The four main layers of the atmosphere are classified according to changes in temperature. These layers are the troposphere, the stratosphere, the mesosphere, and the thermosphere.
- Rain, snow, storms, and most clouds occur in the troposphere.
- Ozone in the stratosphere absorbs energy from the sun.
- Most meteoroids burn up in the mesosphere, producing meteor trails.
- The aurora borealis occurs in the ionosphere.
- Communications satellites orbit Earth in the exosphere.

Key Terms
troposphere   thermosphere   aurora borealis
stratosphere   ionosphere   exosphere
mesosphere

Organizing Information

Concept Map Copy the air pressure concept map onto a separate sheet of paper. Then complete it and add a title. (For more on concept maps, see the Skills Handbook.)

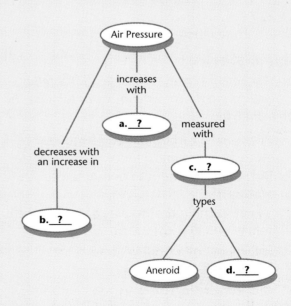

Reviewing Content

 For more review of key concepts, see the Interactive Student Tutorial CD-ROM.

Multiple Choice

Choose the letter of the answer that best completes each statement.

1. The most abundant gas in the atmosphere is
   a. ozone.   b. carbon dioxide.
   c. oxygen.   d. nitrogen.

2. Most air pollution is caused by
   a. dust and pollen.
   b. acid rain.
   c. erupting volcanoes.
   d. the burning of fossil fuels.

3. A barometer is used to measure
   a. temperature.   b. smog.
   c. air pressure   d. density.

4. The layers of the atmosphere are classified according to changes in
   a. altitude.
   b. temperature.
   c. pressure.
   d. density.

5. The inner layer, or "weather layer," of the atmosphere is called the
   a. mesosphere.
   b. troposphere.
   c. thermosphere.
   d. stratosphere.

True or False

If the statement is true, write true. If it is false, change the underlined word or words to make the statement true.

6. Plants need <u>carbon dioxide</u> from the atmosphere to make food.

7. Burning fuels add <u>nitrogen</u> to the atmosphere.

8. When sulfur and nitrogen oxides mix with water in the air, they form <u>smog</u>.

9. If the mass of a fixed volume of air increases, it becomes <u>less</u> dense.

10. Air pressure <u>increases</u> as you climb from land at sea level to the top of a mountain.

Checking Concepts

11. Name two ways in which carbon dioxide is added to the atmosphere.

12. Explain why it is difficult to include water vapor in a graph that shows the percentages of various gases in the atmosphere.

13. What is the difference between photo-chemical smog and London-type smog?

14. Describe some of the problems caused by acid rain.

15. List the following layers of the atmosphere in order moving up from Earth's surface: thermosphere, stratosphere, troposphere, mesosphere.

16. Describe the temperature changes that occur as you move upward through the troposphere.

17. **Writing to Learn** You are a scientist who has a chance to join a research mission to explore the atmosphere. To win a place on this mission, write a persuasive letter telling which layer of the atmosphere you want to research and why you chose it.

Thinking Critically

18. **Predicting** Describe the changes in the atmosphere that you would experience while climbing a mountain four or more kilometers high. How might these changes affect you physically?

19. **Applying Concepts** Why can an aneroid barometer be used to measure elevation as well as air pressure?

20. **Relating Cause and Effect** How can burning high-sulfur coal in a power-generating plant harm a forest hundreds of kilometers away?

21. **Classifying** Which sources of air pollution occur naturally, and which are caused by humans?

Applying Skills

The table below shows the temperature at various altitudes above Omaha, Nebraska, on a day in January. Use the table to answer the questions that follow.

Altitude (kilometers)	0	1.6	3.2	4.8	6.4	7.2
Temperature (°C)	0	−4	−9	−21	−32	−40

22. Graphing Make a line graph of the data in the table. Put temperature on the horizontal axis and altitude on the vertical axis. Label your graph.

23. Interpreting Graphs At about what height above the ground was the temperature −15°C?

24. Interpreting Graphs What was the approximate temperature 2.4 kilometers over Omaha?

25. Calculating Suppose an airplane was about 6.8 kilometers above Omaha on this day. What was the approximate temperature at 6.8 kilometers? How much colder was the temperature at 6.8 kilometers above the ground than at ground level?

Performance CHAPTER PROJECT Assessment

Present Your Project For your class presentation, prepare a display of your weather observations. Include drawings, graphs, and tables that summarize the weather you observed. Practice presenting your project to your group. Do you need to make any improvements? If so, make them now.

Reflect and Record In your journal, write how you might improve your weather log. What weather conditions would you like to know more about? What factors could you have measured more accurately using instruments?

Test Preparation

Use these questions to prepare for standardized tests.

Study the graph. Then answer Questions 26–29.

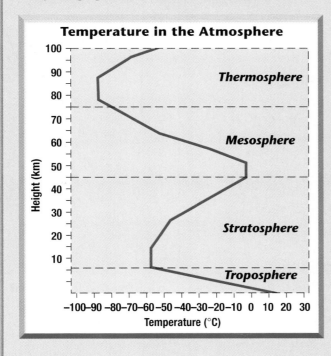

Temperature in the Atmosphere

26. Name the layer of the atmosphere that is closest to Earth's surface.
  a. thermosphere   **b.** troposphere
  c. stratosphere   **d.** mesosphere

27. Which layer of the atmosphere has the lowest temperature?
  a. thermosphere   **b.** troposphere
  c. stratosphere   **d.** mesosphere

28. The range of temperatures found in the stratosphere is about ____ Celsius degrees.
  a. 100   **b.** 0
  c. 30   **d.** 60

29. Which of the following best describes how temperature changes as altitude increases in the troposphere?
  a. steadily increases
  b. increases then decreases
  c. steadily decreases
  d. decreases then increases

CHAPTER 16 Weather Factors

WEB ACTIVITY www.phschool.com

 SECTION 1 **Energy in the Atmosphere**

Discover **Does a Plastic Bag Trap Heat?**
Science at Home **Heating by Radiation**
Skills Lab **Heating Earth's Surface**

Integrating Physics

 SECTION 2 **Heat Transfer**

Discover **What Happens When Air Is Heated?**
Try This **Temperatures at Two Heights**

 SECTION 3 **Winds**

Discover **Which Way Does the Wind Turn?**
Try This **Build a Wind Vane**
Real-World Lab **Where's the Wind?**

524

CHAPTER 16 PROJECT

Your Own Weather Station

Adrenching spring rain is just what the flowers need! As the weather gets warmer, the garden will bloom. Warm days, soft winds, and plenty of rain—all of these are weather factors that affect growing things. In this chapter, you will learn about a variety of weather factors, including air pressure, temperature, wind speed and direction, relative humidity, precipitation, and the amount and types of clouds.

Your Goal To measure and record weather conditions using instruments. You will look for patterns in your data that can be used to predict the next day's weather.

In completing your project, you will
- ◆ develop a plan for measuring weather factors
- ◆ record your data in a daily log
- ◆ display your data in a set of graphs
- ◆ use your data and graphs to try to predict the weather
- ◆ follow the safety guidelines in Appendix A

Get Started Begin by previewing the chapter to see what weather factors you want to measure. Discuss with a group of your classmates what instruments you might use. Brainstorm what observations you should make each day.

Check Your Progress You'll be working on the project as you study this chapter. To keep your project on track, look for Check Your Progress boxes at the following points.

Section 2 Review, page 535: Prepare to make observations.
Section 3 Review, page 544: Collect and record data.
Section 5 Review, page 554: Graph your data and look for patterns.

Present Your Project At the end of the chapter (page 557), present your weather observations and explain how well you predicted the weather.

Spring rains are an important factor in helping these tulips grow.

SECTION 4 Water in the Atmosphere

Discover **How Does Fog Form?**
Sharpen Your Skills **Interpreting Data**
Science at Home **Condensation on Glass**

SECTION 5 Precipitation

Discover **How Can You Make Hail?**
Sharpen Your Skills **Calculating**

1 Energy in the Atmosphere

DISCOVER ······························ACTIVITY····

Does a Plastic Bag Trap Heat?

1.  Record the initial temperatures on two thermometers. (You should get the same readings.)

2. Place one of the thermometers in a plastic bag. Put a small piece of paper in the bag so that it shades the bulb of the thermometer. Seal the bag.

3. Place both thermometers on a sunny window ledge or near a light bulb. Cover the bulb of the second thermometer with a small piece of paper. Predict what you think will happen.

4. Wait five minutes. Then record the temperatures on the two thermometers.

Think It Over
Measuring Were the two temperatures the same? How could you explain any difference?

GUIDE FOR READING

◆ In what form does energy from the sun travel to Earth?

◆ What happens to energy from the sun when it reaches Earth?

Reading Tip Before you read, skim the section for boldfaced words that are unfamiliar to you. As you read, find their meanings and write them down in your notebook.

Think of a sunny summer day. When you get up in the morning, the sun is low in the sky and the air is cool. As the sun rises, the temperature increases. By noon it is quite hot. As you will see in this chapter, heat is a major factor in the weather. The movement of heat in the atmosphere causes temperatures to change, winds to blow, and rain to fall.

Energy from the Sun

INTEGRATING PHYSICS Nearly all the energy in Earth's atmosphere comes from the sun. This energy travels to Earth as **electromagnetic waves,** a form of energy that can travel through space. Electromagnetic waves are classified according to wavelength, or distance between waves. The direct transfer of energy by electromagnetic waves is called **radiation.**

Most of the energy from the sun reaches Earth in the form of visible light and infrared radiation, and a small amount of ultraviolet radiation. Visible light is a mixture of all of the colors that you see in a rainbow: red, orange, yellow, green, blue, and violet. The different colors are the result of different wavelengths

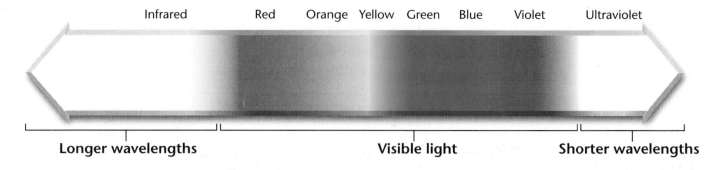

| Infrared | Red | Orange | Yellow | Green | Blue | Violet | Ultraviolet |

Longer wavelengths   **Visible light**   **Shorter wavelengths**

of visible light. Red and orange light have the longest wavelengths, while blue and violet light have the shortest wavelengths.

Infrared radiation is a form of energy with wavelengths that are longer than red light. Infrared radiation is not visible, but can be felt as heat. Heat lamps used to keep food warm in restaurants give off both visible red light and invisible infrared radiation. The sun also gives off **ultraviolet radiation,** which has wavelengths that are shorter than violet light. Sunburns are caused by ultraviolet radiation. This radiation can also cause skin cancer and eye damage.

☑ *Checkpoint* Which color of visible light has the longest wavelengths?

Figure 1 Electromagnetic waves include infrared radiation, visible light, and ultraviolet radiation.
Interpreting Diagrams What type of radiation has wavelengths that are shorter than visible light? What type has wavelengths that are longer?

Energy in the Atmosphere

Before the sun's rays can reach Earth's surface, they must pass through the atmosphere. The path of the sun's rays is shown in *Exploring Energy in the Atmosphere* on the following page.

Some of the energy from the sun is absorbed within the atmosphere. Water vapor and carbon dioxide absorb some infrared radiation. The ozone layer in the stratosphere absorbs most of the ultraviolet radiation. Clouds, dust, and other gases also absorb energy from the sun.

Some of the sun's rays are reflected. Clouds in the atmosphere act like mirrors, reflecting some solar energy back into space. In addition, dust particles and molecules of gases in the atmosphere reflect light from the sun in all directions.

Reflection of light in all directions is called **scattering**. When you look at the sky, the light you see has been scattered by gas molecules in the atmosphere. Gas molecules scatter short wavelengths of visible light (blue and violet) more than long wavelengths (red and orange). Scattered light is therefore bluer than ordinary sunlight, which is why the daytime sky looks blue.

When the sun is rising or setting, light from the sun passes through a greater thickness of the atmosphere than when the sun is higher in the sky. More light from the blue end of the spectrum is removed by scattering before it reaches your eyes. The remaining light from the sun contains mostly red and orange light. The sun looks red, and clouds around it become very colorful.

☑ *Checkpoint* *Why would particles from volcanic eruptions make sunsets and sunrises more red?*

EXPLORING *Energy in the Atmosphere*

Most of the energy that keeps Earth warm comes from the sun. Some of this energy is reflected or absorbed in the atmosphere. The rest of the energy reaches Earth's surface, where it is reflected or absorbed.

Solar energy is mostly visible light and infrared radiation, with a small amount of ultraviolet radiation.

Clouds, dust, and gases in the atmosphere reflect and scatter light.

Gases and particles in the atmosphere absorb solar energy.

Some energy that reaches the surface is reflected back into the atmosphere.

Earth's surface absorbs solar energy. This energy heats the land and water.

Some of the absorbed energy is then radiated back into the atmosphere.

Energy at Earth's Surface

Some of the sun's energy reaches Earth's surface and is reflected back into the atmosphere. Some of the energy, however, is absorbed by the land and water and changed into heat.

When Earth's surface is heated, it radiates some of the energy back into the atmosphere as infrared radiation. This infrared radiation cannot travel all the way through the atmosphere back into space. Instead, much of it is absorbed by water vapor, carbon dioxide, methane, and other gases in the air. The energy from the absorbed radiation heats the gases in the air. These gases form a "blanket" around Earth that holds heat in the atmosphere. The process by which gases hold heat in the air is called the **greenhouse effect.**

Have you ever been inside a greenhouse during the winter? Even on a cold day, a greenhouse is warm. Greenhouses trap heat in two ways. First, infrared radiation given off in the interior cannot easily pass through glass and is trapped inside. Second, warm air inside the greenhouse cannot escape because the glass blocks the movement of air. What happens in Earth's atmosphere is similar to the first way that greenhouses trap heat.

The greenhouse effect is a natural process that keeps Earth's atmosphere at a temperature that is comfortable for most living things. Human activities over the last 200 years, however, have increased the amount of carbon dioxide in the atmosphere, which may be warming the atmosphere. You will learn more about the greenhouse effect in Chapter 18.

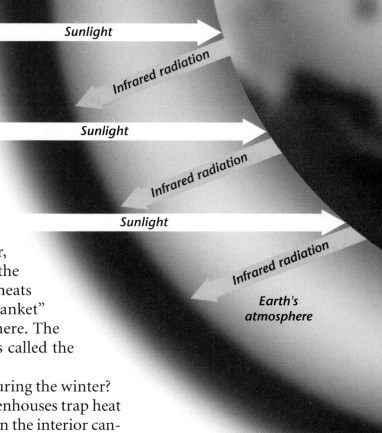

Figure 2 Sunlight travels through the atmosphere to Earth's surface. Earth's surface then gives off infrared radiation. Much of this energy is held by the atmosphere, warming it.

Section 1 Review

1. List three forms of radiation from the sun. How are these alike? How are they different?
2. What happens to the energy from the sun that is absorbed by Earth's surface?
3. Why is the sky blue? Why are sunsets often red?
4. **Thinking Critically** **Applying Concepts** What might conditions on Earth be like without the greenhouse effect?

Science at Home

Heating by Radiation With an adult family member, explore the role radiation plays in heating your home. Are some rooms warmer and sunnier in the morning? Are other rooms warmer and sunnier in the afternoon? How does opening and closing curtains or blinds affect the temperature of a room? Explain your observations to your family.

Heating Earth's Surface

In this lab, you will develop and test a hypothesis about how quickly different materials absorb radiation.

Problem

How do the heating and cooling rates of sand and water compare?

Materials

2 thermometers ring stand and ring clamp
2 beakers, 400 mL sand, 300 mL
water, 300 mL lamp with 100-W bulb
metric ruler clock or stopwatch
string graph paper

Procedure

1. Do you think sand or water will heat up faster? Record your hypothesis in the form of an "If . . . then. . . ." statement. Explain what information you used to form your hypothesis. Then follow these steps to test your hypothesis.
2. Copy the data table into your notebook. Add enough rows to record data for 15 minutes.
3. Fill one beaker with 300 mL of dry sand.
4. Fill the second beaker with 300 mL of water at room temperature.
5. Arrange the beakers beneath the ring stand.
6. Place one thermometer in each beaker.
7. Suspend the thermometers from the ring stand with string. This will hold the thermometers in place so they do not fall.

8. Adjust the height of the clamp so that the bulb of each thermometer is covered by about 0.5 cm of sand or water in a beaker.
9. Position the lamp so that it is about 20 cm above the sand and water. There should be no more than 8 cm between the beakers. **CAUTION:** *Be careful not to splash water onto the hot light bulb.*
10. Record the temperature of the sand and water in your data table.
11. Turn on the lamp. Read the temperature of the sand and water every minute for 15 minutes. Record the temperatures in the Light On column in the data table.
12. Which material do you think will cool off more quickly? Record your hypothesis. Again, give reasons why you think your hypothesis is correct.
13. Turn the light off. Read the temperature of the sand and water every minute for another 15 minutes. Record the temperatures in the Light Off column (16–30 minutes).

DATA TABLE

Temperature with Light On (°C)			Temperature with Light Off (°C)		
Time (min)	Sand	Water	Time (min)	Sand	Water
Start			16		
1			17		
2			18		
3			19		
4			20		
5			21		

Analyze and Conclude

1. Draw two line graphs to show the data for the temperature change in sand and water over time. Label the horizontal axis from 0 to 30 minutes and the vertical axis in degrees Celsius. Draw both graphs on the same piece of graph paper. Use a dashed line to show the temperature change in water and a solid line to show the temperature change in sand.

2. Calculate the total change in temperature for each material.

3. Based on your data, which material had the greater increase in temperature?

4. What can you conclude about which material absorbed heat faster? How do your results compare with your hypothesis?

5. Review your data again. In 15 minutes, which material cooled faster?

6. How do these results compare to your second hypothesis?

7. **Think About It** If your results did not support either of your hypotheses, why do you think the results differed from what you expected?

8. **Apply** Based on your results, which do you think will heat up more quickly on a sunny day: the water in a lake or the sand surrounding it? Which will cool off more quickly after dark?

More to Explore

Do you think all solid materials heat up as fast as sand? For example, consider gravel, crushed stone, or different types of soil. Write a hypothesis about their heating rates as an "If . . . then. . ." statement. With the approval and supervision of your teacher, develop a procedure to test your hypothesis. Was your hypothesis correct?

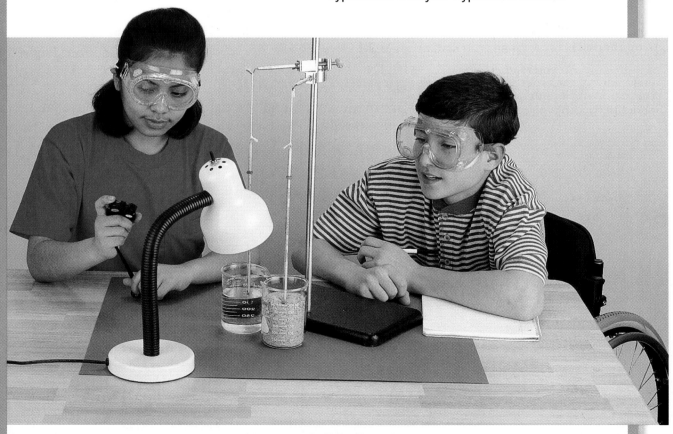

SECTION
②Heat Transfer

What Happens When Air Is Heated?

1. Use heavy scissors to cut the flat part out of an aluminum pie plate. Use the tip of the scissors to poke a small hole in the middle of the flat part.

2. Cut the part into a spiral shape, as shown in the photo. Tie a 30-centimeter piece of thread to the middle of the spiral.

3. Hold the spiral over a source of heat, such as a candle, hot plate, or incandescent light bulb.

Think It Over
Inferring What happened to the spiral? Why do you think this happened?

GUIDE FOR READING

◆ How is temperature measured?

◆ In what three ways is heat transferred?

Reading Tip As you read, make a list of the types of heat transfer. Write a sentence about how each type occurs.

You know that energy from the sun is absorbed by Earth's surface. Some energy is then transferred from the surface to the atmosphere in the form of heat. The heat then moves from place to place within the atmosphere. But how does heat move in the atmosphere?

Energy and Temperature

Gases are made up of small particles, called molecules, that are constantly moving. The faster the molecules are moving, the more energy they have. Figure 3 shows how the motion of

Figure 3 The lemonade is cold, so the molecules move slowly. The herbal tea is hot, so the molecules move faster than the molecules in the lemonade. *Inferring* Which liquid has a higher temperature?

Herbal Tea

532

molecules is related to the amount of energy they hold. The total energy of motion in the molecules of a substance is called **thermal energy.** On the other hand, **temperature** is the *average* amount of energy of motion of each molecule of a substance. That means that temperature is a measure of how hot or cold a substance is.

Measuring Temperature

Ask someone what the weather is like. The answer will probably include the temperature. Temperature is one of the most important elements of weather. **Air temperature is usually measured with a thermometer.** A **thermometer** is a thin glass tube with a bulb on one end that contains a liquid, usually mercury or colored alcohol.

Thermometers work because liquids expand when they are heated and contract when they are cooled. When the air temperature increases, the liquid in the bulb expands and rises up the column. What happens when the temperature decreases? The liquid in the bulb contracts and moves down the tube.

Temperature is measured in units called degrees. The two most common scales are shown in Figure 4. Scientists use the Celsius scale. On the Celsius scale, the freezing point of pure water is 0°C (read "zero degrees Celsius"). The boiling point of pure water is 100°C. Weather reports in the United States use the Fahrenheit scale. On the Fahrenheit scale, the freezing point of water is 32°F and the boiling point is 212°F.

✓ *Checkpoint* *How many degrees Celsius are there between the freezing point of water and the boiling point of water?*

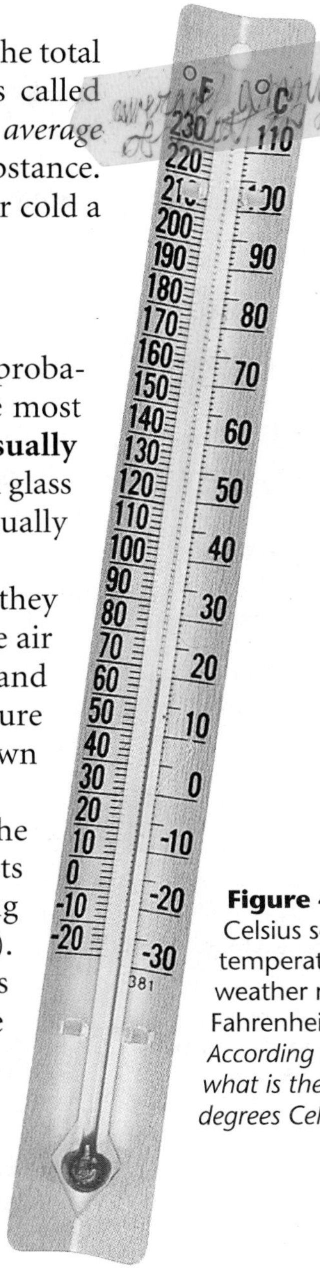

Figure 4 Scientists use the Celsius scale to measure temperature. However, weather reports use the Fahrenheit scale. *Measuring According to this thermometer, what is the air temperature in degrees Celsius?*

How Heat Is Transferred

The energy transferred from a hotter object to a cooler one is referred to as **heat.** The types of heat transfer are shown in Figure 5 on page 535. **Heat is transferred in three ways: radiation, conduction, and convection.**

Radiation Have you ever felt the warmth of the sun's rays on your face? You were feeling energy coming directly from the sun as radiation. Recall that radiation is the direct transfer of energy by electromagnetic waves. The heat you feel from the sun or a campfire travels directly to you as infrared radiation. You cannot see infrared radiation, but you can feel it as heat.

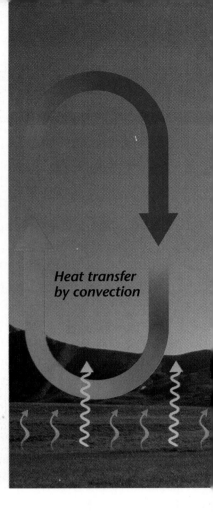

Heat transfer by convection

Conduction

Have you ever walked barefoot on hot sand? Your feet felt hot because heat moved directly from the sand into your feet. When a fast-moving molecule bumps into a nearby slower-moving molecule, it transfers some of its energy. The direct transfer of heat from one substance to another substance that it is touching is called **conduction.** The molecules that gain energy can in turn pass the energy along to other nearby molecules. When you walk on hot sand, the fast-moving molecules in the sand transfer heat into the slower-moving molecules in your feet.

The closer together the molecules in a substance are, the more effectively they can conduct heat. Conduction works well in some solids, such as metals, but not as well in liquids and gases. Air and water do not conduct heat very well.

Convection

How can you dry your boots over a hot-air vent, even though the furnace is in another room? Air from the furnace carries the heat to your boots. In fluids (liquids and gases), molecules can move from place to place. As the molecules move, they take their heat along with them. The transfer of heat by the movement of a fluid is called **convection.**

☑ *Checkpoint* *Give at least one example each of radiation, conduction, and convection in your daily life.*

Heat Transfer in the Troposphere

Radiation, conduction, and convection work together to heat the troposphere. When Earth's surface absorbs solar energy during the day, the surface of the land becomes warmer than the air. Air near Earth's surface is warmed by radiation and conduction of heat from the surface to the air. However, heat is not easily conducted from one air molecule to another. Only the first few meters of the troposphere are heated by conduction. Thus, the air close to the ground is usually warmer than the air a few meters up.

Convection causes most of the heating of the troposphere. When the air near the ground is heated, the molecules have more energy. Because they have more energy, the molecules move

Analyze and Conclude

1. Draw two line graphs to show the data for the temperature change in sand and water over time. Label the horizontal axis from 0 to 30 minutes and the vertical axis in degrees Celsius. Draw both graphs on the same piece of graph paper. Use a dashed line to show the temperature change in water and a solid line to show the temperature change in sand.

2. Calculate the total change in temperature for each material.

3. Based on your data, which material had the greater increase in temperature?

4. What can you conclude about which material absorbed heat faster? How do your results compare with your hypothesis?

5. Review your data again. In 15 minutes, which material cooled faster?

6. How do these results compare to your second hypothesis?

7. **Think About It** If your results did not support either of your hypotheses, why do you think the results differed from what you expected?

8. **Apply** Based on your results, which do you think will heat up more quickly on a sunny day: the water in a lake or the sand surrounding it? Which will cool off more quickly after dark?

More to Explore

Do you think all solid materials heat up as fast as sand? For example, consider gravel, crushed stone, or different types of soil. Write a hypothesis about their heating rates as an "If . . . then. . ." statement. With the approval and supervision of your teacher, develop a procedure to test your hypothesis. Was your hypothesis correct?

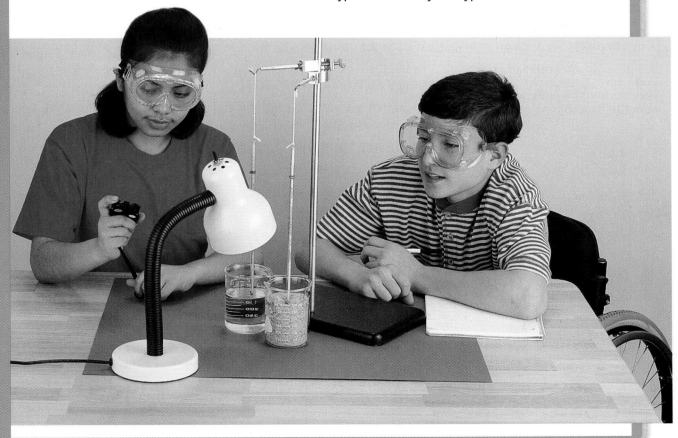

SECTION 2 Heat Transfer

DISCOVER •••••••••••••••••••••••••••••••••• ACTIVITY

What Happens When Air Is Heated?

1. Use heavy scissors to cut the flat part out of an aluminum pie plate. Use the tip of the scissors to poke a small hole in the middle of the flat part.

2. Cut the part into a spiral shape, as shown in the photo. Tie a 30-centimeter piece of thread to the middle of the spiral.

3. Hold the spiral over a source of heat, such as a candle, hot plate, or incandescent light bulb.

Think It Over

Inferring What happened to the spiral? Why do you think this happened?

GUIDE FOR READING

◆ How is temperature measured?

◆ In what three ways is heat transferred?

Reading Tip As you read, make a list of the types of heat transfer. Write a sentence about how each type occurs.

You know that energy from the sun is absorbed by Earth's surface. Some energy is then transferred from the surface to the atmosphere in the form of heat. The heat then moves from place to place within the atmosphere. But how does heat move in the atmosphere?

Energy and Temperature

Gases are made up of small particles, called molecules, that are constantly moving. The faster the molecules are moving, the more energy they have. Figure 3 shows how the motion of

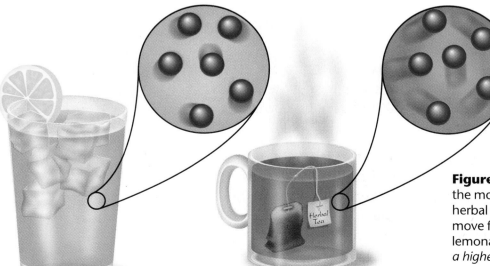

Figure 3 The lemonade is cold, so the molecules move slowly. The herbal tea is hot, so the molecules move faster than the molecules in the lemonade. *Inferring* Which liquid has a higher temperature?

532

molecules is related to the amount of energy they hold. The total energy of motion in the molecules of a substance is called **thermal energy.** On the other hand, **temperature** is the *average* amount of energy of motion of each molecule of a substance. That means that temperature is a measure of how hot or cold a substance is.

Measuring Temperature

Ask someone what the weather is like. The answer will probably include the temperature. Temperature is one of the most important elements of weather. **Air temperature is usually measured with a thermometer.** A thermometer is a thin glass tube with a bulb on one end that contains a liquid, usually mercury or colored alcohol.

Thermometers work because liquids expand when they are heated and contract when they are cooled. When the air temperature increases, the liquid in the bulb expands and rises up the column. What happens when the temperature decreases? The liquid in the bulb contracts and moves down the tube.

Temperature is measured in units called degrees. The two most common scales are shown in Figure 4. Scientists use the Celsius scale. On the Celsius scale, the freezing point of pure water is 0°C (read "zero degrees Celsius"). The boiling point of pure water is 100°C. Weather reports in the United States use the Fahrenheit scale. On the Fahrenheit scale, the freezing point of water is 32°F and the boiling point is 212°F.

☑ *Checkpoint* *How many degrees Celsius are there between the freezing point of water and the boiling point of water?*

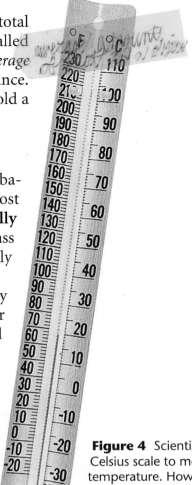

Figure 4 Scientists use the Celsius scale to measure temperature. However, weather reports use the Fahrenheit scale. *Measuring According to this thermometer, what is the air temperature in degrees Celsius?*

How Heat Is Transferred

The energy transferred from a hotter object to a cooler one is referred to as **heat.** The types of heat transfer are shown in Figure 5 on page 535. **Heat is transferred in three ways: radiation, conduction, and convection.**

Radiation Have you ever felt the warmth of the sun's rays on your face? You were feeling energy coming directly from the sun as radiation. Recall that radiation is the direct transfer of energy by electromagnetic waves. The heat you feel from the sun or a campfire travels directly to you as infrared radiation. You cannot see infrared radiation, but you can feel it as heat.

How much difference do you think there is between air temperatures near the ground and air temperatures higher up? Give reasons for your prediction.

1. Take all of your measurements at a location that is sunny all day.

2. Early in the morning, measure the air temperature 1 cm and 1.25 m above the ground. Record the time of day and the temperature for both locations. Repeat your measurements late in the afternoon.

3. Record these measurements in the morning and afternoon for two more days.

4. Graph your data for each height with temperature on the vertical axis and time on the horizontal axis. Draw both lines on the same piece of graph paper using the same axes. Label both lines.

Interpreting Data At which height did the temperature vary the most? How can you explain the difference?

Conduction Have you ever walked barefoot on hot sand? Your feet felt hot because heat moved directly from the sand into your feet. When a fast-moving molecule bumps into a nearby slower-moving molecule, it transfers some of its energy. The direct transfer of heat from one substance to another substance that it is touching is called **conduction.** The molecules that gain energy can in turn pass the energy along to other nearby molecules. When you walk on hot sand, the fast-moving molecules in the sand transfer heat into the slower-moving molecules in your feet.

The closer together the molecules in a substance are, the more effectively they can conduct heat. Conduction works well in some solids, such as metals, but not as well in liquids and gases. Air and water do not conduct heat very well.

Convection How can you dry your boots over a hot-air vent, even though the furnace is in another room? Air from the furnace carries the heat to your boots. In fluids (liquids and gases), molecules can move from place to place. As the molecules move, they take their heat along with them. The transfer of heat by the movement of a fluid is called **convection.**

☑ *Checkpoint* *Give at least one example each of radiation, conduction, and convection in your daily life.*

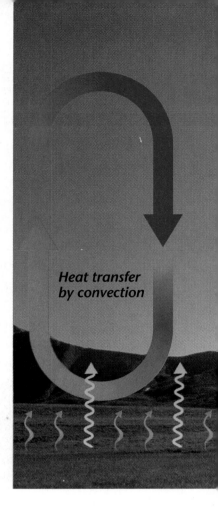

Heat transfer by convection

Heat Transfer in the Troposphere

Radiation, conduction, and convection work together to heat the troposphere. When Earth's surface absorbs solar energy during the day, the surface of the land becomes warmer than the air. Air near Earth's surface is warmed by radiation and conduction of heat from the surface to the air. However, heat is not easily conducted from one air molecule to another. Only the first few meters of the troposphere are heated by conduction. Thus, the air close to the ground is usually warmer than the air a few meters up.

Convection causes most of the heating of the troposphere. When the air near the ground is heated, the molecules have more energy. Because they have more energy, the molecules move

Analyze and Conclude

1. Draw two line graphs to show the data for the temperature change in sand and water over time. Label the horizontal axis from 0 to 30 minutes and the vertical axis in degrees Celsius. Draw both graphs on the same piece of graph paper. Use a dashed line to show the temperature change in water and a solid line to show the temperature change in sand.
2. Calculate the total change in temperature for each material.
3. Based on your data, which material had the greater increase in temperature?
4. What can you conclude about which material absorbed heat faster? How do your results compare with your hypothesis?
5. Review your data again. In 15 minutes, which material cooled faster?
6. How do these results compare to your second hypothesis?
7. **Think About It** If your results did not support either of your hypotheses, why do you think the results differed from what you expected?
8. **Apply** Based on your results, which do you think will heat up more quickly on a sunny day: the water in a lake or the sand surrounding it? Which will cool off more quickly after dark?

More to Explore

Do you think all solid materials heat up as fast as sand? For example, consider gravel, crushed stone, or different types of soil. Write a hypothesis about their heating rates as an "If . . . then. . ." statement. With the approval and supervision of your teacher, develop a procedure to test your hypothesis. Was your hypothesis correct?

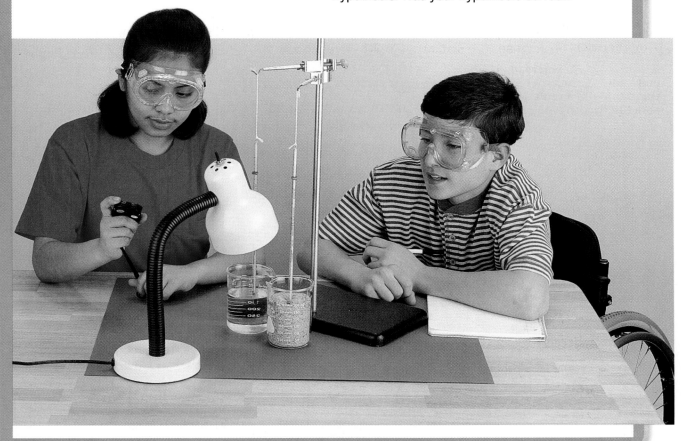

SECTION 2 Heat Transfer

DISCOVER .... ACTIVITY

What Happens When Air Is Heated?

1. Use heavy scissors to cut the flat part out of an aluminum pie plate. Use the tip of the scissors to poke a small hole in the middle of the flat part.

2. Cut the part into a spiral shape, as shown in the photo. Tie a 30-centimeter piece of thread to the middle of the spiral.

3. Hold the spiral over a source of heat, such as a candle, hot plate, or incandescent light bulb.

Think It Over

Inferring What happened to the spiral? Why do you think this happened?

GUIDE FOR READING

◆ How is temperature measured?

◆ In what three ways is heat transferred?

Reading Tip As you read, make a list of the types of heat transfer. Write a sentence about how each type occurs.

Y ou know that energy from the sun is absorbed by Earth's surface. Some energy is then transferred from the surface to the atmosphere in the form of heat. The heat then moves from place to place within the atmosphere. But how does heat move in the atmosphere?

Energy and Temperature

Gases are made up of small particles, called molecules, that are constantly moving. The faster the molecules are moving, the more energy they have. Figure 3 shows how the motion of

Figure 3 The lemonade is cold, so the molecules move slowly. The herbal tea is hot, so the molecules move faster than the molecules in the lemonade. *Inferring* Which liquid has a higher temperature?

molecules is related to the amount of energy they hold. The total energy of motion in the molecules of a substance is called **thermal energy.** On the other hand, **temperature** is the *average* amount of energy of motion of each molecule of a substance. That means that temperature is a measure of how hot or cold a substance is.

Measuring Temperature

Ask someone what the weather is like. The answer will probably include the temperature. Temperature is one of the most important elements of weather. **Air temperature is usually measured with a thermometer.** A thermometer is a thin glass tube with a bulb on one end that contains a liquid, usually mercury or colored alcohol.

Thermometers work because liquids expand when they are heated and contract when they are cooled. When the air temperature increases, the liquid in the bulb expands and rises up the column. What happens when the temperature decreases? The liquid in the bulb contracts and moves down the tube.

Temperature is measured in units called degrees. The two most common scales are shown in Figure 4. Scientists use the Celsius scale. On the Celsius scale, the freezing point of pure water is 0°C (read "zero degrees Celsius"). The boiling point of pure water is 100°C. Weather reports in the United States use the Fahrenheit scale. On the Fahrenheit scale, the freezing point of water is 32°F and the boiling point is 212°F.

☑ *Checkpoint* *How many degrees Celsius are there between the freezing point of water and the boiling point of water?*

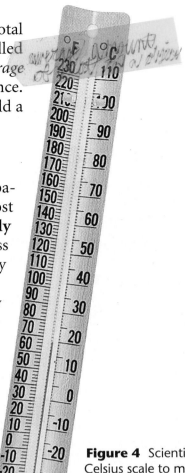

Figure 4 Scientists use the Celsius scale to measure temperature. However, weather reports use the Fahrenheit scale. *Measuring According to this thermometer, what is the air temperature in degrees Celsius?*

How Heat Is Transferred

The energy transferred from a hotter object to a cooler one is referred to as **heat.** The types of heat transfer are shown in Figure 5 on page 535. **Heat is transferred in three ways: radiation, conduction, and convection.**

Radiation Have you ever felt the warmth of the sun's rays on your face? You were feeling energy coming directly from the sun as radiation. Recall that radiation is the direct transfer of energy by electromagnetic waves. The heat you feel from the sun or a campfire travels directly to you as infrared radiation. You cannot see infrared radiation, but you can feel it as heat.

Temperatures at Two Heights

ACTIVITY

How much difference do you think there is between air temperatures near the ground and air temperatures higher up? Give reasons for your prediction.

1. Take all of your measurements at a location that is sunny all day.

2. Early in the morning, measure the air temperature 1 cm and 1.25 m above the ground. Record the time of day and the temperature for both locations. Repeat your measurements late in the afternoon.

3. Record these measurements in the morning and afternoon for two more days.

4. Graph your data for each height with temperature on the vertical axis and time on the horizontal axis. Draw both lines on the same piece of graph paper using the same axes. Label both lines.

Interpreting Data At which height did the temperature vary the most? How can you explain the difference?

Conduction Have you ever walked barefoot on hot sand? Your feet felt hot because heat moved directly from the sand into your feet. When a fast-moving molecule bumps into a nearby slower-moving molecule, it transfers some of its energy. The direct transfer of heat from one substance to another substance that it is touching is called **conduction.** The molecules that gain energy can in turn pass the energy along to other nearby molecules. When you walk on hot sand, the fast-moving molecules in the sand transfer heat into the slower-moving molecules in your feet.

The closer together the molecules in a substance are, the more effectively they can conduct heat. Conduction works well in some solids, such as metals, but not as well in liquids and gases. Air and water do not conduct heat very well.

Convection How can you dry your boots over a hot-air vent, even though the furnace is in another room? Air from the furnace carries the heat to your boots. In fluids (liquids and gases), molecules can move from place to place. As the molecules move, they take their heat along with them. The transfer of heat by the movement of a fluid is called **convection.**

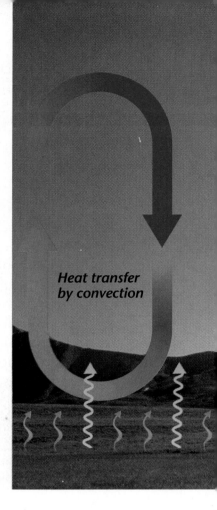

Heat transfer by convection

☑ *Checkpoint* *Give at least one example each of radiation, conduction, and convection in your daily life.*

Heat Transfer in the Troposphere

Radiation, conduction, and convection work together to heat the troposphere. When Earth's surface absorbs solar energy during the day, the surface of the land becomes warmer than the air. Air near Earth's surface is warmed by radiation and conduction of heat from the surface to the air. However, heat is not easily conducted from one air molecule to another. Only the first few meters of the troposphere are heated by conduction. Thus, the air close to the ground is usually warmer than the air a few meters up.

Convection causes most of the heating of the troposphere. When the air near the ground is heated, the molecules have more energy. Because they have more energy, the molecules move

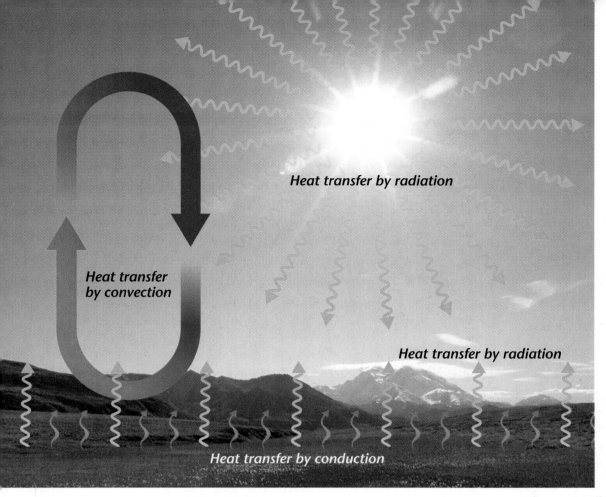

Heat transfer by radiation

Heat transfer by convection

Heat transfer by radiation

Heat transfer by conduction

Figure 5 All three types of heat transfer—radiation, convection, and conduction—occur near Earth's surface.

faster. As the molecules in the heated air move, they bump into each other and move farther apart. The air becomes less dense. Cooler, denser air sinks, forcing the warmer, less dense air to rise.

The upward movement of warm air and the downward movement of cool air form convection currents. Convection currents move heat throughout the troposphere.

Section 2 Review

1. What is temperature?
2. Describe how a thermometer works.
3. Name three ways that heat can be transferred. Briefly explain how the three work together to heat the troposphere.
4. **Thinking Critically** **Applying Concepts** When you light a fire in a fireplace, warm air rises by convection and goes up the chimney. How, then, does a fireplace heat a room? Why do only the people directly in front of the fireplace feel the warmth of the fire?

Check Your Progress CHAPTER PROJECT
Gather the instruments you will need to measure the weather factors. (*Hint:* Make sure you know how to take accurate measurements.) Plan when and where to measure weather factors. Be sure to take your measurements at the same location and at the same time of day.

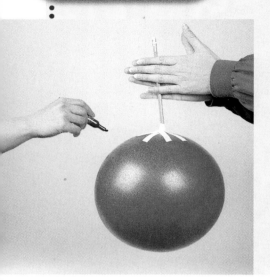

Which Way Does the Wind Turn?

Do this activity with a partner. Think of the ball as a model of Earth and the marker as representing wind.

1. Using heavy-duty tape, attach a pencil to a large smooth ball so that you can spin the ball from the top without touching it.

2. One partner should hold the pencil. Slowly turn the ball counterclockwise when seen from above.

3. While the ball is turning, the second partner should use a marker to try to draw a straight line from the "North Pole" to the "equator" of the ball. What shape does the line form?

Think It Over
Making Models If cold air were moving south from Canada into the United States, how would its movement be affected by Earth's rotation?

GUIDE FOR READING

◆ What causes winds?

◆ What are local winds and global winds?

◆ Where are the major global wind belts located?

Reading Tip Before you read, preview the illustrations and read their captions. Write down any questions you have about winds. As you read, look for answers to your questions.

The highest point in the northeastern United States, at 1,917 meters above sea level, is Mount Washington in New Hampshire. On April 12, 1934, instruments at the weather observatory atop Mount Washington measured a wind speed of 370 kilometers per hour. That's the greatest wind speed ever measured at Earth's surface apart from a fierce storm such as a tornado. What causes this incredible force?

What Causes Winds?

Because air is a fluid, it can move easily from place to place. The force that makes air move is caused by a difference of air pressure. Fluids tend to move from areas of high pressure to areas of low pressure. A **wind** is the horizontal movement of air from an area of high pressure to an area of lower pressure. **All winds are caused by differences in air pressure.**

Most differences in air pressure are caused by unequal heating of the atmosphere. As you learned in the previous section, convection currents form when an area of Earth's surface is heated by the sun's rays. Air over the heated surface expands and becomes less dense. As the air becomes less dense, its air pressure decreases. If a nearby area is not heated as much, the air above the less-heated area will be cooler and denser. The cool, dense air has a higher air pressure so it flows underneath the warm, less dense air. This process forces the warm air to rise.

Measuring Wind

Winds are described by their direction and speed. Wind direction is determined with a wind vane. The wind swings the wind vane so that one end points into the wind. The name of a wind tells you where the wind is coming from. For example, a south wind blows from the south toward the north. A north wind blows to the south.

Wind speed is measured with an **anemometer** (an uh MAHM uh tur). An anemometer has three or four cups mounted at the ends of spokes that spin on an axle. The force of the wind against the cups turns the axle. A speedometer attached to the axle shows the wind speed.

A cool breeze can be very refreshing on a warm day. However, during the winter, a similar breeze can make you feel uncomfortably cold. The wind blowing over your skin removes body heat. The stronger the wind, the colder you feel. The increased cooling that a wind can cause is called the **wind-chill factor.** Thus a weather report may say, "The temperature is 20 degrees Fahrenheit. But with a wind speed of 30 miles per hour, the wind-chill factor makes it feel like 18 degrees below zero."

☑ *Checkpoint* *Toward what direction does a west wind blow?*

Build a Wind Vane

Here's how to build your own wind vane.

1. ✂ Use scissors to cut out a pointer and a slightly larger tail fin from construction paper.
2. Make a slit 1 cm deep in each end of a soda straw.
3. Slide the pointer and tail fin into place on the straw, securing them with small pieces of tape.

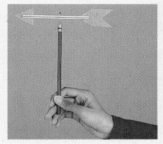

4. Hold the straw on your finger to find the point at which it balances.
5. Carefully push a pin through the balance point and into the eraser of a pencil. Move the wind vane back and forth to make sure it can spin freely.

Observing How can you use your wind vane to tell the direction of the wind?

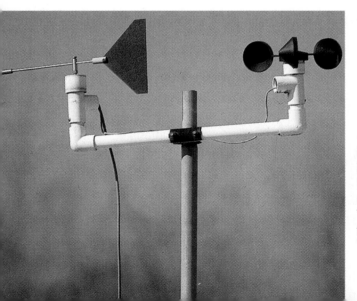

Figure 6 The wind vane on the left points in the direction the wind is blowing from. The anemometer on the right measures wind speed. The cups catch the wind, turning faster when the wind blows faster.

Local Winds

Have you ever flown a kite at the beach on a hot summer day? Even if there is no wind inland, there may be a cool breeze blowing in from the water toward the beach. This breeze is an example of a local wind. **Local winds** are winds that blow over short distances. **Local winds are caused by unequal heating of Earth's surface within a small area.** Local winds form only when no winds are blowing from farther away.

WHERE'S THE WIND?

Your city is planning to build a new community center. You and your classmates want to be sure that the doors will not be hard to open or close on windy days. You need to know which side of the building will be sheltered from the wind. You decide to measure wind speeds around a similar building.

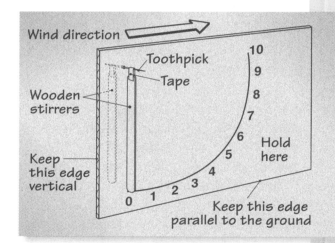

Problem

How can you determine wind patterns around a building?

Skills Focus

measuring, interpreting data, drawing conclusions

Materials

pen	round toothpick
wind vane	2 wooden coffee stirrers
meter stick	narrow masking tape
corrugated cardboard sheet, 15 cm x 20 cm	

Procedure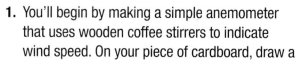

1. You'll begin by making a simple anemometer that uses wooden coffee stirrers to indicate wind speed. On your piece of cardboard, draw a curved scale like the one shown in the diagram. Mark it in equal intervals from 0 to 10.
2. Carefully use the pen to make a small hole where the toothpick will go. Insert the toothpick through the hole.
3. Tape the wooden coffee stirrers to the toothpick as shown in the diagram, one on each side of the cardboard.
4. Copy the data table into your notebook.
5. Take your anemometer outside the school. Stand about 2–3 m away from the building and away from any corners or large plants.

Unequal heating often occurs on land that is next to a large body of water. It takes more energy to warm up a body of water than it does to warm up an equal area of land. This means that as the sun heats Earth's surface during the day, the land warms up faster than the water. The air over the land becomes warmer than the air over the water. The warm air expands and rises, creating a low-pressure area. Cool air blows inland from the water and moves underneath the warm air. A wind that blows

DATA TABLE		
Location	Wind Direction	Wind Speed

6. Use the wind vane to find out what direction the wind is coming from. Hold your anemometer so that the card is straight, vertical, and parallel to the wind direction. Observe which number the wooden stirrer is closest to. Record your data.
7. Repeat your measurements on all the other sides of the building. Record your data.

Analyze and Conclude

1. Was the wind stronger on one side of the school building than the other sides? How can you explain your observation?
2. Do your classmates' results agree with yours? What might account for any differences?
3. **Apply** Based on your data, which side of the building provides the best location for a door?

More to Explore

What effect do plants have on the wind speed in an area? Could bushes and trees be planted so that they reduce the wind speed near the doors? What measurements could you make to find out?

Warmer air rising

Cooler air moving to take warmer air's place

Warmer air rising

Cooler air moving to take warmer air's place

Figure 7 A. During the day, cool air moves from the sea to the land, creating a sea breeze. B. At night, cooler air moves from the land to the sea. *Forming Operational Definitions What type of breeze occurs at night?*

from an ocean or lake onto land is known as a **sea breeze** or a lake breeze. Figure 7A shows a sea breeze.

At night, the situation is reversed. Land cools more quickly than water, so the air over the land becomes cooler than the air over the water. As the warmer air over the water rises, cooler air moves from the land to take its place. The flow of air from land to a body of water is called a **land breeze.**

Monsoons

A process similar to land and sea breezes can occur over wider areas. In the summer in South and Southeast Asia, the land gradually gets warmer than the ocean. A large "sea breeze" blows steadily inland from the ocean all summer, even at night. In the winter, the land cools and becomes colder than the ocean. A "land breeze" blows steadily from the land to the ocean.

Sea and land breezes over a large region that change direction with the seasons are called **monsoons.** The summer monsoon in South Asia and Southeast Asia is very important for the crops grown there. The air blowing from the ocean during the rainy season is very warm and humid. As the humid air rises over the land, the air cools, producing heavy rains that supply the water needed by rice and other crops.

Figure 8 This heavy rain in Nepal is part of the summer monsoon, which blows from the ocean to the land. In the winter, the monsoon reverses and blows from the land to the ocean.

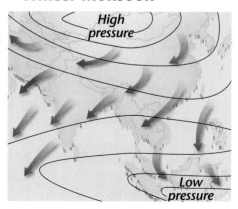

Summer Monsoon

Low pressure

High pressure

Winter Monsoon

High pressure

Low pressure

Global Winds

Winds that blow steadily from specific directions over long distances are called **global winds.** Like local winds, global winds are created by unequal heating of Earth's surface. Refer to Figure 9 to see how sunlight strikes Earth's surface. In the middle of the day near the equator, the sun is almost directly overhead. The direct rays from the sun heat Earth's surface intensely. Near the North Pole or South Pole, the sun's rays strike Earth's surface at a lower angle, even at noon. The sun's energy is spread out over a larger area, so it heats the surface less. As a result, temperatures near the poles are much lower than they are near the equator.

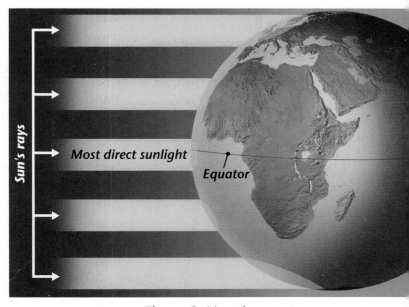

Figure 9 Near the equator, energy from the sun strikes Earth almost directly. Near the poles, the same amount of energy is spread out over a larger area.

Global Convection Currents Temperature differences between the equator and the poles produce giant convection currents in the atmosphere. Warm air rises at the equator, and cold air sinks at the poles. Therefore air pressure tends to be lower near the equator and greater near the poles, causing winds at Earth's surface to blow from the poles toward the equator. Higher in the atmosphere, air flows away from the equator toward the poles. **The movement of air between the equator and the poles produces global winds.**

The Coriolis Effect If Earth did not rotate, global winds would blow in a straight line from the poles toward the equator. Because Earth is rotating, global winds do not follow a straight path. As the winds move, Earth rotates from west to east underneath them, making it seem as if the winds have curved. The way Earth's rotation makes winds curve is called the **Coriolis effect** (kawr ee OH lis). It is named for the French mathematician who studied and explained it in 1835.

In the Northern Hemisphere, all global winds gradually turn toward the right. As you can see in Figure 10, a wind blowing toward the north gradually turns toward the northeast. In other words, a south wind gradually changes to a southwest wind. In the Southern Hemisphere, winds curve toward the left. A south wind becomes an southeast wind, and a north wind becomes a northwest wind.

Figure 10 As Earth rotates, the Coriolis effect turns winds in the Northern Hemisphere toward the right. *Interpreting Diagrams Which way do winds turn in the Southern Hemisphere?*

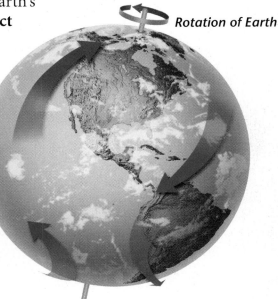

Rotation of Earth

☑ *Checkpoint* *What happens to a wind blowing toward the south in the Northern Hemisphere? What would you call this wind?*

From colonial days to the late 1800s, American merchants traded new ships, lumber, cotton, tobacco, and furs for manufactured goods, such as textiles, from England. The eastbound voyage in the early 1800s took about three weeks. However, the westbound passage took almost twice as long—five to six weeks.

In Your Journal

Imagine that you are a sea captain making the voyage to England and back to America. Your family doesn't understand why your journey home takes almost twice as long as your journey to England. Write a letter to your family explaining why you have to travel farther south to take advantage of the prevailing winds on your return voyage.

Global Wind Belts

The Coriolis effect and other factors combine to produce a pattern of calm areas and wind belts around Earth. The calm areas include the doldrums and the horse latitudes. **The major global wind belts are the trade winds, the prevailing westerlies, and the polar easterlies.** As you read about each area, find it in *Exploring Global Winds*.

Doldrums Near the equator, the sun heats the surface strongly. Warm air rises steadily, creating an area of low pressure. Cool air moves into the area, but is warmed rapidly and rises before it moves very far. There is very little horizontal motion, so the winds near the equator are very weak. Regions near the equator with little or no wind are called the doldrums.

Horse Latitudes Warm air that rises at the equator divides and flows both north and south. **Latitude** is the distance from the equator, measured in degrees. At about 30° north and south latitudes, the air stops moving toward the poles and sinks. In each of these regions, another belt of calm air forms. Hundreds of years ago, sailors becalmed in these waters ran out of food and water for their horses and had to throw the horses overboard. Because of this, the latitudes 30° north and south of the equator are called the horse latitudes.

Trade Winds When the cold air over the horse latitudes sinks, it produces a region of high pressure. This high pressure causes surface winds to blow both toward the equator and away from it. The winds that blow toward the equator are turned west by the Coriolis effect. As a result, winds in the Northern Hemisphere between 30° north latitude and the equator blow generally from the northeast. In the Southern Hemisphere between 30° south latitude and the equator, the winds blow from the southeast. These steady easterly winds are called the trade winds. For hundreds of years, sailors relied on them to carry cargoes from Europe to the West Indies and South America.

Figure 11 The bark *Patriot*, built in 1809, carried goods to many parts of the world. *Applying Concepts How much effect do you think the prevailing winds have on shipping today?*

EXPLORING Global Winds

A series of wind belts circles Earth. Between the wind belts are calm areas where air is rising or falling.

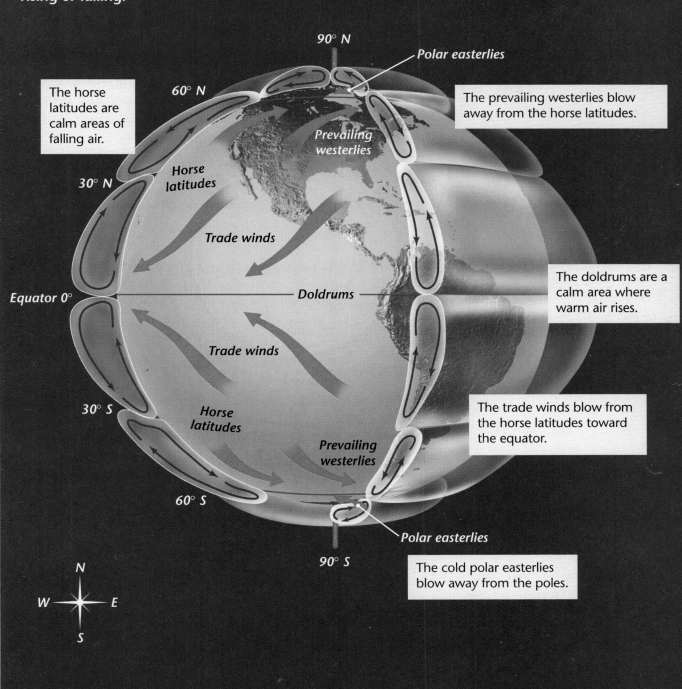

The horse latitudes are calm areas of falling air.

The prevailing westerlies blow away from the horse latitudes.

The doldrums are a calm area where warm air rises.

The trade winds blow from the horse latitudes toward the equator.

The cold polar easterlies blow away from the poles.

90° N
60° N
30° N
Equator 0°
30° S
60° S
90° S

Polar easterlies
Prevailing westerlies
Horse latitudes
Trade winds
Doldrums
Trade winds
Horse latitudes
Prevailing westerlies
Polar easterlies

N
W   E
S

Prevailing Westerlies In the mid-latitudes, winds that blow toward the poles are turned toward the east by the Coriolis effect. Because they blow from the west to the east, they are called prevailing westerlies. The prevailing westerlies blow generally from the southwest between 30° and 60° north latitudes and from the northwest between 30° and 60° south latitudes. The prevailing westerlies play an important part in the weather of the United States.

Polar Easterlies Cold air near the poles sinks and flows back toward lower latitudes. The Coriolis effect shifts these polar winds to the west, producing winds called the polar easterlies. The polar easterlies meet the prevailing westerlies at about 60° north and 60° south latitudes, along a region called the polar front. The mixing of warm and cold air along the polar front has a major effect on weather changes in the United States.

☑ *Checkpoint* *In what region do the polar easterlies meet the prevailing westerlies?*

Figure 12 By traveling east in a jet stream, pilots can save time and fuel. *Predicting What would happen if a plane flew west in a jet stream?*

Jet Streams

About 10 kilometers above Earth's surface are bands of high-speed winds called **jet streams.** These winds are hundreds of kilometers wide but only a few kilometers deep. Jet streams blow from west to east at speeds of 200 to 400 kilometers per hour. As jet streams travel around Earth, they wander north and south along a wavy path.

Airplanes are aided by a jet stream when traveling east. Pilots can save fuel and time by flying east in a jet stream. However, airplanes flying at jet stream altitudes are slowed down when traveling west against the jet stream winds.

Section 3 Review

1. How does the unequal heating of Earth's surface cause winds?
2. How are local winds and global winds similar? How are they different?
3. Name and draw the three major wind belts.
4. **Thinking Critically Applying Concepts** Imagine you are flying from Seattle to San Francisco, which is almost exactly due south of Seattle. Should the pilot set a course due south? Explain your answer.

Check Your Progress CHAPTER PROJECT
Check with your teacher to be sure you are using the weather instruments correctly. Are you recording units for each measurement? Collect and record measurements each day.

SECTION 4 Water in the Atmosphere

During a rainstorm, the air feels moist. On a clear, cloudless day, the air may feel dry. As the sun heats the land and oceans, the amount of water in the atmosphere changes. Water is always moving between the atmosphere and Earth's surface.

As you learned in Chapter 11, this movement of water between the atmosphere and Earth's surface is called the water cycle. This cycle is shown in Figure 13. Water vapor enters the air by evaporation from the oceans and other bodies of water. **Evaporation** is the process by which water molecules in liquid water escape into the air as water vapor. Water vapor is also added to the air by living things. Water enters the roots of plants, rises to the leaves, and is released as water vapor.

As part of the water cycle, some of the water vapor in the atmosphere condenses to form clouds. Rain and other forms of precipitation fall from the clouds toward the surface. The water then runs off the surface, or moves through the ground, back into the oceans, lakes, and streams.

The Water Cycle

Condensation

Precipitation

Evaporation from plants

Evaporation from oceans, lakes, and streams

Surface runoff

Figure 13 In the water cycle, water moves from lakes and oceans into the atmosphere and falls back to Earth.

Humidity

Humidity is a measure of the amount of water vapor in the air. The percentage of water vapor in the air compared to the maximum amount the air could hold is called the **relative humidity.** For example, at 10°C, 1 cubic meter of air can hold a maximum of 8 grams of water vapor. If there actually were 8 grams of water vapor in the air, then the relative humidity of the air would be 100 percent. If the air held 4 grams of water vapor, the relative humidity would be half, or 50 percent. The amount of water vapor that the air can hold depends on its temperature. Warm air can hold more water vapor than cool air.

 **INTEGRATING LIFE SCIENCE** "It's not the heat, it's the humidity." What does this common expression mean? Even on a hot day, you can still feel comfortable if the air is dry. Evaporation of moisture from your skin removes heat and helps to keep your body's temperature comfortable. You feel less comfortable on a hot day if the relative humidity is high. When the relative humidity is high, evaporation slows down. Evaporation therefore has less cooling effect on your body.

Measuring Relative Humidity

Relative humidity can be measured with a psychrometer. A **psychrometer** (sy KRAHM uh tur) has two thermometers, a wet-bulb thermometer and a dry-bulb thermometer. The bulb of the wet-bulb thermometer has a cloth covering that is moistened with water. Air is then blown over both thermometers. Because the wet-bulb thermometer is cooled by evaporation, its reading drops below that of the dry-bulb thermometer.

Relative Humidity					
Dry-Bulb Reading (°C)	Difference Between Wet- and Dry-Bulb Readings (°C)				
	1	2	3	4	5
10	88	76	65	54	43
12	88	78	67	57	48
14	89	79	69	60	50
16	90	80	71	62	54
18	91	81	72	64	56
20	91	82	74	66	58
22	92	83	75	68	60
24	92	84	76	69	62
26	92	85	77	70	64
28	93	86	78	71	65
30	93	86	79	72	66

Figure 14 A sling psychrometer is used to measure relative humidity. First, find the wet-bulb and dry-bulb temperatures. Then find the dry-bulb temperature in the left column of the table. Find the difference between the wet- and dry-bulb temperatures across the top of the table. The number in the table where these two readings intersect indicates the relative humidity in percent.

If the relative humidity is high, the water on the wet bulb will evaporate slowly and the wet-bulb temperature will not change much. If the relative humidity is low, the water on the wet bulb will evaporate rapidly and the wet-bulb temperature will drop. The relative humidity can be found by comparing the temperatures of the wet-bulb and dry-bulb thermometers on a table like the one in Figure 14.

☑ *Checkpoint* *What is the difference between humidity and relative humidity?*

How Clouds Form

What do clouds remind you of? They can look like people, animals, countries, and a thousand other fanciful forms. Of course, not all clouds are fluffy and white. Storm clouds can be dark and cover the whole sky.

Clouds of all kinds form when water vapor in the air becomes liquid water or ice crystals. The process by which molecules of water vapor in the air become liquid water is called **condensation.** How does water condense? As you know, cold air can hold less water vapor than warm air. As air cools, the amount of water vapor it can hold decreases. Some of the water vapor in the air condenses to form droplets of liquid water.

The temperature at which condensation begins is called the **dew point.** If the dew point is below the freezing point, the water vapor may change directly into ice crystals. When you look at a cloud, you are seeing millions of tiny ice crystals or water droplets.

For water vapor to condense, tiny particles must be present so the water has a surface on which to condense. Most of these particles are salt crystals, dust from soil, and smoke. Sometimes water vapor condenses onto solid surfaces, such as blades of grass, instead of particles. Water that condenses from the air onto a cold surface is called dew. Frost is ice that has been deposited directly from the air onto a cold surface.

Clouds form whenever air is cooled to its dew point and particles are present. But why does the air cool? If air is warmed near the ground, it

Sharpen your Skills

Interpreting Data

ACTIVITY

At lunchtime you use a psychrometer and get readings of 26°C on the dry-bulb thermometer and 21°C on the wet-bulb thermometer. Use Figure 14 to find the relative humidity.

Later in the day you use the psychrometer again and this time get readings of 20°C on the dry-bulb thermometer and 19°C on the wet-bulb thermometer. Find the new relative humidity. Is the relative humidity increasing or decreasing?

Figure 15 Dew forms when water vapor condenses out of the air onto a solid surface, such as this flower.

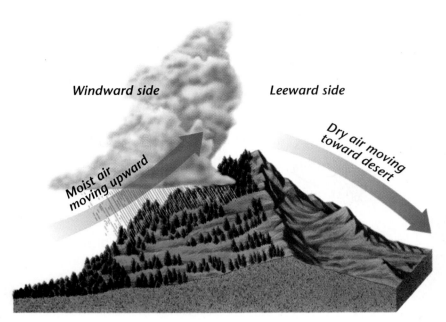

Windward side

Leeward side

Moist air moving upward

Dry air moving toward desert

Figure 16 Humid air cools as it is blown up the side of a mountain. *Predicting What happens when water vapor condenses out of the air?*

becomes less dense and rises in a convection current. When the rising air expands and becomes cooler, clouds may form.

When wind strikes the side of a hill or mountain, the air is forced upward. As the air rises along the slope, the air cools. Rain or snow falls on the windward side of the mountains, the side facing the on-coming wind.

By the time the air reaches the other side of the mountains, it has lost much of its water vapor. The air is cool and dry. The land on the leeward side of the mountains—downwind—is in a rain shadow. Just as very little light falls in a sun shadow, very little rain falls in a rain shadow. Not only has the air lost its water vapor while crossing the mountains, but the air has also grown warmer while flowing down the mountainside. This warm, dry air often creates a desert on the leeward side of the mountains.

✓ *Checkpoint* *Why are the tops of some mountains almost always covered by clouds?*

Types of Clouds

As you know, clouds come in different shapes. **Meteorologists classify clouds into three main types: cumulus, stratus, and cirrus.** Clouds are also classified by their altitude. Each type of cloud is associated with a different type of weather.

Clouds that look like fluffy, rounded piles of cotton are called **cumulus** (KYOO myuh lus) clouds. The word *cumulus* means "heap" or "mass." Cumulus clouds form less than 2 kilometers above the ground, but may grow in size and height until they extend upward as much as 18 kilometers. Cumulus clouds usually indicate fair weather. Towering clouds with flat tops, called cumulonimbus clouds, often produce thunderstorms. The suffix *-nimbus* comes from a Latin word meaning "rain."

Clouds that form in flat layers are called **stratus** (STRAT us) clouds. *Strato* means "spread out." Stratus clouds usually cover all or most of the sky. As stratus clouds thicken, they may produce drizzle, rain, or snow. They are then called nimbostratus clouds.

Wispy, feathery clouds are called **cirrus** (SEER us) clouds. Cirrus clouds form only at high levels, above about 6 kilometers, where temperatures are very low. As a result, cirrus clouds are made mostly of ice crystals.

EXPLORING Clouds

The main types of clouds are cumulus, stratus, and cirrus. A cloud's name contains clues about its height and structure.

Cirrus

Cirrocumulus

Altocumulus

Cirrus clouds
Cirrus, cirrostratus, and cirrocumulus clouds are made up mostly of ice crystals.

Cumulonimbus clouds
Thunderstorms come from cumulonimbus clouds. For this reason cumulonimbus clouds are also called thunderheads.

Altostratus

Cumulonimbus

Nimbostratus clouds
Nimbostratus clouds may produce rain or snow.

Nimbostratus

Cumulus clouds
Cumulus clouds are usually a sign of fair weather.

Stratus

Cumulus

Fog

Figure 17 Fog often forms at night over cool lakes. *Predicting What will happen as the sun rises and warms the air above the lake?*

Cirrus clouds that have feathery "hooked" ends are sometimes called mare's tails. Cirrocumulus clouds, which look like rows of cotton balls, often indicate that a storm is on its way.

Part of a cloud's name may be based on its height. The names of clouds that form between about 2 and 6 kilometers above Earth's surface have the prefix *alto-*, which means "high." The two main types of these clouds are altocumulus and altostratus.

Clouds that form at or near the ground are called fog. Fog often forms when the ground cools at night after a warm, humid day. The ground cools the air just above the ground to the air's dew point. The next day the heat of the morning sun "burns" the fog off as its water droplets evaporate.

Section 4 Review

1. What instrument is used to measure relative humidity? How does it work?
2. What conditions are needed for clouds to form?
3. Describe each of the three main types of clouds.
4. **Thinking Critically** **Classifying** Classify each of the following cloud types as low-level, medium-level, or high-level: altocumulus, altostratus, cirrostratus, cirrus, cumulus, fog, nimbostratus, and stratus.

Science at Home

Condensation on Glass Fill a large glass half-full with cold water. Show your family members what happens as you add ice cubes to the water. Explain to your family that the water that appears on the outside of the glass comes from water vapor in the atmosphere. Also explain why the water on the outside of the glass only appears after you add ice to the water in the glass.

550

SECTION 5 Precipitation

In Arica, Chile, the average rainfall is less than 1 millimeter per year. Many years pass with no precipitation at all. On the other hand, the average rainfall on Mount Waialeale on the island of Kauai in Hawaii is about 12 meters per year. That's more than enough to cover a three-story house! As you can see, rainfall varies greatly around the world.

Water evaporates into the air from every water surface on Earth and from living things. This water eventually returns to the surface as precipitation. **Precipitation** (pree sip uh TAY shun) is any form of water that falls from clouds and reaches Earth's surface.

Precipitation always comes from clouds. But not all clouds produce precipitation. For precipitation to occur, cloud droplets or ice crystals must grow heavy enough to fall through the air. One way that cloud droplets grow is by colliding and combining with other cloud droplets. As the droplets grow larger, they fall faster and collect more droplets. Finally, the droplets become heavy enough to fall out of the cloud as raindrops.

Types of Precipitation

In warm parts of the world, precipitation is almost always rain or drizzle. In colder regions, precipitation may fall as snow or ice. **Common types of precipitation include rain, sleet, freezing rain, hail, and snow.**

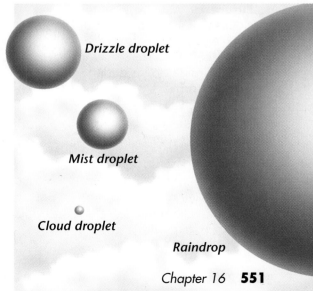

Figure 18 Droplets come in many sizes. Believe it or not, a raindrop has about one million times as much water in it as a cloud droplet.

Drizzle droplet

Mist droplet

Cloud droplet

Raindrop

Figure 19 A. Snowflakes form in clouds that are colder than 0°C. B. Freezing rain coats objects with a layer of ice. C. Hailstones are formed inside clouds during thunderstorms.

Rain The most common kind of precipitation is rain. Drops of water are called rain if they are at least 0.5 millimeter in diameter. Precipitation made up of smaller drops of water is called mist or drizzle. Mist and drizzle usually fall from nimbostratus clouds.

Sleet Sometimes raindrops fall through a layer of air below 0°C, the freezing point of water. As they fall, the raindrops freeze into solid particles of ice. Ice particles smaller than 5 millimeters in diameter are called sleet.

Freezing Rain At other times raindrops falling through cold air near the ground do not freeze in the air. Instead, the raindrops freeze when they touch a cold surface. This is called freezing rain. In an ice storm, a smooth, thick layer of ice builds up on every surface. The weight of the ice may break tree branches onto power lines, causing power failures. Freezing rain and sleet can make sidewalks and roads slippery and dangerous.

Hail Round pellets of ice larger than 5 millimeters in diameter are called hailstones. Hail forms only inside cumulonimbus clouds during thunderstorms. A hailstone starts as an ice pellet inside a cold region of a cloud. Strong updrafts in the cloud carry the hailstone up and down through the cold region many times. Each time the hailstone goes through the cold region, a new layer of ice forms around the hailstone. Eventually the hailstone becomes heavy enough to fall to the ground. If you cut a hailstone in half, you can often see shells of ice, like the layers of an onion. Because hailstones can grow quite large before finally falling to the ground, hail can cause tremendous damage to crops, buildings, and vehicles.

Snow Often water vapor in a cloud is converted directly into ice crystals called snowflakes. Snowflakes have an endless number of different shapes and patterns, all with six sides or branches. Snowflakes often join together into larger clumps of snow in which the six-sided crystals are hard to see.

☑ *Checkpoint* *How do hailstones form?*

Measuring Precipitation

Meteorologists measure rainfall with a rain gauge. A rain gauge is an open-ended can or tube that collects rainfall. The amount of rainfall is measured by dipping a ruler into the water or by reading a marked scale. To increase the accuracy of the measurement, the top of a rain gauge may have a funnel that collects ten times as much rain as the tube alone. The funnel collects a greater depth of water that is easier to measure. But to get the actual depth of rain, it is necessary to divide by ten.

Snowfall is measured using a ruler or by melting collected snow and measuring the depth of water it produces. On average, 10 centimeters of snow contains about the same amount of water as 1 centimeter of rain. Of course, light, fluffy snow contains far less water than heavy, wet snow.

Collecting funnel

1 centimeter of rain

10 centimeters in measuring tube

Measuring tube
$\frac{1}{10}$ area of funnel

Figure 20 A rain gauge measures the depth of rain that falls. *Observing How much rain was collected in the measuring tube of this rain gauge?*

Figure 21 The corn in this photo was damaged by a long drought. *Applying Concepts How can cloud seeding be used to reduce the effect of droughts?*

Controlling Precipitation

In some regions, there may be periods that are much drier than usual. Long periods of unusually low precipitation are called **droughts.** Droughts can cause great hardship. In the farming regions of the Midwest, for example, droughts may cause entire crops to fail. The farmers suffer from lost income and consumers suffer from high food prices. In some less-developed countries, droughts can cause widespread hunger, or famine.

INTEGRATING TECHNOLOGY In recent years, scientists have been trying to produce rain during droughts. The most common method is called cloud seeding. In cloud seeding, tiny crystals of dry ice (solid carbon dioxide) and silver iodide are sprinkled into clouds from airplanes. Many clouds contain supercooled water droplets, which are actually below 0°C. The droplets don't freeze because there aren't enough particles around which ice crystals can form. Water vapor can condense on the particles of silver iodide, forming rain or snow. Dry ice works by cooling the droplets even further, so that they will freeze without particles being present.

Cloud seeding has also been used with some success to clear fog from airports. Dry ice is sprinkled into the fog, causing ice crystals to form. This removes some of the fog so pilots can see the runways. Unfortunately, cloud seeding clears only cold fogs, so its use for this purpose is limited.

Section 5 Review

1. Name the five common types of precipitation.
2. What device is used to measure precipitation?
3. What must happen before precipitation can fall from a cloud?
4. What kind of cloud produces hail?
5. **Thinking Critically Applying Concepts** If two open cans of different diameters were left out in the rain, how would the amount of water they collected compare? How would the depth of water in the cans compare?

Check Your Progress **CHAPTER PROJECT**
Now you should be ready to begin graphing your weather data. Look for patterns in your graphs. Use your data to predict what the next day's weather will be. Compare your predictions with what actually happens the next day. Are you able to predict the weather with confidence?

SECTION 1 Energy in the Atmosphere

Key Ideas

◆ Energy from the sun travels to Earth as electromagnetic waves—mostly visible light, infrared radiation, and ultraviolet radiation.

◆ When Earth's surface is heated, it radiates some of the energy back into the atmosphere in the form of longer-wavelength radiation.

Key Terms

electromagnetic waves   ultraviolet radiation
radiation   scattering
infrared radiation   greenhouse effect

SECTION 2 Heat Transfer

INTEGRATING PHYSICS

Key Ideas

◆ The energy of motion in the molecules of a substance is called thermal energy.

◆ Three forms of heat transfer—radiation, conduction, and convection—work together to heat the troposphere.

Key Terms

thermal energy   thermometer   conduction
temperature   heat   convection

SECTION 3 Winds

Key Ideas

◆ All winds are caused by differences in air pressure, which are the result of unequal heating of Earth's surface.

◆ Local winds are caused by unequal heating of Earth's surface within a small area.

◆ The movement of air between the equator and the poles produces global winds.

Key Terms

wind   monsoon
anemometer   global wind
wind-chill factor   Coriolis effect
local wind   latitude
sea breeze   jet stream
land breeze

SECTION 4 Water in the Atmosphere

Key Ideas

◆ Relative humidity is the percentage of water vapor in the air compared to the amount of water vapor the air could hold. It can be measured with a psychrometer.

◆ Clouds of all kinds form when water vapor in the air becomes liquid water or solid ice.

◆ Meteorologists classify clouds into three main types: cumulus, stratus, and cirrus.

Key Terms

evaporation   psychrometer   cumulus
humidity   condensation   stratus
relative humidity   dew point   cirrus

SECTION 5 Precipitation

Key Ideas

◆ Common types of precipitation include rain, sleet, freezing rain, hail, and snow.

◆ Rain is measured with a rain gauge.

◆ Scientists have used cloud seeding to produce rain and to clear fog from airports.

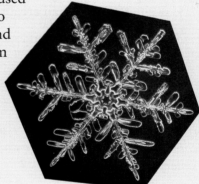

Key Terms

precipitation
rain gauge
drought

Organizing Information

Concept Map Construct a concept map about winds on a separate sheet of paper. Be sure to include the following terms: local winds, global winds, monsoons, sea breezes, land breezes, prevailing westerlies, polar easterlies, tradewinds, and the two types of monsoon. (For more on concept maps, see the Skills Handbook.)

Reviewing Content

 For more review of key concepts, see the Interactive Student Tutorial CD-ROM.

Multiple Choice

Choose the letter of the best answer.

1. Energy from the sun travels to Earth's surface by
   a. radiation.
   b. convection.
   c. evaporation.
   d. conduction.
2. Rising warm air transports heat energy by
   a. conduction.
   b. convection.
   c. radiation.
   d. condensation.
3. A psychrometer is used to measure
   a. rainfall.
   b. relative humidity.
   c. temperature.
   d. humidity.
4. Clouds form because water vapor in the air
   a. warms.   b. conducts.
   c. condenses.   d. evaporates.
5. Rain, sleet, and hail are all forms of
   a. evaporation.
   b. condensation.
   c. precipitation.
   d. convection.

True or False

If the statement is true, write true. If it is false, change the underlined word or words to make the statement true.

6. Infrared radiation and <u>ultraviolet radiation</u> make up most of the energy Earth receives from the sun.
7. The process by which gases hold heat in the atmosphere is called the <u>wind-chill factor</u>.
8. Water molecules in liquid water escape into the atmosphere as water vapor in the process of <u>evaporation</u>.
9. The instrument used to measure wind speed is a <u>thermometer</u>.
10. Clouds that form near the ground are called <u>fog</u>.

Checking Concepts

11. What causes the greenhouse effect? How does it affect Earth's atmosphere?
12. What form of heat transfer is most important in heating the troposphere?
13. What are monsoons? How are they like land and sea breezes? How are they different?
14. Describe how the movements of hot air at the equator and cold air at the poles produce global wind patterns.
15. Why are deserts often found on the leeward side of mountain ranges?
16. Why do clouds usually form high in the air instead of near Earth's surface?
17. Describe sleet, hail, and snow in terms of how each one forms.
18. **Writing to Learn** Imagine you are a drop of water in the ocean. Write a diary describing your journey through the water cycle. How do you become a cloud? What type of conditions cause you to fall as precipitation? Use descriptive words to describe your journey.

Thinking Critically

19. **Relating Cause and Effect** What circumstances could cause a night-time land breeze in a city near the ocean?
20. **Problem Solving** If you use a psychrometer and get the same reading on both thermometers, what is the relative humidity?
21. **Comparing and Contrasting** How are hail and sleet alike? How are they different?
22. **Classifying** Classify the different types of clouds by the kind of weather associated with each type.
23. **Relating Cause and Effect** What is the source of the energy that powers Earth's winds?

Applying Skills

Use the table below to answer Questions 24–27.

Average Monthly Rainfall

Month	Rainfall	Month	Rainfall
January	1 cm	July	49 cm
February	1 cm	August	57 cm
March	1 cm	September	40 cm
April	2 cm	October	20 cm
May	25 cm	November	4 cm
June	52 cm	December	1 cm

24. Graphing Use the information in the table to draw a bar graph that shows the rainfall each month at this location.

25. Calculating What is the total amount of rainfall each year at this location?

26. Classifying Which months of the year would you classify as "dry"? Which months would you classify as "wet"?

27. Drawing Conclusions The place represented by the rainfall data is in Southeast Asia. What do you think accounts for the extremely heavy rainfall that occurs during some months?

Performance ▼CHAPTER PROJECT Assessment

Present Your Project Develop a way to present your findings to the class. For example, you could put your graphs and predictions on a poster. Are your graphs neatly drawn and easy to understand? Practice your presentation and make any needed improvements.

Reflect and Record How could you improve the accuracy of your observations? What did you learn about how easy or difficult it is to predict the weather?

Test Preparation

Use these questions to prepare for standardized tests.

Study the graph. Then answer Questions 28–31.

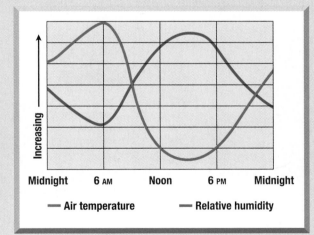

— Air temperature   — Relative humidity

28. The greatest change in air temperature occurred during the period from
 a. midnight to 6 A.M.
 b. 6 A.M. to noon.
 c. noon to 6 P.M.
 d. 6 P.M. to midnight.

29. The graph indicates that as air temperature increases, relative humidity
 a. increases.
 b. sometimes increases and sometimes decreases.
 c. decreases.
 d. stays about the same.

30. Condensation is most likely to occur at approximately
 a. 6 A.M.   **b.** noon.
 c. 3 P.M.   **d.** 6 P.M.

31. Assuming that the amount of water vapor in the air stayed constant through the day, one could infer from the graph that
 a. cool air can hold more water vapor than warm air.
 b. cool air can hold less water vapor than warm air.
 c. cool air and warm air can hold the same amount of water vapor.
 d. cool air cannot hold water vapor.

A lightning bolt tears
through the dark sky,
illuminating a field
of wheat.

WEB ACTIVITY
www.phschool.com

 SECTION 1 **Air Masses and Fronts**

Discover **How Do Fluids of Different Densities Behave?**
Sharpen Your Skills **Classifying**

 SECTION 2 **Storms**

Discover **Can You Make a Tornado?**
Try This **Lightning Distances**
Science at Home **Storm Experiences**
Real-World Lab **Tracking a Hurricane**

Integrating Health

 SECTION 3 **Floods**

Discover **What Causes Floods?**
Sharpen Your Skills **Communicating**

The Weather Tomorrow

When the sky turns dark and threatening, it's not hard to predict the weather. A storm is on its way. But wouldn' you rather know about an approaching storm before it actually arrives?

In this chapter you will learn about weather patterns, including the kinds of patterns that cause strong thunderstorms like this one. As you work through this chapter, you will get a chance to make your own weather forecasts and compare them to the forecasts of professionals. Good luck!

Your Goal To predict the weather for your own community and two other locations in the United States.

To complete the project you will
◆ compare weather maps for several days at a time
◆ look for repeating patterns in the weather
◆ draw maps to show your weather predictions

Get Started Begin by previewing Section 4 to learn about weather maps and symbols. Start a project folder to hold daily national weather maps from your local newspaper and a description of the symbols used on the maps. Choose two locations in the United States that are at least 1,000 kilometers away from your community and from each other.

Check Your Progress You'll be working on this project as you study this chapter. To keep your project on track, look for Check Your Progress boxes at the following points.
Section 1 Review, page 566: Collect weather maps and look for patterns.
Section 3 Review, page 582: Predict the next day's weather.
Section 4 Review, page 589: Compare your predictions to professional forecasts and to the actual weather.

Present Your Project At the end of the chapter (page 593), you will present your weather maps and discuss how well you predicted the weather.

SECTION 4 Predicting the Weather

Discover **What's the Weather?**
Sharpen Your Skills **Interpreting Data**
Skills Lab **Reading a Weather Map**

1 Air Masses and Fronts

How Do Fluids of Different Densities Behave?

1. Put on your apron. Place a cardboard divider across the middle of a plastic shoe box.

2. Add a few drops of red food coloring to a liter of warm water. Pour the red liquid, which represents low-density warm air, into the shoe box on one side of the divider.

3. Add about 100 mL of table salt and a few drops of blue food coloring to a liter of cold

water. Pour the blue liquid, which represents high-density cold air, into the shoe box on the other side of the divider.

4. What do you think will happen if you remove the divider?

5. Now quickly remove the divider. Watch carefully from the side. What happens?

Think It Over

Developing Hypotheses Based on this activity, write a hypothesis stating what would happen if a mass of cold air ran into a mass of warm air.

GUIDE FOR READING

◆ What are the major types of air masses that affect the weather in North America?

◆ What are the main types of fronts?

◆ What are cyclones and anticyclones?

Reading Tip Before you read, use the headings to make an outline about air masses and fronts. Leave space to fill in details as you read.

L isten to the evening news and you may hear a weather fore-cast like this: "A huge mass of Arctic air is moving our way, bringing freezing temperatures." Today's weather is influ-enced by air from thousands of kilometers away—perhaps from Canada or the Caribbean Sea. A huge body of air that has simi-lar temperature, humidity, and air pressure throughout it is called an **air mass.** A single air mass may spread over an area of millions of square kilometers and be up to 10 kilometers high.

Types of Air Masses

Scientists classify air masses according to two characteristics: temperature and humidity. Whether an air mass is warm or cold depends on the temperature of the region over which the air mass forms. **Tropical,** or warm, air masses form in the tropics and have low air pressure. **Polar,** or cold, air masses form north of 50° north latitude and south of 50° south latitude. Polar air masses have high air pressure.

Whether an air mass is humid or dry depends on whether it forms over water or land. **Maritime** air masses form over oceans. Water evaporates from the oceans, so the air can become very humid. **Continental** air masses form over land, in the middle of continents, and are dry.

Today

Four major types of air masses influence the weather in North America: maritime tropical, continental tropical, maritime polar, and continental polar. *Exploring North American Air Masses* on the next page shows where these air masses come from and what parts of North America they affect.

Maritime Tropical Warm, humid air masses form over oceans near the tropics. Maritime tropical air masses that form over the Gulf of Mexico and the Atlantic Ocean move first into the southeastern United States. These air masses then move north and northeast, where they influence weather in the central and eastern United States. In the west, maritime tropical air masses form over the Pacific Ocean. They affect mainly the weather on the West Coast. As they cross the coastal mountain ranges, the Pacific air masses lose moisture. They bring dry air to the eastern slopes.

In summer, maritime tropical air masses usually bring hot, humid weather. Most summer showers and thunderstorms in the United States develop in air masses that have formed over the Gulf of Mexico. In winter, a humid air mass can bring heavy rain or snow.

Maritime Polar Cool, humid air masses form over the icy cold North Pacific and North Atlantic oceans. Maritime polar air masses affect the West Coast more than the East Coast. Even in summer, these masses of cool, humid air often bring fog, rain, and cool temperatures to the West Coast.

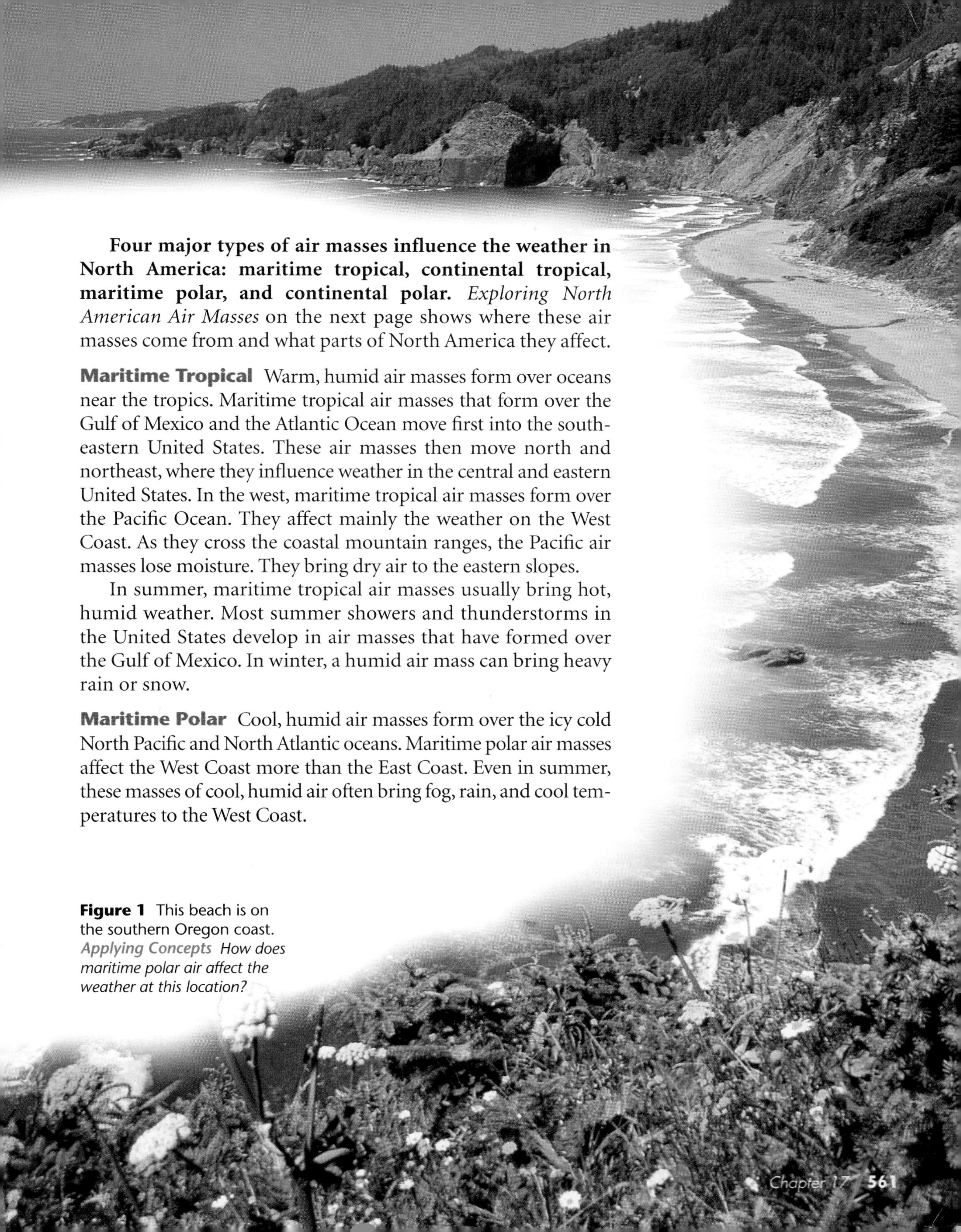

Figure 1 This beach is on the southern Oregon coast. *Applying Concepts How does maritime polar air affect the weather at this location?*

EXPLORING North American Air Masses

A ir masses can be warm or cold, and humid or dry. As an air mass moves into an area, it changes the weather there.

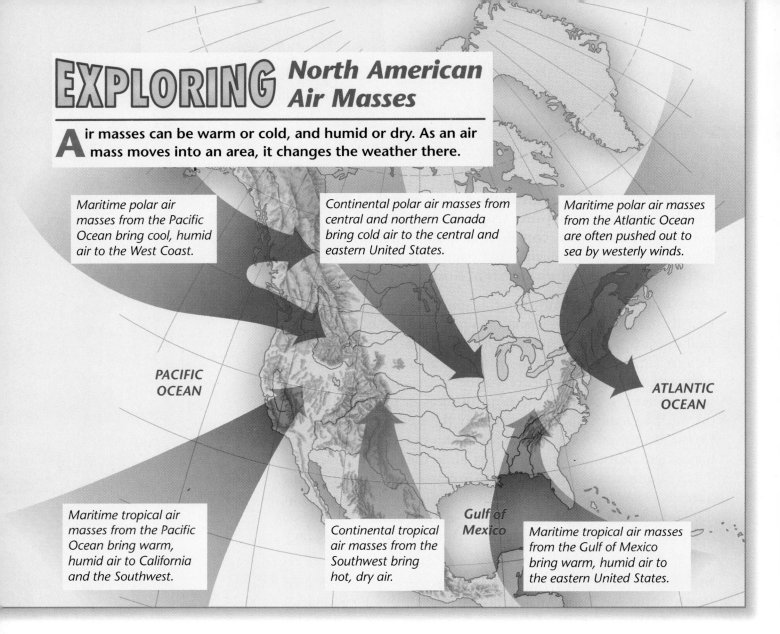

Maritime polar air masses from the Pacific Ocean bring cool, humid air to the West Coast.

Continental polar air masses from central and northern Canada bring cold air to the central and eastern United States.

Maritime polar air masses from the Atlantic Ocean are often pushed out to sea by westerly winds.

PACIFIC OCEAN

ATLANTIC OCEAN

Maritime tropical air masses from the Pacific Ocean bring warm, humid air to California and the Southwest.

Continental tropical air masses from the Southwest bring hot, dry air.

Gulf of Mexico

Maritime tropical air masses from the Gulf of Mexico bring warm, humid air to the eastern United States.

Continental Tropical Hot, dry air masses form only in summer over dry areas of the Southwest and northern Mexico. Continental tropical air masses cover a smaller area than other air masses. They occasionally move northeast, bringing hot, dry weather to the southern Great Plains.

Continental Polar Large continental polar air masses form over central and northern Canada and Alaska. As you would expect, continental polar air masses bring cool or cold air. In winter, continental polar air masses bring clear, cold, dry air to much of North America. Air masses that form near the Arctic Circle can bring bitterly cold weather with very low humidity. In summer, storms may occur when continental polar air masses move south and meet maritime tropical air masses moving north.

☑ *Checkpoint* *Where do continental polar air masses come from?*

How Air Masses Move

Recall that the prevailing westerlies are the major wind belts in the continental United States. The prevailing westerlies generally push air masses from west to east. For example, maritime polar air masses from the Pacific Ocean are blown onto the West Coast, bringing heavy rain or snow. Continental polar air masses from central Canada enter the United States between the Rocky Mountains and the Great Lakes. These cold, dry air masses are then blown east, where they affect the weather of the central and eastern United States.

Fronts

As huge masses of air move across the land and the oceans, they bump into each other. But the air masses do not easily mix. Why don't they? Think about a bottle of oil-and-vinegar salad dressing. The less dense oil floats on top of the more dense vinegar.

Something similar happens when two air masses with different temperatures and densities collide. The area where the air masses meet and do not mix becomes a **front.** The term *front,* which is borrowed from military language, means a battle area where opposing armies meet to fight. When air masses meet at a front, the collision often causes storms and changeable weather. A front may be 15 to 200 kilometers wide and extend as much as 10 kilometers up into the troposphere.

There are four types of fronts: cold fronts, warm fronts, stationary fronts, and occluded fronts. The kind of front that develops depends on the characteristics of the air masses and how they are moving. How does each type of front affect your local weather?

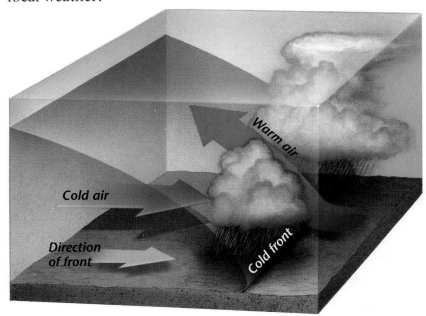

Figure 2 A cold front forms when cold air moves underneath warm air, forcing the warm air to rise.

Warm air

Cold air

Direction of front

Cold front

Cold Fronts As you know, cold air is dense and tends to sink. Warm air is less dense and tends to rise. When a rapidly moving cold air mass runs into a slowly moving warm air mass, the denser cold air slides under the lighter warm air. The warm air is pushed upward, as shown in Figure 2. The front that forms is called a cold front.

As the warm air rises, it cools. Remember that warm air can hold more water vapor than cool air. The rising air soon reaches the dew point, the temperature at which the water vapor in the air condenses into droplets of liquid water. Clouds form. If there is a lot of water vapor in the warm air, heavy rain or snow may fall. What will happen if the warm air mass contains only a little water vapor? In this case, the cold front may be accompanied by only cloudy skies.

Cold fronts move quickly, so they can cause abrupt weather changes, including violent thunderstorms. After a cold front passes through an area, cool, dry air moves in, often bringing clear skies and cooler temperatures.

Warm Fronts Clouds, storms, and rain also accompany warm fronts. At a warm front, a moving warm air mass collides with a slowly moving cold air mass. Because cold air is more dense than warm air, the warm air moves over the cold air, as shown in Figure 3. If the warm air is humid, showers and light rain fall along the front where the warm and cold air meet. If the warm air is dry, scattered clouds form. Because warm fronts move more slowly than cold fronts, the weather may be rainy or foggy for several days. After a warm front passes through an area, the weather is likely to be warm and humid. In winter, warm fronts bring snow.

Figure 3 A warm front forms when warm air moves over cold air. *Interpreting Diagrams* *What kind of weather forms at a warm front?*

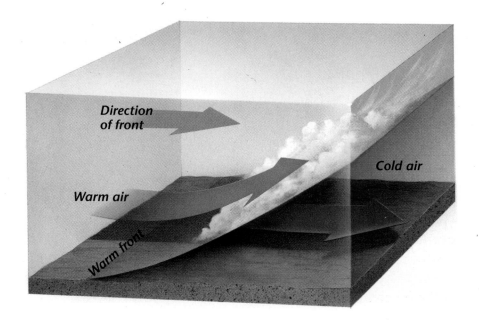

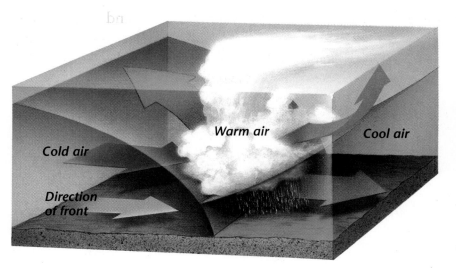

Figure 4 When a cold air mass and a cool air mass come together, the warm air caught between them is forced upward. The result is an occluded front.

Cold air

Warm air

Cool air

Direction of front

Stationary Fronts Sometimes cold and warm air masses meet, but neither one has enough force to move the other. The two air masses face each other in a "standoff." In this case, the front is called a stationary front. Where the warm and cool air meet, water vapor in the warm air condenses into rain, snow, fog, or clouds. If a stationary front remains stalled over an area, it may bring many days of clouds and precipitation.

Occluded Fronts The most complex weather situation occurs at an occluded front, shown in Figure 4. At an occluded front, a warm air mass is caught between two cooler air masses. The denser cool air masses move underneath the less dense warm air mass and push it upward. The two cooler air masses meet in the middle and may mix. The temperature near the ground becomes cooler. The warm air mass is cut off, or **occluded,** from the ground. As the warm air cools and its water vapor condenses, the weather may turn cloudy and rainy or snowy.

☑ *Checkpoint* *What type of front forms when two air masses meet and neither one can move?*

Cyclones and Anticyclones

If you look at a weather map, you will see areas marked with an L. The L is short for "low," and indicates an area of relatively low air pressure. A swirling center of low air pressure is called a **cyclone,** from a Greek word meaning "wheel."

As warm air at the center of a cyclone rises, the air pressure decreases. Cooler air blows toward this low-pressure area from nearby areas where the air pressure is higher. Winds spiral inward toward the center of the system. Recall that in the Northern Hemisphere the Coriolis effect deflects winds to the right.

Sharpen your **Skills**

Classifying

ACTIVITY

At home, watch the weather forecast on television. Make a note of each time the weather reporter mentions a front. Classify the fronts mentioned or shown as cold, warm, stationary, or occluded. Also, note what type of weather is predicted to occur when the front arrives. Is each type of front always associated with the same type of weather?

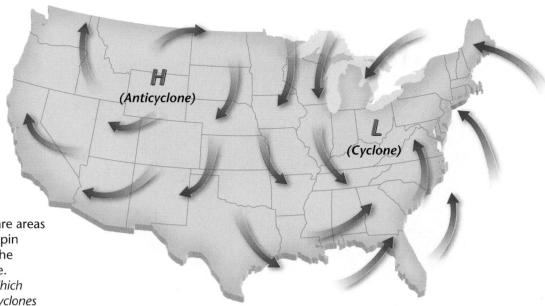

Figure 5 Cyclones are areas of low pressure that spin counterclockwise in the Northern Hemisphere.
Interpreting Maps Which way do winds in anticyclones spin?

Because of this, winds in a cyclone spin counterclockwise in the Northern Hemisphere, as shown in Figure 5.

Cyclones play a large part in the weather of the United States. As air rises in a cyclone, the air cools, forming clouds and precipitation. **Cyclones and decreasing air pressure are associated with storms and precipitation.**

As its name suggests, an anticyclone is the opposite of a cyclone in most ways. **Anticyclones** are high-pressure centers of dry air. Anticyclones are also called "highs"—H on a weather map. Winds spiral outward from the center of an anticyclone, moving toward areas of lower pressure. Because of the Coriolis effect, winds in an anticyclone spin clockwise in the Northern Hemisphere. Because air moves out from the center of the anticyclone, cool air moves downward from higher in the troposphere. As the cool air falls, it warms up, so its relative humidity drops. The descending air in an anticyclone causes dry, clear weather.

Section 1 Review

1. What two main characteristics are used to classify air masses?
2. What is a front? Name and describe four types of fronts.
3. What is a cyclone? What type of weather does it bring?
4. Why do maritime polar air masses have more effect on the West Coast than the East Coast?
5. **Thinking Critically** **Classifying** Classify the four major types of air masses according to whether they are dry or humid.

Check Your Progress

CHAPTER PROJECT

Collect newspaper weather maps for about a week, and arrange them in order. Look carefully at how symbols on the map have moved from one day to the next. What patterns do you see from day to day in different weather factors? How does the weather in your community differ from the weather in the two other locations you selected?

2 Storms

Can You Make a Tornado?

1. Fill a large plastic jar three-quarters full with water. Add a drop of liquid dish detergent and a penny or marble.

2. Put the lid on the jar tightly. Now move the jar in a circle until the water inside begins to spin.

Think It Over

Observing What happens to the water in the jar? Describe the pattern that forms. How is it like a tornado? Unlike a tornado?

Early in 1998, a series of powerful tornadoes roared through central Florida. With winds as high as 210 miles per hour, the tornadoes dropped cars into living rooms, crumpled trailers, and destroyed businesses and school buildings. They were the deadliest tornadoes ever to hit Florida. These tornadoes were not the only violent weather that year. In California the problem was rain. Record rainfalls brought devastating floods and mudslides.

What was causing these disasters? Meteorologists had an answer: El Niño. El Niño is a weather pattern related to the temperature of the water in the tropical Pacific Ocean. When temperatures there rise, they set off a series of events that can influence weather half a world away.

Have you ever experienced a tornado, hurricane, or other severe storm? When rain pours down, thunder crashes, or snow-drifts pile up, it may be hard to think about the actions of air pressure and air masses. Yet these are the causes of severe storms as well as the weather you experience every day.

A **storm** is a violent disturbance in the atmosphere. Storms involve sudden changes in air pressure, which in turn cause rapid air movements. Conditions that bring one kind of storm often cause other kinds of storms in the same area. For example, the conditions that cause thunderstorms can also cause tornadoes.

GUIDE FOR READING

◆ What are the main kinds of storms? How do they form?

◆ What measures can you take to ensure safety in a storm?

Reading Tip As you read, create a table comparing thunderstorms, tornadoes, hurricanes, and snowstorms. Include temperature, precipitation, and safety rules.

Figure 6 Tornadoes caused tremendous damage in Florida and other parts of the southeastern United States in 1998.

Figure 7 The anvil shape of this cloud is typical of cumulonimbus clouds that produce thunderstorms. *Applying Concepts Why do cumulonimbus clouds often form along cold fronts?*

TRY THIS

Lightning Distances

Because light travels faster than sound, you see a lightning flash before you hear the clap of thunder. Here's how to calculate your distance from a thunderstorm.
CAUTION: *Do this activity inside a building only.*

1. Count the number of seconds between the moment when you see the lightning and when you hear the thunder.

2. Divide the number of seconds you counted by three to get the distance in kilometers. Example:

$$\frac{15 \text{ s}}{3 \text{ s/km}} = 5 \text{ km}$$

Calculating Wait for another flash of lightning and calculate the distance again. How can you tell whether a thunderstorm is moving toward you or away from you?

Thunderstorms

Do you find thunderstorms frightening? Exciting? A little of both? As you watch the brilliant flashes of lightning and listen to long rolls of thunder, you have probably wondered what caused them.

How Thunderstorms Form Thunderstorms are heavy rainstorms accompanied by thunder and lightning. **Thunderstorms form within large cumulonimbus clouds, or thunderheads.** Most cumulonimbus clouds and thunderstorms form when warm air is forced upward at a cold front. Cumulonimbus clouds also form on hot, humid afternoons in the spring and summer. In both cases, the warm, humid air rises rapidly. As the air rises, it cools, forming dense thunderheads. Heavy rain falls, sometimes along with hail.

Thunderstorms produce strong upward and downward winds—updrafts and downdrafts—inside clouds. When a downdraft strikes the ground, the air spreads out in all directions, producing bursts of wind called wind shear. Wind shear has caused a number of airplane accidents during takeoff or landing.

Lightning and Thunder During a thunderstorm, areas of positive and negative electrical charges build up in the storm clouds. **Lightning** is a sudden spark, or energy discharge, as these charges jump between parts of a cloud, between nearby clouds, or between the cloud and the ground. Lightning is similar to the shocks you sometimes feel when you touch a metal object on a very dry day, but on a much larger scale.

What causes thunder? A lightning bolt can heat the air near it to as much as 30,000°C, much hotter than the surface of the sun. The rapidly heated air expands suddenly and explosively. Thunder is the sound of the explosion. Because light travels faster than sound, you see lightning before you hear thunder.

Thunderstorm Safety When lightning strikes

the ground, the hot, expanding air can start forest fires. When lightning strikes people or animals, it acts like a powerful electric shock. Being struck by lightning can cause unconsciousness, serious burns, or even heart failure.

What should you do to remain safe if you are caught outside during a thunderstorm? **During thunderstorms, avoid touching metal objects because they can conduct electricity from lightning into your body.** Lightning usually strikes the tallest nearby object, such as a tree, house, or flagpole. To protect buildings from lightning, people install metal lightning rods at the highest point on a roof. Lightning rods intercept a lightning stroke and conduct the electricity through cables safely into the ground.

In open spaces, such as a golf course, people can be in danger because they are the tallest objects in the area. It is equally dangerous to seek shelter under a tree, because lightning may strike the tree and you at the same time. Instead, find a low area away from trees, fences, and poles. Crouch with your head down and your hands on your knees. If you are swimming or in a boat, get to shore and find shelter away from the water.

If you are inside a house during a thunderstorm, avoid touching telephones, electrical appliances, or plumbing fixtures, all of which can conduct electricity into the house. It is usually safe to stay in a car with a hard top during a thunderstorm because the electricity will move along the metal skin of the car and jump to the ground. However, do not touch any metal inside the car.

✓ *Checkpoint* **Why is lightning dangerous?**

Figure 8 Lightning occurs when electricity jumps within clouds, between clouds, or between a cloud and the ground.

Tornadoes

A tornado is one of the most frightening and destructive types of storms. A **tornado** is a rapidly whirling, funnel-shaped cloud that reaches down from a storm cloud to touch Earth's surface. If a tornado occurs over a lake or ocean, it is known as a waterspout. Tornadoes are usually brief, but can be deadly. They may touch the ground for 15 minutes or less and be only a few hundred meters across, but wind speeds may approach 480 kilometers per hour.

How Tornadoes Form **Tornadoes develop in low, heavy cumulonimbus clouds—the same clouds that bring thunderstorms.** Tornadoes are most likely to occur when thunderstorms are likely—in spring and early summer, often late in the afternoon when the ground is warm. The Great Plains often have the kind of weather pattern that is likely to create tornadoes: a warm, humid air mass moves north from the Gulf of Mexico into the lower Great Plains. A cold, dry air mass moves south from Canada. When the air masses meet, the cold air moves under the warm air, which rises. A squall line of thunderstorms is likely to form, with storms traveling from southwest to northeast. A single squall line can cause 10 or more tornadoes.

Tornadoes occur more often in the United States than in any other country. About 800 tornadoes occur in the United States

Weather That Changed History

Unanticipated storms have caused incredible damage, killed numbers of people, and even changed the course of history.

1281 Japan

In an attempt to conquer Japan, Kublai Khan, the Mongol emperor of China, sent a fleet of ships carrying a huge army. A hurricane from the Pacific brought high winds and towering waves that sank the ships. The Japanese named the storm *kamikaze*, meaning "divine wind."

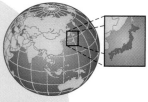

1620 Massachusetts

English Pilgrims set sail for the Americas in the *Mayflower*. They had planned to land near the mouth of the Hudson River, but turned back north because of rough seas and storms. When the Pilgrims landed farther north, they decided to stay and so established Plymouth Colony.

| 1300 | 1400 | 1500 | 1600 |

1588 England

King Philip II of Spain sent the Spanish Armada, a fleet of 130 ships, to invade England. Strong winds in the English Channel trapped the Armada near shore. Some Spanish ships escaped, but storms wrecked most of them.

every year. Weather patterns on the Great Plains result in a "tornado alley," shown in Figure 9, that runs from north-central Texas across central Oklahoma, Kansas, and Nebraska. However, tornadoes can and do occur in nearly every part of the United States.

☑ *Checkpoint* *Where do tornadoes form?*

Tornado Safety A tornado can level houses on one street, but

 INTEGRATING HEALTH

leave neighboring houses standing. Tornado damage comes from both strong winds and flying debris. The low pressure inside the tornado sucks up dust and other objects into the funnel. Tornadoes can move large objects—sheds, trailers, cars—and scatter debris many miles away. One tornado tore off a motel sign in Broken Bow, Oklahoma, and dropped it 30 miles away in Arkansas!

In Your Journal

Some of these events happened before forecasters had the equipment to predict weather scientifically. Choose one of the events in the time line. Write a paragraph describing how history might have been different if the people involved had had accurate weather predictions.

1870 Great Lakes

Learning that more than 1,900 boats had sunk in storms on the Great Lakes in 1869, Congress decided to set up a national weather service, the Army Signal Corps. In 1891 the job of issuing weather warnings and forecasts went to a new agency, the U.S. Weather Bureau.

| 1700 | 1800 | 1900 |

1837 North Carolina

The steamship *Home* sank during a hurricane off Ocracoke, North Carolina. In one of the worst storm-caused disasters at sea, 90 people died. In response, the U.S. Congress passed a law requiring seagoing ships to carry a life preserver for every passenger.

1915 Texas

When a hurricane struck the port city of Galveston in 1900, it killed 6,000 people and destroyed much of the city. As a result, a seawall 5 meters high and 16 kilometers long was built. When another hurricane struck in 1915, the seawall greatly reduced the amount of damage.

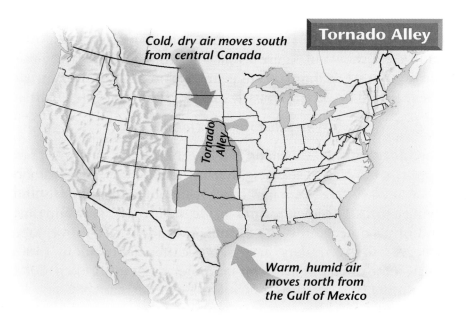

Tornado Alley

Cold, dry air moves south from central Canada

Tornado Alley

Warm, humid air moves north from the Gulf of Mexico

Figure 9 A tornado can cause a lot of damage in a short period of time. The map shows where tornadoes are most likely to occur in the United States.
Interpreting Maps Which states are partially located in "tornado alley"?

What should you do if a tornado is predicted in your area? A "tornado watch" is an announcement that tornadoes are possible in your area. Watch for approaching thunderstorms. A "tornado warning" is an announcement that a tornado has been seen in the sky or on weather radar. If you hear a tornado warning, move to a safe area as soon as you can. Do not wait until you actually see the tornado.

The safest place to be during a tornado is in the basement of a well-built building. If the building you are in does not have a basement, move to the middle of the ground floor. Stay away from windows and doors that could break and fly through the air. Lie on the floor under a sturdy piece of furniture, such as a large table. If you are outdoors or in a car or mobile home, move to a building or lie flat in a ditch.

✓ *Checkpoint* What is the difference between a tornado watch and a tornado warning?

Hurricanes

Between June and November, people who live in the eastern United States hear weather reports much like this: "A hurricane warning has been issued for the Atlantic coast from Florida to North Carolina. Hurricane Michael has winds of over 160 kilometers per hour and is moving north at about 65 kilometers per hour." A **hurricane** is a tropical storm that has winds of 119 kilometers per hour or higher. A typical hurricane is about 600 kilometers across.

Hurricanes also form in the Pacific and Indian oceans. In the western Pacific Ocean, hurricanes are called typhoons. Although hurricanes may be destructive, they bring much-needed rainfall to South Asia and Southeast Asia.

How Hurricanes Form A typical hurricane that strikes the United States forms in the Atlantic Ocean north of the equator in August, September, or October. **A hurricane begins over warm water as a low-pressure area, or tropical disturbance.** If the tropical disturbance grows in size and strength, it becomes a tropical storm, which may then become a hurricane.

A hurricane gets its energy from the warm, humid air at the ocean's surface. As this air rises and forms clouds, more air is drawn into the system. As with other storm systems, winds spiral inward toward the areas of low pressure. Inside the storm are bands of very high winds and heavy rains. The lowest air pressure and warmest temperatures are at the center of the hurricane. The lower the air pressure at the center of a storm, the faster the winds blow toward the center. Hurricane winds may be as strong as 320 kilometers per hour.

The Eye of the Hurricane The center of a hurricane is a ring of clouds surrounding a quiet "eye," as shown in Figure 10. If you were in the path of a hurricane, you would notice that the wind gets stronger as the eye approaches. When the eye arrives, the weather changes suddenly. The winds grow calm and the sky may clear. After the eye passes, the storm resumes, but the wind blows from the opposite direction.

How Hurricanes Move Hurricanes last longer than other storms, usually a week or more. Hurricanes that form in the Atlantic Ocean are steered by easterly trade winds toward the Caribbean islands and the southeastern United States. After a hurricane passes over land, it no longer has warm, moist air to draw energy from. The hurricane gradually slows down and loses strength, although heavy rainfall may continue for a number of days.

Figure 10 In a hurricane, air moves rapidly around a low-pressure area called the eye. *Observing* Where is the eye of the hurricane in the photograph?

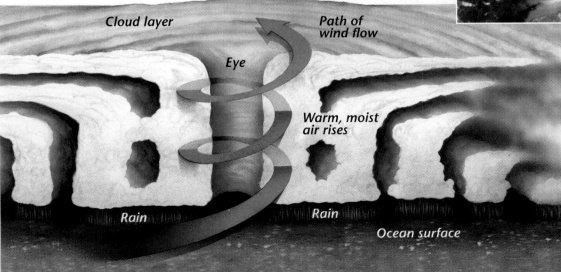

Cloud layer

Path of wind flow

Eye

Warm, moist air rises

Rain

Rain

Ocean surface

Hurricane Damage When a hurricane comes ashore, it brings high waves and severe flooding as well as wind damage. Hurricanes uproot trees, smash buildings, and destroy power lines. Heavy rains flood roads.

One of the most dangerous features of a hurricane is the storm surge. The low pressure and high winds of the hurricane over the ocean raise the level of the water up to six meters above normal sea level. The result is a **storm surge,** a "dome" of water that sweeps across the coast where the hurricane lands. As the hurricane comes onshore, the water comes with it. Storm surges can cause great damage, washing away beaches and destroying buildings along the coast.

Hurricane Safety Until the 1950s, a fast-moving hurricane

INTEGRATING HEALTH could strike with little warning. Since then, advances in communications and satellite tracking have made hurricanes less deadly. People now receive information well in advance of an approaching hurricane.

A "hurricane watch" is an announcement that hurricane conditions are *possible* in your area within the next 36 hours. People should be prepared to **evacuate** (ee VAK yoo ayt), or move away temporarily.

A "hurricane warning" means that hurricane conditions are *expected* within 24 hours. **If you hear a hurricane warning and are told to evacuate, leave the area immediately.** If you must stay in a house, move to the interior of the building, away from windows.

☑ *Checkpoint* *What is a storm surge?*

Winter Storms

In the winter in the northern United States, much precipitation falls as snow. **Snow falls when humid air cools below 0°C.** Heavy snowfalls can block roads, trapping people in their homes and making it hard for emergency vehicles to move. Extreme cold can damage crops and cause water pipes to freeze and burst.

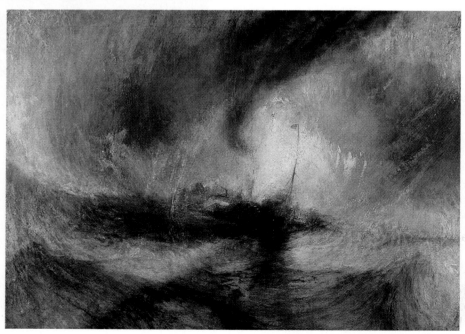

Figure 11 The British artist J.M.W. Turner painted "Snow Storm" in 1842.

574

Lake-effect Snow Two of the snowiest cities in the United States are Buffalo and Rochester in upstate New York. On average, nearly three meters of snow falls on each of these cities every winter. Why do Buffalo and Rochester get so much snow?

Study Figure 12. Notice that Buffalo is located to the east of Lake Erie, and Rochester is located to the south of Lake Ontario. In the fall and winter, the land near these lakes cools much more rapidly than the water in the lakes. Although the water in these lakes is cold, it is still much warmer than the surrounding land and air. When a cold, dry air mass moves from central Canada southeast across one of the Great Lakes, it picks up water vapor and heat from the lake. As soon as the air mass reaches the other side of the lake, the air rises and cools again. The water vapor condenses and falls as snow, usually within 40 kilometers of the lake.

Great Lakes Snow Belts

KEY

Snow belt

Cold, dry air

Figure 12 As cold dry air moves across the warmer water, it picks up water vapor. When the air reaches land and cools, lake-effect snow falls. *Interpreting Maps* *Which two cities receive large amounts of snow?*

Snowstorm Safety Imagine being out in a snowstorm when

INTEGRATING HEALTH the wind suddenly picks up. High winds can blow falling snow sideways or pick up snow from the ground and suspend it in the air. This situation can be extremely dangerous because the blowing snow makes it easy to get lost. Also, strong winds cool a person's body rapidly. **If you are caught in a snowstorm, try to find shelter from the wind.** Cover exposed parts of your body and try to stay dry. If you are in a car, the driver should keep the engine running only if the exhaust pipe is clear of snow.

Section 2 Review

1. What weather conditions are most likely to cause thunderstorms and tornadoes?
2. What is the most common path for the hurricanes that strike the United States?
3. What safety precautions should you take if a tornado is predicted in your area? If a hurricane is predicted?
4. **Thinking Critically** **Applying Concepts** In the winter, cool, humid air from the Pacific Ocean blows across the cold land of southern Alaska. What kind of storm do you think this causes?

Science at Home

Storm Experiences Interview a family member or other adult about a dramatic storm that he or she has experienced. Before the interview, make a list of questions you would like to ask. For example, how old was the person when the storm occurred? When and where did the storm occur? Write up your interview in a question-and-answer format, beginning with a short introduction.

Tracking a Hurricane

Hurricane alert! You work at the National Hurricane Center. It is your job to track the paths of hurricanes and try to predict when and where a hurricane is likely to strike land. Then you must decide whether to warn people in the area to evacuate.

Problem

How can you predict when and where a hurricane will come ashore?

Skills Focus

interpreting data, predicting

Materials

ruler
red, blue, green, and brown pencils
tracing paper

Procedure

1. Look at the plotted path of the hurricane on the map. Each dot represents the location of the eye of the hurricane at six-hour intervals. The last dot shows where the hurricane was located at noon on August 30.

2. Predict the path you think the hurricane will take. Place tracing paper over the map below. Using a red pencil, place an X on your tracing paper where you think the hurricane will first reach land. Next to your X, write the date and time you think the hurricane will come ashore.

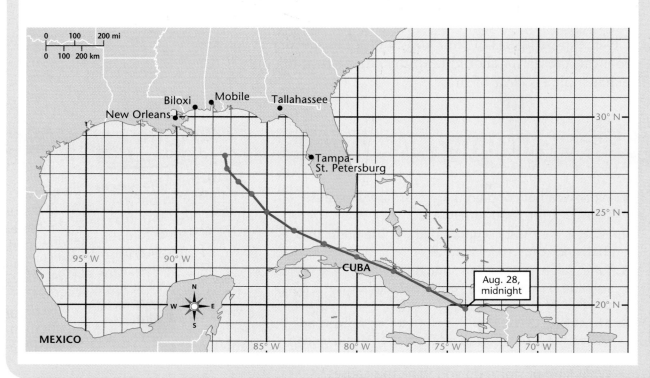

3. Hurricane warnings are issued for an area that is likely to experience a hurricane within 24 hours. On your tracing paper, shade in red the area for which you would issue a hurricane warning.

4. Using the following data table, plot the next five positions for the storm using a blue pencil. Use your ruler to connect the dots to show the hurricane's path.

Date and Time	Latitude	Longitude
August 30, 6:00 P.M.	28.3° N	86.8° W
August 31, midnight	28.4° N	86.0° W
August 31, 6:00 A.M.	28.6° N	85.3° W
August 31, noon	28.8° N	84.4° W
August 31, 6:00 P.M.	28.8° N	84.0° W

5. Based on the new data, decide if you need to change your prediction of where and when the hurricane will come ashore. Mark your new predictions in blue pencil on your tracing paper.

6. During September 1, you obtain four more positions. (Plot these points only after you have completed Step 5.) Based on these new data, mark in green pencil when and where you now think the hurricane will come ashore.

Date and Time	Latitude	Longitude
September 1, midnight	28.8° N	83.8° W
September 1, 6:00 A.M.	28.6° N	83.9° W
September 1, noon	28.6° N	84.2° W
September 1, 6:00 P.M.	28.9° N	84.8° W

7. The next day, September 2, you plot four more positions using a brown pencil. (Plot these points only after you have completed Step 6.)

Date and Time	Latitude	Longitude
September 2, midnight	29.4° N	85.9° W
September 2, 6:00 A.M.	29.7° N	87.3° W
September 2, noon	30.2° N	88.8° W
September 2, 6:00 P.M.	31.0° N	90.4° W

Analyze and Conclude

1. Describe in detail the complete path of the hurricane you tracked. Include where it came ashore and identify any cities that were in the vicinity.
2. How did your predictions in Steps 2, 5, and 6 compare to what actually happened?
3. What was unusual about your hurricane's path?
4. How do you think hurricanes with a path like this one affect the issuing of hurricane warnings?
5. Why do you have to be so careful when issuing warnings? What problems might be caused if you issued an unnecessary hurricane warning? What might happen if a hurricane warning were issued too late?
6. **Think About It** In this activity you only had data for the hurricane's position. If you were tracking a hurricane and issuing warnings, what other types of information would help you make decisions about the hurricane's path?

More to Explore

With your teacher's help, search the Internet for more hurricane tracking data. Map the data and try to predict where the hurricane will come ashore.

Hurricane Alert: To Stay or Not To Stay?

When a hurricane sweeps in from the ocean, the National Hurricane Center tracks the storm's course. Radio stations broadcast warnings. Sirens blow, and people in the storm path take steps to protect their homes and families.

State and local governments may try to keep people safe by closing state offices, setting up emergency shelters, and alerting the National Guard. As the danger increases, a state's governor can order the evacuation of people from dangerous areas. These actions are meant to protect public safety.

But not everyone wants to evacuate. Some people believe they have the right to stay. And officials cannot make people obey an evacuation order. How much can—or should—the government do to keep people safe?

The Issues

Why Play It Safe? Hurricanes can be extremely dangerous. High winds blow off roofs and shatter windows. Flash floods and storm surges can wash away houses. Even after the storm blows away, officials may need to keep people from returning home because of flooded sewers or broken power lines and gas mains.

In recent years, earlier and more accurate forecasts have saved lives. People now have time to prepare and to get out of the hurricane's path. Emergency officials urge people—especially the elderly, sick, or disabled—to leave early while the weather is still good. Most casualties happen when people are taken by surprise or ignore warnings. Those who decide to stay may later have to be rescued by boat or helicopter. These rescues add to the expense of the storm and may put the lives of rescuers in danger.

Why Ride Out the Storm? People have different reasons for not wanting to evacuate. Some want to protect their homes or businesses. Others don't want to leave pets or farm animals or go to public shelters. Store owners may stay open to sell disaster supplies. In addition, warnings may exaggerate the potential danger, urging people to leave when they might actually be safe. Since leaving can be expensive and disruptive, residents have to carefully evaluate the risks.

Is It a Matter of Rights? Should a government have the power to make people evacuate? Some citizens argue that the government should not tell them what to do as long as they are not harming others. They believe that individuals should have the right to decide for themselves. What do you think?

You Decide

1. Identify the Problem

In your own words, explain the controversy around hurricane evacuations.

2. Analyze the Options

Review and list the pros and cons of forcing people to evacuate. What people benefit? Who might be harmed? What more, if anything, should government officials do? What more could citizens do?

3. Find a Solution

Imagine that the radio has broadcast a hurricane warning. Write a dialogue in which you and members of your family discuss the options and decide whether or not to evacuate.

SECTION 3 Floods

DISCOVER · ACTIVITY · · · ·

What Causes Floods?

1. Fill a cup with water. Hold a funnel above a basin and pour the water very slowly into the funnel.

2. Refill the cup with the same amount of water you used in Step 1. Hold the funnel above the basin and this time pour the water rapidly into the funnel. What happens?

Think It Over

Inferring How is a funnel like a river valley? What do you think would happen if a large amount of water entered a river valley in a short period of time?

A ntelope Canyon in the northern Arizona desert is only a few meters wide in places. On August 12, 1997, a group of 12 hikers entered the dry, narrow canyon. That after-noon a severe thunderstorm dropped several inches of rain on the Kaibeto Plateau, 24 kilometers away. Dry stream channels that drain into Antelope Canyon quickly filled with rainwater. The water rushed into the canyon, creating a wall of water over 3 meters high. Tourists at the top of the canyon watched in hor-ror as the water swept the hikers away. Only one hiker survived.

Are you surprised that floods can occur in a desert? Actually, floods like this are more common in the dry Southwest than in areas with more rain.

GUIDE FOR READING

◆ What causes flooding?

◆ How can the dangers of floods be reduced?

Reading Tip As you read, draw a flowchart showing what can happen during a flood and how people should respond to it.

Figure 13 From the top, Antelope Canyon looks like a narrow slit in the ground.

① *Heavy rain falls on the plateau.*

② *Instead of soaking into the hard soil, the water runs into the canyon.*

③ *The rainwater is funneled into the narrow canyon and floods it.*

Figure 14 Flash floods occur when large amounts of rain are funneled into a narrow valley. This drawing shows what happened in the Antelope Canyon flood.

Flash Floods

Although movies feature the violent winds of tornadoes and hurricanes, floods are the most dangerous weather-related events in the United States. **Floods occur when so much water pours into a stream or river that it overflows its banks and covers the land on either side of the channel.** People who live along certain rivers know that melting snow and spring rains are likely to bring floods.

Unexpected floods are the most dangerous. Floods like the Antelope Canyon flood are called flash floods because the water rises very rapidly—"in a flash"—after it begins to rain heavily. A **flash flood** is a sudden, violent flood that occurs within a few hours, or even minutes, of a storm.

Most flash floods are due to large amounts of rain. For example, a line of thunderstorms may remain over an area, dropping heavy rain for several hours or days. Hurricanes or tropical storms bring downpours that quickly fill stream channels. A flash flood can also be caused by a dam breaking, releasing millions of liters of water all at once. Similarly, if ice that has jammed a river breaks free, the sudden rush of water can cause a flash flood.

✓ *Checkpoint* *Why are flash floods so dangerous?*

Flood Safety Measures

If you've never been in a flood, it's hard to imagine the awesome power of rushing water. What can people do to protect themselves and their homes?

Predicting Floods Advance warnings can help reduce flood damage and loss of life. Weather satellites supply information about snow cover so that scientists can estimate how much water will run into rivers when the snow melts. Radar can track and measure the size of an approaching rainstorm. Scientists check river gauges that measure water levels. With this information, forecasters can predict flood heights at different points along a river. Their goal is to issue warnings early enough to help people prepare and evacuate if necessary.

Sharpen your Skills

Communicating

Write a script for a 30-second public service radio announcement in which you tell about the dangers of floods. Include recommended safety steps to follow in case of a flood.

ACTIVITY

1️⃣ The car stalls in the water.

2️⃣ Moving water pushes against the car.

3️⃣ As the water rises, the car begins to float.

4️⃣ Sixty centimeters of water can wash a car away.

Figure 15 These drawings show what can happen to a car in a flood. *Applying Concepts Why is it dangerous to stay in a car in a flood?*

A "flood watch" is an announcement describing the area in which flooding is possible. Stay alert for more news. A "flood warning" is an announcement that floods have already been reported or are about to occur. It's time to take action!

Emergency Safety What should *you* do in case of a flood? When the danger becomes too great or the water rises too high, people are usually evacuated. **The first rule of flood safety: Move to higher ground and stay away from flood waters.** Don't try to cross streams and rivers that look as if they're flooded. Playing in flood waters may look like fun, but it's dangerous. A few centimeters of fast-moving water can sweep you off your feet. Even the storm drain on a city street can draw you in.

If your family is in a car, the driver shouldn't try to drive on a flooded road. Sometimes less than 60 centimeters of fast-moving water can sweep a car away, as shown in Figure 15. Everyone should leave the car and move to higher ground.

Figure 16 In the spring of 1997, the Red River of the North flooded regions of North Dakota and Minnesota. A large part of flooded downtown Grand Forks burned down because fire trucks could not get to the scene of the fire or connect to any fire hydrants.

Other Flood Hazards High water is not the only hazard in a flood. Floods can knock down electrical poles and wires, cutting off power supplies. Flood waters can also saturate soil, causing landslides or mudslides. If roads have been flooded or washed away, emergency vehicles such as fire trucks and ambulances may not be able to get through.

Flood waters can wash into wells and water treatment plants, polluting the water. Therefore, be careful with food and water that flood waters have touched. Boil water before drinking it to be sure it is safe.

Section 3 Review

1. How can precipitation cause flooding?
2. What should you do to stay safe during a flood?
3. What is the difference between a flood watch and a flood warning?
4. Name three tools that supply information used in forecasting floods and providing flood information.
5. **Thinking Critically** Predicting Describe two weather situations in which you would expect floods to occur.

Check Your Progress *CHAPTER PROJECT*

Now you are ready to predict tomorrow's weather. Look at today's weather map. Then predict tomorrow's weather both where you live and in the two other locations you selected. (*Project Hint:* Refer to the weather patterns you have been observing.) Decide what symbols you will need to use. Then, on an outline map of the United States, draw symbols to show what you think tomorrow's weather will be. Continue to make predictions every day for at least a week.

DISCOVER

What's the Weather?

1. Look at the weather report in your local newspaper. Note what weather conditions are predicted for your area today, including temperature, precipitation, and wind speed.

2. Look out the window or think about what it was like the last time you were outside. Write down the actual weather conditions where you are.

Think It Over

Observing Does the weather report match what you observe? What is the same? What is different?

For centuries, people have tried to predict the weather. Every nation's folklore includes weather sayings. Many of these sayings are based on long-term observations. Sailors, pilots, farmers, and others who work outdoors are usually careful observers of clouds, winds, and other signs of coming changes in the weather. Here are two examples:

> *Evening red and morning gray*
> *Will send the traveler on his way;*
> *Evening gray and morning red*
> *Will bring down rain upon his head.*

> *Red sky in the morning,*
> *sailors take warning;*
> *Red sky at night, sailor's delight.*

GUIDE FOR READING

◆ How does technology help forecasters predict the weather?

◆ What types of information are shown on weather maps?

Reading Tip Before you read, preview Figure 19 and *Exploring Newspaper Weather Maps.* Write a list of any questions you have about weather maps.

Why do these two weather sayings agree that a red morning sky means bad weather? Recall that in the United States storms usually move from west to east. Clouds in the west may indicate an advancing low-pressure area, bringing stormy weather. If there are high clouds in the west in the morning, the rising sun in the east turns these clouds red. The reverse is true at sunset. As the sun sets in the west, it turns clouds in the east red. Clouds in the east may indicate that a storm is moving away to the east.

Weather Forecasting

You can make many predictions from your own observations. For example, if a barometer shows that the air pressure is falling, you can expect a change in the weather. Falling air pressure usually indicates an approaching low-pressure area, possibly bringing rain or snow.

You can read weather signs in the clouds, too. Cumulus clouds often form on warm afternoons when warm air rises. If you see these clouds growing larger and taller, you can expect them to become cumulonimbus clouds, which may bring a thunderstorm. If you see thin cirrus clouds high in the sky, a low-pressure area may be approaching.

Even careful weather observers often turn to professional meteorologists for television weather information. You may hear the person who gives the television weather report referred to as a meteorologist. Despite their name, meteorologists don't study meteors. **Meteorologists** (mee tee uh RAWL uh jists) are scientists who study the causes of weather and try to predict it.

Meteorologists interpret information from a variety of sources, including local weather observers, instruments carried by balloons, satellites, and weather stations around the world. They use maps, charts, and computers to analyze the data and to prepare weather forecasts. Meteorologists use radar to track areas of rain or snow, so that forecasters can follow the path of a storm system.

Where do television and radio weather reporters get their information? A lot of weather information comes from the National Weather Service. However, weather forecasts for the general public may not have enough detail to be useful to farmers and pilots. There are also private weather-forecasting services, many of which use advanced, high-technology equipment. Private forecasting services are useful to people who need to answer questions like these: "Will the frost hurt the oranges in my orchard?" "Will the airport be fogged in?" "Will the trucks need to spread sand on the roads today?"

✓ *Checkpoint* *Where do meteorologists get weather information?*

Figure 17 These meteorologists are releasing a weather balloon. The box attached to the balloon contains instruments that will record weather data—such as temperature, pressure, and humidity—high in the troposphere.

Figure 18 This satellite photo shows an intense storm over the North Atlantic Ocean. *Observing* What weather-related information can you see in the photo?

Warmer   Colder

Weather Technology

Techniques for predicting weather have changed rapidly in recent years. Short-range forecasts—forecasts for up to five days—are now fairly reliable. Meteorologists can also make long-range predictions that were once impossible. **Changes in technology have occurred in two areas: gathering weather data and using computers to make forecasts.**

Weather Balloons and Satellites As you learned in Chapter 15, weather balloons carry instruments high into the troposphere and stratosphere. The instruments measure temperature, air pressure, and humidity.

The first weather satellite was launched in 1960. Cameras on weather satellites in the exosphere can photograph Earth's surface, clouds, storms, and ice and snow cover. These images are then transmitted to meteorologists on Earth, who interpret the information.

Computer Forecasts Computers are widely used to help forecast weather. Instruments can now gather thousands of bits of data about temperature, air pressure, wind speed, and other factors. Computers process large amounts of information quickly to help forecasters make predictions. To make a forecast, the computer starts with weather conditions reported from weather stations over a large area. Conditions reported include wind speed and direction, humidity, sunlight, temperature, and air pressure. Then the computer works through thousands of calculations and makes forecasts for 12 hours, 24 hours, 36 hours, and so on. Each forecast builds on the previous forecast. When new weather data come in, the computer revises its forecasts.

INTEGRATING TECHNOLOGY

El Niño

Some long-term weather patterns may be caused by changes in ocean currents and global winds. Periodically, a warm-water event known as **El Niño** occurs in the tropical Pacific Ocean. During an El Niño event, winds shift and push warm surface water toward the west coast of South America. The warm water replaces the cold water that usually rises from the deep ocean near the coast.

El Niño events occur once every two to seven years. They can cause dramatic climate changes around the Pacific Ocean and in other places. In the winter of 1997 and 1998, a strong El Niño current caused droughts in Asia and Brazil, heavy rains and floods in California and Peru, and tornadoes in Florida and other parts of the southeastern United States.

Scientists have looked for clues and warnings to help predict the return of El Niño. One signal is rising surface temperatures in the tropical part of the Pacific Ocean. Using data gathered during past El Niño events, scientists were able to predict many of the results of the 1997–1998 El Niño.

☑ *Checkpoint* **What evidence do scientists use to predict an El Niño?**

Reading Weather Maps

A weather map is a "snapshot" of conditions at a particular time over a large area. There are many different types of weather maps. Television forecasters often present maps generated by computers from radar information.

Weather Service Maps Data from more than 300 local weather stations all over the country are assembled into weather maps at the National Weather Service. The information collected by a typical reporting station is summarized in the key to Figure 19. The weather map, which has been simplified, includes most of the weather station data shown in the key.

On some weather maps, you see curved lines. These lines connect places where certain conditions—temperature or air pressure—are the same. **Isobars** are lines joining places on the map that have the same air pressure. (*Iso* means "equal" and *bar* means "pressure.") The numbers on the isobars are the pressure readings. Air pressure readings may be given in inches of mercury or in millibars or both. Figure 19 has isobars.

Isotherms are lines joining places that have the same temperature. The isotherm may be labeled with the temperature in degrees Fahrenheit, degrees Celsius, or both.

Interpreting Data

Use the key to Figure 19 to help you answer the questions about this weather station data.

1. What is the temperature at this station?
2. What is the wind speed?
3. Which way is the wind blowing?
4. What is the air pressure?
5. What percent of the sky is covered by clouds?
6. What type of precipitation, if any, is falling?

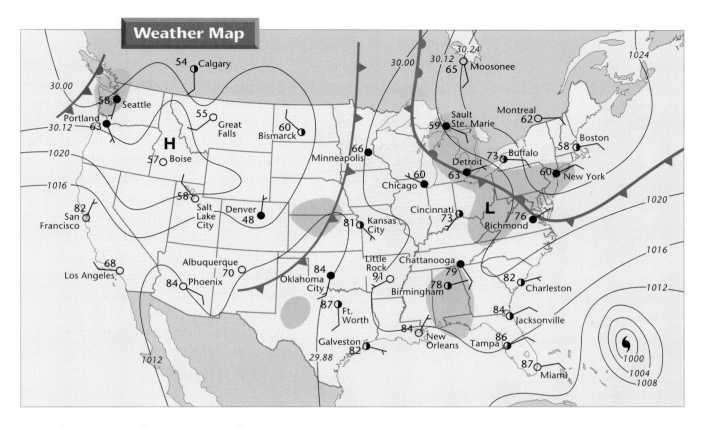

Weather Map

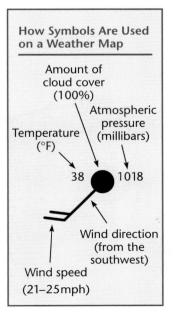

EXPLANATION OF FRONTS

▼▼▼ Cold Front
Boundary between a cold air mass and a warm air mass. Brings brief storms and cooler weather.

⏜⏜⏜ Warm Front
Boundary between a warm air mass and a cold air mass. Usually accompanied by precipitation.

⏜▼ Stationary Front
Boundary between a warm air mass and a cold air mass when no movement occurs. Brings long periods of precipitation.

⏜▲ Occluded Front
Boundary on which a warm front has been overtaken by a cold front. Brings precipitation.

Weather	Symbol
Drizzle	
Fog	
Hail	
Haze	
Rain	
Shower	
Sleet	
Smoke	
Snow	
Thunderstorm	
Hurricane	

Wind Speed (mph)	Symbol
1–2	
3–8	
9–14	
15–20	
21–25	
26–31	
32–37	
38–43	
44–49	
50–54	
55–60	
61–66	
67–71	
72–77	

Cloud Cover (%)	Symbol
0	
10	
20–30	
40	
50	
60	
70–80	
90	
100	

How Symbols Are Used on a Weather Map

Amount of cloud cover (100%)

Atmospheric pressure (millibars)

Temperature (°F)

38   1018

Wind direction (from the southwest)

Wind speed (21–25mph)

Figure 19 This weather map shows data collected from weather stations all over the country. Below the map is an explanation of what the symbols at each city mean.

Newspaper Weather Maps Maps in newspapers are simplified versions of maps produced by the National Weather Service. *Exploring Newspaper Weather Maps* shows a typical newspaper weather map. From what you have learned in this chapter, you can probably interpret most of the symbols on this map. **Standard symbols on weather maps show fronts, areas of high and low pressure, types of precipitation, and temperatures.** Note that the high and low temperatures are given in degrees Fahrenheit instead of Celsius.

The maps in Figure 20 show the path of a winter storm. If you study the maps carefully, you can track this storm and its effects. With practice, you can use information from weather maps to help you predict the weather in your area.

The Butterfly Effect

Even with current technology, weather forecasting is tricky. The main reason is that weather patterns do not follow an orderly, step-by-step process.

A forecast for the weather six days from now is based on forecasts for all the days between now and then. A small change in the weather today can mean a larger change in the weather a week later! This is the so-called butterfly effect. The name refers to a scientist's suggestion that even the flapping of a butterfly's wings causes a tiny disturbance in the atmosphere. This tiny event might cause a larger disturbance that could—eventually—grow into a hurricane.

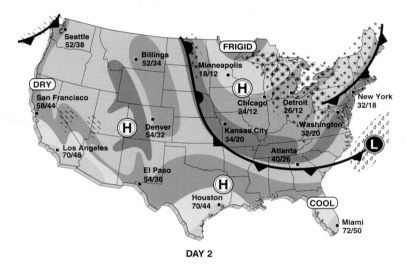

DAY 1

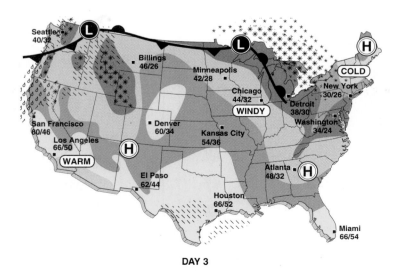

DAY 2

DAY 3

Figure 20 These weather maps show a storm moving from west to east over a three-day period.
Interpreting Diagrams What were the high and low temperatures in Chicago on Day 2? On Day 3?

EXPLORING Newspaper Weather Maps

Weather maps in newspapers use symbols to show fronts, high and low pressure areas, and precipitation. Color bands indicate different temperatures.

Areas in the same temperature range are shown in the same color. For example, light green areas have high temperatures in the 40's.

Major low-pressure areas are shown with an L. High-pressure areas are shown with an H.

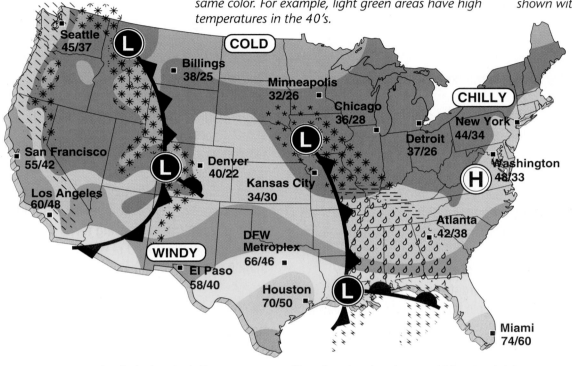

Symbols that look like raindrops or snowflakes show precipitation.

The triangles showing a cold front point in the direction the cold air is moving. The half-circles indicating a warm front show the direction the warm air is moving.

Section 4 Review

1. What kinds of technology do meteorologists use to help predict the weather?
2. Name at least three types of information you could get from a weather map of your area.
3. What lines on a weather map connect points that have the same temperature?
4. **Thinking Critically** **Predicting** If you observe that air pressure is rising, what kind of weather do you think is coming?

CHAPTER PROJECT

Check Your Progress
After a week of predicting the weather, you are ready to compare your predictions to the actual weather that occurred. Then compare your predictions with those made by professional meteorologists. How accurate were your predictions? How accurate were the predictions made by professional meteorologists?

Reading a Weather Map

In this lab, you will interpret data from a weather map to describe weather conditions in various places.

Problem

How does a weather map communicate data?

Procedure

1. Examine the symbols on the weather map below. For more information about the symbols used on the map, refer to Figure 19 on page 587 and to *Exploring Newspaper Weather Maps* on page 589.
2. Observe the different colors on the weather map.
3. Find the symbols for snow and rain.
4. Locate the warm fronts and cold fronts.
5. Locate the symbols for high and low pressure.

Analyze and Conclude

1. What color represents the highest temperatures? What color represents the lowest temperatures?

2. What city has the highest temperature? What city has the lowest temperature?
3. Where on the map is it raining? Where on the map is it snowing?
4. How many different kinds of fronts are shown on the map?
5. How many areas of low pressure are shown on the map? How many areas of high pressure are shown on the map?
6. What season does this map represent? How do you know?
7. **Think About It** The triangles and semicircles on the front lines show which way the front is moving. What front is moving toward Minneapolis? What kind of weather do you think it will bring?

More to Explore

Compare this weather map with the weather map shown in a television news report. Which symbols on these maps are similar? Which symbols are different?

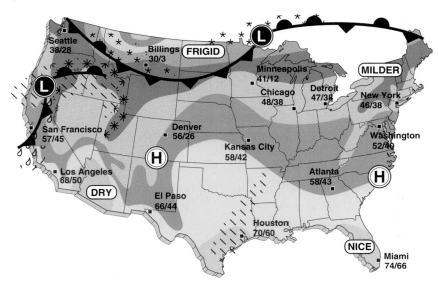

Air Masses and Fronts

SECTION 1

Key Ideas

◆ Four major types of air masses influence the weather in North America: maritime tropical, continental tropical, maritime polar, and continental polar.

◆ When air masses collide, they form four types of fronts: cold fronts, warm fronts, stationary fronts, and occluded fronts.

◆ Cyclones and decreasing air pressure are associated with storms and precipitation.

Key Terms

air mass	maritime	occluded
tropical	continental	cyclone
polar	front	anticyclone

 Storms

SECTION 2

Key Ideas

◆ Thunderstorms and tornadoes form within large cumulonimbus clouds. During thunderstorms, avoid touching metal objects.

◆ A hurricane begins over warm water as a low-pressure area. If you hear a hurricane warning and are told to evacuate, leave the area immediately.

◆ Snow falls when humid air cools below 0°C. If you are caught in a snowstorm, try to find shelter from the wind.

Key Terms

storm	tornado	storm surge
lightning	hurricane	evacuate

 Floods

SECTION 3

INTEGRATING HEALTH

Key Ideas

◆ Floods occur when so much water pours into a stream or river that it overflows its banks on either side of the channel.

◆ The first rule of flood safety: Move to higher ground and stay away from flood waters.

Key Term

flash flood

 Predicting the Weather

SECTION 4

Key Ideas

◆ Meteorologists interpret weather information from local weather observers, instruments carried by balloons, satellites, and weather stations around the world.

◆ Changes in weather technology have occurred in two areas: gathering weather data and using computers to make forecasts.

◆ Standard symbols on weather maps show fronts, areas of high and low pressure, types of precipitation, and temperatures.

Key Terms

meteorologist
El Niño
isobar
isotherm

Organizing Information

Compare/Contrast Table Copy the compare/contrast table about hurricanes and tornadoes onto a separate sheet of paper. Then fill in the empty spaces and add a title. (For more on compare/contrast tables, see the Skills Handbook.)

Type of Storm	Hurricane	Tornado
Where storm forms	Over warm ocean water	a. ?
Size of storm	b. ?	Several hundred meters
How long storm lasts	A week or more	c. ?
Time of year	d. ?	Spring, early summer
Safety rules	Evacuate or move inside a well-built building	e. ?

Reviewing Content

 For more review of key concepts, see the Interactive Student Tutorial CD-ROM.

Multiple Choice

Choose the letter of the answer that best completes each statement.

1. An air mass that forms over an ocean is called
   a. tropical.
   b. continental.
   c. maritime.
   d. polar.

2. Cool, clear weather is usually brought by a
   a. warm front.
   b. cold front.
   c. stationary front.
   d. occluded front.

3. Winds spiraling inward toward a center of low pressure form a(n)
   a. anticyclone.
   b. front.
   c. isobar.
   d. cyclone.

4. Very large tropical storms with high winds are called
   a. hurricanes.   b. tornadoes.
   c. thunderstorms.   d. blizzards.

5. Most flash floods are caused by
   a. hailstorms.   b. heavy rainfall.
   c. high winds.   d. melting snow.

True or False

If the statement is true, write true. If it is false, change the underlined word or words to make it true.

6. Summers in the Southwest are hot and dry because of <u>maritime tropical</u> air masses.

7. A <u>cold front</u> over an area will bring many days of cloudy weather.

8. Foggy, rainy, or humid weather usually follows the passage of a <u>warm front</u> through an area.

9. Low cumulonimbus clouds may bring both thunderstorms and <u>tornadoes</u>.

10. On a weather map, <u>isobars</u> join places on the map with the same temperature.

Checking Concepts

11. What are the basic characteristics used to describe air masses?

12. Describe how wind patterns affect the movement of air masses in North America.

13. How does a cold front form?

14. Describe three hazards associated with floods.

15. What are some of the sources of information that meteorologists use to predict the weather?

16. What is El Niño? How does it influence the weather in certain regions?

17. **Writing to Learn** Imagine you are a meteorologist. Your assignment is to investigate a hurricane by flying into it with a large plane. Describe your experiences in a journal entry. Be sure to include descriptive words. How did the hurricane look? Sound? Feel?

Thinking Critically

18. **Classifying** Classify the major types of air masses that influence weather in the United States in two ways: by temperature and by where they form.

19. **Comparing and Contrasting** Compare and contrast cyclones and anticyclones. What type of weather is associated with each?

20. **Applying Concepts** Would you expect hurricanes to form over the oceans off the northeast and northwest coasts of the United States? Explain.

21. **Relating Cause and Effect** How do differences in air density influence the movement of cold and warm fronts?

22. **Making Judgments** What do you think is the most important thing people should do to reduce the dangers of storms?

Applying Skills

Use the map to answer Questions 23–26.

23. **Interpreting Maps** Does the map show a cyclone or an anticyclone? How can you tell?

24. **Interpreting Data** What do the arrows show about the movement of the winds in this pressure center? What else indicates wind direction?

25. **Making Models** Using this diagram as an example, draw a similar diagram to illustrate a high pressure area. Remember to indicate wind direction in your diagram.

26. **Posing Questions** If you saw a pressure center like this on a weather map, what prediction could you make about the weather? What questions would you need to ask in order to make a better prediction?

Performance ▽ CHAPTER PROJECT Assessment

Present Your Project Prepare your final report and arrange your maps for presentation. You may want to display each of your maps next to the actual newspaper weather map for that day. Practice your presentation, make any needed changes, and then present your report.

Reflect and Record In your journal, describe what you learned. Are there weather factors on the maps to which you should have paid more attention? Do meteorologists have information that isn't in the newspaper? How could you gather more information to improve your forecasting?

Test Preparation

Use these questions to prepare for standardized tests.

Read the passage. Then answer Questions 27–30.

As Hurricane Andrew roared toward the southern Florida coastline, millions of Florida residents evacuated the area, heading toward safety. It was 1992, and forecasters predicted that Andrew would make landfall sometime in the early morning of August 24. Andrew had been rapidly building speed and strength since it was first classified as a tropical storm on August 17. Andrew quickly advanced to a fierce Category 4 hurricane, with sustained wind speeds estimated at 145 m.p.h. The only type of hurricane that is stronger is a Category 5 hurricane—a very rare event.

Andrew pounded South Florida for several hours. In the end, this hurricane caused over $20 billion in damage to Florida, becoming the most expensive natural disaster in U.S. history up to that date.

27. What is the best title for this selection?
   a. Category 4 Hurricanes
   b. August 24, 1992
   c. Hurricane Andrew Pounds Florida
   d. Hurricane Andrew Heads North

28. What kind of storm was Andrew before it was classified as a hurricane?
   a. tropical storm
   b. thunderstorm
   c. rainstorm
   d. monsoon

29. Which category of hurricanes has the greatest wind speed?
   a. category 1
   b. category 4
   c. category 5
   d. none of the above

30. Why did Andrew cause so much damage?
   a. because it traveled so fast
   b. because it traveled in a northward direction
   c. because it had very strong wind speed
   d. because it traveled over water

WEB ACTIVITY
www.phschool.com

Investigating Microclimates

Most of the Mojave Desert is too dry for trees. Only cactus, shrubs, and other hardy plants are able to survive in the parched land. So if you see palm trees, you know there must be water nearby. Palm trees in the desert grow only in a small area with its own climate—a microclimate. As you work through this chapter, you will investigate microclimates in your community.

Your Goal To compare weather conditions from at least three microclimates.

To complete your project, you must

◆ hypothesize how the microclimates in three areas will differ from one another
◆ collect data at the same places and times each day
◆ relate each microclimate to the plants and animals found there
◆ follow the safety guidelines in Appendix A

Get Started Begin by brainstorming a list of nearby places that may have different microclimates. How are the places different? Keep in mind weather factors such as temperature, precipitation, humidity, wind direction, and wind speed. Consider areas that are grassy, sandy, sunny, or shaded. Start thinking about what instruments you will need to do your investigation.

Check Your Progress You'll be working on this project as you study this chapter. To keep your project on track, look for Check Your Progress boxes at the following points.

Section 1 Review, page 603: Measure and record weather data.
Section 3 Review, page 622: Graph your data and look for patterns.

Present Your Project At the end of the chapter (page 629), you will present the data you collected about your microclimates. Include any patterns you observed.

Even in a desert, palm trees can survive if they have enough water.

 Integrating Environmental Science
SECTION 4 Global Changes in the Atmosphere

Discover What Is the Greenhouse Effect?
Try This It's Your Skin!
Science at Home Compare Sunscreens

DISCOVER

ACTIVITY

How Does Earth's Shape Affect Climate Zones?

1. On a globe, tape a strip of cash register paper from the equator to the North Pole. Divide the tape into three equal parts. Label the section near the North Pole *poles*, the section near the equator *equator*, and the middle section *mid-latitudes*.

2. Tape the end of an empty toilet paper roll to the end of a flashlight. Hold the flashlight about 30 cm from the equator. Turn on the flashlight to represent the sun. On the paper strip, have a partner draw the shape of the area the light shines on.

3. Move the flashlight up slightly to aim at the section of the paper marked "mid-latitudes." Keep the flashlight horizontal and at the same distance from the globe. Again have a partner draw the shape of the area that the light shines on.

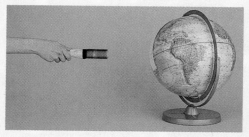

4. Move the flashlight up again to shine on the section of the paper marked "poles." Keep the flashlight horizontal and at the same distance from the globe. Draw the shape of the area that the light shines on.

Think It Over

Observing How does the shape of the area that is illuminated change? Do you think the sun's rays heat Earth's surface evenly?

GUIDE FOR READING

◆ What are the factors that influence temperature and precipitation?

◆ What causes the seasons?

Reading Tip As you read, use the headings to make an outline of the factors that affect climate.

If you telephone a friend in another state and ask, "What's the weather there today?" she might answer: "It's gray, cool, and rainy. It's usually like that this time of year." Your friend has told you something about both weather and climate.

Weather is day-to-day events. The weather may be cloudy and rainy one day and clear and sunny the next. Weather refers to the condition of the atmosphere at a particular place and time. **Climate,** on the other hand, refers to the average, year-after-year conditions of temperature, precipitation, winds, and clouds in an area. How would you describe the climate where you live?

Two main factors—temperature and precipitation—determine the climate of a region. A climate region is a large area with similar climate conditions throughout. For example, the climate in the southeastern United States is humid, with moderate temperatures.

◀ These polar bears— two males and their mother—are taking it easy in the polar zone.

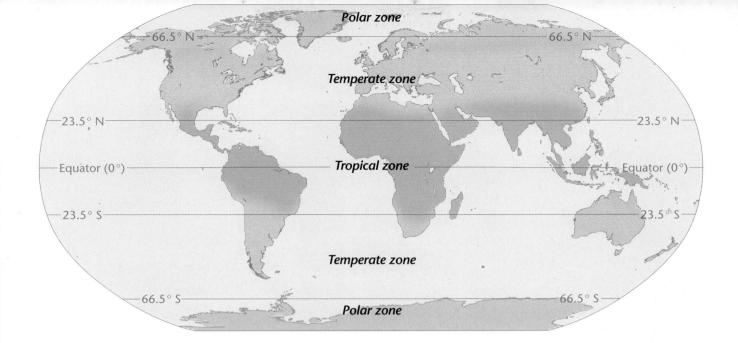

Polar zone

66.5° N   66.5° N

Temperate zone

23.5° N   23.5° N

Equator (0°)   Equator (0°)

Tropical zone

23.5° S   23.5° S

Temperate zone

66.5° S   66.5° S

Polar zone

Figure 1 Earth has three main temperature zones.
Interpreting Maps In which temperature zone is most of the United States located?

Factors Affecting Temperature

Tropical countries, such as Panama, are usually hot. Northern countries, such as Finland, are usually cold. Why are some places warm and others cold? **The main factors that influence temperature are latitude, altitude, distance from large bodies of water, and ocean currents.**

Latitude In general, climates of locations farther from the equator are cooler than climates of areas closer to the equator. Why is this? As you found out if you tried the Discover activity, the sun's rays hit Earth's surface most directly at the equator. At the poles, the same amount of solar radiation is spread out over a larger area, and therefore brings less warmth.

Recall that latitude is the distance from the equator, measured in degrees. Based on latitude, Earth's surface can be divided into the three temperature zones shown in Figure 1. The **tropical zone** is the area near the equator, between about 23.5° north latitude and 23.5° south latitude. The tropical zone receives direct or nearly direct sunlight all year round, making climates there warm.

In contrast, the sun's rays always strike at a lower angle near the North and South poles. As a result, the areas near both poles have cold climates. These **polar zones** extend from about 66.5° to 90° north and 66.5° to 90° south latitudes.

The **temperate zones** are between the tropical and the polar zones—from about 23.5° to 66.5° north and 23.5° to 66.5° south latitudes. In summer, the sun's rays strike the temperate zones more directly. In winter, the sun's rays strike at a lower angle. As a result, the weather in the temperate zones ranges from warm or hot in summer to cool or cold in winter.

Figure 2 Mount Kilimanjaro in Tanzania, Africa, is near the equator. *Applying Concepts Why is there snow on top of the mountain?*

Altitude The peak of Mount Kilimanjaro towers high above the African plains. At nearly 6 kilometers above sea level, Kilimanjaro is covered in snow all year round. Yet it is located near the equator, at 3° south latitude. Why is Mount Kilimanjaro so cold?

In the case of high mountains, altitude is a more important climate factor than latitude. Recall from Chapter 1 that the temperature of the troposphere decreases about 6.5 Celsius degrees for every 1-kilometer increase in altitude. As a result, highland areas everywhere have cool climates, no matter what their latitude. At nearly 6 kilometers, the air at the top of Mount Kilimanjaro is about 39 Celsius degrees colder than the air at sea level at the same latitude.

Distance From Large Bodies of Water Oceans or large lakes can also affect temperatures. Oceans greatly moderate, or make less extreme, the temperatures of nearby land. Water heats up more slowly than land; it also cools down more slowly. Therefore, winds from the ocean keep coastal regions from reaching extremes of hot and cold. Much of the west coasts of North America, South America, and Europe have mild **marine climates,** with relatively warm winters and cool summers.

The centers of North America and Asia are too far inland to be warmed or cooled by the oceans. Most of Canada and Russia, as well as the central United States, have **continental climates.** Continental climates have more extreme temperatures than marine climates. Winters are cold, while summers are warm or hot.

Ocean Currents Many marine climates are influenced by ocean currents, streams of water within the oceans that move in regular patterns. In general, warm ocean currents carry warm water from the tropics toward the poles. Cold currents bring cold water from the polar zones toward the equator. The surface of the water warms or cools the air above it. The warmed or cooled air then moves over the nearby land. So a warm current brings warm air to the land it touches. A cold current brings cool air.

As you read about the following currents, trace their paths on the map in Figure 3. The best-known warm-water current is the Gulf Stream. The Gulf Stream begins in the Gulf of Mexico, then flows north along the east coast of the United States. When it crosses the North Atlantic, it becomes the North Atlantic Drift. This warm current gives Ireland and southern England a mild, wet climate despite their relatively high latitude.

In contrast, the cool California Current flows from Alaska southward down the West Coast. The California Current makes climates of places along the West Coast cooler than you would expect at their latitudes.

✓ *Checkpoint* **What effect do oceans have on the temperatures of nearby land areas?**

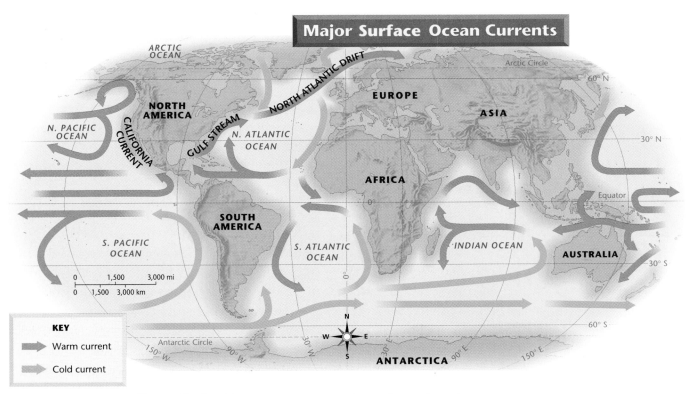

Figure 3 On this map, warm currents are shown in red and cold currents in blue.

Factors Affecting Precipitation

The amount of rain and snow that falls in an area each year determines how wet or dry its climate is. But what determines how much precipitation an area gets? **The main factors that affect precipitation are prevailing winds and the presence of mountains.**

Prevailing Winds As you know, weather patterns depend on the movement of huge air masses. Air masses are moved from place to place by prevailing winds, the directional winds that usually blow in a region. Air masses can be warm or cool, dry or humid. The amount of water vapor in the air mass influences how much rain or snow will fall.

Warm air can carry more water vapor than cold air can. When warm air rises and cools, water comes out of the air as precipitation. For example, surface air near the equator is generally hot and humid. As the air rises and cools, heavy rains fall, nourishing thick tropical forests. In contrast, sinking cold air is usually dry. Because the air becomes warmer as it sinks, it can hold more water vapor. The water vapor stays in the air and little or no rain falls. The result may be a desert.

The amount of water vapor in prevailing winds also depends on where the winds come from. Winds that blow inland from oceans carry more water vapor than winds that blow from over land. For example, the Sahara in Africa is near both the Atlantic Ocean and the Mediterranean Sea. Yet the Sahara is very dry. This is because few winds blow from the oceans toward this area. Instead, the prevailing winds are the dry northeast trade winds. The source of these winds is cool, sinking air from southwest Asia.

Figure 4 The prevailing winds that blow across the Sahara begin far inland. Since the air is dry, the Sahara gets very little rain.

SAHARA

AFRICA

ATLANTIC
OCEAN

Mountain Ranges A mountain range in the path of prevailing winds can also influence where precipitation falls. As you have learned, when humid winds blow from the ocean toward coastal mountains, they are forced to rise up to pass over the mountains. The rising warm air cools and its water vapor condenses, forming clouds. Rain or snow falls on the **windward** side of the mountains, the side the oncoming wind hits.

By the time the air reaches the other side of the mountains, it has lost much of its water vapor, so it is cool and dry. The land on the **leeward** side of the mountains—downwind—is in a rain shadow.

The Owens Valley in California, shown in Figure 5, is in the rain shadow of the Sierra Nevada, about 80 kilometers west of Death Valley. Humid winds blow eastward from the Pacific Ocean. In the photo, you can see that this humid air has left snow on top of the mountains. Then the air flowed down the leeward side of the mountains. As it moved downward, the air became warmer. The desert in the Owens Valley, on the eastern side of the Sierra Nevada, was formed by this hot, dry air.

✓ *Checkpoint* *Why does precipitation fall mainly on the windward sides of mountains?*

Microclimates

Have you ever noticed that it is cooler and more humid in a grove of trees than in an open field? The same factors that affect large climate regions also affect smaller areas. A small area with specific climate conditions may have its own **microclimate.** Inland mountains, lakes, forests, and other natural features can influence climate nearby, resulting in a microclimate.

You might find a microclimate in a downtown area with clusters of tall buildings, or on a windy peninsula jutting out into the ocean. Even a small park, if it is usually sunnier or windier than nearby areas, may have its own microclimate. The grass on a lawn can be covered in dew and produce conditions like a rain forest, while the pavement in the parking lot is dry, like a desert.

Sierra Nevada

Owens Valley

Moist air

Coastal Ranges

Pacific Ocean

Figure 5 The Sierra Nevada runs through eastern California, parallel to the Pacific coast. To the east of the Sierras is the Owens Valley, shown above. *Inferring Is the Owens Valley on the windward or leeward side of the mountains?*

Angles

Light from the sun strikes Earth's surface at different angles. An angle is made up of two lines that meet at a point. Angles are measured in degrees. A full circle has 360 degrees.

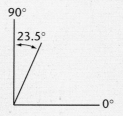

When the sun is directly overhead near the equator, it is at an angle of 90° to Earth's surface. A 90° angle is called a right angle. It is one fourth of a circle.

When the sun is near the horizon, it is at an angle of close to 0° to Earth's surface.

Earth's axis is tilted at an angle of 23.5°. About what fraction of a right angle is this?

The Seasons

INTEGRATING SPACE SCIENCE Although you can describe the average weather conditions of a climate region, these conditions are not constant all year long. Instead, most places on Earth outside the tropics have four seasons: winter, spring, summer, and autumn.

You might think that Earth is closer to the sun during the summer and farther away during winter. If this were true, every place on Earth would have summer at the same time. Actually, when it is summer in the Northern Hemisphere it is winter in the Southern Hemisphere. So the seasons are *not* a result of changes in the distance between Earth and the sun.

Tilted Axis *Exploring the Seasons* on page 603 shows how Earth's axis is tilted in relation to the sun. **The seasons are caused by the tilt of Earth's axis as Earth travels around the sun.** The axis is an imaginary line through Earth's center that passes through both poles. Earth turns, or rotates, around this axis once each day. Earth's axis is not straight up and down, but is tilted at an angle of 23.5°. The axis always points in the same direction—toward the North Star. As Earth travels around the sun, the north end of the axis is pointed away from the sun for part of the year and toward the sun for part of the year.

Winter or Summer Look at *Exploring the Seasons* on the next page. Which way is the north end of Earth's axis tilted in June? Notice that the Northern Hemisphere receives more direct rays from the sun. Also, in June the days in the Northern Hemisphere are longer than the nights. The combination of more direct rays and longer days makes Earth's surface warmer in the Northern Hemisphere than at any other time of the year. It is summer.

In June, when the north end of Earth's axis is tilted toward the sun, the south end of the axis is tilted away from the sun. The Southern Hemisphere receives fewer direct rays from the sun. The days are shorter than the nights. As a result, the Southern Hemisphere is experiencing winter.

Now look at the situation in December, six months later. Which way is the north end of Earth's axis tilted now? The Northern Hemisphere receives fewer direct rays from the sun and has shorter days. It is winter in the Northern Hemisphere and summer in the Southern Hemisphere.

Twice during the year, in March and September, neither end of Earth's axis is tilted toward the sun. At both of these times, one hemisphere has spring while the other has autumn.

EXPLORING *the Seasons*

The seasons are a result of Earth's tilted axis. The seasons change as the amount of energy each hemisphere receives from the sun changes.

December
The south end of Earth's axis is tilted toward the sun. The Southern Hemisphere receives more energy from the sun. It is summer in the Southern Hemisphere and winter in the Northern Hemisphere.

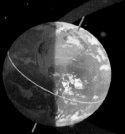

June
As the north end of Earth's axis is tilted toward the sun, the Northern Hemisphere receives more energy. It is summer in the Northern Hemisphere and winter in the Southern Hemisphere.

March and September
Neither end of Earth's axis is tilted toward the sun. Both hemispheres receive the same amounts of energy.

Section 1 Review

1. Name the four main factors that influence the temperature of an area.
2. How do prevailing winds affect the amount of precipitation an area receives?
3. On which side of mountains—leeward or windward—does precipitation fall?
4. How does the tilt of Earth's axis cause the seasons?
5. **Thinking Critically Developing Hypotheses** How might Earth's climates be different if Earth were not tilted on its axis?

CHAPTER PROJECT

Check Your Progress
Have you chosen your microclimate study sites? If your sites are on private property, get permission. Set up a logbook so that you can record your data. How do you think the conditions in these sites will differ? Write down your hypotheses. Now you are ready to measure daily weather conditions for your microclimates. (*Hint:* Be sure to take your measurements at the same time each day.)

Sunny Rays and Angles

In this lab, you will investigate how the angle of the sun's rays affects the amount of energy absorbed by different parts of Earth's surface.

Problem

How does the angle of a light source affect the rate of temperature change of a surface?

Materials

books	graph paper	pencil
scissors	ruler	clear tape
watch or clock	3 thermometers	protractor
100-W incandescent lamp		
black construction paper		

Procedure

1. Cut a strip of black construction paper 5 cm by 10 cm. Fold the paper in half and tape two sides to form a pocket.
2. Repeat Step 1 to make two more pockets.
3. Place the bulb of a thermometer inside each pocket.
4. Place the pockets with thermometers close together, as shown in the photo. Place one thermometer in a vertical position (90° angle), one at a 45° angle, and the third one in a horizontal position (0° angle). Use a protractor to measure the angles. Support the thermometers with books.
5. Position the lamp so that it is 30 cm from each of the thermometer bulbs. Make sure the lamp will not move during the activity.

6. Copy a data table like the one below into your notebook.
7. In your data table, record the temperature on all three thermometers. (All three temperatures should be the same.)
8. Switch on the lamp. In your data table, record the temperature on each thermometer every minute for 15 minutes. **CAUTION:** *Be careful not to touch the hot lampshade.*
9. After 15 minutes, switch off the lamp.

Analyze and Conclude

1. In this experiment, what was the manipulated variable? What was the responding variable? How do you know which is which?
2. Graph your data. Label the horizontal axis and vertical axis of your graph as shown on the sample graph. Use solid, dashed, and dotted lines to show the results from each thermometer, as shown in the key.
3. Based on your data, at which angle did the temperature increase the most?
4. At which angle did the temperature increase the least?

DATA TABLE

Time (min.)	Temperature (°C)		
	0° Angle	45° Angle	90° Angle
Start			
1			
2			
3			
4			
5			

5. What part of Earth's surface does each thermometer represent?

6. Why is air at the North Pole still very cold in the summer even though the Northern Hemisphere is tilted toward the sun?

7. **Think About It** In this experiment, what variables were held constant?

Design an Experiment

Design an experiment to find out how the results of this investigation would change if the lamp were placed farther from the thermometers. Then design another experiment to find out what would happen if the lamp were placed closer to the thermometers.

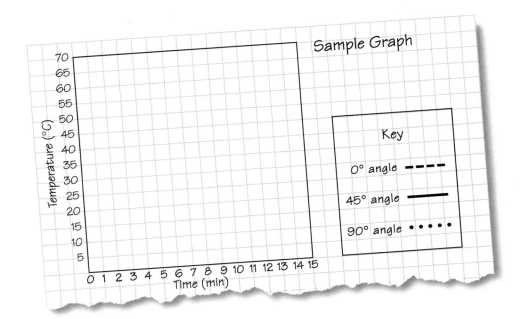

Sample Graph

Temperature (°C)
70
65
60
55
50
45
40
35
30
25
20
15
10
5

0 1 2 3 4 5 6 7 8 9 10 11 12 13 14 15
Time (min)

Key

0° angle – – – –

45° angle ———

90° angle • • • • •

DISCOVER ....**ACTIVITY**...

What Are Different Climate Types?

1. Collect pictures from magazines and newspapers of a variety of land areas around the world.

2. Sort the pictures into categories according to common weather characteristics.

Think It Over
Forming Operational Definitions Choose several words that describe the typical weather for each of your categories. What words would you use to describe the typical weather where you live?

GUIDE FOR READING

◆ What factors are used to define climates?

◆ What are the five main climate regions?

Reading Tip Before you read, preview *Exploring Climate Regions*. Write a list of any questions you have about climate regions.

When the Spanish settlers came to California in the 1700s, they brought with them plants from home. The padres, or priests, who established missions planted vineyards and orchards. They found that grapes, figs, and olives grew as well in California as they had in Spain. What do Spain and California have in common? They have similar climates.

Classifying Climates

The Spanish padres traveled a long distance but found a familiar climate. Suppose you traveled from your home to a place where the weather, the sunlight, and even the plants and trees were very different from what you are used to. Would you know what caused those differences?

Scientists classify climates according to two major factors: temperature and precipitation. They use a system developed around 1900 by Wladimir Köppen (KEP un). This system identifies broad climate regions, each of which has smaller subdivisions.

There are five main climate regions: tropical rainy, dry, temperate marine, temperate continental, and polar. Note that there is only one category of dry climates, whether hot or cold. These climate regions are shown in *Exploring Climate Regions* on pages 608–609.

 Olive trees

Exploring Climate Regions also shows a sixth type of climate: highlands. Recall that temperatures are cooler at the tops of mountains than in the surrounding areas. So a highland climate can occur within any of the other zones.

Maps show boundaries between the climate regions. In the real world, of course, no clear boundaries mark where one climate region ends and another begins. Each region blends gradually into the next.

☑ *Checkpoint* **What are the five main climate regions?**

Tropical Rainy Climates

The tropics have two types of rainy climates: tropical wet and tropical wet-and-dry. Trace the equator on *Exploring Climate Regions* with your finger. Tropical wet climates are found in low-lying lands near the equator. If you look north and south of tropical wet climates on the map, you can see two bands of tropical wet-and-dry climates.

Tropical Wet In areas that have a tropical wet climate, many days are rainy, often with afternoon thunderstorms. With year-round heat and heavy rainfall, vegetation grows lush and green. Dense rain forests grow in these rainy climates. **Rain forests** are forests in which plenty of rain falls all year-round. Tall trees such as teak and mahogany form the top layer, or canopy, while smaller bushes and vines grow near the ground. There are also many animals in the rain forest, including colorful parrots and toucans, bats, insects, frogs, and snakes.

In the United States, only the windward sides of the Hawaiian islands have a tropical wet climate. Rainfall is very heavy—over 10 meters per year on the windward side of the Hawaiian island of Kauai. The rain forests in Hawaii have a large variety of plants, including ferns, orchids, and many types of vines and trees.

Figure 6 Lush tropical rain forests grow in the tropical wet climate. *Relating Cause and Effect What climate factors encourage this growth?*

EXPLORING Climate Regions

Climate regions are classified according to a combination of temperature and precipitation. Climates in highland regions change rapidly as altitude changes.

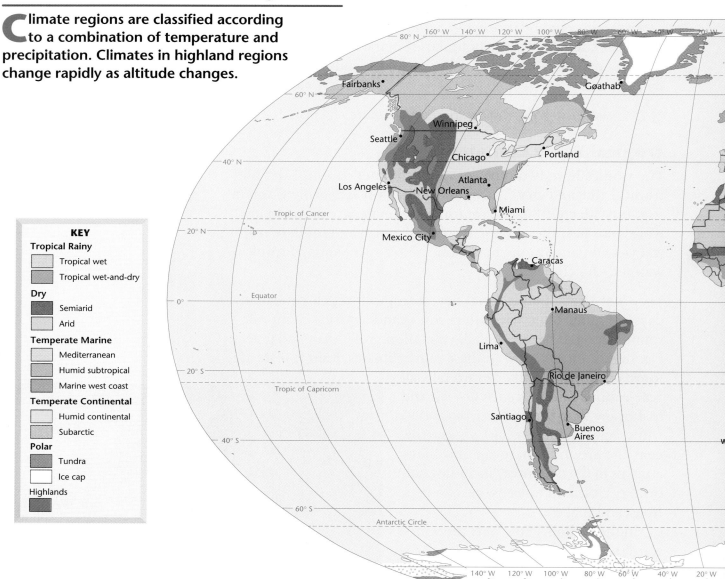

KEY

Tropical Rainy
- Tropical wet
- Tropical wet-and-dry

Dry
- Semiarid
- Arid

Temperate Marine
- Mediterranean
- Humid subtropical
- Marine west coast

Temperate Continental
- Humid continental
- Subarctic

Polar
- Tundra
- Ice cap

Highlands

Tropical Rainy
Temperature always 18°C or above.

Tropical wet *Always hot and humid, with heavy rainfall (at least 6 centimeters a month) all year round.*

Tropical wet-and-dry *Always hot, with alternating wet and dry seasons; heavy rainfall in the wet season.*

Dry
Occurs wherever potential evaporation is greater than precipitation. May be hot or cold.

Arid *Desert, with little precipitation, usually less than 25 centimeters a year.*

Semiarid *Dry but receives about 25 to 50 centimeters of precipitation a year.*

Temperate Marine
Average temperature 10°C or above in the warmest month, between −3° and 18°C in the coldest month.

Mediterranean *Warm, dry summers and rainy winters.*

Humid subtropical *Hot summers and cool winters.*

Marine west coast *Mild winters and cool summers, with moderate precipitation year round.*

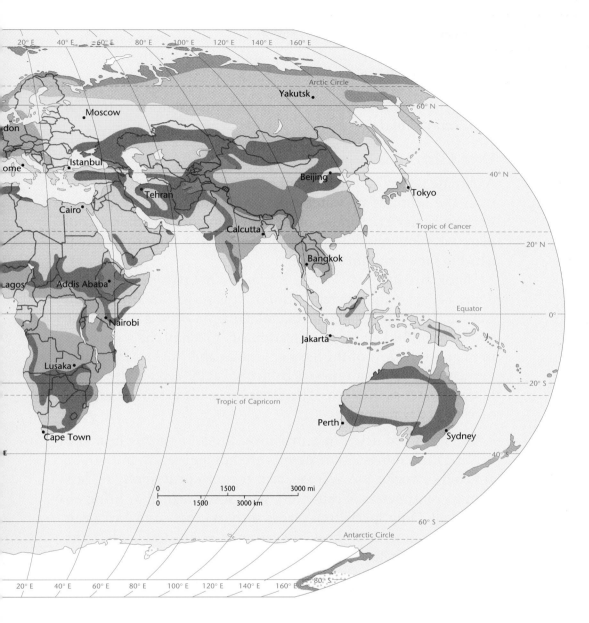

Temperate Continental
Average temperature 10°C or above in the warmest month, −3°C or below in the coldest month.

Humid continental *Hot, humid summers and cold winters, with moderate precipitation year round.*
Subarctic *Short, cool summers and long, cold winters. Light precipitation, mainly in summer.*

Polar
Average temperature below 10°C in the warmest month.

Tundra *Always cold with a short, cool summer—warmest temperature about 10°C.*
Ice cap *Always cold, average temperature at or below 0°C.*

Highlands
Generally cooler and wetter than nearby lowlands, temperature decreasing with altitude.

Figure 7 A reticulated giraffe gazes across the grasses and shrubby trees of the African savanna. Savannas are found in tropical wet-and-dry climates.

Tropical Wet-and-Dry Tropical wet-and-dry climates get slightly less rain than tropical climates and have distinct dry and rainy seasons. Instead of rain forests, there are tropical grasslands called **savannas.** Scattered clumps of trees that can survive the dry season dot the coarse grasses. Only a small part of the United States—the southern tip of Florida—has a tropical wet-and-dry climate.

☑ *Checkpoint* *What parts of the United States have tropical rainy climates?*

Dry Climates

A climate is "dry" if the amount of precipitation that falls is less than the amount of water that could potentially evaporate. Because water evaporates more slowly in cool weather, a cool place with low rainfall may not be as dry as a hotter place that gets the same amount of rain.

Look at *Exploring Climate Regions.* What part of the United States is dry? Why is precipitation in this region so low? As you can see, dry regions often lie inland, far from oceans that are the source of humid air masses. In addition, much of the region lies in the rain shadow of the Sierra Nevadas and Rocky Mountains to the west. Humid air masses from the Pacific Ocean lose much of their water as they cross the mountains. Little rain or snow is carried to dry regions.

Arid The word *desert* may make you think of blazing heat and drifting sand dunes. Some deserts are hot and sandy, but others are cold or rocky. On average, arid regions, or **deserts,** get less than 25 centimeters of rain every year. Some years may bring no rain at all. Only specialized plants such as cactus and yucca can survive the desert's dryness and extremes of hot and cold. In the United States there are arid climates in portions of California, the Great Basin, and the southwest.

Figure 8 Dry-land wheat farming is common in the steppe region of the Great Plains. *Comparing and Contrasting How are steppes similar to savannas, shown in Figure 7? How are they different?*

Semiarid Locate the semiarid regions on *Exploring Climate Regions*. As you can see, large semiarid areas are usually located on the edges of deserts. A steppe is dry but gets enough rainfall for short grasses and low bushes to grow. For this reason, a **steppe** may also be called a prairie or grassland.

The Great Plains are the steppe region of the United States. Many kinds of short grasses and wildflowers grow here, along with scattered forests. Livestock grazing is an important part of the economy of the Great Plains. Beef cattle, sheep, and goats graze on the short grasses of the region. Farm crops include grains, such as wheat and oats, and sunflowers.

Temperate Marine Climates

Look at *Exploring Climate Regions*, along the coasts of continents in the temperate zones. You will find the third main climate region, temperate marine. There are three kinds of temperate marine climates. Because of the moderating influence of oceans, all three are humid and have mild winters.

Marine West Coast The coolest temperate marine climates are found on the west coasts of continents north of 40° north latitude and south of 40° south latitude. Humid ocean air brings cool, rainy summers and mild, rainy winters.

In North America, the marine west coast climate extends from northern California to southern Alaska. In the Pacific Northwest of the United States, humid air from the Pacific Ocean rises as it hits the western slopes of the Coastal Ranges. As the air cools, large amounts of rain or snow fall on the western slopes.

Because of the heavy precipitation, thick forests of tall trees grow in this region, including coniferous, or cone-bearing, trees such as Sitka spruce, Douglas fir, redwoods, and Western red cedar. One of the main industries of this region is harvesting and processing wood for lumber, paper, and furniture.

Modeling a Humid Climate

ACTIVITY

Here's how you can create humidity.

1. Put the same amount of water in each of two small plastic bowls.

2. Place a sheet of transparent plastic wrap over each bowl. Secure each sheet with a rubber band.

3. Place one bowl on a warm, sunny windowsill or near a radiator. Put the other bowl in a cool location.

4. Wait a day and then look at the two bowls. What do you see on the plastic wrap over each bowl?

Inferring Would you expect to find more water vapor in the air in a warm climate or in a cool one? Why? Explain your results in terms of solar energy.

Figure 9 Seattle, Washington, is in the marine west coast climate region. Here the summers are cool and rainy, and winters are wet and mild.

Figure 10 A. Much of Italy has a Mediterranean climate, with warm, dry summers and cool, rainy winters. B. Rice is a major food crop in places with a humid subtropical climate, as in parts of China. *Comparing and Contrasting* How are Mediterranean and humid subtropical climates similar? How do they differ?

Mediterranean A coastal climate that is drier and warmer than west coast marine is known as Mediterranean. Find the Mediterranean climates in *Exploring Climate Regions.* In the United States, the southern coast of California has a Mediterranean climate. This climate is mild, with two seasons. In winter, marine air masses bring cool, rainy weather. Summers are somewhat warmer, with little rain.

Mediterranean climates have two main vegetation types. One is made up of dense shrubs and small trees, called chaparral (chap uh RAL). The other vegetation type includes grasses with a few oak trees.

Agriculture is an important part of the economy of California's Mediterranean climate region. Some crops, including olives and grapes, were originally introduced by Spanish settlers. With the help of irrigation, farmers grow many different crops, including rice, oranges, and many vegetables, fruits, and nuts.

Humid Subtropical The warmest temperate marine climates are on the edges of the tropics. **Humid subtropical** climates are wet and warm, but not as constantly hot as the tropics. Locate the humid subtropical climates in *Exploring Climate Regions.*

The southeastern United States has a humid subtropical climate. Summers are hot, with much more rainfall than in winter. Maritime tropical air masses move inland, bringing tropical weather conditions, including thunderstorms and occasional hurricanes, to southern cities such as Houston, New Orleans, and Atlanta. Winters are cool to mild, with more rain than snow. However, polar air masses moving in from the north can bring freezing temperatures and severe frosts.

Mixed forests of oak, ash, hickory, and pines grow in the humid subtropical region of the United States. Cotton was once the most important crop grown in this region. Other crops, including oranges, grapefruits, peaches, peanuts, sugar cane, and rice, are now more important to the economy.

☑ *Checkpoint* What is the main difference between a humid subtropical climate and a tropical climate?

Temperate Continental Climates

Temperate continental climates are found on continents in the Northern Hemisphere. Because they are not influenced very much by oceans, temperate continental climates have extremes of temperature. Why do continental climates occur only in the Northern Hemisphere? The parts of continents in the Southern Hemisphere south of 40° south latitude are not far enough from oceans for dry continental air masses to form.

Humid Continental Shifting tropical and polar air masses bring constantly changing weather to humid continental climates. In winter, continental polar air masses move south, bringing bitterly cold weather. In summer, tropical air masses move north, bringing heat and high humidity. Humid continental climates receive moderate amounts of rain in the summer. Smaller amounts of rain or snow fall in winter.

What parts of the United States have a humid continental climate? The eastern part of the region—the Northeast—has a range of forest types, from mixed forests in the south to coniferous forests in the north. Much of the western part of this region—the Midwest—was once tall grasslands, but is now farmland. Farmers in the Midwest grow wheat, corn, other grains, and soybeans. These crops are used as food for people and for hogs, poultry, and beef cattle.

Subarctic The **subarctic** climates lie north of the humid continental climates. The world's largest subarctic regions are in Russia, Canada, and Alaska. Summers in the subarctic are short and cool. Winters are long and bitterly cold.

In North America, coniferous trees such as spruce and fir make up a huge northern forest that stretches from Alaska to Canada's east coast. Many large mammals, including bears, wolves, and moose, live in the forest. Small mammals such as beavers, porcupines, and red squirrels, and birds such as grouse and owls also live in the forest. Wood products from the northern forest are an important part of the economy.

Sharpen your Skills

Classifying

ACTIVITY

The table shows some climate data for three cities.

	City A	City B	City C
Average January Temperature (°C)	12.8	18.9	−5.6
Average July Temperature (°C)	21.1	27.2	20
Annual Precipitation (cm)	33	152	109

Describe the climate you would expect each city to have. Identify which city is Miami, which is Los Angeles, and which is Portland, Maine. Use *Exploring Climate Regions* on pages 608–609 to help identify each city's climate.

Figure 11 Subarctic climates have cool summers and cold winters. Parts of this region are called "spruce-moose belts."

Polar Climates

The polar climate is the coldest climate region. Ice cap and tundra climates are found only in the far north and south, near the North and South poles.

Ice Cap As you can see in *Exploring Climate Regions*, ice cap climates are found mainly on Greenland and in Antarctica. With average temperatures always at or below freezing, the land in ice cap climate regions is covered with ice and snow. Intense cold makes the air dry. Lichens and a few low plants may grow on the rocks.

Tundra The **tundra** climate region stretches across northern Alaska, Canada, and Russia. Short, cool summers follow bitterly cold winters. Because of the cold, some layers of the tundra soil are always frozen. This permanently frozen tundra soil is called **permafrost.** Because of the permafrost, water cannot drain away, so the soil is wet and boggy in summer.

It is too cold on the tundra for trees to grow. Despite the harsh climate, during the short summers the tundra is filled with life. Mosquitoes and other insects hatch in the ponds and marshes above the frozen permafrost. Mosses, grasses, lichens, wildflowers, and shrubs grow quickly during the short summers. Herds of caribou and musk oxen eat the vegetation and are in turn preyed upon by wolves. Some birds, such as the white-tailed ptarmigan, live on the tundra year-round. Others, such as the arctic tern and many waterfowl, spend only the summer there.

☑ *Checkpoint* *What type of vegetation is found on the tundra?*

Figure 12 Emperor penguins live on the ice cap of Antarctica.

Figure 13 The tundra is often very cold, but still many plants and animals live there. *Observing How are these musk oxen adapted to the cold climate?*

Highlands

Why are highlands a distinct climate region? Remember that temperature falls as altitude increases, so highland regions are colder than the regions that surround them. Increasing altitude produces climate changes similar to the climate changes you would expect with increasing latitude. In the tropics, highlands are like cold islands overlooking the warm lowlands.

The climate on the lower slopes of a mountain range is like that of the surrounding countryside. The foothills of the Rocky Mountains, for instance, share the semiarid climate of the Great Plains. But as you go higher up into the mountains, temperatures become lower. Climbing 1,000 meters up in elevation is like traveling 1,200 kilometers north. The climate higher in the mountains is like that of the subarctic: cool with coniferous trees. Animals typical of the subarctic zone—such as moose and porcupines—live in the mountain forest.

Above a certain elevation—the tree line—no trees can grow. The climate above the tree line is like that of the tundra. Only low plants, mosses, and lichens can grow there.

Figure 14 The top of this mountain is too cold and windy for trees to grow. *Classifying* What climate zone does this mountaintop resemble?

Section 2 Review

1. What two factors are used to classify climates?
2. Briefly describe each of the five main climate types.
3. Give three examples of how the climate of a region affects what plants and animals can live there.
4. **Thinking Critically** **Applying Concepts** Which of these two places has more severe winters—central Russia or the west coast of France? Why?
5. **Thinking Critically** **Classifying** Classify the main climate regions according to whether or not trees usually grow in each one.

Science at Home

Climate Regions Describe to your family the characteristics of each of the climate regions found in the United States. Which climate region does your family live in? What plants and animals live in your climate region? What characteristics do these plants and animals have that make them well-adapted to living in your climate region?

Cool Climate Graphs

You are a land-use planner who has been hired by a company that builds recreational facilities. Your company is considering buying land near at least one of four cities, all at about the same latitude. Your job is to decide which of the cities would be the best place to build a water park and which is the best place to build a ski-touring center.

Problem

Based on climate data, which city is the best place for each type of recreational facility?

Skills Focus

graphing, interpreting data, drawing conclusions

Materials

calculator
ruler
3 pieces of graph paper
black, blue, red, and green pencils
climate map on pages 608–609
U.S. map with city names and latitude lines

Procedure

1. Work in groups of three. Each person should graph the data for a different city, A, B, or C.
2. On graph paper, use a black pencil to label the axes as on the climate graph below. Title your climate graph City A, City B, or City C.
3. Use your green pencil to make a bar graph of the monthly average amount of precipitation. Place a star below the name of each month that has more than a trace of snow.
4. Use a red pencil to plot the average monthly maximum temperature. Make a dot for the temperature in the middle of each space for the month. When you have plotted data for all 12 months, connect the points into a smooth curved line.
5. Use a blue pencil to plot the average monthly minimum temperature for your city. Use the same procedure as in Step 4.
6. Calculate the total average annual precipitation for this city and include it in your observations. Do this by adding the average precipitation for each month.

Washington, D.C., Climate Averages

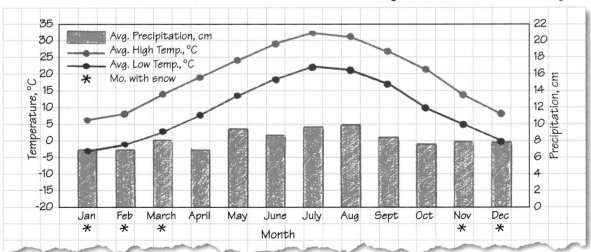

Climate Data

Washington, D.C.	Jan	Feb	Mar	April	May	June	July	Aug	Sept	Oct	Nov	Dec
Average High Temp. (°C)	6	8	14	19	24	29	32	31	27	21	14	8
Average Low Temp. (°C)	-3	-2	3	8	14	19	22	21	17	10	5	0
Average Precipitation (cm)	6.9	6.9	8.1	6.9	9.4	8.6	9.7	9.9	8.4	7.6	7.9	7.9
Months With Snow	*	*	*	trace	—	—	—	—	—	trace	*	*
City A	Jan	Feb	Mar	Apr	May	Jun	July	Aug	Sept	Oct	Nov	Dec
Average High Temp. (°C)	13	16	16	17	17	18	18	19	21	21	17	13
Average Low Temp. (°C)	8	9	9	10	11	12	12	13	13	13	11	8
Average Precipitation (cm)	10.4	7.6	7.9	3.3	0.8	0.5	0.3	0.3	0.8	3.3	8.1	7.9
Months With Snow	trace	trace	trace	—	—	—	—	—	—	—	—	trace
City B	Jan	Feb	Mar	Apr	May	Jun	July	Aug	Sept	Oct	Nov	Dec
Average High Temp. (°C)	5	7	10	16	21	26	29	27	23	18	11	6
Average Low Temp. (°C)	−9	−7	−4	1	6	11	14	13	8	2	−4	−8
Average Precipitation (cm)	0.8	1.0	2.3	3.0	5.6	5.8	7.4	7.6	3.3	2.0	1.3	1.3
Months With Snow	*	*	*	*	*	—	—	—	trace	*	*	*
City C	Jan	Feb	Mar	Apr	May	Jun	July	Aug	Sept	Oct	Nov	Dec
Average High Temp. (°C)	7	11	13	18	23	28	33	32	27	21	12	8
Average Low Temp. (°C)	−6	−4	−2	1	4	8	11	10	5	1	−3	−7
Average Precipitation (cm)	2.5	2.3	1.8	1.3	1.8	1	0.8	0.5	0.8	1	2	2.5
Months With Snow	*	*	*	*	*	trace	—	—	trace	trace	*	*

Analyze and Conclude

Compare your climate graphs and observations. Use all three climate graphs, plus the graph for Washington, D.C., to answer these questions.

1. Which of the four cities has the least change in average temperatures during the year?
2. In which climate region is each city located?
3. Which of the cities listed below matches each climate graph?

Colorado Springs, Colorado	latitude 39° N
San Francisco, California	latitude 38° N
Reno, Nevada	latitude 40° N
Washington, D.C.	latitude 39° N

4. Even though these cities are at approximately the same latitude, why are their climate graphs so different?
5. **Apply** Which city would be the best location for a water slide park? For a cross-country ski touring center? What other factors should you consider when deciding where to build each type of recreational facility? Explain.

More to Explore

What type of climate does the area where you live have? Find out what outdoor recreational facilities your community has. How is each one particularly suited to the climate of *your* area?

SECTION
3 Long-Term Changes in Climate

GUIDE FOR READING

◆ What principle do scientists follow in studying ancient climates?

◆ What changes occur on Earth's surface during an ice age?

◆ What theories have been proposed to explain natural climate change?

Reading Tip Before you read, preview the art and photos and read the captions. Write a prediction about how Earth's climate has changed through time.

One of the greatest Native American cultures in the American Southwest was the Ancestral Pueblos. These farming people built great pueblos, or "apartment houses," of stone and sun-baked clay, with hundreds of rooms. By about the year 1000, the Ancestral Pueblos were flourishing. They grew crops of corn, beans, and squash and traded extensively with other groups of people. But in the late 1200s, the climate became drier, reducing the size of their crops. After a long period of drought, the Ancestral Pueblos migrated to other areas.

Although weather can vary from day to day, climates usually change more slowly. But climates do change, both in small areas and throughout the world. Although climate change is usually slow, its consequences are great. Climate changes have affected many civilizations, including the Ancestral Pueblos.

Figure 15 The Ancestral Pueblos lived in these buildings, now in Mesa Verde National Park in southwestern Colorado, about 1,000 years ago.

Studying Climate Change

In studying ancient climates, scientists follow an important principle: If plants or animals today need certain conditions to live, then similar plants and animals in the past also required those conditions. For example, today magnolia and palm trees grow only in warm, moist climates. Scientists assume that the ancestors of these trees required similar conditions. Thus, 80-million-year-old fossils of these trees in Greenland are good evidence that the climate of Greenland was warm and moist 80 million years ago.

Tree rings can also be used to learn about ancient climates. Every summer, a tree grows a new layer of wood under its bark. These layers form rings when seen in a cross section, as shown in Figure 16. In cool climates, the amount the tree grows—the thickness of a ring—depends on the length of the warm growing season. In dry climates, the thickness of each ring depends on the amount of rainfall. By looking at cross sections of trees, scientists can count backward from the outer ring to see whether previous years were warm or cool, wet or dry. A thin ring indicates that the year was cool or dry. A thick ring indicates that the year was warm or wet.

A third source of information about ancient climates is pollen records. Each type of plant has a particular type of pollen. The bottoms of some lakes are covered with thick layers of mud and plant material, including pollen, that fell to the bottom of the lake over thousands of years. Scientists can drill down into these layers and bring up cores to examine. By looking at the pollen present in each layer, scientists can tell what types of plants lived in the area. The scientists can then infer that the climate that existed when the pollen was deposited was similar to the climate where the same plants grow today.

Figure 16 Scientists have learned about past climates by studying tree rings. They can learn much from giant sequoias, some of which may be 3,000–4,000 years old.

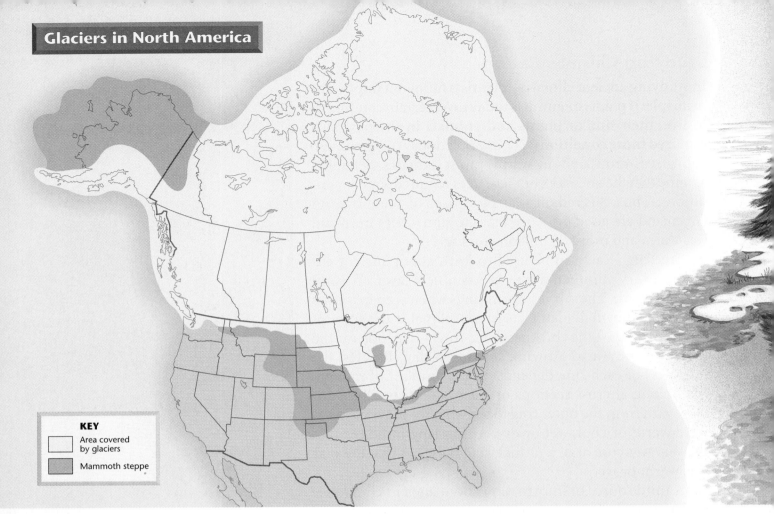

Glaciers in North America

KEY
☐ Area covered by glaciers
☐ Mammoth steppe

Figure 17 The map shows the parts of North America that were covered by glaciers 18,000 years ago. On the steppe near the glaciers lived many mammals that are now extinct, including woolly mammoths and scimitar-toothed cats.

Ice Ages

Throughout Earth's history, climates have gradually changed. Over millions of years, warm periods have alternated with cold periods known as **ice ages,** or glacial episodes. **During each ice age, huge sheets of ice called glaciers covered large parts of Earth's surface.**

From fossils and other evidence, scientists have concluded that in the past two million years there have been at least four major ice ages. Each one lasted 100,000 years or longer. Long, warmer periods known as interglacials occurred between the ice ages. Some scientists think that we are now in a warm period between ice ages.

The most recent major ice age ended only about 10,500 years ago. Ice sheets covered much of northern Europe and North America, reaching as far south as present-day Iowa and Nebraska. In some places, the ice was more than 3 kilometers thick. So much water was frozen in the ice sheets that the average sea level was much lower than it is today. When the ice sheets melted, the rising oceans flooded coastal areas. Inland, large lakes formed.

☑ *Checkpoint* *Why were the oceans lower during the ice ages than they are now?*

Causes of Climate Change

Why do climates change? Scientists have formed several hypotheses. **Possible explanations for major climate changes include variations in the position of Earth relative to the sun, changes in the sun's energy output, and the movement of continents.**

Earth's Position Changes in Earth's position relative to the sun may have affected climates. According to one hypothesis, as Earth revolves around the sun, the time of year when Earth is closest to the sun shifts from January to July and back again over a period of about 26,000 years.

The angle at which Earth's axis tilts and the shape of Earth's orbit around the sun also change slightly over long periods of time. The combined effects of these changes in Earth's movements may be the main cause of ice ages.

INTEGRATING SPACE SCIENCE **Solar Energy** Short-term changes in climate have been linked to changes in the number of **sunspots**—dark, cooler regions on the surface of the sun. Sunspots increase and decrease in regular 11-year cycles. Sunspot cycles could in turn be caused by changes in the sun's energy output.

Social Studies
CONNECTION

Prehistoric people who lived during the last ice age faced a harsh environment. To endure the cold, they learned to make clothing from animal skins. They also used fires for warmth and cooking.

In Your Journal

Make a list of five ways your life would change if the climate suddenly became colder.

225 million years ago

Equator

Pangaea

180–200 million years ago

Equator

Laurasia

Gondwanaland

Figure 18 The continents have moved over millions of years. *Interpreting Maps Which present-day continents broke away from Gondwanaland? Which broke away from Laurasia?*

Recently, satellite measurements have shown that the amount of energy the sun produces increases and decreases slightly from year to year. These changes may cause Earth's temperature to increase and decrease. More observations are needed to test this hypothesis.

Movement of Continents Earth's continents have not always been located where they are now. About 225 million years ago, most of the land on Earth was part of a single continent called Pangaea (pan JEE uh).

As Figure 18 shows, most continents were far from their present positions. Continents that are now in the polar zones were once near the equator. This movement explains how tropical plants such as magnolias and palm trees could once have grown in Greenland.

Over millions of years, the continents broke away and gradually moved to their present positions. The movements of continents over time changed the locations of land and sea. These changes affected the global patterns of winds and ocean currents, which in turn slowly changed climates. And as the continents continue to move, climates will continue to change.

Section 3 Review

1. What types of evidence do scientists use to study changes in climate?
2. How was the climate during an ice age different from the climate today?
3. List three factors that could be responsible for changing Earth's climates.
4. **Thinking Critically** Predicting What kinds of climate changes might be caused by a volcanic eruption? Would these changes be permanent? Explain.

Check Your Progress CHAPTER PROJECT

What types of weather conditions have you measured at each site? Have you been recording all the data in your logbook? You should now be ready to graph and analyze your data. Are the weather conditions at all of your test areas similar, or do you see differences? What do you think causes the different conditions? What organisms did you observe at your sites?

SECTION 4 Global Changes in the Atmosphere

DISCOVER ••• ACTIVITY

What Is the Greenhouse Effect?

1. ✂ Cut two pieces of black construction paper to fit the bottoms of two shoe boxes.

2. 🧤 Place a thermometer in one end of each box. Read the temperatures on the thermometers. (They should be the same.) Cover one box with plastic wrap.

3. Place the boxes together where sunlight or a light bulb can shine on them equally. Make sure the thermometers are shaded by the sides of the boxes.

4. What do think will happen to the temperatures on the thermometers? Wait 15 minutes and read the thermometers again. Record the temperatures.

Think It Over

Inferring How can you explain the temperature difference between the box with the plastic wrap and the open box? Why does the inside of a car left in direct sunlight get so warm?

Have you ever seen a headline like the one below? If you hate cold winters and love summer sports, you may wonder what would be wrong with a slightly warmer world. Some experts agree with you, but many scientists are worried about such climate change.

> **❖ ANYWHERE U.S.A. DAILY NEWS ❖**
> **Earth's Average Temperature Expected to Increase by 3 Celsius Degrees**

Most changes in world climates are caused by natural factors. In the last hundred years, however, human activities have also had an effect on Earth's climate and atmosphere. Two of the most important worldwide issues are global warming and thinning of the ozone layer.

Global Warming

Over the last 120 years, the average temperature of the troposphere has risen by about 0.5 Celsius degree. Was this increase part of natural variations, or was it caused by human activities? What effects could higher temperatures have? Scientists have done a great deal of research to try to answer these questions.

GUIDE FOR READING

◆ How might human activities be affecting the temperature of Earth's atmosphere?

◆ How have human activities affected the ozone layer?

Reading Tip As you read, draw a concept map showing how human activities can cause changes in the atmosphere and climate.

Sunlight

Infrared radiation cannot pass through greenhouse roof

Figure 19 Sunlight enters the greenhouse and is absorbed. The interior of the greenhouse radiates back energy in the form of infrared radiation, or heat. The heat is trapped and held inside the greenhouse, warming it.
Applying Concepts What gases in Earth's atmosphere can trap heat like a greenhouse?

The Greenhouse Effect Recall that gases in Earth's atmosphere hold in heat from the sun, keeping the atmosphere at a comfortable temperature for living things. The process by which gases in Earth's atmosphere trap solar energy is called the greenhouse effect.

Gases in the atmosphere that trap solar energy are called **greenhouse gases.** Water vapor, carbon dioxide, and methane are some of the greenhouse gases. **Human activities that add greenhouse gases to the atmosphere may be warming Earth's atmosphere.** For example, the burning of wood, coal, oil, and natural gas adds carbon dioxide to the air. If the increased carbon dioxide traps more heat, the result could be **global warming,** a gradual increase in the temperature of Earth's atmosphere.

The amount of carbon dioxide in the atmosphere has been steadily increasing. Some scientists predict that if the level of carbon dioxide doubles by the year 2100, the average global temperature could go up by 1.5 to 3.5 Celsius degrees.

Another Hypothesis Not everyone agrees about the causes of global warming. Some scientists think that the 0.5 Celsius degree rise in global temperatures over the past 120 years may be part of natural variations in climate rather than a result of increases in carbon dioxide.

As you learned in Section 3, satellite measurements have shown that the amount of energy the sun produces increases and decreases from year to year. These changes in solar energy could be causing periods of warmer and cooler climates. Or climate change could be a result of changes in both carbon dioxide levels and amounts of solar energy.

Possible Effects Global warming has some potential advantages. Farmers in cool areas could plant two crops a year. Places that are too cold for farming today could become farmland. However, many effects of global warming are likely to be less positive. Higher temperatures would cause water to evaporate from exposed soil, such as plowed farmland. Dry soil blows away easily. Thus some fertile fields might become "dust bowls."

A rise in temperatures of even a few degrees could warm up water in the oceans. As ocean surface temperatures increased, the number of hurricanes might increase.

As the water warmed, it would expand, raising sea levels around the world. Glaciers and polar ice caps might partially melt, which would also increase sea levels. Sea levels have already risen by 10 to 20 centimeters over the last 100 years, and could rise another 25 to 80 centimeters by the year 2100. Even such a small rise in sea levels would flood low-lying coastal areas.

✓ *Checkpoint* *What are three possible effects of global warming?*

Ozone Depletion

Another global change in the atmosphere involves the ozone layer, which you learned about in Chapter 15. Ozone in the stratosphere filters out much of the harmful ultraviolet radiation from the sun.

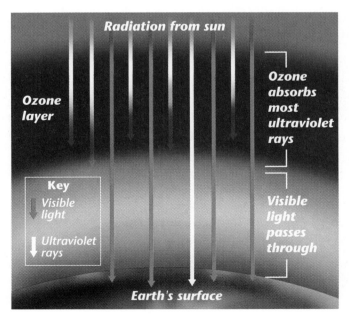

Figure 20 The ozone layer blocks much of the ultraviolet radiation coming from the sun. Visible light can pass through the ozone layer.

It's Your Skin!

How well do sunscreens block out ultraviolet rays? Here's how to compare sunscreens.

ACTIVITY

1. Close the blinds or curtains in the room. Place one square of sun-sensitive paper inside each of three plastic sandwich bags.

2. Place three drops of one sunscreen on the outside of one bag. Spread the sunscreen as evenly as possible. Label this bag with the SPF number of the sunscreen.

3. On another bag, repeat Step 2 using a sunscreen with a different SPF. Wash your hands after spreading the sunscreen. Leave the third bag untreated as a control.

4. Place the bags outside in direct sunlight. Bring them back inside after 3 minutes or after one of the squares of paper has turned completely white.

Drawing Conclusions Did both of the sunscreens block ultraviolet radiation? Did one of the sunscreens block more ultraviolet radiation than the other one? Explain your results.

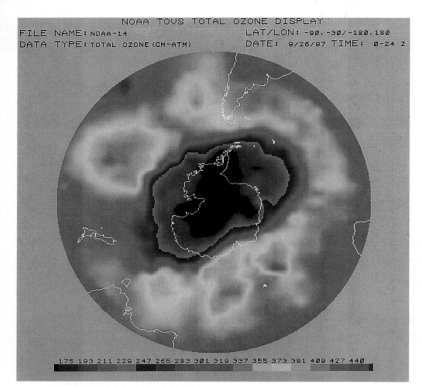

175 193 211 229 247 265 283 301 319 337 355 373 391 409 427 440

Figure 21 This satellite image shows the concentration of ozone in the air over the South Pole. The dark area shows where the ozone layer is the thinnest.

In the 1970s, scientists noticed that the ozone layer over Antarctica was growing thinner each spring. By 1992, the area of thinner ozone was more than twice as large as the continental United States. What created the ozone hole? **Chemicals produced by humans have been damaging the ozone layer.**

The main cause of ozone depletion is a group of chlorine compounds called **chlorofluorocarbons,** or CFCs. CFCs were used in air conditioners and refrigerators, as cleaners for electronic parts, and in spray cans. Most chemical compounds released into the air eventually break down. CFCs, however, can last for decades and rise all the way to the stratosphere. In the stratosphere, ultraviolet radiation breaks down the CFC molecules into atoms, including chlorine. The chlorine atoms then break ozone down into oxygen atoms.

Because ozone blocks ultraviolet radiation, a decrease in ozone means an increase in the amount of ultraviolet radiation that reaches Earth's surface. If you have ever been sunburned, you can understand one effect of stronger ultraviolet radiation! Ultraviolet radiation can also cause eye damage and several kinds of skin cancer.

In the late 1970s, the United States and many other countries banned the use of CFCs in spray cans. In 1990, many nations signed an agreement to ban the use of almost all CFCs by the year 2000. Because ozone depletion affects the whole world, such agreements must be international to be effective.

Section 4 Review

1. What human actions increase the amount of carbon dioxide in Earth's atmosphere?
2. How could increases in carbon dioxide in the air affect world temperatures?
3. What chemicals are the major cause of ozone depletion in the stratosphere?
4. **Thinking Critically Predicting** How might global warming change conditions where you live? How would this affect your life?

Science at Home

Compare Sunscreens Visit a drugstore with your family. Compare the SPF (sun protection factor) of the various sunscreens for sale. Explain why it is important to protect your skin from ultraviolet radiation. Ask your family members to determine the best value for their money in terms of SPF rating and price.

SECTION 1 What Causes Climate?

Key Ideas

◆ The climate of a region is determined by its temperature and precipitation.

◆ The main factors that influence temperature are latitude, altitude, distance from large bodies of water, and ocean currents.

◆ The main factors that affect precipitation are prevailing winds and the presence of mountains.

◆ The different seasons are a result of the tilt of Earth's axis as Earth travels around the sun.

Key Terms

climate   continental climate
tropical zone   windward
polar zone   leeward
temperate zone   microclimate
marine climate

SECTION 2 Climate Regions

Key Ideas

◆ Climates are classified according to temperature and precipitation.

◆ There are five main climate regions: tropical rainy, dry, temperate marine, temperate continental, and polar. Highlands are often considered to be a sixth climate region.

Key Terms

rain forest   steppe   tundra
savanna   humid subtropical   permafrost
desert   subarctic

SECTION 3 Long-Term Changes in Climate

Key Ideas

◆ During each ice age, huge sheets of ice covered much of Earth's surface.

◆ Possible explanations for major climate changes include movement of continents, variations in the position of Earth relative to the sun, and changes in the sun's energy output.

Key Terms

ice age   sunspot

SECTION 4 Global Changes in the Atmosphere

INTEGRATING ENVIRONMENTAL SCIENCE

Key Ideas

◆ Human activities that add greenhouse gases to the atmosphere may be warming Earth's atmosphere.

◆ Chemicals produced by humans have been damaging the ozone layer.

Key Terms

greenhouse gas
global warming
chlorofluorocarbons

Organizing Information

Concept Map Copy the concept map about climate onto a separate sheet of paper. Then complete it and add a title. (For more on concept maps, see the Skills Handbook.)

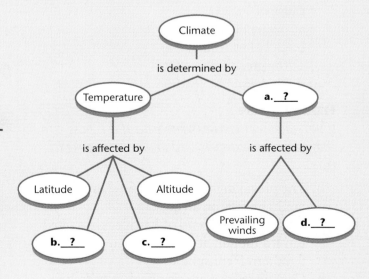

Reviewing Content

 For more review of key concepts, see the Interactive Student Tutorial CD-ROM.

Multiple Choice

Choose the letter of the best answer.

1. Temperatures are highest in the tropical zone because
   a. the land is flat.
   b. the sun's rays strike most directly.
   c. Earth's axis is tilted toward the sun.
   d. ocean currents warm the region.

2. Continental climates are found
   a. on every continent.
   b. only near the equator.
   c. only in the Northern Hemisphere.
   d. only in the Southern Hemisphere.

3. In a wet-and-dry tropical climate, the most common vegetation is
   a. coniferous forests.
   b. savanna grasslands.
   c. tropical rain forest.
   d. steppe grasslands.

4. Extremely cold periods in Earth's history have resulted in huge
   a. tree rings.
   b. sunspots.
   c. pollen deposits.
   d. glaciers.

5. Chlorofluorocarbons, or CFCs, are the main cause of
   a. ozone depletion.
   b. global warming.
   c. the greenhouse effect.
   d. ice ages.

True or False

If the statement is true, write true. If it is false, change the underlined word or words to make it true.

6. The prevailing winds affect how much <u>sunlight</u> falls on an area.

7. When the north end of Earth's axis is tilted toward the sun, it is <u>summer</u> in the Southern Hemisphere.

8. Climate regions are classified according to temperature and <u>precipitation</u>.

9. A <u>thin</u> tree ring indicates that a year was cool or dry.

10. An increase in <u>nitrogen</u> in the atmosphere may be making world temperatures increase.

Checking Concepts

11. Explain how distance from large bodies of water can effect the temperature of nearby land areas.

12. What causes Earth's seasons?

13. Identify the parts of the United States that are located in each of the three temperature zones.

14. How are "dry" climates defined? How do the two types of dry climate differ?

15. How does the movement of continents explain major changes in climate over time?

16. To be effective, why must agreements aimed at preventing or reducing ozone depletion be international?

17. **Writing to Learn** In what climate region do you live? Write a description of your local climate and identify some of the things—such as latitude, bodies of water, or wind patterns—that affect the climate.

Thinking Critically

18. **Relating Cause and Effect** Describe three ways in which water influences climate.

19. **Comparing and Contrasting** How is global warming different from earlier changes in Earth's climate?

20. **Making Judgments** What is the most important thing that needs to be done about global warming?

21. **Relating Cause and Effect** Why do parts of the United States have a semiarid climate while neighboring areas have a humid continental climate?

Applying Skills

Use the map of world temperature zones to answer Questions 22–24.

22. **Interpreting Maps** Name each of the five zones shown on the map.

23. **Measuring** What is the name of the temperature zone that includes the equator? How many degrees of latitude does this zone cover?

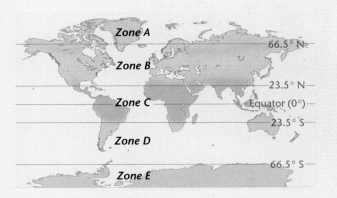

24. **Interpreting Data** Which of the five zones shown on the map has the greatest amount of land area suitable for people to live?

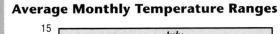

Present Your Project Decide how to present your project. You could use a written report, oral presentation, or a bulletin board. Do your graphs compare the conditions in the different microclimates? What conditions favor plants or animals in some areas? After you present your project to the class, discuss what you think causes different microclimates.

Reflect and Record In your journal, describe how you could improve your investigation. Are there factors you did not study? Did you notice any organisms that live only in certain microclimates? What additional information about microclimates would you like to find?

Test Preparation

Use these questions to prepare for standardized tests.

Study the graph. Then answer Questions 25–30.

25. Which of the following months has the widest range of temperatures during the year?
    a. September   b. June
    c. May   d. April

26. Which month shown on the graph is the warmest on average?
    a. August   b. June
    c. July   d. May

27. Which month is the coldest on average?
    a. January   b. December
    c. March   d. February

28. What is the average temperature in April?
    a. about −21°C   b. about −17°C
    c. about 0°C   d. about −30°C

29. What is the average temperature in December?
    a. about −20°C   b. about −26°C
    c. about 0°C   d. about −30°C

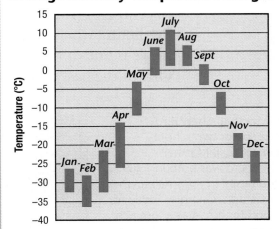

30. What kind of climate is indicated by the graph?
    a. polar
    b. temperate continental
    c. temperate marine
    d. tropical rainy

Eyes On EARTH

At the Kennedy Space Center on the east coast of Florida, a crew prepares to launch a satellite into space. They know that a thunderstorm may be moving toward them. Should they launch the mission or delay? Before deciding, the crew contacts meteorologists for the latest weather forecast.

The Kennedy Space Center is about 100 kilometers east of the center of the state. More summer thunderstorms occur in central Florida than nearly any other area in the world. Predicting when severe storms will develop and where they will move is one of the most demanding jobs for a meteorologist. One of the best people at this job is J. Marshall Shepherd.

J. Marshall Shepherd
The son of two school principals, J. Marshall Shepherd was born in 1969 and raised in the small town of Canton, Georgia. Today he works for NASA as a research meteorologist for Mission to Planet Earth. He's an expert on the development of powerful thunderstorms. He studied meteorology at Florida State University.

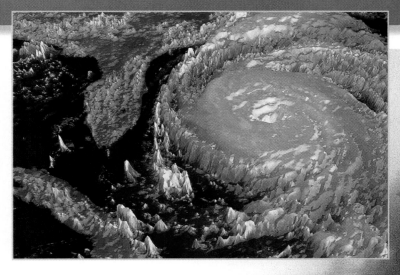

Hurricane Fran roars over the Caribbean Sea near Florida and the island of Cuba. White clouds swirl around the "eye" at the center of the hurricane (upper right).

Getting Started at a Science Fair

Marshall Shepherd is an "old hand" at predicting the weather. He's been at it since sixth grade, when his teacher suggested that he enter a science fair. Marshall titled his science project "Can a Sixth-Grader Predict the Weather?" First he toured the local TV station in Atlanta to see what instruments meteorologists use to measure basic weather variables.

> ❝ **The shape of Florida is part of the reason that so many storms form here.** ❞

"Then I did a little background reading and decided I could build some of those instruments out of basic materials around the house," he recalls.

Using household materials and a few inexpensive items at supply stores, Marshall Shepherd built everything he needed for his project. He constructed a weather station with an anemometer to measure wind speed, a wind vane to measure wind direction, a barometer to measure air pressure, a hair hygrometer to measure humidity, and a rain gauge.

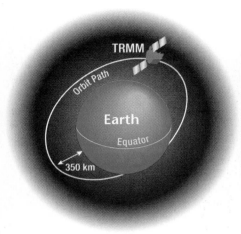

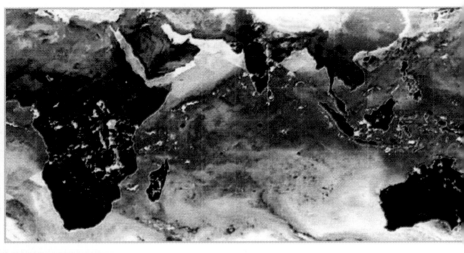

▲ TRMM, a device that records weather conditions from space, orbits Earth at an altitude of 350 kilometers. It flies over each position on Earth at a different time each day.

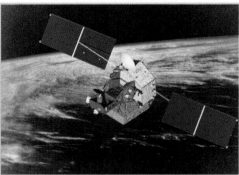

TRMM observatory is about the size of a small room and weighs as much as a medium-sized truck. It contains two solar panels and instruments to record weather data.

"From these basic instruments, I took weather observations around my neighborhood," he explains. "I developed a model of day-to-day weather over a six-month period and found some very interesting and accurate results." Marshall's instruments and scientific work on this project won prizes for him at local, district, and state science fairs.

"From that point on, I was involved with science projects," he recalls. By the time he graduated from high school, he had a definite goal. "One day, I planned to be a research scientist at NASA (National Aeronautics and Space Administration)," he stated.

Predicting Severe Storms

Hurricane Andrew—the most powerful hurricane ever to strike Florida—swept through southern Florida and Louisiana in 1992. Marshall was in college at the time. "My college research paper was on hurricane tracking using radar. I actually did some work with Hurricane Andrew," he says. "That's how I got interested in tropical weather."

In graduate school, Marshall Shepherd investigated the way powerful thunderstorms form and move, especially those in central Florida. The long, narrow shape of Florida is part of the reason that so many storms form there. "When you have land heating faster than water, you get something called sea-breeze circulation," he explains. "On a typical summer day, a sea-breeze forms on both the west coast and the east coast of Florida. They tend to move toward the center. When they collide, you get intense thunderstorm development."

Designing New Instruments

Now Marshall Shepherd works at NASA, where his projects contribute to NASA's Mission to Planet Earth.

632

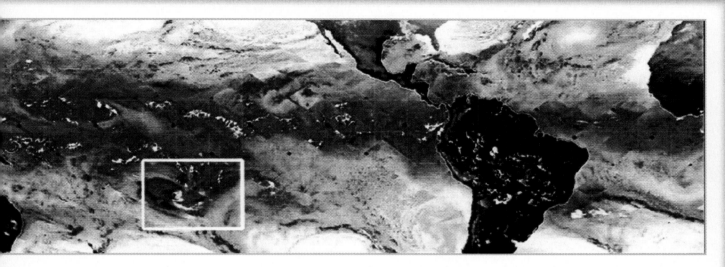

This map was generated by TRMM. The white rectangle identifies a cyclone.

This long-term program uses information from satellites, aircraft, and ground studies to explore environmental changes around the world.

Marshall Shepherd's knowledge of thunderstorms is especially valuable in interpreting data from TRMM (Tropical Rainfall Measuring Mission), a device that measures tropical and subtropical rainfall. Rainfall cycles in tropical regions affect weather throughout the world.

Marshall Shepherd's work involves both observation and calculation. As he did in sixth grade, he designs and builds instruments. But now his devices are some of the most advanced in the world. He no longer takes his instruments into a neighborhood to measure weather conditions directly. Instead, his specialty is "remote sensing"—making observations of weather conditions (rainfall, water vapor, and so on) from a distance.

After collecting data, Marshall uses a computer to analyze it. He and others have designed a computer program that uses the data to predict the development of severe storms. So when a crew at the Kennedy Space Center must decide whether or not to launch a rocket, they rely on predictions from programs similar to ones that Marshall Shepherd has worked on.

Looking Ahead

Marshall Shepherd's personal goals go beyond Mission to Planet Earth. "With the upcoming international space station, scientists are going to have the opportunity to do research from space. My goal is to conduct Earth-directed meteorological research from the space station as well as from the ground. I'll use some of the new instruments we are currently developing." He describes another important goal back home on Earth—"to reach out, inspire, and expose students to science."

In Your Journal

Marshall Shepherd credits his success to having detailed goals. "I always write down goals, and check them off as they happen," he says. Think of an important task that you would like to accomplish over the next year. Identify the steps and note target dates you will need to meet in order to reach your goal. How do those steps help bring you closer to achieving your goal?

Earth, Moon, and Sun

www.phschool.com

Where's the Moon?

What a view! Though you would have to be in orbit around the moon to see this kind of Earthrise, you don't have to travel at all to see the moonrise from Earth. All you have to do is look in the right direction at the right time and you will see the moon rise in front of you!

In this chapter, you will explore relationships among Earth, the moon, and the sun. In your project, you will observe the position of the moon in the sky every day. These observations will show you the changing positions of Earth and the moon with respect to each other and to the sun.

Your Goal To observe the shape of the moon and its position in the sky every day for one month.

To complete the project you will
◆ observe and record every day the compass direction in which you see the moon and its height above the horizon
◆ use your observations to explain the phases of the moon
◆ develop rules you can use to predict where and when you might see the moon each day throughout a month

Get Started Begin by preparing an observation log. You will want to record the date and time of each observation, the direction and height of the moon, a sketch of its shape, and notes about the cloud cover or other conditions. You can also keep track of the time of moonrise each day.

Check Your Progress You'll be working on this project as you study this chapter. To keep your project on track, look for Check Your Progress boxes at the following points.

Section 1 Review, page 643: Make a map to help you determine the direction of the moon.
Section 2 Review, page 654: Observe the moon every day.
Section 4 Review, page 664: Look for patterns in your observations.

Present Your Project At the end of the chapter (page 667), you will present your observations of the moon using words, drawings, and graphs.

This amazing Earthrise above the moon's horizon was seen by astronaut Michael Collins in the *Apollo 11* moon orbiter *Columbia*.

SECTION 4 Earth's Moon

Discover Why Do Craters Look Different From One Another?
Sharpen Your Skills Calculating

DISCOVER •••**ACTIVITY**••••

Why Does Earth Have Day and Night?

1. Place a lamp with a bare bulb in the middle of a table to represent the sun. Put a globe at the end of the table about 1 meter away to represent Earth.

2. Turn the lamp on and darken the room. Which parts of the globe have light shining on them? Which parts are in shadow?

3. Find your location on the globe. Take about 5 seconds to turn the globe once. Notice when it is lit—day—at your location and when it is dark—night.

Think It Over

Making Models How does one complete turn of the globe represent one day? In this model, how many seconds represent one day? How could you use the model to represent a year?

GUIDE FOR READING

◆ What causes day and night?

◆ What causes the cycle of seasons on Earth?

Reading Tip Before you read, preview the figures and captions in the section. List any terms that are not familiar to you. Then write their definitions as you read about them.

Ancient Egyptian farmers eagerly awaited the annual spring flood of the Nile River. For thousands of years, their planting was ruled by it. As soon as the Nile's floodwaters withdrew, the farmers had to be ready to plow and plant their fields along the banks of the river. Because of this, the Egyptians wanted to predict when the flood would occur. Around 3000 B.C., people noticed that the bright star Sirius first became visible in the early morning sky every year shortly before the flood began. The Egyptians used this knowledge to predict each year's flood.

Egyptian farmers ▶

Rotation

N

Axis —

S

Earth

Revolution

Earth

Sun

Figure 1 Earth rotates on its axis and revolves around the sun.
Applying Concepts What is one full rotation called? What is one complete revolution called?

Days and Years

The ancient Egyptians were among the first people to study the stars. The study of the moon, stars, and other objects in space is called **astronomy.**

Ancient astronomers also studied the movements of the sun and the moon as they appeared to travel across the sky. It seemed to them as though Earth were standing still and the sun and moon were moving around it. Actually, the sun and moon seem to move across the sky each day mainly because Earth is rotating on its axis.

Rotation The imaginary line that passes through Earth's center and the North and South poles is called Earth's **axis.** The north end of the axis currently points toward a point in space near Polaris, the North Star. Earth's spinning on its axis is called its **rotation.** A point on the equator rotates at about 1,600 kilometers per hour. Even most commercial jet planes can't fly this fast!

Earth's rotation on its axis causes day and night. As Earth rotates eastward, the sun appears to move westward across the sky. It is day on the side of Earth facing the sun. As Earth continues to turn to the east, the sun appears to set in the west. Sunlight can't reach the side of Earth facing away from the sun, so it is night there. It takes Earth about 24 hours to rotate once on its axis. As you know, each 24-hour cycle of day and night is called a day.

Revolution In addition to rotating on its axis, Earth travels around the sun. The movement of one object around another object is called **revolution.** One complete revolution around the sun is called a year. Earth's path as it revolves around the sun is called its **orbit.** As it travels around the sun, Earth's orbit is not quite a circle. It is a slightly flattened circle, or oval shape.

✓ *Checkpoint* **Why do the sun and moon seem to move each day?**

Sharpen your Skills

Calculating

ACTIVITY

Earth moves at a speed of about 30 km/sec as it travels around the sun. What distance, in kilometers, does Earth travel in a minute? An hour? A day? A year?

Calendars The Egyptian astronomers counted the number of days between each first appearance of the star Sirius. In this way, they found that there were about 365 days in each year. By dividing the year into 365 days, the ancient Egyptians had created one of the first calendars.

People of many different cultures have struggled to come up with workable calendars. Earth's orbit around the sun takes about $365\frac{1}{4}$ days. Four years of about $365\frac{1}{4}$ days each can be approximated by taking 3 years of 365 days and a fourth year of 366 days. You know this fourth year as a "leap year." During a leap year, an extra day is added to February, giving it 29 days instead of its usual 28.

Tracking the Cycle of the Year

For thousands of years, people have used observations of the sky to keep track of the time of year.

1500 B.C.
British Isles

Ancient peoples complete Stonehenge, a monument with giant stones that mark the directions in which the sun rises and sets on the longest day of the year.

1500 B.C.	900 B.C.	300 B.C.

1300 B.C.
China

During the Shang dynasty, Chinese astronomers made detailed observations of the sun, planets, and other objects they saw in the night sky. Chinese astronomers calculated that the length of a year is 365.25 days.

300 B.C.
Egypt

Astronomers in Alexandria, Egypt, learned to use an instrument called an astrolabe. Astrolabes were used to find the positions of stars and planets.

Dividing the year into smaller parts was difficult also. Early people used moon cycles as a sort of calendar. The time between one full moon and the next one is about $29\frac{1}{2}$ days. A year of 12 of these "moonths" only adds up to 354 days. The ancient Egyptians worked out a calendar that had 12 months of 30 days each, with an extra 5 days that were not part of any month. The Romans borrowed this calendar and made changes to it. With more changes, it eventually became the calendar we know: 11 months having 30 or 31 days each, plus one month (February) having 28 or 29 days.

In Your Journal

Research one of the accomplishments discussed in the time line. Write a dialogue in which two people from the culture that made the discovery or observation discuss its importance in their lives.

Wyoming

A.D. 1450
Wyoming

The Big Horn Medicine Wheel was built by Native Americans. Individual stones are aligned with the rising and setting sun and several bright stars. The rising of these specific stars may have indicated to people when it was time to move south for the winter.

A.D. 300 **A.D. 900** **A.D. 1500**

A.D. 900
Mexico

The Mayas studied the movement of the sun, the moon, and the planet Venus. They had two different calendars, one with 365 days for everyday use and the other with 260 days for religious uses. These calendars combined to make a 52-year cycle. The Mayas were able to predict astronomical events 3,000 years into the future.

Figure 2 It is warm near the equator because sunlight hits Earth's surface more directly and is less spread out.
Interpreting Diagrams Why is it colder near the poles?

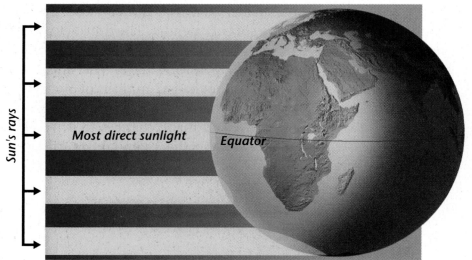

Most direct sunlight

Equator

Sun's rays

What's Your Angle?

An angle is formed when two lines meet at a point. Angles are measured in degrees (symbol°).

Earth's axis currently points near Polaris, the North Star. As a result, the angle of the North Star above the horizon at any point in the Northern Hemisphere equals the latitude of a person observing from that point. For example, at the equator, which has a latitude of 0°, Polaris would be seen at an angle of 0°, which is on the horizon. What is your latitude if you observe that Polaris is 41° above the horizon? If Polaris is directly overhead?

Seasons on Earth

Most places outside the tropics have four distinct seasons: winter, spring, summer, and autumn. But there are great differences in temperature from place to place. For instance, it is warmer near the equator than near the poles. Why is this so?

How Sunlight Hits Earth Figure 2 shows how sunlight hits Earth's surface. Notice that at the equator, sunlight hits Earth's surface more directly. Closer to the poles, sunlight hits Earth's surface at an angle. Near the poles, energy from the sun is spread out over a greater area. That is why it is warmer near the equator than near the poles.

Earth's Tilted Axis If Earth's axis were straight up and down relative to the sun, as in Figure 2, temperatures would remain constant year-round. There would be no seasons. **Earth has seasons because its axis is tilted as it moves around the sun.**

Look at Earth's position in space in *Exploring the Seasons* on the next page. Notice that Earth's axis is tilted at an angle of 23.5° from the vertical. As Earth revolves around the sun, its axis is tilted away from the sun for part of the year and toward the sun for part of the year.

When the north end of Earth's axis is tilted toward the sun, the Northern Hemisphere has summer. At the same time, the south end of Earth's axis is tilted away from the sun. As a result, the Southern Hemisphere has winter.

Summer and winter are not affected by changes in Earth's distance from the sun. In fact, when the Northern Hemisphere is having summer, Earth is at its greatest distance from the sun.

Checkpoint How is Earth's axis tilted when the Northern Hemisphere has summer?

EXPLORING Solstices and Equinoxes

The yearly cycle of the seasons is caused by the tilt of Earth's axis as it revolves around the sun.

March Equinox

Late December—Solstice The south end of Earth's axis is tilted toward the sun. It is summer in the Southern Hemisphere and winter in the Northern Hemisphere.

June Solstice

December Solstice

September Equinox

Late June—Solstice The north end of Earth's axis is tilted toward the sun. It is summer in the Northern Hemisphere and winter in the Southern Hemisphere.

Late March and Late September—Equinoxes Neither end of Earth's axis is tilted toward the sun. Both hemispheres receive the same amount of energy.

June Solstice

N

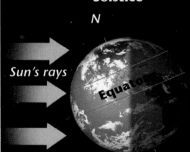

Sun's rays

Equator

S

Noon sun vertical at 23.5° N

March Equinox

N

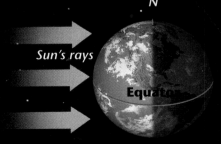

Sun's rays

Equator

S

Noon sun vertical at equator

December Solstice

N

Sun's rays

Equator

S

Noon sun vertical at 23.5° S

Earth in June In June, the north end of Earth's axis is tilted toward the sun. The noon sun is directly overhead at 23.5° north latitude. **Latitude** is a measurement of distance from the equator, expressed in degrees north or south. (The equator has latitude 0° and the North Pole has latitude 90° north.)

The hemisphere that is tilted toward the sun also has more hours of daylight than the hemisphere that is tilted away from the sun. The combination of direct rays and more hours of sunlight heats the surface more than at any other time of the year. It is summer in the Northern Hemisphere.

At the same time, for any place on Earth south of the equator, the sun's energy is spread over a large area. There are also fewer hours of daylight. The combination of indirect rays and fewer hours of sunlight heats Earth's surface less than at any other time of the year. It is winter in the Southern Hemisphere.

Earth in December Look again at *Exploring the Seasons.* Around December 21, the noon sun is overhead at 23.5° south latitude. People in the Southern Hemisphere receive the most direct sunlight, so it is summer there. At the same time, the sun's rays in the Northern Hemisphere are indirect and there are fewer hours of daylight. So it is winter in the Northern Hemisphere.

Both June and December On two days each year, the noon sun is overhead at either 23.5° south or 23.5° north. Each of these days is known as a **solstice** (SAHL stis). The day when the noon sun is overhead at 23.5° south is the winter solstice in the Northern Hemisphere. It is the summer solstice in the Southern Hemisphere. This solstice occurs around December 21 each year, and is the shortest day of the year in the Northern Hemisphere. At

Figure 3 Spring is the season between the vernal equinox and the summer solstice. The warming temperatures of spring make it the best time to plant flowers like these pansies.

the same time, it is close to the longest day of the year in the Southern Hemisphere.

Similarly, around June 21, the noon sun is overhead at 23.5° north. This is the summer solstice in the Northern Hemisphere and the winter solstice in the Southern Hemisphere.

Earth in March and September Halfway between the solstices, neither hemisphere is tilted toward or away from the sun. This situation occurs on only two days of the year. On these days, the noon sun is directly overhead at the equator.

Each of these days is known as an **equinox,** which means "equal night." During an equinox, the lengths of nighttime and daytime are about the same. The **vernal equinox,** or spring equinox, occurs around March 21, and marks the beginning of spring in the Northern Hemisphere. The **autumnal equinox** occurs around September 23. It marks the beginning of fall in the Northern Hemisphere.

INTEGRATING LIFE SCIENCE In much of the United States, seasonal changes affect living things. In spring and summer, the sun shines for more hours each day and is higher in the sky. The warmer days and additional sunlight allow many plants to begin growing leaves and flowers. Because plants grow more, animals that feed on the plants, from tiny insects to large deer, get more food.

In the fall, the nights get longer, signaling the plants to stop growing and some plants to lose their leaves. With less food available, black bears and some other animals go into a dormant state in which they use very little energy. Others, like many songbirds and waterfowl, travel to warmer climates where food is still available.

Figure 4 This hungry bear has spent the long winter in a dormant state in a cave in Alaska. *Applying Concepts* Why didn't this bear remain active all winter?

Section 1 Review

1. Explain the process that causes day and night.
2. What two factors cause the cycle of the seasons?
3. Compare rotation and revolution.
4. What do the words *solstice* and *equinox* mean? How are they related to the position of Earth's axis?
5. **Thinking Critically Relating Cause and Effect** Are changes in the distance between Earth and the sun important in causing the cycle of the seasons? Explain.

Check Your Progress CHAPTER PROJECT
Begin recording your daily observations of the moon. Sketch a map of the site from which you will be making observations. Which way is north? East? South? West? Each night, observe and record the moon's direction. You should also estimate the moon's altitude, or height in degrees from the horizon. You can do this by making a fist and holding it at arm's length. One fist above the horizon is 10°, two fists are 20°, and so on.

Skills Lab

REASONS FOR THE SEASONS

In this lab, you will use an Earth-sun model to make observations about factors that contribute to the seasons.

Problem

What effect does the tilt of Earth's axis have on the heat and light received by Earth as it revolves around the sun?

Materials (per pair of students)

books   flashlight   paper
pencil   protractor   toothpick
acetate sheet with thick grid lines drawn on it
plastic foam ball marked with poles and equator

Procedure

1. Make a pile of books about 15 cm high. Dim the room lights.
2. Tape the acetate sheet to the head of the flashlight. Place the flashlight on the pile of books.
3. Carefully push a pencil into the South Pole of the plastic foam ball, which represents Earth.
4. Use the protractor to measure a 23.5° tilt of the axis of your Earth away from your "flashlight sun," as shown in the first diagram. This represents winter.
5. Hold the pencil so that Earth is steady at this 23.5° angle and about 15 cm from the flashlight head. Turn the flashlight on.
6. The squares on the acetate should show up on Earth. Move the ball closer if necessary or dim the room lights more. Observe and record the shape of the squares at the equator and at the poles.

7. Carefully stick the toothpick straight into Earth about halfway between the equator and the North Pole. Observe and record the length of the shadow.
8. Without changing the tilt, turn the pencil to rotate Earth once on its axis. Observe and record how the shadow of the toothpick changes.
9. Tilt Earth 23.5° toward the flashlight, as shown in the second diagram. This is summer. Observe and record the shape of the squares at the equator and at the poles. Observe how the toothpick's shadow changes.
10. Rotate Earth and note the shadow pattern.

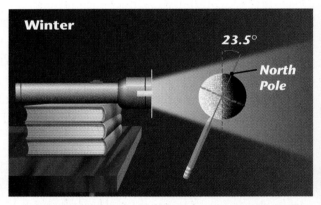

Winter 23.5° North Pole

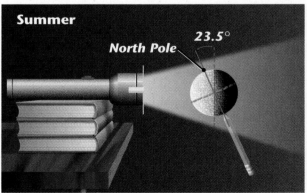

Summer North Pole 23.5°

Analyze and Conclude

1. When it is winter in the Northern Hemisphere, which areas on Earth get the most concentrated amount of light? Which areas get the most concentrated light when it is summer in the Northern Hemisphere?

2. Compare your observations of how the light hits the area halfway between the equator and the North Pole during winter (Step 6) and during summer (Step 9).

3. If the squares projected on the ball from the acetate become larger, what can you conclude about the amount of heat distributed in each square?

4. According to your observations, which areas on Earth are consistently coolest? Which areas are consistently warmest? Why?

5. What time of year will the toothpick's shadow be longest? When will the shadow be shortest?

6. How are the amounts of heat and light received in a square related to the angle of the sun's rays?

7. **Think About It** How can you use your observations of an Earth-sun model to explain what causes the seasons?

More to Explore

You can measure how directly light from the sun hits Earth's surface by making a shadow stick. You need a stick or pole about 1 m long. With the help of your teacher, push the stick partway into the ground where it will not be disturbed. Make sure the stick stays vertical. At noon on the first day of every month, measure the length of the stick's shadow. The shorter the shadow, the more directly the sun's rays are hitting Earth. At what time of the year are the shadows longest? Shortest? How do your observations help explain the seasons?

SECTION 2 Phases, Eclipses, and Tides

DISCOVER  ACTIVITY

How Does the Moon Move?

1. Put a quarter flat on your desk to represent Earth. Use a penny flat on your desk to represent the moon.

2. One side of the moon always faces Earth. Move the moon through one revolution around Earth, keeping Lincoln's face always looking at Earth. How many times did the penny make one complete rotation?

Think It Over

Inferring From the point of view of someone on Earth, does the moon seem to rotate? Explain your answer.

GUIDE FOR READING

◆ What causes the phases of the moon?

◆ What causes solar and lunar eclipses?

◆ What causes the tides?

Reading Tip As you read, write a sentence to describe what causes each of the following: phases, solar eclipses, lunar eclipses, tides.

The moon is Earth's closest neighbor in space—much closer than any planet. In fact, the average distance from Earth to the moon is only about 30 times Earth's diameter. Even so, it is quite far away. On average, the moon is 384,400 kilometers from Earth. If there were a highway to the moon and you could travel at 100 kilometers per hour, it would take you more than five months to get there.

The moon moves in space just as Earth does. As the moon revolves around Earth and Earth revolves around the sun, the relative positions of the moon, Earth, and sun change. **The positions of the moon, Earth, and the sun cause the phases of the moon, eclipses, and tides.**

Motions of the Moon

The moon revolves around Earth and rotates on its own axis. It takes the moon about 27.3 days to revolve around Earth. Like Earth's orbit around the sun, the moon's orbit around Earth is a flattened circle or oval shape.

The moon rotates slowly on its own axis once every 27.3 days. Because the moon also revolves around Earth every 27.3 days, a "day" and a "year" on the moon are the same length. As you saw if you

◀ Crescent moon over Fire Island, New York

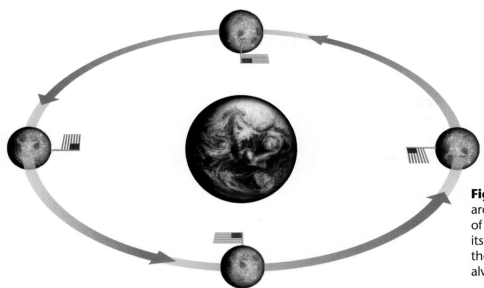

Figure 5 The moon revolves around Earth in the same amount of time the moon takes to rotate on its axis. As a result, the near side of the moon (shown with a flag) always faces Earth.

tried the Discover activity, the same side of the moon, the "near side," always faces Earth. The "far side" of the moon always faces away from Earth, so you never see it from Earth.

☑ *Checkpoint* *How many days does it take the moon to revolve once around Earth?*

Phases of the Moon

On a clear night when the moon is full, the bright moonlight can keep you awake. But the moon does not produce the light you see. Instead, it reflects light from the sun. Imagine taking a flashlight into a dark room. If you were to shine the flashlight on a chair, you would see the chair because the light from your flashlight would bounce, or reflect, off the chair. In the same way that the chair wouldn't shine by itself, the moon doesn't give off light by itself. You see the moon because sunlight reflects off it.

When you see the moon in the sky, sometimes it appears round. Other times you see only a thin sliver, or crescent. The different shapes of the moon you see from Earth are called **phases.** The moon goes through its whole set of phases each time it revolves around Earth, that is, about once a month.

What Causes Phases? Phases are caused by changes in the relative positions of the moon, Earth, and the sun. Because the sun lights the moon, half the moon is almost always in sunlight. However, since the moon revolves around Earth, you see the moon from different angles. The half of the moon that faces Earth is not always the half that is sunlit. **The phase of the moon you see depends on how much of the sunlit side of the moon faces Earth.** To understand the changing phases, refer to *Exploring Phases of the Moon* on the next page.

Social Studies CONNECTION

Before there was artificial lighting, the phases of the moon were important in planning activities. For example, the full moon nearest the autumnal equinox is called the harvest moon, and the following full moon is called the hunter's moon.

In Your Journal

Find out about an event that is determined by the phases of the moon, such as the Jewish Passover, the Christian Easter, or the Islamic fast of Ramadan. How is the date of the event calculated?

EXPLORING Phases of the Moon

The diagram in the center shows a view of Earth and the moon phases from above. The sun is shining from the right. The outer ring of photos shows the different amounts of the sunlit side of the moon that an observer on Earth sees as the moon revolves around Earth.

First Quarter
You see half of the lighted side of the moon.

Waxing Crescent
You see more and more of the lighted side of the moon. This is called a waxing crescent moon.

Waxing Gibbous
The moon continues to wax. The moon is called gibbous.

New Moon
The sun lights the side of the moon facing away from Earth. The side of the moon that faces Earth is dark.

Full Moon
You see the whole lighted side of the moon.

Waning Gibbous
The fraction of the lighted side of the moon that you see gets smaller each day.

Third Quarter
You can see half of the moon's lighted side.

Waning Crescent
You see a crescent again.

The Cycle of the Phases During the new moon, the side of the moon facing Earth is not lit. As the moon revolves around Earth, you see more and more of the lighted side of the moon every day, until the side of the moon you see is fully lit. As the moon continues in its orbit, you see less and less of the lighted side of the moon. About 29.5 days after the last new moon, the cycle is complete, and you see a new moon again.

☑ *Checkpoint* *Since the moon does not produce light, how can you see it?*

Eclipses

What would you think if you were walking home from school on a sunny afternoon and the sun began to disappear? Would you be frightened? On rare occasions, the moon completely blocks the sun. The sky grows as dark as night even in the middle of a clear day. The air gets cool and the sky becomes an eerie color. If you don't know what is happening, you can become very frightened.

The moon doesn't usually go directly between Earth and the sun or directly behind Earth. As Figure 6 shows, the moon's orbit around Earth is slightly tilted with respect to Earth's orbit around the sun. As a result, in most months the moon revolves completely around Earth without the moon moving into Earth's shadow or the moon's shadow hitting Earth.

When the moon's shadow hits Earth or Earth's shadow hits the moon, an eclipse occurs. An **eclipse** (ih KLIPS) occurs when an object in space comes between the sun and a third object, and casts a shadow on that object. There are two types of eclipses: solar eclipses and lunar eclipses. (The words *solar* and *lunar* come from the Latin words for "sun" and "moon.")

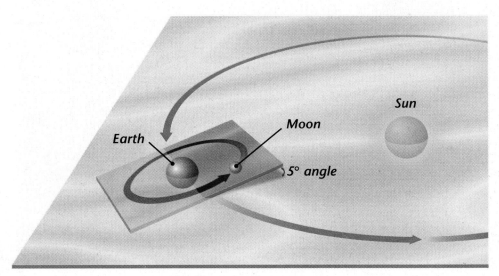

Figure 6 The moon's orbit is tilted with respect to Earth's orbit. So the moon rarely goes directly between Earth and the sun. *Interpreting Diagrams How large is the angle between Earth's orbit and the moon's orbit?*

Solar Eclipses

During a new moon, the moon is almost exactly between Earth and the sun. But most months, as you have seen, the moon travels a little above or below the sun in the sky. A **solar eclipse** occurs when the moon passes between Earth and the sun, blocking the sunlight from reaching Earth. The moon's shadow then hits Earth, as shown in Figure 7. So a solar eclipse is really just a new moon in which the moon blocks your view of the sun.

Total Solar Eclipses The darkest part of the moon's shadow, the **umbra** (UM bruh), is cone-shaped. From any point in the umbra, light from the sun is completely blocked by the moon. The moon's umbra happens to be long enough so that the point of the cone can just reach a small part of Earth's surface. Only the people within the umbra experience a total solar eclipse. During a total solar eclipse, the sky is dark. You can see the stars and the solar corona, which is the faint outer atmosphere of the sun.

Partial Solar Eclipses In Figure 7, you can see that the moon casts another shadow that is less dark than the umbra. In this larger part of the shadow, called the **penumbra** (pih NUM bruh), part of the sun is visible from Earth. During a solar eclipse, people in the penumbra see only a partial eclipse. Since part of the sun remains visible, it is not safe to look directly at the sun during a partial solar eclipse (just as you wouldn't look directly at the sun at any other time).

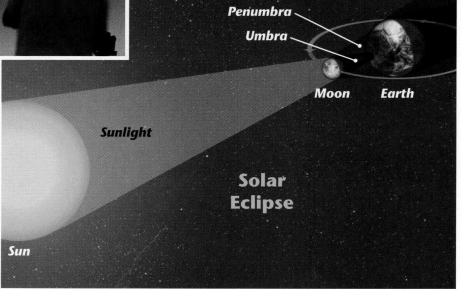

Figure 7 During a solar eclipse, right, the moon blocks light from the sun, preventing the light from reaching Earth's surface. The solar corona, which surrounds the dark disk of the moon, above, is visible during a solar eclipse.

Penumbra

Umbra

Moon   Earth

Sunlight

Solar Eclipse

Sun

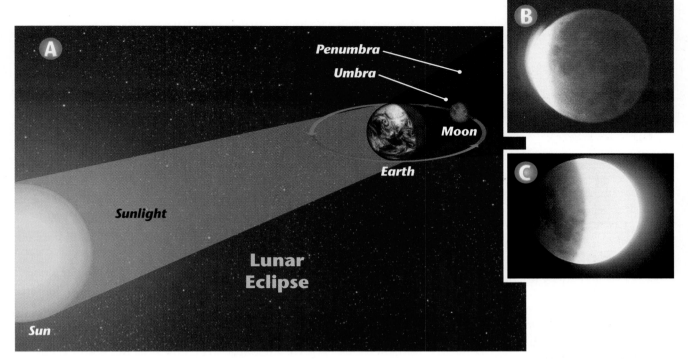

Figure 8 A. During a lunar eclipse, Earth blocks sunlight from reaching the moon's surface. B. This photo of the moon was taken during a total lunar eclipse. C. This photo was taken during a partial lunar eclipse. *Interpreting Diagrams What is the difference between Earth's umbra and penumbra?*

Lunar Eclipses

During most months, the moon goes near Earth's shadow but not quite into it. A **lunar eclipse** occurs at a full moon when Earth is directly between the moon and the sun. You can see a lunar eclipse in Figure 8. During a lunar eclipse, Earth blocks sunlight from reaching the moon. The moon is then in Earth's shadow and looks dark from Earth. Because the moon is closest to Earth's shadow during the full moon, lunar eclipses occur only at full moon.

Total Lunar Eclipses Like the moon's shadow, Earth's shadow has an umbra and a penumbra. When the moon is in Earth's umbra, you see a total lunar eclipse. You can see Earth's shadow on the moon before and after the total part of a lunar eclipse.

Unlike a solar eclipse, a lunar eclipse can be seen anywhere on Earth that the moon is visible. So you are more likely to see a total lunar eclipse than a total solar eclipse.

Partial Lunar Eclipses For most lunar eclipses, Earth, the moon, and the sun are not quite in line, and a partial lunar eclipse results. A partial lunar eclipse occurs when the moon passes partly into the umbra of Earth's shadow. The edge of the shadow appears blurry, and you can watch it pass across the moon for up to two or three hours.

☑ *Checkpoint* *Why do lunar eclipses occur only at full moon?*

Making Models

A "Moonth" of Phases

In this lab, you will use a model of the Earth-moon-sun system to explore how the phases of the moon occur.

Problem

What causes the phases of the moon?

Materials

floor lamp with 150-watt bulb
extension cord
pencils
plastic foam balls

Procedure

1. Place a lamp in the center of the room. Remove the lampshade.
2. Close the doors and shades to darken the room, and switch on the lamp.
3. Carefully stick the point of a pencil into the plastic foam ball so that the pencil can be used as a "handle."
4. Draw 8 circles on a sheet of paper. Number them 1–8.
5. Have your partner hold the plastic foam ball at arm's length in front and slightly above his or her head so that the ball is between him or her and the lamp. **CAUTION:** *Do not look directly at the bulb.*
6. The ball should be about 1 to 1.5 m away from the lamp. Adjust the distance between the ball and the lamp so that the light shines brightly on the ball.

7. Stand directly behind your partner and observe what part of the ball facing you is lit by the lamp. If light is visible on the ball, draw the shape of the lighted part of the ball in the first circle.
8. Have your partner turn 45° to the left while keeping the ball in front and at arm's length.
9. Repeat Step 7. Be sure you are standing directly behind your partner.
10. Repeat Steps 8 and 9 six more times until your partner is facing the lamp again. See the photograph for the 8 positions.
11. Change places and repeat Steps 4–10.

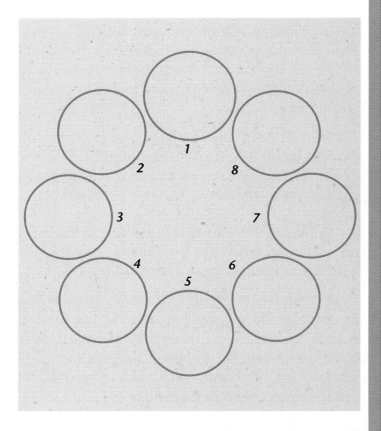

Analyze and Conclude

1. In your model, what represents Earth? The sun? The moon?
2. Refer back to your 8 circles. How much of the lighted part of the ball did you see when facing the lamp?
3. Label your drawings with the names of the phases of the moon. Which drawing represents a full moon? A new moon? Which represents a waxing crescent? A waning crescent?
4. How much of the lighted part of the ball did you see after each turn?
5. Whether you could see it or not, how much of the ball's surface was always lit by the lamp? Was the darkness of the new moon caused by an eclipse? Explain your answer.
6. **Think It Over** How did making a model help you understand the phases of the moon? What are some disadvantages of using models? What is another way to make a model to represent the moon's phases?

More to Explore

Design a model to show a lunar eclipse and a solar eclipse. What objects would you use for Earth, the sun, and the moon? Use the model to demonstrate why there isn't an eclipse every full moon and new moon.

45°

Figure 9 The Hopewell Rocks in New Brunswick, Canada, are partly covered at high tide. At low tide, people can walk along the beach between the rocks. *Predicting What would happen if these people stayed on the beach too long?*

Tides

Have you ever built a sand castle at an ocean beach? Was it washed away by the rising water? People who spend time near the ocean see the effects of **tides,** the rise and fall of water, every 12.5 hours or so. The water rises for about six hours, then falls for about six hours, in a regular cycle.

The force of **gravity** pulls the moon and Earth (including the water on Earth's surface) toward each other. The force of gravity between two objects depends on the masses of the objects and the distance between them. **Tides occur mainly because of differences in how much the moon pulls on different parts of Earth.** As discussed in Chapter 13, the position of the sun also influences the height of the tides.

As Earth rotates, the moon's gravity pulls water toward the point on Earth's surface closest to the moon. If that were the only cause, there would be only one high tide at a time, at the point on Earth closest to the moon. Actually, there is a second high tide on the opposite side of Earth, so the explanation must be more complex. The two high tides occur because of the difference in the force of gravity between one place and another. There are also two low tides on Earth located halfway between the high tides. As Earth rotates, tides occur in a 25-hour cycle.

Not every place on Earth has two regular tides every day. The shapes of bays, inlets, and the ocean floor can affect the flow of water, so that the height and timing of the tides can vary even in places that are close to each other.

Section 2 Review

1. Why does the moon change its phases as the month progresses?
2. Describe the relative positions of Earth, the sun, and the moon during a solar eclipse and during a lunar eclipse.
3. Why are a "day" and a "year" on the moon the same length?
4. **Thinking Critically Interpreting Diagrams** Make a diagram to show what phase the moon is in during a lunar eclipse.

CHAPTER PROJECT

Check Your Progress
Bring your log sheet to class so you can share your observations with classmates. Check the newspaper every day to find the times of moonrise and moonset and record this information. If you can, look for the moon at moonrise or moonset, even during daylight hours. Use your map to keep track of the direction in which you can see the moon.

SECTION 3 Rockets and Satellites

DISCOVER

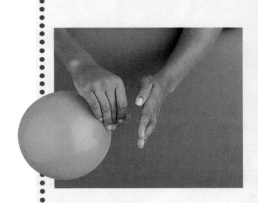

How Do Rockets Work?

1. Put on your goggles. Blow up a balloon and hold its neck closed with your fingers.

2. Point the balloon toward an area where there are no people. Put your free hand behind the neck of the balloon, so the air will push against your hand. Let go of the balloon.

3. Repeat Steps 1 and 2 without your free hand behind the balloon.

Think It Over

Observing In which direction does the air rush out? In which direction does the balloon go? Does the balloon need to push against something in order to move? Explain your answer.

Curiosity about Earth's "neighborhood" in space has led to moon missions, space shuttle missions, space stations, and Mars missions. But without rockets, none of these accomplishments would have been possible.

How Rockets Work

A rocket works in much the way that a balloon is propelled through the air by releasing gas. **A rocket moves forward when gases expelled from the rear of the rocket push it in the opposite direction.** It's a basic law of physics that for every force, or action, there is an equal and opposite force, or reaction. For example, the force of the air going out the back of a balloon is an action force. An equal force, the reaction, pushes the balloon forward.

In a rocket, fuel is burned to make a hot gas. This hot gas is forced out of narrow nozzles in the back of the rocket, propelling the rocket forward.

GUIDE FOR READING

◆ How do rockets travel in space?

◆ What are satellites and space stations used for?

Reading Tip Before you read, rewrite the headings in the section as *how, why,* or *what* questions. As you read, look for answers to those questions.

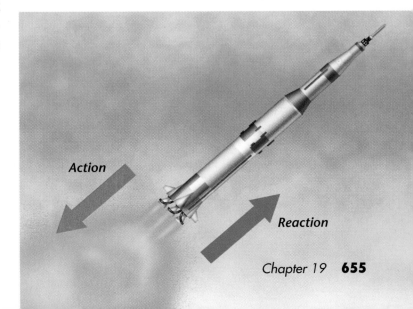

Figure 10 Hot gas is propelled out of the back of a rocket engine. The force of the gas in one direction (action) produces an opposing force (reaction) that propels the rocket forward.

Action

Reaction

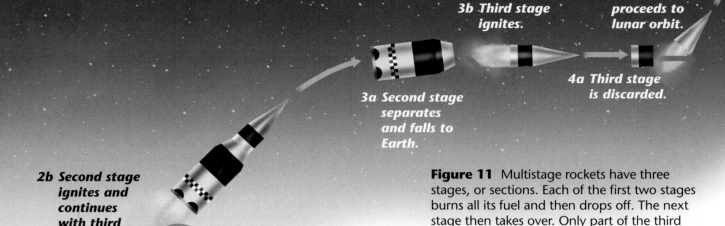

4b Lunar vehicle proceeds to lunar orbit.

3b Third stage ignites.

4a Third stage is discarded.

3a Second stage separates and falls to Earth.

2b Second stage ignites and continues with third stage.

2a First stage separates and falls to Earth.

Figure 11 Multistage rockets have three stages, or sections. Each of the first two stages burns all its fuel and then drops off. The next stage then takes over. Only part of the third stage reaches the rocket's destination.

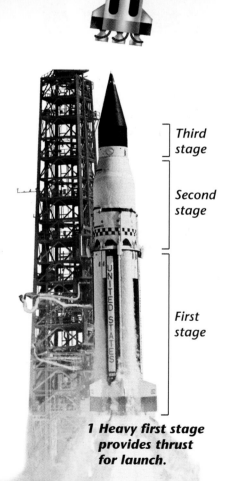

Third stage

Second stage

First stage

1 Heavy first stage provides thrust for launch.

Multistage Rockets

Early rockets, built by the Chinese around the year 1000, used gunpowder as fuel. But gunpowder burns quickly and explosively. A rocket designed to travel out of Earth's atmosphere needs a different sort of fuel that burns slowly and continuously. The American scientist Robert H. Goddard experimented with liquid fuels in the 1920s. He showed that a liquid fuel can provide continuous power. Some solid fuels also burn slowly and continuously.

Another problem remained, however. A rocket can carry only so much fuel. Once the fuel is used up, the rocket falls back to Earth. In 1903, a Russian named Konstantin Tsiolkovsky came up with the idea of multistage rockets. As each stage, or section, of a rocket uses up its fuel, the empty fuel container drops off. Then the next stage ignites and continues up toward the rocket's destination.

The development of powerful multistage rockets in the 1950s and 1960s made it possible to send rockets to the moon and farther into space. Figure 11 shows a rocket similar to the Saturn V that carried the astronauts to the moon. You will learn more about the moon landings in Section 4.

Artificial Satellites

The world was astounded on October 4, 1957, when the Soviet Union launched the first artificial satellite into orbit around Earth. A **satellite** is any natural or artificial object that revolves around an object in space, just as the moon revolves around Earth. This satellite, *Sputnik 1*, revolved around Earth every 96 minutes. Three months later, the United States launched *Explorer 1* into orbit. On April 12, 1961, Yuri Gagarin, a Soviet cosmonaut, orbited Earth, becoming the first person in space.

Since 1957, thousands of artificial satellites, including space stations, have been launched into orbit. **Satellites and space stations are used for communications, navigation, collecting weather data, and research.**

Satellites Artificial satellites are used to relay telephone calls, to measure Earth's atmosphere, and to photograph weather systems, crops, troops, and ships. In addition, two dozen Global Positioning Satellites give off signals that can be picked up by small receivers on Earth. The receiver can then tell you where you are on Earth's surface.

Some satellites are in **geosynchronous orbits,** which means they revolve around Earth at the same rate that Earth rotates. Geosynchronous satellites above the equator seem to hover over a given point on Earth. Geosynchronous satellites are used to relay television signals and to map weather patterns.

Space Stations A space station is a large satellite in which people can live for long periods. The first space station, the Soviet Union's *Salyut,* was launched in 1971. In 1973, the United States launched *Skylab,* which carried a series of telescopes and medical, geological, and astronomical experiments. The former Soviet Union, of which Russia was part, launched the *Mir* space station in 1986. The word *mir* is Russian for "peace." Astronauts from many countries, including Americans, have visited *Mir.* Sixteen countries, including the United States and Russia, are now cooperating to build the International Space Station.

✓ *Checkpoint* **What is a geosynchronous orbit?**

Be a Rocket Scientist
You can build a rocket.

1. Use a plastic or paper cup as the rocket body. Cut out a paper nose cone and tape it to the closed end of the cup.
2. Obtain an empty film canister with a lid that snaps on inside the canister. Go outside to do Steps 3–5.
3. Fill the canister about one-quarter full with water.
4. Put on your goggles. Now add half of a fizzing antacid tablet to the film canister and quickly snap on the lid.
5. Place the canister on the ground with the lid down. Place your rocket over the canister and stand back.

Observing
What action happened inside the film canister? What was the reaction of the rocket?

Figure 12 The International Space Station is a cooperative project involving 16 countries, including the United States, Russia, Japan, and Canada. This is an artist's conception of the station in orbit over Florida.

Figure 13 The Space Shuttle *Discovery* is launched into space by its own rockets as well as by rockets attached to it. *Inferring What is one advantage of a reusable space vehicle?*

Space Shuttles

The Saturn V rockets that carried astronauts to the moon in the 1960s and 1970s were very expensive. In addition, they could not be reused because each stage burned up as it fell back through Earth's atmosphere. In the late 1970s, the National Aeronautics and Space Administration (NASA) developed the reusable space shuttles. They are called shuttles because they can go back and forth, or shuttle, between Earth and space. Since the first shuttle was launched in 1981, space shuttles have been the main way that the United States launches astronauts and equipment into space.

NASA is studying several ideas for building better and less expensive ways of launching people and cargo into space. The ideal vehicle would be an aerospace plane that could take off from a runway, travel into space, and land again on a runway.

Section 3 Review

1. How does a rocket work?
2. Describe three uses of satellites and space stations.
3. Which stage of a multistage rocket reaches the final destination?
4. **Thinking Critically Comparing and Contrasting** What is one way that Saturn V rockets and space shuttles are different?

Science at Home

Landmarks in Space Flight Interview someone who remembers the space programs of the 1950s and 1960s. Prepare your questions in advance, such as: How did you feel when you heard that *Sputnik* was in orbit? How did you feel when the first Americans went into space? Did you watch any of the space flights on television? You may want to record your interview, then write it out in a question-and-answer format.

DISCOVER · ACTIVITY

Why Do Craters Look Different From One Another?

The moon's surface has pits in it, called craters.

1. Put on your goggles. Fill a large plastic basin with 2 cm of sand.

2. Drop marbles of different masses from about 20 cm high. Take the marbles out and view the craters they left.

3. Predict what will happen if you drop marbles from a higher point. Smooth out the sand. Now drop marbles of different masses from about 50 cm high.

4. Take the marbles out and view the craters they left.

Think It Over

Developing Hypotheses In which step do you think the marbles were moving faster when they hit the sand? If objects hitting the moon caused craters, how did the speeds of the objects affect the sizes of the craters? How did the masses of the objects affect the sizes of the craters?

Would you want to take a vacation on the moon? Before you answer, think about these facts. There is no air or liquid water on the moon. Temperatures on the moon's surface range from 100°C, the boiling point of water, to –170°C, well below freezing.

To stay at a comfortable temperature and carry an air supply, the astronauts who landed on the moon had to wear bulky spacesuits. Each spacesuit had a mass of 90 kilograms, about as much as the astronaut himself! Because the moon's gravity is only about one-sixth as strong as Earth's, however, the astronauts were able to leap about like basketball stars despite their heavy spacesuits. What do you think now? Do you still want to go?

GUIDE FOR READING

◆ What features of the moon can be seen with a telescope?

◆ How did the Apollo landings help scientists learn about the moon?

Reading Tip As you read, write down ways in which the moon's surface is similar to Earth's surface.

Figure 14 Astronaut John W. Young jumps up from the moon's surface as he salutes the flag on April 21, 1972. The machine on the left is the *Apollo 16* lunar lander.

The Structure and Origin of the Moon

The moon is 3,476 kilometers in diameter, a little less than the distance across the United States. This diameter is only one fourth Earth's diameter. However, the moon contains only one eightieth as much mass as Earth. Though Earth has a very dense core, the outer layers are less dense. The moon's average density is about the same as the density of Earth's outer layers.

People have long wondered how the moon formed. Scientists have suggested many possible hypotheses. For example, did Earth at one time spin so fast that the material the moon is made of was thrown off? Was the moon formed elsewhere in the solar system and captured by Earth's gravitational pull as it came near? Was the moon formed near Earth at the same time that Earth formed? Scientists have found reasons to reject all of these ideas.

The theory of the moon's origin that best fits the evidence is called the collision theory. It is illustrated in Figure 16. About 4.5 billion years ago, when Earth was very young, an object at least as large as Mars collided with Earth. Material from the object and Earth's outer layers was thrown into orbit around Earth. Eventually, this material combined to form the moon.

Looking at the Moon From Earth

For thousands of years, people could see shapes on the surface of the moon, but didn't know what caused them. The ancient Greeks thought that the moon was perfectly smooth. It was not until about 400 years ago that scientists could study the moon more closely.

Figure 15 The diameter of the moon is a little less than the distance across the United States.

Figure 16 This computer simulation shows the collision theory of the moon's origin. In this theory, a large object struck Earth. The resulting debris formed the moon.

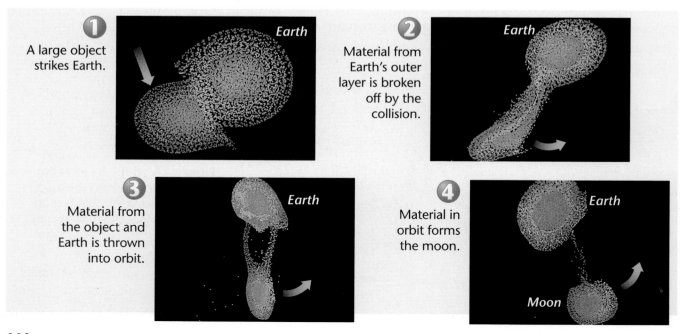

① A large object strikes Earth.

② Material from Earth's outer layer is broken off by the collision.

③ Material from the object and Earth is thrown into orbit.

④ Material in orbit forms the moon.

Earth

Earth

Earth

Earth

Moon

Labels on moon image: Plato, Sea of Rains, Archimedes, Sea of Serenity, Copernicus, Sea of Tranquillity

Figure 17 Astronomers have given names to many of the moon's craters and maria. Copernicus, named after the 16th-century astronomer, is one of the largest craters.

In 1609, the Italian astronomer Galileo Galilei heard about a device that made distant objects appear closer. Galileo soon made his own **telescope** by putting two lenses in a wooden tube. The lenses focused the light coming through the tube, making distant objects seem closer. When Galileo pointed his telescope at the moon, he was able to see much more detail than anyone had ever seen before. **Features on the moon's surface include craters, highlands, and maria.**

Galileo saw that much of the moon's surface is covered with round pits called **craters.** Some craters are hundreds of kilometers across. For 300 years, scientists thought that the craters on the moon had been made by volcanoes. But about 50 years ago, scientists concluded that the craters on the moon were caused by the impacts of meteoroids, rocks from space.

Galileo inferred that some of the other features he saw were highlands, or mountains. The peaks of the highlands and the rims of the craters cast dark shadows, which Galileo could see.

The moon's surface also has dark, flat areas, which Galileo called **maria** (MAH ree uh), the Latin word for "seas." Each one is a "mare" (MAH ray). Galileo thought that the maria might be oceans. Scientists now know that there are no oceans on the moon. The maria are low, dry areas that were flooded with molten material billions of years ago. Since you always see the same maria and craters from Earth, you can tell that the moon always shows the same face to Earth.

☑ Checkpoint What are maria?

Visual Arts
CONNECTION

When Galileo observed the moon, he drew pictures like the one below. Galileo had been trained as an artist, so he interpreted his observations as an artist would. Light and shadow are used in art to create the appearance of three-dimensional forms.

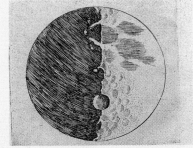

Galileo saw the areas of light and shadow on the moon and concluded that the surface of the moon was not smooth.

In Your Journal

Under a bright light, set up an arrangement of objects. Sketch the outline of the objects. Then observe where the shadows fall. Shade in those areas. Notice how adding shading makes your drawing look more real.

Missions to the Moon

"I believe that this nation should commit itself to achieving the goal, before this decade is out, of landing a man on the moon and returning him safely to Earth." With these words from a May 1961 speech, President John F. Kennedy launched an enormous program of space exploration and scientific research.

Exploring the Moon Between 1964 and 1972, the United States and the Soviet Union sent dozens of rockets to explore the moon. Until spacecraft went to the moon, no one knew what its surface was like. Would spacecraft landing on the moon sink deep into thick dust and be lost? When *Surveyor* spacecraft landed on the moon, they didn't sink in, thus showing that the surface was solid. Lunar orbiters then photographed the moon's surface, so scientists could find a flat, safe spot for a rocket to land.

The Moon Landings In July 1969 three astronauts circled the moon in *Apollo 11*. Once in orbit around the moon, Neil Armstrong and Buzz Aldrin got into a tiny Lunar Module called *Eagle*, leaving Michael Collins in orbit in the Command Module. On July 20, 1969, the *Eagle* descended toward a flat area on the moon's surface called the Sea of Tranquillity. Armstrong and Aldrin were running out of fuel, so they had to find a safe landing spot fast. Billions of people held their breaths as they waited to learn if the astronauts had landed safely on the moon. Finally, a red light flashed on the control panel. "Contact light! Houston, Tranquillity Base here. The *Eagle* has landed," Armstrong radioed to Earth.

After the landing, Armstrong and Aldrin left the *Eagle* to explore the moon. When Armstrong first set foot on the moon, he said, "That's one small step for man, one giant leap for mankind." Armstrong meant to say "That's one small step for *a* man," meaning himself, but in his excitement he never said the "a."

Figure 18 On July 20, 1969, *Apollo 11* astronaut Neil Armstrong became the first person to walk on the moon. He took this photo of Buzz Aldrin, the second person to walk on the moon. *Inferring Why was it important for the lunar module to land on a flat spot?*

Figure 19 Astronauts on later missions had a lunar buggy to help them explore the moon's surface.

On the Surface of the Moon Everything the *Apollo 11* astronauts found was new and exciting. Even looking at their footprints taught the astronauts lessons about the moon's soil. The astronauts bounded around the surface, picking up samples of rocks to bring back to Earth for scientists to study.

In later missions, the astronauts were able to stay on the moon for days instead of hours. They even had a lunar buggy to ride around in. The astronauts were also able to land near the highlands, which were more interesting to study than the flat mare where *Apollo 11* landed.

Moon Rocks and Moonquakes The astronauts brought back to Earth 382 kilograms of moon rocks, about half the mass of a small car. **Much of what scientists have learned about the moon came from detailed study of the moon rocks gathered by astronauts.** Almost all of the rocks were formed from the cooling of molten material, so the moon's surface must once have been very hot. Some of the rocks showed that they had been broken apart by impacts and then reformed. So scientists concluded that meteoroids had bombarded the moon's surface.

The astronauts brought measuring instruments to the moon to record some of the meteoroid impacts. One type of device, known as a seismometer, is used to detect earthquakes on Earth. The seismometers on the moon detected extremely weak moonquakes, the result of changes deep under the moon's surface.

Until the *Apollo* astronauts landed, scientists knew very little about the moon's interior. Another kind of instrument the astronauts left behind measured the amount of heat flowing out from the moon's interior, in order to study what the inside of the moon is like. This instrument showed that the moon has cooled almost completely since it was formed.

✓ *Checkpoint* **What did scientists discover about the interior of the moon as a result of the moon landings?**

Sharpen your **Skills**

Calculating ACTIVITY
If you went to the moon for a vacation, your weight would only be about one sixth of your weight on Earth. To find your weight on the moon, divide your weight by 6.

If you had to wear a spacesuit that weighed as much as you do, what would be your total weight on the moon?

Figure 20 The far side of the moon is much rougher than the side that faces Earth.
Observing What are the round features in this photograph called?

Photographs of the Moon The *Apollo* astronauts circled the moon by rocket and photographed its surface. The pictures show that the far side of the moon is rougher than the near side and has very few maria.

The American *Clementine* spacecraft went to the moon in 1994. It took photographs of the moon through different filters chosen to show what types of minerals are on the moon. The name *Clementine* was chosen because it is the name of the prospector's daughter in the old song "My Darlin' Clementine."

In 1998, the American *Lunar Prospector* spacecraft went to the moon. *Lunar Prospector* mapped the entire moon from an altitude of only 100 kilometers. *Lunar Prospector* found evidence that there is ice frozen into the lunar soil near the moon's poles.

Section 4 Review

1. Name the three kinds of features that Galileo saw on the moon's surface.
2. What did the *Apollo* astronauts do on the moon?
3. How did the craters form on the moon?
4. **Thinking Critically Inferring** Why did scientists once think there were volcanoes on the moon? What evidence from the *Apollo* landings makes this unlikely?

Check Your Progress

CHAPTER PROJECT

Compare your observations of the moon early in the day with observations later that day. How does the moon appear to move in the sky during the course of the day? What happens to the appearance of the moon between earlier and later observations? Is there a pattern for each day? (*Hint:* See whether the same pattern holds true for observations later in the month.)

SECTION 1 Earth in Space

Key Ideas

◆ Astronomy is the study of the moon, stars, and other objects in space.
◆ Earth's rotation on its axis causes day and night.
◆ One complete revolution of Earth around the sun is called a year.
◆ Earth has seasons because its axis is tilted as it revolves around the sun.

Key Terms

astronomy	latitude
axis	solstice
rotation	equinox
revolution	vernal equinox
orbit	autumnal equinox

 SECTION 2 Phases, Eclipses, and Tides

Key Ideas

◆ The moon revolves around Earth and rotates on its own axis.
◆ The phase of the moon you see depends on how much of the sunlit side of the moon faces Earth.
◆ A solar eclipse occurs when the moon passes between Earth and the sun, blocking the sunlight from reaching Earth.
◆ A lunar eclipse occurs when Earth is directly between the moon and the sun, blocking the sunlight from reaching the moon.
◆ Tides occur mainly because of differences in how much the moon pulls on different parts of Earth.

Key Terms

phase	penumbra
eclipse	lunar eclipse
solar eclipse	tide
umbra	gravity

 SECTION 3 Rockets and Satellites

INTEGRATING TECHNOLOGY

Key Ideas

◆ A rocket moves in one direction when gases are expelled from it in the opposite direction.
◆ Satellites and space stations are used for communications, navigation, collecting weather data, and research.

Key Terms

satellite   geosynchronous orbit

SECTION 4 Earth's Moon

Key Ideas

◆ Features on the moon's surface include craters, highlands, and maria.
◆ Much of what scientists have learned about the moon came from detailed study of the moon rocks.

Key Terms

telescope   crater   maria

Organizing Information

Concept Map Copy the concept map about how Earth moves in space onto a sheet of paper. Then complete it and add a title. (For more on concept maps, see the Skills Handbook.)

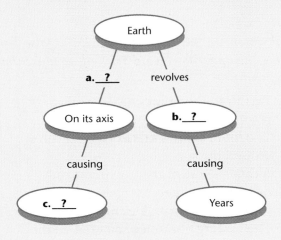

Reviewing Content

 For more review of key concepts, see the Interactive Student Tutorial CD-ROM.

Multiple Choice

Choose the letter of the answer that best completes each statement.

1. The movement of Earth around the sun once a year is Earth's
   a. orbit.
   b. rotation.
   c. revolution.
   d. axis.
2. The darkest part of a shadow is the
   a. umbra.
   b. penumbra.
   c. eclipse.
   d. phase.
3. When Earth's shadow falls on the moon, the shadow causes a
   a. new moon.
   b. solar eclipse.
   c. full moon.
   d. lunar eclipse.
4. A satellite in geosynchronous orbit revolves around Earth once each
   a. hour.
   b. week.
   c. month.
   d. day.
5. The craters on the moon were caused by
   a. highlands.   b. volcanoes.
   c. meteoroid impacts.   d. maria.

True or False

If the statement is true, write true. If it is false, change the underlined word or words to make the statement true.

6. Earth's spinning on its axis is called <u>revolution</u>.
7. The tilt of Earth's axis as Earth revolves around the sun causes <u>eclipses</u>.
8. A total eclipse of the <u>sun</u> occurs only during a new moon.
9. Many <u>artificial satellites</u> orbit Earth.
10. The cooling of molten material on the moon formed the <u>craters</u>.

Checking Concepts

11. Describe the shape of Earth's orbit.
12. Mars's axis is tilted at about the same angle as Earth's axis. Do you think Mars has seasons? Explain your answer.
13. How does the time it takes the moon to rotate on its axis compare with the time it takes the moon to revolve around Earth?
14. Why isn't there a lunar eclipse every month?
15. Why do more people see a total lunar eclipse than a total solar eclipse?
16. Why is there a high tide on the side of Earth closest to the moon? On the side of Earth furthest from the moon?
17. What basic law of physics explains how a rocket moves forward?
18. Describe the events that formed the moon, according to the collision theory.
19. What did scientists learn by studying the rocks astronauts brought back from the moon?
20. **Writing to Learn** Imagine that trips to the moon are resuming. You are an astronaut going to the moon. Write a paragraph describing what you see as you arrive. What does the sky look like? What could the rocks you find help scientists learn?

Thinking Critically

21. **Relating Cause and Effect** How does the position of the moon cause high and low tides on Earth?
22. **Applying Concepts** At what time does the full moon rise? Is it visible in the eastern sky or the western sky?
23. **Posing Questions** Suppose you were assigned to design a spacesuit for astronauts to wear on the moon. What questions about the moon would you need to have answered in order to design the spacesuit?

Applying Skills

Use the illustration below to answer Questions 24–26. (Hint: The tilt of the Earth's axis is 23.5°.)

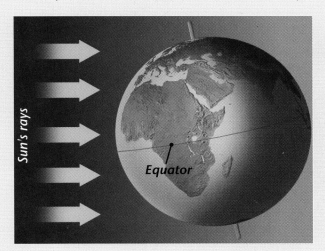

Sun's rays

Equator

24. Interpreting Diagrams On which hemisphere are the sun's rays falling most directly?

25. Inferring In the Northern Hemisphere, is it the summer solstice, winter solstice, or one of the equinoxes? How do you know?

26. Predicting Six months after this illustration, Earth will have revolved halfway around the sun. Show in a sketch which end of Earth's axis will be tilted toward the sun.

Performance ▽ Assessment
CHAPTER PROJECT

Present Your Project Now you are ready to present your log, map, and drawings. Here are some ways you can graph your data: time of moonrise for each date; how often you saw the moon at each compass direction; how often you saw the moon at a specific time. Display your graphs. Discuss any patterns you discovered with your classmates. With your classmates, predict when and where you can see the moon.

Reflect and Record In your journal, write about the easiest and hardest parts of this project. What would you do differently if you observed the moon for another month? What observation(s) surprised you? Why?

Test Preparation
Use these questions to prepare for standardized tests.

Study the diagram. Then answer Questions 27–30. Numbers 1, 2, 3, and 4 on the diagram indicate locations of the moon in its orbit around Earth.

27. About how much time does it take the moon to revolve once around Earth?
  a. one day
  b. 7 days
  c. 27 days
  d. one year

28. Which of the following phases is the moon in at location 1?
  a. new   **b.** crescent
  c. half   **d.** full

29. At which location(s) could a lunar eclipse occur?
  a. 1 only   **b.** 3 only
  c. 1 and 3   **d.** 2 and 4

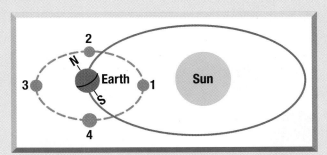

30. Only one side of the moon is visible from Earth because
  a. the moon does not rotate on its axis.
  b. the moon does not revolve around Earth.
  c. the moon is in a geosynchronous orbit around Earth.
  d. the moon revolves once and rotates once in the same period of time.

CHAPTER 20 The Solar System

This artist's conception shows the *Cassini* space probe arriving near Saturn's rings in 2004.

WEB ACTIVITY www.phschool.com

SECTION **1** Observing the Solar System

Discover How Do Mass and Speed Affect an Object's Motion?
Try This A Loopy Ellipse

SECTION **2** The Sun

Discover How Can You Safely Observe the Sun?
Try This Viewing Sunspots
Science at Home Solar Symbols
Real-World Lab Stormy Sunspots

SECTION **3** The Inner Planets

Discover How Does Mars Look From Earth?
Sharpen Your Skills Graphing
Try This Remote Control

668

CHAPTER 20 PROJECT

Model of the Solar System

I f you could drive from Earth to the sun at 100 kilometers per hour, your trip would take 170 years. And most distances in the solar system are even greater! The *Cassini* space probe left Earth for Saturn in 1997 traveling much faster than highway speed, but will not arrive at Saturn's rings until 2004. Sizes in the solar system can be huge, too. Compared with some of the other planets in the solar system, Earth is very small. Saturn, for example, is about 10 times Earth's diameter.

In this chapter, you will get to know many of the objects in the solar system. To help you understand the huge distances and sizes, you will design three different scale models of the solar system.

Your Goal To design scale models of the solar system.

To complete this project, you will
◆ design a model to show the planets' distances from the sun
◆ design a model to show the planets' sizes relative to the sun
◆ test different scales to see if you can use the same scale for both size and distance in one model

Get Started Begin by previewing the tables with distances and diameters on pages 683 and 691. Brainstorm with a group of classmates how you will build your models. Prepare a data sheet to record your calculations of scaled-down distances and diameters.

Check Your Progress You will be working on this project as you study this chapter. To keep your project on track, look for Check Your Progress boxes at the following points.
Section 1 Review, page 675: Design a model to show distances.
Section 3 Review, page 689: Design a model to show diameters.
Section 4 Review, page 697: Design one scale model that shows both sizes and distances.

Present Your Project At the end of the chapter (page 711), you will present your design to the class.

SECTION 4 The Outer Planets

Discover How Large Are the Outer Planets?
Try This Model Saturn
Skills Lab Speeding Around the Sun

SECTION 5 Comets, Asteroids, and Meteors

Discover Which Way Do Comet Tails Point?
Science at Home Watch a Meteor Shower

Integrating Life Science

SECTION 6 Is There Life Beyond Earth?

Discover Is Yeast Alive or Not?
Sharpen Your Skills Communicating
Science at Home Message to E.T.

SECTION 1 Observing the Solar System

DISCOVER  ACTIVITY

How Do Mass and Speed Affect an Object's Motion?

1. Have your partner push a toy truck across the table toward you. Stop the truck with your hands.

2. Repeat Step 1, but have your partner push the truck a little faster. Was it easier or harder to stop the truck than in Step 1?

3. Now add some rocks or other heavy objects to the truck and repeat Step 1. Your partner should push the truck at the same speed as in Step 1. How hard was it to stop the truck this time compared to Step 1?

4. Repeat Step 2 with the rocks still in the truck. How hard was it to stop the truck this time?

Think It Over
Predicting How hard would it be to stop the truck if your partner pushed it more slowly? If you added more mass to the truck?

GUIDE FOR READING

◆ How do the heliocentric and geocentric descriptions of the solar system differ?

◆ What did Kepler discover about the orbits of the planets?

◆ What two factors keep the planets in their orbits?

Reading Tip As you read, make a list of the evidence that supports the heliocentric system.

Have you ever lain outdoors on a starry night, gazing up at the stars? As you watch, the stars seem to move across the sky. The sky seems to be rotating right over your head. In fact, from the Northern Hemisphere, the sky appears to rotate around a point near Polaris, the North Star, once every 24 hours.

Now think about what you see every day. During the day, the sun appears to move across the sky. From here on Earth, it seems as if Earth is stationary and that the sun, moon, and stars are all moving around Earth. But is the sky really moving above you? Centuries ago, before there were space shuttles or even telescopes, there was no easy way to find out.

Figure 1 This photo was made by exposing the camera film for several hours. Each star appears as part of a circle, and all the stars seem to revolve around a single point.

Wandering Stars

When the ancient Greeks watched the stars move across the sky, they noticed that the patterns of most of the stars didn't change. Although the stars seemed to move, they stayed in the same position relative to one another. For example, the constellations kept the same shapes from night to night and from year to year.

As they observed the sky more carefully, the Greeks noticed something surprising. Five points of light seemed to wander among the stars. The Greeks called these objects *planets*, from the Greek word meaning "wandering star." The Greeks made very careful observations of the motions of the five planets they could see. You know these planets by the names the ancient Romans later gave them: Mercury, Venus, Mars, Jupiter, and Saturn.

Greek Ideas: Earth at the Center

When you look up at the sky, you can almost imagine that you are under a rotating dome with the stars pasted on it. The Greeks thought that they were inside a rotating dome they called the celestial sphere. Most Greek astronomers believed that the universe is perfect and unchangeable and that Earth is stationary in the center of the celestial sphere. Since *geo* is the Greek word for Earth, an Earth-centered explanation is known as a **geocentric** (jee oh SEN trik) system. **In a geocentric system, Earth is at the center of the revolving planets.**

In A.D. 140, the Greek astronomer Ptolemy (TAHL uh mee) explained the motion of the planets in another way. Like the earlier Greeks, Ptolemy thought that Earth is at the center of the system of planets. Ptolemy also thought that the moon, Mercury, Venus, the sun, Mars, Jupiter, and Saturn revolve around Earth.

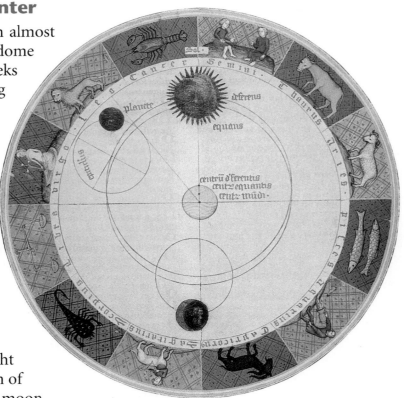

Figure 2 In the 1500s, an astronomy book published this illustration of Ptolemy's system. *Interpreting Diagrams Where is Earth located in this illustration?*

In Ptolemy's explanation, however, the planets move on little circles that move on bigger circles. Ptolemy thought that this explained why the planets seem to move at different speeds, and even backwards, among the stars. For the next 1,400 years, people believed that Ptolemy's ideas were correct.

☑ *Checkpoint* **What is a geocentric system?**

Copernicus's Idea: Sun at the Center

In the early 1500s, the Polish astronomer Nicolaus Copernicus developed another explanation for the motions of the planets. Copernicus thought that the sun is at the center of the system of planets. His sun-centered system is called a **heliocentric** (hee lee oh SEN trik) system. *Helios* is Greek for "sun." **In a heliocentric system, Earth and the other planets revolve around the sun.** Copernicus's explanation included the six planets he knew about: Mercury, Venus, Earth, Mars, Jupiter, and Saturn.

Galileo's Observations

In the 1500s and 1600s, most people still believed Ptolemy's geocentric explanation. However, the Italian astronomer Galileo Galilei, who lived nearly 100 years after Copernicus, thought that the heliocentric explanation was correct.

Recall from Chapter 19 that Galileo was the first scientist to use a telescope to look at objects in the sky. With his telescope, Galileo made two discoveries that supported the heliocentric model. First, Galileo saw four moons revolving around Jupiter. Galileo's observations of Jupiter's moons showed that not everything in the sky revolves around Earth.

Galileo's observations of Venus also supported Copernicus's heliocentric system. Galileo discovered that Venus goes through phases similar to those of Earth's moon. Galileo reasoned that the phases of Venus could not be explained if Earth were at the center of the system of planets. So Ptolemy's geocentric system could not be correct.

Galileo's evidence gradually convinced others that Copernicus's explanation was correct. Today, people talk about the "solar system" rather than the "Earth system." This shows that people accept Copernicus's idea that the sun is at the center.

☑ Checkpoint What two discoveries made by Galileo supported the heliocentric description of the solar system?

Brahe and Kepler

Copernicus and Galileo had correctly identified the sun as the center of the system of planets. But Copernicus, like Ptolemy, assumed that the orbits of the planets are circles.

Copernicus's ideas were based on observations made by the ancient Greeks. In the late 1500s, Tycho Brahe (TEE koh BRAH uh), a Danish astronomer, made

Figure 3 From this observatory, Tycho Brahe made accurate observations of the planets for nearly 20 years. His data became the basis for many important discoveries.

much more accurate observations. Brahe carefully observed the positions of the planets for almost 20 years.

In 1600, a German mathematician, Johannes Kepler, went to work analyzing Brahe's data. Kepler tried to figure out the shape of the planets' orbits. At first, he assumed that the orbits are circles. When Kepler tried to figure out the exact orbit of Mars, however, no circle fit the observations.

Kepler had discovered that the orbit of each planet is an ellipse. An **ellipse** is an elongated circle, or oval shape. Kepler found that if he assumed that Mars's orbit is an ellipse, his calculations fit Brahe's observations better.

Inertia and Gravity

Kepler had discovered the correct shape of the planets' orbits. But he could not explain why the planets stay in orbit. The work of the English scientist Isaac Newton provided the answer to that puzzle. **Newton concluded that two factors—inertia and gravity—combine to keep the planets in orbit.**

Galileo had discovered that a moving object will continue to move until some force acts to stop its motion. This tendency of a moving object to continue in a straight line or a stationary object to remain in place is the object's **inertia.** The more mass an object has, the more inertia it has. As you found if you did the Discover activity, an object with greater inertia is more difficult to start or stop.

Isaac Newton picked up where Galileo had left off. Late in his life, Newton told the story of how watching an apple fall from a tree in 1665 had made him think about motion. He hypothesized that the same force that pulls the apple to the ground also pulls the moon toward Earth. This force, called gravity, attracts all

Figure 4 Newton was a man of many achievements. Among them was the invention of this telescope.

Chapter 20 **673**

A Loopy Ellipse

You can draw an ellipse.

1. ✂ Carefully stick two pushpins about 10 cm apart through a sheet of white paper on top of corrugated cardboard.

2. Tie the ends of a 30-cm piece of string together. Place the string around the pushpins.

3. Keeping the string tight, move a pencil around inside the string.

4. Now place the pushpins 5 cm apart. Repeat Step 3.

Predicting How does changing the distance between the pushpins affect the ellipse's shape? What shape would you draw if you used only one pushpin?

Mercury 58,000,000 km
Venus 108,000,000 km
Earth 150,000,000 km
Mars 228,000,000 km

Jupiter
778,000,000 km

Saturn
1,427,000,000 km

objects toward one another. The strength of gravity depends on the masses of the objects and the distance between them.

Newton figured out that Earth keeps pulling the moon toward it with gravity. At the same time, the moon keeps moving ahead because of its inertia. Earth curves away as the moon falls toward it, so the moon winds up in orbit around Earth.

In the same way, the planets are in orbit around the sun because the sun's gravity pulls on them while their inertia keeps them moving ahead. Therefore, the planets keep moving around the sun and end up in orbit.

Figure 5 If there were no force of gravity, inertia would make a planet travel in a straight line. But because gravity pulls the planet toward the sun, the planet actually travels in an elliptical orbit around the sun. *Interpreting Diagrams What would happen if a planet had no inertia?*

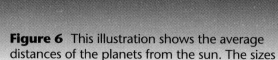

Uranus
2,871,000,000 km

Neptune
4,497,000,000 km

Pluto
5,913,000,000 km

Figure 6 This illustration shows the average distances of the planets from the sun. The sizes of the planets and the sun are not to scale.

More to Discover

Since Newton's time, our knowledge about the solar system has increased dramatically. Newton knew of the same six planets the ancient Greeks had known—Mercury, Venus, Earth, Mars, Jupiter, and Saturn. Now astronomers know three more planets—Uranus, Neptune, and Pluto. Astronomers have also identified many other objects in the solar system, such as comets and asteroids, that you will learn about later in this chapter.

Galileo and Newton used telescopes on Earth to observe the solar system. Astronomers still use telescopes on Earth, but they have also made close-up observations of the planets from space probes sent far into the solar system. Our understanding of the solar system continues to change every day. Who knows what new discoveries will be made in your lifetime!

Section 1 Review

1. How is Copernicus's description of the system of planets different from Ptolemy's description?
2. How did Galileo's observations of Jupiter's moons help to show that the geocentric explanation is incorrect?
3. What shape are the orbits of the planets? How was the discovery of this orbit shape made?
4. What two factors act together to keep the planets in orbit around the sun?
5. **Thinking Critically Applying Concepts** People usually say that the sun rises in the east, moves across the sky, and sets in the west. Is this description literally correct? Explain.

Check Your Progress

CHAPTER
PROJECT

Begin by making a table that shows the distances of the planets from the sun. To help visualize the solar system, you can reduce all the distances by the same amount: for example, divide all distances by 100,000 or 1,000,000. You can use the resulting smaller numbers to design a scale model of the solar system. Record your calculations on your data sheet. Now choose a different scale and repeat your calculations. Which scale makes it easier to see the relative distances between the planets and the sun?

The Sun

DISCOVER

ACTIVITY

How Can You Safely Observe the Sun?

1. Clamp a pair of binoculars to a ring stand.

2. Cut a hole in a 20-cm by 28-cm sheet of thin cardboard so that it will fit over the binoculars, as shown in the photo. The cardboard should cover one lens, but allow light through the other lens. Tape the cardboard on securely. **CAUTION:** *Never look directly at the sun. You will hurt your eyes if you do.*

3. Use the binoculars to project an image of the sun onto a sheet of white paper. The cardboard will shade the paper. Change the focus and move the paper back and forth until you get a sharp image.

Think It Over
Observing Draw what you see on the paper. What do you see on the surface of the sun?

GUIDE FOR READING

◆ **How does the sun get its energy?**

◆ **What are the layers of the sun's atmosphere?**

◆ **What are some features of the sun's surface?**

Reading Tip As you read, write a sentence defining each boldfaced term in your own words.

The sun's gravity is by far the most powerful force in the solar system—strong enough to hold all of the planets and comets in orbit! The sun's gravity is so strong because the sun's mass is very large. In fact, 99.8 percent of the mass of the solar system is in the sun.

Like Earth, the sun has an interior and an atmosphere. Unlike Earth, however, the sun does not have a solid surface. The sun is a ball of glowing gas. About three fourths of the sun's mass is hydrogen, one fourth is helium, and very small amounts are other chemical elements.

The Sun's Interior

The interior of the sun is like a giant furnace. Like furnaces in houses, the sun produces energy. But the sun does not get its energy from burning fuels such as oil. **Instead, the sun's energy comes from nuclear fusion.** In the process of **nuclear fusion,** hydrogen atoms join together to form helium. Nuclear fusion occurs only under conditions of extremely high temperature and pressure. The temperature inside the sun's **core,** or center, reaches about 15 million degrees Celsius, high enough for nuclear fusion to occur.

The total mass of the helium produced by nuclear fusion is slightly less than the total mass of the hydrogen that goes into it. The change in mass occurs because some of the matter is converted into energy, including light and heat. The light and heat gradually move from the core of the sun to its atmosphere and escape into space. Some of this light and heat reach Earth, becoming Earth's main source of energy.

There is enough hydrogen fuel in the core of the sun to last for a total of 10 billion years. The sun is now only about 5 billion years old, so you don't have to worry about the sun "burning out" any time soon!

✓ *Checkpoint* *Where in the sun does nuclear fusion occur?*

The Sun's Atmosphere

The sun's atmosphere has three layers: the photosphere, the chromosphere, and the corona. There are no boundaries between the layers of the sun.

The Photosphere The inner layer of the sun's atmosphere is called the **photosphere** (FOH tuh sfeer). The Greek word *photo* means "light," so *photosphere* means the sphere that makes light. When you look at an image or photograph of the sun, you are looking at the photosphere.

The Chromosphere During a total solar eclipse, the moon blocks light from the photosphere. The photosphere no longer provides the glare that keeps you from seeing the sun's faint, outer layers. At the beginning and end of a total eclipse, you can see a reddish glow just around the photosphere. This glow comes from the middle layer of the sun's atmosphere, the **chromosphere.** The Greek word *chromo* means "color," so the chromosphere is the "color sphere."

The Corona In the middle of a total solar eclipse, the moon also blocks light from the chromosphere. At these times an even fainter layer of the sun becomes visible, as you can see in Figure 7. This outer layer, which looks like a white halo around the sun, is called the **corona,** which means "crown" in Latin. From Earth's surface, the corona is only visible during eclipses or from special telescopes. But astronomers can use telescopes in space to observe the corona all the time and to study how it changes.

Figure 7 During a total solar eclipse, you can see light from the corona, the outer layer of the sun's atmosphere. *Inferring Why is it easiest to photograph the sun's outer layers during a solar eclipse?*

Viewing Sunspots

You can observe changes in the number of sunspots.

1. Make a data table to record the average number of sunspots you see each day.

2. Decide on a time to look for sunspots each day.

3. View the sun in the way described in the Discover activity. **CAUTION:** *Never look directly at the sun. You will hurt your eyes if you do.*

4. Make and record your observations.

Interpreting Data How much did the average number of sunspots change from day to day?

The corona sends out a stream of electrically charged particles called **solar wind.** Normally Earth's atmosphere and magnetic field block these particles. However, near the North and South poles, the particles can enter Earth's atmosphere, where they hit gas molecules and cause them to glow. The result is rippling sheets of light in the sky called auroras.

☑ *Checkpoint* During what event could you see the sun's corona?

Features on the Sun

For hundreds of years, scientists have used telescopes to look at the sun. (To protect their eyes, they used a filter or projected the sun onto a white surface, as in the Discover activity.) The dark spots that they saw on the sun's surface became known as sunspots. The spots seemed to move across the sun's surface, which showed that the sun rotates on its axis, just as Earth does. **Features on or above the sun's surface include sunspots, prominences, and solar flares.**

Sunspots As you can see in Figure 8, sunspots look like small, dark areas on the sun's surface. But in fact, they can be as large as Earth. **Sunspots** are areas of gas on the sun that are cooler than the gases around them. Cooler gases don't give off as much light as hotter gases, which is why sunspots look darker than the rest of the photosphere.

Figure 8 Sunspots are areas of gas on the sun that are cooler than the gas around them. Many of the sunspots in these photos are about as large as Earth.

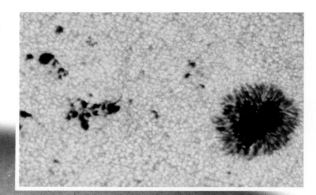

The number of sunspots on the sun varies over a period of 10 or 11 years. Some scientists have hypothesized that short-term changes in climate on Earth may be related to sunspot cycles. Satellites have recently collected data that show that the amount of energy the sun produces changes slightly from year to year. Some scientists think that these increases and decreases, which may be linked to the number of sunspots, may cause changes in Earth's temperature. Scientists need to make more observations in order to test this hypothesis.

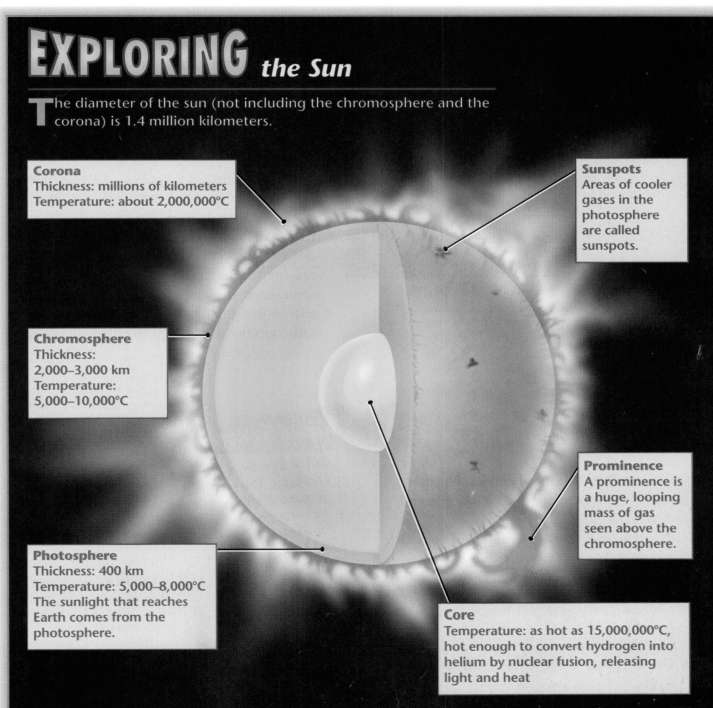

EXPLORING *the Sun*

The diameter of the sun (not including the chromosphere and the corona) is 1.4 million kilometers.

Corona
Thickness: millions of kilometers
Temperature: about 2,000,000°C

Sunspots
Areas of cooler gases in the photosphere are called sunspots.

Chromosphere
Thickness: 2,000–3,000 km
Temperature: 5,000–10,000°C

Prominence
A prominence is a huge, looping mass of gas seen above the chromosphere.

Photosphere
Thickness: 400 km
Temperature: 5,000–8,000°C
The sunlight that reaches Earth comes from the photosphere.

Core
Temperature: as hot as 15,000,000°C, hot enough to convert hydrogen into helium by nuclear fusion, releasing light and heat

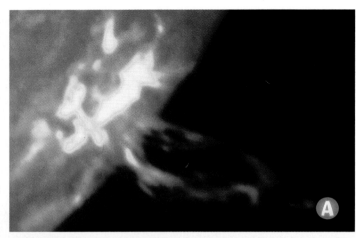

Figure 9 **A.** Prominences are huge loops of gas that connect different parts of sunspot regions. **B.** Solar flares on the sun release large amounts of energy. *Relating Cause and Effect How can solar flares affect communications on Earth?*

Prominences Sunspots usually occur in pairs or groups. Reddish loops of gas called **prominences** link different parts of sunspot regions. When a group of sunspots is near the edge of the sun as seen from Earth, these loops can stick out over the edge of the sun. If an eclipse hides the sun's photosphere, astronomers are able to see these loops. Prominences are about the same temperature as the sun's chromosphere, about 10,000 degrees Celsius.

Solar Flares Sometimes the loops in sunspot regions suddenly connect, releasing large amounts of energy. The energy heats gas on the sun to millions of degrees Celsius, causing the hydrogen gas to explode out into space. These explosions are known as **solar flares.**

Solar flares can greatly increase the solar wind from the corona, resulting in an increase in the number of particles reaching Earth's atmosphere. These solar wind particles can affect Earth's upper atmosphere, causing magnetic storms. Magnetic storms sometimes disrupt radio, telephone, and television signals. Magnetic storms can also cause electrical power problems for homes and businesses.

Section 2 Review

1. How is energy produced in the sun's core?
2. Name the layers of the sun's atmosphere.
3. What is the solar wind?
4. Describe three features found on or above the surface of the sun.
5. Why do sunspots look darker than the rest of the sun's photosphere?
6. How does the number of sunspots change over time?
7. **Thinking Critically Comparing and Contrasting** What is the difference between a prominence and a solar flare?

Science at Home

Solar Symbols As the source of heat and light, the sun is an important symbol in many cultures. With family members, look around your home and neighborhood for illustrations of the sun on signs, flags, clothing, and in artwork. Which parts of the sun's atmosphere do the illustrations show? Describe the layers of the sun's atmosphere to your family.

STORMY SUNSPOTS

Problem

How are magnetic storms on Earth related to sunspot activity?

Skills Focus

graphing, interpreting data

Materials

graph paper   pencil   straightedge

Procedure

1. Use the data in the table to make a line graph of sunspot activity between 1967 and 1997.
2. On the graph, label the *x*-axis "Year." Use a scale with 2-year intervals, from 1967 to 1997.
3. Label the *y*-axis "Sunspot Number." Use a scale of 0 through 160 in intervals of 10.
4. Graph a point for the Sunspot Number for each year.
5. Complete your graph by drawing lines to connect the points.

Sunspots			
Year	**Sunspot Number**	**Year**	**Sunspot Number**
1967	93.8	1983	66.6
1969	105.0	1985	17.9
1971	66.6	1987	29.4
1973	38.0	1989	157.6
1975	15.5	1991	145.7
1977	27.5	1993	54.6
1979	155.4	1995	17.5
1981	140.4	1997	23.4

Analyze and Conclude

1. Based on your graph, which years had the highest Sunspot Numbers? The lowest Sunspot Numbers?
2. How often does the cycle of maximum and minimum activity repeat?
3. When was the most recent maximum sunspot activity? The most recent minimum sunspot activity?
4. Compare your sunspot graph with the magnetic storms graph. What relationship can you infer between periods of high sunspot activity and magnetic storms? Explain.
5. **Apply** During which years do you think electrical disturbances on Earth were most common?

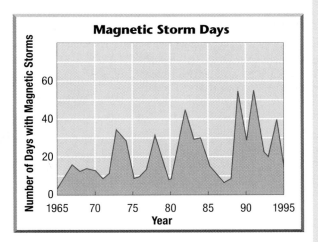

Magnetic Storm Days

More to Explore

Using the pattern of sunspot activity you found, predict the number of peaks you would expect in the next 30 years. Around which years would you expect the peaks to occur?

SECTION 3 The Inner Planets

DISCOVER ·············· ACTIVITY

How Does Mars Look From Earth?

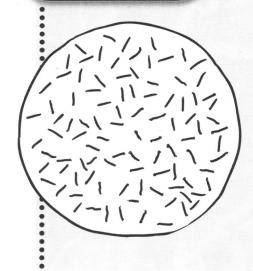

1. Work in pairs. On a sheet of paper, draw a circle 20 cm across to represent Mars. Draw about 100 small lines, each about 1 cm long, at random places inside the circle.

2. Have your partner look at your drawing of Mars from the other side of the room. Your partner should draw what he or she sees.

3. Compare your original drawing with what your partner drew. Then look at your own drawing from across the room.

Think It Over

Observing Did your partner draw any connecting lines that were not actually on your drawing? What can you conclude about the accuracy of descriptions of other planets as observed from Earth?

GUIDE FOR READING

◆ What are the main characteristics of the inner planets?

Reading Tip As you read about each planet, write down the similarities and differences between that planet and Earth.

Where could you find a planet whose surface is hot enough to melt lead? How about a planet whose atmosphere has almost entirely leaked away? And how about a planet with volcanoes higher than any on Earth? Finally, what about a planet with oceans of water brimming with fish and other life? These are descriptions of the four planets closest to the sun, known as the inner planets

Earth and the other three inner planets—Mercury, Venus, and Mars—are more similar to each other than they are to the five outer planets. **The four inner planets are small and have rocky surfaces.** These planets are often called the **terrestrial planets,** from the Latin word *terra,* which means "Earth." Figure 10 gives a summary of information about the inner planets.

Earth

Our planet's atmosphere extends more than 100 kilometers above Earth's surface. The oxygen you need to live makes up about 20 percent of the gases in Earth's atmosphere. Almost all the rest is nitrogen gas, with small amounts of argon and other gases. Earth's atmosphere also contains water vapor and clouds of water droplets. From space, astronauts can usually see past the clouds to Earth's surface.

Most of Earth, about 70 percent, is covered with water. Perhaps the planet should be named "Water" instead of "Earth"! No other planet in our solar system has oceans like Earth's.

682

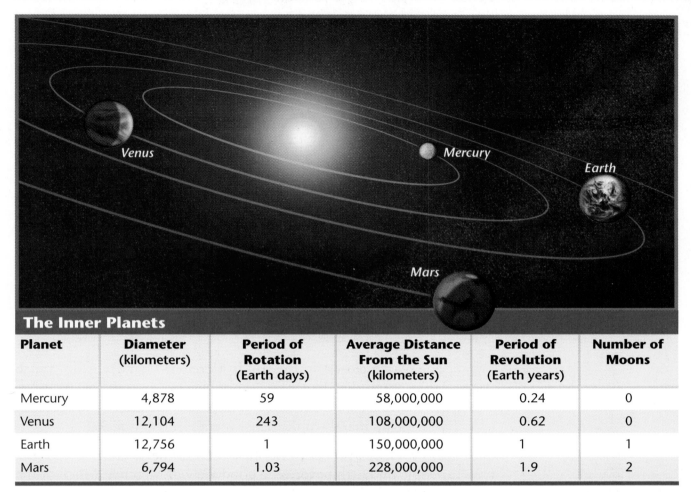

The Inner Planets

Planet	Diameter (kilometers)	Period of Rotation (Earth days)	Average Distance From the Sun (kilometers)	Period of Revolution (Earth years)	Number of Moons
Mercury	4,878	59	58,000,000	0.24	0
Venus	12,104	243	108,000,000	0.62	0
Earth	12,756	1	150,000,000	1	1
Mars	6,794	1.03	228,000,000	1.9	2

Figure 10 The inner planets take up only a small part of the solar system. The diameter of the entire solar system is more than 25 times the diameter of Mars's orbit.

INTEGRATING EARTH SCIENCE As you recall from Chapter 4, Earth has three main layers—a crust, a mantle, and a core. The crust includes the solid rocky surface. Under the crust is the mantle, a layer of hot molten rock. When volcanoes erupt, this hot material rises to the surface. Earth has a dense inner core made up mainly of iron and nickel. The outer core is liquid, but the inner core is probably solid.

Scientists have been studying Earth for many years. They use what they know about Earth to make inferences about the other planets. For example, when astronomers find volcanoes on other planets, they infer that these planets have or once had hot material inside them. As we continue to learn more about our own planet, scientists will be able to apply that new knowledge to the study of the other planets.

Figure 11 Earth has a solid, rocky surface. *Interpreting Diagrams What are Earth's three main layers?*

Crust
Mantle
Outer core
Inner core

Figure 12 This photo of Mercury and the closeup view of some of its craters (inset) were taken by the *Mariner 10* space probe.

Mercury

The planet closest to the sun is Mercury. Mercury is not much larger than Earth's moon and has no moons of its own. Astronomers have been able to infer that the interior of Mercury is made up mainly of the dense metals iron and nickel.

Exploring Mercury Because Mercury is so close to the sun, people on Earth never get a good view of Mercury. Much of the knowledge that astronomers have about Mercury's surface came from a single probe, *Mariner 10,* in 1974. *Mariner 10* photographed only half of Mercury's surface, so astronomers still don't know what the rest of Mercury is like.

Mariner 10's photographs show that, like the moon, Mercury has many flat plains and many craters on its surface. The craters on Mercury have been named for artists, writers, and musicians, including the composers Bach and Mozart.

Mercury's Atmosphere Mercury has an extremely thin atmosphere. Apparently the gases Mercury once had were heated so much that the gas particles moved very fast. Since they were moving so fast, the gas particles escaped from Mercury's weak gravity into space. However, astronomers have detected small amounts of sodium and other gases in Mercury's atmosphere.

Mercury is a planet of extremes. It is so close to the sun that during the day, the side facing the sun reaches temperatures of 430°C. Because Mercury has almost no atmosphere, at night all the heat escapes into space. The temperature drops to −170°C. Mercury thus has a greater range of temperatures than any other planet in the solar system.

☑ *Checkpoint* *Why is it difficult for astronomers to learn about Mercury?*

Venus

Whenever you see a bright object in the west after sunset, it is probably Venus. When Venus shines brightly like that, it is known as the "evening star," though of course it really isn't a star. Stars shine with their own light, while Venus shines because it is reflecting light from the sun, just as the other planets and moons do. At other times, you see Venus rise before the sun in the morning. It is then known as the "morning star." At still other times, Venus is too close to the sun in the sky for you to see it from Earth.

Venus is so similar in size to Earth that it is sometimes called Earth's twin. Astronomers also think that the density and internal structure of Venus are similar to Earth's. However, in many other ways, Venus is very different from Earth.

Venus's Rotation   Venus takes about 7.5 Earth months to revolve around the sun. It takes about 8 months for Venus to rotate on its axis. Venus rotates so slowly that its "day" is longer than its "year." Oddly, Venus rotates from east to west, the opposite direction from most other planets and moons. This type of rotation is called **retrograde rotation,** from the Latin words for "moving backward." One hypothesis proposed by astronomers to explain this unusual rotation is that Venus was struck by a very large object billions of years ago. Such a collision could have caused the direction of its rotation to change.

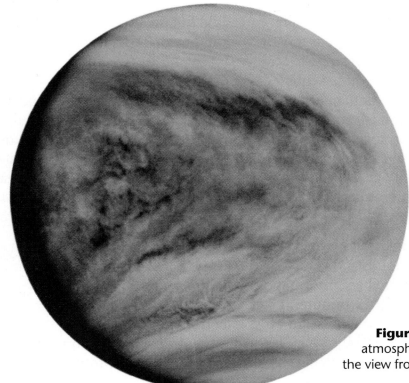

Figure 13 The thick atmosphere of Venus makes the view from space a cloudy one.

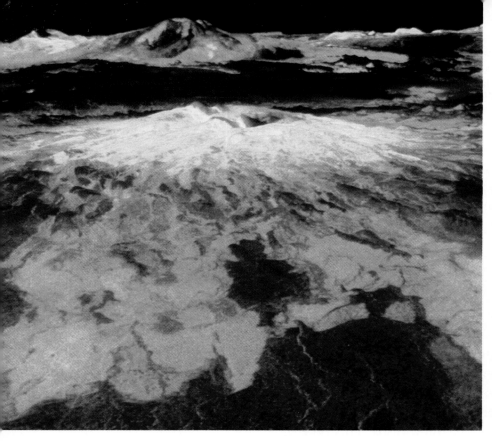

Figure 14 The *Magellan* spacecraft used radar to penetrate Venus's clouds. This three-dimensional image of a volcano on Venus was created by a computer using radar data. The height of the mountains is exaggerated to make them stand out.

Venus's Atmosphere The atmosphere of Venus is so thick that every day is a cloudy one. Venus never has a sunny day. From Earth, astronomers see only a smooth cloud cover over Venus all the time.

If you could stand on the surface of Venus, you would quickly be crushed by the weight of its atmosphere. The pressure of Venus's atmosphere is 90 times greater than the pressure of Earth's atmosphere. You could not breathe on Venus because its atmosphere is mostly carbon dioxide. Also, its clouds are partly made of sulfuric acid.

Because Venus is closer to the sun than Earth, it gets more solar energy than Earth does. Ordinary light from the sun can penetrate Venus's atmosphere and hit its surface. The surface heats up and then gives off heat. Carbon dioxide traps this heat in the atmosphere. So Venus's surface becomes hotter and hotter, until it is about 460°C—hot enough to melt lead. This trapping of heat by the atmosphere is called the **greenhouse effect.**

Exploring Venus About 20 spacecraft have visited Venus, more than have visited any other planet. Some have even penetrated its clouds and landed on its surface. The first spacecraft to land and send back information, *Venera 7,* landed in 1970 but survived for only 23 minutes. Later spacecraft were more durable and sent back pictures and other data from Venus's surface.

Scientists have learned most of what they know about Venus's surface from data collected by the *Magellan* probe. The *Magellan* probe reached Venus in 1990, carrying radar instruments. Radar works through clouds, so *Magellan* was able to map Venus's entire surface.

The *Magellan* views are so detailed that computers can be used to figure out what Venus would look like if you could fly just above its surface. Figure 14 shows one of these radar images. Venus is covered with rock, similar to many rocky areas on Earth. Venus has volcanoes with lava flows, many craters, and strange domes not found on other planets.

☑ *Checkpoint* **Why is the surface of Venus so hot?**

Mars

Mars is called the "red planet" because it has a slightly reddish tinge when you see it in the sky. The atmosphere of Mars is mostly carbon dioxide and has only 1 percent the pressure of Earth's atmosphere. You could walk around on Mars, but you would have to wear an airtight suit and carry your own air, like a scuba diver. Mars has clouds but they are very thin compared to the clouds on Earth.

Canals on Mars? In 1877, an Italian astronomer, Giovanni Schiaparelli (sky ah puh REL ee), announced that he had seen long, straight lines on Mars. He called them *canale,* or channels. In the 1890s and early 1900s, Percival Lowell, an American astronomer, convinced many people that these lines were canals that had been built by intelligent Martians to carry water. Astronomers now know that Schiaparelli and Lowell were mistaken. There are no canals on Mars, or even channels that can be seen from Earth.

Astronomers have found that some water remains on Mars in the form of ice at its north pole, as shown in Figure 15. Mars' south pole has an ice cap made mostly of frozen carbon dioxide. Unlike Earth's ice caps, Mars' polar ice caps are covered by a layer of frozen carbon dioxide during each hemisphere's winter.

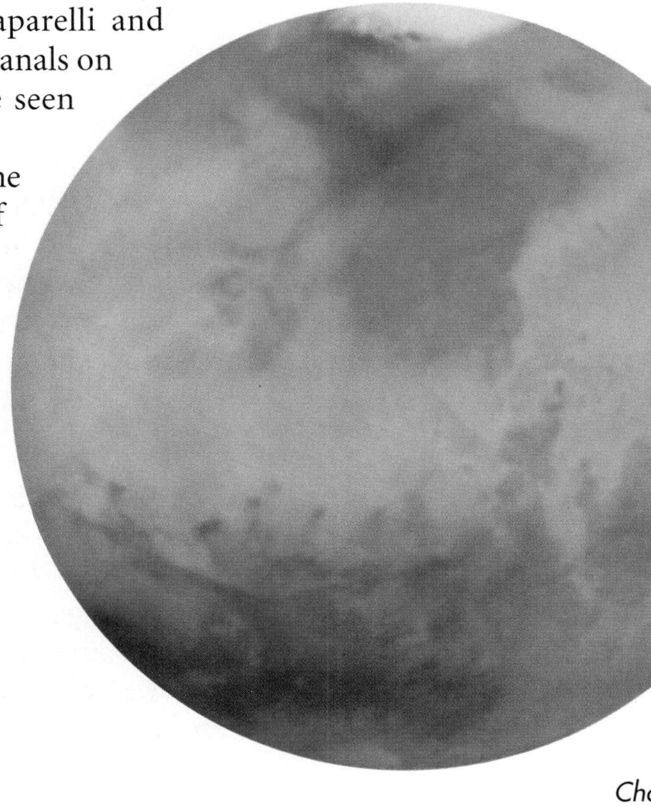

Figure 15 Because of its thin atmosphere and its distance from the sun, Mars is quite cold. Mars has ice caps at both poles.

Seasons on Mars Because the axis of Mars is tilted, Mars has seasons just as Earth does. As the seasons change on the dusty surface of Mars, wind storms arise and blow the dust around. Since the dust is blown off some regions, these regions look darker. A hundred years ago, some people thought these regions looked darker because plants were growing there. Astronomers now realize that it is just that wind storms blow dust off the surface.

Exploring Mars The United States has sent many spacecraft to Mars. The first ones, in the 1960s, seemed to show that Mars is barren and covered with craters like the moon. Later spacecraft showed that regions of Mars have giant volcanoes. Astronomers see signs that hot material flowed down the volcanoes in the past, but they don't think the volcanoes are active now.

In 1976, two NASA spacecraft, *Viking 1* and *Viking 2*, landed on Mars. They sent back close-up pictures from Mars's surface. The pictures showed that the rocks look red because they are covered with a rusty dust. Other parts of the *Viking* spacecraft went into orbit around Mars, sending back detailed pictures.

In 1997, *Mars Pathfinder* landed on Mars. As Figure 16 shows, close-up photographs from *Mars Pathfinder* show no oceans or even puddles of water. Photographs taken from space do show evidence that water flowed on Mars millions of years ago.

Figure 16 The surface of Mars is rugged and rocky. The object at the bottom of the photo is the *Mars Pathfinder* lander. You can see the remote-control rover *Sojourner* in the middle of the photo.

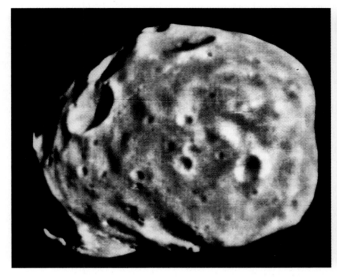

Figure 17 Phobos (left) and Deimos (right) are Mars's two small, crater-covered moons.

Mars Pathfinder carried a microwave-sized remote-control rover, called *Sojourner*, that investigated rocks on Mars. Also in 1997, another probe, *Mars Global Surveyor*, arrived in orbit around Mars, where it began mapping and photographing all of the planet's surface in detail.

Mars's Moons Mars has two very small moons. Phobos, the larger moon, is only 27 kilometers in diameter, about the distance a car can travel on the highway in 15 minutes. Deimos is even smaller, only 15 kilometers in diameter. Close-up views from space show that, like Earth's moon, Phobos and Deimos are covered with craters.

Section 3 Review

1. What features do all of the inner planets have in common?
2. What is Mercury's atmosphere like? Explain.
3. Why can astronomers see the surface of Mars clearly, but not the surface of Venus?
4. How have astronomers been able to study the surface of Venus?
5. What evidence do astronomers have that water once flowed on Mars?
6. **Thinking Critically Relating Cause and Effect** Venus is much farther from the sun than is Mercury. Yet temperatures on Venus are as high as those on the sunny side of Mercury. Explain why.

Check Your Progress CHAPTER PROJECT
Now you will design a model that shows the relative diameters of the planets. Try several different scales to find one for which the smallest planet is clearly visible but the sun would still fit into your classroom. Convert the sun's and planets' diameters to scaled-down diameters and record your results on your data sheet. Compare your scaled-down diameters to objects you are familiar with, such as coins. Include your comparisons in your data sheet.

4 The Outer Planets

DISCOVER

How Large Are the Outer Planets?

The table shows the diameters of the outer planets compared to Earth. For example, Jupiter's diameter is 11 times Earth's diameter.

Planet Diameters

Planet	Diameter
Earth	1
Jupiter	11
Saturn	9.4
Uranus	4.0
Neptune	3.9
Pluto	0.17

1. Measure the diameter of a quarter in millimeters. This represents Earth's diameter. Trace the quarter to represent Earth.

2. If Earth were the size of a quarter, calculate how large Jupiter would be. Now draw a circle to represent Jupiter.

3. Repeat Step 2 for each of the other outer planets.

Think It Over

Classifying List the planets in order from largest to smallest. What is the largest outer planet? Which outer planet is much smaller than Earth?

GUIDE FOR READING

◆ What are the main characteristics of the gas giant planets?

◆ How is Pluto different from the other outer planets?

Reading Tip Before you read, preview the photos and captions in this section. Then write down any questions you have. Look for answers as you read.

Most of what astronomers know about the outer planets has come from visits by NASA space probes. *Voyager 1* and *Voyager 2* reached Jupiter in 1979 and sent back close-up views of the planet. *Voyager 1* went on to visit Saturn in 1980. *Voyager 2* also visited Saturn, but then moved on to explore Uranus and Neptune. In 1995, the spacecraft *Galileo* reached Jupiter and dropped a probe into Jupiter's atmosphere.

Structure of the Gas Giants

Compared to Earth, some planets are huge. The largest planet, Jupiter, has a diameter that is 11 times Earth's diameter. Jupiter's mass is more than 300 times Earth's mass. If you could put Earth next to Jupiter, Earth would look like a tiny Chihuahua next to an enormous Great Dane. If Earth were the height of an average student, Jupiter would be as tall as a six-story building.

Jupiter and the other planets farthest from the sun, as seen in Figure 19, are called the outer planets. **The first four outer planets—Jupiter, Saturn, Uranus, and Neptune—are much larger than Earth, and do not have solid surfaces.** Because these four planets are all so large, they are also called the **gas giants.** The fifth outer planet, Pluto, is small and rocky like the terrestrial planets.

Figure 18 If the tiny Chihuahua were Earth's size, the Great Dane would be about half Jupiter's size.

The Outer Planets

Planet	Diameter (kilometers)	Period of Rotation (Earth days)	Average Distance From the Sun (kilometers)	Period of Revolution (Earth years)	Number of Moons
Jupiter	142,800	0.41	778,000,000	12	17
Saturn	120,540	0.43	1,427,000,000	29	19
Uranus	51,200	0.72	2,871,000,000	84	18
Neptune	49,500	0.67	4,497,000,000	165	8
Pluto	2,200	6.4	5,913,000,000	248	1

Figure 19 The outer planets are much farther apart than the inner planets. At this scale, the inner planets are so small and close to the sun that they cannot be shown. *Observing Which outer planet is closest to the sun?*

Atmospheres Because the gas giants have so much mass, they exert a much stronger gravitational force than the terrestrial planets. The strong gravity keeps the giant planets' gases from escaping, so they have deep atmospheres. The composition of their atmospheres is similar to the gases in the sun. They average about 75 percent hydrogen, 24 percent helium, and 1 percent other elements.

None of the giant planets has a well-defined surface. If you could parachute into Jupiter's atmosphere, you would sink into denser and denser gas. You would be crushed by the enormous pressure long before you got to the center, or core, of the planet.

Solid Cores Astronomers think that each of the giant planets has a partly solid core made of rock, ice, frozen carbon dioxide, and other compounds. Each of these cores may have several times as much mass as Earth. But they are buried so deep inside the planets that it has been hard to find out much about them.

☑ *Checkpoint* Why do the gas giants have large atmospheres?

Jupiter

Jupiter is the most massive planet. In fact, Jupiter is more than 300 times as massive as Earth.

Jupiter's Atmosphere Like all of the gas giant planets, Jupiter has a thick atmosphere made up mainly of hydrogen and helium. Jupiter's atmosphere contains many colorful bands and swirls of thick clouds. An especially interesting feature in Jupiter's atmosphere is its Great Red Spot, a giant area of swirling clouds many times bigger than Earth. The Great Red Spot, shown in Figure 20, appears to be an ongoing storm similar to a hurricane on Earth.

Jupiter's Moons Recall that the astronomer Galileo discovered four of Jupiter's moons. These moons are named Io (EYE oh), Europa, Ganymede, and Callisto. These four moons are Jupiter's largest. Three of them, Io, Ganymede, and Callisto, are larger than Earth's own moon. Since Galileo's time, astronomers have discovered 13 more moons revolving around Jupiter, for a total of 17.

The *Voyager* and *Galileo* probes sent back images that showed detailed views of Jupiter's moons. Jupiter's moons are very different from one another, as you can see in Figure 21.

Figure 20 The larger photo of Jupiter was taken by the *Voyager 1* spacecraft. The small objects in front of Jupiter are two of Jupiter's moons, Io (left) and Europa (right). The Great Red Spot, shown in the inset, is a giant storm much larger in size than Earth.

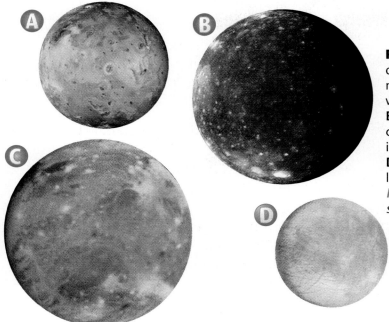

Figure 21 The astronomer Galileo discovered Jupiter's four largest moons. **A.** Io's surface is covered with large, active volcanoes. **B.** Callisto's surface is icy and covered with craters. **C.** Ganymede is the largest of Jupiter's moons. **D.** Europa's icy crust may have liquid water underneath.
Inferring Why was Galileo able to see only Jupiter's largest moons?

Io is covered with volcanoes. Over a dozen huge volcanoes are erupting all the time, so Io's surface changes from year to year because of the flows of hot material. The sulfur in the flows gives a variety of colors to Io's surface. From space, Io looks like a giant pizza. Europa has an icy crust that may have liquid water underneath. You will learn more about Europa in Section 6.

Ganymede is the largest of Jupiter's moons and has about twice the mass of Earth's moon. Ganymede's surface is icy and partly covered with craters. Other parts of the surface show giant grooves in the ice. Callisto also has an icy surface. It is so heavily cratered that no part of its surface is free of craters.

✓ *Checkpoint* *What are Jupiter's four largest moons?*

Saturn

The second-largest planet in the solar system is Saturn. Saturn is slightly smaller than Jupiter, but including its beautiful rings it has a greater overall diameter. The *Voyager* probes showed that Saturn, like Jupiter, has a thick atmosphere made up mainly of hydrogen and helium. Saturn's atmosphere also contains clouds and storms, but they are less dramatic than those on Jupiter. Saturn is the only planet that is less dense than water.

Saturn's Rings When Galileo first looked at Saturn with a telescope, he could see that something was sticking out on the sides, but he didn't know what it was. A few decades later, another astronomer using a better telescope discovered that Saturn had rings around it. Astronomers later found that these rings are made of chunks of ice and rock, each traveling in its own orbit around Saturn.

Model Saturn

Here's how you can build a scale model of Saturn.

ACTIVITY

1. Use a plastic foam sphere 8 cm in diameter to represent Saturn.

2. ✂ Use an overhead transparency to represent Saturn's rings. Cut a circle 18 cm in diameter out of the transparency. Cut a hole 9 cm in diameter out of the center of the circle.

3. Stick five toothpicks into Saturn, spaced equally around its equator. Put the transparency on the toothpicks and tape it to them. Sprinkle baking soda on the transparency.

4. Use a peppercorn to represent Titan. Place the peppercorn 72 cm away from Saturn on the same plane as the rings.

Making Models What do the particles of baking soda represent?

Figure 22 Saturn's rings are made up of ice chunks and rocks of many different sizes. The smaller photo shows that there are actually many small rings. The colors in this photo have been added by a computer. *Observing* *Why might it be hard to see Saturn's rings when their edges are facing Earth?*

From Earth, it looks as though Saturn has only a few rings, and that they are divided from each other by narrow, dark regions. The *Voyager* spacecraft discovered that each of these obvious rings is divided into dozens of smaller rings. In all, Saturn has hundreds of rings.

Saturn's rings are broad and thin, like a compact disc. Sometimes the rings are tipped so that observers see them at an angle. Occasionally, they are on edge, and then, because they are so thin, astronomers can't see them at all.

In the last few decades, rings have been discovered around the other three gas giants as well. But the rings around Jupiter, Uranus, and Neptune are not as spectacular as Saturn's.

Saturn's Moons Saturn's largest moon, Titan, is larger than Earth's own moon. Titan was discovered in 1665 but was known only as a point of light until the *Voyager*s went by. The probes showed that Titan has an atmosphere so thick that little light can get through it. Astronomers studying Hubble Space Telescope images can barely see Titan's surface.

Four other moons of Saturn are each over 1,000 kilometers in diameter. They are named Tethys (TEE this), Iapetus (eye AP uh tus), Dione, and Rhea. *Voyager* images show craters and canyons on these moons.

✓ *Checkpoint* *What are Saturn's rings made of?*

Figure 23 This image of Saturn and six of its moons combines photos taken by *Voyager 1* and *Voyager 2*.

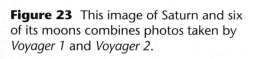

Uranus

Although the gas giant Uranus (YOOR uh nus) is about four times the diameter of Earth, it is still much smaller than Jupiter and Saturn. Uranus is twice as far from the sun as Saturn, so it is much colder. Uranus looks bluish because of traces of methane in its atmosphere.

Discovery of Uranus In 1781, Uranus became the first new planet discovered since ancient times. Astronomer William Herschel, in England, found an object in the sky that did not look like a star. At first he thought it might be a comet. But other astronomers soon calculated its orbit and realized that it was a planet beyond Saturn. The discovery made Herschel famous and started an era of solar system exploration.

Exploring Uranus In 1986, about 200 years after Herschel's discovery, *Voyager 2* arrived at Uranus and sent back our only close-up views of that giant planet. Images from *Voyager 2* show only a few clouds on Uranus's surface, but even these few allowed astronomers to calculate that Uranus rotates in about 17 hours.

Strangely, Uranus's axis is tilted at an angle of about 90° from the vertical, as shown in Figure 24. Viewed from Earth, Uranus is rotating from top to bottom instead of from side to side, the way most of the other planets do. Astronomers think that billions of years ago Uranus was hit by an object that knocked it on its side.

Uranus's Moons Photographs from *Voyager 2* showed that Uranus's five largest moons have icy, cratered surfaces. The craters show that the moons have been hit by rocks from space. Uranus's moons also have lava flows on their surfaces, suggesting that material has erupted from inside each moon. *Voyager 2* images revealed ten moons that had never been seen before. In 1999, astronomers discovered another moon, for a total of 18.

Figure 24 A. This composite image of *Voyager 2* photos includes Uranus and five of its 18 moons. **B.** Unlike most other planets, Uranus rotates on its side.

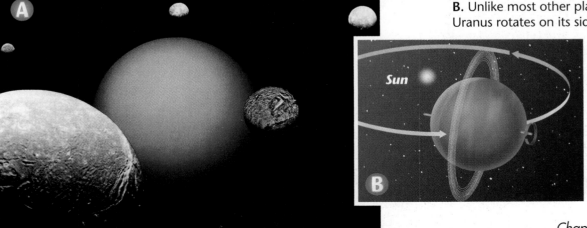

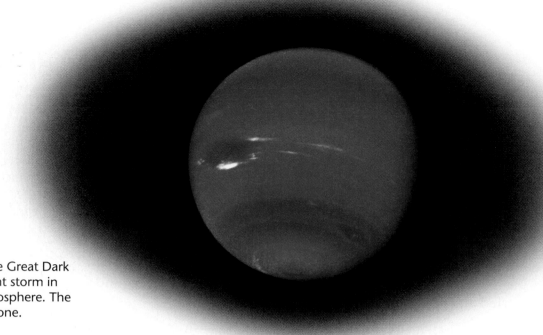

Figure 25 The Great Dark Spot was a giant storm in Neptune's atmosphere. The storm is now gone.

Neptune

Neptune is even farther from the sun than Uranus—in fact, it is 30 times Earth's distance from the sun. Unlike Uranus's nearly featureless blue atmosphere, Neptune's atmosphere contains visible clouds.

Discovery of Neptune The planet Neptune was discovered as a result of a mathematical prediction. Uranus was not quite following the orbit astronomers predicted for it. Astronomers hypothesized that there must be another, unseen planet whose gravity was affecting Uranus's orbit. By 1846, mathematicians in both England and France had calculated the orbit of this new planet. A few months later, an observer in Germany saw an unknown object in the sky. It was the new planet, now called Neptune.

Figure 26 Neptune's largest moon, Triton, is covered with ridges and craters.

Exploring Neptune In 1989 *Voyager 2* flew by Neptune, where it photographed a Great Dark Spot, as shown in Figure 25, about the size of Earth. Like the Great Red Spot on Jupiter, the Great Dark Spot probably was a giant storm. But the storm didn't last long. Images from the Hubble Space Telescope taken five years later showed that the Great Dark Spot was gone. Other, smaller spots and regions of clouds on Neptune seem to come and go.

Neptune's Moons Astronomers have discovered eight moons revolving around Neptune. Neptune's largest moon is Triton. The *Voyager* photos show that the region near Triton's south pole is covered with a cap of ice, and that dark material erupts from underneath.

Checkpoint *Before they could see Neptune, what evidence led scientists to conclude that it existed?*

Pluto and Charon

Pluto and its single moon Charon are very different from the gas giants. **Pluto and Charon have solid surfaces and masses much less than that of Earth.** In fact, Pluto is less than two thirds the size of Earth's moon. Since Charon is more than half the size of Pluto, astronomers often consider them to be a double planet instead of a planet and a moon.

Pluto and Charon are so far from the sun that they revolve around the sun only once every 248 Earth years. Because Pluto and Charon are so small and far away, astronomers have been unable to learn much about them.

Discovery of Pluto and Charon The American astronomer Clyde Tombaugh discovered Pluto in 1930. He had been searching for a large object he thought might be affecting Neptune's orbit. Tombaugh spent 10 months looking at hundreds of thousands of images before he found Pluto. Charon was not discovered until 1978, by the astronomer James Christy. Christy was studying photographs of Pluto when he noticed that Pluto seemed to have a "bump." The bump turned out to be Charon.

Is Pluto Really a Planet? Pluto is so small that many astronomers do not think it should be called a planet at all. Pluto may be merely the largest of thousands of objects revolving around the sun out beyond Neptune. If astronomers had found these other objects before they found Pluto, they might not have called Pluto a planet.

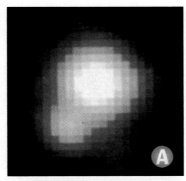

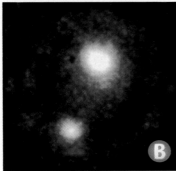

Figure 27 A. The space between Pluto and Charon couldn't be clearly seen from Earth until 1999, when they were observed by new telescopes in Hawaii. **B.** This photo, taken with the Hubble Space Telescope, clearly shows them as two objects. *Inferring Why do astronomers often call Pluto and Charon a double planet?*

Section 4 Review

1. How are the gas giants similar to each other? How are they different?
2. How is Pluto different from the gas giants?
3. What is the most prominent feature of Jupiter's surface? What causes this feature?
4. Why do astronomers think Uranus may have been hit by another object billions of years ago?
5. **Thinking Critically** **Predicting** Do you think astronomers have found all of the moons of the outer planets? Explain.

Check Your Progress
Once you have models that show size and distance separately, design another scale model of the solar system. This time, use the same scale for both size and distance. If your chalkboard is the sun, which planets would be in your classroom? Where would the other planets be with respect to your classroom, school grounds, and town?

Discuss with classmates any problems that would come up in building a model using the same scale for both size and distance. Revise your model as needed.

CHAPTER PROJECT

SPEEDING AROUND THE SUN

In this lab, you will make and test a hypothesis about how a planet's distance from the sun is related to its period of revolution.

Problem

How does a planet's distance from the sun affect its period of revolution?

Materials

string, 1.5 m
plastic tube, 6 cm
meter stick

one-hole rubber stopper
stopwatch
weight or several washers

Procedure

1. What do you think is the relationship between a planet's distance from the sun and its period of revolution? Write your hypothesis in the form of an "If . . . then . . ." statement.

2. To test your hypothesis, you need to make a model planet.

   a. Thread the string through the rubber stopper hole. Tie the end of the string to the main part of the string. Pull tightly to make sure that the knot will not become untied.

   b. Thread the other end of the string through the plastic tube and tie a weight to that end. Have your teacher check both knots.

   c. Hold the plastic tube in your hand above your head. Swing the stopper around above your head. Practice keeping the stopper moving at a constant speed. The circle represents the planet's orbit. **CAUTION:** *Stand away from other students. Make sure the swinging stopper will not hit students or objects. Do not let go of the string.*

3. Before you try different distances for your model planet, copy the data table into your notebook.

DATA TABLE				
Distance (cm)	Period of Revolution (seconds)			
	Trial 1	Trial 2	Trial 3	Average
20				
40				
60				

4. Pull the string so the stopper is 20 cm away from the plastic tube. Swing the stopper just fast enough to keep the stopper moving.

5. Have your partner time how long it takes for the stopper to make 10 revolutions. Divide by 10 to find the period of revolution. Record this number as Trial 1.

6. Repeat Steps 4–5 two more times. Record your results as Trials 2 and 3. Add the results of the three trials together and divide by three to find the average period of revolution.

7. If you pull the stopper out to 40 cm, do you think the period of revolution will increase or decrease? To find out, pull the stopper out to 40 cm and repeat Steps 4–6.

8. Based on your results in Step 7, do you want to revise your hypothesis? Make any needed changes. Then pull the stopper out to 60 cm and repeat Steps 4–6.

Analyze and Conclude

1. Which object in your model represented the sun? Which represented the planet?

2. What force did the pull on the string represent?

3. When you pulled the stopper out to make the orbit larger, did the string then represent a stronger or weaker force of gravity? Why?

4. What happened to the period of revolution when you made the orbit larger in Steps 7 and 8?

5. Did your observations support your hypothesis? Summarize your conclusions based on your observations.

6. Which planets take less time to revolve around the sun—those closer to the sun or those farther away? Use the model to support your answer.

7. **Think About It** What information did you consider when you made your hypothesis? How did having some experimental data help you modify your hypothesis?

Design an Experiment

Write a hypothesis relating the mass of a planet to its period of revolution. Then, using a stopper with a different mass, modify the activity to test your hypothesis. Before you swing the stopper, have your teacher check your knots.

5 Comets, Asteroids, and Meteors

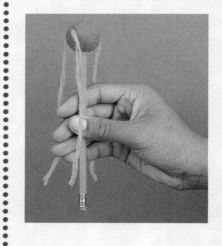

Which Way Do Comet Tails Point?

1. Form a small ball out of modeling clay to represent a comet.

2. Using a pencil point, push three 10-cm lengths of string into the ball. The strings represent the comet's tail. Stick the ball onto the pencil point, as shown in the photo.

3. Hold the ball about 1 m in front of a fan. The air from the fan represents the solar wind. Move the ball toward the fan, away from the fan, and from side to side.
CAUTION: *Keep your fingers away from the fan blades.*

Think It Over

Inferring How does moving the ball affect the direction in which the strings point? What determines which way the tail of a comet points?

GUIDE FOR READING

◆ What are the characteristics of comets and asteroids?

◆ Where do meteoroids come from?

Reading Tip As you read, make an outline of this section using the headings as the main topics.

I magine watching a cosmic collision! That's exactly what happened in July 1994. Eugene and Carolyn Shoemaker and David Levy discovered a new comet in 1993 that had previously broken into pieces near Jupiter. In 1994, the fragments returned and crashed into Jupiter. On Earth, astronomers were fascinated to see the huge explosions—some were as large as Earth!

As this story shows, the sun, planets, and moons aren't the only objects in the solar system. There are also millions of smaller objects, most of which are classified as comets and asteroids.

Comets

One of the most glorious things you can see in the night sky is a comet. A bright comet may be visible only for days or weeks or months, but is well worth seeing. In April 1997, for example, Comet Hale-Bopp and its bright dust tail were clearly visible even without a telescope.

You can think of a **comet** as a "dirty snowball" about the size of an Earth mountain. **Comets are chunks of ice and dust whose orbits are usually very long, narrow ellipses.** Because their orbits are so

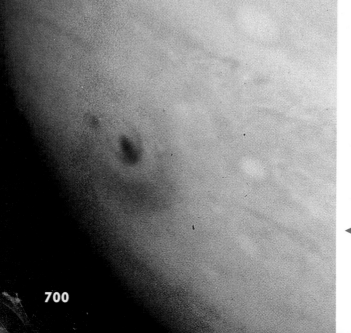

◀ A dark ring on Jupiter caused by comet Shoemaker-Levy 9

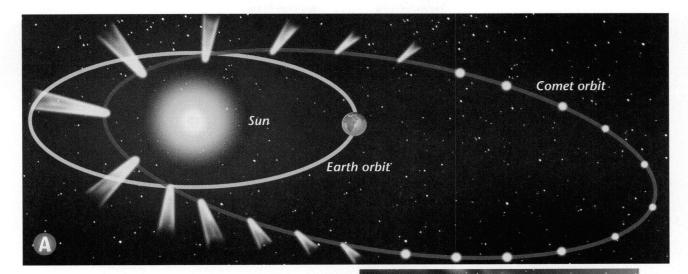

Comet orbit

Sun

Earth orbit

A

B

Tail

Nucleus

Coma

Figure 28 A. Most comets revolve around the sun in very long, narrow orbits. B. The main parts of a comet are the nucleus, the coma, and the tail. *Observing* What shape is a comet's orbit?

elliptical, few of them pass near Earth. They can usually then be seen only briefly. When a comet gets close enough to the sun, the energy in the sunlight turns the ice into gas, releasing dust. The gas and dust form an outer layer called the coma. Figure 28 shows the inner layer of the comet, which is then called the nucleus. The brightest part of a comet, the comet's head, is made up of the nucleus and coma.

Remember that the sun's corona produces a stream of particles called the solar wind. Solar wind pushes the gas from a comet away from the sun. Gas and dust form the comet's tail. The tail looks like hair; in fact, the name *comet* means "long-haired star" in Greek.

A comet's tail can be hundreds of millions of kilometers long and stretch across most of the sky. The material is stretched out very thinly, however, so there isn't much mass in a comet tail.

In 1705, Edmond Halley, an English astronomer, calculated the orbits of 24 comets that people had observed over hundreds of years. Halley realized that several of the comets seemed to have the same orbit and suggested that they were actually the same comet. Halley calculated that this comet appeared about every 76 years, and predicted that it would reappear in 1758. When this prediction came true, the comet was named Halley's Comet. In 1986, the last time Halley's Comet appeared in our sky, the European Space Agency's *Giotto* spacecraft flew within a few hundred kilometers of it.

☑ *Checkpoint* How did Halley's Comet get its name?

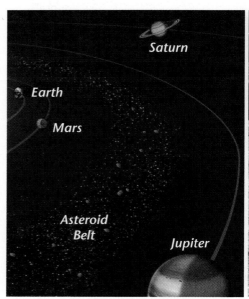

Figure 29 The asteroid belt (left) lies between Mars and Jupiter. Asteroids come in many sizes and shapes, as shown in this artist's depiction (center). NASA's *Near Earth Asteroid Rendezvous* mission photographed the asteroid Mathilde (right) in 1997.

Asteroids

Between 1801 and 1807, astronomers discovered four small objects between the orbits of Mars and Jupiter. They named the objects Ceres, Pallas, Juno, and Vesta. Over the next 80 years, astronomers found 300 more. These objects, called **asteroids,** are too small and too numerous to be considered full-fledged planets. **Most asteroids revolve around the sun between the orbits of Mars and Jupiter.** This region of the solar system, shown in Figure 29, is known as the **asteroid belt.**

Astronomers have discovered more than 10,000 asteroids, and more are found every month. Ceres, Pallas, Juno, and Vesta are among the dozen that are over 250 kilometers across.

INTEGRATING EARTH SCIENCE Some asteroids come near the orbit of Earth. Someday, one of these near-Earth asteroids could hit Earth. When a large asteroid hit Earth 65 million years ago, it exploded, making a crater 200 kilometers in diameter near the Yucatán Peninsula of Mexico. The explosion almost certainly raised trillions of tons of dust into the atmosphere, blocking the light from the sun for months. Debris from the explosion probably started huge fires that destroyed much of Earth's forests and grass. Scientists hypothesize that as a result many species of organisms, including the dinosaurs, became extinct.

Meteors

Imagine being outside in the country on a clear night, looking up at the sky. Suddenly, you see a streak of light flashing across the sky. Within seconds, you see another streak. For an hour or so, you see a streak at least once a minute. You are watching a meteor shower. Meteor showers happen regularly, several times a year.

Even when there is no meteor shower, you frequently can see meteors if you are far from city lights and the sky is free of clouds. On average, a meteor streaks overhead every 10 minutes.

A **meteoroid** is a chunk of rock or dust in space. **Meteoroids usually come from comets or asteroids.** Comets leave dust behind as they move through the solar system. When Earth passes through one of these dust clouds, bits of dust enter Earth's atmosphere.

When a meteoroid enters Earth's atmosphere, friction makes it burn up and produce the streak of light you see in the sky—a **meteor.** If the meteoroid is large, it may not burn up completely. Meteoroids that pass through the atmosphere and hit Earth's surface are called **meteorites.** The craters on the moon and on other objects in the solar system were caused by meteoroids.

Meteorites fall all over Earth. Most of them look just like stones, so nobody notices them. A few meteorites are made almost entirely of iron and nickel, and so are unusually heavy for their size. This makes them more likely to be identified as meteorites than as Earth rocks.

Figure 30 A. Meteor Crater in Arizona is the best-known meteorite crater on Earth. It was formed when a meteorite hit Earth about 40,000 years ago. **B.** Meteoroids make streaks of light, like the one above, as they burn up in the atmosphere.

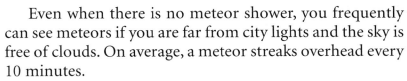

Section 5 Review

1. What is a comet made of?
2. Where are most asteroids found?
3. What are the main sources of meteoroids?
4. What is the difference between a meteor and a meteorite?
5. **Thinking Critically Predicting** Describe what might happen if an asteroid the size of the one that hit Earth 65 million years ago hit Earth today.

Science at Home

Watch a Meteor Shower Meteor showers occur regularly on specific dates. (The Perseids meteor shower, for example, occurs every August 12.) Look in the newspaper or almanac for information about the next meteor shower. With adult family members, go outside on that night and look for meteors. Explain to your family what causes the glow.

INTEGRATING LIFE SCIENCE

Is There Life Beyond Earth?

SECTION 6

DISCOVER ·····································ACTIVITY····

Is Yeast Alive or Not?

1. Open a package of yeast and pour it into a bowl.

2. Look at the yeast carefully. Make a list of your observations.

3. Fill the bowl about halfway with warm water (about 20°C). Add a spoonful of sugar. Stir the mixture with the spoon. Wait five minutes.

4. Now look at the yeast again and make a list of your observations.

Think It Over
Forming Operational Definitions Which of your observations seem to suggest that yeast is not alive? Which observations suggest that yeast is alive? How can you tell if something is alive?

GUIDE FOR READING

◆ What conditions do living things need to exist on Earth?

◆ Why do scientists think Mars and Europa are good places to look for signs of life?

Reading Tip As you read, write down evidence to support this statement: Life may exist in other parts of the solar system.

Figure 31 Dr. Ursula Marvin (lying down) studies meteorites such as this one in Antarctica.

Most of Antarctica is covered with snow and ice. You would not expect to see rocks lying on top of the whiteness. But surprisingly, in some places people have found rocks lying on the surface. When scientists examined the rocks, they found that the rocks are meteorites. A few of the meteorites came from Mars. Astronomers think that meteoroids hitting the surface of Mars must have blasted chunks of rock into space. The rocks eventually entered Earth's atmosphere and landed in Antarctica.

Recently a team of scientists announced that a meteorite from Mars found in Antarctica shows tiny shapes that look like fossils—the remains of ancient life preserved in rock. Many scientists doubt that the shapes really are fossils. But if they are, it would be a sign that life forms similar to bacteria once existed on Mars. Life other than that on Earth would be called **extraterrestrial life**.

The "Goldilocks Conditions"

If you did the Discover activity, you saw that it can be hard to tell whether something is alive or not. But all living things on Earth have several characteristics in common. Living things are made up of one or more cells. Living things take in energy and use it to grow and develop. They reproduce, producing new living things of the same type. Living things also give off waste.

704

A yeast cell, for example, is a living thing. Each yeast organism has one cell. Yeast cells take in sugar for energy. They reproduce and make new yeast cells. And yeast cells produce carbon dioxide as waste. A yeast cell, then, fulfills all the requirements for a living thing.

Nobody knows whether life exists anywhere other than Earth. Scientists often talk about the conditions needed by "life as we know it." **Earth has liquid water and a suitable temperature range and atmosphere for living things to survive.** Other planets do not have such favorable conditions, which scientists sometimes call the "Goldilocks conditions." That is, the temperature is not too hot and not too cold. It is just right. If Earth were hotter, water would always be a gas—water vapor. If Earth were colder, water would always be solid ice. On Earth, water exists as a liquid as well as a solid and a gas.

Are these the conditions necessary for life? Or are they just the conditions that Earth's living things happen to need? Scientists have only one example of life to study: life on Earth. Unless scientists find life somewhere else, there will be no way to answer these questions.

☑ *Checkpoint* *What are some characteristics of all living things?*

Life on Earth

In recent years, astounding discoveries have been made deep under the ocean. Sunlight never penetrates there. But deep-diving submarines have discovered giant tube worms and other animals that live at very high pressure in the dark. Single-celled forms of life have been discovered that are different from plants, animals, or bacteria. These newly discovered life forms get their energy not from sunlight, but from chemicals. Other scientists have found tiny life forms in caves and deep inside solid rocks. Still other scientists have found life surviving in hot springs that had been thought to be too hot to support life.

The range of conditions in which life can exist is much greater than scientists once thought. Perhaps life forms exist that do not even need the "Goldilocks conditions"!

Sharpen your Skills

Communicating

You are writing a letter to a **ACTIVITY** friend who lives on another planet. Your friend has never been to Earth and has no idea what the planet is like. Explain in your letter why the conditions on Earth make it the ideal place for living things.

Figure 32 These colonies of microorganisms were discovered deep in a cave in Mexico. *Inferring* *How does studying unusual organisms like these help scientists predict what extraterrestrial life might be like?*

Life on Mars?

Recall that Mars is the planet most similar to Earth. That makes Mars the most obvious place to look for living things similar to those on Earth.

The *Viking* Missions In 1970, a spacecraft found regions on the surface of Mars that look like stream beds with criss-crossing paths of water. These shapes, shown in Figure 33, were almost certainly formed by flowing water. **Since life as we know it requires water, scientists hypothesize that Mars may have once had the conditions needed for life to exist.**

Twin *Viking* spacecraft reached Mars in 1976. Each had one part that landed on Mars's surface and another part that stayed in orbit, taking pictures of most of the surface. Each of the *Viking* landers carried a compact biology laboratory meant to search for life forms.

The biology laboratories on the landers tested the Martian air and soil for signs of life. Each laboratory was designed to see if there were life forms that used oxygen and gave off carbon dioxide, as many living things on Earth do. A robot scoop brought some soil from Mars's surface into the lab and added water to see if the sample gave off oxygen. None of these tests showed any evidence of life.

☑ *Checkpoint* *What evidence shows that there may once have been running water on Mars?*

Meteorites From Mars Interest in life on Mars was increased by the report in 1996 about the meteorite from Mars that may contain fossils. The scientists' report started a huge debate. What were the tubelike things in the meteorite? Many scientists have suggested that the tiny shapes found in the meteorite do not prove that life forms once existed on Mars. Perhaps the shapes came from natural processes on Mars and are just lumps of hardened clay. Perhaps the shapes came from snow that got into cracks in the meteorite after it landed on Earth. Were the shapes

Figure 33 These patterns on the surface of Mars are probably evidence that liquid water once flowed on Mars. *Applying Concepts Why does this evidence make it more likely that there may once have been life on Mars?*

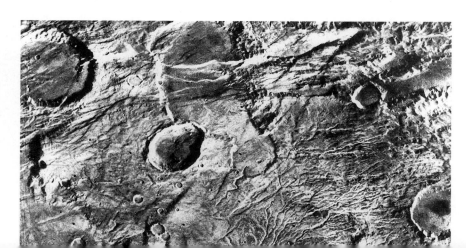

too deep inside the rocks to be from Earth? Perhaps the shapes are too small to be the remains of life forms. They are only one-hundredth the size of any other known life forms.

The most effective way to answer these questions is to send more probes to Mars. Future Mars missions should be able to bring samples of rocks and soil back to Earth for detailed analysis. Scientists may not yet have evidence of life on Mars, but hope is growing that we can soon solve the mystery.

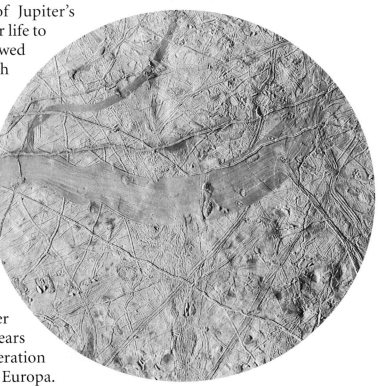

Figure 34 Europa is covered with a layer of ice similar to the ice covering Earth's Arctic Ocean. There may be liquid water under the ice.

Life on Europa?

Many scientists think that Europa, one of Jupiter's moons, may have the conditions necessary for life to develop. Photos from *Voyager* and *Galileo* showed that Europa has a very smooth, icy crust with giant cracks in it.

Close-up views from *Galileo* show that Europa's ice has broken up and re-formed, resulting in twisted, house-sized blocks of ice. Similar patterns occur in the ice crust over Earth's Arctic Ocean. Could this mean that there is a liquid ocean under Europa's ice? The water in the ocean could possibly be kept liquid by heat coming from inside Europa. **If there is liquid water on Europa, there might also be life.**

How can scientists study conditions under Europa's ice sheet? Such studies are many years off. People will have to wait for the next generation of space probes to search for liquid water on Europa.

Section 6 Review

1. What conditions does life on Earth need to survive?
2. Why do astronomers think there could be life on Europa?
3. How did the *Viking* missions search for life on Mars?
4. **Thinking Critically Applying Concepts** Do you think there could be life as we know it on Venus? Explain. (*Hint:* Review page 686.)

Science at Home

Message to E.T. Imagine that scientists have found intelligent extraterrestrial life. With family members, make up a message to send to the extraterrestrials. Remember that they will not understand English, so you should use only symbols and drawings in your message.

SCIENCE AND SOCIETY

Space Exploration—Is It Worth the Cost?

Imagine that your spacecraft has just landed on Mars after a two-month journey from Earth. You've spent years planning for this moment. Canyons, craters, and distant plains stretch out before you. You check your spacesuit and prepare to step out onto the rocky red surface of Mars.

Is such a trip likely? Would it be worthwhile? How much is space flight really worth to human society? Scientists and politicians have already started to debate such questions. Space exploration can help us learn more about the universe. But exploration is risky and expensive. Sending people into space costs billions of dollars and risks human lives. How can we balance the costs and benefits of space exploration?

The Issues

Should Humans Travel Into Space? Many Americans think that Neil Armstrong's walk on the moon in 1969 was one of the great moments in history. Also, learning how to keep people alive in space has led to improvements in everyday life. Safer equipment for firefighters, easier ways to package frozen food, and effective heart monitors have all come out of space program research.

What Are the Alternatives? Space exploration can involve a project to put a person on Mars. It also can involve a more limited use of scientific instruments near Earth, such as the Hubble Space Telescope. Instead of sending people, we could send space probes like *Mars Pathfinder* to other planets.

Is Human Space Exploration Worth the Cost? Scientists who favor human travel into space say that only people can collect certain kinds of information. And using simpler space vehicles that are cheaper to build can also save money. But no one knows if research in space really provides information quicker than research that can be done on Earth. Many critics of space research think that other needs are more important. One United States senator said, "Every time you put money into the space station, there is a dime that won't be available for our children's education or for medical research."

You Decide

1. **Identify the Problem**
   In your own words, list the costs and benefits of space exploration.

2. **Analyze the Options**
   Make a chart of three different approaches to space exploration: sending humans to another planet, doing only Earth-based research, and one other option. What are the benefits and drawbacks of each approach?

3. **Find a Solution**
   Imagine that you are a member of Congress who has to vote on a new budget. There is a fixed amount of money to spend, so you have to decide which needs are most important. Make a list of your top ten priorities. Explain your decisions.

SECTION 1 Observing the Solar System

Key Ideas
◆ Ptolemy thought that Earth is at the center of the system of planets.
◆ Copernicus thought that the sun is at the center of the planets. Galileo's observations supported Copernicus's theory.
◆ Kepler discovered that the orbits of the planets are ellipses.
◆ Newton concluded that two factors—inertia and gravity—combine to keep the planets in orbit.

Key Terms
geocentric   ellipse
heliocentric   inertia

SECTION 2 The Sun

Key Ideas
◆ The sun's energy comes from nuclear fusion.
◆ The sun's atmosphere has three layers: the photosphere, the chromosphere, and the corona.
◆ Features on or above the sun's surface include sunspots, prominences, and solar flares.

Key Terms
nuclear fusion   solar wind
core   sunspot
photosphere   prominence
chromosphere   solar flare
corona

SECTION 3 The Inner Planets

Key Idea
◆ The four inner planets—Mercury, Venus, Earth, and Mars—are small and have rocky surfaces. They are often called the terrestrial planets.

Key Terms
terrestrial planets
retrograde rotation
greenhouse effect

SECTION 4 The Outer Planets

Key Ideas
◆ Four outer planets—Jupiter, Saturn, Uranus, and Neptune—are much larger than Earth.
◆ Pluto and Charon have solid surfaces and masses much less than that of Earth.

Key Term
gas giant

SECTION 5 Comets, Asteroids, and Meteors

Key Ideas
◆ Comets are chunks of ice and dust that usually have long, elliptical orbits.
◆ Most asteroids revolve around the sun between the orbits of Mars and Jupiter.

Key Terms
comet   asteroid belt   meteor
asteroid   meteoroid   meteorite

SECTION 6 Is There Life Beyond Earth?

INTEGRATING LIFE SCIENCE

Key Ideas
◆ Earth has liquid water and a suitable temperature range and atmosphere for living things to survive.
◆ Since life as we know it requires water, scientists hypothesize that Mars may have once had the conditions for life to exist.

Key Term
extraterrestrial life

Organizing Information

Compare/Contrast Table On a separate piece of paper, make a table comparing and contrasting the geocentric and heliocentric systems. Include information on the following: object at the center of the system; objects that move around the center; who the system was first proposed by; and who supported the system. (For more on compare/contrast tables, see the Skills Handbook.)

Reviewing Content

 For more review of key concepts, see the Interactive Student Tutorial CD-ROM.

Multiple Choice

Choose the letter of the answer that best completes each statement.

1. Copernicus thought that the solar system was
   a. celestial.
   b. elliptical.
   c. geocentric.
   d. heliocentric.

2. The part of the sun where nuclear fusion occurs is the
   a. photosphere.   b. chromosphere.
   c. corona.   d. core.

3. Planets with atmospheres composed mostly of carbon dioxide include
   a. Earth and Mercury.
   b. Venus and Mercury.
   c. Venus and Mars.
   d. Mercury and Mars.

4. The Great Red Spot is a huge storm on
   a. Jupiter.   b. Neptune.
   c. Saturn.   d. Pluto.

5. Most asteroids orbit the sun
   a. between the sun and Mercury.
   b. between Earth and Mars.
   c. between Mars and Jupiter.
   d. between Neptune and Pluto.

True or False

If the statement is true, write true. If it is false, change the underlined word or words to make the statement true.

6. The shape of the orbit of each planet is a <u>circle</u>.

7. Sunspots are regions of <u>cooler</u> gases on the sun.

8. The atmosphere of Venus has <u>higher</u> pressure than the atmosphere of Earth.

9. Aside from the sun, <u>Saturn</u> is the largest source of gravity in the solar system.

10. Conditions favorable to life as we know it are sometimes called the <u>Goldilocks conditions</u>.

Checking Concepts

11. How did Galileo's observations support the heliocentric system?

12. How did Newton's work on orbits add to the work Kepler had done?

13. Why is it usually impossible to see the sun's corona?

14. What are sunspots?

15. Why does Mercury have only a thin atmosphere?

16. How do astronomers explain that Venus rotates in the opposite direction from most planets and moons?

17. What are the major characteristics of the terrestrial planets? How do they differ from the gas giants?

18. Why do some astronomers think that Pluto should not be called a planet?

19. Why does a comet's tail always stream away from the sun?

20. Do living things have to live on the surface of a planet or moon? Where else on a planet or moon could scientists look for evidence of life?

21. **Writing to Learn** Imagine you are an astronaut on a mission to explore the solar system. Write a trip journal telling the story of your trip from Earth to another terrestrial planet and to a gas giant. Include a description of each planet.

Thinking Critically

22. **Relating Cause and Effect** How would Earth move if the sun (including its gravity) suddenly disappeared? Explain your answer.

23. **Applying Concepts** Explain why Venus is hotter than it would be without its atmosphere.

24. **Comparing and Contrasting** Compare and contrast meteoroids, meteors, and meteorites.

25. **Making Generalizations** Why would the discovery of liquid water on another planet be important?

Applying Skills

Use the diagram of an imaginary, newly discovered planetary system around Star X to answer Questions 26–28. The periods of revolution of planets A, B, and C are 75 Earth days, 200 Earth days, and 300 Earth days.

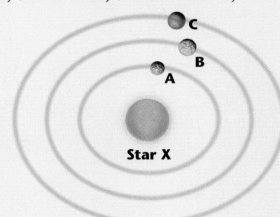

Star X

26. **Interpreting Data** Which planet in this new planetary system revolves around Star X in the shortest amount of time?

27. **Making Models** In 150 days, how far will each planet have revolved around Star X? Copy the diagram and sketch the positions of the three planets to find out. How far will each planet have revolved around Star X in 400 days? Sketch their positions.

28. **Drawing Conclusions** Can planet C ever be closer to planet A than to planet B? Study your drawings to figure this out.

Performance [CHAPTER PROJECT] Assessment

Present Your Project Now you are ready to present your solar system. Explain how you were able to work with large distances. Display your data tables showing how you did the calculations and how you checked them for accuracy. Compare the distances in your models to distances inside and outside your classroom.

Reflect and Record In your journal, explain what you would change in your model of the solar system. What would you do to improve the model? How effectively did you use computers or calculators to get the data?

Test Preparation

Use these questions to prepare for standardized tests.

Study the table. Then answer Questions 29–32.

Planet	Period of Rotation (Earth days)	Period of Revolution (Earth years)	Average Distance From the Sun (million kilometers)
Mars	1.03	1.9	228
Jupiter	0.41	12	778
Saturn	0.43	29	1,427
Uranus	0.72	84	2,871
Neptune	0.67	165	4,497

29. Which of these planet's orbits is farthest from Earth's orbit?
    a. Mars   b. Jupiter
    c. Uranus   d. Neptune

30. Which planet has a "day" that is most similar in length to a day on Earth?
    a. Mars   b. Jupiter
    c. Uranus   d. Neptune

31. Light takes about 8 minutes and 20 seconds to travel from the sun to the Earth, 150 million kilometers away. About how long does it take light to travel from the sun to Jupiter?
    a. 10 minutes   b. 25 minutes
    c. 43 minutes   d. 112 minutes

32. Which one of the following conclusions about planets is supported by the information in the table?
    a. As distance from the sun increases, period of rotation increases.
    b. As distance from the sun increases, period of revolution increases.
    c. As distance from the sun increases, period of revolution decreases.
    d. There is no relationship between distance from the sun and period of revolution.

Stars, Galaxies, and the Universe

www.phschool.com

Integrating Physics

CHAPTER 21 PROJECT

Star Stories

In the spring of 1997, you could easily see comet Hale-Bopp, shown here, without any special equipment. But many of the objects astronomers study just look to you like tiny pinpoints of light—that is, if you can see them at all. However, astronomers have found many ways to learn about these "pinpoints."

In this chapter, you will discover how astronomers study the universe and what they have learned about the stars. In your project, you will find out how people in the past created stories to explain the patterns they saw in the sky. You'll learn how the names of constellations reflect the cultures of the people who named them.

Your Goal To recognize major constellations, learn the stories behind their names, and create your own star myth.

To complete the project you will
◆ learn the star patterns of at least three major constellations
◆ research the myths that gave one constellation its name
◆ write a new star myth

Get Started Begin your project by previewing page 94 to learn what a constellation is. With a group of your classmates, make a list of constellations you have heard about. Then look at the star charts in Appendix C. From the chart for the current season, choose three or four constellations to explore further.

Check Your Progress You'll be working on this project as you study this chapter. To keep your project on track, look for Check Your Progress boxes at the following points.
Section 1 Review, page 720: Locate constellations and research one.
Section 3 Review, page 736: Draw a new picture for the star pattern in your constellation and give it a name.
Section 5 Review, page 744: Write a story about your constellation.

Present Your Project At the end of the chapter (page 747), you will present your constellation along with a story that explains its name.

These telescopes on top of Mauna Kea, a mountain in Hawaii, are used to study distant stars and galaxies.

SECTION 4 Star Systems and Galaxies

Discover **Why Does the Milky Way Look Hazy?**
Try This **A Spiral Galaxy**
Science at Home **Stargazing**

SECTION 5 History of the Universe

Discover **How Does the Universe Expand?**

SECTION 1 Tools of Modern Astronomy

Are Those Stars Really a Group?

1. Cut ten pieces of thread to different lengths between 5 cm and 25 cm. Tape a 1-cm plastic foam ball to the end of each piece of thread.

2. Obtain a piece of cardboard about 50 cm by 50 cm. Tape the free ends of the thread pieces to various points on the cardboard.

3. Turn the cardboard over so the balls hang down. While your partner holds the cardboard horizontally, look at the balls from the side.

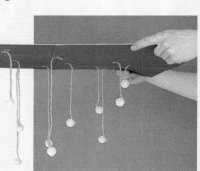

4. Imagine that the balls are stars in a constellation. With one eye closed, sketch the pattern the balls make.

Think It Over
Observing Can you tell which balls are farther away and which are closer? Do you think you can tell how close to one another the stars in a constellation are?

GUIDE FOR READING

◆ What is the electromagnetic spectrum?

◆ What is the main purpose of a telescope?

◆ Why do astronomers use spectrographs?

Reading Tip Before you read, rewrite the main headings of the section as *how, why,* or *what* questions.

Before the Civil War, thousands of enslaved African Americans fled north to freedom. Traveling in secret by night, they looked to the stars for direction. They told one another to "follow the drinking gourd"—the star pattern that points to the North Star. Most Americans today call this pattern the Big Dipper.

Patterns of stars in the sky are called **constellations.** Stars in a constellation can look as if they are close together, even though they are at very different distances from Earth. For example, the star at the end of the handle in the Big Dipper is about twice as far from Earth as most of the other stars in the Big Dipper. So the stars in a constellation are not, in fact, all close together. Constellations are just patterns formed by stars that happen to be in the same direction in the sky.

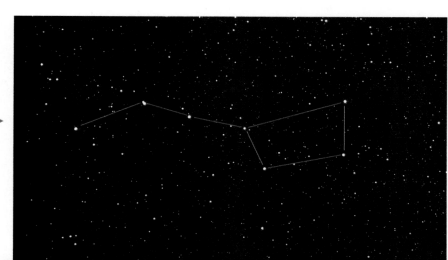

Big Dipper ▶

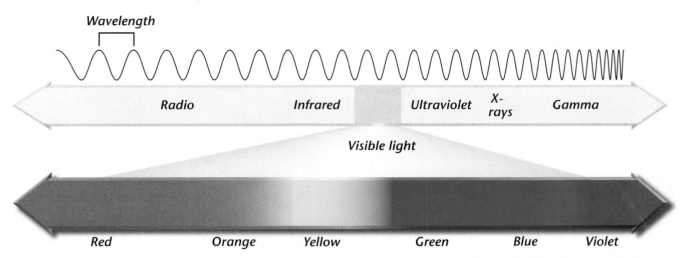

Wavelength

Radio   Infrared   Ultraviolet   X-rays   Gamma

Visible light

Red   Orange   Yellow   Green   Blue   Violet

Figure 1 The electromagnetic spectrum ranges from long-wavelength radio waves through short-wavelength gamma rays. *Interpreting Diagrams Are infrared waves longer or shorter than ultraviolet waves?*

Electromagnetic Radiation

The stars in constellations appear as tiny points of light. In fact, stars are huge spheres of hot glowing gas, like the sun. By using telescopes to study the light from stars, astronomers have learned a great deal about stars and other objects in the sky.

Types of Electromagnetic Radiation Scientists call the light you see with your eyes **visible light.** Light is a form of **electromagnetic radiation** (ih lek troh mag NET ik), or energy that can travel directly through space in the form of waves.

Visible light is only one type of electromagnetic radiation. Many objects give off radiation that you can't see. For example, the glowing coils of an electric heater give off infrared radiation, which you feel as heat. Radio waves carry signals to radios and televisions.

The Electromagnetic Spectrum As you can see in Figure 1, the distance between the crest of one wave and the crest of the next wave is called the **wavelength.** Visible light has very short wavelengths, less than one millionth of a meter. Some electromagnetic waves have even shorter wavelengths. Other waves are much longer, even several meters long.

If you shine white light through a prism, the light spreads out to make a range of different colors with different wavelengths, called a **spectrum.** The spectrum of visible light is composed of the colors red, orange, yellow, green, blue, and violet. **The electromagnetic spectrum includes radio waves, infrared radiation, visible light, ultraviolet radiation, X-rays, and gamma rays.** All these different kinds of electromagnetic waves make up the electromagnetic spectrum, shown in Figure 1.

✓ *Checkpoint* *Give two examples of electromagnetic waves that you might use or experience every day.*

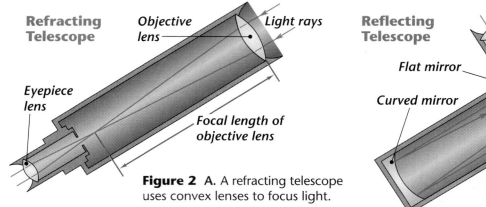

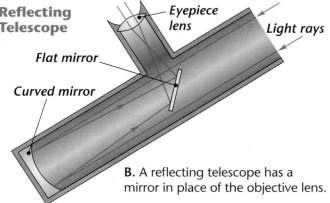

Refracting Telescope — *Objective lens*, *Light rays*, *Eyepiece lens*, *Focal length of objective lens*

Figure 2 **A.** A refracting telescope uses convex lenses to focus light.

Reflecting Telescope — *Eyepiece lens*, *Light rays*, *Flat mirror*, *Curved mirror*

B. A reflecting telescope has a mirror in place of the objective lens.

Locating Radio Waves

You can use an umbrella to focus radio waves.

ACTIVITY

1. Line the inside of an umbrella with aluminum foil.
2. Turn on a small radio and tune it to a station.
3. Move the radio up and down along the umbrella handle. Find the position where the station is clearest. Radio waves reflecting off the foil focus at this point. Tape the radio to the handle.

4. Hold the umbrella at different angles. At which angle is the station the clearest?

Inferring In which direction do you think the radio station is located? Explain.

Telescopes

Objects in space give off all types of electromagnetic radiation. Many telescopes produce images using visible light. But much of modern astronomy is based on detection of other types of electromagnetic radiation. **Most telescopes collect and focus different types of electromagnetic radiation, including visible light.**

Visible Light Telescopes In 1609, Galileo used a refracting telescope to look at objects in the sky. A **refracting telescope** uses convex lenses to gather a large amount of light and focus it onto a small area. A **convex lens** is a piece of transparent glass, curved so that the middle is thicker than the edges.

Galileo's telescope, like the refracting telescope in Figure 2, used two lenses—an eyepiece lens and an objective lens. When light passes through the objective lens, the lens focuses the light at a certain distance away from the lens. This distance is called the focal length of the lens. Different lenses have different focal lengths. The larger the objective lens, the more light it can collect, making it easier for astronomers to see faint objects.

Isaac Newton built the first **reflecting telescope** in 1668. It used a mirror instead of an objective lens. Like the lenses in a refracting telescope, the mirror in a reflecting telescope focuses a large amount of light onto a small area. The larger the mirror, the more light the telescope can collect. The largest visible light telescopes are now all reflecting telescopes.

Radio Telescopes Devices used to detect radio waves from objects in space are called **radio telescopes.** Most radio telescopes have curved, reflecting surfaces—up to 305 meters in diameter. These surfaces focus radio waves the way the mirror in a reflecting telescope focuses light waves. The surfaces of radio telescopes concentrate the faint radio waves from outer space onto small antennas like those on radios. As with visible light telescopes, the larger a radio telescope is, the more radio waves it can collect.

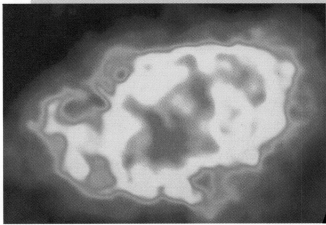

Figure 3 The Crab Nebula is the remains of a star that exploded about 1,000 years ago. The top image was photographed using visible light. The lower image was made using radio waves.

Other Telescopes Some telescopes detect infrared radiation, which has longer wavelengths than visible light. There are also telescopes that detect the shortest wavelengths—ultraviolet radiation, X-rays, and gamma rays.

☑ *Checkpoint* *What are two types of visible light telescopes?*

Observatories

A building that contains one or more telescopes is called an **observatory.** Most large observatories are located on mountaintops. Why have astronomers built the largest visible light telescopes on the tops of mountains? Earth's atmosphere makes objects in space look blurry. The sky on some mountaintops is clearer and is not brightened much by city lights.

The best observatory site on Earth is probably the top of Mauna Kea, an ancient volcano on the island of Hawaii. Mauna Kea is so tall—4,200 meters above sea level—that it is above 40 percent of Earth's atmosphere. The sky there is very dark at night, and many nights are free of clouds.

To collect data from visible light telescopes on Earth, astronomers must stay awake all night. Radio telescopes, however, can be used 24 hours a day and do not have to be on mountaintops.

Satellites

 INTEGRATING TECHNOLOGY Most ultraviolet radiation, X-rays, and gamma rays are blocked by Earth's atmosphere. To detect these wavelengths, astronomers have placed telescopes on satellites.

The Hubble Space Telescope is a reflecting telescope with a mirror 2.4 meters in diameter. Because it is above the atmosphere, it makes images in visible light that are about seven times more detailed than the best images from telescopes on Earth. The Hubble Space Telescope can also collect ultraviolet and infrared radiation. The Chandra X-ray Observatory, similar in size to Hubble, makes images in the X-ray portion of the spectrum.

SCIENCE & History

Development of Modern Telescopes

During the last century, astronomers have built larger telescopes, which can collect more light and other types of radiation. Today's astronomers use tools that could not have been imagined 100 years ago.

1897

Yerkes Telescope

The 1-meter-diameter telescope at Yerkes Observatory in Wisconsin is the largest refracting telescope ever built. Because its main lens is so large, the Yerkes telescope can collect more light than any other refracting telescope.

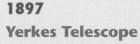

1900   **1920**   **1940**

1931

Beginning of Radio Astronomy

Karl Jansky, an American engineer, was trying to find the source of static that was interfering with radio communications. Using a large antenna, he discovered that the static was coming from objects in space giving off radio waves. Jansky's accidental discovery led to the beginning of radio astronomy.

Spectrographs

Most large telescopes today have spectrographs. A **spectrograph** (SPEK truh graf) breaks the light from an object into colors and photographs the resulting spectrum. **Astronomers use spectrographs to get information about stars, including their chemical compositions and temperatures.**

Chemical Compositions Chemical elements in a star's atmosphere absorb light from the star. Each element absorbs light at different wavelengths, and each absorbed wavelength is shown as a dark line on a spectrum. Just as each person has a unique set of fingerprints, each element has a unique set of lines. By comparing

In Your Journal

Research one of these telescopes or another large telescope. Create a publicity brochure in which you describe the telescope's features, when and where it was built, and what types of research it is used for.

1963
Arecibo Radio Telescope

This radio telescope in Puerto Rico was built in a natural bowl in the ground. It is 305 meters in diameter, more than three times the size of the next-largest radio telescope.

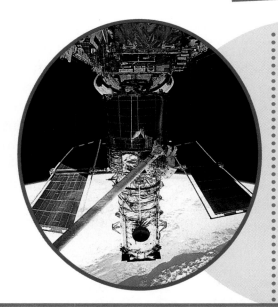

1990
Hubble Space Telescope

The Hubble Space Telescope can see objects in space more clearly than any other telescope. Astronauts have visited the telescope several times to repair or replace equipment.

1960   **1980**   **2000**

1980
Very Large Array

The Very Large Array is a set of 27 radio telescopes in New Mexico. The telescopes can be moved close together or far apart. The telescopes are linked, so they can be used as if they were one giant telescope 25 kilometers in diameter.

1999
Chandra X-ray Observatory

The hottest objects in space give off X-rays. NASA launched the Chandra X-ray Observatory into orbit to make detailed images in that part of the spectrum. Chandra X-ray images match Hubble visible-light images in detail.

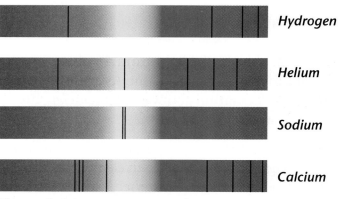

Figure 4 Astronomers can use line spectrums to find the temperatures of stars.

Hydrogen

Helium

Sodium

Calcium

Sharpen your Skills

Inferring ACTIVITY

The lines on the spectrums below are from three different stars. Each of these star spectrums is made up of an overlap of spectrums from the individual elements shown in Figure 4. In star A, which elements have the strongest lines? Which are the strongest in star B? In star C?

A

B

C

a star's spectrum with the known spectrums of different elements, such as those shown in Figure 4, astronomers can infer which elements are found in a star.

Temperatures Most stars have a chemical composition similar to the sun, about 73% hydrogen, 25% helium, and 2% other elements. The amount of energy each of these elements absorbs depends on the temperature of the star. Because of this, stars at different temperatures produce different line spectrums. By comparing a star's spectrum with the known spectrums of elements at different temperatures, astronomers can infer how hot the star is. Hydrogen, for example, produces very strong spectral lines when it is at about 10,000 degrees Celsius. If astronomers do not see a strong hydrogen line on a spectrum, this does not mean there is no hydrogen in the star. It just means that the star is much cooler or hotter than 10,000 degrees Celsius.

Section 1 Review

1. What are the main types of electromagnetic waves, from longest wavelength to shortest?
2. For what purpose are most telescopes designed?
3. What can astronomers tell from looking at a star's spectrum?
4. How are the stars in a constellation related to each other in space?
5. **Thinking Critically Applying Concepts** Why are images from the Hubble Space Telescope clearer than images from telescopes on Earth?

Check Your Progress

CHAPTER PROJECT

Using the star charts in Appendix B, try to locate constellations in the night sky. (*Hint:* Remember that you may be looking at a constellation upside down. Also, light conditions may affect how many stars you can see.) Sketch the constellations you can locate and compare them with the ones your classmates saw. Now choose one constellation and research the myths or legends that gave it its name. Find as many stories as you can about your constellation and make notes about them.

Make Your Own Telescope

In this lab you will learn how to construct and use a simple refracting telescope. You can then try out your telescope.

Problem

How can you build a telescope?

Skill Focus

making models, observing, drawing conclusions

Materials

2 paper towel tubes of slightly different diameters
plastic objective lens (43-mm diameter, 400-mm focal length)
plastic eyepiece lens (17.5-mm diameter, 25-mm focal length)
foam holder for eyepiece
transparent tape
meter stick

Procedure

1. Fit one of the paper towel tubes inside the other. Make sure you can move the tubes but that they will not slide on their own.

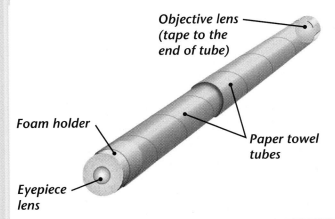

Objective lens (tape to the end of tube)

Foam holder

Eyepiece lens

Paper towel tubes

2. Place the large objective lens flat against the end of the outer tube. Tape the lens in place. Try to block as little of the lens with the tape as possible.

3. Make sure the center of the foam holder is free of foam. Insert the small eyepiece lens into the opening in the holder.

4. Place the foam eyepiece lens holder into the inner tube at the end of the telescope opposite to the objective lens.

5. Tape a meter stick to the wall. Look through the eyepiece at the meter stick from 5 m away. Slide the tubes in and out to focus your telescope so that you can clearly read the numbers on the meter stick.

6. Use your telescope to look at other objects at different distances, both in your classroom and through the window. **CAUTION:** *Do not look at the sun. You will damage your eyes.*

Analyze and Conclude

1. Why do you need two tubes?
2. If you focus on a nearby object and then focus on something farther away, do you have to move the tubes together or apart?
3. How does this telescope compare to the telescopes astronomers use?
4. **Apply** How could you improve on the design of your telescope? What effects would different lenses or tubes have?

More to Explore

With an adult, go outside in the evening a few days after the first-quarter phase and observe the moon. Point the telescope at the moon and draw a circle with all the features you see. Label the maria (lowlands) and highlands.

SCIENCE AND SOCIETY

Light Pollution

Imagine you are in a dark theater watching a movie when the lights come on. You can still see the movie, but it seems dull and faded. For the same reason, you may not see very many stars if you live in or near a city. Light from street lights and advertising signs masks much of the starlight. Artificial light that makes it difficult to see the night sky clearly is known as light pollution.

Astronomers build modern observatories far from cities and outdoor lights. But light pollution is still a problem for older observatories and for amateur astronomers like the one in this photo. If light pollution increases, how will you see glittering stars in the night sky, the broad Milky Way, meteor showers, or an occasional passing comet?

The Issues

How Important Are Outdoor Lights?
Artificial lighting is one of the great advantages of the modern age. Street lights make it easier to drive safely, reducing accidents. Night lighting allows businesses to stay open later. In addition, lighting helps people feel safer in their homes and on the streets.

What Can Be Done?
Street lights are the biggest cause of light pollution. However, some types of street lights cause more light pollution than others. The three types of street light bulbs are mercury vapor bulbs, high-pressure sodium bulbs, and low-pressure sodium bulbs. Low-pressure sodium lights cause the least problem for astronomers because they shine in only a very narrow range of wavelengths. A simple filter on a telescope can eliminate this light from the telescope's view. In addition, street lights of all types can be shielded so they don't shine upward. They can also be pointed only where the light is needed.

Would Reducing Light Pollution Save Money?
Mercury vapor lights are the most common type of street light. High-pressure sodium and low-pressure sodium lights use less electricity, however.

Modifying street lights to reduce light pollution would initially cost a lot of money. However, reducing unneeded light and using light bulbs that require less electricity would also reduce energy usage, which could save money.

You Decide

1. **Identify the Problem**
   In your own words, explain the problem of light pollution.

2. **Analyze the Options**
   List possible solutions. What procedures are involved in each solution? List the advantages and disadvantages of each solution.

3. **Find a Solution**
   Find out what types of street lights your town or city has. Are the lights shielded? Write a letter to your city council proposing a solution to light pollution in your city or town.

SECTION 2 Characteristics of Stars

DISCOVER ······ ACTIVITY ····

How Does Your Thumb Move?

1. Stand facing a wall, at least an arm's length away. Stretch your arm out with your thumb up and your fingers curled.

2. Close your right eye and look at your thumb with your left eye. Line your thumb up with something on the wall.

3. Now close your left eye and open your right eye. How does your thumb appear to move along the wall?

4. Bring your thumb closer to your eye, about half the distance as before. Repeat Steps 2 and 3.

Think It Over

Observing How does your thumb appear to move in Step 4 compared to Step 3? How are these observations related to how far away your thumb is at each step? How could you use this method to estimate distances?

Imagine you could travel to the stars at the speed of light. To travel from Earth to the sun would take about 8 minutes, not very long for such a long trip! Yet the next nearest star, Proxima Centauri, is much farther away—a trip to Proxima Centauri would take 4.2 years!

Most stars are much farther away than Proxima Centauri. Our sun and Proxima Centauri are only two of the stars that make up the Milky Way. The Milky Way is a cluster of stars, called a **galaxy.** It contains hundreds of billions of stars. At the speed of light, it would take you 25,000 years to travel the 250 million billion kilometers to the center of our galaxy. If you left our galaxy and traveled at the speed of light for about 2 million years, you would eventually reach another galaxy, the Andromeda Galaxy.

There are billions of galaxies in the **universe,** which astronomers define as all of space and everything in it. Since galaxies are so far apart, most of the universe is empty space. If our galaxy were the size of a dime, the Andromeda Galaxy would be about half a meter away. The rest of the universe, as far as astronomers can see, would extend for about 2 kilometers in all directions.

GUIDE FOR READING

◆ How do astronomers measure distances to nearby stars?

◆ How are stars classified?

Reading Tip As you read, make a list of the characteristics of stars. Write a sentence describing each characteristic.

Distances to Stars

Distances on Earth are often measured in kilometers. However, as you have seen, distances to stars are so large that the kilometer is not a very practical unit. Instead of kilometers, astronomers use a unit called the light-year. In space, light travels at a speed of 300,000 kilometers per second. A **light-year** is the distance that light travels in one year, or about 9.5 million million kilometers. Note that the light-year is a unit of distance, not time.

To help you understand what a light-year is, consider an everyday example. If you bicycle at 10 kilometers per hour, it would take you 1 hour to go to a mall 10 kilometers away. You could say that the mall is "1 bicycle-hour" away.

It takes light about 4.2 years to reach Earth from Proxima Centauri, so Proxima Centauri is 4.2 light-years, or 40 million million kilometers, away.

☑ *Checkpoint* *How many kilometers are in three light-years?*

Measuring Distances to Stars

Standing on Earth looking up at the sky, it seems as if there is no way to tell how far away the stars are. However, astronomers have found a way to measure those distances. **Astronomers often use parallax to measure distances to nearby stars.**

Parallax is the apparent change in position of an object when you look at it from different places. For example, imagine that you and a friend have gone to a movie. After you sit down, a woman with a large hat sits down in front of you. Because you and your friend are sitting in different positions, the woman's hat blocks different parts of the screen. If you are sitting on her left, the woman's hat appears to be in front of the dinosaur. But to your friend, who is sitting on her right, she appears to be in front of the bird.

Have the woman and her hat moved? No. But because of your relative positions, she appears to have moved. This apparent movement is parallax.

Astronomers use parallax to measure the distances to nearby stars. They look at a star when Earth is on one side of the sun. Then they

Figure 5 You and your friend are sitting behind a woman with a large hat.
Applying Concepts Why is your view of the screen different from your friend's view?

Your view

Your friend's view

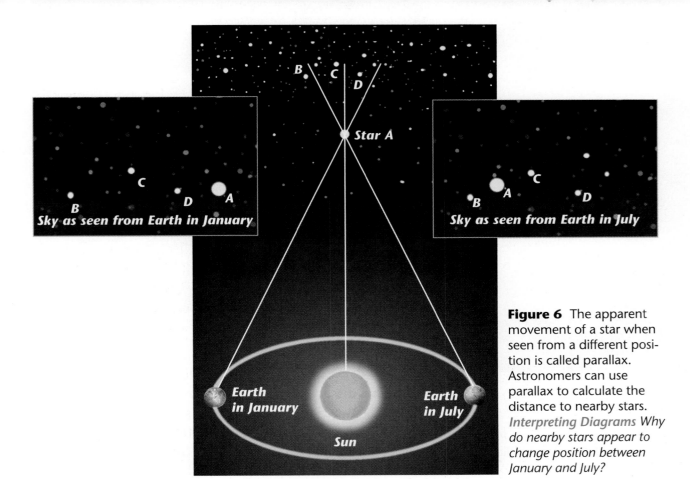

Figure 6 The apparent movement of a star when seen from a different position is called parallax. Astronomers can use parallax to calculate the distance to nearby stars. *Interpreting Diagrams* Why do nearby stars appear to change position between January and July?

look at the same star again six months later, when Earth is on the other side of the sun. Astronomers measure how much the star appears to move against a background of stars that are much farther away. They can then use this measurement, called the parallax shift, to calculate how far away the star is. The less the star appears to move, the farther away it is.

Parallax cannot be used to measure distances any greater than 1,000 light-years. The distance that a star that far away would appear to move when seen from opposite sides of Earth's orbit is too small to measure accurately.

Classifying Stars

Like the sun, all stars are huge spheres of glowing gas. They are made up mostly of hydrogen, and they make energy by nuclear fusion. This energy makes stars shine brightly. The sun is only an average-brightness star. However, the sun is much closer to Earth than any other star. Because it is so close, the sun appears much brighter and much larger than any other star. But the sun is neither the brightest nor the largest star in the galaxy.

Astronomers classify stars according to their physical characteristics. **The main characteristics used to classify stars are size, temperature, and brightness.**

Neutron star

(Sun)
Medium-sized star

White dwarf star

Giant star

Supergiant star

Figure 7 **A.** Stars range in size from tiny neutron stars to enormous supergiants. **B.** The brighter star is Sirius A. The fainter star circled in yellow, Sirius B, is a white dwarf. *Observing What size star is the sun?*

Sizes of Stars

When you look at stars in the sky, they all appear to be the same size. Many stars are actually about the size of the sun, which is a medium-sized star. However, some stars are much larger than the sun. Very large stars are called **giant stars** or supergiant stars. If the supergiant star Betelgeuse (BAY tul jooz) were located where our sun is, it would be large enough to fill the solar system as far out as Jupiter.

Some stars are much smaller than the sun. White dwarf stars are about the size of Earth. Neutron stars are even smaller, only about 20 kilometers in diameter.

✓ *Checkpoint* *Name five sizes of stars, in order from largest to smallest.*

Color and Temperature of Stars

If you look around the sky at night, you can see slight differences in the colors of the stars. Figure 8 shows the constellation known as Orion the Hunter. The red star in Orion's shoulder is Betelgeuse. The blue-white star in Orion's heel is called Rigel.

A star's color reveals its temperature. Hot objects on Earth display the same range of colors as stars. If you watch a toaster heat up, you can see the wires glow red-hot. The wires inside a light bulb are even hotter and glow white. Similarly, the coolest stars—about 3,200 degrees Celsius—appear reddish in the sky. Reddish Betelgeuse is a cool star. With a surface temperature of about 5,500 degrees Celsius, the sun glows white. The hottest stars in the sky—over 10,000 degrees Celsius—appear slightly bluer than the sun. Blue-white Rigel is a very hot star, more than 15,000 degrees Celsius.

726

Brightness of Stars

Stars also differ in brightness, the amount of light they give off. The brightness of a star depends upon its size and temperature. Recall from Chapter 20 that the photosphere is the layer of a star that gives off light. Betelgeuse is fairly cool, so each square meter of its photosphere doesn't give off much light. But Betelgeuse is very large, so it shines brightly. Rigel, on the other hand, is very hot, so each square meter of Rigel's photosphere gives off a lot of light. Even though it is much smaller than Betelgeuse, Rigel also shines brightly.

How bright a star looks from Earth depends on both how far the star is from Earth and how bright the star actually is. Because of these two factors, the brightness of a star can be described in two different ways: apparent magnitude and absolute magnitude.

Apparent Magnitude A star's **apparent magnitude** is its brightness as seen from Earth. Astronomers can measure apparent magnitude fairly easily using electronic devices.

Astronomers cannot tell how much light a star gives off just from the star's apparent magnitude. Just as a flashlight looks brighter the closer it is to you, a star looks brighter the closer it is to Earth. For example, the sun looks very bright. This does not mean that the sun gives off more light than all other stars. The sun looks so bright simply because it is so close to Earth.

Social Studies
CONNECTION

During the Middle Ages Arab astronomers in Southwest Asia and North Africa named many stars. For example, the star name Algol comes from the Arabic words *Ras al Ghul*, which mean "the demon's head." Other Arabic star names include Aldebaran ("the follower of the Pleiades"), Vega ("swooping eagle"), and Rigel ("the left leg of the giant").

In Your Journal

Many other words used in astronomy and mathematics come from Arabic. Find *zenith*, *nadir*, *algorithm*, and *algebra* in a dictionary. Write their definitions in your own words.

Figure 8 The constellation Orion includes the red supergiant star Betelgeuse and the blue supergiant star Rigel.

Figure 9 The stars in a globular cluster are all about the same distance from Earth.

Star Bright ACTIVITY

Here's how you can compare absolute and apparent magnitudes.

1. Dim the lights. Put two equally bright flashlights next to each other on a table. Turn them on.

2. Look at the flashlights from the other side of the room. Think of the flashlights as two stars. Then compare them in terms of absolute and apparent magnitudes.

3. Move one of the flashlights closer to you and repeat Step 2.

4. Replace one of the flashlights with a brighter one. Repeat Step 1 with the unequally bright flashlights. Then repeat Step 2.

Making Models How could you place the flashlights in Step 4 so that they have the same apparent magnitude? Try it.

Absolute Magnitude A star's **absolute magnitude** is the brightness the star would have if it were at a standard distance from Earth. Finding a star's absolute magnitude is more complicated than finding its apparent magnitude. An astronomer must first find out the star's apparent magnitude and its distance from Earth. The astronomer can then calculate the star's brightness if it were at a standard distance from Earth.

Figure 9 shows a globular cluster, a group of 10,000 to 1,000,000 stars that are close together. The stars in a globular cluster are all at about the same distance from Earth. So astronomers study globular clusters to compare the brightnesses of stars. If one star in a globular cluster appears brighter than another star, it really is brighter than that other star.

The Hertzsprung-Russell Diagram

Two of the most important characteristics of stars are temperature and absolute magnitude. About 100 years ago, Ejnar Hertzsprung (EYE nahr HURT sprung) in Denmark and Henry Norris Russell in the United States each made graphs to find out if temperature and brightness are related. They plotted the temperatures of stars on the x-axis and their brightness on the y-axis. The points formed a pattern.

The graph they made is still used by astronomers. It is called the **Hertzsprung-Russell diagram,** or H-R diagram. As you can see in Figure 10, most of the stars in the H-R diagram form a diagonal band called the **main sequence.** In the main sequence, surface temperature increases as brightness increases. More than 90% of all stars are main-sequence stars. The sun is among the stars on the main sequence. Giant and supergiant stars are higher and farther to the right on the H-R diagram. White dwarfs are hot, but not very bright, so they appear at the bottom center of the diagram.

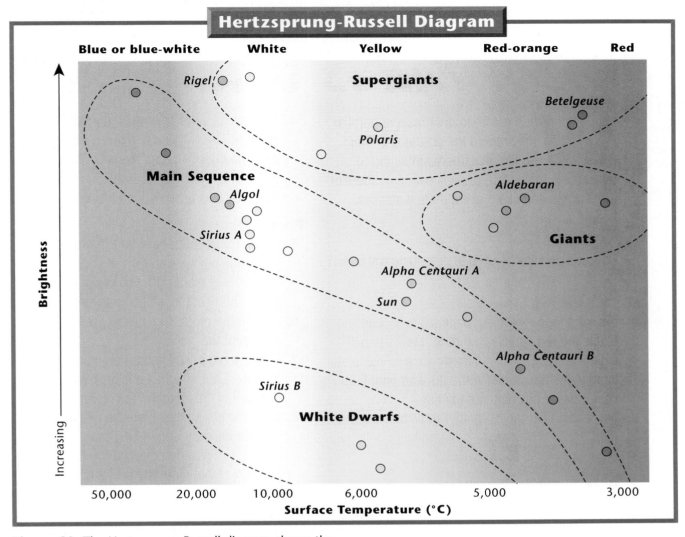

Hertzsprung-Russell Diagram

Blue or blue-white   White   Yellow   Red-orange   Red

Rigel

Supergiants

Betelgeuse

Polaris

Main Sequence

Algol

Aldebaran

Sirius A

Giants

Alpha Centauri A

Sun

Alpha Centauri B

Sirius B

White Dwarfs

Brightness

Increasing

50,000   20,000   10,000   6,000   5,000   3,000

Surface Temperature (°C)

Figure 10 The Hertzsprung-Russell diagram shows the relationship between surface temperature and brightness.
Interpreting Diagrams Which star is hotter: Rigel or Aldebaran?

Section 2 Review

1. What is parallax? How is it useful in astronomy?
2. List three characteristics used to classify stars.
3. Which is hotter—a red star or a blue star? Why?
4. **Thinking Critically Applying Concepts** Stars A and B have about the same apparent magnitude, but Star A is about twice as far from Earth as Star B. Which star has the greater absolute magnitude? Explain your answer.

Science at Home

View Orion With adult family members, go outside on a clear, dark night. Determine which way is north, south, east, and west. Using the star chart for the correct season in Appendix C, look for the constellation Orion. Find the stars Betelgeuse and Rigel in Orion and explain to your family why they are different colors.

HOW FAR IS THAT STAR?

When astronomers measure parallax, they record the positions of stars on film in cameras attached to telescopes. In this lab, you will set up a model of a telescope and use it to estimate distances.

Problem

How can parallax be used to determine distances?

Materials

masking tape	paper clips	pen
black and red pencils	metric ruler	paper
extension cord	meter stick	calculator

lamp without a shade, with 100-watt light bulb
copier paper box (without the lid)
flat rectangular table, about 1 m wide

Procedure

Part 1 Telescope Model

1. Place the lamp on a table in the middle of the classroom.
2. Carefully use the tip of the pen to make a small hole in the middle of one end of the box. The box represents a telescope.
3. At the front of the classroom, place the box on a flat table so the hole points toward the light. Line the left side of the box up with the left edge of the table.

4. Put a small piece of tape on the table below the hole. Use the pen to make a mark on the tape directly below the hole. The mark represents the position of the telescope when Earth is on one side of its orbit.

Part 2 Star 1

5. Label a sheet of paper Star 1 and place it inside the box as shown in the drawing. Hold the paper in place with two paper clips. The paper represents the film in a telescope.
6. Darken the room. Turn on the light to represent the star.
7. With the red pencil, mark the paper where you see a dot of light. Label this dot A. Dot A represents the image of the star on the film.
8. Move the box so the right edge of the box lines up with the right edge of the table. Repeat Step 4. The mark on the tape represents the position of the telescope six months later, when Earth is on the other side of its orbit.
9. Repeat Step 7, and use a black pencil to mark the second dot B. Dot B represents the image of the star as seen 6 months later from the other side of Earth's orbit.
10. Remove the paper. Before you continue, copy the data table into your notebook.
11. Measure and record the distance in millimeters between dots A and B. This distance represents the parallax shift for Star 1.

DATA TABLE

Star	Parallax Shift (mm)	Focal Length (mm)	Diameter of Orbit (mm)	Calculated Distance to Star (mm)	Calculated Distance to Star (m)	Actual Distance to Star (m)

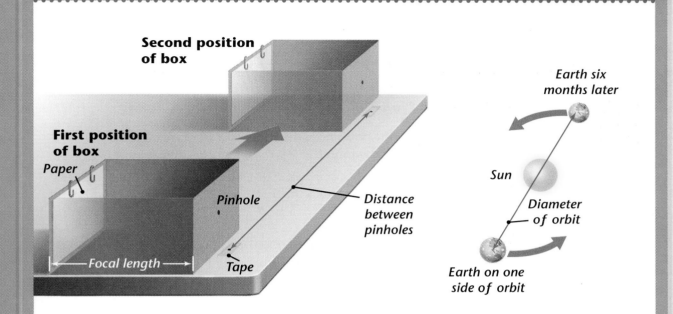

First position of box
Paper
Pinhole
Focal length
Tape

Second position of box

Distance between pinholes

Earth six months later
Sun
Diameter of orbit
Earth on one side of orbit

12. Measure and record the distance from the hole (lens) to the paper (film) at the back of the box in millimeters. This distance represents the focal length of your telescope.

13. Measure and record the distance in millimeters between the marks on the two pieces of masking tape. This distance represents the diameter of Earth's orbit.

Part 3 Stars 2 and 3

14. Move the lamp away from the table—about half the distance to the back of the room. The bulb now represents Star 2. Predict what you think will happen to the light images on your paper.

15. Repeat Steps 6–11 with a new sheet of paper to find the parallax shift for Star 2.

16. Move the lamp to the back of the classroom. The bulb now represents Star 3. Repeat Steps 6–11 with a new sheet of paper to find the parallax shift for Star 3.

Analyze and Conclude

1. What happened to the dot of light for each star when you moved your model telescope from one side of Earth's orbit to the other?

2. What caused the apparent change in position of the dots of light for each star? Explain.

3. Use the following formula to calculate the distance from the telescope to Star 1.

$$\text{Distance} = \frac{\text{Diameter} \times \text{Focal length}}{\text{Parallax shift}}$$

4. Divide your result from Question 3 by 1,000 to get the distance to the light bulb in meters.

5. Repeat Questions 3 and 4 for Stars 2 and 3.

6. Was your prediction in Step 14 correct? Why or why not?

7. Is the parallax shift greater or smaller the farther away the star is? Relate each star's parallax shift to its distance from Earth.

8. **Think About It** Use a meter stick to measure the actual distance from the box to the bulb. How did your calculation for Star 3 compare with the actual distance? What could you do to improve your results?

Design an Experiment

What would happen if you kept moving the lamp away from the box? Is there a distance at which you can no longer find the distance to the star? Design an experiment to find out.

SECTION 3 Lives of Stars

DISCOVER ACTIVITY

What Determines How Long Stars Live?

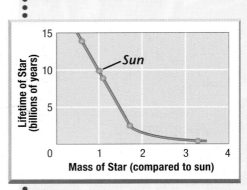

1. This graph shows how the mass of a star is related to its lifetime—how long the star lives before it runs out of fuel.

2. How long does a star with 0.8 times the mass of the sun live? How long does a star with 1.7 times the mass of the sun live?

Think It Over

Drawing Conclusions Describe the general relationship between a star's mass and its lifetime.

GUIDE FOR READING

◆ How does the life of a star begin?

◆ What determines how long a star will live?

◆ What happens to a star when it runs out of fuel?

Reading Tip As you read, make a flowchart showing the stages in the life of a medium-sized star.

Jocelyn Bell today ▼

In 1967, Jocelyn Bell, a British astronomy student, detected an object in space that appeared to give off regular pulses of radio waves. Some astronomers hypothesized that the pulses might be a signal from an extraterrestrial civilization. At first, astronomers even named the source LGM, for the "Little Green Men" in early science-fiction stories. Eventually, astronomers concluded that the source of the radio waves was a neutron star. A neutron star is a tiny star left over when a giant star explodes. Neutron stars like the one Bell discovered are called **pulsars**—pulsating radio sources.

Studying the Lives of Stars

Stars do not last forever. Each star is born, goes through its life cycle, and eventually dies. (Of course, stars are not really alive. The words *born, live,* and *die* are just helpful comparisons.) How did astronomers figure out that the neutron star Bell discovered had been a larger star earlier in its life?

Imagine that you want to study how people age. You wish you could watch a few people for 50 years, but your assignment is due next week! You have to study a lot of people for a short time, and classify the people into different age groups. You may come up with groups like *babies, children, teenagers, young adults, middle-aged people,* and *elderly people.* You don't have time to see a single person go through all these stages, but you know the stages exist.

Astronomers have a similar problem with stars. They can't watch a single star for billions of years, so they study many stars and see how they differ from one another.

A Star Is Born

A star is made up of a large amount of gas in a relatively small volume. A **nebula,** on the other hand, is a large amount of gas and dust spread out in an immense volume. All stars begin their lives as parts of nebulas.

Gravity can pull some of the gas and dust in a nebula together. The contracting cloud is then called a protostar. *Proto* means "earliest" in Greek, so a **protostar** is the earliest stage of a star's life. **A star is born when the contracting gas and dust become so hot that nuclear fusion starts.** Recall from Chapter 20 that nuclear fusion is the process by which atoms of hydrogen are combined to form helium. During fusion, enormous amounts of energy are released.

Lifetimes of Stars

Before they can tell how old a star is, astronomers must determine its mass. **How long a star lives depends on how much mass it has.**

You might think that stars with more mass would last longer than stars with less mass. However, the reverse is true. You can think of stars as being like cars. A small car has a small gas tank, but it also has a small engine that burns gas slowly. A large car, on the other hand, has a larger gas tank, but it also has a larger engine that burns gas rapidly. So the small car might be able to travel farther on one small tank of gas than the larger car can on one large tank of gas. Small stars use up their fuel more slowly than large stars, so they have much longer lives.

Generally, stars that have less mass than the sun use their fuel slowly, and can live for up to 200 billion years. Medium-mass stars like the sun live for about 10 billion years. Astronomers think the sun is about 4.6 billion years old, so it is almost halfway through its lifetime.

Stars that have more mass than the sun have shorter lifetimes. A star that is 15 times as massive as the sun may live only about ten million years. That may seem like a long time, but it is only one tenth of one percent of the lifetime of the sun.

✓ *Checkpoint* *If a star is twice as massive as the sun, will it have a longer or shorter life than the sun?*

Figure 11 The Orion Nebula, top, is a giant cloud of gas and dust. The Hubble Space Telescope took this photo of a protostar, bottom, in the Orion Nebula. A protostar is a star in the earliest stage of its life. *Applying Concepts How do some of the gas and dust in a nebula become a protostar?*

Figure 12 Supernova 1987A was the brightest supernova seen in hundreds of years. The arrow in the photo at the left points to the original star, before it exploded. *Making Generalizations Why were ancient astronomers able to see supernovas?*

Deaths of Stars

When a star begins to runs out of fuel, the center of the star shrinks and the outer part of the star expands. The star becomes a red giant or supergiant.

All main sequence stars eventually become red giants or supergiants. However, what happens next depends on the mass of the star, as *Exploring the Lives of Stars* shows. **When a star runs out of fuel, it becomes a white dwarf, a neutron star, or a black hole.**

White Dwarfs Small and medium stars take 10 billion or more years to use up their nuclear fuel. Then their outer layers expand, and they become red giants. Eventually, the outer parts grow bigger still and drift out into space. The blue-white hot core of the star that is left behind is a **white dwarf.**

White dwarfs are only about the size of Earth, but they have about as much mass as the sun. Since a white dwarf has the same mass as the sun but only one millionth the volume, it is one million times as dense as the sun. A spoonful of material from a white dwarf has as much mass as a large truck. White dwarfs have no fuel, but they glow faintly from leftover energy. When a white dwarf stops glowing, it is dead. Then it is called a black dwarf.

Neutron Stars A dying giant or supergiant star can suddenly explode. Within hours, the star blazes millions of times brighter. The explosion is called a **supernova.** You can see a supernova in Figure 12. After a supernova, some of the material from the star expands into space. This material may become part of a nebula. The nebula can then contract to form a new, "recycled" star. Astronomers think the sun began as a nebula that contained material from a supernova explosion.

After the star explodes, some of the material from the star is left behind. This material forms a neutron star. **Neutron stars** are even smaller and denser than white dwarfs. A neutron star may contain as much as three times the mass of the sun but be only about 20 kilometers in diameter, the size of a large asteroid or a town on Earth.

Sharpen your Skills

Predicting ACTIVITY

Find Algol, Polaris, and Sirius B in the H-R diagram on page 729. For each star, write a sentence predicting what the next stages in its life will be.

Black Holes The most massive stars—those having more than 40 times the mass of the sun—become **black holes** when they die. After this kind of star becomes a supernova, more than five times the mass of the sun may be left. The gravity of this mass is so strong that the gas is pulled inward, packing the gas into a smaller and smaller space. Eventually five times as much mass as the sun becomes packed within a sphere 30 kilometers in diameter. At that point, the gravity is so strong that nothing can escape, not even light. The remains of the star become a black hole.

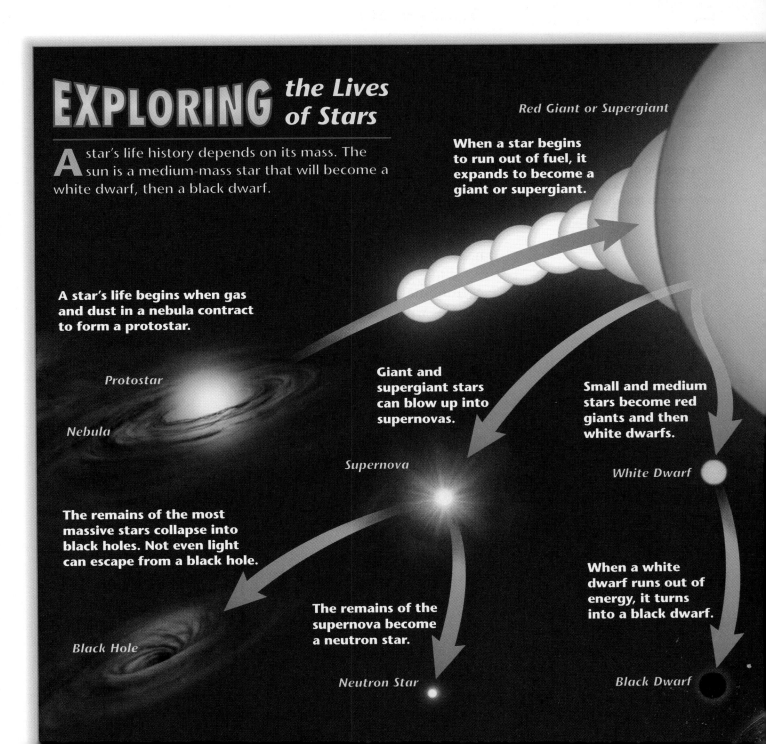

EXPLORING the Lives of Stars

A star's life history depends on its mass. The sun is a medium-mass star that will become a white dwarf, then a black dwarf.

Red Giant or Supergiant

When a star begins to run out of fuel, it expands to become a giant or supergiant.

A star's life begins when gas and dust in a nebula contract to form a protostar.

Protostar

Nebula

Giant and supergiant stars can blow up into supernovas.

Small and medium stars become red giants and then white dwarfs.

Supernova

White Dwarf

The remains of the most massive stars collapse into black holes. Not even light can escape from a black hole.

When a white dwarf runs out of energy, it turns into a black dwarf.

The remains of the supernova become a neutron star.

Black Hole

Neutron Star

Black Dwarf

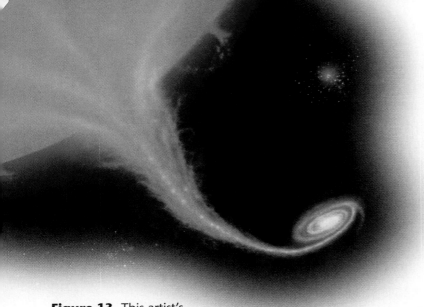

Figure 13 This artist's impression shows a black hole pulling matter from a companion star. The material glows as it is pulled into the black hole. *Applying Concepts If it is impossible to detect a black hole directly, how do astronomers find them?*

No light, radio waves, or any other form of radiation can ever get out of a black hole, so it is not possible to detect a black hole directly. But astronomers can detect black holes indirectly.

For example, gas near a black hole is pulled so strongly that it rotates faster and faster around the black hole. Friction heats the gas up. Astronomers can detect X-rays coming from the hot gas and infer that a black hole is present. Similarly, if another star is near a black hole, astronomers can calculate the mass of the black hole from the effect of its gravity on the star. The Chandra X-ray Observatory is looking for black holes by studying sources of X-rays.

Quasars In the 1960s, astronomers discovered objects that are unusual because they are very bright, but also very far away. Many of these objects are about 12 billion light-years away, making them among the most distant objects in the universe. These distant bright objects looked almost like stars. Since *quasi* means "something like" in Latin, these objects were given the name **quas**i-stell**ar** objects, or **quasars.**

What could be so bright even though it is so far away? Astronomers have concluded that quasars are actually distant galaxies with giant black holes at their centers. Each black hole has a mass a billion times or more as great as that of the sun. As enormous amounts of gas revolve around such a black hole, the gas heats up and shines brightly.

Section 3 Review

1. What is the earliest stage in the life of a star?
2. Why do small stars have longer lifetimes than large stars?
3. What is the difference between stars that become white dwarfs and stars that become neutron stars?
4. What evidence do astronomers use to detect black holes?
5. **Thinking Critically Inferring** What will happen to the sun when it dies? Explain your answer.

Check Your Progress CHAPTER PROJECT

Draw and label the stars in your constellation *without* the connecting lines that form the usual image. What different patterns can you see? (*Hint:* Use a pencil to "doodle" different connections among the stars.) What does each pattern look like? Choose one pattern, and use it to name your constellation. Then write an outline of a brief story that explains why this constellation is in the sky.

736

4 Star Systems and Galaxies

Why Does the Milky Way Look Hazy?

1. Using a pencil, carefully poke at least 20 holes close together in a sheet of white paper.

2. Tape the paper to a chalkboard or dark-colored wall.

3. Go to the other side of the room and look at the paper. From the far side of the room, what do the dots look like? Can you see individual dots?

Think It Over

Making Models How is looking at the paper from the far side of the room like trying to see many very distant stars that are close together? How does your model compare to the photograph of the Milky Way below?

On a clear, dark summer night in the country, you can see a hazy band of light stretched across the sky. This band of stars is called the Milky Way. It looks as if the Milky Way is very far away from Earth. Actually, though, Earth is inside the Milky Way! How is this possible? Before you can understand the answer to this question, you need to know more about how stars are grouped together.

Star Systems and Planets

Our solar system has only one star, the sun. **But more than half of all stars are members of groups of two or more stars, called star systems.** If you were on a planet in one of these star systems, you would probably see two or more suns in the sky.

Double and Triple Stars Star systems with two stars are called double stars or **binary stars.** (The prefix *bi* means "two.") Those with three stars are called triple stars. Proxima Centauri is probably part of a triple star system close to our sun. The other two stars in the system, Alpha Centauri A and Alpha Centauri B, form a double star. Scientists are not sure whether Proxima Centauri is really part of the system or is just passing close to the other two stars temporarily.

Astronomers can sometimes detect a binary star even if only one of the stars in the pair can be seen from Earth. For example, the darker star in the pair may pass in front of the other star and eclipse the other star. A system in which one star blocks the light from another is

GUIDE FOR READING

◆ What is a star system?

◆ What are the three types of galaxies?

Reading Tip Before you read, preview the boldfaced terms. As you read, look for a photograph or diagram that illustrates each term.

The Milky Way ▶

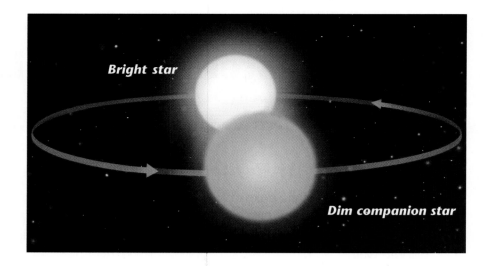

Figure 14 Algol is an eclipsing binary star system, consisting of a bright star and a dim companion star. Each time the dimmer star passes in front of the brighter one, Algol becomes less bright. *Interpreting Diagrams When does Algol become brighter?*

Bright star

Dim companion star

Figure 15 If you saw someone dancing but couldn't see a partner, you could infer that the partner was there by watching the dancer you could see. Astronomers use a similar method to detect faint stars in star systems.

called an **eclipsing binary.** As Figure 14 shows, the star Algol is actually part of an eclipsing binary.

Often astronomers can tell that there is a second star in a system only by observing the effects of its gravity. As the second star revolves around the first star, the second star's gravity makes the first star move back and forth. Imagine you are watching a pair of dancers twirling each other around. Even if one dancer were invisible, you could tell that the invisible dancer was there from watching the motion of the visible dancer.

Planets Around Other Stars In 1995, astronomers discovered a planet revolving around a star using a method similar to the one they use to detect binary stars. The star the astronomers were observing, 51 Pegasi, moved back and forth only very slightly. Therefore, they knew the invisible object could not have enough mass to be a star. They deduced that it must be a planet.

Before this discovery, there was no way to know whether stars other than the sun had planets revolving around them. Now astronomers are fairly sure that our solar system is not the only one. All of the planets found beyond our solar system so far are very large, at least half Jupiter's mass. A small planet would be difficult to detect because it would have little gravitational effect on the star it revolved around.

Astronomers are trying to find new ways to use telescopes to see planets directly. Seeing a planet around another star is like trying to see a firefly near a street light. The glare of the light makes it hard to see anything near the light. To see a planet directly, astronomers will have to shield their view from the glare of the star that the planet revolves around. This may not be possible for many decades.

Some scientists hypothesize that life may exist on planets revolving around other stars. A few astronomers are using radio telescopes to search for signals that could not have come from natural sources. Such a signal might be evidence that an extraterrestrial civilization existed and was sending out radio waves.

☑ Checkpoint **What evidence have astronomers used to conclude that there are planets around other stars?**

Galaxies

Now you are ready to learn about the Milky Way. The Milky Way is the galaxy in which our solar system is located. Like other galaxies, it contains single stars, double stars, star systems, and lots of gas and dust between the stars. The Milky Way Galaxy, often just called "our galaxy," looks milky or hazy because the stars are too close together for your eyes to see them individually. The dark blotches in the Milky Way are clouds of dust that block light coming from stars behind them.

There are billions of galaxies in the universe. **Astronomers have classified most galaxies into three main categories: spiral galaxies, elliptical galaxies, and irregular galaxies.**

Side view

Sun's location

Top view

Sun's location

About 100,000 light-years

A Spiral Galaxy

You can make a model of our galaxy.

1. Using pipe cleaners, make a pinwheel with two spirals.

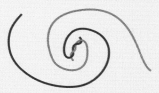

2. View the spirals along the surface of the table. Sketch what you see. Can you see the spiral shape?

3. Next, view the spirals from above the table and sketch them.

Observing The sun is inside a flat spiral galaxy. From Earth's position on the flat surface, is it possible to get a good view of stars in the spiral arms? Why or why not?

Figure 16 From the side, the Milky Way Galaxy appears to be a narrow disk. The spiral structure would be visible only from above the galaxy.

Figure 17 **A.** This spiral galaxy is similar to our galaxy. **B.** An elliptical galaxy looks like a flattened ball. **C.** The Large Magellanic Cloud is an irregular galaxy.

Spiral Galaxies   Figure 17A shows a galaxy that has the shape of twin spirals, called a **spiral galaxy.** Astronomers can see other spiral galaxies from different angles. These views show that spiral galaxies have arms that spiral outward, like pinwheels.

Our galaxy has the same spiral, pinwheel shape. It is hard for us to see the spiral shape of our galaxy because our solar system is inside the galaxy, about two thirds of the way out in one of the spiral arms. The Milky Way you see in the sky is the view people on Earth get when they look toward the part of our galaxy that is visible from Earth. The center of our galaxy is about 25,000 light-years from the sun. However, we cannot see the center of our galaxy. The center is hidden from our view by the dust associated with massive clouds of gas between the sun and the center.

Elliptical Galaxies   Not all galaxies have spiral arms. **Elliptical galaxies** look like flattened balls. These galaxies contain billions of stars but have little gas and dust between the stars. Because of the lack of gas and dust, new stars cannot form in elliptical galaxies. So elliptical galaxies contain only old stars.

Irregular Galaxies   Some galaxies do not have regular shapes. Because of this, they are known as **irregular galaxies.** The Large Magellanic Cloud is an irregular galaxy about 160,000 light-years away from our galaxy. At this distance it is one of the closest neighboring galaxies in the universe.

Section 4 Review

1. What is a star system?
2. Describe the three main types of galaxies.
3. Where is the sun in our galaxy?
4. **Thinking Critically** **Applying Concepts** Some binary stars are called eclipsing binaries. Explain why this term is appropriate. (*Hint:* Think about Algol as you come up with an answer.)

Science at Home

Stargazing Plan an evening of stargazing with adult family members. Choose a dark, clear night. Use binoculars if available and the star charts in Appendix C to locate the Milky Way and some interesting stars you have learned about. Explain to your family what you know about the Milky Way and each star you observe.

The Andromeda Galaxy is the most distant object you can see with your unaided eyes. Light from this galaxy has traveled for 2 million years before reaching your eyes. When that light finally reaches your eye, you are seeing what the galaxy looked like 2 million years ago. It is as though you are looking back in time.

Astronomers have photographed galaxies that are billions of light-years away. Light from these galaxies traveled for billions of years before it reached telescopes on Earth. From these observations, astronomers have inferred that the universe is incredibly old—billions of years old.

Moving Galaxies

To study how and when the universe formed, astronomers use information about how galaxies are moving. Astronomers can measure how far away different galaxies are. By examining the spectrum of a galaxy, astronomers can tell how fast the galaxy is moving and whether it is moving toward our galaxy or away from it. Only a few nearby galaxies are moving toward our galaxy. All of the other galaxies are moving away from our galaxy.

In the 1920s, Edwin Hubble, an American astronomer, discovered that the farther away a galaxy is from us, the faster it is moving away from us. The Hubble Space Telescope was named after Hubble in honor of this and other important discoveries.

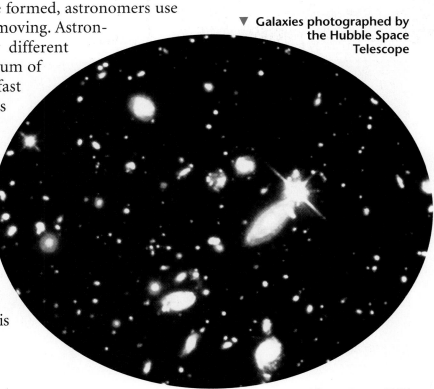

▼ Galaxies photographed by the Hubble Space Telescope

Figure 18 The galaxies in the expanding universe are like the raisins in rising bread dough. *Making Models How does rising raisin bread dough model the expanding universe?*

To understand how the galaxies are moving, think of raisin bread dough that is rising. If you could shrink yourself to sit on a raisin, you would see all the other raisins moving away from you as the bread dough rose. The farther away a raisin was from you, the faster it would move away, because there would be more bread dough to expand between you and the raisin. No matter which raisin you sat on, all the other raisins would seem to be moving away from you. You could tell that the bread dough was expanding by watching the other raisins.

The universe is like the raisin bread dough. The galaxies in the universe, like the raisins in the dough, are moving away from each other. In the universe it is space that is expanding, like the dough between the raisins.

The Big Bang Theory

To understand how the galaxies moved in the past, imagine you could run time backward. All of the galaxies would then be moving together instead of apart. All of the matter in the universe would eventually come together at a single point. At that time, billions of years ago, the universe was small, hot, and dense. The universe then exploded in what astronomers call the **big bang.**

According to the big bang theory, the universe formed in an enormous explosion about 10 to 15 billion years ago. Since the big bang, the universe has been expanding rapidly. Because of the big bang, the universe is billions of times larger than it was billions of years ago. To understand this change in size, picture a

Figure 19 All of the distant galaxies astronomers have observed are moving away from our galaxy.

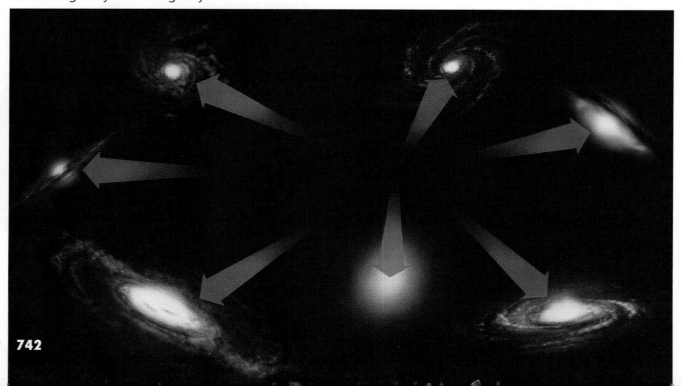

Figure 20 The solar system formed from a collapsing cloud of gas and dust.

Within the image panels:

A cloud of gas and dust formed a spinning disk.

Gas in the center of the disk collapsed to form the sun.

The remaining gas and dust formed the planets.

The solar system includes the sun, planets, and belts of rock, ice, and dust.

tiny pea. Pretend you can blow it up to be as big as Earth. You would be inflating the pea by about two billion times. Like the pea, the universe in which you live was once very small. The universe has been growing rapidly ever since the big bang. Astronomers have concluded that the galaxies are moving away from each other as a result of the big bang.

Since astronomers know approximately how fast the universe is expanding now, they can infer how long it has been expanding. Astronomers estimate that the universe has been expanding for 10 billion to 15 billion years.

☑ *Checkpoint* *Which way are most galaxies moving relative to each other?*

Formation of the Solar System

After the big bang, matter in the universe separated into galaxies. Gas and dust spread throughout space in our galaxy. Where the solar system is now, there was only cold, dark gas and dust.

About five billion years ago, a giant cloud of gas and dust, or nebula, collapsed to form the solar system. Slowly the nebula shrank to form a spinning disk. As gravity pulled some of the gas into the center of the disk, the gas became hot and dense enough for nuclear fusion to begin. The sun was born.

Figure 21 This engineer is checking data from the Hubble Space Telescope. The telescope can be controlled from this room.

Elsewhere in the disk, gas and dust formed solid spheres smaller than the sun. The spheres closest to the sun lost most of their gases and became the inner planets Mercury, Venus, Earth, and Mars. The spheres farthest from the sun became the gas giants Jupiter, Saturn, Uranus, and Neptune. Between the inner planets and the gas giants, the asteroids formed. Beyond the gas giants, a huge cloud of ice and other substances formed. This cloud is probably the main source of comets. Pluto also formed in this region.

The Future of the Universe

What will happen to the universe in the future? One possibility is that the universe will continue to expand, as it is doing now. All of the stars will eventually run out of fuel and burn out, and the universe will be cold and dark. Another possibility is that the force of gravity will begin to pull the galaxies back together. The result will be a reverse big bang, or "big crunch." All of the matter in the universe will be crushed into an enormous black hole.

Which of these possibilities is more likely? The answer depends on how strong the total force of gravity pulling the galaxies together is. This force depends on the total mass of the universe. It is very difficult for astronomers to estimate this mass because much of it is in the form of particles that do not give off electromagnetic radiation. The evidence so far suggests that the total mass of the universe is not great enough to pull the galaxies back together again. However, more research needs to be done to solve this problem.

Astronomy is one of the oldest sciences, but there are still many discoveries to be made and puzzles to be solved about this universe of ours!

 Section 5 Review

1. What was the big bang?
2. Describe how the solar system formed.
3. What observations show that the universe is expanding?
4. **Thinking Critically** **Inferring** What can astronomers infer from the fact that other galaxies are moving away from ours?

Check Your Progress CHAPTER PROJECT

Now you are ready to write the first draft of a story that explains your constellation's name. After you have written a first draft, read it over carefully and look for ways to improve it. Here are things to look for as you edit your first draft. Does the beginning grab the reader's interest? Does your story make sense? Should you add more details? Should you rethink your choice of words? Rewrite and revise as much as necessary.

SECTION 1 — Tools of Modern Astronomy

INTEGRATING PHYSICS

Key Ideas

◆ The electromagnetic spectrum includes radio waves, infrared radiation, visible light, ultraviolet radiation, X-rays, and gamma rays.
◆ Telescopes collect and focus different types of electromagnetic radiation.
◆ Astronomers use spectrographs to get information about stars.

Key Terms

constellation	refracting telescope
visible light	convex lens
electromagnetic radiation	reflecting telescope
wavelength	radio telescope
spectrum	observatory
	spectrograph

SECTION 2 — Characteristics of Stars

Key Ideas

◆ Astronomers use parallax to measure distances to nearby stars.
◆ The main characteristics used to classify stars are size, temperature, and brightness.

Key Terms

galaxy	apparent magnitude
universe	absolute magnitude
light-year	Hertzsprung-Russell diagram
parallax	main sequence
giant star	

SECTION 3 — Lives of Stars

Key Ideas

◆ A star is born when nuclear fusion starts.
◆ The length of a star's life depends on its mass.
◆ When a star runs out of fuel, it becomes a white dwarf, a neutron star, or a black hole.

Key Terms

pulsar	white dwarf	black hole
nebula	supernova	quasar
protostar	neutron star	

SECTION 4 — Star Systems and Galaxies

Key Ideas

◆ More than half of all stars are members of groups of two or more stars, called star systems.
◆ There are three types of galaxies: spiral galaxies, elliptical galaxies, and irregular galaxies.

Key Terms

binary star	elliptical galaxy
eclipsing binary	irregular galaxy
spiral galaxy	

SECTION 5 — History of the Universe

Key Ideas

◆ According to the big bang theory, the universe formed in an enormous explosion about 10 to 15 billion years ago.
◆ About five billion years ago, a cloud of gas and dust collapsed to form the solar system.

Key Term

big bang

Organizing Information

Concept Map Copy the concept map about telescopes onto a separate sheet of paper. Then complete it and add a title. (For more on concept maps, see the Skills Handbook.)

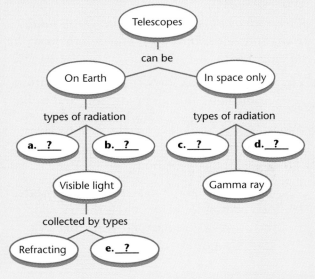

Reviewing Content

 For more review of key concepts, see the Interactive Student Tutorial CD-ROM.

Multiple Choice

Choose the letter of the answer that best completes each statement.

1. The Hubble Space Telescope is a
   a. gamma ray telescope.
   b. reflecting telescope.
   c. refracting telescope.
   d. radio telescope.

2. The most common chemical element in a star is
   a. hydrogen.
   b. helium.
   c. carbon.
   d. sodium.

3. To measure the distance to a nearby star, an astronomer would use
   a. visible light.
   b. quasars.
   c. parallax.
   d. a spectrograph.

4. Stars more massive than the sun
   a. live longer than the sun.
   b. are redder than the sun.
   c. have shorter lives than the sun.
   d. live as long as the sun.

5. The sun formed out of a
   a. pulsar.   b. supergiant star.
   c. black hole.   d. nebula.

True or False

If the statement is true, write true. If it is false, change the underlined word or words to make the statement true.

6. Gamma rays, X-rays, ultraviolet radiation, visible light, infrared radiation, and radio waves make up the <u>Hertzsprung-Russell diagram</u>.

7. The sun is a <u>main-sequence</u> star.

8. Pulsars are a <u>kind of</u> <u>neutron star</u>.

9. More than half of all stars are <u>single</u> stars.

10. Acccording to the <u>big bang</u> theory, the universe has been growing for 10–15 billion years.

Checking Concepts

11. What types of radiation are included in the electromagnetic spectrum?

12. What kinds of information can astronomers obtain by studying the spectrum of a star?

13. Describe what will happen to the sun when it runs out of fuel.

14. Why can astronomers see the spiral arms of the Andromeda Galaxy more clearly than the spiral arms of the Milky Way Galaxy?

15. Describe the process by which the sun was formed.

16. **Writing to Learn** Imagine you have a spaceship that can travel much faster than the speed of light. Write a letter describing your three-part trip from Earth: to the nearest star other than the sun, to the center of our galaxy, and to the next nearest spiral galaxy.

Thinking Critically

17. **Relating Cause and Effect** Once every three days a small, bright star becomes much dimmer, only to return to its original brightness within six hours. Based on this information, what is causing the small star to become dimmer?

18. **Applying Concepts** Describe a real-world situation involving absolute and apparent magnitudes. (*Hint:* Think about riding in a car at night.)

19. **Comparing and Contrasting** Compare the life histories of a medium-sized star and a giant star. How are they similar? How are they different?

20. **Making Generalizations** What does knowing the rate at which the universe is expanding tell astronomers about the big bang?

21. **Applying Concepts** Is a light-year a unit of distance or a unit of time? Explain.

Applying Skills

Use the data about moving galaxies in the table below to answer Questions 22–24.

Cluster of Galaxies	Distance (millions of light-years)	Speed (kilometers per second)
Virgo	80	1,200
Ursa Major	980	15,000
Bootes	2,540	39,000
Hydra	3,980	61,000

22. **Graphing** Make a line graph showing how each cluster's distance from our galaxy is related to its speed. Put distance on the *x*-axis and speed on the *y*-axis.

23. **Interpreting Data** How are the distance and speed of a galaxy related?

24. **Drawing Conclusions** Does your graph indicate that the universe is expanding, contracting, or staying the same size? Explain.

CHAPTER PROJECT

Performance Assessment

Present Your Project Check the final draft of your story for correct spelling, grammar, punctuation, and usage. Make any necessary changes. Then decide how you will present your new constellation story. For example, you can make a poster showing the constellation, its star pattern, and your story. You can read your story aloud or perform it as a skit or play.

Reflect and Record This project has given you a chance to research information and then present it in writing. In your journal, write what you found easiest and hardest about researching and writing.

Test Preparation
Use these questions to prepare for standardized tests.

Study the diagram. Then answer Questions 25–29.

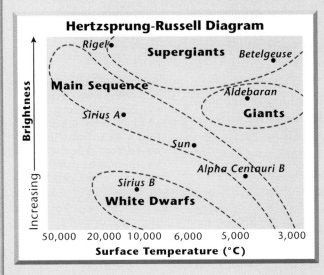

25. To which group do most stars belong?
    a. supergiants   b. giants
    c. main sequence   d. white dwarfs

26. **Which star is hotter than the sun?**
    a. Betelgeuse
    b. Aldebaran
    c. Alpha Centauri B
    d. Sirius B

27. **Which star is most likely to be red?**
    a. Rigel
    b. Sirius A
    c. Sirius B
    d. Betelgeuse

28. **Compared to Rigel, Alpha Centauri B is**
    a. cooler and brighter.
    b. cooler and dimmer.
    c. hotter and brighter.
    d. hotter and dimmer.

29. **Which star has a greater absolute magnitude?**
    a. Rigel
    b. Betelgeuse
    c. Sirius B
    d. Aldebaran

JOURNEY TO
MARS

The little six-wheeled rover inched down
the steep ramp of the lander and onto the surface of Mars.
Scientists on Earth held their breaths.
Then, Sojourner hummed into action.

Sojourner became the star of the 1997 *Pathfinder* mission. Engineers at the Jet Propulsion Laboratory in Pasadena, California, guided the rover from remote controls on Earth. It rolled from rock to rock, collecting scientific data and checking the mineral content of each rock. Back on Earth, the *Pathfinder* team named the rocks after cartoon characters—Barnacle Bill, Scooby Doo, and Casper. They named a bear-shaped rock Yogi.

Pathfinder had landed in a region of Mars that no one had seen closely before. The lander took photographs of Martian landscapes, sunrises, and sunsets. Running on energy from solar panels, *Pathfinder's* instruments sent back huge amounts of information for scientists on Earth to analyze. This mission was just one of many that would study the Martian landscape.

Sojourner—about the size of a microwave oven—explores the rocky surface of Mars. Here it bumps into a rock that scientists called Yogi. The electronic image was transmitted by *Pathfinder* from Mars to Earth.

Honor in a Name

Would you like to name a spacecraft? A 13-year-old student from Connecticut got that chance. Valerie Ambroise chose the name *Sojourner* for the small Pathfinder rover that explored the Martian surface in 1997. In a contest sponsored by NASA and The Planetary Society, Valerie wrote the winning essay for the best name. There were 3,500 student entries.

Valerie named *Sojourner* after Sojourner Truth, an African American reformer in the 1840s and 1850s. Here is Valerie Ambroise's essay.

Sojourner Truth (above), a powerful speaker against slavery, and Valerie Ambroise (right).

The name of the Pathfinder should be Sojourner Truth. I chose Sojourner because she was a heroine to Blacks, slaves, and women. She acted on her strong feelings about life and the way it should be. Her greatest companions were God and her beliefs. Her greatest achievements included the book of her life written through her by a friend, meeting President Lincoln, meeting President Grant, her speeches and tours, her work at hospitals for soldiers during the Civil War, and her intellect (considering that she was illiterate). She went on many journeys and told many truths. She spoke with such eloquence that she moved people with simple words and understandings.

It's only logical that the Pathfinder be named Sojourner Truth, because she is on a journey to find truths about Mars. The Pathfinder should be able to have strong personalities in order to go under harsh conditions like that on Mars. Truth, while on tours, went under many harsh conditions. Even before, she went under harsh conditions as a slave.

Like Sojourner, the Pathfinder should be able to survive with what she already has. She should not need any extra equipment for surviving. The Pathfinder could use its feet like wheels, for transportation. Sojourner used her feet to travel a lot.

To research Mars, first, Sojourner would find out all she could about it. She always tried to understand further about what she was fighting for. When she got her information; she would use this information in Mars to study it more and add it to hers. She would act quickly to get what she wanted or what she felt was needed. Her talents in her work would be the same on Mars. She would use her eloquent voice and powerful actions.

You must admit, Sojourner and the Pathfinder are important.

Language Arts Activity

You have the chance to name the first research station on Mars, honoring an important person in scientific exploration or discovery. Research your hero or heroine. Then write a persuasive essay explaining why the research station should be named after him or her.

An artist imagines a scene in the future in which humans walk on the rocky plains of Mars.

Essentials for Survival

You step out of your spacecraft onto a dusty red landscape under a pinkish-red sky. Now you know why Mars is called the "red planet." Water vapor in the air forms thin clouds, even fog. Because the air is so thin, the sun glares down. It's windy, too. Thick clouds of reddish dust, rich in iron, blow around you.

Without a pressurized spacesuit, you would not survive in the thin Martian air. Unlike the thick layers of atmosphere around Earth, this atmosphere gives almost no protection against harmful ultraviolet radiation. You also must carry oxygen. Martian air is about 95 percent carbon dioxide, which humans can't breathe.

Your spacesuit must keep you warm. Even at the Martian equator, daytime temperatures are rarely above freezing. At night they plunge to about −100°C. Walk carefully, too, because Martian gravity is weak. You'll feel only 38 percent of your Earth weight!

This is a 360-degree image taken from *Pathfinder.* On the rugged Martian landscape, sand and dust storms have carved rocks into fantastic shapes. Deep canyons and huge volcanoes also shape the surface.

Science Activity

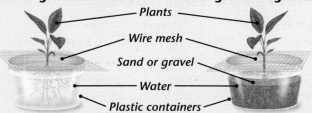

Plants grown in water   Plants grown in gravel

— Plants —
— Wire mesh —
— Sand or gravel —
— Water —
— Plastic containers —

Any human settlement on Mars would have to grow some of its own food. Experiment with a method called hydroponics—growing plants mainly in water, without soil. Set up two plant containers to grow tomatoes or peppers.

◆ Decide what variables to control.

◆ In one container, use just water and plant food, with a wire mesh support.

◆ In the other, add sand or gravel to root plants; add water and plant food.

◆ Record the rate of growth and strength of each plant over a two-to three-week period.

Which technique worked the best? How do you think hydroponics would work on Mars?

Astronaut Shannon Lucid and a Russian cosmonaut examine food bins on *Mir* (left).

A cosmonaut, floating in space, repairs equipment on *Mir* (above).

Partners in Space

Many engineers and scientists are sure that humans will travel to Mars sometime in the next 25 years. Meanwhile, people have gotten a preview of a space voyage from astronauts and cosmonauts traveling on space shuttles and on *Mir*, Russia's space station. *Mir* was launched in 1986.

For years, the United States and the Soviet Union competed in the race to send missions into space. Recently, Russia and the United States have cooperated on *Mir*. In 1997, Americans became full members of the *Mir* crew with specific jobs. They worked with the cosmonauts to solve problems, make repairs, take space walks, and run the ship's computers.

What's it like for crew members from different backgrounds to live and work together in a cramped spacecraft? Besides having cultural and language differences,

Russian and American crews have different training and different equipment. Even spacesuits are not the same.

Because *Mir* is an old station, space crews have gotten used to dealing with emergencies. On a long flight, such as one to Mars, those skills would be essential.

All this experience on *Mir* is a first step toward the International Space Station, now being built—and possibly an expedition to Mars.

Social Studies Activity

The first trips to Mars will probably take at least 6 to 8 months. Think about the difficulties you would have spending 7 months in a spacecraft about the size of a school bus. Set up rules and guidelines for your voyage. Plan for 5 astronauts from 2 different countries. Consider these issues:

◆ who will make decisions and give orders

◆ how you will communicate

◆ how you'll adjust for different living habits and backgrounds

◆ how you'll avoid getting bored

◆ how you'll resolve conflicts among crew members or with mission control scientists on Earth.

Sols of Mars

Mars is the planet most like Earth. But its smaller size, greater distance from the sun, and different orbit cause some immense differences. A Martian day, called a sol, is only about 40 minutes longer than an Earth day. The Martian year, however, is much longer—669 sols.

Mars, like Earth, tilts on its axis, so it has seasons. Each Martian season lasts longer than an Earth season because the Martian year is longer. The shape of Mars's orbit makes the seasons unequal in length (see table below).

The climate in the southern hemisphere is more extreme than in the northern hemisphere. Winters in the south are longer and colder, while summers are shorter and warmer. Winter in the south, for instance, lasts 177 sols. In the northern hemisphere, winter lasts only 156 sols.

Seasonal changes affect Mars's north and south poles, which are covered with polar ice caps made of water and carbon dioxide. During winter in the southern hemisphere, the polar cap covers almost half the hemisphere. Here the ice cap is mainly frozen carbon dioxide—like dry ice. In spring, the ice cap partially melts, releasing carbon dioxide into the air. In a similar way, when spring comes in the northern hemisphere, the north polar cap melts. But in the north, the frozen core is made mainly of water ice.

Northern Hemisphere of Mars

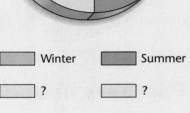

23%

27%

☐ Winter   ☐ Summer

☐ ?   ☐ ?

An ice cap covers the northern polar region of Mars.

Martian Seasons in Sols (Martian Days)

	Northern Hemisphere	Southern Hemisphere
Winter	156	177
Spring	194	142
Summer	177	156
Fall	142	194

The sun rises on Mars.

Southern Hemisphere of Mars

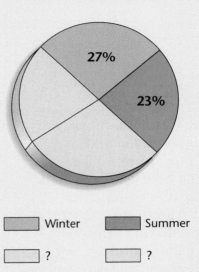

27%

23%

▢ Winter	▢ Summer
▢ ?	▢ ?

Math Activity

People working on Mars would probably go by Martian time. You know that there are 669 sols (Martian days) in a Martian year. Knowing the number of sols in a season, you can figure the percent of the year that's winter. For example, winter in the northern hemisphere is 156 sols ÷ 669 sols ≈ 0.233 ≈ 23%.

- Use the table on page 752 to figure out what percent of the Martian year in each hemisphere is winter, spring, summer, and fall. Round to the nearest hundredth.

- Make two circle graphs like those on pages 752 and 753. Label, color, and write the percent for each season in the northern and southern hemispheres.

- Choose a different color for each.

If you had a choice, which hemisphere would you choose to live in?

Tie It Together

Plan a Martian Station

At last, you will be going to Mars to set up the first human research station. For an expedition this long, good planning is essential. Review the major problems that Mars presents to humans, such as thin atmosphere, no oxygen, extreme temperatures, and so on. Remember that it's too expensive to send most supplies to Mars. Work in groups to make a plan for setting up Earth's research station. Include maps and drawings. As you make your plan, consider questions such as these:

- How will you supply oxygen? Water? Fuel?

- What site will you choose for your settlement? Consider the landscape and climate on Mars.

- What supplies will you bring with you?

- What will you use for building materials?

- What kinds of food will you get? How will you get food?

This painting shows how one artist imagined a human home on another planet.

Think Like a Scientist

Although you may not know it, you think like a scientist every day. Whenever you ask a question and explore possible answers, you use many of the same skills that scientists do. Some of these skills are described on this page.

Observing

When you use one or more of your five senses to gather information about the world, you are **observing.** Hearing a dog bark, counting twelve green seeds, and smelling smoke are all observations. To increase the power of their senses, scientists sometimes use microscopes, telescopes, or other instruments that help them make more detailed observations.

An observation must be an accurate report of what your senses detect. It is important to keep careful records of your observations in science class by writing or drawing in a notebook. The information collected through observations is called evidence, or data.

Inferring

When you interpret an observation, you are **inferring,** or making an inference. For example, if you hear your dog barking, you may infer that someone is at your front door. To make this inference, you combine the evidence—the barking dog—and your experience or knowledge—you know that your dog barks when strangers approach— to reach a logical conclusion.

Notice that an inference is not a fact; it is only one of many possible explanations for an observation. For example, your dog may be barking because it wants to go for a walk. An inference may turn out to be incorrect even if it is based on accurate obser- vations and logical reasoning. The only way to find out if an inference is correct is to investigate further.

Predicting

When you listen to the weather forecast, you hear many predictions about the next day's weather—what the temperature will be, whether it will rain, and how windy it will be. Weather forecasters use observations and knowledge of weather patterns to predict the weather. The skill of **predicting** involves making an inference about a future event based on current evidence or past experience.

Because a prediction is an inference, it may prove to be false. In science class, you can test some of your predictions by doing experiments. For example, suppose you predict that larger paper airplanes can fly farther than smaller airplanes. How could you test your prediction?

ACTIVITY Use the photograph to answer the questions below.

Observing Look closely at the photograph. List at least three observations.

Inferring Use your observations to make an inference about what has happened. What experience or knowledge did you use to make the inference?

Predicting Predict what will happen next. On what evidence or experience do you base your prediction?

Classifying

Could you imagine searching for a book in the library if the books were shelved in no particular order? Your trip to the library would be an all-day event! Luckily, librarians group together books on similar topics or by the same author. Grouping together items that are alike in some way is called **classifying.** You can classify items in many ways: by size, by shape, by use, and by other important characteristics.

Like librarians, scientists use the skill of classifying to organize information and objects. When things are sorted into groups, the relationships among them become easier to understand.

Classify the objects in the photograph into two groups based on any characteristic you choose. Then use another characteristic to classify the objects into three groups.

ACTIVITY

Making Models

Have you ever drawn a picture to help someone understand what you were saying? Such a drawing is one type of model. A model is a picture, diagram, computer image, or other representation of a complex object or process. **Making models** helps people understand things that they cannot observe directly.

Scientists often use models to represent things that are either very large or very small, such as the planets in the solar system, or the parts of a cell. Such models are physical models—drawings or three-dimensional structures that look like the real thing. Other models are mental models—mathematical equations or words that describe how something works.

This student is using a model to demonstrate what causes day and night on Earth. What do the flashlight and the tennis ball in the model represent?

ACTIVITY

Communicating

Whenever you talk on the phone, write a letter, or listen to your teacher at school, you are communicating. **Communicating** is the process of sharing ideas and information with other people. Communicating effectively requires many skills, including writing, reading, speaking, listening, and making models.

Scientists communicate to share results, information, and opinions. Scientists often communicate about their work in journals, over the telephone, in letters, and on the Internet. They also attend scientific meetings where they share their ideas with one another in person.

On a sheet of paper, write out clear, detailed directions for tying your shoe. Then exchange directions with a partner. Follow your partner's directions exactly. How successful were you at tying your shoe? How could your partner have communicated more clearly?

ACTIVITY

Making Measurements

When scientists make observations, it is not sufficient to say that something is "big" or "heavy." Instead, scientists use instruments to measure just how big or heavy an object is. By measuring, scientists can express their observations more precisely and communicate more information about what they observe.

Measuring in SI

The standard system of measurement used by scientists around the world is known as the International System of Units, which is abbreviated as SI (in French, *Système International d'Unités*). SI units are easy to use because they are based on multiples of 10. Each unit is ten times larger than the next smallest unit and one tenth the size of the next largest unit. The table lists the prefixes used to name the most common SI units.

Common SI Prefixes		
Prefix	**Symbol**	**Meaning**
kilo-	k	1,000
hecto-	h	100
deka-	da	10
deci-	d	0.1 (one tenth)
centi-	c	0.01 (one hundredth)
milli-	m	0.001 (one thousandth)

Length To measure length, or the distance between two points, the unit of measure is the **meter (m).** One meter is the approximate distance from the floor to a doorknob. Long distances, such as the distance between two cities, are measured in kilometers (km). Small lengths are measured in centimeters (cm) or millimeters (mm). Scientists use metric rulers and meter sticks to measure length.

Common Conversions

1 km = 1,000 m
1 m = 100 cm
1 m = 1,000 mm
1 cm = 10 mm

Liquid Volume To measure the volume of a liquid, or the amount of space it takes up, you will use a unit of measure known as the **liter (L).** One liter is the approximate volume of a medium-sized carton of milk. Smaller volumes are measured in milliliters (mL). Scientists use graduated cylinders to measure liquid volume.

Common Conversion

1 L = 1,000 mL

The graduated cylinder in the picture is marked in milliliter divisions. Notice that the water in the cylinder has a curved surface. This curved surface is called the *meniscus.* To measure the volume, you must read the level at the lowest point of the meniscus. What is the volume of water in this graduated cylinder? **ACTIVITY**

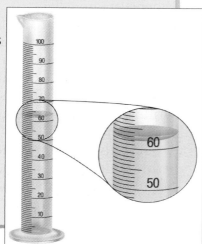

The larger lines on the metric ruler in the picture show centimeter divisions, while the smaller, unnumbered lines show millimeter divisions. How many centimeters long is the shell? How many millimeters long is it? **ACTIVITY**

Mass To measure mass, or the amount of matter in an object, you will use a unit of measure known as the **gram (g).** One gram is approximately the mass of a paper clip. Larger masses are measured in kilograms (kg). Scientists use a balance to find the mass of an object.

Common Conversion

1 kg = 1,000 g

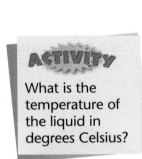

The electronic balance displays the mass of an apple in kilograms. What is the mass of the apple? Suppose a recipe for applesauce called for one kilogram of apples. About how many apples would you need?

ACTIVITY

Temperature To measure the temperature of a substance, you will use the **Celsius scale.** Temperature is measured in degrees Celsius (°C) using a Celsius thermometer. Water freezes at 0°C and boils at 100°C.

ACTIVITY

What is the temperature of the liquid in degrees Celsius?

Converting SI Units

To use the SI system, you must know how to convert between units. Converting from one unit to another involves the skill of **calculating,** or using mathematical operations. Converting between SI units is similar to converting between dollars and dimes because both systems are based on multiples of ten.

Suppose you want to convert a length of 80 centimeters to meters. Follow these steps to convert between units.

1. Begin by writing down the measurement you want to convert—in this example, 80 centimeters.

2. Write a conversion factor that represents the relationship between the two units you are converting. In this example, the relationship is *1 meter = 100 centimeters.* Write this conversion factor as a fraction, making sure to place the units you are converting from (centimeters, in this example) in the denominator.

3. Multiply the measurement you want to convert by the fraction. When you do this, the units in the first measurement will cancel out with the units in the denominator. Your answer will be in the units you are converting to (meters, in this example).

Example

80 centimeters = ___?___ meters

$$80 \text{ centimeters} \times \frac{1 \text{ meter}}{100 \text{ centimeters}} = \frac{80 \text{ meters}}{100}$$

$$= 0.8 \text{ meters}$$

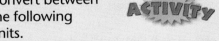

Convert between the following units.

ACTIVITY

1. 600 millimeters = _?_ meters
2. 0.35 liters = _?_ milliliters
3. 1,050 grams = _?_ kilograms

757

Conducting a Scientific Investigation

In some ways, scientists are like detectives, piecing together clues to learn about a process or event. One way that scientists gather clues is by carrying out experiments. An experiment tests an idea in a careful, orderly manner. Although all experiments do not follow the same steps in the same order, many follow a pattern similar to the one described here.

Posing Questions

Experiments begin by asking a scientific question. A scientific question is one that can be answered by gathering evidence. For example, the question "Which freezes faster—fresh water or salt water?" is a scientific question because you can carry out an investigation and gather information to answer the question.

Developing a Hypothesis

The next step is to form a hypothesis. A **hypothesis** is a possible explanation for a set of observations or answer to a scientific question. In science, a hypothesis must be something that can be tested. A hypothesis can take the form of an *If . . . then . . .* statement. For example, a hypothesis might be *"If I add salt to fresh water, then the water will take longer to freeze."* A hypothesis worded this way serves as a rough outline of the experiment you should perform.

Designing an Experiment

Next you need to plan a way to test your hypothesis. Your plan should be written out as a step-by-step procedure and should describe the observations or measurements you will make.

Two important steps involved in designing an experiment are controlling variables and forming operational definitions.

Controlling Variables In a well-designed experiment, you need to keep all variables the same except for one. A **variable** is any factor that can change in an experiment. The factor that you change is called the **manipulated variable.** In this experiment, the manipulated variable is the amount of salt added to the water. Other factors, such as the amount of water or the starting temperature, are kept constant.

The factor that changes as a result of the manipulated variable is called the responding variable. The **responding variable** is what you measure or observe to obtain your results. In this experiment, the responding variable is how long the water takes to freeze.

An experiment in which all factors except one are kept constant is a **controlled experiment.** Most controlled experiments include a test called the control. In this experiment, Container 3 is the control. Because no salt is added to Container 3, you can compare the results from the other containers to it. Any difference in results must be due to the addition of salt alone.

Forming Operational Definitions
Another important aspect of a well-designed experiment is having clear operational definitions. An **operational definition** is a statement that describes how a particular variable is to be measured or how a term is to be defined. For example, in this experiment, how will you determine if the water has frozen? You might decide to insert a stick in each container at the start of the experiment. Your operational definition of "frozen" would be the time at which the stick can no longer move.

EXPERIMENTAL PROCEDURE

1. Fill 3 containers with 300 milliliters of cold tap water.

2. Add 10 grams of salt to Container 1; stir. Add 20 grams of salt to Container 2; stir. Add no salt to Container 3.

3. Place the 3 containers in a freezer.

4. Check the containers every 15 minutes. Record your observations.

Interpreting Data

The observations and measurements you make in an experiment are called data. At the end of an experiment, you need to analyze the data to look for any patterns or trends. Patterns often become clear if you organize your data in a data table or graph. Then think through what the data reveal. Do they support your hypothesis? Do they point out a flaw in your experiment? Do you need to collect more data?

Drawing Conclusions

A conclusion is a statement that sums up what you have learned from an experiment. When you draw a conclusion, you need to decide whether the data you collected support your hypothesis or not. You may need to repeat an experiment several times before you can draw any conclusions from it. Conclusions often lead you to pose new questions and plan new experiments to answer them.

How is a plant's growth affected by the amount of **ACTIVITY** water it receives? Using the steps just described, plan a controlled experiment to investigate this problem.

Thinking Critically

Has a friend ever asked for your advice about a problem? If so, you may have helped your friend think through the problem in a logical way. Without knowing it, you used critical-thinking skills to help your friend. Critical thinking involves the use of reasoning and logic to solve problems or make decisions. Some critical-thinking skills are described below.

Comparing and Contrasting

When you examine two objects for similarities and differences, you are using the skill of **comparing and contrasting.** Comparing involves identifying similarities, or common characteristics. Contrasting involves identifying differences. Analyzing objects in this way can help you discover details that you might otherwise overlook.

Compare and contrast the two animals in the photo. First list all the similarities that you see. Then list all the differences.

ACTIVITY

Applying Concepts

When you use your knowledge about one situation to make sense of a similar situation, you are using the skill of **applying concepts.** Being able to transfer your knowledge from one situation to another shows that you truly understand a concept. You may use this skill in answering test questions that present different problems from the ones you've reviewed in class.

You have just learned that lightning can travel through metal and water. Use this knowledge to decide which objects in your home could act as conductors and therefore be dangerous during a thunderstorm.

ACTIVITY

Interpreting Illustrations

Diagrams, photographs, and maps are included in textbooks to help clarify what you read. These illustrations show processes, places, and ideas in a visual manner. The skill called **interpreting illustrations** can help you learn from these visual elements. To understand an illustration, take the time to study the illustration along with all the written information that accompanies it. Captions identify the key concepts shown in the illustration. Labels point out the important parts of a diagram or map, while keys identify the symbols used in a map.

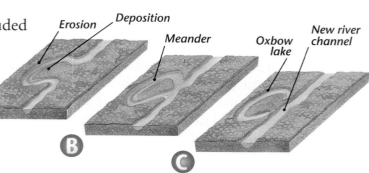

Erosion Deposition Meander Oxbow lake New river channel

A B C

▲ An oxbow lake begins to form as erosion and deposition create a meander, or bend, in a river.

Study the diagrams above. Then write a short paragraph explaining what you have learned.

ACTIVITY

Relating Cause and Effect

If one event causes another event to occur, the two events are said to have a cause-and-effect relationship. When you determine that such a relationship exists between two events, you use a skill called **relating cause and effect.** For example, if you notice an itchy, red bump on your skin, you might infer that a mosquito bit you. The mosquito bite is the cause, and the bump is the effect.

It is important to note that two events do not necessarily have a cause-and-effect relationship just because they occur together. Scientists carry out experiments or use past experience to determine whether a cause-and-effect relationship exists.

> **ACTIVITY** It is a hot day. You go to the freezer for ice and find only water in the trays. List some possible reasons for the missing ice. How would you determine which cause-and-effect relationship has left you without a cool drink?

Making Generalizations

When you draw a conclusion about an entire group based on information about only some of the group's members, you are using a skill called **making generalizations.** For a generalization to be valid, the sample you choose must be large enough and representative of the entire group. You might, for example, put this skill to work at a farm stand if you see a sign that says, "Sample some grapes before you buy." If you sample a few sweet grapes, you may conclude that all the grapes are sweet—and purchase a large bunch.

> **ACTIVITY** A team of scientists needs to determine whether the water in a large reservoir is safe to drink. How could they use the skill of making generalizations to help them? What should they do?

Making Judgments

When you evaluate something to decide whether it is good or bad, or right or wrong, you are using a skill called **making judgments.** For example, you make judgments when you decide to eat healthful foods or to pick up litter in a park. Before you make a judgment, you need to think through the pros and cons of a situation, and identify the values or standards that you hold.

> **ACTIVITY** Should children and teens be required to wear helmets when bicycling? Explain why you feel the way you do.

Problem Solving

When you use critical-thinking skills to resolve an issue or decide on a course of action, you are using a skill called **problem solving.** Some problems, such as how to convert a fraction into a decimal, are straightforward. Other problems, such as figuring out why your computer has stopped working, are complex. Some complex problems can be solved using the trial and error method—try out one solution first, and if that doesn't work, try another. Other useful problem-solving strategies include making models and brainstorming possible solutions with a partner.

Organizing Information

As you read this textbook, how can you make sense of all the information it contains? Some useful tools to help you organize information are shown on this page. These tools are called *graphic organizers* because they give you a visual picture of a topic, showing at a glance how key concepts are related.

Concept Maps

Concept maps are useful tools for organizing information on broad topics. A concept map begins with a general concept and shows how it can be broken down into more specific concepts. In that way, relationships between concepts become easier to understand.

A concept map is constructed by placing concept words (usually nouns) in ovals and connecting them with linking words. Often, the most general concept word is placed at the top, and the words become more specific as you move downward. Often the linking words, which are written on a line connecting the two ovals, describe the relationship between the two concepts they connect. If you follow any string of concepts and linking words down the map, it should read like a sentence.

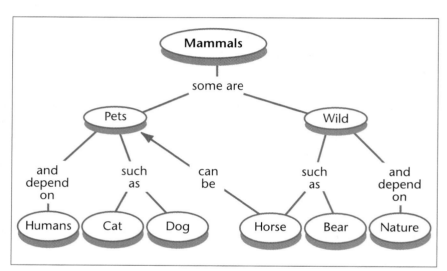

Some concept maps include linking words that connect a concept on one branch of the map to a concept on another branch. These linking words, called cross-linkages, show more complex interrelationships among concepts.

Compare/Contrast Tables

Compare/contrast tables are useful tools for sorting out the similarities and differences between two or more items. A table provides an organized framework in which to compare items based on specific characteristics that you identify.

To create a compare/contrast table, list the items to be compared across the top of a table. Then list the characteristics that will form the basis of your comparison in the left-hand

Characteristic	Baseball	Basketball
Number of Players	9	5
Playing Field	Baseball diamond	Basketball court
Equipment	Bat, baseball, mitts	Basket, basketball

column. Complete the table by filling in information about each characteristic, first for one item and then for the other.

Venn Diagrams

Another way to show similarities and differences between items is with a Venn diagram. A Venn diagram consists of two or more circles that partially overlap. Each circle represents a particular concept or idea. Common characteristics, or similarities, are written within the area of overlap between the two circles. Unique characteristics, or differences, are written in the parts of the circles outside the area of overlap.

To create a Venn diagram, draw two overlapping circles. Label the circles with the names of the items being compared. Write the

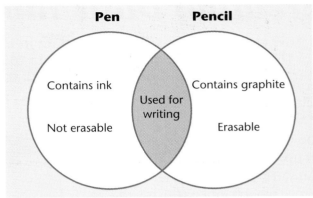

unique characteristics in each circle outside the area of overlap. Then write the shared characteristics within the area of overlap.

Flowcharts

A flowchart can help you understand the order in which certain events have occurred or should occur. Flowcharts are useful for outlining the stages in a process or the steps in a procedure.

To make a flowchart, write a brief description of each event in a box. Place the first event at the top of the page, followed by the second event, the third event, and so on. Then draw an arrow to connect each event to the one that occurs next.

Preparing Pasta

Boil water
↓
Cook pasta
↓
Drain water
↓
Add sauce

Cycle Diagrams

A cycle diagram can be used to show a sequence of events that is continuous, or cyclical. A continuous sequence does not have an end because, when the final event is over, the first event begins again. Like a flowchart, a cycle diagram can help you understand the order of events.

To create a cycle diagram, write a brief description of each event in a box. Place one event at the top of the page in the center. Then, moving in a clockwise direction around an imaginary circle, write each event in its proper sequence. Draw arrows that connect each event to the one that occurs next, forming a continuous circle.

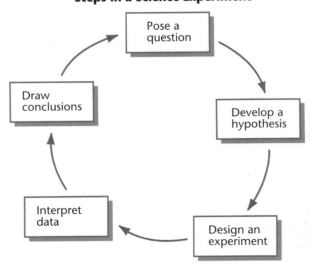

Steps in a Science Experiment

Pose a question → Develop a hypothesis → Design an experiment → Interpret data → Draw conclusions → (Pose a question)

Creating Data Tables and Graphs

How can you make sense of the data in a science experiment? The first step is to organize the data to help you understand them. Data tables and graphs are helpful tools for organizing data.

Data Tables

You have gathered your materials and set up your experiment. But before you start, you need to plan a way to record what happens during the experiment. By creating a data table, you can record your observations and measurements in an orderly way.

Suppose, for example, that a scientist conducted an experiment to find out how many Calories people of different body masses burn while doing various activities. The data table shows the results.

Notice in this data table that the manipulated variable (body mass) is the heading of one column. The responding variable (for Experiment 1, the number of Calories burned while bicycling) is the heading of the next column. Additional columns were added for related experiments.

CALORIES BURNED IN 30 MINUTES OF ACTIVITY			
Body Mass	Experiment 1 Bicycling	Experiment 2 Playing Basketball	Experiment 3 Watching Television
30 kg	60 Calories	120 Calories	21 Calories
40 kg	77 Calories	164 Calories	27 Calories
50 kg	95 Calories	206 Calories	33 Calories
60 kg	114 Calories	248 Calories	38 Calories

Bar Graphs

To compare how many Calories a person burns doing various activities, you could create a bar graph. A bar graph is used to display data in a number of separate, or distinct, categories. In this example, bicycling, playing basketball, and watching television are three separate categories.

To create a bar graph, follow these steps.

1. On graph paper, draw a horizontal, or *x*-, axis and a vertical, or *y*-, axis.
2. Write the names of the categories to be graphed along the horizontal axis. Include an overall label for the axis as well.
3. Label the vertical axis with the name of the responding variable. Include units of measurement. Then create a scale along the axis by marking off equally spaced numbers that cover the range of the data collected.
4. For each category, draw a solid bar using the scale on the vertical axis to determine the

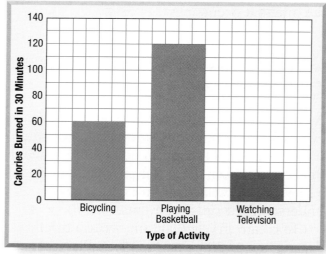

Calories Burned by a 30-kilogram Person in Various Activities

appropriate height. For example, for bicycling, draw the bar as high as the 60 mark on the vertical axis. Make all the bars the same width and leave equal spaces between them.

5. Add a title that describes the graph.

Line Graphs

To see whether a relationship exists between body mass and the number of Calories burned while bicycling, you could create a line graph. A line graph is used to display data that show how one variable (the responding variable) changes in response to another variable (the manipulated variable). You can use a line graph when your manipulated variable is *continuous*, that is, when there are other points between the ones that you tested. In this example, body mass is a continuous variable because there are other body masses between 30 and 40 kilograms (for example, 31 kilograms). Time is another example of a continuous variable.

Line graphs are powerful tools because they allow you to estimate values for conditions that you did not test in the experiment. For example, you can use the line graph to estimate that a 35-kilogram person would burn 68 Calories while bicycling.

To create a line graph, follow these steps.

1. On graph paper, draw a horizontal, or *x*-, axis and a vertical, or *y*-, axis.
2. Label the horizontal axis with the name of the manipulated variable. Label the vertical axis with the name of the responding variable. Include units of measurement.
3. Create a scale on each axis by marking off equally spaced numbers that cover the range of the data collected.
4. Plot a point on the graph for each piece of data. In the line graph above, the dotted lines show how to plot the first data point (30 kilograms and 60 Calories). Draw an imaginary vertical line extending up from the horizontal axis at the 30-kilogram mark. Then draw an imaginary horizontal line extending across from the vertical axis at the 60-Calorie mark. Plot the point where the two lines intersect.

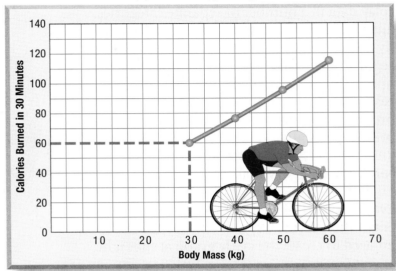

Effect of Body Mass on Calories Burned While Bicycling

5. Connect the plotted points with a solid line. (In some cases, it may be more appropriate to draw a line that shows the general trend of the plotted points. In those cases, some of the points may fall above or below the line.)
6. Add a title that identifies the variables or relationship in the graph.

ACTIVITY
Create line graphs to display the data from Experiment 2 and Experiment 3 in the data table.

ACTIVITY
You read in the newspaper that a total of 4 centimeters of rain fell in your area in June, 2.5 centimeters fell in July, and 1.5 centimeters fell in August. What type of graph would you use to display these data? Use graph paper to create the graph.

Circle Graphs

Like bar graphs, circle graphs can be used to display data in a number of separate categories. Unlike bar graphs, however, circle graphs can only be used when you have data for *all* the categories that make up a given topic. A circle graph is sometimes called a pie chart because it resembles a pie cut into slices. The pie represents the entire topic, while the slices represent the individual categories. The size of a slice indicates what percentage of the whole a particular category makes up.

The data table below shows the results of a survey in which 24 teenagers were asked to identify their favorite sport. The data were then used to create the circle graph at the right.

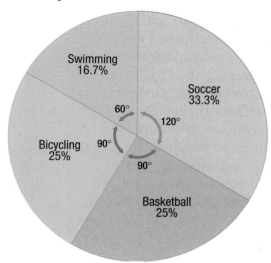

Sports That Teens Prefer

Swimming 16.7%

Soccer 33.3%

Bicycling 25%

Basketball 25%

FAVORITE SPORTS

Sport	Number of Students
Soccer	8
Basketball	6
Bicycling	6
Swimming	4

To create a circle graph, follow these steps.

1. Use a compass to draw a circle. Mark the center of the circle with a point. Then draw a line from the center point to the top of the circle.

2. Determine the size of each "slice" by setting up a proportion where x equals the number of degrees in a slice. (NOTE: A circle contains 360 degrees.) For example, to find the number of degrees in the "soccer" slice, set up the following proportion:

$$\frac{\text{students who prefer soccer}}{\text{total number of students}} = \frac{x}{\text{total number of degrees in a circle}}$$

$$\frac{8}{24} = \frac{x}{360}$$

Cross-multiply and solve for x.

$$24x = 8 \times 360$$
$$x = 120$$

The "soccer" slice should contain 120 degrees.

3. Use a protractor to measure the angle of the first slice, using the line you drew to the top of the circle as the 0° line. Draw a line from the center of the circle to the edge for the angle you measured.

4. Continue around the circle by measuring the size of each slice with the protractor. Start measuring from the edge of the previous slice so the wedges do not overlap. When you are done, the entire circle should be filled in.

5. Determine the percentage of the whole circle that each slice represents. To do this, divide the number of degrees in a slice by the total number of degrees in a circle (360), and multiply by 100%. For the "soccer" slice, you can find the percentage as follows:

$$\frac{120}{360} \times 100\% = 33.3\%$$

6. Use a different color to shade in each slice. Label each slice with the name of the category and with the percentage of the whole it represents.

7. Add a title to the circle graph.

ACTIVITY

In a group of 32 students, 24 are right-handed, 6 are left-handed and 2 use both hands equally. Create a circle graph to display these data.

Laboratory Safety

Safety Symbols

These symbols alert you to possible dangers in the laboratory and remind you to work carefully.

Safety Goggles Always wear safety goggles to protect your eyes in any activity involving chemicals, flames or heating, or the possibility of broken glassware.

Lab Apron Wear a laboratory apron to protect your skin and clothing from damage.

Breakage You are working with materials that may be breakable, such as glass containers, glass tubing, thermometers, or funnels. Handle breakable materials with care. Do not touch broken glassware.

Heat-resistant Gloves Use an oven mitt or other hand protection when handling hot materials. Hot plates, hot glassware, or hot water can cause burns. Do not touch hot objects with your bare hands.

Heating Use a clamp or tongs to pick up hot glassware. Do not touch hot objects with your bare hands.

Sharp Object Pointed-tip scissors, scalpels, knives, needles, pins, or tacks are sharp. They can cut or puncture your skin. Always direct a sharp edge or point away from yourself and others. Use sharp instruments only as instructed.

Electric Shock Avoid the possibility of electric shock. Never use electrical equipment around water, or when the equipment is wet or your hands are wet. Be sure cords are untangled and cannot trip anyone. Disconnect the equipment when it is not in use.

Corrosive Chemical You are working with an acid or another corrosive chemical. Avoid getting it on your skin or clothing, or in your eyes. Do not inhale the vapors. Wash your hands when you are finished with the activity.

Poison Do not let any poisonous chemical come in contact with your skin, and do not inhale its vapors. Wash your hands when you are finished with the activity.

Physical Safety When an experiment involves physical activity, take precautions to avoid injuring yourself or others. Follow instructions from your teacher. Alert your teacher if there is any reason you should not participate in the activity.

Animal Safety Treat live animals with care to avoid harming the animals or yourself. Working with animal parts or preserved animals also may require caution. Wash your hands when you are finished with the activity.

Plant Safety Handle plants in the laboratory or during field work only as directed by your teacher. If you are allergic to certain plants, tell your teacher before doing an activity in which those plants are used. Avoid touching harmful plants such as poison ivy, poison oak, or poison sumac, or plants with thorns. Wash your hands when you are finished with the activity.

Flames You may be working with flames from a lab burner, candle, or matches. Tie back loose hair and clothing. Follow instructions from your teacher about lighting and extinguishing flames.

No Flames Flammable materials may be present. Make sure there are no flames, sparks, or other exposed heat sources present.

Fumes When poisonous or unpleasant vapors may be involved, work in a ventilated area. Avoid inhaling vapors directly. Only test an odor when directed to do so by your teacher, and use a wafting motion to direct the vapor toward your nose.

Disposal Chemicals and other laboratory materials used in the activity must be disposed of safely. Follow the instructions from your teacher.

Hand Washing Wash your hands thoroughly when finished with the activity. Use antibacterial soap and warm water. Lather both sides of your hands and between your fingers. Rinse well.

General Safety Awareness You may see this symbol when none of the symbols described earlier appears. In this case, follow the specific instructions provided. You may also see this symbol when you are asked to develop your own procedure in a lab. Have your teacher approve your plan before you go further.

Science Safety Rules

To prepare yourself to work safely in the laboratory, read over the following safety rules. Then read them a second time. Make sure you understand and follow each rule. Ask your teacher to explain any rules you do not understand.

Dress Code

1. To protect yourself from injuring your eyes, wear safety goggles whenever you work with chemicals, burners, glassware, or any substance that might get into your eyes. If you wear contact lenses, notify your teacher.
2. Wear a lab apron or coat whenever you work with corrosive chemicals or substances that can stain.
3. Tie back long hair to keep it away from any chemicals, flames, or equipment.
4. Remove or tie back any article of clothing or jewelry that can hang down and touch chemicals, flames, or equipment. Roll up or secure long sleeves.
5. Never wear open shoes or sandals.

General Precautions

6. Read all directions for an experiment several times before beginning the activity. Carefully follow all written and oral instructions. If you are in doubt about any part of the experiment, ask your teacher for assistance.
7. Never perform activities that are not assigned or authorized by your teacher. Obtain permission before "experimenting" on your own. Never handle any equipment unless you have specific permission.
8. Never perform lab activities without direct supervision.
9. Never eat or drink in the laboratory.
10. Keep work areas clean and tidy at all times. Bring only notebooks and lab manuals or written lab procedures to the work area. All other items, such as purses and backpacks, should be left in a designated area.
11. Do not engage in horseplay.

First Aid

12. Always report all accidents or injuries to your teacher, no matter how minor. Notify your teacher immediately about any fires.
13. Learn what to do in case of specific accidents, such as getting acid in your eyes or on your skin. (Rinse acids from your body with lots of water.)
14. Be aware of the location of the first-aid kit, but do not use it unless instructed by your teacher. In case of injury, your teacher should administer first aid. Your teacher may also send you to the school nurse or call a physician.
15. Know the location of emergency equipment, such as the fire extinguisher and fire blanket, and know how to use it.
16. Know the location of the nearest telephone and whom to contact in an emergency.

Heating and Fire Safety

17. Never use a heat source, such as a candle, burner, or hot plate, without wearing safety goggles.
18. Never heat anything unless instructed to do so. A chemical that is harmless when cool may be dangerous when heated.
19. Keep all combustible materials away from flames. Never use a flame or spark near a combustible chemical.
20. Never reach across a flame.
21. Before using a laboratory burner, make sure you know proper procedures for lighting and adjusting the burner, as demonstrated by your teacher. Do not touch the burner. It may be hot. And never leave a lighted burner unattended!
22. Chemicals can splash or boil out of a heated test tube. When heating a substance in a test tube, make sure that the mouth of the tube is not pointed at you or anyone else.
23. Never heat a liquid in a closed container. The expanding gases produced may blow the container apart.
24. Before picking up a container that has been heated, hold the back of your hand near it. If you can feel heat on the back of your hand, the container is too hot to handle. Use an oven mitt to pick up a container that has been heated.

Using Chemicals Safely

25. Never mix chemicals "for the fun of it." You might produce a dangerous, possibly explosive substance.

26. Never put your face near the mouth of a container that holds chemicals. Never touch, taste, or smell a chemical unless you are instructed by your teacher to do so. Many chemicals are poisonous.

27. Use only those chemicals needed in the activity. Read and double-check labels on supply bottles before removing any chemicals. Take only as much as you need. Keep all containers closed when chemicals are not being used.

28. Dispose of all chemicals as instructed by your teacher. To avoid contamination, never return chemicals to their original containers. Never simply pour chemicals or other substances into the sink or trash containers.

29. Be extra careful when working with acids or bases. Pour all chemicals over the sink or a container, not over your work surface.

30. If you are instructed to test for odors, use a wafting motion to direct the odors to your nose. Do not inhale the fumes directly from the container.

31. When mixing an acid and water, always pour the water into the container first and then add the acid to the water. Never pour water into an acid.

32. Take extreme care not to spill any material in the laboratory. Wash chemical spills and splashes immediately with plenty of water. Immediately begin rinsing with water any acids that get on your skin or clothing, and notify your teacher of any acid spill at the same time.

Using Glassware Safely

33. Never force glass tubing or thermometers into a rubber stopper or rubber tubing. Have your teacher insert the glass tubing or thermometer if required for an activity.

34. If you are using a laboratory burner, use a wire screen to protect glassware from any flame. Never heat glassware that is not thoroughly dry on the outside.

35. Keep in mind that hot glassware looks cool. Never pick up glassware without first checking to see whether it is hot. Use an oven mitt. See rule 24.

36. Never use broken or chipped glassware. If glassware breaks, notify your teacher and dispose of the glassware in the proper broken-glassware container. Never handle broken glass with your bare hands.

37. Never eat or drink from lab glassware.

38. Thoroughly clean glassware before putting it away.

Using Sharp Instruments

39. Handle scalpels or other sharp instruments with extreme care. Never cut material toward you; cut away from you.

40. Immediately notify your teacher if you cut your skin when working in the laboratory.

Animal and Plant Safety

41. Never perform experiments that cause pain, discomfort, or harm to mammals, birds, reptiles, fishes, or amphibians. This rule applies at home as well as in the classroom.

42. Animals should be handled only if absolutely necessary. Your teacher will instruct you as to how to handle each animal species brought into the classroom.

43. If you know that you are allergic to certain plants, molds, or animals, tell your teacher before doing an activity in which these are used.

44. During field work, protect your skin by wearing long pants, long sleeves, socks, and closed shoes. Know how to recognize the poisonous plants and fungi in your area, as well as plants with thorns, and avoid contact with them.

45. Never eat any part of an unidentified plant or fungus.

46. Wash your hands thoroughly after handling animals or the cage containing animals. Wash your hands when you are finished with any activity involving animal parts, plants, or soil.

End-of-Experiment Rules

47. After an experiment has been completed, clean up your work area and return all equipment to its proper place.

48. Dispose of waste materials as instructed by your teacher.

49. Wash your hands after every experiment.

50. Always turn off all burners or hot plates when they are not in use. Unplug hot plates and other electrical equipment. If you used a burner, check that the gas-line valve to the burner is off as well.

Physical Map: United States

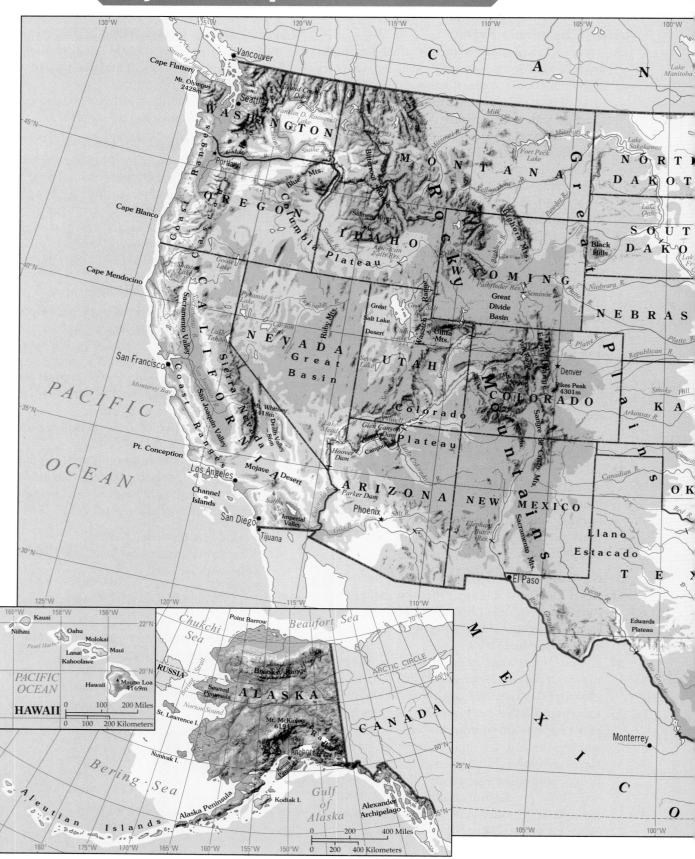

UNITED STATES
Physical

International boundary
State boundary
⊛ Washington, D.C. National capital
★ Atlanta State capital
● Detroit Major city

ELEVATION

Meters		Feet
Over 3000		Over 10,000
1500 to 3000		5,000 to 10,000
600 to 1500		2,000 to 5,000
300 to 600		1,000 to 2,000
150 to 300		500 to 1,000
0 to 150		0 to 500
Below sea level		Below sea level

WATER DEPTH

Less than 200   Less than 600
Greater than 200   Greater than 600

0   100   200   300 Miles

0   100   200   300 Kilometers

Star Charts

Autumn Sky

To use this chart, hold it up in front of you and turn it so that the direction you are facing is at the bottom of the chart. This chart works best at 34° north latitude, but can be used at other times and latitudes within the continental United States. It works best at the following times: 10:00 P.M. on September 1; 9:00 P.M. on September 15; 8:00 P.M. on September 30.

NORTHERN HORIZON

EASTERN HORIZON

WESTERN HORIZON

SOUTHERN HORIZON

Winter Sky

To use this chart, hold it up in front of you and turn it so that the direction you are facing is at the bottom of the chart. This chart works best at 34° north latitude, but can be used at other times and latitudes within the continental United States. It works best at the following times: 10:00 P.M. on December 1; 9:00 P.M. on December 15; 8:00 P.M. on December 30.

NORTHERN HORIZON

EASTERN HORIZON

WESTERN HORIZON

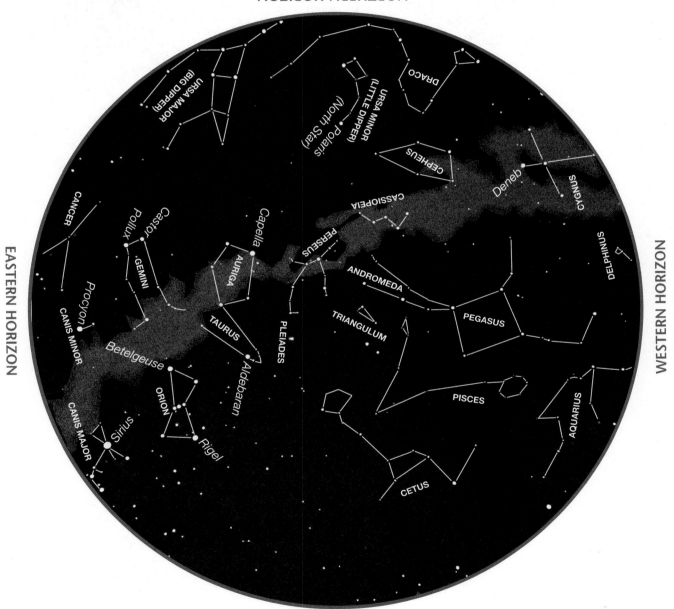

SOUTHERN HORIZON

Spring Sky

To use this chart, hold it up in front of you and turn it so that the direction you are facing is at the bottom of the chart. This chart works best at 34° north latitude, but can be used at other times and latitudes within the continental United States. It works best at the following times: 10:00 P.M. on March 1; 9:00 P.M. on March 15; 8:00 P.M. on March 30.

NORTHERN HORIZON

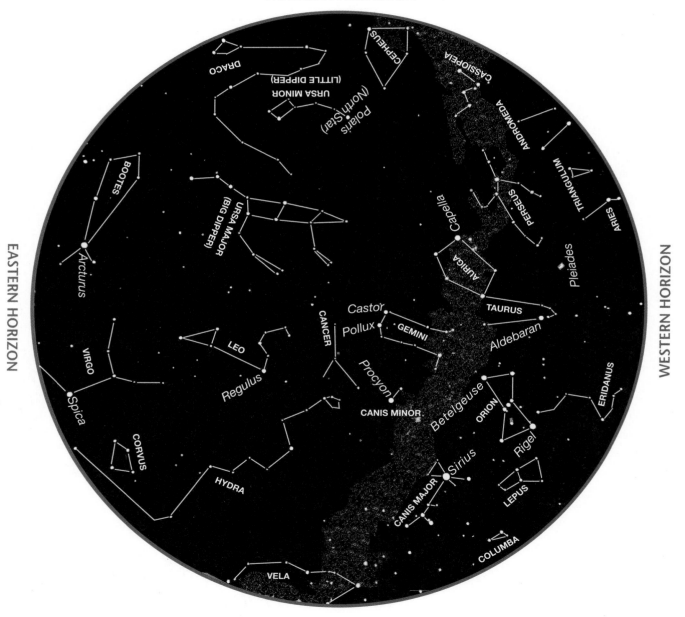

EASTERN HORIZON

WESTERN HORIZON

SOUTHERN HORIZON

Summer Sky

To use this chart, hold it up in front of you and turn it so that the direction you are facing is at the bottom of the chart. This chart works best at 34° north latitude, but can be used at other times and latitudes within the continental United States. It works best at the following times: 10:00 P.M. on June 1; 9:00 P.M. on June 15; 8:00 P.M. on June 30.

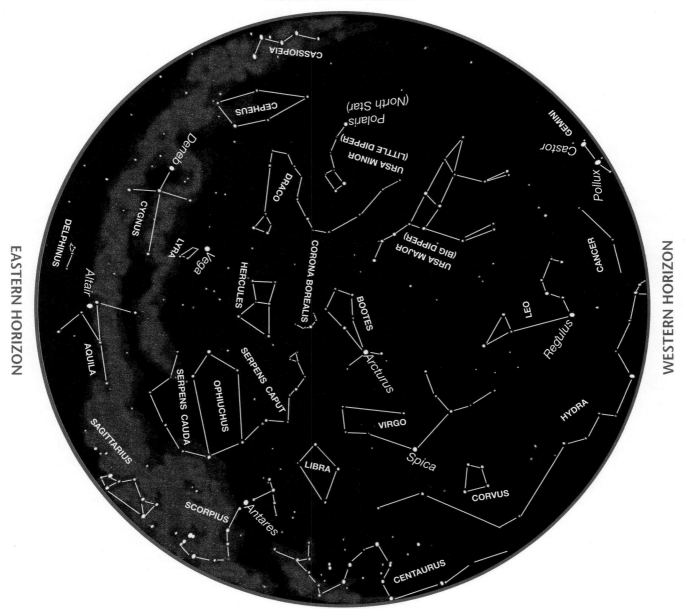

Identifying Common Minerals

GROUP 1
Metallic Luster, Mostly Dark-Colored

Mineral/ Formula	Hardness	Density (g/cm³)	Luster	Streak	Color	Other Properties/Remarks
Pyrite FeS_2	6–6.5	5.0	Metallic	Greenish, brownish black	Light yellow	Harder than chalcopyrite and pyrrhotite; called "fool's gold," but harder than gold and very brittle
Magnetite Fe_3O_4	6	5.2	Metallic	Black	Iron black	Very magnetic; important iron ore; some varieties known as "lodestone"
Hematite Fe_2O_3	5.5–6.5	4.9–5.3	Metallic or earthy	Red or red brown	Reddish brown to black; also steel gray crystals	Most important ore of iron; known as "red ocher"; often used as red pigment in paint.
Pyrrhotite FeS	4	4.6	Metallic	Gray black	Brownish bronze	Less hard than pyrite: slightly magnetic
Sphalerite ZnS	3.5–4	3.9–4.1	Resinous	Brown to light yellow	Brown to yellow	Most important zinc ore
Chalcopyrite $CuFeS_2$	3.5–4	4.1–4.3	Metallic	Greenish black	Golden yellow, often tarnished	Most important copper ore; softer than pyrite and more yellow; more brittle than gold
Bornite Cu_5FeS_4	3	4.9–5.4	Metallic	Gray black	Copper, brown; turns to purple and black	Important copper ore; known as "peacock ore" because of iridescent purple color when exposed to air for a time
Copper Cu	2.5–3	8.9	Metallic	Copper red	Copper red to black	Can be pounded into various shapes and drawn into wires; used in making electrical wires, coins, pipes
Gold Au	2.5–3	19.3	Metallic	Yellow	Rich yellow	Can be pounded into various shapes and drawn into wires; does not tarnish; used in jewelry, coins, dental fillings
Silver Ag	2.5–3	10.0–11.0	Metallic	Silver to light gray	Silver white, tarnishes to black	Can be pounded into various shapes and drawn into wires; used in jewelry, coins, electrical wire
Galena PbS	2.5	7.4–7.6	Metallic	Lead gray	Lead gray	Main ore of lead; used in shields against radiation
Graphite C	1–2	2.3	Metallic to dull	Black	Black	Feels greasy; very soft; used as pencil "lead" and as a lubricant

GROUP 2
Nonmetallic Luster, Mostly Dark-Colored

Mineral/ Formula	Hardness	Density (g/cm³)	Luster	Streak	Color	Other Properties/Remarks
Corundum Al_2O_3	9	3.9–4.1	Brilliant to glassy	White	Usually brown	Very hard; used as an abrasive; transparent crystals used as gems called "ruby" (red) and "sapphire" (blue and other colors)
Garnet $(Ca,Mg,Fe)_3$ $(Al,Fe,Cr)_2(SiO_4)_3$	7–7.5	3.5–4.3	Glassy to resinous	White, light brown	Red, brown, black, green	A group of minerals used in jewelry, as a birthstone, and as an abrasive
Olivine $(Mg,Fe)_2SiO_4$	6.5–7	3.3–3.4	Glassy	White or gray	Olive green	Found in igneous rocks; sometimes used as a gem
Augite $Ca(Mg,Fe,Al)$ $(AlSi)_2O_6$	5–6	3.2–3.4	Glassy	Greenish gray	Dark green to black	Found in igneous rocks
Hornblende $NaCa_2(Mg,Fe,Al)_5$ $(Si,Al)_8O_{22}(OH)_2$	5–6	3.0–3.4	Glassy, silky	White to gray	Dark green to brown, black	Found in igneous and metamorphic rocks
Apatite $Ca_5(PO_4)_3F$	5	3.1–3.2	Glassy	White	Green, brown, red, blue, violet, yellow	Sometimes used as a gem; source of the phosphorus needed by plants
Azurite $Cu_3(CO_3)_2(OH)_2$	3.5–4	3.8	Glassy to dull	Pale blue	Intense blue	Ore of copper; used as a gem
Biotite $K(Mg,Fe)_3AlSiO_{10}$ $(OH)_2$	2.5–3	2.8–3.4	Glassy or pearly	White to gray	Dark green, brown, or black	A type of mica, sometimes used as a lubricant
Serpentine $Mg_6Si_4O_{10}(OH)_8$	2–5	2.2–2.6	Greasy, waxy, silky	White	Usually green	Once used in insulation but found to cause cancer; used in fireproofing; can be in the form of asbestos
Limonite Mixture of hydrous iron oxides	1–5.5	2.8–4.3	Glassy to dull	Yellow brown	Brown black to brownish yellow	Ore of iron, also known as "yellow ocher," a pigment; a mixture that is not strictly a mineral
Bauxite Mixture of hydrous aluminum oxides	1–3	2.0–2.5	Dull to earthy	Colorless to gray	Brown, yellow, gray, white	Ore of aluminum, smells like clay when wet; a mixture that is not strictly a mineral

GROUP 3
Nonmetallic Luster, Mostly Light-Colored

Mineral/ Formula	Hardness	Density (g/cm³)	Luster	Streak	Color	Other Properties/Remarks
Diamond C	10	3.5	Brilliant	White	Colorless and varied	Hardest known substance; used in jewelry; as an abrasive; in cutting instruments
Topaz $Al_2SiO_4(F,OH)_2$	8	3.5–3.6	Glassy	White	Straw yellow, pink, bluish, greenish	Valuable gem
Quartz SiO_2	7	2.6	Glassy, greasy	White	Colorless, white; any color when not pure	The second most abundant mineral; many varieties are gems (amethyst, cat's-eye, bloodstone, agate, jasper, onyx); used in making glass
Feldspar (K,Na,Ca) $(AlSi_3O_8)$	6	2.6	Glassy	Colorless, white	Colorless, white, various colors	As a family, the most abundant of all minerals; the different types of feldspar make up over 60 percent of Earth's crust
Fluorite CaF_2	4	3.0–3.3	Glassy	Colorless	Purple, light, green, yellow, bluish green, other colors	Some types are fluorescent (glow when exposed to ultraviolet light); used in making steel
Dolomite $CaMg(CO_3)_2$	3.5–4	2.8	Glassy or pearly	White	Colorless, white, pinkish, or light tints	Used in making concrete and cement; fizzes slowly in dilute hydrochloric acid
Calcite $CaCO_3$	3	2.7	Glassy	White to grayish	Colorless, white, pale tints	Easily scratched; bubbles in dilute hydrochloric acid; frequently fluorescent
Halite $NaCl$	2.5	2.1–2.6	Glassy	White	Colorless or white	Occurs as perfect cubic crystals; has salty taste
Gypsum $CaSO_4 \cdot 2H_2O$	2	2.3	Glassy, pearly, silky	White	Colorless, white, light tints	Very soft; used in manufacture of plaster of Paris; form known as alabaster used for statues
Sulfur S	2	2.0–2.1	Resinous to greasy	White	Yellow to yellowish brown	Used in making many medicines, in production of sulfuric acid, and in vulcanizing rubber
Talc $Mg_3Si_4O_{10}(OH)_2$	1	2.7–2.8	Pearly to greasy	White	Gray, white, greenish	Very soft; used in talcum powder; found mostly in metamorphic rocks; also called "soapstone"

Glossary

aa A slow-moving type of lava that hardens to form rough chunks; cooler than pahoehoe. (p. 187)

abrasion The grinding away of rock by other rock particles carried in water, ice, or wind. (pp. 266, 213)

absolute age The age of a rock given as the number of years since the rock formed. (p. 293)

absolute magnitude The brightness of a star if it were a standard distance from Earth. (p. 728)

abyssal plain A smooth, nearly flat region of the deep ocean floor. (p. 463)

acid rain Rain that is more acidic than normal, caused by the release of molecules of sulfur dioxide and nitrogen oxide into the air. (pp. 415, 507)

active Said of a volcano that is erupting or has shown signs of erupting in the near future. (p. 188)

active solar system A method of capturing the sun's energy and distributing it using pumps and fans. (p. 335)

aftershock An earthquake that occurs after a larger earthquake in the same area. (p. 163)

air mass A huge body of air that has similar temperature, pressure, and humidity throughout. (p. 560)

air pressure A force that is the result of the weight of a column of air pushing down on an area. (p. 510)

alloy A solid mixture of two or more metals. (p. 66)

alluvial fan A wide, sloping deposit of sediment formed where a stream leaves a mountain range. (p. 257)

altitude Elevation above sea level. (p. 512)

amphibian A vertebrate that lives part of its life on land and part of its life in water. (p. 310)

anemometer An instrument used to measure wind speed. (p. 537)

aneroid barometer An instrument that measures changes in air pressure without using a liquid. Changes in the shape of an airtight metal box cause a needle on the barometer dial to move. (p. 511)

anticline An upward fold in rock formed by compression of Earth's crust. (p. 150)

anticyclone A high-pressure center of dry air. (p. 566)

apparent magnitude The brightness of a star as seen from Earth. (p. 727)

aquaculture The farming of saltwater and freshwater organisms. (p. 481)

aquifer An underground layer of rock or soil that holds water. (p. 380)

artesian well A well in which water rises because of pressure within the aquifer. (p. 381)

asteroid belt The region of the solar system between the orbits of Mars and Jupiter, where many asteroids are found. (p. 702)

asteroids Objects revolving around the sun that are too small and too numerous to be considered planets. (p. 702)

asthenosphere The soft layer of the mantle on which the lithosphere floats. (p. 111)

astronomy The study of the moon, stars, and other objects in space. (p. 637)

astronomer A scientist who studies the universe beyond Earth. (p. 11)

atmosphere The mixture of gases that surrounds Earth. The outermost of the four spheres into which scientists divide Earth. (pp. 22, 498)

atoll A ring-shaped coral island found far from land. (pp. 89, 474)

atom The smallest unit of an element that retains the properties of that element. (p. 299)

aurora borealis A colorful, glowing display in the sky caused when particles from the sun strike oxygen and nitrogen atoms in the ionosphere; also called the Northern Lights. (p. 520)

autumnal equinox The day of the year that marks the beginning of fall in the Northern Hemisphere. (p. 643)

axis An imaginary line that passes through Earth's center and the North and South poles, about which Earth rotates. (p. 637)

barometer An instrument used to measure changes in air pressure. (p. 510)

basalt A dark, dense, igneous rock with a fine texture, found in oceanic crust. (p. 79)

base-isolated building A building mounted on bearings designed to absorb the energy of an earthquake. (p. 166)

batholith A mass of rock formed when a large body of magma cooled inside the crust. (p. 197)

beach Wave-washed sediment along a coast. (p. 277)

bedrock The solid layer of rock beneath the soil. (p. 221)

benthos Organisms that live on the bottom of the ocean or another body of water. (p. 467)

big bang The initial explosion that resulted in the formation and expansion of the universe. (p. 742)

binary star A star system that contains two stars. (p. 737)

bioluminescence The production of light by living things. (p. 477)

biomass fuel Fuel made from things that once were alive. (p. 337)

biosphere All living things. One of the four spheres into which scientists divide Earth. (p. 22)

black hole The remains of an extremely massive star pulled into a small volume by the force of gravity. (p. 735)

brackish Water that is partly salty and partly fresh, characteristic of estuaries. (p. 470)

caldera The large hole at the top of a volcano formed when the roof of a volcano's magma chamber collapses. (p. 194)

carbon film A type of fossil consisting of an extremely thin coating of carbon on rock. (p. 289)

cast A fossil that is a copy of an organism's shape, formed when minerals seep into a mold. (p. 288)

cementation The process by which dissolved minerals crystallize and glue particles of sediment together into one mass. (p. 83)

chemical rock Sedimentary rock that forms when minerals crystallize from a solution. (p. 86)

chemical weathering The process that breaks down rock through chemical changes. (p. 215)

chlorofluorocarbons Chlorine compounds formerly used in air conditioners, refrigerators, and spray cans; also called CFCs. (p. 626)

chromosphere The middle layer of the sun's atmosphere. (p. 677)

cinder cone A steep, cone-shaped hill or mountain made of volcanic ash, cinders, and bombs piled up around a volcano's opening. (p. 194)

cirrus Wispy, feathery clouds made mostly of ice crystals that form at high levels, above about 6 kilometers. (p. 548)

clastic rock Sedimentary rock that forms when rock fragments are squeezed together under high pressure. (p. 84)

cleavage A mineral's ability to split easily along flat surfaces. (p. 53)

climate The average, year-after-year conditions of temperature, precipitation, winds, and clouds in an area. (pp. 448, 596)

coagulation The process by which particles in a liquid clump together; a step in the water treatment process. (p. 399)

combustion The burning of a fuel. (p. 327)

comet A ball of ice and dust whose orbit is a long, narrow ellipse. (p. 700)

compaction The process by which sediments are pressed together under their own weight. (p. 83)

composite volcano A tall, cone-shaped mountain in which layers of lava alternate with layers of ash and other volcanic materials. (p. 194)

compound A substance in which two or more elements are chemically joined. (p. 48)

compression Stress that squeezes rock until it folds or breaks. (p. 145)

concentration The amount of one substance in a certain volume of another substance. (p. 398)

condensation The process by which a gas, such as water vapor, changes to a liquid, such as water. (p. 547)

conduction The transfer of heat by from one substance to another by direct contact of particles of matter. (pp. 116, 534)

conservation The process of using a resource wisely so it will not be used up. (p. 406)

conservation plowing Soil conservation method in which the dead stalks are left in the ground to hold the soil in place. (p. 233)

constellation A pattern of stars in the sky. (p. 714)

continental (air mass) A dry air mass that forms over land. (p. 560)

continental climate The climate of the centers of continents, with cold winters and warm or hot summers. (p. 598)

continental drift The hypothesis that the continents slowly move across Earth's surface. (pp. 119)

continental glacier A glacier that covers much of a continent or large island. (p. 269)

continental shelf A gently sloping, shallow area of the ocean floor that extends outward from the edge of a continent. (p. 462)

continental slope An incline leading down from the edge of the continental shelf. (p. 462)

contour interval The difference in elevation from one contour line to the next. (p. 37)

contour line A line on a topographic map that connects points of equal elevation. (p. 37)

contour plowing Plowing fields along the curves of a slope to prevent soil loss. (p. 233)

control rod Cadmium rod used in a nuclear reactor to absorb neutrons from fission. (p. 342)

controlled experiment An experiment in which all factors except one are kept constant. (pp. 6, 759)

convection The transfer of heat by movements of a fluid. (pp. 116, 536)

convection current The movement of a fluid, caused by differences in temperature, that transfers heat from one part of the fluid to another. (p. 116)

convergent boundary A plate boundary where two plates move toward each other. (p. 136)

convex lens A piece of transparent glass curved so that the middle is thicker than the edges. (p. 716)

coral reef A structure of calcite skeletons built up by coral animals in warm, shallow ocean water. (p. 88)

core Earth's dense center, made up of the solid inner core and the molten outer core (p. 22); also, the central part of the sun, where nuclear fusion occurs. (p. 676)

Coriolis effect The way Earth's rotation makes winds in the Northern Hemisphere curve to the right and winds in the Southern Hemisphere curve to the left. (pp. 447, 541)

corona The outer layer of the sun's atmosphere. (p. 677)

crater A bowl-shaped area that forms around a volcano's central opening (p. 184); A round pit on the moon's surface. (p. 661)

crest The highest point of a wave. (p. 430)

crop rotation The planting of different crops in a field each year. (p. 234)

crust The layer of rock that forms Earth's outer surface. (pp. 23, 110)

crystal A solid in which the atoms are arranged in a pattern that repeats again and again. (p. 48)

cumulus Clouds that form less than 2 kilometers above the ground and look like fluffy, rounded piles of cotton. (p. 548)

current A large stream of moving water that flows through the ocean. (p. 447)

cyclone A swirling center of low air pressure. (p. 565)

data The facts, figures, and other evidence gained through observation. (p. 7)

decomposer An organism that breaks down wastes and dead organisms. (p. 225)

deep-ocean trench A deep valley along the ocean floor through which oceanic crust slowly sinks towards the mantle. (p. 128)

deflation Wind erosion that removes surface materials. (p. 279)

deformation A change in the volume or shape of Earth's crust. (p. 145)

degree A unit used to measure distances around a circle. One degree equals 1/360 of a full circle. (p. 28)

delta A landform made of sediment that is deposited where a river flows into an ocean or lake. (p. 257)

density The amount of mass in a given space; mass per unit volume. (pp. 116, 509)

deposition The process by which sediment settles out of the water or wind that is carrying it, and is deposted in a new location. (pp. 83, 247)

desalination The process of obtaining fresh water from salt water by removing the salt. (p. 408)

desert A region that receives less than 25 centimeters of rain a year. (p. 610)

desertification The advance of desertlike conditions into areas that previously were fertile. (p. 231)

development The construction of buildings, roads, dams, and other structures. (p. 230)

dew point The temperature at which condensation begins. (p. 547)

digitizing Converting information to numbers for use by a computer. (p. 34)

dike A slab of volcanic rock formed when magma forces itself across rock layers. (p. 196)

divergent boundary A plate boundary where two plates move away from each other. (p. 135)

divide A ridge of land that separates one drainage basin or watershed from another. (pp. 255, 369)

dormant Said of a volcano that does not show signs of erupting in the near future. (p. 188)

drainage basin The land area from which a river and its tributaries collect their water. (p. 255)

drought A water shortage caused by long periods of low precipitation in a particular area. (pp. 405, 554)

Dust Bowl The area of the Great Plains where wind erosion caused soil loss during the 1930s. (p. 232)

earthquake The shaking that results from the movement of rock beneath Earth's surface. (p. 144)

Earth science The science that focuses on planet Earth and its place in the universe. (p. 10)

eclipse The partial or total blocking of one object by another. (p. 649)

eclipsing binary A star system in which one star periodically blocks the light from another. (p. 738)

efficiency The percentage of energy that is used by a device to perform work. (p. 348)

El Niño An abnormal climate event that occurs every 2 to 7 years in the Pacific Ocean, causing changes in winds, currents, and weather patterns that can lead to dramatic climate changes. (pp. 451, 586)

electromagnetic radiation Energy that travels through space in the form of waves. (p. 715)

electromagnetic wave A form of energy that can travel through space. (p. 526)

element A substance composed of a single kind of atom. (p. 48, 299)

elevation Height above sea level. (p. 19)

ellipse An elongated circle, or oval shape; the shape of the planets' orbits. (p. 673)

elliptical galaxy A galaxy shaped like a flattened ball, containing only old stars. (p. 740)

energy The ability to do work or cause change. (p. 265)

energy conservation The practice of reducing energy use. (p. 347)

environmental scientist A scientist who studies the effects of human activities onEarth's land, air, water, and living things and also tries to solve problems relating to the use of resources. (p. 11)

epicenter The point on Earth's surface directly above an earthquake's focus. (p. 154)

epochs Subdivisions of the periods of the geologic time scale. (p. 305)

equinox The two days of the year on which neither hemisphere is tilted toward or away from the sun. (p. 643)

equator An imaginary line halfway between the North and South poles that circles Earth. (p. 27)

era One of the three long units of geologic time between the Precambrian and the present. (p. 304)

erosion The process by which water, ice, wind, or gravity moves fragments of rock and soil. (pp. 83, 247)

estuary A coastal inlet or bay where fresh water mixes with salty ocean water. (p. 470).

eutrophication The process by which nutrients in a lake build up over time, causing an increase in the growth of algae. (p. 375)

evacuate To move away temporarily. (p. 574)

evaporation The process by which molecules at the surface of a liquid, such as water, absorb enough energy to change to a gaseous state, such as water vapor. (pp. 545, 362)

evolution The process by which all the different kinds of living things have changed over time. (p. 290)

exosphere The outer layer of the thermosphere, extending outward into space. (p. 520)

extinct Said of a volcano that is unlikely to erupt again (p. 188); describes a type of organism that no longer exists anywhere on Earth. (p. 290)

extraterrestrial life Life that arises outside of Earth. (p. 704)

extrusion An igneous rock layer formed when lava flows onto Earth's surface and hardens. (p. 295)

extrusive rock Igneous rock that forms from lava on Earth's surface. (p. 79)

fallow Left unplanted with crops. (p. 234)

fault A break or crack in Earth's lithosphere along which the rocks move. (pp. 134, 146)

fault-block mountain A mountain that forms where a normal fault uplifts a block of rock. (p. 148)

filtration The process of passing water through a series of screens that allow the water through, but not larger solid particles. (p. 399)

flash flood A sudden, violent flood that occurs within a few hours, or even minutes, of a heavy rainstorm. (p. 580)

flocs Sticky globs created by adding a chemical such as alum during water treatment. (p. 399)

flood plain A broad, flat valley through which a river flows. (p. 256)

fluorescence The property of a mineral in which the mineral glows under ultraviolet light. (p. 54)

focus The point beneath Earth's surface where rock breaks under stress and causes an earthquake. (p. 154)

fold A bend in rock that forms where part of Earth's crust is compressed. (p. 149)

foliated Term used to describe metamorphic rocks whose grains are arranged in parallel layers or bands. (p. 91)

food web The pattern of overlapping food chains in a habitat or ecosystem. (p. 467)

footwall The block of rock that forms the lower half of a fault. (p. 146)

fossil The preserved remains or traces of living things. (pp. 120, 286)

fossil fuel An energy-rich substance (such as coal, oil, or natural gas) formed from the remains of organisms. (p. 328)

fracture The way a mineral looks when it breaks apart in an irregular way. (p. 53)

frequency The number of waves that pass a specific point in a given amount of time. (p. 430)

friction The force that opposes the motion of one surface as it moves across another surface. (p. 267)

front The area where air masses meet and do not mix. (p. 563)

fuel rod Uranium rod that undergoes fission in a nuclear reactor. (p. 342)

galaxy A giant structure that contains hundreds of billions of stars. (p. 723)

gas giants The name given to the first four outer planets: Jupiter, Saturn, Uranus, and Neptune. (p. 690)

gasohol A mixture of gasoline and alcohol. (p. 337)

gemstone A hard, colorful mineral that has a brilliant or glassy luster. (p. 63)

geocentric A description of the solar system in which all of the planets revolve around Earth. (p. 671)

geologic time scale A record of the geologic events and life forms in Earth's history. (p. 303)

geologist A scientist who studies the forces that make and shape planet Earth. (p. 10)

geology The study of the solid Earth. (p. 23)

geosynchronous orbit The orbit of a satellite that revolves around Earth at the same rate that Earth rotates. (p. 657)

geothermal energy Heat energy in Earth's interior from water or steam that has been heated by magma. (pp. 189, 337)

geyser A type of hot spring that builds up pressure underground and erupts at regular intervals as a fountain of water and steam. (p. 189)

giant star A very large star, much larger than the sun. (p. 726)

glacier A huge mass of ice and snow that moves slowly over the land. (p. 269)

Global Positioning System A method of finding latitude and longitude using satellites. (p. 39)

global warming A gradual increase in the temperature of Earth's atmosphere. (p. 624)

global winds Winds that blow steadily from specific directions over long distances. (p. 541)

globe A sphere that represents Earth's surface. (p. 25)

grain A particle of mineral or other rock that gives a rock its texture. (p. 75)

granite A usually light-colored rock that is found in continental crust. (p. 151)

gravity The attractive force between two objects; its magnitude depends on their masses and the distance between them. (p. 654)

greenhouse effect The process by which heat is trapped in the atmosphere by water vapor, carbon dioxide, methane, and other gases that form a "blanket" around Earth. (pp. 529, 686)

greenhouse gases Gases in the atmosphere that trap heat. (p. 624)

groin A stone or concrete wall built out from a beach to reduce erosion. (p. 433)

groundwater Water that fills the cracks and pores in underground soil and rock layers. (pp. 260, 361)

gully A large channel in soil formed by erosion. (p. 253)

habitat The place where an organism lives and that provides the things it needs to survive. (p. 366)

half-life The time it takes for half of the atoms of a radioactive element to decay. (p. 300)

hanging wall The block of rock that forms the upper half of a fault. (p. 146)

hardness The level of the minerals calcium and magnesium in water. (p. 398)

hazardous waste A material that can be harmful if it is not properly disposed of. (p. 239)

heat The energy transferred from a hotter object to a cooler one. (p. 533)

heat transfer The movement of energy from a warmer object to a cooler object. (p. 115, 533)

heliocentric A description of the solar system in which all of the planets revolve around the sun. (p. 672)

hemisphere One half of the sphere that makes up Earth's surface. (p. 27)

Hertzsprung-Russell diagram A graph relating the temperature and brightness of stars. (p. 728)

holdfast A bundle of rootlike strands that attaches algae to the rocks. (p. 474)

hot spot An area where magma from deep within the mantle melts through the crust above it. (p. 181)

hot spring A pool formed by groundwater that has risen to the surface after being heated by a nearby body of magma. (p. 189)

humid subtropical A wet and warm climate area on the edge of the tropics. (p. 612)

humidity A measure of the amount of water vapor in the air. (p. 546)

humus Dark-colored organic material in soil. (p. 222)

hurricane A tropical storm that has winds of 119 kilometers per hour or higher; typically about 600 kilometers across. (p. 572)

hydrocarbon A compound that contains carbon and hydrogen atoms. (p. 328)

hydroelectric power Electricity produced by the kinetic energy of water moving over a waterfall or dam. (pp. 336, 420)

hydrosphere Earth's water and ice. One of the four spheres into which scientists divide Earth. (p. 22)

hydrothermal vent An area where ocean water sinks through cracks in the ocean floor, is heated by the underlying magma, and rises again through the cracks. (p. 478)

hypothesis A possible explanation for a set of observations or answer to a scientific question. (pp. 6, 758)

ice ages Cold time periods in Earth's history, during which glaciers covered large parts of the surface. (pp. 270, 620)

ice wedging Process that splits rock when water seeps into cracks, then freezes and expands. (p. 214)

igneous rock A type of rock that forms from the cooling of molten rock at or below the surface. (p. 77)

impermeable Characteristic of materials through which water does not easily pass, such as clay and granite. (p. 379)

incineration The burning of solid waste. (p. 237)

index fossils Fossils of widely distributed organisms that lived during only one short period. (p. 296)

inertia The tendency of a moving object to continue in a straight line or a stationary object to remain in place. (p. 673)

inference An interpretation based on observation and prior knowledge. (p. 5)

infrared radiation A form of energy with wavelengths that are longer than visible light. (p. 527)

inner core A dense sphere of solid iron and nickel in the center of Earth. (p. 111)

inorganic Not formed from living things or the remains of living things. (p. 47)

insulation Building material that blocks heat transfer between the air inside and outside. (p. 349)

intertidal zone The area that stretches from the highest high-tide line on land out to the point on the continental shelf exposed by the lowest low tide. (p. 468)

intrusion An igneous rock layer formed when magma hardens beneath Earth's surface. (p. 295)

intrusive rock Igneous rock that forms when magma hardens beneath Earth's surface. (p. 79)

invertebrate An animal without a backbone. (p. 304)

ionosphere The lower part of the thermosphere, where electrically charged particles called ions are found. (p. 520)

irregular galaxy A galaxy that does not have a regular shape. (p. 740)

irrigation The process of supplying water to areas of land to make them suitable for growing crops. (p. 364)

island arc A string of islands formed by the volcanoes along a deep ocean trench. (p. 180)

isobars Lines on a map joining places that have the same air pressure. (p. 586)

isotherms Lines on a map joining places that have the same temperature. (p. 586)

jet streams Bands of high-speed winds about 10 kilometers above Earth's surface. (p. 544)

karst topography A type of landscape in rainy regions where there is limestone near the surface, characterized by caverns, sinkholes, and valleys. (p. 261)

kettle A small depression that forms when a chunk of ice is left in glacial till. (p. 272)

key A list of the symbols used on a map. (p. 26)

kinetic energy The form of energy an object has because of its motion. (pp. 265, 420)

land breeze The flow of air from land to a body of water. (p. 540)

landform A feature of topography formed by the processes that shape Earth's surface. (p. 19)

landform region A large area of land where the topography is similar. (p. 19)

land reclamation The process of restoring land to a more natural state. (p. 234)

latitude The distance north or south from the equator, measured in degrees. (pp. 28, 542)

lava Magma that reaches the surface; also the rock formed when liquid lava hardens. (p. 57, 178)

lava flow The area covered by lava as it pours out of a volcano's vent. (p. 184)

law of superposition The geologic principle that states that in horizontal layers of sedimentary rock, each layer is older than the layer above it and younger than the layer below it. (p. 294)

leachate Water that has passed through buried wastes in a landfill. (p. 235)

leach field The ground area around a septic tank through which wastewater filters after leaving the tank. (p. 403)

leeward The downwind side of mountains. (p. 601)

levee A long ridge formed by deposits of sediments alongside a river channel. (p. 371)

lightning A sudden spark, or energy discharge, caused when electrical charges jump between parts of a cloud or between a cloud and the ground. (p. 568)

light-year The distance that light travels in one year. (p. 724)

liquefaction The process by which an earthquake's violent movement suddenly turns loose soil into liquid mud. (p. 163)

lithosphere A rigid layer made up of the uppermost part of the mantle and the crust. One of four spheres into which scientists divide Earth. (pp. 22, 110)

litter The loose layer of dead plant leaves and stems on the surface of the soil. (p. 224)

load The amount of sediment that a river or stream carries. (p. 266)

loam Rich, fertile soil that is made up of about equal parts of clay, sand, and silt. (p. 222)

local winds Winds that blow over short distances. (p. 538)

loess A wind-formed deposit made of fine particles of clay and silt. (p. 280)

longitude The distance in degrees east or west of the prime meridian. (p. 29)

longshore drift The movement of water and sediment along a beach caused by waves coming into shore at an angle. (pp. 277, 432)

lunar eclipse The blocking of sunlight to the moon that occurs when Earth is directly between the sun and moon. (p. 651)

luster The way a mineral reflects light from its surface. (p. 51)

magma The molten mixture of rock-forming substances, gases, and water that makes up part of Earth's mantle. (pp. 57, 178)

magma chamber The pocket beneath a volcano where magma collects. (p. 184)

magnitude The measurement of an earthquake's strength based on seismic waves and movement along faults. (p. 157)

main sequence An area on the Hertzsprung-Russell diagram that runs from the upper left to the lower right and includes more than 90 percent of all stars. (p. 728)

mammal A warm-blooded vertebrate that feeds its young milk. (p. 317)

manipulated variable The one factor that a scientist changes during an experiment; also called the independent variable. (pp. 7, 759)

mantle The layer of hot, solid material between Earth's crust and core. (pp. 22, 110)

map A model of all or part of Earth's surface as seen from above. (p. 25)

map projection A framework of lines that helps to show landmasses on a flat surface. (p. 30)

maria Dark, flat regions on the moon's surface. (p. 661)

marine climate The climate of some coastal regions, with relatively warm winters and cool summers. (p. 598)

maritime (air mass) A humid air mass that forms over oceans. (p. 560)

mass extinction When many types of living things become extinct at the same time. (p. 311)

mass movement Any one of several processes by which gravity moves sediment downhill. (p. 247)

meander A looping curve formed in a river as it winds through its flood plain. (p. 256)

mechanical weathering The type of weathering in which rock is physically broken into smaller pieces. (p. 213)

meltdown A dangerous condition caused by overheating inside a nuclear reactor. (p. 343)

Mercalli scale A scale that rates earthquakes according to their intensity and how much damage they cause. (p. 157)

mercury barometer An instrument that measures changes in air pressure, consisting of a glass tube part filled with mercury, with its open end resting in a dish of mercury. Air pressure pushing on the mercury in the dish forces the mercury in the tube higher. (p. 510)

mesosphere The middle layer of Earth's atmosphere; the layer in which most meteoroids burn up. (p. 516)

metamorphic rock A type of rock that forms from an existing rock that is changed by heat, pressure, or chemical reactions. (p. 77)

meteor A streak of light in the sky produced by the burning of a meteoroid in Earth's atmosphere. (p. 703)

meteorite A meteoroid that has hit Earth's surface. (p. 703)

meteoroid A chunk of rock or dust in space. (p. 703)

meteorologists Scientists who study the causes of weather and try to predict it. (pp. 11, 584)

microclimate The climate characteristic of a small, specific area; it may be different from the climate of the surrounding area. (p. 601)

mid-ocean ridge The undersea mountain chain where new ocean floor is produced; a divergent plate boundary. (pp. 124, 463)

mineral A naturally occurring, inorganic solid that has a crystal structure and a definite chemical composition. (p. 47)

Mohs hardness scale A scale ranking ten minerals from softest to hardest; used in testing the hardness of minerals. (p. 49)

mold A fossil formed when an organism buried in sediment dissolves, leaving a hollow area. (p. 288)

moment magnitude scale A scale that rates earthquakes by estimating the total energy released by an earthquake. (p. 158)

monsoons Sea and land breezes over a large region that change direction with the seasons. (p. 540)

moraine A ridge formed by the till deposited at the edge of a glacier. (p. 271)

mountain A landform with high elevation and high relief. (p. 20)

mountain range A series of mountains that have the same general shape and structure. (p. 20)

municipal solid waste Waste produced in homes, businesses, and schools. (p. 235)

neap tide A tide with the least difference between low and high tide that occurs when the sun and moon pull at right angles to each other. (p. 437)

nebula A large amount of gas and dust in space, spread out in an immense volume. (p. 733)

nekton Free-swimming animals that can move throughout the water column. (p. 467)

neritic zone The region of shallow water in the ocean that extends from the low-tide line out to the edge of the continental shelf. (p. 473)

neutron star A tiny star that remains after a supernova explosion. (p. 734)

nodule A black, potato-shaped lump formed when metals build up around pieces of shell on the ocean floor. (p. 481)

nonpoint source A widely spread source of pollution, such as road runoff, that is difficult to link to a specific point of origin. (p. 413)

nonrenewable resource A natural resource that is not replaced as it is used. (p. 332)

normal fault A type of fault where the hanging wall slides downward; caused by tension in the crust. (p. 146)

nuclear fission The splitting of an atom's nucleus into smaller nuclei. (p. 341)

nuclear fusion The combining of two atomic nuclei into a single larger nucleus, as when two hydrogen atoms join together to form helium, releasing energy. (p. 344, 676)

nucleus The central core of an atom that contains the protons and neutrons. (p. 341)

observation Using all five senses to gather information. (p. 5)

observatory A building that contains one or more telescopes. (p. 717)

oceanographer A scientist who studies Earth's oceans. (p. 11)

occluded Cut off, as the warm air mass at an occluded front is cut off from the ground by cooler air beneath it. (p. 565)

open-ocean zone The area of the ocean beyond the edge of the continental shelf. (p. 473)

operational definition A statement that describes how a particular variable is to be measured or a term is to be defined. (p. 759)

orbit The path of an object as it revolves around another object in space. (p. 637)

ore Rock that contains a metal or economically useful mineral. (p. 63)

organic rock Sedimentary rock that forms where remains of organisms are deposited in thick layers. (p. 85)

outer core A layer of molten iron and nickel that surrounds the inner core of Earth. (p. 111)

oxbow lake The crescent-shaped, cutoff body of water that remains after a river carves a new channel. (p. 256)

ozone A form of oxygen that has three oxygen atoms in each molecule instead of the usual two. (p. 500)

P wave A type of seismic wave that compresses and expands the ground. (p. 155)

pahoehoe A hot, fast-moving type of lava that hardens to form smooth, ropelike coils. (p. 187)

paleontologist A scientist who studies fossils to learn about organisms that lived long ago. (p. 286)

Pangaea The name of the single landmass that broke apart 225 million years ago and gave rise to today's continents. (p. 119)

parallax The apparent change in position of an object when seen from different places. (p. 724)

passive solar system A method of converting solar energy into heat without pumps or fans. (p. 335)

penumbra The part of a shadow surrounding the darkest part. (p. 650)

period One of the units of geologic time into which geologists divide eras. (p. 305)

permafrost Permanently frozen soil found in the tundra climate region. (p. 614)

permeable Characteristic of materials such as sand and gravel which allow water to pass easily through them. (pp. 217, 379)

pesticide A chemical intended to kill insects and other organisms that damage crops. (p. 416)

petrified fossil A fossil in which minerals replace all or part of an organism. (p. 287)

petrochemical Compound made from oil. (p. 331)

petroleum Liquid fossil fuel; oil. (p. 330)

pH How acidic or basic a substance is, measured on a scale of 1 (very acidic) to 14 (very basic). (p. 397)

phase One of the different shapes of the moon as seen from Earth. (p. 647)

photochemical smog A brownish haze that is a mixture of ozone and other chemicals, formed when nitrogen oxides, hydrocarbons, and other pollutants react with one another in the presence of sunlight. (p. 506)

photosphere The inner layer of the sun's atmosphere. (p. 677)

photosynthesis The process by which plants use water, plus carbon dioxide and energy from the sun, to make food. (p. 366)

pipe A long tube through which magma moves from the magma chamber to Earth's surface. (p. 184)

pixels The tiny dots in a satellite image. (p. 33)

plain A landform made up of flat or gently rolling land with low relief. (p. 20)

plankton Tiny algae and animals that float in water and are carried by waves and currents. (p. 467)

plate A section of the lithosphere that slowly moves over the asthenosphere, carrying pieces of continental and oceanic crust. (p. 132)

plate tectonics The theory that pieces of Earth's lithosphere are in constant motion, driven by convection currents in the mantle. (p. 133)

plateau A landform that has a more or less level surface and is elevated high above sea level. (pp. 21, 151)

plucking The process by which a glacier picks up rocks as it flows over the land. (p. 270)

point source A specific source of pollution that can be identified, such as a pipe. (p. 413)

polar (air mass) A cold air mass that forms north of 50° north latitude or south of 50° south latitude and has high air pressure. (p. 560)

polar zones The areas near both poles, from about 66.5° to 90° north and 66.5° to 90° south latitudes. (p. 597)

pollutants Harmful substances in the air, water, or soil. (p. 504)

pores Tiny openings in and between particles of rock and soil which may contain air or water. (p. 379)

porphyritic texture An igneous rock texture in which large crystals are scattered on a background of much smaller crystals. (p. 79)

potential energy Energy that is stored and available to be used later. (pp. 265, 420)

precipitation Forms of water such as rain, snow, sleet, or hail that fall from clouds and reach Earth's surface. (pp. 551, 362)

pressure The amount of force pushing on a surface or area. (pp. 109, 509)

prime meridian The line that makes a half circle from the North Pole to the South Pole, passing through Greenwich, England. (p. 28)

prominence A loop of gas that protrudes from the sun's surface, linking parts of sunspot regions. (p. 680)

protostar A contracting cloud of gas and dust; the earliest stage of a star's life. (p. 733)

psychrometer An instrument used to measure relative humidity, consisting of a wet-bulb thermometer and a dry-bulb thermometer. (p. 546)

pulsar A neutron star that produces radio waves. (p. 732)

pyroclastic flow The expulsion of ash, cinders, bombs, and gases during an explosive volcanic eruption. (p. 188)

quasar A distant galaxy with a black hole at its center. (p. 736)

radiation The direct transfer of energy through empty space by electromagnetic waves. (pp. 115, 526)

radioactive decay The breakdown of a radioactive element, releasing particles and energy. (p. 300)

radio telescope A device used to detect radio waves from objects in space. (p. 716)

rain forest A forest in the tropical wet climate zone that gets plenty of rain all year. (p. 607)

rain gauge An instrument used to measure the amount of precipitation, consisting of an open-ended can topped by a collecting funnel and having a collecting tube and measuring scale inside. (p. 553)

reactor vessel The part of a nuclear reactor where nuclear fission occurs. (p. 342)

recharge New water that enters an aquifer from the surface. (p. 381)

recycling The process of reclaiming and reusing raw materials. (p. 237)

refinery A factory where crude oil is separated into fuels and other products. (p. 331)

reflecting telescope A telescope that uses one or more mirrors to gather light. (p. 716)

refracting telescope A telescope that uses convex lenses to gather and focus light. (p. 716)

relative age The age of a rock compared to the ages of rock layers. (p. 293)

relative humidity The percentage of water vapor in the air compared to the maximum amount the air can hold at that temperature. (p. 546)

relief The difference in elevation between the highest and lowest parts of an area. (p. 19)

renewable resource A resource that is naturally replaced in a relatively short time. (p. 333)

reptile A vertebrate with scaly skin that lays eggs with tough, leathery shells. (p. 311)

reserve A known deposit of fuels. (p. 329)

reservoir A natural or artificial lake that stores water for human use. (p. 374)

responding variable The factor that changes as a result of changes to the manipulated variable in an experiment; also called the dependent variable. (pp. 7, 759)

retrograde rotation The spinning motion of a planet from east to west, opposite to the direction of rotation of most planets and moons. (p. 685)

reverse fault A type of fault where the hanging wall slides upward; caused by compression in the crust. (p. 147)

revolution The movement of an object around another object. (p. 637)

Richter scale A scale that rates seismic waves as measured by a mechanical seismograph. (p. 157)

rift valley A deep valley that forms where two plates move apart. (p. 135)

rill A tiny groove in soil made by flowing water. (p. 253)

Ring of Fire A major belt of volcanoes that rims the Pacific Ocean. (p. 179)

rip current A rush of water that flows rapidly back to sea through a narrow opening. (p. 432)

river A large stream. (pp. 254, 432)

rock The material that forms Earth's hard surface. (p. 23)

rock cycle A series of processes on the surface and inside Earth that slowly changes rocks from one kind to another. (p. 94)

rotation The spinning motion of a planet about its axis. (p. 637)

runoff Water that flows over the ground surface rather than soaking into the ground. (p. 253)

S wave A type of seismic wave that moves the ground up and down or side to side. (p. 155)

salinity The total amount of dissolved salts in a water sample. (p. 439)

sand dune A deposit of wind-blown sand. (p. 278)

sandbar A ridge of sand deposited by waves as they slow down near shore. (p. 432)

sanitary landfill A landfill that holds nonhazardous waste such as municipal solid waste and construction debris. (p. 236)

satellite Any object that revolves around another object in space. (p. 656)

satellite images Pictures of the land surface based on computer data collected from satellites. (p. 32)

saturated zone A layer of permeable rock or soil in which the cracks and pores are completely filled with water. (p. 379)

savanna A tropical grassland with scattered clumps of trees; found in the tropical wet-and-dry climate zone close to the equator. (p. 610)

scale Used to compare distance on a map or globe to distance on Earth's surface. (p. 25)

scattering Reflection of light in all directions. (p. 528)

science A way of learning about the natural world and the knowledge gained through that process. (p. 4)

scientific inquiry The diverse ways in which scientists explore problems and seek to answer questions about the natural world. (p. 4)

scientific theory A well-tested concept that explains a wide range of observations. (pp. 8, 133)

sea breeze The flow of air from an ocean or lake to the land. (p. 540)

sea-floor spreading The process by which molten material adds new oceanic crust to the ocean floor. (pp. 125)

seamount A mountain on the ocean floor that is completely underwater. (p. 463)

sediment Small, solid particles of material from rocks or organisms which are moved by water or wind, resulting in erosion and deposition. (pp. 82, 247)

sedimentary rock A type of rock that forms when particles from other rocks or the remains of plants and animals are pressed and cemented together. (pp. 77, 287)

seismic wave A vibration that travels through Earth carrying the energy released during an earthquake. (pp. 108, 154)

seismograph A device that records ground movements caused by seismic waves as they move through Earth. (p. 156)

septic tank An underground tank containing bacteria that treats wastewater as it passes through. (p. 403)

sewage Water containing human wastes. (p. 401)

shearing Stress that pushes a mass of rock in opposite directions. (p. 145)

shield volcano A wide, gently sloping mountain made of layers of lava and formed by quiet eruptions. (p. 194)

silica A material that is formed from the elements oxygen and silicon; silica is found in magma. (pp. 80, 186)

sill A slab of volcanic rock formed when magma squeezes between layers of rock. (p. 196)

sludge Deposits of fine solids that settle out from wastewater during the treatment process. (p. 402)

smelting The process by which ore is melted to separate the useful metal from other elements. (p. 66)

sod A thick mass of grass roots and soil. (p. 232)

soil The loose, weathered material on Earth's surface in which plants can grow. (p. 221)

soil conservation The management of soil to prevent its destruction. (p. 233)

soil horizon A layer of soil that differs in color and texture from the layers above or below it. (p. 223)

solar eclipse The blocking of sunlight to Earth that occurs when the moon is between the sun and Earth. (p. 650)

solar flare An explosion of hydrogen gas from the sun's surface that occurs when loops in sunspot regions suddenly connect. (p. 680)

solar wind A stream of electrically charged particles produced by the sun's corona. (p. 678)

solstice The two days of the year on which the noon sun is directly overhead at either 23.5° South or 23.5° North. (p. 642)

solution A mixture in which one substance is dissolved in another. (p. 58)

sonar A system that determines the distance of an object under water by recording echoes of sound waves; gets its name from sound navigation and ranging. (pp. 124, 461)

spectrograph An instrument that separates light into colors and photographs the resulting spectrum. (p. 719)

spectrum The range of wavelengths of electromagnetic waves. (p. 715)

spiral galaxy A galaxy whose arms curve outward in a pinwheel pattern. (p. 740)

spit A beach formed by longshore drift that projects like a finger out into the water. (p. 277)

spring A place where groundwater bubbles or flows out of cracks in the rocks. (p. 380)

spring tide A tide with the greatest difference between high and low tide that occurs when the sun and the moon are aligned in a line with Earth. (p. 436)

stalactite A calcite deposit that hangs from the roof of a cave. (p. 261)

stalagmite A cone-shaped calcite deposit that builds up from the floor of a cave. (p. 261)

steppe A prairie or grassland found in the semiarid climate region. (p. 611)

storm A violent disturbance in the atmosphere. (p. 567)

storm surge A dome of water that sweeps across the coast where a hurricane lands. (p. 574)

stratosphere The second-lowest layer of Earth's atmosphere; the ozone layer is located in the upper stratosphere. (p. 516)

stratus Clouds that form in flat layers. (p. 548)

streak The color of a mineral's powder. (p. 50)

stream A channel through which water is continually flowing downhill. (p. 254)

stress A force that acts on rock to change its shape or volume. (p. 144)

strike-slip fault A type of fault where rocks on either side move past each other sideways with little up-or-down motion. (p. 146)

subarctic A climate zone that lies north of the humid continental climate zone, with short, cool summers and long, bitterly cold winters. (p. 613)

subduction The process by which oceanic crust sinks beneath a deep-ocean trench and back into the mantle at a convergent plate boundary. (p. 128)

submersible An underwater vehicle built of strong materials to resist pressure at depth. (p. 443)

subsoil The layer of soil beneath the topsoil that contains mostly clay and other minerals. (p. 223)

sunspots Dark, cooler regions on the surface of the sun. (pp. 621, 678)

supernova The explosion of a dying giant or supergiant star. (p. 734)

surface wave A type of seismic wave that forms when P waves and S waves reach Earth's surface. (p. 156)

symbols On a map, pictures used by mapmakers to stand for features on Earth's surface. (p. 26)

syncline A downward fold in rock formed by compression in Earth's crust. (p. 150)

telescope A device built to study distant objects by making them appear closer. (p. 661)

temperate zones The area between the tropical and polar zones, from about 23.5° to 66.5° north and 23.5° to 66.5° south latitudes. (p. 597)

temperature The average amount of energy of motion in the molecules of a substance. (p. 533)

tension Stress that stretches rock so that it becomes thinner in the middle. (p. 145)

terrestrial planets The name given to the four inner planets: Mercury, Venus, Earth, and Mars. (p. 682)

texture The size, shape, and pattern of a rock's grains. (p. 75)

thermal energy The energy of motion in the molecules of a substance. (p. 533)

thermometer An instrument used to measure temperature, consisting of a thin, glass tube with a bulb on one end that contains a liquid (usually mercury or alcohol). (p. 533)

thermosphere The outermost layer of Earth's atmosphere. (p. 519)

tides The daily rise and fall of Earth's waters on shores. (pp. 435, 654)

till The sediments deposited directly by a glacier. (p. 271)

topographic map A map that shows the surface features of an area. (p. 35)

topography The shape of the land determined by elevation, relief, and landforms. (p. 18)

topsoil Mixture of humus, clay, and other minerals that forms the crumbly, topmost layer of soil. (p. 223)

tornado A rapidly whirling, funnel-shaped cloud that reaches down from a storm cloud to touch Earth's surface, usually leaving a destructive path. (p. 569)

trace fossils A type of fossil that provides evidence of the activities of ancient organisms. (p. 289)

transform boundary A plate boundary where two plates move past each other in opposite directions. (p. 134)

transpiration The process by which plants release water vapor through their leaves. (p. 362)

trench A deep canyon in the ocean floor. (p. 464)

tributary A stream that flows into a larger stream. (pp. 254, 368)

tropical (air mass) A warm air mass that forms in the tropics and has low air pressure. (p. 560)

tropical zone The area near the equator, between about 23.5° north latitude and 23.5° south latitude. (p. 597)

troposphere The lowest layer of Earth's atmosphere, where weather occurs. (p. 515)

trough The lowest point of a wave. (p. 431)

tsunami A giant wave caused by an earthquake on the ocean floor. (p. 164)

tundra A polar climate region, found across northern Alaska, Canada, and Russia, with short, cool summers and bitterly cold winters. (p. 614)

turbulence A type of movement of water in which, rather than moving downstream, the water moves every which way. (p. 268)

ultraviolet radiation A form of energy with wavelengths that are shorter than visible light. (p. 527)

umbra The darkest part of a shadow. (p. 650)

unconformity A place where an old, eroded rock surface is in contact with a newer rock layer. (p. 296)

universe All of space and everything in it. (p. 723)

unsaturated zone A layer of rocks and soil above the water table in which the pores contain air as well as water. (p. 379)

upwelling An upward flow of cold water from the ocean depths. (p. 449)

valley glacier A long, narrow glacier that forms when snow and ice build up in a mountain valley. (p. 269)

variable Any factor that can change in an experiment. (pp. 7, 759)

vein A narrow slab of a mineral that is sharply different from the surrounding rock. (p. 58)

vent The opening through which molten rock and gas leave a volcano. (p. 184)

vernal equinox The day of the year that marks the beginning of spring in the Northern Hemisphere. (p. 643)

vertebrate An animal with a backbone. (p. 310)

visible light Electromagnetic radiation that can be seen with the unaided eye. (p. 715)

volcanic neck A deposit of hardened magma in a volcano's pipe. (p. 196)

volcano A weak spot in the crust where magma has come to the surface. (p. 178)

water cycle The continuous process by which water moves from Earth's surface to the atmosphere and back, passing through the living and nonliving parts of the environment. (p. 362)

water pollution The addition of any substance that has a negative effect on water or the living things that depend on the water. (p. 411)

water quality The degree of purity of water, determined by measuring the substances in water, besides water molecules. (p. 396)

water table The top of the saturated zone, or depth to the groundwater in an aquifer. (p. 379)

water vapor The invisible, gaseous form of water. (pp. 360, 501)

watershed The land area that supplies water to a river system. (p. 369)

wave The movement of energy through a body of water. (p. 429)

wave height The vertical distance from the crest of a wave to the trough. (p. 431)

wavelength The horizontal distance between two wave crests. (pp. 430, 715)

weather The condition of Earth's atmosphere at a particular time and place. (p. 498)

weathering The chemical and physical processes that break down rock at Earth's surface. (p. 212)

wetland An area of land that is covered with a shallow layer of water during some or all of the year. (p. 384)

white dwarf The remaining hot core of a star after its outer layers have expanded and drifted out into space. (p. 734)

wind The horizontal movement of air from an area of high pressure to an area of lower pressure. (p. 536)

wind-chill factor Increased cooling caused by the wind. (p. 537)

windward The side of mountains that faces the oncoming wind. (p. 601)

Index

Index

Acknowledgments

Staff Credits

The people who made up the *Life, Earth, and Physical Science* team—representing design services, editorial, editorial services, electronic publishing technology, manufacturing & inventory planning, marketing, marketing services, market research, online services & multimedia development, production services, product planning, project office, publishing processes—are listed below. Bold type denotes core team members.

Carolyn Belanger, Barbara Bertell, Kristen Braghi, **Roger Calado, Jonathan Cheney, Lisa Clark,** Ed Cordero, Patricia Cully, Patricia Dambry, **Kathleen Dempsey,** Jim Fellows, Joel Gendler, Robert Graham, Joanne Hudson, Don Manning, Brent McKenzie, Paul W. Murphy, **Cindy Noftle,** Julia Osborne, **Caroline M. Power,** Shelley Ryan, **Robin Santel,** Helen Young

Additional Credits

Peggy Bliss, Barnard Gage, Julia Gecha, Adam Goldberg, Jessica Gould, Anne Jones, Dorothy Kavanaugh, Toby Klang, Jay Kulpan, Danny Marcus, Jeanne Maurand, Shilo McDonald, Carolyn McGuire, Tania Mlawer, Angela Sciaraffa

Illustrations

AccuWeather: 588, 589, 590
Peter Brooks: 391b, 644, 652, 681, 698, 721, 730
Warren Cutler: 372–373, 386–387b, 468–469
Kathleen Dempsey: 31, 40, 55, 68, 93, 96, 130, 138, 152, 160, 182, 198, 218, 228, 250, 262, 298, 306, 667b
Julia Gecha: 590
Andrea Golden: 367bl, 380, 382t, 586
JB Woolsey Associates: 7, 146b, 146t, 147, 148b, 149, 175, 214, 243, 253, 294inset, 297, 298b, 312, 313, 314, 315, 323b, 328–329b, 425, 489b, 548, 581, 629b, 716tl, 716tr
John Edwards & Associates: 23, 28tl, 28tr, 29tl, 29tr, 37tl, 37tr, 164, 216, 266, 267, 271, 275, 287t, 296, 327, 337, 343, 413, 430tr, 431, 432, 435tr, 437, 449, 473, 514, 528, 540t, 565, 573bl, 624, 641, 647,648overlay, 650r, 651l, 674b, 674–675t, 683t, 691,726t, 735, 738, 739, 742b, 743
Jared D. Lee: 724bl, 104, 105
MapQuest.com,Inc.: 19t, 19b, 29b, 30l, 30r, 60, 119, 120, 124, 133, 141t, 148t, 159, 160, 171, 172, 179, 207, 227, 231, 232, 255t, 257, 270, 278, 330t, 356bl, 369, 387t, 447, 480, 572tr, 575, 576b, 587t, 593, 599, 601, 608–609, 620
Martucci Studio: 36, 161, 205, 222b, 229, 347b, 361, 489t, 499, 527, 587b, 616, 681, 715, 720t, 720b, 732t
Matt Mayerchak: 41, 52m, 69, 97, 139, 173, 203, 321, 323t, 423br, 521, 627, 629t, 665,
Paul Mirocha: 477t,
Morgan Cain & Associates: 21, 39, 43b, 80, 83tl, 83tm, 83tr, 99, 112–113, 114, 116t, 116b, 117, 125, 126, 128, 134–135b, 141b, 145, 150, 155t, 156, 166, 167t, 167b, 169–170, 181, 185, 195t, 195m, 195b, 196, 197, 209, 222t, 224–225b, 246, 248, 249, 255b, 268, 279, 300t, 300b, 302, 303, 304, 331, 342, 400, 407, 416, 420, 430bl, 460bl, 475t, 492b, 510b, 511tl, 512, 523, 529, 532, 534, 538, 541t, 541b, 543, 551bl, 553, 557, 625, 637, 640, 644, 649, 655b, 656t, 657r, 667t, 679, 683b, 695r, 701t, 701m, 702l, 721, 725, 729, 731, 742t, 742m, 747, 750m
Ortelius Design: 6bl, 26bl, 26br, 26t, 27bl, 27bl, 27tr, 64t, 64bl, 64br, 65t, 65br, 102l, 102r, 136–137, 190tl, 190tr, 190br, 191t, 191bl, 191br, 207, 316, 364tl, 364bl, 364br, 365tl, 365bl, 365br, 375, 410, 434tl, 451, 459inset, 465, 490r, 501inset, 540b, 566, 570tl, 570tr, 570br, 571t, 571bl, 571br, 593m, 597, 600, 622, 638
Matthew Pippin: 58, 67, 155b, 165, 180, 223bl, 223bm, 223br, 258–259, 272–273, 363, 379, 381, 391t, 399, 402, 403, 421t, 442, 492t, 510t, 517, 549, 580t
Rossi Illustration and Design: 376t
John Sanderson: 562
Walter Stuart: 354–355, 357t, 621
U.S.G.S.: 38

Photography

Photo Research Sue McDermott, PoYee Oster, Paula Wehde
Cover image Artville

Front Matter: Page i,ii, Artville; **iiil,** Courtesy of Michael J. Padilla, Ph.D.; **iiir,** Courtesy of Martha Cyr, Ph.D. and Ioannis, Miaoulis, Ph.D.; **viiit,** Gregory G. Dimijian/Photo Researchers; **viiib,** Jean-Marc Truchet/Tony Stone Images; **ix,** Linde Waidhofer/Liaison Agency; **x,** Yamada Toshiro/Tony Stone Images; **xi,** Fred Bavendam; **xiit,** Grant V. Faint/Image Bank; **xiim,** Art Wolfe/Tony Stone Images; **xiib** Duncan Wherrett/Tony Stone Images; **xiiiml,** NASA/Mark Marten/Photo Researchers; **xiiib,** Digital Vision; **xiii inset,** Anglo-Australian Observatory; **xivt,** Schuster/Superstock; **xivm,** Mark Kelley/Stock Boston; **xivb,** Margaret Gowan/Tony Stone Images; **xvt,** Richard Haynes, **xvb,** David Muench Photography; **xvii,** Richard Haynes; **xvir,** Russ Lappa; **xvii both, xviii, xix,** Richard Haynes; **xxit,** Alberto Garcia/Saba Press; **xxib,** Herb Swanson.

What Is Science?
Page 4t, John Sanford/Science Photo Library/Photo Researchers; **4b,** The Granger Collection, NY; **5,** Robert E. Daemmrich/Tony Stone Images; **6,** Manfred Gottschalk/Tom Stack & Associates; **8,** Tsado/NCDC/NOAA/Tom Stack & Associates; **9,** Richard Haynes; **10,** Charles Cupton/The Stock Market; **11,** NASA; **12–13t,** M.W.Franke/Peter Arnold; **12l,** L. Gould/OSF/Animals Animals; **12br,** M. W. Franke/Peter Arnold; **13tr,** Peter Menzel/Stock Boston; **13bl,** Frank Pederick/The Image Works; **13br,** Bob Crandall/Stock Boston; **14,** Tsado/NCDC/NOAA/Tom Stack & Associates.

Chapter 1
Pages 16–17, Tom Bean; **18,** The Granger Collection, NY; **20t,** Tom Bean; **20b,** David Muench Photography; **22,** ESA/PLI/The Stock Market; **24,** Gardar Palsson/Mats Wibe Lund; **25t,b,** Russ Lappa; **26t,** Bodleian Library, Oxford, U.K.; **26b,** The Granger Collection, NY; **27t,** The Granger Collection, NY; **27bl,** British Library, London/Bridgeman Art Library, London/Superstock; **27br,** The Granger Collection, NY; **32t,** Russ Lappa; **32b,** Earth Satellite Corporation/Science Photo Library/Photo Researchers; **33l,** Earth Satellite Corporation/Science Photo Library/Photo Researchers; **33r,** Earth Satellite Corporation/Science Photo Library/Photo Researchers; **34l,** Geographix; **34r,** Bob Daemmrich/Stock Boston; **35t,** Richard Haynes; **35b,** Robert Rathe/Stock Boston; **37,** Paul Rezendes; **39,** Ken M. Johns/Photo Researchers; **40,** Richard Haynes.

Chapter 2
Pages 44–45, Thomas R. Taylor/Photo Researchers; **46t,** Richard Haynes; **46b,** Richard B. Levine; **47t,** Mark A. Schneider/Visuals Unlimited; **47m,** Ben Johnson/Science Photo Library/Photo Researchers; **47b,** E. R. Degginger; **48l,** Richard Treptow/Visuals Unlimited; **48m,** McCutcheon/Visuals Unlimited; **48r,** Gregory G. Dimijian/Photo Researchers; **49l,** Arne Hodalic/Corbis; **49m,** Charles D. Winters/Photo Researchers; **49r,** Ken Lucas/Visuals Unlimited; **50,** Paul Silverman/Fundamental Photographs; **51l,** Breck P. Kent; **51r,** Breck P. Kent; **52 sulfer,** E. R. Degginger; **52 the rest,** Breck P. Kent; **53l,** Paul Silverman/Fundamental Photographs; **53tr,** A. J. Copley/Visuals Unlimited; **53br,** Runk/Schoenberger/Grant Heilman Photography; **54l,** E. R. Degginger; **54r,** E. R. Degginger; **56t,** Richard Haynes; **56b,** Gerhard Gscheidle/Peter Arnold; **57,** Jeffrey Scovil; **58l,** Ken Lucas/Visuals Unlimited; **58r,** Ted Clutter/Photo Researchers; **59,** Jay Syverson/Stock Boston; **61,** Nautilus Minerals Corp.; **62,** C.M.Dixon; **63,** Mike Husar/DRK photo; **64t,** C.M. Dixon; **64bl,** Scala/Art Resource, NY; **64br,** C.M. Dixon; **65,** The Granger Collection, NY; **66t,** Charles D. Winters/Photo Researchers; **66b,** Russ Lappa; **67,** Visuals Unlimited; **68,** Richard Haynes; **69t,b, 71,** Breck P. Kent.

Chapter 3
Pages 72–73, Jim Nelson/Adventure Photo; **74t,m,** Breck P. Kent; **74b,** Jeff Zaroda/The Stock Market; **75tl,bl,** E. R. Degginger; **75m,tr,** Breck P. Kent; **75br,** Barry L. Runk/Grant Heilman Photography; **76tl,** E. R. Degginger; **76ml both,** Breck P. Kent; **76bl,** Specimen from North Museum/Franklin and Marshall College/Grant Heilman Photography; **76 breccia,** Breck P. Kent; **76br,** E. R. Degginger; **77,** Martin Rogers/Stock Boston; **78t,** Breck P. Kent; **78m,** Doug Martin/Photo Researchers; **78b,** Greg Vaughn/Tom Stack & Associates; **79l,m,** Breck P. Kent; **79r,** E. R. Degginger; **80,** Alfred Pasieka/Science Photo Library/Photo Researchers; **81,** Michele & Tom Grimm/Tony Stone Images; **82,** Clyde H. Smith/Peter Arnold; **84,** Specimen from North Museum/Franklin and Marshall College/Grant Heilman Photography; **85t,** E. R. Degginger; **85b,** Kevin Sink/Midwestock; **86,** Grant Heilman/Grant Heilman Photography; **87t,** Richard Haynes; **87b,** Stephen Frink/Waterhouse; **88t,** Norbert Wu/The Stock Market; **88b,** Jean-Marc Truchet/Tony Stone Images; **89,** Grant Heilman/Grant Heilman Photography; **90l,** Barry L. Runk/ Grant Heilman Photography; **90r,** Andrew J. Martinez/Photo Researchers; **91tl,** E. R. Degginger; **91bl,**

Andrew J. Martinez/Photo Researchers; **91tr,** Jeff Scovil; **91br,** Jeff Scovil; **92,** David Hosking/Photo Researchers; **94l,** Jeff Scovil; **94m,** Breck P. Kent; **94r,** Jeff Scovil; **96 all,** Russ Lappa; **99tl,** Andrew J. Martinez/Photo Researchers; **99m,** E. R. Degginger; **99tr,** Breck P. Kent; **100tl,** Rosenfeld Images Ltd/Rainbow;**100br,** C.M. Dixon; **100–101,** B. Daemmrich/The Image Works; **101 inset,** NASA/The Image Works; **102 border,** Corel Corp.; **104,** John Coletti/ Stock Boston.

Chapter 4
Pages 106–107, Earth Satellite Corporation/Science Photo Library/Photo Researchers; **109,** Michael Nichols/Magnum Photos; **110–111t,** Linde Waidhofer/Liaison Agency; **110m,** E. R. Degginger; **110b,** Breck P. Kent; **114,** Runk/Schoenberger/Grant Heilman Photography; **115,** Richard Haynes; **118t,** Russ Lappa; **118b,** The Granger Collection, NY; **120,** Breck P. Kent; **121,** Tom Bean; **122,** Bildarchiv Preussischer Kulturbesitz; **123,** Emory Kristof/National Geographic Image Collection; **126l,** Woods Hole Oceanographic Institute/Sygma; **126r,** USGS/HVO 3cp/U.S. Geological Survey; **127,** SCRIPPS Oceanographic Institute; **129,** Norbert Wu; **130 all,131,** Richard Haynes; **132,** Gerry Ellis/ENP Images; **136,** Emil Muench/Photo Researchers; **138,** Tim Davis/Photo Researchers.

Chapter 5
Pages 142–143, Science Museum/Michael Holford; **144,** Ben S. Kwiatkowski/Fundamental Photographs; **146t,** David Parker/Science Photo Library/Photo Researchers; **146b,** David Muench Photography; **147,** Sharon Gerig/Tom Stack & Associates; **148,** Stan Osolinski/Tony Stone Images; **149,** Phillips Petroleum; **150,151,** Tom Bean; **153 both,154,** Richard Haynes; **156t,** Richard Haynes; **156b,** Russell D. Curtis/Photo Researchers; **157,** Leonetto Medici/AP Photo; **158,** EERC/Berkeley; **162t,** Richard Haynes; **162b,** Sipa Press; **163,** EERC/Berkeley; **166,** Esbin-Anderson/The Image Works; **168,** Terraphotographics/BPS.

Chapter 6
Pages 176–177, Soames Summerhays/Photo Researchers; **178,** Savino/Sipa Press; **183all,** Breck P. Kent; **184,** E. R. Degginger; **185,** B. Ingalls/NASA/Liaison Agency; **186t,** Ed Reschke/Peter Arnold; **186b,** E. R. Degginger; **187l,** Dave B. Fleetham/Tom Stack & Associates; **187r,** William Felger/Grant Heilman Photography; **188tl,tr,** Alberto Garcia/Saba Press; **188b,** Robert Frerck/Woodfin Camp & Associates; **189tl,tr,** Alberto Garcia/Saba Press;**189b,** Norbert Rosing/Animals Animals/Earth Scenes; **190tl,** North Wind; **190tr,** Kim Heacox/Peter Arnold; **190b,** Robert Fried Photography; **191,** Alberto Garcia/Saba Press; **192l,** Pat Roqua/AP/Wide World Photos; **192r,** Antonio Emerito/Sipa Press; **193t,** Richard Haynes; **193b,** Hela Lade/Peter Arnold; **194,** Greg Vaughn/Tom Stack & Associates; **195t,** Picture Perfect; **195m,** Manfred Gottschalk/Tom Stack & Associates; **195b,** Chris Hamilton/The Stock Market; **196t,** Brownie Harris/The Stock Market; **196bl,** Tom Bean/DRK Photo; **196br,** David Hosking/Photo Researchers; **197,** Bob Newman/Visual Unlimited; **199,** Richard Haynes; **200t,m,** NASA; **200b,** Chris Bjornberg/Photo Researchers; **201 both, 202,** NASA; **206,** Paul Mann; **207,** Carol Prentice/U.S. Geological Survey; **208,** Paul Mann.

Chapter 7
Pages 210–211, Mike Mazzaschi/Stock Boston; **212,** Russ Lappa; **213l,** Ron Watts/Westlight; **213r,** Jerry D. Greer; **214l,** Breck P. Kent/Animals Animals/Earth Scenes; **214r,** Susan Rayfield/Photo Researchers; **215l,** John Sohlden/Visuals Unlimited; **215tr,** Gerald & Buff Corsi/Visuals Unlimited; **215br,** E. R. Degginger/Photo Researchers; **217t,** Chromosohm/Sohm/Photo Researchers; **217b,** Breck P. Kent/Animals Animals/Earth Scenes; **219,** Richard Haynes; **220,** John G. Ross/Photo Researchers; **221t,** Richard Haynes; **221b,** Rod Planck/Tony Stone Images; **226,** J.M. Labat/Jacana/Photo Researchers; **228,** Richard T. Nowitz/Photo Researchers; **229,** Richard Haynes; **230l,** Bertrand Rieger/Tony Stone Images; **230m,** Chad Slattery/Tony Stone Images; **230r,** Jacques Jangoux/Tony Stone Images; **231t,** Corbis; **231b,** Chris Sattleberger/Panos Pictures; **232,** AP/Wide World Photos; **233tl,** Kevin Horan/Tony Stone Images; **233tr,** Tom Bean 1994/DRK Photo; **233bl,** Larry Lefever/Grant Heilman Photography; **233br,** Martin Benjamin/The Image Works; **234 both,** Wally McNamee/Woodfin Camp & Associates; **235,** Russ Lappa; **237,** Hank Morgan/Science Source/Photo Researchers; **238,** Ray Pfortner/Peter Arnold; **239 all,** Russ Lappa; **240,** Stephen Agricola/The Image Works.

Chapter 8
Pages 244–245, Jim Steinberg/Photo Researchers; **246,** Jim Steinberg/Photo Researchers; **247,** Paul Sequeira/Photo Researchers; **248t,** Eric Vandeville/Liaison Agency; **248b,** Thomas G. Rampton/Grant Heilman Photography; **249,** Steven Holt; **250, 251,** Richard Haynes; **252t,** PhotoDisc, Inc.; **252–253b,** Walter Bibikow/The Viesti Collection; **253t,** Runk Schoenberger/Grant Heilman Photography; **254,** Inga Spence/Tom Stack & Associates; **255,** David Ball/The Stock Market; **256l,** Glenn M. Oliver/Visuals Unlimited; **256r,** Index Stock Imagery, Inc.; **257t,** Gerald & Buff Corsi/Visuals Unlimited; **257b,** NASA/SADO/Tom Stack & Associates; **260,** Chuck O'Rear/Westlight; **261,** St. Petersburg Times/Liaison Agency; **262,** Russ

Lappa; **263,** Richard Haynes; **264,** Doug McKay/Tony Stone Images; **265t,** Richard Haynes; **265b,** Eliot Cohen; **269t,** Richard Haynes; **269b,** Mark Kelley/ Stock Boston; **271,** Grant Heilman Photography; **274,** Craig Tuttle/The Stock Market; **276,** Randy Wells/Tony Stone Images; **277,** E. R.I.M./Tony Stone Images; **278t,** Richard Haynes; **278b,** Jess Stock/Tony Stone Images; **279,** Breck P. Kent; **280,** Connie Toops.

Chapter 9
Page 284–285, Phil Degginger; **286t,** John Cancalosi/Stock Boston; **286b,** Flowers & Newman/Photo Researchers; **287,** Francois Gohier/Photo Researchers; **288 both,** Runk/Schoenberger/Grant Heilman Photography; **289t,** Breck P. Kent; **289b,** Tom Bean; **290,** Howard Grey/Tony Stone Images; **291tl,** Khalid Ghani/Animals Animals/Earth Scenes; **291bl,** John Sibbick; **291tr,** Frans Lanting/Minden Pictures; **291mr,** The National History Museum, London; **292,** Sinclair Stammers/Science Photo Library/Photo Researchers; **293,** Richard Haynes; **294,** Jeff Greenberg/Photo Researchers; **295l,** G.R. Roberts/Photo Researchers; **295r,** Tom Bean; **296,** Breck P. Kent; **299,** Mitsuaki Iwago/Minden Pictures; **301,** James King-Holmes/Science Photo Library/Photo Researchers; **305,** Fletcher & Baylis/Photo Researchers; **305 inset,** John Cancalosi/Tom Stack & Associates; **307,** Richard Haynes; **308l,** Breck P. Kent; **308r,** Runk/Schoenberger/ Grant Heilman Photography; **309l,** John Sibbick; **309 inset,** The Natural History Museum, London; **310,** John Sibbick; **311t,** (c)The Field Museum, Neg.#CSGEO 75400c.; **311b,** Natural History Museum/London; **317,** 1989 Mark Hallett; **318l,** Jane Burton/Bruce Coleman; **318r,** David M. Dennis/Tom Stack Associates; **319t,** D. Van Ravenswaay/Photo Researchers; **319b,** C.M. Dixon ; **320,** John Reader/Science Photo Library/Photo Researchers.

Chapter 10
Pages 324–325, Yamada Toshiro/Tony Stone Images; **326,** M. L. Sinibaldi/The Stock Market; **329t,** Mike Abrahams/Tony Stone Images; **329b,** Paul Harris/Tony Stone Images; **330,** Jbboykin Oil Prod./The Stock Market; **332,** UPI/Corbis-Bettmann; **333,** Chad Ehlers/International Stock; **334,** Nadia MacKenzie/Tony Stone Images; **336,** A & L Sinibaldi/Tony Stone Images; **338,** NASA; **339,** Richard Haynes; **340,** Herb Swanson; **341t,** Russ Lappa; **341b,** Photograph by Johan Hagemeyer, courtesy AIP Emilio Segre Visual Archives; **344,** Y. Arthus-Bertrand/Peter Arnold; **345,** U.S. Dept. of Energy/Science Photo Library/Photo Researchers; **347,** Richard Haynes; **348l,** Mitch Kezar/Tony Stone Images; **348r,** Leonard Lessin/Peter Arnold; **349,** Yves Marcoux/Tony Stone Images; **350,** Wolf/Monkmeyer; **351,** Nadia MacKenzie/Tony Stone Images; **354,** University of Wyoming Public Relations; **356 both,** Courtesy of Kelli Trujillo; **357,** University of Wyoming Public Relations.

Chapter 11
Pages 358–359, Randy Linchs/Sharpshooters; **360t,** Richard Haynes; **364t,** O. Louis Mazzatenta/National Geographic Image Collection; **364b,** Liba Taylor/Corbis; **365t,** Tom Bean/Tony Stone Images; **365b,** Gianni Dagli Orti/Corbis; **368t,** Russ Lappa; **368 binoculars,** Superstock; **368 reflection,** Wernher Krutein/Liaison Agency; **370,** Bill Gillette/Liaison Agency; **370 inset,** Gregory Foster/Liaison Agency; **371,** Les Stone/Sygma; **374l,** David L. Brown/The Stock Market; **374r,** John Shaw/Tom Stack & Associates; **375,** George Holton/Photo Researchers; **376l,** Hulton Getty/Tony Stone Images; **376r,** Superstock; **377,** Ralph A. Clevenger/Westlight; **378t,** Richard Haynes; **378b,** Tim Olive/SharpShooters; **383,** Mark Thayer; **384,** Russ Lappa; **385t,** Breck P. Kent/Animals Animals/Earth Scenes; **385bl,** Greg Vaughn/Tom Stack & Associates; **385br,** John Eastcott /Yva Momatiuk/Animals Animals/Earth Scenes; **388,** Patrick M. Rose/Save the Manatee.

Chapter 12
Pages 392–393, Jeremy Horner/Corbis; **394,** Russ Lappa; **395,** Guy Marche/Tony Stone Images; **396,** Michael Newman/PhotoEdit; **401t,** Ted Horowitz/The Stock Market; **401b,** Deborah Davis/PhotoEdit; **404t,** Russ Lappa; **404b,** Laura Sikes/Sygma; **405,** Calvin Larsen/Photo Researchers; **406,** Russ Lappa; **408t,** Peter Skinner/Photo Researchers; **408b,409,411t,** Russ Lappa; **411b,** Seth Resnick/Stock Boston; **414,** Corbis-Bettmann; **415t,** Mugshots/Stock Market; **415b,** Wayne Eastep/Tony Stone Images; **417t,** Carson Baldwin/Animals Animals/Earth Scenes; **417b,** John Eastcott/Yva Momatiuk/Stock Boston; **418,** Peter Essick/Aurora; **419t,** Russ Lappa; **419b,** I. Burgum/P. Boorman/Tony Stone Images; **421,** Robert K. Grubbs/Photo Network; **422,** George Gerster/Photo Researchers; **423,** Deborah David/PhotoEdit.

Chapter 13
Pages 426–427, Siegried Layda/Tony Stone Images; **428t,** Richard Haynes; **428–429,** Aaron Chang/The Stock Market; **433,** (c)1996 The Art Institute of Chicago, Clarence Buckingham Collection; **434,435,** Gene Ahrens/Bruce Coleman; **438,** Maher Attar/Sygma; **439t,** Richard Haynes; **439b,** Russ Lappa; **440,** Alon Reininger/The Stock Market; **441,** Corel Corp.; **443,** Russ Lappa; **445,** Mark Thayer; **446t,** Richard Haynes; **446b,** Russ Lappa; **448,** Raven/Explorer/Photo Researchers; **449,** Carol Roessler/Animals Animals/Earth Scenes; **452,** Ryan Ott/ AP Photo; **453,** Art Institute of Chicago.

Chapter 14
Pages 456–457, Fred Bavendam; **458t,** Russ Lappa; **458b,** The Granger Collection, NY; **459,** Courtesy, Peabody Essex Museum, Salem, MA; **460,** Norbert Wu/The Stock Market; **461t,** SCRIPPS Oceanographic Institute; **461b,** Scott Camanzine/Photo Researchers; **464t,** Ted Streshinsky/Corbis; **464b,** Russ Lappa; **466,** Richard Dunoff/The Stock Market; **467t,** E. R. Degginger/Photo Researchers; **467m,** Tim Heller/Mo Yung Productions; **467bl,** F. Stuart Westmorland/Photo Researchers; **467br,** Doug Perrine/Innerspace Visions; **470l,** Maresa Pryor/Animals Animals/Earth Scenes; **470r,** Peter Weiman/Animals Animals/Earth Scenes; **471t,** Lynda Richardson/Corbis; **471b,** Andy Martinez/Photo Researchers; **472t,** Richard Haynes; **472b,** Jeff Foott/Tom Stack & Associates; **474l,** Chuck Davis/Tony Stone Images; **474r,** Randy Morse/Tom Stack & Associates; **475,** Mike Bacon/Tom Stack & Associates; **476,** Norbert Wu; **478,** D. Foster/WHOI/Visuals Unlimited; **479t,** Richard Haynes; **479b,** Nathan Benn/Stock Boston; **481,** Russ Lappa; **482,** Arnulf Husmo/Tony Stone Images; **483l,** Bob Torrez/Tony Stone Images; **483r,** Bill Nation/Sygma; **484t,** Jake Evans/Tony Stone Images; **484b,** Richard Haynes; **485,** Tim Hauf/Visuals Unlimited; **487,** Doug Perrine/Innerspace Visions; **491t,** The Granger Collection, NY; **491m,** 1998 North Wind Picture Archives; **491b,** Hippolyte Sebron (born France 1801–1879) Giant Steamboats on the Levee at New Orleans, 1853. Oil on canvas, Tulane. University Art Collection, Gift of D.H. Holmes Company; **493,** Richard Pasley/Liaison Agency; **494t,** National Portrait Gallery, Smithsonian Institution/Art Resource, NY; **494b,** Chromo Sohm/Sohm/Photo Researchers; **495t,** 1998 North Wind Picture Archives; **495b,** Chromo Sohm/Sohm/Photo Researchers.

Chapter 15
Pages 496–497, Jay Simon/Tony Stone Images; **498t,** Russ Lappa; **498b,** NASA/Photo Researchers; **500t,** Richard Haynes; **500b,** Russ Lappa; **501,** George G. Dimijian/Photo Researchers; **502,** Eric Horan/Liaison Agency; **503,** Richard Haynes; **504t,** Russ Lappa; **504b,** Aaron Haupt/Photo Researchers; **505t,** Biophoto Associates/Photo Researchers; **505b,** Paul Lowe/Magnum Photos; **507,** Will McIntyre/Photo Researchers; **508,** Steve Casimiro/Liaison Agency; **509l,** Russ Lappa; **509b,** Eric A. Kessler; **511,** Ivan Bucher/Photo Researchers; **513, 515t,** Russ Lappa; **515b,** Steve Vidler/Superstock; **516,** Mark C. Burnett/Photo Researchers; **518t,** The Granger Collection, NY; **518b,** Corbis-Bettmann; **519t,** The National Archives/Corbis; **519b,** NASA; **520,** Jack Finch/Science Photo Library/Photo Researchers.

Chapter 16
Pages 524–525, William Johnson/Stock Boston; **526–527,** Photo Researchers; **531,** Richard Haynes; **532, 533, 536t,** Russ Lappa; **536b,** Victoria Hurst/Tom Stack & Associates; **537l,** Gary Retherford/Photo Researchers; **537r, 539,** Richard Haynes; **540,** Steve McCurry/Magnum Photos; **542,** Scala/Art Resource, NY; **544,** Ken McVey/Tony Stone Images; **545,** Russ Lappa; **546,** E.J. Tarbuck; **547,** Peter Arnold; **549t,** Michael Gadomski/GADOM/Bruce Coleman; **549tm,** Phil Degginger/Bruce Coleman; **549bm,** E. R. Degginger; **549b,** John Shaw/Bruce Coleman; **550,** Wendy Shattil/Bob Rozinski/Tom Stack & Associates; **551,** Richard Haynes; **552t,** AP/Wide World Photos; **552 inset,** Gerben Oppermans/Tony Stone Images; **552b,** Nuridsany et Perennou/Photo Researchers; **554,** Bill Frantz/Tony Stone Images; **555,** Gerben Oppermans/Tony Stone Images.

Chapter 17
Pages 558–559, Pete Turner/Image Bank; **560 both,** Russ Lappa; **561,** Jim Corwin/Tony Stone Images; **567t,** Russ Lappa; **567b,** Dirck Halstead/Liaison Agency; **568,** Dan Sudia/Photo Researchers; **569,** Schuster/Superstock; **570t,b,** The Granger Collection, NY; **571,** North Wind Picture Archives; **572,** Sheila Beougher/Liaison Agency; **573,** NASA Goddard Laboratory for Atmospheres; **574,** Clore Collection, Tate Gallery, London/Art Resource, NY; **576,** NOAA; **578,** Tony Freeman/PhotoEdit; **579t,** Richard Haynes; **579bl,** Keith Kent/Science Photo Library/Photo Researchers; **579br,** Grant V. Faint/Image Bank; **582,** David J. Phillip/AP/Wide World Photos; **583t,** Larry Lawfer; **583b,** Corel Corp.; **584,** David Umberger/AP Photo; **585,** NOAA; **588, 589, 590,** AccuWeather, Inc.; **591,** Schuster/Superstock.

Chapter 18
Pages 594–595, David Muench Photography; **596t,** Richard Haynes; **596b,** Thomas D. Mangelsen/Peter Arnold; **598,** David Madison/Bruce Coleman; **600,** Duncan Wherrett/Tony Stone Images; **601,** Chris Cheadle/Tony Stone Images;

605, Richard Haynes; **606t,** Russ Lappa; **606b,** Charlie Waite/Tony Stone Images; **607,** Geogory G. Dimigian/Photo Researchers; **610t,** Thomas D. Mangelsen/Peter Arnold; **610b,** Alex S. MacLean/Peter Arnold; **611,** Stephen Johnson/Tony Stone Images; **612t,** Ann Duncan/Tom Stack & Associates; **612b,** Margaret Gowan/Tony Stone Images; **613,** Corbis-Bettmann; **614t,** Art Wolfe/Tony Stone Images; **614b,** Thomas Kitchin/Tom Stack & Associates; **615,** Photodisc, Inc.; **618,** 1996 Ira Block; **619,** Tony Craddock/Science Photo Library/Photo Researchers; **619 inset,** George Godfrey/Animals Animals/Earth Scenes; **626,** NOAA; **627,** Tony Craddock/Science Photo Library/Photo Researchers; **630,** Jane Love /NASA; **631l,** NASA/Photo Researchers; **631r,** Jose L. Pelaez/The Stock Market; **632 both, 633,** NASA.

Chapter 19
Pages 634–635, NASA; **636t,** Russ Lappa; **636b,** Eric Lessing/Art Resource; **638,** Corel Corp.; **639t,** Courtney Milne/Masterfile; **639b,** Hazel Hankin/Stock Boston; **642,** Palmer/Kane/Tony Stone Images; **643,** Art Wolfe/Tony Stone Images; **645,** Richard Haynes; **646t,** Richard Haynes; **646b,** Larry Landolfi/Photo Researchers; **648 all,** John Bova/Photo Researchers; **650, 651 both,** Jay M. Pasachoff; **653,** Richard Haynes; **654 both,** Nancy Dudley/Stock Boston; **655,** Richard Haynes; **656, 657, 658,** NASA; **659t,** Richard Haynes; **659b,** NASA; **660t,** John Bova/Photo Researchers; **660 the rest,** Courtesy of Alastair G.W. Cameron, Center for Astrophysics at Harvard University; **661t,** NASA; **661b,** Jay M. Pasachoff; **662,** N. Armstrong/The Stock Market; **663,** Tony Stone Images; **664,** NASA.

Chapter 20
Pages 668–669, NASA; **670t,** Russ Lappa; **670b,** Anglo-Australian Observatory, photograph by David Malin; **671,** The Granger Collection, NY; **672,** The Granger Collection, NY; **673t,** Richard Haynes; **673b,** The Granger Collection, NY; **676,** Richard Haynes; **677,** Digital Vision; **678,** National Solar Observatory; **678 inset,** Space Telescope Science Institute; **680t,** Space Telescope Science Institute; **680b,** National Solar Observatory; **684,** NASA; **684 inset,** A.S.P./Science Source/Photo Researchers; **685, 686,** Digital Vision; **687,** NASA; **688,** Jet Propulsion Laboratory; **689 both,** NASA; **690,** Tony Stone Images; **692 both,** NASA; **693, 694t,** Jet Propulsion Laboratory; **694 inset,** Digital Vision; **694b, 695, 696 both, 697 both,** NASA; **698, 699, 700t,** Richard Haynes; **700b,** Space Telescope Science Institute; **702,** Jet Propulsion Laboratory; **703l,** U.S. Geological Survey; **703r,** Jerry Schad/Photo Researchers; **704,** Ghislaine Grozaz; **705,** James Pisarowicz; **706,** U.S. Geological Survey; **707,** NASA; **708, 709,** Jet Propulsion Laboratory.

Chapter 21
Pages 712–713, David Nunuk/Science Photo Library/Photo Researchers; **714t,** Richard Haynes; **714b,** John Sanford/Science Photo Library/Photo Researchers; **716,** Russ Lappa; **717t,** Malin/Pasachoff/Caltech 1992; **717b,** NRAO/Science Photo Library/Photo Researchers; **718tl,** Yerkes Observatory; **718–719tr,** National Astronomy and Ionosphere Center; **718–719b,** John Sanford/Astrostock; **719t,** NASA; **722,** Silver, Burdett & Ginn Publishing; **723t,** Richard Haynes; **723b,** Roger Harris/Science Photo Library/Photo Researchers; **726,** UCO/Lick Observatory; **727,** Luke Dodd/Science Photo Library/Photo Researchers; **728,** Anglo-Australian Observatory, photograph by David Malin; **732,** Open University, UK; **733,** National Optical Astronomy Observatories; **733 inset,** Space Telescope Science Institute; **734 both,** Anglo-Australian Observatory, photograph by David Malin; **736,** Photo Researchers; **737,** Dennis Di Cicco/Peter Arnold; **738 both,** Richard Haynes; **740t,** Anglo-Australian Observatory; **740m,** Anglo-Australian Observatory, photograph by David Malin; **740b,** Royal Observatory, Edinburgh/AATB/Science Photo Library/Photo Researchers; **741,** NASA; **744,** David Parker/Science Photo Library/Photo Researchers; **748t,** Jet Propulsion Laboratory; **748b,** U.S. Geological Survey; **749l,** Corbis-Bettmann; **749r,** Valerie Ambroise; **750t,** Pat Rawlings/NASA; **750–751b,** Jet Propulsion Laboratory; **751 tl, tr,** NASA; **752 inset,** U.S. Geological Survey; **752b,** NASA/Peter Arnold; **753,** Pat Rawlings/NASA.

Skills Handbook
Page 754, PhotoDisc, Inc.; **755t,** Breck P. Kent; **755m,** Richard Haynes; **755b,** Russ Lappa; **758,** Richard Haynes; **760,** Ron Kimball; **761,** Renee Lynn/Photo Researchers.

Appendix
Pages 770–771, Bilderberg/The Stock Market; **772, 773, 774, 775,** Griffith Observer, Griffith Observatory, Los Angeles.